# Social Networking and Community Behavior Modeling:

## Qualitative and Quantitative Measures

Maytham Safar
*Kuwait University, Kuwait*

Khaled A. Mahdi
*Kuwait University, Kuwait*

Information Science
REFERENCE

| Managing Director: | Lindsay Johnston |
|---|---|
| Senior Editorial Director: | Heather Probst |
| Book Production Manager: | Sean Woznicki |
| Development Manager: | Joel Gamon |
| Development Editor: | Michael Killian |
| Acquisitions Editor: | Erika Gallagher |
| Typesetters: | Milan Vracarich, Jr. |
| Print Coordinator: | Jamie Snavely |
| Cover Design: | Nick Newcomer, Greg Snader |

Published in the United States of America by
Information Science Reference (an imprint of IGI Global)
701 E. Chocolate Avenue
Hershey PA 17033
Tel: 717-533-8845
Fax: 717-533-8661
E-mail: cust@igi-global.com
Web site: http://www.igi-global.com

Library of Congress Cataloging-in-Publication Data

Social networking and community behavior modeling: qualitative and quantitative measures / Maytham Safar and Khaled A. Mahdi, editors.
     p. cm.
  Includes bibliographical references and index.
  Summary: "This book provides a clear and consolidated view of current social network models, exploring new methods for modeling, characterizing, and constructing social networks"--Provided by publisher.
  ISBN 978-1-61350-444-4 (hardcover) -- ISBN 978-1-61350-445-1 (ebook) -- ISBN 978-1-61350-446-8 (print & perpetual access) 1. Social networks. I. Safar, Maytham. II. Mahdi, Khaled A., 1970-
  HM741.S6343 2012
  302.3--dc23
                        2011038336

British Cataloguing in Publication Data
A Cataloguing in Publication record for this book is available from the British Library.

All work contributed to this book is new, previously-unpublished material. The views expressed in this book are those of the authors, but not necessarily of the publisher.

# Table of Contents

Foreword ............................................................................................................................. xv

Preface ............................................................................................................................... xvii

Acknowledgment .............................................................................................................. xxii

## Section 1
### Social Networks and Communities

**Chapter 1**

Social Networks and Communities: From Traditional Society to the Virtual Sphere ........................... 1
*Francesca Odella, University of Trento, Italy*

**Chapter 2**

Network Perspective on Structures Related to Communities ........................................................ 26
*Alvin Wolfe, University of Southern Florida, USA*

**Chapter 3**

Civic Engagement and Communication Technology Networks ....................................................... 51
*Philip J. Salem, Texas State University, USA*

## Section 2
### Modeling and Developing Social Networks and Online Communities

**Chapter 4**

The Social Construction of New Cultural Models through Information and Communication
Technologies ............................................................................................................................. 68
*Almudena Moreno, Universidad de Valladolid, Spain*

**Chapter 5**

From Virtual to the Simulated World: An Agent-Based Model of Friendship Network in
Second Life ............................................................................................................................... 85
*Sadaf Alvi, University of Karachi, Pakistan*
*Shah Jamal Alam, University of Michigan, USA*

**Chapter 6**
Analysis of Success Factors in Social Networking Website Development ........................................ 103
    *Zanita Zahari, La Trobe University, Australia*
    *Eric Pardede, La Trobe University, Australia*

**Section 3**
**Information-Knowledge Discovery and Diffusion in Social Networks and Online Communities**

**Chapter 7**
Knowledge Discovery from Online Communities ........................................................................ 123
    *Luca Cagliero, Politecnico di Torino, Italy*
    *Alessandro Fiori, Politecnico di Torino, Italy*

**Chapter 8**
Information Diffusion in Social Networks.................................................................................... 146
    *Dmitry Zinoviev, Suffolk University, USA*

**Chapter 9**
Social Network, Information Flow and Decision-Making Efficiency: A Comparison of
Humans and Animals .................................................................................................................... 164
    *Cédric Sueur, Free University of Brussels, Belgium & Kyoto University, Japan*

**Chapter 10**
Extracting and Measuring Relationship Strength in Social Networks............................................ 178
    *Steven Gustafson, GE Global Research, USA*
    *Abha Moitra, GE Global Research, USA*

**Chapter 11**
Bringing Qualitative and Quantitative Data Together: Collecting Network Data with the
Help of the Software Tool VennMaker ........................................................................................ 193
    *Markus Gamper, University Trier, Germany*
    *Michael Schönhuth, University Trier, Germany*
    *Michael Kronenwett, University Trier, Germany*

**Section 4**
**Evolution of Social Networks and Online Communities**

**Chapter 12**
Observing the Evolution of a Learning Community Using Social Network Analysis ...................... 215
    *Francesca Grippa, University of Salento, Italy*
    *Marco De Maggio, University of Salento, Italy*
    *Angelo Corallo, University of Salento, Italy*

**Chapter 13**

Social Networks and Terrorism..............................................................................................232

    *David Knoke, University of Minnesota, USA*


**Section 5**
**Business Impact of Social Networks and Online Communities**

**Chapter 14**

Social Network Sites: Modeling the New Business-Customer Relationship .....................248

    *Pedro Isaías, Universidade Aberta, Portugal*

    *Sara Pífano, Information Society Research Lab, Portugal*

    *Paula Miranda, Polytechnic Institute of Setubal, Portugal*

**Chapter 15**

Community Structure Extraction for Social Networks.............................................................266

    *Helen Hadush, North Carolina Central University, USA*

    *Gaolin Zheng, North Carolina Central University, USA*

    *Chung-Hao Chen, North Carolina Central University, USA*

    *E-Wen Huang, National Central University, Taiwan*

**Chapter 16**

Towards a Bespoke Framework for Eliciting Consumer Satisfaction in Second Life.........................283

    *Mitul Shukla, University of Bedfordshire, UK*

    *Marc Conrad, University of Bedfordshire, UK*

    *Nik Bessis, University of Bedfordshire, UK and University of Derby, UK*

**Chapter 17**

Finding Similar Users in Facebook.............................................................................................304

    *Pasquale De Meo, University of Messina, Italy*

    *Emilio Ferrara, University of Messina, Italy*

    *Giacomo Fiumara, University of Messina, Italy*


**Compilation of References** .............................................................................................324

**About the Contributors** .................................................................................................365

**Index**.................................................................................................................................373

# Detailed Table of Contents

**Foreword**.................................................................................................................... xv

**Preface**...................................................................................................................... xvii

**Acknowledgment**......................................................................................................... xxii

### Section 1
### Social Networks and Communities

*Different meanings and definitions of offline and online communities are found in social network analysis. This section aims to demonstrate the intrinsic capability of communication technologies enabled through the Internet and mobile applications in the form of exchange of messages over sms, emails, blogs, and social network sites. It emphasizes those technologies' expansion in both speed and number in the creation of virtual online social networks and communities as opposed to the traditional local/nation civic communities and social groups that are usually created by traditional forms of communications; face-to-face, telephone, or mail.*

**Chapter 1**

Social Networks and Communities: From Traditional Society to the Virtual Sphere ............................ 1
   *Francesca Odella, University of Trento, Italy*

The author introduces a critical view of the community concept in social network analysis and in particular to the study of complex interaction environments, such as Internet and mobile media. The development of the field of network analysis is described by means of case studies and scholarly examples form various fields of empirical network research (political science, communication sciences and technology studies). In particular, the chapter explores the research process that evolved from the first ethnographic studies of social groups, and proceeds to exploration of new forms of interaction in online and computer mediated environments.

**Chapter 2**

Network Perspective on Structures Related to Communities............................................................. 26
   *Alvin Wolfe, University of Southern Florida, USA*

The application of network perspectives to communities requires some appreciation of the variety of ways people are now writing about communities. From the 1940s well into the 1960s the local community was the recognized social unit that sociologists and anthropologists studied. People who write about communities nowadays are using terms in a wide variety of ways. The "little communities" that anthropologist Robert Redfield (1960) wrote about fifty years ago have very little in common with the present-day "community of nations, the community of Jamaica Plain, the gay community, the IBM community, the Catholic Community, the Yale Community, the African American community, the 'virtual' community of cyberspace," all mentioned by Robert Putnam (2000). In the decade since Putnam, electronic connections have expanded logarithmically in both number and speed, and the community problem is even more vexing.

## Chapter 3

Civic Engagement and Communication Technology Networks ........................................................... 51
*Philip J. Salem, Texas State University, USA*

Individuals address public issues by becoming involved with civic groups and performing civic activities such as charity and political work. Changes in communication technology have led to changes in civic engagement, and it is now possible to perform civic activities digitally. Actors develop social networks as they use various communication technologies, and the resultant networks act as passive constraints on individual activities. This chapter investigated face-to-face, telephone, email, private electronic, and public electronic communication networks. Private electronic communication networks develop through text messaging, instant messaging, and private chat, and public electronic communication networks emerge through the exchange of messages over blogs, social network sites, and Twitter.

## Section 2
## Modeling and Developing Social Networks and Online Communities

*This section outlines some models of social networks that describe how online social networks and communities are formed, developed and analyzed. Analytical tools are used to provide an adequate interpretation of these newly created social networks such as the famous friendship network in Second Life. In addition, the chapter concludes with key success factors for the development for social networking websites.*

## Chapter 4

The Social Construction of New Cultural Models through Information and Communication
Technologies ....................................................................................................................................... 68
*Almudena Moreno, Universidad de Valladolid, Spain*

This chapter contains a theoretical reflection on the meaning of the new forms of social relations in this ICT-based culture, as well as on the need to define new analytical tools to enable an adequate interpretation of this new cultural context within the framework of globalization and digitalization. The work analyzes the cultural significance of the new concept of cyberculture and the new socio-cultural concepts regarding to ICTs.

## Chapter 5

From Virtual to the Simulated World: An Agent-Based Model of Friendship Network in
Second Life ......................................................................................................................................... 85
*Sadaf Alvi, University of Karachi, Pakistan*
*Shah Jamal Alam, University of Michigan, USA*

A prototype agent-based model of the friendship network in Second Life is presented. Second Life is a 3D virtual world that allows users to engage in various social activities, meet friends, form communities, attend events of interests and trade online with other users represented through their virtual 3D avatars. For social and behavioral scientists, this provides an opportunity to investigate the dynamics of social interaction and formation of interpersonal and group affiliation ties. Initial results from the model concerning friendship ties are reported.

**Chapter 6**
Analysis of Success Factors in Social Networking Website Development ........................................ 103
    *Zanita Zahari, La Trobe University, Australia*
    *Eric Pardede, La Trobe University, Australia*

The popularity and rapid growth of social networking Websites is undeniable. Unfortunately, it is hard to guarantee the success and sustainability of these Websites. This chapter focuses on identifying the key success factors for each phase in agile iteration development for social networking Websites. Qualitative and quantitative analysis were adopted using Web analytical tools to gather and measure these success factors. This chapter will benefit Website designers and developers by suggesting the success factors for each agile iteration development phase.

**Section 3**
**Information-Knowledge Discovery and Diffusion in Social Networks and Online Communities**

*The growth of the Internet and online communities has led to an increasing importance for understanding the social network structure of communities, the relationships between members, and how information is discovered and diffused in such virtual networks. This section overviews the gathering of network data by means of both qualitative and quantitative methodologies. It describes the state-of-the-art data mining algorithms and tools oriented to knowledge discovery, collective decision-making, information diffusion, and identifying relationships from online communities.*

**Chapter 7**
Knowledge Discovery from Online Communities ............................................................ 123
    *Luca Cagliero, Politecnico di Torino, Italy*
    *Alessandro Fiori, Politecnico di Torino, Italy*

The chapter overviews the most notable research trends and application systems concerning data mining and knowledge discovery from user-generated content. It first introduces the most popular social media features. Secondly, it overviews the most appealing approaches to social network analysis and user behavior modeling. Finally, it categorizes and thoroughly describes the state-of-the-art data mining algorithms and tools oriented to knowledge discovery from online communities. A particular attention is focused on semantic knowledge inference and automatic understanding of the user-generated content.

**Chapter 8**
Information Diffusion in Social Networks............................................................................ 146
    *Dmitry Zinoviev, Suffolk University, USA*

The chapter provides an overview of information and innovation diffusion in scale-free, small-world social networks. The material is suitable for network science specialists, as well as for interested professionals in the fields of Sociology, Psychology, and Marketing. Both static and dynamic aspects are discussed, as well as message taxonomies. The text addresses the role and the strategic position of influential spreaders of information; the pathways in the social networks that serve as conduits for communication and information flow; mathematical models describing proliferation processes; short-term and long-term dynamics of information diffusion, and secrecy of information diffusion.

**Chapter 9**

Social Network, Information Flow and Decision-Making Efficiency: A Comparison of
Humans and Animals .................................................................................................................. 164
*Cédric Sueur, Free University of Brussels, Belgium & Kyoto University, Japan*

In animals, including humans, group or community members not only have to take decisions satisfying the majority of individuals (i.e. decision accuracy) but also have a relatively short period to do so (i.e. decision speed). The decision efficiency will vary according to the way individuals are inter-connected, namely according to the social network. However, the traditional approach used in management and decision sciences has been revealed to be insufficient to fully explain decision-making efficiency. This chapter addresses the question of how social network may enhance collective decision-making by increasing both the accuracy and the speed of decisions.

**Chapter 10**

Extracting and Measuring Relationship Strength in Social Networks ............................................... 178
*Steven Gustafson, GE Global Research, USA*
*Abha Moitra, GE Global Research, USA*

The growth of the Internet and online communities has led to increasing importance for understanding the social network structure of communities and the relationships between members. The mapping from online communications and behaviors to relationships should identify valid relationships so that the structural properties of the resulting social network are stable in the face of incomplete or inaccurate data. This chapter shows how slight variations in data processing steps for identifying relationships can lead to very different networks. It considers a number of design choices and the network structure variability they introduce and measures its effectiveness in performance on a prediction task.

**Chapter 11**

Bringing Qualitative and Quantitative Data Together: Collecting Network Data with the
Help of the Software Tool VennMaker ............................................................................................ 193
*Markus Gamper, University Trier, Germany*
*Michael Schönhuth, University Trier, Germany*
*Michael Kronenwett, University Trier, Germany*

This chapter describes the gathering of network data by means of both qualitative and quantitative methodologies. An overview of the important visual approaches (e.g. network pictures and network maps) is given. Following, an example of a migration-network study was inverstigated with the aid of the software program VennMaker. Finally, the advantages and disadvantages of data collection based on digital network maps are discussed.

## Section 4
## Evolution of Social Networks and Online Communities

*This section introduces two case studies of actual social networks with an objective to analyze their formation and evolution in time. Dynamic social network analysis was applied to a learning community built around a Master's Program in an Italian University, and some international terror networks to help in detecting, or modifying the created/evolved networks.*

### Chapter 12

Observing the Evolution of a Learning Community Using Social Network Analysis ...................... 215

*Francesca Grippa, University of Salento, Italy*
*Marco De Maggio, University of Salento, Italy*
*Angelo Corallo, University of Salento, Italy*

This chapter proposes an empirical correlation between the stages of development of a learning community and a set of social network metrics. Social Network Analysis was applied to observe a learning community built around a Master's Program in an Italian University. It was found that the evolution of social network metrics - such as Density, Betweenness Centrality, Contribution Index, Core/Periphery Structure – matched the formal stages of community development, with a clear identification of forming, norming and storming phases.

### Chapter 13

Social Networks and Terrorism................................................................................................ 232

*David Knoke, University of Minnesota, USA*

This chapter explains how international terror networks, consisting of individuals and organizations spanning countries and continents, form and evolve. Terrorism is violence committed by groups with political goals, targeted against civilians, and intended to create fear in a population. Social network analysis, which uses visual and matrix algebra methods to study such networks, can help counterterrorist organizations to detect, disrupt, and dismantle terrorist groups.

## Section 5
## Business Impact of Social Networks and Online Communities

This section focuses on the methods, frameworks and approaches that study the relationship between social network users/customers and businesses and analyses the important role that social network sites can play in market penetration. It identifies the mechanisms to to extract useful information from the community structure, and how this information can be used to improve business efficiency and customer satisfaction. An overview of how the proposed frameworks and approaches can be used by others is given along with the wider context of its use.

### Chapter 14

Social Network Sites: Modeling the New Business-Customer Relationship ..................................... 248

*Pedro Isaías, Universidade Aberta, Portugal*
*Sara Pífano, Information Society Research Lab, Portugal*
*Paula Miranda, Polytechnic Institute of Setubal, Portugal*

This chapter focuses on the new facets of the relationship between customers and businesses and analyses the important role that Social Network Sites (SNSs) can play in its strengthening. The era of Web 2.0 has empowered consumers, by amplifying their voices and providing them with venues for information search and sharing. SNSs represent one of the most successful examples of social technology and since the business sector needs to adapt to customers' changing profile and behaviour, SNSs have proven to be important tools in terms of upholding the business-consumer relationship. Nonetheless, their primordial social and informal nature recommends thoroughness in order to maximise their potential, while avoiding their perils.

**Chapter 15**
Community Structure Extraction for Social Networks .................................................................... 266
*Helen Hadush, North Carolina Central University, USA*
*Gaolin Zheng, North Carolina Central University, USA*
*Chung-Hao Chen, North Carolina Central University, USA*
*E-Wen Huang, National Central University, Taiwan*

This chapter applied two graph partition approaches to extract community structures from social networks. The spectral approach is based on the minimization of balanced cut and its resulting solution comes from the spectral decomposition of the graph Laplacian. The modularity-based approach is based on the maximization of modularity and implemented in a hierarchical fashion. The method is able to extract useful information from the community structure, such as what is the most influential component in a given community. This information can be used to improve marketing efficiency by customized advertisement. Network visualization and navigation can also benefit from the community structural information.

**Chapter 16**
Towards a Bespoke Framework for Eliciting Consumer Satisfaction in Second Life......................... 283
*Mitul Shukla, University of Bedfordshire, UK*
*Marc Conrad, University of Bedfordshire, UK*
*Nik Bessis, University of Bedfordshire, UK and University of Derby, UK*

This chapter focuses on the development of a framework for eliciting consumer satisfaction perceptions in the context of the social virtual world Second Life. An introduction to Second Life is followed by an overview of the relevant literature. The framework and the inter-related component parts that it is made up from are then described in detail. This is followed by an evaluation of the framework through semi-structured in-world interviews as well as the refinement of the framework as a consequence of our evaluation. Finally an overview of how the framework can be used by others is given along with the wider context of its use.

**Chapter 17**
Finding Similar Users in Facebook.................................................................................................. 304
*Pasquale De Meo, University of Messina, Italy*
*Emilio Ferrara, University of Messina, Italy*
*Giacomo Fiumara, University of Messina, Italy*

A crucial aspect in the analysis of Online Social Networks is to determine whether two users of the network can be considered similar, or not. This reflects in several interesting applications, such as the possibility of finding social aggregations or targeting commercial promotions with proficiency. This chapter provides an approach to estimate the similarity among users of a network using information about their social ties and the analysis of their activities. It draws several local measures of similarity considering different indicators, and combines them obtaining a global measure of similarity, by applying metrics introduced in Social Sciences combined with techniques as the linear regression.

**Compilation of References** ................................................................................. 324

**About the Contributors** ..................................................................................... 365

**Index** ................................................................................................................ 373

# Foreword

Social networks represent aspects of human relationships and behaviors existing and happening around us in the real physical world. In the past decade, they have come along in the cyber digital world with the rapid development of emerging information and communication technology, such as web 2.0, ubiquitous computing, cloud services, and smart phones. Social networking services, including a variety of micro blogging services and so-called social media, have moved into the limelight in the recent years. They have made a lasting influence on an individual's daily life, an enterprise's business process, and even a nation's economic and political system.

*Social Networking and Community Behavior Modeling: Qualitative and Quantitative Measures*, edited by Professors Maytham Safar and Khaled Mahdi, with an Editorial Advisory Board of famous scholars from different parts of the world, has been published at a very opportune time. The volume encompasses a variety of interdisciplinary topics, which have carefully selected and well discussed from a multidisciplinary perspective. It provides socio-technical views on modeling and developing social networks and online communities, and a comprehensive discussion of the core issues, integrated approaches, and practical visions of its trend in the field.

The book begins with the theoretical issues on the formation of social networks and online communities, transformation from traditional society to virtual world, social construction and network structure, civic engagement and cultural model, and analysis of success factors. It goes further into application issues on knowledge discovery, information diffusion, decision-making, customer relationship management, and learning support in or through social networking and online communities. It presents methodologies and describes solutions related to these difficult issues in the field. This book offers a comprehensive viewpoint of the upcoming evolution and trend of social networks, and the potential impact it may bring to the business and society.

Research on social network modeling and analysis relates to a lot of cross-disciplinary, interdisciplinary, and trans-disciplinary issues. It is a continuously and rapidly evolving field. This book is highly expected to help researchers to become aware of the very wide range of social network issues from the perspectives of both computer science and social science. It can serve as a reference work for domain researchers interested in social networking and online community behavior modeling and analysis, and a text for novice social networkers looking for an overview of the field. It can lead the interested readers to a brand new starting point of the research field.

*Qun Jin*
*Waseda University, Japan*

**Qun Jin** *is a Computer Science Professor at the Networked Information Systems Lab, Department of Human Informatics and Cognitive Sciences, Faculty of Human Sciences, Waseda University, Japan. He has been engaged extensively in research works on computer science, Information Systems, and Internet computing. His recent research interests include human-centric Information Systems, contextaware ubiquitous personal media, human-media interaction, socially intelligent agents, semantic P2P networking and applications, groupware, scalable knowledge information sharing systems, and e-learning support. He received a BSc in process control from Zhejiang University, China, a MSc in Computer Science from Hangzhou Institute of Electronic Engineering, and the Fifteenth Research Institute of Ministry of Electronic Industry, China, and a PhD in Computer Science from Nihon University, Japan, in 1982, 1984, and 1992, respectively. He worked at Hangzhou Institute of Electronic Engineering (1984–1989), INES Corporation (1992–1995), Tokushima University (1995–1999), and the University of Aizu (1999–2003). During the summer of 1997, he was a short-term scholar in the Department of Electrical and Computer Engineering, Boston University, USA. Since April 2003, he has been at the current position. Contact him at jin@waseda.jp.*

# Preface

Sociality is the most unique characteristic of human beings. Humans usually strive to create relations with others by sharing their thoughts, emotions, and even their actions. Sometimes, it is not necessary to even have a direct interaction between actors to say that there is a social relation between them. It is enough that one of them is acting under the assumption that the others shared the same meanings that caused him to act. This uniqueness implied an important philosophical question that was considered centuries ago, "How do people communicate?" What are the rules that really control these communications? Half a century ago, it was almost impossible to provide qualitative or quantitative assessment to help providing accurate answers to these questions. However, as the population of the world is growing day by day, the importance of answering this question is increasing. That's because the spread of news, rumors, and even the diseases have become very hard to be controlled.

Sociology is the branch of social sciences that considers investigating empirically the social activities of the human being. Its concerns include both micro and macro levels of the human-to-human interactions. In other words, it considers both the face-to-face human interaction and the overall society behavior. After the technological advancement in the communication field and the creation of the Internet and mobiles, the ability to provide an insight has grown tremendously. Fortunately, the ability to study the human society and answer the questions mentioned has grown.

Social networks are how any community is modeled. They have emerged as a major trend of computing and social paradigms in the past few years. The social network model helps the study of the community behavior and thus leverages social networks to researchers' demands.

Social networks in most works are treated like any complex network with modeled sociological features. The social actor is a simple node, and the relationships are simple links connecting the nodes with specific and non-specific directions. This book's contributors hypothesize that understanding the information flow, patterns, and distribution in social networks and online communities will lead to characteristic finding of the nature of those networks.

An essential characteristic of any network is its resilience to failures or attacks, or what is known as the robustness of a network. The definition of a robust network is rather debatable. One interpretation of a robust network assumes that social links connecting people together can experience dynamic changes, as is the case with many friendship networks such as Facebook, Hi5, et cetera. Individuals can easily delete a friend or add a new one, with and without constraints. Other networks, however, have rigid links that are not allowed to experience changes with time such in strong family networks. Hence, it is vital to find a quantitative measure of a networks' robustness.

This book is designed for professionals, researchers, and graduate students working in the field of social networks, both from theoretical and practical point of views. The book will also provide insights to the executives responsible for understanding the technology and utilizing it to have a positive impact on their business.

The audience for the book include, but are not limited to researchers, computer scientists, physicists, chemists, sociologists, computer network designers, chatters, bloggers, social networkers, web developers, and people and enterprises involved in marketing/advertising using the internet and mobile systems.

Chapter 1, "*Social Networks and Communities: From Traditional Society to the Virtual Sphere*," describes the different meaning and operational definitions that the concept of community covered in Social Network Analysis. The aim is to introduce the readers to a critical view of the use of the concept of community in social network analysis and in particular to the study of complex interaction environments, such as Internet and mobile media. The development of the field of network analysis is described by means of case studies and scholarly examples from various fields of empirical network research (political science, communication sciences and technology studies). In particular, the chapter explores the research process that evolved from the first ethnographic studies of social groups, and proceeds to exploration of new forms of interaction in online and computer mediated environments.

Chapter 2, "*Network Perspective on Structures Related to Communities*." The application of network perspectives to communities requires some appreciation of the variety of ways people are now writing about communities. From the 1940s well into the 1960s the local community was the recognized social unit that sociologists and anthropologists studied. People who write about communities nowadays are using terms in a wide variety of ways. The "little communities" that anthropologist Robert Redfield (1960) wrote about fifty years ago have very little in common with the present-day "community of nations, the community of Jamaica Plain, the gay community, the IBM community, the Catholic Community, the Yale Community, the African American community, the 'virtual' community of cyberspace," all mentioned by Robert Putnam (2000). In the decade since Putnam, electronic connections have expanded logarithmically in both number and speed, and the community problem is even more vexing.

In chapter 3, "*Civic Engagement and Communication Technology Networks*," individuals address public issues by becoming involved with civic groups and performing civic activities such as charity and political work. Changes in communication technology have led to changes in civic engagement, and it is now possible to perform civic activities digitally. Actors develop social networks as they use various communication technologies, and the resultant networks act as passive constraints on individual activities. This chapter investigated face-to-face, telephone, email, private electronic, and public electronic communication networks. Private electronic communication networks develop through text messaging, instant messaging, and private chat, and public electronic communication networks emerge through the exchange of messages over blogs, social network sites, and Twitter.

Chapter 4, "*The Social Construction of New Cultural Models through Information and Communication Technologies*," contains a theoretical reflection on the meaning of the new forms of social relations in this ICT-based culture, as well as on the need to define new analytical tools to enable an adequate interpretation of this new cultural context within the framework of globalization and digitalization. The work analyzes the cultural significance of the new concept of cyberculture and the new socio-cultural concepts regarding to ICTs.

Chapter 5, "*From Virtual to the Simulated World: An Agent-Based Model of Friendship Network in Second Life*." A prototype agent-based model of the friendship network in Second Life is presented. Second Life is a 3D virtual world that allows users to engage in various social activities, meet friends, form communities, attend events of interests, and trade online with other users represented through their virtual 3D avatars. For social and behavioral scientists, this provides an opportunity to investigate the dynamics of social interaction and formation of interpersonal and group affiliation ties. Initial results from the model concerning friendship ties are reported.

Chapter 6 is titled *"Analysis of Success Factors in Social Networking Website Development."* The popularity and rapid growth of social networking Websites is undeniable. Unfortunately, it is hard to guarantee the success and sustainability of these Websites. This chapter focuses on identifying the key success factors for each phase in agile iteration development for social networking Websites. Qualitative and quantitative analysis were adopted using Web analytical tools to gather and measure these success factors. This chapter will benefit Website designers and developers by suggesting the success factors for each agile iteration development phase.

Chapter 7, *"Knowledge Discovery from Online Communities,"* overviews the most notable research trends and application systems concerning data mining and knowledge discovery from user-generated content. It first introduces the most popular social media features. This chapter also overviews the most appealing approaches to social network analysis and user behavior modeling. Finally, it categorizes and thoroughly describes the state-of-the-art data mining algorithms and tools oriented to knowledge discovery from online communities. A particular attention is focused on semantic knowledge inference and automatic understanding of the user-generated content.

Chapter 8, *"Information Diffusion in Social Networks,"* provides an overview of information and innovation diffusion in scale-free, small-world social networks. The material is suitable for network science specialists, as well as for interested professionals in the fields of Sociology, Psychology, and Marketing. Both static and dynamic aspects are discussed, as well as message taxonomies. The text addresses the role and the strategic position of influential spreaders of information; the pathways in the social networks that serve as conduits for communication and information flow; mathematical models describing proliferation processes; short-term and long-term dynamics of information diffusion, and secrecy of information diffusion.

Chapter 9, *"Social Network, Information Flow and Decision-Making Efficiency: A Comparison of Humans and Animals."* In animals, including humans, group or community members not only have to take decisions satisfying the majority of individuals (i.e. decision accuracy), but also have a relatively short period to do so (i.e. decision speed). The decision efficiency will vary according to the way individuals are inter-connected, namely according to the social network. However, the traditional approach used in management and decision sciences has been revealed to be insufficient to fully explain decision-making efficiency. This chapter addresses the question of how social network may enhance collective decision-making by increasing both the accuracy and the speed of decisions.

Chapter 10 is titled *"Extracting and Measuring Relationship Strength in Social Networks."* The growth of the Internet and online communities has led to increasing importance for understanding the social network structure of communities and the relationships between members. The mapping from online communications and behaviors to relationships should identify valid relationships so that the structural properties of the resulting social network are stable in the face of incomplete or inaccurate data. This chapter shows how slight variations in data processing steps for identifying relationships can lead to very different networks. It considers a number of design choices and the network structure variability they introduce and measures its effectiveness in performance on a prediction task.

Chapter 11, *"Bringing Qualitative and Quantitative Data Together: Collecting Network Data With the Help of the Software Tool VennMaker,"* describes the gathering of network data by means of both qualitative and quantitative methodologies. An overview of the important visual approaches (e.g. network pictures and network maps) is given. Following, an example of a migration-network study was investigated with the aid of the software program VennMaker. Finally, the advantages and disadvantages of data collection based on digital network maps are discussed.

Chapter 12 is *"Observing the Evolution of a Learning Community using Social Network Analysis."* This chapter proposes an empirical correlation between the stages of development of a learning community and a set of social network metrics. Social Network Analysis was applied to observe a learning community built around a Master's Program in an Italian University. It was found that the evolution of social network metrics - such as Density, Betweenness Centrality, Contribution Index, Core/Periphery Structure – matched the formal stages of community development, with a clear identification of forming, norming, and storming phases.

Chapter 13 is *"Social Networks and Terrorism."* This chapter explains how international terror networks, consisting of individuals and organizations spanning countries and continents, form and evolve. Terrorism is violence committed by groups with political goals, targeted against civilians, and intended to create fear in a population. Social network analysis, which uses visual and matrix algebra methods to study such networks, can help counterterrorist organizations to detect, disrupt, and dismantle terrorist groups.

Chapter 14 is titled *"Social Network Sites: Modeling the New Business-Customer Relationship."* This chapter focuses on the new facets of the relationship between customers and businesses and analyses the important role that Social Network Sites (SNSs) can play in its strengthening. The era of Web 2.0 has empowered consumers, by amplifying their voices and providing them with venues for information search and sharing. SNSs represent one of the most successful examples of social technology and since the business sector needs to adapt to customers' changing profile and behaviour, SNSs have proven to be important tools in terms of upholding the business-consumer relationship. Nonetheless, their primordial social and informal nature recommends thoroughness in order to maximise their potential, while avoiding their perils.

Chapter 15 is called*"Community Structure Extraction for Social Networks."* This chapter applied two graph partition approaches to extract community structures from social networks. The spectral approach is based on the minimization of balanced cut and its resulting solution comes from the spectral decomposition of the graph Laplacian. The modularity-based approach is based on the maximization of modularity and implemented in a hierarchical fashion. The method is able to extract useful information from the community structure, such as what is the most influential component in a given community. This information can be used to improve marketing efficiency by customized advertisement. Network visualization and navigation can also benefit from the community structural information.

Chapter 16 is titled *"Towards a Bespoke Framework for Eliciting Consumer Satisfaction in Second Life."* This chapter focuses on the development of a framework for eliciting consumer satisfaction perceptions in the context of the social virtual world Second Life. An introduction to Second Life is followed by an overview of the relevant literature. The framework and the inter-related component parts that it is made up from are then described in detail. This is followed by an evaluation of the framework through semi-structured in-world interviews as well as the refinement of the framework as a consequence of our evaluation. Finally, an overview of how the framework can be used by others is given along with the wider context of its use.

Chapter 17 is *"Finding Similar Users in Facebook."* A crucial aspect in the analysis of Online Social Networks is to determine whether two users of the network can be considered similar, or not. This reflects in several interesting applications, such as the possibility of finding social aggregations or targeting commercial promotions with proficiency. This chapter provides an approach to estimate the similarity among users of a network using information about their social ties and the analysis of their activities. It draws several local measures of similarity considering different indicators, and combines them obtaining a global measure of similarity by applying metrics introduced in Social Sciences combined with techniques as the linear regression.

Social networks and online communities are complex networks with minimal sociological features modeled. The objective of this work is to provide a clear and consolidated view of current online communities and social networks' models and their accuracy in representing real life social networks. This book seeks to explore the new methods to model, characterize, and build such networks and communities. The book addresses the need to explore the critical issues (cultural, security, threats, legal, and technical) confronting social networking, the emergence of new mobile social networking devices and applications, and how social networks impact the business aspects of organizations. Network robustness is also a vital property that needs to be addressed.

The concepts, models, and algorithms outlined in the book would provide useful information about social behavior and how well the network is connected. It would analyze how social networks and online communities can disseminate information in the existing networks. Contributors hypothesize that understanding the patterns of information distribution in the network will lead to characteristic finding of the nature of those networks, the capacity of this social network to store information, and accurately study the state of the network using information equilibrium.

*Maytham Safar*
*Kuwait University, Kuwait*

*Khaled A. Mahdi*
*Kuwait University, Kuwait*

# Acknowledgment

The work presented in this book could not have been possible without the guidance and support of many people. First, and foremost, I would like to acknowledge and thank the help of my co-editor, Dr. Khaled Mahdi, who has provided me with substantial assistance. He helped me in taking the opportunity of pursuing this work and directing my efforts to complete it. I wish to thank our Assistant Development Editor, Mike Killian, at IGI Global Publisher, for his confidence and patience in working with us on the project.

We are gratefully thankful for the authors of these book chapters and all the reviewers. They have paved the way to produce such a book with their continuous support, patience, and endless efforts to help finishing the writing of the content of the book and meeting all the milestones and deadlines.

Last, but not least, I would like to thank my Synergy Research Group (http://synergy.ku.edu.kw) faculty members, students, external collaborators, and alumnus for their encouragement, support, and faith in our abilities to accomplish anything we set out to do. Would also like to thank them for being a source of motivation and encouragement.

*Maytham Safar*
*Kuwait University, Kuwait*

*Khaled A. Mahdi*
*Kuwait University, Kuwait*

# Section 1
# Social Networks and Communities

*Different meanings and definitions of offline and online communities are found in social network analysis. This section aims to demonstrate the intrinsic capability of communication technologies enabled through the Internet and mobile applications in the form of exchange of messages over SMS, emails, blogs, and social network sites. It emphasizes those technologies' expansion in both speed and number in the creation of virtual online social networks and communities as opposed to the traditional local/nation civic communities and social groups that are usually created by traditional forms of communications; face-to-face, telephone, or mail.*

# Chapter 1
# Social Networks and Communities:
## From Traditional Society to the Virtual Sphere

**Francesca Odella**
*University of Trento, Italy*

## ABSTRACT

*The concept of community has been used in social sciences to describe several types of relatively stable relations among individuals, in a variety of contexts, from small rural villages to metropolitan and multicultural cities and for different forms of interaction from economic exchanges to leisure and political expression. Emerging outcomes of communitarian relations such as cohesion and cooperation, exchange of resources and communication efficiency have fostered and stimulated theory advancements and investigation of these relational contexts. The following chapter focuses on the concept of community in social network studies and describes the main theoretical approaches and research strategies adopted by network analysts to study social groupings. The review surveys classical network studies and the theoretical debate that involved the concept of community during the last century, exploring the perspective of contemporary research on communities. The theoretical implications of the study of communitarian relations and social participation will be addressed describing main community detection strategies and the debate on social capital. The third section of the chapter depicts network studies that deal with the social impact of new forms of societal communication and special types of communities in the virtual world. In the conclusions, the text outlines the challenges that social research on virtual and natural communities is expected to face in the next decade. The complete list of references is provided at the end of the chapter.*

DOI: 10.4018/978-1-61350-444-4.ch001

## DEFINING COMMUNITIES: NETWORKS AND PERSONAL CONNECTIONS

The use of the concept of community is at the origin of social network analysis, with the first empirical studies carried on by sociologists and anthropologists in European and non-European contexts. The original framework for community theory dates back to the theory of German sociologist F. Tonnies (1887), who interpreted the rise of the modern industrial civilization in old traditional European societies as the juxtaposition of Gesellshaft to Gemeinshaft, with public associations taking the place of community bonds.' *In classical sociology the concept of community'*, as Piselli (2007) synthesizes, *'referred to significant social relations that involved the individual as a whole. These solidarity relations based on kinship and common residence, a shared mode of feeling, and a spontaneous willingness to cooperate.'* (2007: 867).

The first network studies to adopt this idea of community were carried on by British social anthropologists (the so called Manchester Group) in the fifties and sixties of last century; researchers analyzed the social and political changes that were transforming African and Asian countries (Rhodesia/Zambia and Malawi, India) and related them to modification of relations among tribal members in terms of solidarity and kinship bonds induced by urbanization and new economic activities. However, the first formal systematization of network perspective was provided in the studies by researchers John Barnes (1954) and Elizabeth Bott (1955) on European traditional communities. Barnes's study of a small Norwegian fishery town highlighted the presence of personal links among the inhabitants that could not be summarized by localization (neighbourhood) or economic relations. According to Barnes, informal relations among members of the community, partially related to kinship or family, reproduce a class structure; a 'hidden' class structure that in an egalitarian culture like the one of Norway would not have been visible on the bases of observations limited to economic or territorial relations. Subsequent studies of English working class families by Elizabeth Bott (1971) extended the concept of community reconstructing the personal relations of couples beyond the urban and social class boundaries, and relating their networks with family organization. The researches of Barnes and Bott put in evidence that people tended to connect and share immaterial and material resources (mutual help and support, friendship, pastimes) with others that were similar in terms of income and lifestyle preferences (a social propensity defined as homofily). These relatively stable sets of personal relations constituted a community; the same relations were also the bases for coordination in collective actions and decision-making, either in village, kin or family organization.

Since the first anthropological studies, network analysts developed specific techniques and original procedures to collect, analyze and describe significant relations among members of a community. In the study of Bott, for example, the principal indicators for community detection where size and density of contacts in personal networks and the percentage of restricted or large family members included in the individual circle, obtained by face to face interviews. According to this early theoretical perspective a community is identified by the presence of two main types of relations: social support (economic or information resources) and emotional or affective support. Other indicators, such as the presence of individuals' multiple relations (multiplexity), and the rate of differences among members of the same community (heterogeneity) in terms of social rank, education, ethnical provenience, linguistic group or residence, were introduced in subsequent researches (Thompson, 1973).

Following researches described thus communities through the contents of members' networks (types, frequency and intensity of personal relationships), and in terms of resources and communication sharing with other groups, or internally. Most of these studies contributed to discuss sociological theories relating the decline of solidarity relations to modernization processes and changes in the structure of the family. The network oriented survey carried on by Fisher (1977; 1982) at the end of the seventies, among new urbanized population in northern California Bay area is an example of how enquiry of communities can give support for new theories about socialization and social change.

The enquiry of Fisher compared the relationships of new urban population to the ones of individuals living in small towns and put in evidence that the opportunities provided by large urban centres in terms of personal relationships were equal, if not more satisfactory, than those in small communities. Networks of urbanites displayed the presence of closed friends' groups with similar interests and lifestyle preferences (or homophile bonds), but also more variety in acquaintances and friends (in terms of attributes such as ethnicity, age and gender). The structure of the personal contacts of urbanites was qualitatively different from the one of those living in rural or small urban areas and according to Fisher urban environment was not deprived of socializing opportunities, as personal relations could be emotionally intense and socially relevant also outside the kinship circle. The typical process of network formation in new urban settings was influenced by education, gender and social class position of the individual, as well as in small urban areas. Other personal characteristics (such as profession and ethnic origin), however, implied large differences for social participation and inclusion in the newly formed local community (Fisher, 1982). The author concluded that reciprocal influence of social structure and spatial location and their interaction with the presence of ethnic diversities in a densely populated area such as metropolitan areas, had not generated a single multiethnic community, but a denser ethnicity based '*constellation of communities*'.

The acknowledgement that communities had been changing since the early studies was relevant for the evolution of network studies because the concept acquired new meaning; new methodological instruments were also designed for exploring different dimensions of social interaction (ex. study of professional and linguistic groups, associative and 'elective' bonds communities). During the seventies, in particular, the theoretic definition of the concept of community itself was subject to interdisciplinary debates, revised and declined in the plural form of communities, to signify the variety that communitarian relationships can assume in different cultures and societal contexts, such as politics and work.

A particular critique was addressed to those scholars that interpreted as communitarian social relations exclusively those which were organised according to social and demographic attributes of subjects such as ethnic origins, age, gender and geographical location. This attitude produced, according to some authors (Wellman, 1999; Piselli, 2007), a space-localized conception of community, where neighbourhood and other spatial attributes (block, district) are considered as central issues for defining community boundaries. According to these critics' societal global changes such as cross-national migration, internationalization of economic and production aspects, secularization and new cultural values were gradually modifying collective experiences of individuals and transforming their aggregative bonds. Results from studies of personal connections through time and in non-Western countries confirmed the criticizing (Schweitzer et al., 1998; Bastani, 2007; Grossetti, 2007).

Among the few studies that analyzed the time-related changes of kinship and friendship relations is the follow-up study of a Canadian community carried out by Barry Wellman's group (Wellman, 1979; Wellman et al., 1997). Starting originally at the beginning of the sixties, the extensive project of Wellman analyzed the personal relationships of a Canadian community for over thirty years and collected personal network data on long-term relationships. At the end of the eighties the project was also improved in its content, involving an extensive research activity on the impact of technological innovation (use of PC, Internet and new forms of territorial mobility) on community and personal bonds (Wellman et al., 1996). Comparing the results of surveys of personal relations in the eighties and in the nineties, Wellman and his collaborators analyzed how time and life events affect the dimensions and structure of personal networks. The results showed that the composition of the personal network and the level of intimacy with kinship changes dramatically with aging and changes in family bonds (Wellman et al., 1997). *'Just as in biological evolution* - observed Wellman - *personal community networks may experience gradual mutation that is punctuated by intense rapid shifts.(..) changes reflect combination of adaptation to outside circumstances, random variations, evolutionary differentiation, and normal wear-and-tear.'* (Wellman, 1997: 47).

A space-based definition of community is consequently not fitted for contemporary social environments where personal relations could be expanded in distance by communication media, and some resources obtained by means of institutionalized channels (social services, personal services on demand). Authors define thus contemporary personal communities as characterised by *'a mode of relating in dense, multiplex and relatively autonomous networks for social relations'* (Caulhon, 1998: 391). This description includes a variety of social bonds, from family, neighbours and friends to members of associations and participation networks (virtual communities), and includes individual interactions that are based purely on cultural and activity interests (online groups). In the following paragraphs, these new forms of communitarian bonds and the main methodological innovations in network analysis research (detection techniques and indexes) will be explored and connected with a notable debate

in the social sciences, involving social capital and social participation.

## THE DEBATE ON COMMUNITIES SURVIVAL

Several theories concerning the social evolution of Western societies and the impact of changes in social and family structure, question the survival of traditional forms of communitarian experience. The debate on 'community survival' dates back to the sixties and seventies of the last century when increasing loosening of family relationships and residential mobility in the United State were interpreted as causes for a progressive decrease in social support to the nuclear family and a diminishing interest in social participation. The terms of the debate are well synthesized by the query *'community lost, restored or liberated?'* which puts in evidence the three main assumptions concerning community that were presented in the sociological literature (Wellman et al., 1997; 1999; Henning, 2007). According to the theorist of the 'community lost' thesis, the bonding and solidarity relations that hold together individuals in traditional societies were disappearing and western societies were evolving towards individualistic and interest-based forms of associations.

The theorists of the 'community restored' thesis, instead, described the formation of communitarian contexts on the bases of different principles from the past and were more positive about the impact of industrial and economic factors in the family and collective sphere. Network research on communities propose a new perspective, the 'community liberated' one, which foresee the modification of old bonding relations and the emergence of new forms of solidarity and identity sharing as effects of increasing opportunities to move and communicate across geographical and generational distances. According to Wellman (1999) contemporary communities are 'liberated' from old ascribed forms of association (family, neighbourhood, class), and offer to individuals innovative opportunities of meeting, connecting and exchanging resources across circles of different social composition (friends, associates and other types of connections). Some factors such as increased residential mobility; new communication opportunities and changes in family structure have multiplied the forms of communitarian experiences that individuals could experiment in their life course. Since the boundaries that define the members of a community, are sometimes not clearly defined by effect of geographical dispersion, political transition, and diversity in cultural frameworks, networks of personal relations are also becoming more individual-centred and less dependent on traditional socializing contexts (family or kin, where the individual is one of the subjects). Therefore, the analysis of communitarian relations is transformed into the study of 'personal communities', where individuals are considered as active members of multiple and diverse socializing experiences (Wellman, 1988; 2007).

Support for the perspective of personal communities was provided by the study of migration biographies of individuals and families, where personal relationships link people across space and time. When an individual moves to a new urban setting or to a new country, the ethnic community frequently provides access to practical resources such as employment, temporary work and housing provisions, and emotional support. Studies of migrant communities put also in evidence the duplicity that characterizes family or ethnic networks, as the ties to family and friends can also represent both a chain of opportunities or a network of exploitation, preventing successful integration in the new country (Grieco, 1982; Cranford, 2005).

Specifically, empirical studies on migration chains reinforced the idea that the enquiry of personal networks can provide clues on large-scale phenomena, such as social selective processes (ethnic and gender discrimination, elite formation and occupational mobility) and diffusion processes (cultural and values change, political mobilization). An interesting theoretical result, for example, is found in the study of Schweizer and colleagues (Schweizer et al., 1998), which at the end of the nineties replicated Fisher's enquiry (1973), comparing Hispanic and Anglo-Saxon communities in a new residential area in southern California. The results of the survey of personal networks showed that over 40% of the relations reported by respondents were kinship type, in both ethnic groups. Cultural differences among Hispanics and Anglo-Saxons explained only the different social roles that are attributed to members of networks (which typically vary according to occupational and marital status of respondents) and not the composition of personal communities. As the researchers concluded the two groups were living mostly in '*ethnically segregated social worlds*' (Schweizer et al., 1998:17) and both were fully integrated in the large metropolitan area. The social organization of personal networks is thus becoming more complex than the traditional framework of community studies had foreseen, with the appearance of a 'fragmentation effect' that makes possible in contemporary communities the co-existence of old and new forms of solidarity bonds, creating transversal forms of differentiation along the axes of family and social class.

In conclusion, the theoretical shift towards the study of personal communities induced a change in network analysis research practice and its results were effective in two main areas.

- First, the analysis of personal networks provided support for theoretical hypothesis concerning the relationship between micro level social interactions (those that mostly occur in communities) and collective by-products, such as trust, group identity and social capital. Since communities have a fundamental role in mobilizing social resources, as well as in diffusing political values and civic participation, scholars of collective action frequently study the network of connections of political actors (parties, movements, lobbies, and other organizations). Analyzing the composition of the network and their capacity to use communitarian resources (social support, personal contacts, information diffusion and fundraising and so on) has thus become a promising research strategy in political and historical research for reconstructing the political role of grassroots organizations and groups (Knocke, 1990; Diani, 2009).

- Second, studies focused on personal networks were a spring to researchers to improve the quality of network analysis data collection (either via interviews or questionnaires) with specialized techniques and expert software, and to perform comparative studies. Methodological improvements in sampling and data collection have been experimented in large surveys to study social capital and social inclusion (Flap and Volker, 2004), applying refined techniques for collecting information about the social position of an individual in her social life (intensity, type and characteristics of personal connections) and put them in relation to the type of resources that are exchanged with other community members (Lin et al. 2008). Studies of local entrepreneurship networks, also, offered an opportunity to investigate how specific social mechanisms, and in particular those that favoured the diffusion of successful economic practices, operate through communitarian bonds (Portes and Sensenbrenner, 1993).

## SOCIAL CAPITAL AND SOCIAL PARTICIPATION IN COMMUNITIES

Since the eighties, the progressive urbanization and change of daily life organization in the US and most West European countries together with the progressive modification of family and generational relationships, favoured a loosening of traditional cohesive values (among them religious and political affiliation) and a crisis of democratic institutions in the European and American communities. Sociologists and political science scholars interpreted these phenomena as a result of the rise of market-type relations in the private sphere, with the deterioration of intense social relations and a diminishing relevance of solidarity and communitarian bonds in advanced economies. To describe this global social effect they spoke of a crisis of 'social capital', as a synthetic expression for describing the presence of solidarity type relations (social support) that embrace members of a community, as well as collective subjects (associations, groups) and institutions that promote communication, egalitarian instances and mutual societal support (Putnam, 1993).

The study of social capital gave rise to a great intensification of studies on communities and community- like forms of relations (from social support to political participation), and in different contexts of economic development from capitalist to post-socialist and semi-planned economies (Dasgupta and Seralgeldin, 1999). In particular, the combination of the more 'classical' theoretical framework on social capital, the one consistent to the theories of established sociologists as James Coleman (1988) and Pierre Bourdieu (1986), with the methodology of social support network researchers such as Nan Lin (2001), kicked off projects on the creation of social capital in communities. Studies analysed the problem of civic culture in small rural and large metropolitan settlements, highlighting the role played by community bonds in establishing positive feedback and trustful expectations about the collective use of individual and family social capital. Social capital research on informal work and ethnic entrepreneurship in urban settings, in fact describe communitarian bonds as a mix of reciprocity obligations and trust, which can provide access to social and economic resources that favours business opportunities and upward mobility, as well as a mechanism that tend to reproduce inequalities inside closed communities (Grieco, 1982; Portes, 1998, Lin, 2001). To depict these social mechanisms network analysts developed dimensional and structural measures of social capital and clarified the variety of effects that intense, interconnected and selective social links can produce in the social sphere from egalitarian and solidaristic to mafia-type and discriminatory bonds (Portes and Sensenbrenner, 1993).

Specifically, comparative methodological designs and large-scale surveys for collecting data concerning personal contacts were suggested as strategies to measure social capital and detect its formation in different organizational context. The opportunity for social capital scholars to analyze the dynamics of exchange for social resources is offered, in particular, by the study of new residential areas, ethnic sub-groups and other local communities developed in the last twenty years in most European countries as result of migration and social mobility. The enquires based on the Survey of the Social Networks of the Dutch population (Flapp and Volker, 2004) and correlated case studies in social housing (Pinkster and Volker, 2009), for example, focused on measurement of the degree to which social resources are provided though local relationships. Similar interest for the participatory elements of social capital are to be found in studies concerning groups' involvement in civil society, from ethnic and political associations to grassroots activism (Fenneman and Tillie, 2001). Indentifying the connections between identity and social participation in communitarian and institutional contexts (parties, civil society organizations, cultural associations) becomes thus a primary goal also for political scholars and all those interested in the formation of collective movements (Knoke, 1990; Diani, 2009).

As a result of societal and economic changes in the last decade the orientation of most recent social capital enquiries is evolving, while indicators connected to institutional dimensions of social action (such as associative membership, adhesion to collective protests, interest's coalitions and lobbying) and traditional forms of economic and social mobilization (such as parties, trade unions and organized political participation) are reducing their theoretical significance. In particular, the fast transformation of personal communications and socializing agents (family, education systems) is shifting attention to new forms of connectedness among individuals that are based on information technologies and new forms of social mobilization, with implications in the participatory and relational spheres.

## DESCRIBING COMMUNITIES: MEASUREMENT AND RESEARCH APPROACHES

Since the early network studies on communities, researchers revised the terms for describing forms of grouping and clustering of individuals; specifically, the critical aspect from the methodological point of view was how to approach the differences between the type of connections that tie community members. Other than the difference between kin and non-kin members in fact, empirical studies illustrated that communitarian relations could originate from different types of social relations. Communities are based on various types of connections: those that are 'visible' in terms of stable and culturally defined relationships (typically kin relations, such as family bonds), and those that are based on occasional and elective bonds between individuals (acquaintances, friends, mediators, associates). Traditional communities are based mostly on the first type of connections, while social interaction in modern societies involves both types of relations, generating individual networks with multiple connections.

Early network analysts detected communitarian relations analyzing the number and the composition of the personal circles of community members, and looked for the presence of sub-groups *(clicques)* or the extension of personal connections outside the neighbourhood or the local dimension. Barnes (1954), for example, in order to understand the meaning of social class in a small Norwegian fishing village conjugated relational data on land property, economic and associative relations of the residents. The relations among members of the community, as Barnes reported, were organized on the bases of three '*social fields*' or grouping principles. The first was related to territorial belonging that structured administrative aspects such as child education, church attendance and other forms of social participation; the second grouping principle related members of the community across economic activities and industrial production (fishing vessels, factories for fish products and other activities collateral to fishing). The third grouping principle was based on kinship relations, friends or acquaintances that happen to have similar status and preferences in lifestyle. Barnes indentified in this third circle of personal and informal ties the class system of the village; according to his interpretation '*this network runs across the whole society and does not stop at the village boundary', and has no clear –cut internal division'* (Barnes, 1954:237).

Following the model of Barnes other researchers observed and registered an ulterior differentiation between those 'formal relations' that constitute social institutions, such as a family, organizations or professional groups; and the 'informal relations' that originate from neighbourhood, personal contacts, encounters. These grouping criteria have been adopted for detecting relevant forms of social groupings, such as political participation (Laumann and Pappi, 1976), voluntary associations (Knocke, 1988) and immigrants economy (Adler Lomnitz, 1988) and integrated in further network community studies. One of the clearest example of a research framework designed for detecting community networks that explores both the dimensions of formal/informal and kinship/associative relations is provided in the works of Wellman. According to his theoretical perspective differences in content and structure of a personal network are expressive not only

of individual traits or preferences, but can be considered as indicators for social organization of a community. Consequently, in his researches he used individual network structure indicators (intensity and frequency of relations, extension of personal connections though time and geographical location, weak and strong connections) and content of relations' indicators (type of personal relations, role of connections in personal networks) to summarize the multiplicity and multidimensionality of human relations. The application of this method to personal ties produced a typology of communitarian relations applied for comparative research in both real and virtual communities (Wellman, 1999), and European and non-European countries (Bastani, 2007; Grossetti, 2007).

Since the application of graph theory to sociometrics in the late sixties, the contribution of network analysts to the creation of indicators for the presence of communitarian bonds has been constant, involving an increasing investment in algorithms modelling and theoretical innovation (Alba, 1981; Knoke and Rogers, 1979; Galaskiewicz, 1979). This advancement, however, has not been easy and theorists and researchers frequently found themselves on opposite sides when aspects related to connectivity in groups (such as social cohesion, but also information flow) had to be systematized in formal models of social structure based either on informal relations (personal contacts), or formal ones (grouping on the bases of social characteristics). Differences in data collection techniques, in fact, prevented for a long time a complete integration of methodological perspectives that deal with personal and social networks and the merging of indexes and measurement procedures.

In general, the main differentiation in network community studies has been between enquiries that were based on ego-centred networks (each network corresponds to a subject, a community member), and those surveying the complete network (where the network corresponds to the whole community or members of a specific group, selected on the bases of specific criteria). With the first type of enquires (ego-centred studies) it was possible to 'create' the relational circle of the members of a personal community and subsequently compare the individual networks in terms of properties (size, % of kin members, density, % of co-workers, etc.), but it was difficult to visualize the structure of the whole community for issues such as power or information flow. The second type of enquiry (complete network), instead, was suitable for highlighting roles and differentiates among members of a community (*cliques*) in terms of influence, power or other hierarchical properties. The disadvantage of this research method is its limitation to 'closed' social environments, where members share characteristics such as residential area, organizational or associative affiliation; homophile relations that are commonly an expression of a communitarian bond were thus pre-selected by the research design.

Integration of methodological prospective in network studies is not common, but special data collection procedures such as small world and snowball sampling may favour an approach that takes in count both the micro (personal ties) and the macro (aggregate of ties in groups and communities) dimensions of connections (Wasserman and Faust, 1993; Snjiders at al., 1995). In the last decade research designs of large-scale surveys concerning personal contacts, such as social capital studies, also contributed to innovate data collection and to combine different strategies of investigation. Indicators and strategies for detecting relevant relations among the respondent (Ego) and the alleged members of a community (Alters), for example, can vary depending of the aim of the research (Van Der Gaag and Snjiders, 2003), focusing on social capital that derives from personal contacts (name generator approach), acquaintances (position generator approach), or instruments (resource generator approach).

## NETWORK TYPES: AN EXAMPLE OF INTEGRATION IN DATA COLLECTION

In the case of special data collection techniques (such as snowball design and territorial survey), the comparison of the two types of networks concerning individual community members and community structure could be facilitated. In Figure 1, for example, the senior population of a neighbourhood is represented as a complete network: the connections of nodes illustrating relations, from acquaintances to further levels of intimacy, among the subjects that share a localized social space. The network in Figure 1 is derived from the questionnaires filled in by the elders, asked to cite the persons living in the same block that he/she knows personally. Since these space-limited connections are considered not exhaustive of the real personal circle of contacts, the subjects were also personally interviewed, providing detailed information about the persons they receive help from in daily activities. As a result Figure 2 depicts the support exchange relations of Subject N.1 as an individual network (ego-network). Her personal network includes those individuals that provide daily support, like relatives and friends that do not live in the same neighbourhood, as well as some subjects living in the same neighbourhood that are reported also in Figure 1. We can see that despite her central position in the neighbourhood network (Figure 1), Subject N.1 receives most of the practical help for her daily activities from relatives (strong ties) and friends that do not live in the same area (weak ties), having similar social characteristics (gender and age). The combination of the two networks is an example of nested connectivity, showing how Subject N.1 is linked through Subject N. 41(described as friend_m1 in Figure 2) to a larger group of other old people (clicque). The bridging relation between Subject N.1 and Subject N. 41 increases the formers' opportunity to participate to community life and share socializing activities with other people alike.

*Figure 1. Network of friends among old people living in block Alfa - (blue/red= male/female). The shape of the nodes represents age (square/ circle = more/less than 65 years old; triangle= under 45 years old).* © *[2011 - Odella –licensed under CC –BY ND].*

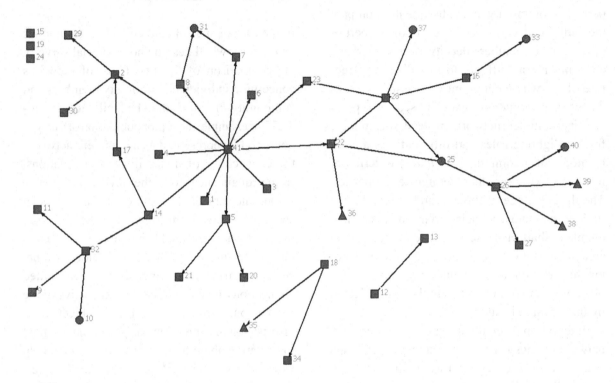

The integration of relational data in measurement issues has been, also, complicated by the fact that nodes (subjects) with multiple affiliations have special properties that make standardized index interpretation more difficult. Moreover, studies that deal with informal relations (such as social support or economic networks) frequently make use of indexes purposely created for the survey, to put in evidence those aspects of multiplexity relations that are of interest for the research (Wellman, 1979; Fisher, 1982; Grossetti, 2007; Bellotti, 2008). The theoretical systematization of network relationships, and a partial solution of the problem concerning multiplexity in personal connections were first solved by the contribution of Granovetter (1973), which shed light on social implications of positional roles of individuals in a network. His theory was also

relevant to bridging the distance that had been growing in community studies among approaches (mistakenly identified as qualitative and quantitative research) centred on individual personal networks and approaches centred on formal community groupings.

Two areas of research, specifically, have contribute to the advancement of methods and theory applicable to community network studies; first, the problem of the differentiation among the type of relations in networks or multiplexity problem and second, the implications of hierarchical techniques for identifying community relations within large networks, such as organizational connections, personal communications and online interactions.

*Figure 2. Personal contacts of Subject N.1: Support network for daily activities (Size of node = strength of support). © [2011 - Odella –licensed under CC –BY ND].*

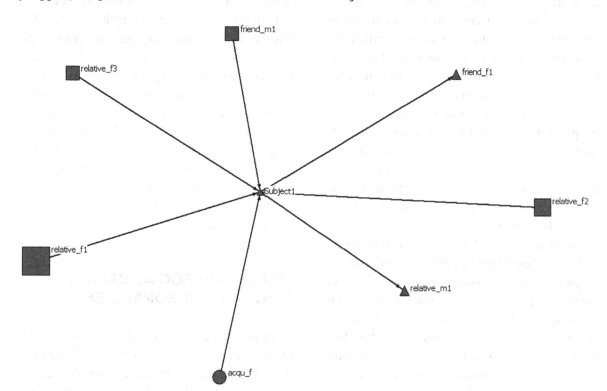

## WEAK AND STRONG TIES AND COMMUNITY BONDS

The difference of personal relations in terms of structural influence was the subject of Granovetter's theory of weak and strong ties: his aim was to put in relation reciprocal expectation in dyadic relations to the creation of common goods and trust in communities. According to Granovetters' perspective, not only the personal network of an individual involved in a communitarian setting has a specific composition, but also the web of relations that link the members of the community show a distinct pattern. Strong ties between two subjects imply a certain amount of homofily and an emotional intensity; when the flow of information is to be considered, however, relationships that are based on strong ties (for example kinship or family relations) are less efficient than

weak ties. A weak tie, characterized by a lesser degree of emotional intensity and homofily, instead, can act as a bridge between the subject and other subjects which are not directly part of her personal network. As Granovetter stated: *'Intuitively speaking, this means that whatever is to be diffused can reach a larger number of people, and traverse greater social distance (i.e., path length), when passed through weak ties rather than strong ones. If one tells a rumour to all his close friends, and they do likewise, many will hear the rumour a second and third time, since those linked by strong ties tend to share friends. If the motivation to spread the rumour is dampened a bit on each wave of retelling, then the rumour moving through strong ties is much more likely to be limited to a few cliques than that going via weak ones; bridges will not be crossed'*.(Granovetter, 1973: 1364).

Since weak ties could have an impact too in terms of increasing possibilities to mobilize resources (personal connections and access to information), they become relevant when the collective dimension is considered. Moreover, the opportunities for individuals to have benefits from weak ties were quite evident in the case analyzed by Granovetter when rumours concerned the post for a job; but the fact that the benefits of social networking and weak connections are not immediately tangible or measurable may create problems when performance of public actions focused on networking is to be evaluated and designed across time.

Specifically considered, informal dimensions of resource exchange that rely on weak ties are frequently the more stable and durable in time, but more dependent on contextual elements (such as local resources, neighbourhood services or geographical location). Strong homophile ties instead reinforce social cohesion, but in the long run this prevents community renewal by confrontation with institutional policies and other social groups. A community fragmented in tightly closed *clicques* may appear more efficient in terms of social control and distribution of resources but, affirms Granovetter (1973), its survival is dependent on a complex dialectic process involving several subjects. On the contrary, weak connections among dissimilar members (for social role or status position) of the same community and between members of different communities (such as in associative affiliations) may create bridges that favour communication and participation to innovation in social practices. So, it is the openness of the informal relations of reciprocity to non-kinship bonds that assures a community success in terms of public usefulness.

Consequently, the implications of the weak ties-strong ties differentiation proposed by Granovetter are significant both from the theoretical, and the methodological point of view. His classification allows researcher to put in relations the micro structure (job seekers' personal networks) with macro-level (labour market structure), taking into account not only formalized links (connections with previous employer, colleagues and family), but also informal links (connections with friends, indirect personal contacts and acquaintances) that had contributed to personal and collective e outcomes. This change in prospective impacted subsequent comparative researches, and in particular quantitative surveys, which now include frequently network modules in their questionnaires to investigate social capital, social and occupational mobility and more in general micro and macro dimensions of community connectedness (McPherson, et al., 1992).

## MEASURING SOCIAL CAPITAL THROUGH PERSONAL TIES

To provide an example of how network analysis of communities can be representative of multiplicity and complexity of social relations this section describes methodologies detecting personal bonds and resource exchanges in social capital research. Several indicators of relational dimension of social capital have been proposed and adopted in empirical research on individuals (Lin et al. 2008), groups (Burt, 1987; Flap and Volker, 2004) and populations (Snijder and Van Der Gaag, 2003). Specifically, as Table 1 illustrate, social capital of the individuals can be inferred by different types of relations and personal ties of Ego (the subject), which provide access to opportunities of re-enforcing the position of the individual in the community (bonding social capital) or of crossing limits of the community (bridging social capital) to take advantage of new resources and links. Personal contacts can involve weak or strong ties with several Alters, members of the community/individuals that the subject (Ego) knows and can access to obtain specific resources (information, financial and emotional support, etc.).

A personal network, however, consists of descriptive aspects (people I know) and dynamic

*Table 1. Social capital measures in personal networks*

| Dimensions of Social Capital | Description | Indicators |
|---|---|---|
| Type of social relations | Weak ties= relation characterized by low emotional intensity, low intimacy, contingent to the context (acquaintances); Strong ties= relation with high emotional intensity, frequency of contacts and intimacy, characterized by reciprocity and time spacing (friendship). | Frequency of contacts, intensity of contacts, time of contacts (I have been knowing X *since year...*) |
| Openness/ closure of personal networks | Density of ego-network with values from 1 (maximum of closure) to zero (maximum openness). | Reciprocity of knowledge between Alters (matrix). |
| Size of personal networks | Size of network as a proxy of accessible social capital of ego. | Total number of Alters in the personal network. |
| Heterogeneity / Homogeneity of networks | Contents of the personal networks. Resources and people Ego can mobilize though personal contacts. | Status, gender, occupation of Alters. |

Source: adapted from Odella F. (2006) .

or collective aspects (how the people I know relate among them). So, the circle of Alters that develops from Ego can be constituted of individuals that mostly know each other (a closed circle). And they share similar or different characteristics in terms of socio-demographic descriptors (age, gender, ethnicity), cultural tastes or values (political and religious preferences), as well as by people that do not display these similarities (an open circle). The relative homogeneity of personal networks is related to bonding social capital, while heterogeneity is a prerequisite for bridging social capital, which favour flow of resources and information across social groups.

By means of such measures, the social capital of an individual can be compared with the one of another individual, and this procedure holds valid also for the social capital of a whole community, or groups. The research of Chiu, Hsu and Wang (2006), for example, analysed the social capital of members of a professional virtual community, by means of a detailed questionnaire that surveyed members' vision and expectations about knowledge sharing and participation in community life. Bellotti's study of single people (2008), instead, adopted social capital measures to evaluate their social integration and their capacity to re-create a community-like personal sphere in a large urban context; while Uzzi (1998), analyses the develop-

ment and success of small garment industries using social capital indicators to describe processes of mobilization of resources through small entrepreneurs' personal contacts.

## COMMUNITY DETECTION AND BLOCK MODELLING TECHNIQUES

The methodological orientation in community studies was further enhanced by theory systematizations such as the relevant distinction introduced by Burt between positional and role related strategies for identifying groups (Burt, 1978; 1987). While positional strategies use indirect and direct connections to indentify member of a group, relational or role related strategies seek patterns of similarity among subjects (nodes) of a network. This second strategy was further developed by Burt as structural equivalence and generated techniques for selecting groups of subjects that show similar profiles in terms of social distance, influence and status in very large networks (such as organizations). The two approaches highlight dimensions of social relations that are relevant for understanding the performance and the hidden structure that ties communities, being one more interested in hierarchical relations (positional strategy) and the other more focused on cohesiveness (relational strategy). The analysis of complete networks, specifically, could be carried out with either the two types of analysis depending on the perspective of the researcher; while direct comparison among strategies may not be fruitful in terms of results and easiness of calculus (Borgatta and Baker, 1981).

An example of utilizing positional strategy is the study of Koksal (2008), carried out on archival data of the Ottoman Empire (19th century). The researcher, according to a perspective that is adopted in political studies, juxtaposed the concept of community, a local based social activity, to central institutions like the state or government and analyzed the political role of two specific communities in a twenty year period. Koksal (2008) compared two administrative networks of two Turkish provinces and measured the intensity of community relations in the two provinces. She adopted multiple indicators extracted from historical archives, such as the presence of formal and collaborative relationships among local elites (such as in trade organization), interethnic cooperation for public resources (petitions to the central government for infrastructures such as roads) and indicators of social and cultural climate (public events organized by local groups). The indicators of density of connections, degree centrality and the presence of *clicques* and other positional indicators are used to support hypothesis concerning the strength and form of relations among these actors. The complete network thus synthesized these different types of relations between the state and the provinces; the final results reported that the local communities of the two provinces had a different grade of centralization and a dissimilar relationship with the national state, shading light on historical processes of economic and social evolution of the two areas.

Block modelling methods, on the contrary, are specifically suitable for highlighting the interconnectedness of organizations and to explore the flow of resources among groups in complete networks; the study of Galaskiewicz and Krohn (1984) on the service and business organizations of two middle size US towns, compared the type of influence exercised on the local communities. The blocks exemplified the connections among different types of organizations, and their availability of resources such as funds, information and political support. The researchers graduated organizations into separate categories on the bases of their intensity of activities and social intrusiveness and discover that communality of interests and values (such as religious or political affiliation) was a strong predictor of the type of involvement that organizations had in the local community. The hierarchical structure of the networks, comparing the position of the organizations in blocks, however, showed that involvement of business, institutions and voluntary associations in community life was a common pattern in both the towns, regardless of their different political and religious orientation.

Recent developments in the computational area enrich and multiply the algorithms that can be used for community detection (Lewis at al., 2008); furthermore the opportunity to investigate large datasets concerning relations in communicative dimensions (telephone calls, emails, social networking and blogging) provide new empirical fields to test explicatory theories about human relations in organizations and collective contexts. In recent studies involving the analysis of social networking sites (Adamic and Adar, 2005; Ganley and Lampe, 2009), the identification of members of a community is frequently based on multiple indicators involving the strength of the relation (frequency of contacts, type of contact and time elapse between contacts), or structural properties of the relation (betweeness, reciprocity loops), but also on so-called local properties (co-residence, similarity in educational or cultural background). An analogous interest for the network study of groupings in the physical and socio-biological sciences has stimulated the elaboration of structural typologies and strategies of community detection that could advance exploratory research on basic principles of human organization in groups (Girvan and Newman, 2002; Arenas et al., 2004; Palla et al., 2007). Several of these works, however, use methodologies that are hardly applicable outside the area of virtual communication research, requiring very large database and providing complex modelling with limited validity in the social sphere.

## COMMUNICATION AND COMMUNITIES IN THE DIGITAL SOCIETY

With the opening of the digitalized millennium the concept of community has been adopted to describe the new forms of social connectedness that take place in social networking sites and in new media (Reihgold, 1998). Communities in the communication sphere, however, appear to have a different role from the ones present in daily life and are characterized by diverse social properties; these aspects solicited scholars to originate the idea of virtual community (Rheingold, 1993), as a new form of social and emotional experience, generated by the integration of digital and tele-communication technologies in daily life.

Several studies put in evidence that virtual communities, compared to the 'natural' ones (family and neighbourhood based, or extended such as in the case of migrants) seem to replicate their patterns of relationships providing members shared identity, emotional support and access to common resources. However, it is in someway contested that they could substitute face-to-face relations and mutual friendship connections that spring from participation in socializing groups (school, fraternities, and voluntary association) and life experiences. Some authors criticize the weakness of the definition of online communities in aspects such as membership, relationships, commitment, shared values, collective goods and duration of relationships and propose new indicators more suitable for analysing virtual world relations (Castells, 1996). In the follow-

ing paragraphs the chapter concentrates on three relevant areas of research on virtual communities, to highlight the elements of continuity with recent network research and the theoretical changes induced by the social impact of digital and mobile communication technologies.

Network analysis contributed to sociological analysis of the new forms of virtual communities either in the work-related sphere, or in the personal and relational one (Wellman, Salaff et al, 1996; Hampton and Wellman, 1999 and 2001). To redefine the terms of the debate on virtual communities, the specific viewpoint of network analysis assert that social proximity that establish communitarian bonds is not limited to spatial closeness, but can arise also from participation in associative or collaborative contexts such as the ones provided by computer mediated communications (CMC), or other forms of virtual socialization (social networking, chat and forums, online gaming, blogging). Since the earliest scholars review of computer supported social networks (or CSSNs, as in Wellman, Salaff et al, 1996), the opportunities for social and individual involvement in on line communitarian-like experiences are increasing faster and faster and this has amplified the opportunities for researchers to explore personal relations.

Empirically, the analysis of virtual forms of bonding and relating among individuals has required specific research strategies and the application of new technical devices in network analysis, such as the use of automated data collection that make it possible to compare the personal networks of thousands of members of community-like meeting places on the Internet (Petróczi, Nepusz and Bazsó, 2008; Mika, 2005; Lewis et al. 2008). These research procedures, however, are also ethically problematic (Molina and Borgatti, 2005; Acquisti and Gross, 2006), since the gathering of data on communications and personal relations available on social networking site scrutinizes aspect of social life having relevant implications for privacy issues (collection of individual data without consent, traceability and anonymization of data) and security concerns (databases of individuals and social profiling).

Finally, new forms of digital communication (mobile or internet based) expanded and complicated the boundary definitions for community detection and introduced in the theoretical debates aspects concerning technology design and institutional control on digital socialization and diffused online participation. Recently, the debate whether virtual communities are real communities has been moving across the boundaries of the social sciences and the new research area of social informatics is now systematizing typologies of virtual communities, based on the passive or active role of participants, the approach to technology (modifiable by users or determined by the media) and the social intent of the interaction set (learning communities, communities oriented to activate actions, such as shopping, or to exchange opinions and information).

## NETWORK STUDIES OF ONLINE COMMUNITIES

Main features of online communities can be described on the bases of the experience of the so-called 'Netville' research project (Hampton, 2010; 2003; Hampton and Wellman, 2001). This project was originally developed at the end of the nineties and involved a two-year study of the social connectivity of the residents in a Toronto suburb, Netville, whose homes were built with advanced digital communication technologies (high-speed Internet). The researchers analyzed both offline and online residents' community ties looking at them globally, from those involving other Netville residents, the ones with institutions and associations (civic involvement) and those involving residents' contacts outside the neighbourhood. With the aid of ethnographic observations and a survey, the study analyzed the changes in social

contacts and exchange of support between the residents and their friends and relatives.

The first results showed that relationships were rarely only computer mediated, and residents tended to combine online and offline or face-to-face connections (Hampton and Wellman, 2001; Hampton 2003). However, comparing two groups of residents in Netville (those benefitting from built in wired connections and those who had not yet access to this facility) the researchers noticed that the use of computer-mediated communication had helped the new residents to keep contacts and receive support from previous personal contacts (friends, former neighbours and acquaintances). Since the relocation, the personal network of wired residents had of course modified, but principal effects due to Internet were the larger increase in relations with long distance personal contacts (strong ties) and the intensification of local contacts (weak ties), providing new channels of communication with other residents (ex. forum on Internet pages, exchange of emails on practical problems).

The community of Netville, in this sense, represents according to Hampton and Wellman (2001) a possible evolution of communitarian relations, where neighbourhood and geographical proximity mix together with global social change factors (urban mobility, Information Technology applied to personal communication), and as such can promote new expressions of civic participation and forms of collective mobilization (Hampton, 2003). The findings of Hampton are confirmed by the research of Stern and Adams (2010) on rural communities in the US. The researchers report that online communication in rural areas facilitated social participation. Despite the fact that only a fraction of population in rural areas uses intensively the Internet (and finds it 'complex to use'), rural community members use their internet connections to get involved at the local level and to maintain local social networks (social capital), as much as to connect and find information about global issues and shared interests (cultural capital).

Easy access to digital communication, can thus favour sharing of interests and the creation of a similar cultural capital, which support socializing practices and social integration in groups and communities. In this sense, new virtual communities may constitute a new form of socialization, but their structural features at the current state of research seem to be similar to previously known communitarian experiences, with time and use related fragmentation processes. Current research on online communities is debating in particular the issues correlated with action orientation and coordination in online groups.

On one side, network researches on internet based communities support the idea that virtual forms of reciprocity are structurally different from friends support, despite the fact that content of relations is similar to non-virtual ones (Adamic and Adar, 2005; Lewis et al., 2008). At initial stage of social integration of new communication technologies, the form of relations among members of virtual communities (intensity and frequency of contacts, emotional response, reciprocity) tends, in fact, to reflect social characteristics of members (sharing of sub-cultures and languages, collective goal). Relying on databases that concern participation limited to the virtual sphere, also, bears the risk of elaborating complex structural modelling of community, which forget about the different impact that formal and informal relations have in face-to-face social life and in public environments such as the Internet (Giarchi, 2001).

On the other side, research carried on strictly defined virtual communities show that their members perceive a substantial similitude between online and offline communitarian relationships and act correspondingly. In virtual communities the ties that link members is frequently described as a general form of reciprocity; most of their actions are in fact coordinated by this cognitive assumption so that *'posting a message on a listserver, an electronic board or initiating a new topic in a discussion forum environment pleading for help is sufficient to solicit advice, help or even emotional*

*support'* (Petróczi, Nepusz and Bazsó, 2007: 48). Forms of virtual reciprocity are essential for creating a community and constitute the base for creation of common resources and maintenance of significant and capable online social connections; a finding that is also established by social exchange theory and cognitive theories that deal with prerequisites of human social organization. The progressive integration of technological and communicative areas of interaction (such as with friendly user devices and public access to IT) may thus activate new social processes that could evolve in unpredictable directions and produce new forms of virtual social participation.

## KNOWLEDGE CREATION AND LEARNING IN W.2 COMMUNITIES

Another interesting contribution from network analysis of virtual communitarian relations concerns the study of knowledge creation and scientific collaboration. Applications of network analysis techniques for community detection to publications dates back to first studies in the discipline (La Solla Price, 1965); its contemporary application to digitalized scientific knowledge and to other forms of knowledge diffusion (ex. conference participation) has contributed to shed a light on collaborative teams and to the social and collective process of knowledge construction in the sciences (Newman, 2001; Boyack, Klavans and Borner, 2004).

Bibliographical and information studies typically apply network analysis to digitalized sources of knowledge (books, articles and other grey literature in the sciences and humanities) to explore the semantic structure of knowledge and draw differences between disciplines and areas of study. The study of Wikipedia collaborations, for example, is giving a lot of information both on the social aspects of virtual relationships (co-operation, in particular) and the semantic space of knowledge on the Web (Holloway, Bozicevic and Borner, 2007). Communitarian relations are suggested by dense and cohesive cliques of authors and joint scientific production, while in the case of wikis and others participative forms of knowledge creation, the researchers analyze the exchange of messages on the Web and in specialized forums, with the intent to put in evidence solidarity and competitive activities that make possible the creation and survival of virtual commons (non-exclusive public resources).

Finally, the studies of learning communities (such as virtual communities of practice) have given further insight about the mechanisms that motivate individuals to share knowledge with other members and provide/seek help online. According to recent studies (Tsai, 2002), the quantity of interaction ties and the presence of reciprocity and identification with other members of a virtual community seem to be essential for providing enduring relations that are based on trust and thus may conduce to knowledge sharing. In a virtual learning community the quality of information provided is not improved by density and connectedness of members, but *'knowledge contributors are more concerned about the successful functioning, survival, and growth of the virtual communities than the benefits that will produce to themselves'* (Chiu, Hsu and Wang, 2006:1883).

Quality of information and knowledge thus seem to acquire different properties when analyzed in the virtual or in the direct day-to-day experience. Aspects that concern the participants in their real life like personal interests, values and affiliations, in particular, influence the participation to dedicated websites and platforms in organizations. Results of recent studies (Di Micco et al., 2008), put in evidence that social network sites inside large organizations can fulfil both work related needs (career, knowledge and project sharing), and personal needs (grouping on the bases of interests), integrating with daily life of employees. Other investigation questioned, on the contrary, the efficacy of virtual relations

in favouring the diffusion of personal connections: the results of a one-year monitoring of the relations mediated by an Enterprise 2.0 showed that employees tend to use the platform to keep up with close colleagues, giving preference to 'strong ties' connections, and to reinforce and strengthen already present relationships (Ferron et al., 2009). The impact of technologies applied to work environments in terms of formation of new relations among employees and evolution of their connections (quantity, intensity of contacts, share of knowledge and interests) is in fact influenced by organizational values and embedded in organizational practices that are not directly modifiable solely with technology implementation.

## VIRTUAL PARTICIPATION AND DYNAMIC OF SOCIAL RELATIONS

The plurality of findings and results on socializing patterns and grouping criteria in the virtual sphere puts in evidence the fact that despite the general acknowledgment of usefulness of work and social networking websites and other IT based resources, the implications of these new forms of connectedness are still to be explored and categorized theoretically. Virtual participation is indeed a recent phenomenon to be explored and engagement in social activities on the Internet is influenced by structural aspects of societies such as digital divide and access to technology, as well as by the level of digital literacy and cultural preferences.

The most recent approaches tend to integrate these aspects and explore the use of information technology communication devices in sub-cultures, developing countries and other social context where virtual relations acquire a special meaning and are used to re-establish contested identities or express values and lifestyle orientations. Instead of looking for similarities between online and real life relations, researchers emphasize the differences from face to face communities and affirm that the bases of the virtual community lie in the presence of cultural forms that allow individuals to recognize themselves as participants in a community, or in *'human imagination of an individual and in public imagination, which is conducted by media'* (Saarinen, 2010:53). Compared to other types of community, in virtual ones the interconnection of social participation, identity and personal relations appear therefore to be built 'inside technology' and not favoured or prevented by it anymore. Virtual communities in this sense could provide several types of socialization whose implications are not obviously evident to researchers.

In a study on Web.2 organizations Ganley and Lampe (2009) show that the structure of the network can have a direct impact on participants, modifying their perception of benefits and costs in participation in the site's communitarian life. Their analysis of the involvement process of new and experienced members in the virtual community reveals that newer members to the site find more personal benefit from connecting to individuals in different circles, while people already involved in the community tend to connect to tight networks of individuals. The authors conclude that since online communities depend on a strong core of very active and experienced users, the risk is to implicitly generate closure mechanisms that mimic real communities dynamics (Ganley and Lampe, 2009).

Furthermore, in virtual communities quality and quantity of resources (time, emotion, effort) and personal investment (privacy disclosure, preference and interest sharing) are central features that may influence the survival and success of a virtual community and influence its future social organization. The medium, being an internet site, a chat or other interactive option, facilitates social and political interaction, or as in the case of recent Web.2 applications could be part of the interaction, offering to its members the opportunity to perform their virtual identity(ies). The functioning of the site, its opportunities of social participation and the general climate of relationships (Strater

and Lipford, 2008) that keep members connected can be improved by programmers' design (Boyd and Ellison, 2008), as well as evolve according to the members preferences (Stutzman, 2006) and direct involvement in the technology design (Open Source Philosophy).

For all these reasons participation in online communities is partially mediated by technical features that enable the members to interact and control their performance (subjectivity emphasized or reduced), and partially mediated by social features as the design of each medium (such as a website, or virtual game) has a direct consequence for members' prospect to get involved in the evolution of a virtual community itself. Future research on virtual communities should pay more attention to these aspects and evolve on both technical and theoretical aspects concerning collection and interpretation of connections among members of social networking sites and other forms of grouping on the Internet (Matzat, 2009).

Specifically, integration with information and decision science may prove useful for developing models of enquiry specifically tailored for online interactions and huge amount of network data; in particular, theoretical attention to cultural aspects (especially among the youngest users) could improve the level of explanation and the significance of results from the study of virtual participation. An example of such perspective is in the longitudinal study of Szell and Thurner (2010) on participants to MMSG (massive multiplayer online games); their analysis explores the dynamics of friendship and negative relationships, looking for evidence of the theory of Granovetter concerning weak and strong ties. The results of their first descriptive analysis report actually that the overlap of friendship networks among players seems to be related to the presence of strong ties, characteristics of sub-groups of allied players or that act as friends. The similarity of virtual world dynamics to natural social ones, the authors conclude, is surprising and more extensive studies on similar contexts could provide lab-like experiments that are comparable to the ones in natural sciences.

## FINAL REMARKS

Since the first empirical studies adopting the network perspective the advancement of research has been remarkable and new forms of interactions that are emerging from digital technologies anticipate that this area of study will not get exhausted or diminish in relevance over the following decades. Nevertheless, 'old' enquires still have a role as guidance and theoretical reference for researchers. Contemporary studies on communities in fact are characterized by a progressive fragmentation of the theoretical perspective and by the emergence of new approaches and multidisciplinary contributes that may require field systematization.

Firstly, the methodological questions posed by investigation of forms of human grouping are to be addressed by future research agenda paying attention to basic social organization principles such as homophily (McPherson, Smith-Lovin and Cook, 2001), shared knowledge and multiplicity of forms of communication (Carley, 2002). Community social networks seem to include original features that make risky comparison among different levels of social organization, therefore suggesting to invest more in research designs oriented to comparative studies and multiple setting enquires. Recent developments which explore more deeply the co-variability of structural and local context in the formation and evolution of rural community social networks (in the case analyzed were forms of kinship help during harvest time and household organization patterns) confirmed that social connections act as mechanisms of transmission of local-based characteristics (Entwistle et al. 2007). Moreover, extended researches in urban communities put in evidence that willingness and interest in exchange of social support and resources with other individu-

als, is more frequent among those subjects that are emotionally close (friendship relations, shared values) or have comparable lifestyles; the bases for community development are thus to be found both in kinship and no-kinship relations (Hampton and Wellman, 1999; Adamic and Adar, 2005).

Secondly, the new communicative forms of interaction based on networks; such as the ones explored in online and technology mediated communities are increasingly becoming subject of scientific enquiry. Their impact on research and theory on communities' structure is still to be evaluated, but is expected to stimulate innovation, not only on the technical side (sampling, collection and filtering of relational and social network data) but also theoretically. According to researchers new forms of social participation, different from the usual one will emerge with the progressive implementation of mobile technologies of communication from e-government to shopping and cultural life.

Frontier research is currently exploring the social implications of the 'migration' of virtual communities from the fixed Internet to physical spaces interfaced by mobile technologies. Specifically, mobile communication technologies such as smartphones will re-define collective events as multiuser environments, fostering a new definition of identity, and new forms of communitarian experience. Researchers describe these new forms with the ad hoc category of hybrid participation and foresee its increase in the next years. In hybrid participation *'the idea of digital spaces as instances disconnected from physical spaces no longer applies'* (De Souza e Silva, 2010); communitarians experiences in such space are characterized also by multiplicity, inducing people to look in a different way to social participation when realizing that participants do not 'belong' to homogenous groups (class, gender, ethnic group). Hybrid participation can assume the forms of political spreads (where mobilization is activated by text messaging exchange among personal networks), 'flash mobs' (mobile-organized gatherings of people, that - often not knowing each other - suddenly perform some specific but innocuous act such as embracing, or standing still, and then promptly disappear), as well as participation in location-based mobile games (where members of virtual communities meet in public space to play one-shot role contest in a short span of time, a single day or night). Pioneering research practices are needed to approach these social phenomena and network analysts are called to respond to these problems with openness to contributions from other social sciences, such as the media and cultural studies, as well as results of enquiries in social physics and quantitative enquires of personal communications and virtual social interactions.

# REFERENCES

Acquisti, A., & Gross, R. (2006). Imagined communities: Awareness, information sharing, and privacy on the Facebook. *Privacy Enhancing Technologies, 4258,* 36–58. doi:10.1007/11957454_3

Adamic, L., & Adar, E. (2005). How to search a social network. *Social Networks, 27,* 187–203. doi:10.1016/j.socnet.2005.01.007

Adler Lomnitz, L. (1988). Informal exchange networks in formal systems: A theoretical model. *American Anthropologist, 90*(1), 42–55. doi:10.1525/aa.1988.90.1.02a00030

Alba, R. D. (1981). From small groups to social networks. Mathematical approaches to the study of group structure. *The American Behavioral Scientist, 24*(5), 681–694. doi:10.1177/000276428102400506

Arenas, A., Danon, L., Dıaz-Guilera, A., Gleiser, P. M., & Guimer, R. (2004). Community analysis in social networks. *European Physical Journal, 38,* 373–380.

Barnes, J. (1954). Class and committee in a Norwegian island parish. *Human Relations, 7,* 39–58. doi:10.1177/001872675400700102

Bastani, S. (2007). Family comes first: Men's and women's personal networks in Teheran. *Social Networks, 29,* 357–374. doi:10.1016/j.socnet.2007.01.004

Bellotti, E. (2008). What are friends for? Elective communities of single people. *Social Networks, 30,* 318–329. doi:10.1016/j.socnet.2008.07.001

Borgatta, E. F., & Baker, P. M. (1981). Introduction: Updating small group research and theory [Special issue]. *The American Behavioral Scientist, 24.*

Bott, E. (1955). Urban families: Conjugal roles and social networks. *Human Relations, 8,* 345–384. doi:10.1177/001872675500800401

Bott, E. (1971). *Family and social network.* New York, NY: Free Press.

Bourdieu, P. (1986). Forms of capital. In Richardson, J. G. (Ed.), *Handbook of theory and research for the sociology and education* (pp. 241–258). Greenwood, NY.

Boyack, K., Klavans, R., & Borner, K. (2005). Mapping the backbone of science. *Scientometrics, 64*(3), 351–374. doi:10.1007/s11192-005-0255-6

Boyd, D. M., & Ellison, N. (2008). Social network sites: Definition, history, and scholarship. *Journal of Computer-Mediated Communication, 13,* 210–230. doi:10.1111/j.1083-6101.2007.00393.x

Burt, R. (1978). Cohesion versus structural equivalence as a basis for network subgroups. *Sociological Methods & Research, 7,* 189–212. doi:10.1177/004912417800700205

Burt, R. S. (1987). Social contagion and innovation: Cohesion versus structural equivalence. *American Journal of Sociology, 92,* 1287–1355. doi:10.1086/228667

Calhoun, C. (1998). Community without propinquity revisited: Communications technology and the transformation of the urban public sphere. *Sociological Inquiry, 63*(3), 373–397. doi:10.1111/j.1475-682X.1998.tb00474.x

Carley, K. M. (2002). Smart agents and organizations of the future. In Lievrouw, L., & Livingstone, S. (Eds.), *The handbook of new media*. London, UK: Sage.

Castells, M. (1996). *The rise of the network society*. Cambridge, MA: Blackwell.

Chiu, C. M., Hsu, M., & Wang, E. (2006). Understanding staring in virtual communities: an integration of social capital and social cognitive theories. *Decision Support Systems*, *42*, 1872–1888. doi:10.1016/j.dss.2006.04.001

Coleman, J. S. (1988). Social capital in the creation of human capital. *American Journal of Sociology*, *4*(34) 95-120.

Cranford, C. J. (2005). Networks of exploitation: Immigrant labour and the restructuring of the Los Angeles janitorial industry. *Social Problems*, *52*(3), 379–397. doi:10.1525/sp.2005.52.3.379

Dasgupta, P., & Serageldin, I. (Eds.). (1999). *Social capital: A multifaceted perspective*. Washington, DC: The World Bank.

De Solla Price, D. J. (1965). Networks of scientific papers. *Science*, *149*, 510–515. doi:10.1126/science.149.3683.510

de Souza e Silva, A. (2006). From cyber to hybrid: Mobile technologies as interfaces of hybrid spaces. *Space and Culture*, *9*, 261–278. doi:10.1177/1206331206289022

Diani, M. (2009). The structural bases of protest events: Multiple memberships and civil society networks in the 15th February 2003 anti-war demonstrations. *Acta Sociologica*, *52*(1), 63–83. doi:10.1177/0001699308100634

DiMicco, J., Millen, D. R., Geyer, W., Dugan, C., Brownholtz, B., & Muller, M. (2008). Motivations for social networking at work. *Proceedings of CSCW*, *08*(November), 8–12.

Entwistle, B., Faust, K., Rindfuss, R., & Kaneda, T. (2007). Networks and contexts: Variations in the structure of social ties. *American Journal of Sociology*, *112*(5), 1495–1533. doi:10.1086/511803

Fenneman, M., & Tillie, J. (2001). Civic community, political participation and political trust of ethnic groups. *Connections*, *24*(1), 26–41.

Ferron, M., Massa, P., & Odella, F. (2011). Analyzing collaborative networks emerging in Enterprise 2.0: The Taolin Platform. *Procedia Social and Behavioural Science*, *10*, 68–78. doi:10.1016/j.sbspro.2011.01.010

Fisher, C. (1977). *Network and places. Social relations in the urban setting*. New York, NY: The Free Press.

Fisher, C. (1982). *To dwell among friends. Personal networks in town and city*. Chicago, IL: University of Chicago Press.

Flap, H. D., & Volker, B. (Eds.). (2004). *Creation and returns of social capital*. London, UK: Routledge.

Galaskiewicz, J. (1979). The structure of community organizational networks. *Social Forces*, *57*, 1346–1364.

Galaskiewicz, J., & Krohn, K. R. (1984). Positions, roles, and dependencies in a community interorganization system. *The Sociological Quarterly*, *25*(4), 527–550. doi:10.1111/j.1533-8525.1984.tb00208.x

Ganley, D., & Lampe, C. (2009). The ties that bind: Social network principles in online communities. *Decision Support Systems*, *47*, 268–274. doi:10.1016/j.dss.2009.02.013

Giarchi, G. G. (2001). Caught in the nets: A critical examination of the use of the concept of networks in community development studies. *Community Development Journal*, *36*(1), 63–71. doi:10.1093/cdj/36.1.63

Girvan, M., & Newman, M. E. J. (2002). Community structure in social and biological networks. *Proceedings of the National Academy of Sciences of the United States of America, 99*(12), 7821–7826. doi:10.1073/pnas.122653799

Granovetter, M. S. (1973). Strength of weak ties. *American Journal of Sociology, 78*(6), 1360–1380. doi:10.1086/225469

Grieco, M. S. (1982). Family structure and industrial employment: The role of information and migration. *Journal of Marriage and the Family, 44*(3), 701–707. doi:10.2307/351590

Grossetti, M. (2007). Are French networks unique? *Social Networks, 29*, 391–404. doi:10.1016/j.socnet.2007.01.005

Hampton, K., & Wellman, B. (1999). Netville online and offline: Observing and surveying a wired suburb. *The American Behavioral Scientist, 43*, 475–492. doi:10.1177/00027649921955290

Hampton, K., & Wellman, B. (2001). Long distance community in the network society: Contact and support beyond Netville. *The American Behavioral Scientist, 45*, 476–495. doi:10.1177/00027640121957303

Hampton, K. N. (2003). Grieving for a lost network: Collective action in a wired suburb. *Special Issue: ICTs and Community Networking. The Information Society, 19*(5), 417–428. doi:10.1080/714044688

Hampton, K. N. (2010). Internet use and the concentration of disadvantage: Glocalization and the urban underclass. *The American Behavioral Scientist, 53*, 1111–1132. doi:10.1177/0002764209356244

Henning, M. (2007). Re-evaluating the community question from a German perspective. *Social Networks, 29*, 375–390. doi:10.1016/j.socnet.2007.01.008

Holloway, T., Bozicevic, M., & Borner, K. (2007). Analyzing and visualizing the semantic coverage of Wikipedia and its authors. *Complexity, 12*(3), 30–40. doi:10.1002/cplx.20164

Knoke, D. (1988). Incentives in collective action organizations. *American Sociological Review, 53*, 311–329. doi:10.2307/2095641

Knoke, D. (1990). Networks of political action: Toward theory construction. *Social Forces, 68*(4), 1041–1063.

Knoke, D., & Rogers, D. L. (1979). A blockmodel analysis of interorganizational networks. *Sociology and Social Research, 64*, 28–52.

Köksal, Y. (2008). Rethinking nationalism: State projects and community networks in 19th century Ottoman empire. *The American Behavioral Scientist, 51*(10). doi:10.1177/0002764208316352

Laumann, E., & Pappi, F. (1976). *Networks of collective action: A perspective on community influence systems.* New York, NY: Academic Press.

Lewis, K., Kaufman, J., Gonzales, M., Wimmer, A., & Christakis, N. (2008). Tastes, ties and time: A new social network dataset using Facebook.com. *Social Networks, 30*, 330–342. doi:10.1016/j.socnet.2008.07.002

Lin, N. (2001). Building a network theory of social capital. In Lin, N., Cook, K., & Burt, R. S. (Eds.), *Social capital: Theory and research.* New York, NY: Aldine De Gruyter.

Lin, N., Son, J., & George, L. K. (2008). Cross-national comparison of social support structures between Taiwan and the United States. *Journal of Health and Social Behavior, 49*, 104–126. doi:10.1177/002214650804900108

Matzat, U. (2009). A theory of relational signals in online groups. *New Media & Society, 11*, 375–394. doi:10.1177/1461444808101617

McPherson, M., Popielarz, P., & Drobnic, S. (1992). Social networks and organizational dynamics. *American Sociological Review, 57,* 153–170. doi:10.2307/2096202

McPherson, M., Smith-Lovin, L., & Cook, J. M. (2001). Birds of a feather: Homophily in social networks. *Annual Review of Sociology, 27,* 415–444. doi:10.1146/annurev.soc.27.1.415

Mika, P. (2005). Flink: Semantic Web technology for the extraction and analysis of social networks. *Web Semantics: Science. Services and Agents on the World Wide Web, 3,* 211–223. doi:10.1016/j.websem.2005.05.006

Molina, J. L., & Borgatti, S. (2005). Toward ethical guidelines for network research in organizations. *Social Networks, 27*(2), 107–117. doi:10.1016/j.socnet.2005.01.004

Newman, M. E. J. (2001). The structure of scientific collaboration network. *PNA, 98*(16), 404–409. doi:10.1073/pnas.021544898

Odella, F. (2006). *Using ego-network in surveys: Methodological and empirical research issues.* Paper presented at NETSCI 06 International Conference on Network Sciences, Bloomington Indiana, USA.

Palla, G., Barabasi, A. L., & Vicsek, T. (2007). Quantifying social group evolution. *Nature, 446*(5), 664–667. doi:10.1038/nature05670

Petroczi, A., Nepusz, T., & Baszo, F. (2007). Measuring tie-strength in virtual social networks. *Connections, 27*(2), 39–52.

Pinkster, F., & Volker, B. (2009). Local social networks and social resources in two Dutch neighbourhoods. *Housing Studies, 24*(2), 225–242. doi:10.1080/02673030802704329

Piselli, F. (2007). Communities, places and social networks. *The American Behavioral Scientist, 50*(7), 867–878. doi:10.1177/0002764206298312

Portes, A. (1998). Social capital: Its origins and applications in modern sociology. *Annual Review of Sociology, 24,* 2. doi:10.1146/annurev.soc.24.1.1

Portes, A., & Sensenbrenner, J. (1993). Embeddedness and immigration: Notes on the social determinants of economic action. *American Journal of Sociology, 98,* 1320–1350. doi:10.1086/230191

Putnam, R. (1993). *Making democracy work: Civic traditions in modern Italy.* Princeton, NJ: Princeton University Press.

Rheingold, H. (1993). *The virtual community.* New York, NY: Harper.

Saarinen, L. (2002). Imagined community and death. *Digital Creativity, 13*(1), 53–61. doi:10.1076/digc.13.1.53.3212

Schweizer, T., Schnegg, T., & Berzborn, S. (1998). Personal networks and social support in a multiethnic community of southern California. *Social Networks, 20,* 1–21. doi:10.1016/S0378-8733(96)00304-8

Snjiders, T., Spreen, M., & Zwaagstra, R. (1995). The use of multilevel modelling for analysing personal networks of cocaine users in a urban area. *Journal of Quantitative Anthropology, 5,* 85–105.

Stern, M. J., & Adams, A. E. (2010). Do rural residents really use the internet to build social capital? An empirical investigation. *The American Behavioral Scientist, 53,* 1389–1422. doi:10.1177/0002764210361692

Strater, K., & Lipford, H. R. (2008). Strategies and struggles with privacy in an online social networking community. Paper published online by the British Computer Society.

Stutzman, F. (2006). An evaluation of identity-sharing behavior in social network communities. *Journal of the International Digital Media and Arts Association, 3*(1), 10–18.

Szell, M., & Thurner, S. (2010). Measuring social dynamics in a massive multiplayer online game. *Social Networks*, *32*, 313–329. doi:10.1016/j.socnet.2010.06.001

Thompson, R. A. (1973). A theory of instrumental social networks. *Journal of Anthropological Research*, *29*(4), 244–265.

Tsai, W. (2002). Social structure of "competition" within a multiunit organization: coordination and intra organizational knowledge sharing. *Organization Science*, *13*(2), 179–190. doi:10.1287/orsc.13.2.179.536

Uzzi, B. (1998). The sources and consequences of embeddedness for the economic performance of organizations: The network effect. *American Sociological Review*, *61*(4), 674-698.

Van Der Gaag, M., & Snijders, T. A. B. (2003). *A comparison of measures for individual social capital. ICS paper for the Research Program SCALE.* Groningen University.

Wasserman, S., & Faust, K. (1994). *Social network analysis: Methods and applications.* Cambridge, UK: Cambridge Univ. Press.

Wellman, B. (1979). The community question: The intimate networks of East Yorkers. *American Journal of Sociology*, *84*(5), 1201–1231. doi:10.1086/226906

Wellman, B. (1999). *Networks in the global village: Life in contemporary communities.* New York, NY: Westview Press.

Wellman, B. (2007). The network is personal: Introduction to a special issue of *Social Networks*. *Social Networks*, *29*, 349–356. doi:10.1016/j.socnet.2007.01.006

Wellman, B., Carrington, P. J., & Hall, A. (1988). Networks as personal communities. In Wellman, B., & Berkovitz, S. D. (Eds.), *Social structures* (pp. 130–184). Cambridge, UK: Cambridge University Press.

Wellman, B., Salaff, J., Dimitrova, D., Garton, L., & Gulia, M. (1996). Computer networks: Collaborative work, telework and virtual community. *Annual Review of Sociology*, *22*, 213–238. doi:10.1146/annurev.soc.22.1.213

Wellman, B., Wong, R. Y., Tindall, D., & Nazer, N. (1997). A decade of network change: Turnover, persistence and stability in personal communities. *Social Networks*, *19*, 27–50. doi:10.1016/S0378-8733(96)00289-4

## KEY TERMS AND DEFINITIONS

**Community Detection Strategies:** Methods and logical reasoning that allow to individuate inside a network of personal or collective relations a specific set of relations that are similar in terms of structural properties (such as homogeneity, intensity, and connectivity) and that theoretically consent significant social interactions.

**Network Structure:** The set of links and nodes that define the main properties of a network in terms of dimensions, internal articulation and connectedness.

**Online Communities:** Forms of social organization that take place in the virtual sphere (Internet), mostly based on mediated communications, and involving forms of social exchange among individuals or their virtual representatives (avatar).

**Personal Networks:** A network that represents the individual relationships by means of links and nodes; a personal network may include other individuals or representatives of collective entities (institutions, organizations, groups, etc.).

**Social Participation:** The social relationships that connect individuals to groups, associations or institutional activity and favour expression of interest, values and cultural preferences.

# Chapter 2
# Network Perspective on Structures Related to Communities

**Alvin Wolfe**
*University of Southern Florida, USA*

## ABSTRACT

*The application of network perspectives to communities requires some appreciation of the variety of ways people are now writing about communities. Some scholars and practitioners have drifted toward the view that a community is composed very largely of the personal networks of the individuals who are members of the community. But the whole community is more than the sum of those related parts, and the structure of a community must include not only those direct interpersonal relations but also the relations among the clusters and groups and corporate entities that interact in and about this whole. If scientific knowledge about these matters is to accumulate, comparing findings among various studies is of vital importance. From the 1940s well into the 1960s, the local community was the recognized social unit that sociologists and anthropologists studied. Linton wrote of the necessity of the local group. Many sociologists and anthropologists gave their full attention to this local level of social integration through a field called "community studies." The work of Conrad Arensberg, Sol Kimball, Robert Redfield, Carl Taylor, Eric Wolf, and others had views of communities that had a network cast to them. The category "community" includes a wide range of social formations, generally local systems of fairly densely connected persons in households and organizations, systems on a scale somewhere between those domestic households and wider society.*

DOI: 10.4018/978-1-61350-444-4.ch002

## INTRODUCTION

Asked to write a chapter on network analysis and community behavior modeling, I thought that would be simple enough. No problem! My anthropological work for fifty-some years focused largely on communities (e.g., Wolfe 1961), except for my forays into studying the networks of multinational companies in the African mineral industry (Wolfe 1963, 1977). As far as network perspective is concerned, I have always, since the 1960s anyway viewed everything as a network (e.g. Wolfe 1968, 1970). Every community has a network structure.

Ah, but it turned out to be more difficult than I had imagined. People who write about communities nowadays are using terms in a wide variety of ways. The "little communities" that anthropologist Robert Redfield (1960) wrote about fifty years ago have very little in common with the present-day "community of nations, the community of Jamaica Plain, the gay community, the IBM community, the Catholic Community, the Yale Community, the African American community, the 'virtual' community of cyberspace," all mentioned by Robert Putnam (2000). In the decade since Putnam, electronic connections have expanded logarithmically in both number and speed, and the community problem is even more vexing. Do urban villagers raise children differently than do rural villagers? What kind of village does it take to raise a child? Is this talk about a global village to be taken seriously? We anthropologists once got all our data simply by talking to people in their communities. Now, like economists and engineers, we also have to mine in data warehouses.

In 2003, a group of 33 "children's doctors, research scientists, and mental health and youth service professionals" prepared a report with the title "Hardwired to Connect, The New Scientific Case for Authoritative Communities" (Commission on Children at Risk 2003). They introduced the concept "authoritative communities" in the hope that it would "help youth service professionals, policy makers, and the entire (U.S.) society do a better job of addressing the crisis. .. (they saw). .. in the deteriorating mental and behavioral health of U.S. children" (5).

Some scholars and practitioners have drifted toward the view that a community is composed entirely or at least very largely of the personal networks of the individuals who are members of the community. That seems to me an inadequate view in that it suggests that a community so defined is nothing more than the sum of the personal networks that make it up. A whole community is more than the sum of those parts, but also, the structure of a community must include not only those direct interpersonal relations but also the relations among the clusters and groups and corporate entities that interact in and about this whole.

I am not one to tell other scholars how they should think or what terms they should use. Still, if knowledge about these matters is to accumulate, as it should in science, we must be able to compare findings among various studies. Comparison requires some clarification about what communities might be, or, put differently, about what social formations might be appropriately labeled communities.

## ON DEFINING COMMUNITIES

The editors of the Encyclopedia of Community, From the Village to the Virtual World (Christiansen and Levinson 2003) tell us that Robert Putnam's book, Bowling Alone (2000) was by far the work most cited by the hundreds of authors in their four-volume encyclopedia. Carrying the subtitle "The Collapse and Revival of American Community," Bowling Alone (2000) should be a good source in which a curious student might look to find a definition of community.

It turns out Putnam is quite cavalier about a definition, "Community means different things to different people. We speak of the community of nations, the community of Jamaica Plain, the gay community, the IBM community, the Catholic Community, the Yale Community, the African American community, the 'virtual' community of cyberspace, and so on. Each of us derives some sense of belonging from among the various communities to which we might in principle belong. For most of us, our deepest sense of belonging is to our most intimate social networks, especially family and friends. Beyond that perimeter lie work, church, neighborhood, civic life, and an assortment of other 'weak ties' that constitute our personal stock of social capital" (2000, 273).

Speaking of social capital, Putnam had earlier said, "Sometimes 'Social Capital,' like its conceptual cousin 'community,' sounds warm and cuddly" (21). His point was not necessarily the looseness of definition alone, but the multivalent nature of the consequences of interpersonal ties despite their association with intimacy and reciprocity and sense of community.

Still lacking an "authoritative" definition, why not turn to the Encyclopedia itself – that is, the four-volume Encyclopedia of Community (2003)? It begins, "Community is a concept, an experience, and a central part of being human" (p. xxxi). That sounds important, but what is it? Editors Karen Christensen and David Levinson continue, "We explore hundreds of different communities, the human webs that provide essential feelings of connectedness, belonging, and meaning. Communities are indeed the core and essence of humanity, around which everything else is woven or spun" (p. xxxi).

That characterization of the subject of the Encyclopedia is certainly appropriate to the purposes of this paper on the application of network perspectives on communities. Nine hundred pages later, Barry Wellman, one of the hundreds of authors in the encyclopedia, stated this network issue with considerable more clarity, "Those who study network communities treat communities as embedded in social networks rather than in places.

Traditionally, analysts have looked for community by asking if neighborhoods are sociable, are supportive and provide social identity. Communities began to be studied as social networks when urbanists realized that many neighborhoods were not thick with community ties, and that many community ties extended beyond the neighborhood. This led to a shift in perspective, especially among sociologists, from thinking about community in place (neighborhoods) to thinking about it in relationships (networks)" (p. 983).

Years ago, anthropologists and sociologists were concerned with defining community not only in terms of location but also in terms of a level of integration in society. There was a time, from the 1940s and well into the 1960s, when the local community was the recognized social unit that sociologists and anthropologists studied. And for good reason.

Ralph Linton, in his 1936 masterpiece entitled "The Study of Man," argued that there are only two social units that appear to be as old as the human species itself – the "basic family group" and the "local group, an aggregation of families." The latter "served as the starting point for the development of all the current types of combined political and territorial units such as tribes and nations" (1936, 209).

Linton lamented that social scientists had paid much more attention to the family than to that form he called the local group. "This focusing of interest upon the family may have been due in part to the European culture pattern of extreme interest in everything connected with mating and reproduction and to the greater variety of the social institutions which have been evolved from the family" (1936, 209).

"Local groups, on the other hand, are as familiar to us as any social institution of universal occurrence can be. They are, or at least have been until very recent times, as characteristic of European societies as of any others. They are still the basis of most of our political organization even though they are losing some of their former importance as functional social units. Moreover, their qualities are so much the same everywhere in the world that these qualities can be studied almost as effectively fifty miles from any large city as in the wilds of Australia" (1936, 209-210).

Linton states explicitly "an understanding of the local group is vitally necessary to the understanding of any social system" (1936, 210). Partly because they have not sufficiently been studied, "There is not even any general agreement on a term for localized, socially integrated groups of fairly constant membership. They have been variously referred to as hordes, villages, and bands. Horde at once brings to mind the promiscuous hordes posited by the evolutionary sociologists as the starting point for the development of all social institutions or, worse yet, an unorganized mass of savages. Village suggests permanent habitations and settled life" (1936, 210).

While Linton, for purposes of his discussion in 1936, settled on the term band because it carried the fewest connotations for the average individual, I settle on the term community for purposes of our discussion here. We are discussing essentially local social formations at levels of scale somewhere between that of family or household and that of state, nation, or society.

With that change of gloss, substituting "community" or "local community" for "band," what Linton said seventy years ago, in 1936, still makes a lot of sense. We need to hear it,

"In spite of its superficial differences from one culture to another, the [local community] is the most constant of all social phenomena and, in many respects, the most uniform. It lies at the very foundation of all existing political and social systems. Its disintegration is one of the most revolutionary results of the rise of modern civilization. With the present ease of travel and communication, both rural and urban local groups are losing their old qualities as closely integrated, self-conscious social units. As a result the patterns of government and social control, which have been evolved through thousands of years of band liv-

ing, are becoming increasingly unworkable. The modern city, with its multiplicity of organizations of every conceivable sort, presents the picture of a mass of individuals who have lost their bands and who are trying, in uncertain and fumbling fashion, to find some substitute. New types of grouping based on congeniality, business association, or community of interest are springing up on all sides, but nothing has so far appeared which seems capable of taking over the primary functions of the local group as these relate to individuals. Membership in the Rotary Club is not an adequate substitute for friendly neighbors.

"Although the disintegration of local groups in our society may progress even further than it has, the author [Linton] is inclined to regard [the disintegration] as a transitory phenomenon. The sudden rise of the machine and of applied science has shattered Western civilization and reduced Western society to something approaching chaos. However, unless all past experience is at fault, the society will once more reduce itself to order. What the new order will be no one can forecast, but the potentialities of the local group both for the control of individuals and for the satisfaction of their psychological needs are so great that it seems unlikely that this unit will be dispensed with" (Linton 1936, 229-230).

After Ralph Linton wrote those words, sociologists and anthropologists gave much more attention to this local level of social integration, and, in fact, developed an entire field called "community studies." Anthropologists had for decades been doing ethnographic work in communities and of communities but they usually thought of them and sold them as studies of societies. Forced to name a genuine community study, many anthropologists would think immediately of Walter Goldschmidt's work in the 1930s of a California farm community, published as As You Sow (1947). Sociologists will think first of Middletown (Lynd 1929) and of Yankee City (Warner 1941, 1942) and of so many community studies that came out of the "Chicago School" of sociology. None of us should ignore the work of Conrad Arensberg and Solon Kimball, especially, Family and Community in Ireland (1940). Rural sociologists, in particular, developed the genre of community studies to a high art, or should I say science. All of this came after Linton's strong statement about the crucial importance of local communities for Homo sapiens.

In a 1944 chapter entitled "Techniques of Community Study and Analysis as Applied to Modern Civilization," Carl Taylor emphasized the importance of defining community,

"An attempt to close the gaps in rural community research demands first a clear conception of what is meant by the term 'rural community.' Cultural anthropologists have constructed concepts as bases for their studies of simple societies. Sociologists have created dogmas which they think are useful concepts by means of which to see the integrating factors, or common denominators, in complex societies. Each of these makes its contribution but none is adequate to the task at hand. Rural sociologists, because they could literally see rural communities in terms of geography and internal patterns of relationships, have gone about analyzing these things as objects of research without an adequate conceptual framework. They have known that the geographic rural community is not a society but apparently have not clearly seen that, to the persons living in these geographic areas, society, almost in its entirety, comes to them through participation in structures, functions, and attitudes, all of which are resident and operative in the local community" (1944, 435-436).

In words that are appropriate still today, Taylor argues that the task of analyzing a community requires a whole group of techniques, Mapping of geographic zones, analyzing attitudes, statistical techniques relating to time and space variations, participant observation to reveal the meaning of significant personal and social experiences.

Speaking of "modern rural man," Taylor says, "The science that would analyze him and his community must be as multiplex as his life"

(1944, 437). "Since the community is where his activities and thoughts occur and since it is an identifiable geographic area which contains all the major institutions, agencies, and instruments of communication through which his contacts flow, it furnishes the laboratory in which to study his society" (1944, 437). Without using the word "network" Taylor nonetheless points to its crucial aspects in saying that the student of community needs to collect "information on the form, nature, and extent of social participation, including formal and informal groupings, leadership, visiting relationships and the like…" (1944, 438).

## ON VARIETIES OF COMMUNITIES

Considering our topic, network perspectives on structures pertaining to communities, we have now become convinced that communities include a wide range of social formations, generally local systems of fairly densely connected persons in households and organizations, systems on a scale somewhere between those domestic households themselves and the wider society – state or nation or supranational world.

During the middle 1950s, when "community studies" were greatly in vogue, there appeared a number of publications that are helpful to our current understanding of the problem. When Eric Wolf (1955) was developing a typology of peasantry in general he was led toward defining types of communities. In taking that direction he seems to have been led by Meyer Fortes' (1953) discussion of the corporate nature of unilineal descent groups. Fortes wrote,

"The most important feature of unilineal descent groups in Africa brought into focus by recent field research is their corporate organization. When we speak of these groups as corporate units we do so in the sense given to the term "corporation" long ago by Maine in his classical analysis of testamentary succession in early law (Maine, 1866). We are reminded also of Max Weber's sociological analysis of the corporate group as a general type of social formation (Weber, 1947), for in many important particulars these African descent groups conform to Weber's definition"(Fortes 1953:25).

Wolf in 1986 described the theoretical context for his two articles -- one on types of Latin American peasantry (Wolf 1955) and the other on closed corporate communities in Mesoamerica and Java (Wolf 1957), as follows:

"The formulation of the closed corporate community. .. responded in part to Meyer Fortes' formulation of the structure of unilineal descent groups (1953), and in part to Julian Steward's attempt to establish what he called cultural types (1949). Fortes' use of the concept of corporation seemed to me applicable in that the Spanish Conquest imposed legal and political institutions on the conquered Amerind population that insisted on administrative, social, and liturgical-religious incorporation."(1986, 325).

Given that our interest here is in structures related to communities, it is important to note that after beginning to speak of "types of peasantry," anthropologist Eric Wolf (1955) glided gradually to "types of groups," and then to "types of communities." Of the seven types Wolf defined, the most interesting and most completely outlined was the "closed corporate community",

"The distinctive characteristic of the corporate peasant community is that it represents a bounded social system with clear-cut limits, in relations to both outsiders and insiders. It has structural identity over time. Seen from the outside, the community as a whole carries on a series of activities and upholds certain 'collective representations.' Seen from within, it defines the rights and duties of its members and prescribes large segments of their behavior"(Wolf 1955, 456).

In addition to the "open" and "closed corporate" community types, Wolf outlined five other types which he thought might deserve further investigation, but I do not believe he himself tried to follow up that line of comparative analysis. Like Fortes, whose comments on corporate lineages piqued his

curiosity, Wolf was really more interested in the structural relations of those community units to the rest of society than to an ethnographic description of the communities themselves.

In the same year that Wolf first described the closed corporate community as a structural type, Conrad Arensberg published a very important work arguing that for each regional cultural variation there is a type of community. Arensberg's (1955) article in the American Anthropologist identified varieties of communities in the United States. As an illustration of his much more general argument. One year later, there was another important publication on varieties of communities. This was a book in which Robert Redfield (1956) contemplates the "little community" as a kind of human whole that can be studied and understood in several different ways. Let us look first at Arensberg's "Types of American Communities."

## ARENSBERG'S TYPES OF AMERICAN COMMUNITIES

Arensberg (1955) found that although it had become traditional to use local communities as samples or microcosms of culture, there had been no independent treatment of whether there was correspondence between specific types of American communities and types of American cultures or subcultures. He set himself the task to discover what sorts of communities are distinguishable in the United States and how these sorts reflect American culture or cultures.

Arensberg saw communities as basic units of organization and transmission within a culture. "They provide for human beings and their cultural adaptation to nature the basic minimum personnel and the basic minimum of social relations through which survival is assured and the content of culture can be passed on to the next generation. Already pan-animal as ecological units, communities are panhuman as transmission units for human culture. It is their function in keeping alive the basic inventory of traits and institutions of the minimal personnel of each kind for which culture provides a role and upon which high-culture specialization and acceptance can be built that makes human communities into cell-like repeated units of organization within human societies and cultures" (1955, 1143).

For Arensberg, "There will be an American community, at least in pattern discernible above accidents of function, size, location, etc., for every American culture. Indeed, conversely, for as many types of communities as we can distinguish from the record there will be so many cultures upon the American scene" (1955, 1144).

In order to make his comparisons among American communities, Arensberg chose to develop models that might have some universal application. Arensberg summarizes his "common terms of description" as follows,

"Thus the models we shall need for American communities must rest on the common terms of description which serve for all others. The terms that we must vary as each successive model of the family represents the changed realities of a common experience of all communities in a new particular one must be terms of universal application. The following are the variable comparative terms, which apply to all human and animal communities, out of which our models can be built,

1. Individuals (persons or animals)
2. Spaces (territory, position, movement)
3. Times (schedules, calendars, time-series)
4. Functions (for individual and group life)
5. Structure and Process" (Arensberg 1955, 1146).

"Communities are, of course, collectivities or 'social systems' of specific individuals. These have identities, and in description we select some and not others, and specify who is member, to be observed, and who is not. Once identified they can be counted, located, and followed. Further, they can be described for the attributes we, observers, select or they, the observed, distinguish, age, sex, color, size, occupation, class, ethnicity, sect, etc. In dealing with human beings and their cultures we learned long ago to treat as significant those categorical attributes which the members of the community and culture inform us they discriminate and to connect these with behavior and organization" (1955, 1146).

"Communities occupy and use space and its contents, have territories the individuals exploit, create boundaries. They use such space and "environment" differentially.... Thereby they produce settlement patterns, land use and property distributions, assembly points and dispersal zones with tracks between, segregations of sex, age, class, occupation, rank, etc., and the things of each of these. ... Obviously intricate connections interlace population and space use" (1955, 1146).

Much more easily now than when Arensberg wrote, we can deal with some of these structural complexities, placement of individuals with respect to their relations over time in multidimensional ways that were not available to him. We also can more realistically deal with space issues, because we are accustomed now, through graph theory and network analysis, to know that adjacency, closeness, and distance, even geodesic distance, do not necessarily entail geographic space. Arensberg seems to have had a "network perspective on communities," but that perspective was not then as nearly realizable as it is now.

"Tables of functions performed for persons and for groups, then, are quite necessary tools for analysis of this unit of organization and continuity in cultural transmission in man, just as they are for physiologists of cells, organs, and organisms. But they are no more so than the maps and time charts we have already cited" (1955, 1147-1148)

Under the rubric of "Structure and Process" Arensberg says, "A model for a community, then ... must put all these things together. It will represent, and help us explore, the characteristic minimal organization of the bearers of a culture in time and space. How will we put these things together; what devices will best represent them and the whole they make? Trial will tell. We cannot predict in advance, in the abstract. Devices for representing empirical structure and process must be invented, searched out of many prior human experiences, tried and fitted to reality again and again" (1955, 1148).

From this perspective, Arensberg convincingly identifies five "types" of American communities, New England town; Southern county; Crossroads hamlet and main street town; Mill town and factory city; Metropolitan mass communication city.

Arensberg, in one brief paper (1955), tried to document for the United States a perception that he felt was emerging from comparative ethnological research wherever community studies have been carried out,

"For every American regional (sub-) culture that we can distinguish in American society and civilization, a particular form of the community is to be found. The ones we have spelled out here, each one quite different according to the measures that serve for all communities, are, as they have been often treated by novelists and historians, quite viable microcosms of the cultures whose florebat they graced, the New England town, the southern county, the open-country neighborhood and crossroads hamlet of the Atlantic region, the frontier and the Appalachians, the Main Street "service-center,". .. the Mormon village, the mill town, the metropolitan conglomeration" (1955, 1160).

## REDFIELD ON VARIATIONS AMONG COMMUNITIES AND HOW TO VIEW THEM

During the same period when Conrad Arensberg was developing his somewhat structural models of American communities, anthropologist Robert Redfield (1960), independently, was giving thought to how best we could describe "little" communities. What he came up with is certainly relevant to our concern about a network perspective on communities.

Redfield points out, as others have as well, that anthropologists and "empirical sociologists" have done most of their field work in little communities – in villages, small towns, and urban neighborhoods.

"What, then, do we mean more particularly by a little community? I put forward, first, the quality of distinctiveness, where the community begins and where it ends is apparent. The distinctiveness is apparent to the outside observer and is expressed in the group-consciousness of the people of the community" (Redfield 1960, 4).

He emphasizes his concern with the "smallness" of community, but our interest here is more in the concept of "community" itself, whether large or small. He himself cited "urban neighborhoods" as, if not typical, at least included. He also states that the communities he discusses "in these chapters" (1960) are homogeneous and "slow-changing." The little community tends to provide for all or most of the activities and needs of the people in it (of course that would be true of an urban neighborhood only in a secondary sense). And the little community is a "cradle-to-the-grave arrangement" (1960, 4).

In Redfield's view, the qualities of distinctiveness, smallness, homogeneity, and all-providing self-sufficiency characterize in different degrees a type of human community that he was writing about under the rubric of "little community." His interest, in the book by that name, was in the little community as a whole, as an ecological system, as a social structure, as a typical biography, as a kind of person, as an outlook on life, as a history, as a community within communities, and as a combination of opposites, as a whole and parts. The "network perspective" that I think he used is most obvious when he discusses social structure in terms of "whole and parts."

## "LOOSELY ORGANIZED" SOCIAL STRUCTURES, AND SO-CALLED "ATOMISTIC SOCIETIES"

In that same period during which community studies played such a prominent role in anthropology and empirical sociology, some scholars were entertaining discussions about the lack of strong institutions at the level of communities. I note especially, a group studying North American Indian societies and cultures (Barnouw 1961, 1974, Hickerson 1967) and another group studying Southeast Asian societies and cultures (Embree 1950, Hans-Dieter Evers 1969).

Some used the phrase "atomistic society" in these discussions. Strangely, there seems to have been no communication between the set of scholars focusing on Southeast Asia and those focusing on indigenous North America. Late in that game, Victor Barnouw attempted to clarify the concept, "The term 'atomism' in my usage refers to a loose form of social organization in which corporate organization and political authority are weak. Ruth Benedict lectured on this concept in courses at Columbia University in the 1940s; it is briefly discussed in her posthumously published lecture notes [Maslow and Honigmann 1970]" (Barnouw 1974, 419).

With regard to Southeast Asia, the atomistic social structure idea seems to have begun with John Embree who used the phrase "loosely structured social system" (1950). He may well have been exposed to Ruth Benedict's views, for he refers to her 1943-mimeographed document entitled "Thai Culture and Behavior." Both Embree and Benedict evaluated the degree to which individual behavior was influenced by membership in local communities by making comparisons with Japan. For example, "The local group in Japan, the hamlet, has a clear-cut social unity with special ceremonies for entry and exit and a whole series of rights and obligations for its members. Each man must sooner or later assume the responsibility of being the representative of the local group, each

must assist on occasions of hamlet cooperation such as road building or funeral preparations. In Thailand the hamlet also has its own identity and its members also have rights and duties, but they are not clearly defined and not strictly enforced. Exchange systems are less clear cut" (Embree 1950, as reprinted in Evers 1969).

What is remarkable to us now about these discussions is how much they would have benefited from using a formal network model. We know that in both of these culture areas (North America and Southeast Asia) little emphasis was put on local institutional organizations. But the scholars lacked ways of measuring that, and even lacked good terminology for talking about it. It was not until Brian Foster (1980) wrote about networks in Thai communities that network models were introduced into the discussion of Southeast Asia. To my knowledge, network structures never were introduced into discussions of the North American woodlands Indians such as the Ojibwa or Chippewa, discussed so extensively by Victor Barnouw (1974) and the others cited above.

There was considerable discussion in those days (1950-1970) about societies that seemed to have minimal local community organizations, minimally stable systems between the household level and the whole "society."

## WELLMAN, AND OTHERS, ON COMMUNITIES LOST, SAVED, AND LIBERATED

In an important chapter entitled "Networks as Personal Communities," Barry Wellman, Peter J. Carrington and Alan Hall looked at "the ways in which networks of informal relations fit persons and households into social structures" (1988, 131). As they studied a residential area of central Toronto labeled East York, they looked for the traditional community identifiers, e.g., "neighbors chatting on front porches, friends relaxing on street corners, cousins gathering for Sunday dinners, and storekeepers retailing local gossip" (1988, 130). When they "found few signs of active neighborhood life," they did not immediately draw the conclusion that community life had vanished in the densely populated town. Instead, they argue that community ties in East York were still robust, but were just represented in ways that were not apparent.

Until the 1960s, scholars were divided into three groups in terms of the extent of community life, which was greatly transformed by the large-scale social changes. Some asserted that community had been "lost," because "individuals had become isolated atoms in a 'mass society' – dependent on large bureaucracies for care and control" (Wellman et. al. 1988, 134). Contrary to this belief, some scholars maintained the "Community Saved" argument, evident by "abundant" and "strong" neighborhood and kinship groups that "acted as buffers against the large-scale forces, filled gaps in contemporary social systems by providing flexible, low-cost aid, and provided secure bases from which residents could powerfully engage the outside world" (p. 134).

Wellman et al. point out the faults of the two dichotomous views, that both arguments defined community as a "solidary," "local," and "kinship-like" group, and disregarded "widespread preindustrial individualism, exploitation, cleavage, and mobility." Going beyond the traditional short-distance community ties, some scholars find "Liberated" community, which is comprised of relationships beyond local areas, made available by cheap and convenient transportation and communication services.

Using a network model, the authors find that despite the empty streets, East Yorkers still maintained community ties in small clusters – "through meetings in private homes and on the telephone" – "and not in large, palpable bodies gathering in public squares, cafes, and meeting halls." Through the strands of ties and networks, the East Yorkers got and expected to get "companionship," "emotional aid," and "small services" both in daily life

and in crisis (Wellman et. al. 1988, 163). The authors analyze the functions of these networks,

First and foremost, the networks provide havens, a sense of being wanted and belonging, and readily available companionship. Second, they provide many "band-aids", emotional aid and small services to help East Yorkers cope with the stresses and strains of their current structural locations. Third, the outward linkages of network provide the East Yorkers with ladders to change their situations (jobs, houses, spouses) and levers (animal welfare, local politics, food additives) to change the world (Wellman et. al. 1988, 174-175).

In conclusion, Wellman et al. argued that the East Yorkers' ties and networks could not be explained with any single model of either Lost, Saved, and Liberated. Their personal networks did not conform to the Lost model, but some community patterns fit with the Saved model (e.g., women maintained close local relations with kin and men with workmates), and some patterns correspond to the Liberated model (e.g. several middle-class men use coworker ties to climb up the occupational ladder). Although the traditional densely knit solidarities are far and few, East Yorkers have managed to maintain their networks and community ties and seems to be satisfied with the support and reciprocity from them.

While none would doubt the existence of those personal support networks – "networks and community ties" – that Wellman and his colleagues describe in Toronto and that others have described for other cities, one should not believe that those social formations are real communities at all. R. B. Driskell and L. Lyon (2002) address this question directly in "Are Virtual Communities True Communities?" They certainly do not conform to the criteria that define communities in most other non-urban places in the world. They are not what Redfield was referring to by his phrase "urban neighborhoods," nor, I think the communities that Herbert Gans (1962) found populated by "Urban Villagers." Do not these networks of personal communities really form another kind of social entity that deserves special consideration or categorization in its own right? These networks that serve primarily the personal ends of individuals and households are indeed social phenomena that lie on the scale between the level of families or households and the level of nations or states, but perhaps they are not communities at all. They may be something akin to the network "action sets" described by Adrian Mayer (1966) and Whitten and Wolfe (1973).

## WHAT IS A COMMUNITY?

Definition remains a problem. What is a community? The question has both scientific and practical importance.

Scientifically, Carl Taylor's comments of 1944 are still relevant. As was pointed out earlier, without using the word "network," Taylor said that one who would study community needs to collect "information on the form, nature, and extent of social participation, including formal and informal groupings, leadership, visiting relationships and the like..." (p.438). It is clear that Taylor, and others of his time were already thinking of networks but did not have the techniques or concepts to put their thoughts into action. While they may not have been perfectly consistent, it seems that many sociologists and anthropologists of that period were not guilty of the charge often leveled at them, that they saw communities as clearly bounded, solidary entities.

Practically, the concept "community" really needs to be defined because it is used in many situations where what it means has real consequences. In the United States, Federal Environmental Laws and Regulations give communities standing, but are very unclear as to what they might be (John Stone 2000). The Magnuson Act includes important references to "fishing-dependent communities," and regulations are implemented somehow, but nobody has defined what that means (Yu Huang 2003). In Florida, privatization of child welfare is touted as "community based," but the system is structured through contracts from the Department of Children and Families at the state level to corporate service providers with no mechanisms for control at the local level, as described in documents on the web site of the Florida Health and Humans Services Board, Inc. http://www.fhhsb.org.

In 1999, in the Preface to Networks in the Global Village, Barry Wellman wrote that communities are far-flung social networks and not neighborhood solidarities. That, of course is not a definition but an important characterization that puts the emphasis on relationships rather than location.

"The thrust of social network analysis has been to reconnect the study of individuals to the relationships and structures of relationships in which they are embedded.... The trick has been to conceive of community as an egocentric network, a 'personal community,' rather than as a neighborhood" (Wellman 1999, xiv).

He continued, "The social network approach enables the authors in this book to study community without necessarily assuming that all communities are local solidarities. They do so by defining community as personal community, a person's set of ties with friends and relatives, neighbors and workmates (1999, xiv-xv).

Wellman identified a "Community Question" that has two parts; one part asks how the structure of large-scale social systems affects the composition, structure, and contents of interpersonal ties within them. The other asks how community networks (these egocentric personal communities or action sets) affect the nature of the large-scale systems in which they are embedded.

I don't feel comfortable defining community in that way. It is as if all social phenomena other than those egocentric networks are not a part of the "community" but exist only as non-community, parts of "large-scale social systems."

I prefer, rather, to envision a whole complex social system as being organized in levels, from a household/family level, upward through a hierarchy of levels, to the national (nation-state) and even beyond that to supranational (above-state) levels. Somewhere among those levels we should be able to identify a structure – even a loose cluster or set of nodes, a set of interlocking circles, a set of equivalent nodes – that is doing what Linton said there would always be a need for, making that connection between the immediate biological realities of humanity and the longer term historical continuity of human institutions. That complex whole, the structured set of phenomena, is what I would call community. The individuals and their apparently egocentric relations are obviously crucial to the relations at all levels, but there is more to the relations among the higher-level formations than just the interpersonal egocentric relations of individuals. Thus, those egocentric sets, while necessary to a community as well as to the individuals, are not in themselves the community.

I have absolutely no criticism of Wellman's statement that the "Community Question stands at a crucial nexus between societal and interpersonal social systems," and that it "juxtaposes the problem of the structural integration of a social system and the interpersonal means by which the members of this social system have access to scarce resources" (1999, 3). That inclusive system, not just the interpersonal system, is what I would call the community.

It is a kind of reductionism to put so much emphasis on individual interpersonal relations when one is trying to understand a community, a society, or other macro-system. We don't come to understand the biological human being by studying only the relations among the cells. Rather, we study the relations among cells in various structures, such as organs. The organs are variously related to one another even though those depend also on inter-cell relations. We will not understand human societies or the social systems of our entire species if we focus on the interpersonal relations among six billion individuals without taking into

account the various structures at intermediate and even global levels.

## NETWORK PERSPECTIVE ON COMMUNITIES

To see a community as a complex network, a first step might well be to collect data on egocentric networks and collate them. The next step should be to recognize the structuring provided when several individuals belong to the same groups. A network perspective on communities – or on structures relating to communities – includes seeing those groups both as networks of the individuals composing them and as nodes related to each other through their common members. Such "affiliation networks" are a little more complex than being just the sum of the personal networks.

The nodes of an affiliation network are not all of one kind; they include both persons and groups. This in itself is complicated enough, but it gets more complex when we recognize that the groups are themselves quite varied both structurally (internal relationships among their members and relationships with other groups and with other kinds of nodes) and functionally (what they do for their members and what they do with respect to persons and groups external to themselves). Edward Laumann and his associates, Galaskiewicz and Marsden, (1978) discussed such complications in "Community Structure as Interorganizational Linkages"

We know these human social networks are almost never "naturally" bounded. At the margins of every egocentric network, relations tend to shade off by degrees rather than being definitely on or off. Adding groups into the sets of relations we are considering does not make the matter of definition any easier. But we can set criteria for recognizing "boundaries," and there may be some regularities that will be discovered as "natural" seams or tears or gaps between segments of the whole seen in network perspective.

A conceptual distinction between Cosmopolitans and Locals, used by Robert K. Merton (1957) with reference to community leadership and by Alvin Gouldner (1957) in an analysis of roles in organizations, could be helpful in showing how the network perspective helps us to recognize a community as some kind of whole without its being an impenetrably bounded entity.

Take two persons who share a number of close, supportive, ties of the kind that Wellman tends to call "community ties" – kinship, frequency of communication by phone or email. They also are common members of a number of groups, working in the same university, serving together on a children's services advisory board, etc. Those two persons, along with other persons similarly connected, would have other ties of different strengths, some in common, some not so. All the ties that collectively define the community are not necessarily what Wellman calls "community" ties. Despite some different ties they have, they are connected in enough ways that we would have no difficulty identifying them as belonging to the same community, and then defining that community in terms of those many common connections including other persons and other groups as well. No perfect boundaries, but sufficient to recognize the "community" system.

Suppose one of those original persons had a brother with whom he is closely tied in terms of kinship and common boyhood experiences and continuing frequent, supportive, communication. But the brothers live far apart physically, and most of the current affiliations of the younger brother are not shared with the original person. Most of the brother's support networks, intimate ties with a number of persons, are not directly linked to the original person. While he provides a strong connection between his own network segment and that of his brother, he is in a different community.

Historically, some ties between different communities have been getting stronger over the years, due to increases in velocity of travel and increases in telecommunications, etc., blurring the boundaries between such network segments and therefore the boundaries between communities.

Each community can be seen as a fairly complex cluster in a larger network. When the gap or seam between the two communities is bridged with numerous ties, the two clusters will, at some point depending on the criteria we choose, be effectively merged. Then what had been two communities will become one. For such a determination, I recommend analysis something like that which Freeman developed in "On Measuring Systematic Integration" (1978), or perhaps something like that used in cultural consensus theory (Romney, Weller and Batchelder 1986).

The network perspective, especially in its graph theoretical aspects, uses "distance" in a different way so that it is no longer tied to geographic space, even though it might be labeled "geodesic." It is important to note that network distances need have very little relation to geographic distances. A "local structure" may include nodes that are not physically close in geographic space. This is a part of the "network perspective" that one has to be reminded of.

Having mentioned a gap or seam between segments or clusters within the larger network brings us to another structural analytic procedure that is applicable to our topic of network perspective on community. Ronald Burt deals with this sort of situation using the concepts of structural equivalence and structural holes (1982, 1992, 2001). Within a community seen as a network, there are sets of nodes (whether the nodes be persons or groups) that have the same or similar relations with others.

The nodes of such a set, whether they are tied to each other or not, are said to have structural equivalence. This is an important thing to know, whether the "local" ties of a set of persons and groups are equivalent. Recall that in network analysis, "local" doesn't have to mean geographical propinquity. But as one observes the current scene, which is still the most likely scenario. Obviously, people or groups who are physically adjacent have a common environment and some degree of common experience, both of which contribute to our conception of community.

Burt goes on to concern himself with the redundancy of ties that the condition of structural equivalence implies. "Structural hole" is the term Burt uses to refer to structural locations where there are few ties between denser segments of a network. Such places would be what I have above called seams or gaps. For me those terms, seams or gaps, evoke a more realistic image of the situation than the term "hole." In any event, Burt (2001) makes the point that while the conventional wisdom seems to have it that dense networks with high redundancy characteristic of cohesive or structurally equivalent sets indicate high social capital, a good argument can be made that the "structural holes" – areas of sparser connections – actually increase social capital by providing the opportunity for competitive advantage. He brings the two seemingly opposing propositions together in a "productive" way, saying, "while brokerage across structural holes is the source of added value, closure can be critical to realizing the value buried in the structural holes" (2001, 52).

If it is not obvious to the reader that structural equivalence and structural holes are crucial to understanding the network aspects of communities, that may be in part because community is not a concept that Burt uses, except quite metaphorically. For example, "Groups can be distinguished on many criteria. I have in mind the two network criteria that define information redundancy (cohesion and structural equivalence), but it is just as well to have in mind a more routine group, a family, a team, a neighborhood, or some broader community such as an industry" (2001, 47). I cannot find an instance where Burt talks about a whole community in the sense that we have been thinking of it. Whatever his conception of community, I believe Burt, like me, would see it as a network, a complex network identifiable through application of network criteria.

Beyond structural equivalence is another kind of equivalence that is perhaps even more important to understanding the network structure of communities. It is called "regular equivalence" (White and Reitz 1983; Borgatti and Everett 1992; Doreian 1999). Regular equivalence is even less dependent on physical or geographical propinquity, but is, in my opinion, crucial to understanding community as a complex network.

The more complex the system of actors, the less does structural equivalence alone, with its local focus, tells us about the whole. Borgatti and Everett put it this way, "The concepts of structural, automorphic, and regular equivalence are listed in order of increasing generalization, Any pair of nodes that is structurally equivalent is also necessarily automorphically and regularly equivalent, and any pair of automorphically equivalent nodes is also regularly equivalent" (1992, 4). Regular equivalencies reveal more general structures beyond the "local" ones found with structural equivalence. As Patrick Doreian puts it, "At a conceptual level, regular equivalence may be more useful than structural equivalence in representing roles and role structures. For each equivalence, a position is occupied by equivalent actors" (1999, p.7). Where the networks are complex – and in any communities, networks are complex – regular equivalence can reveal structures within and between communities.

The regular equivalence algorithm identifies a sort of "pure" structure of relationships with considerable independence from the substantive content of the relationships.

Even beyond that, analysis of the patterns of relationships among persons or corporations or other nodes in a large complex network can tell us the degree to which that network has a hierarchical structure even if this is not apparent to the participants or to outside observers.

These are the kinds of analyses that are necessary in order to define and understand communities.

## SORTING THE SUBSYSTEMS

In such an enterprise, I have used techniques of this kind to try to find the structure of a network of six hundred agencies and organizations, some public and some private, that serve children and families in a multi-county area. In that study, initially funded by National Science Foundation, Grant No. BNS-9023383, 1991-1993, the question for me was whether analysis of their patterns of relationships could identify subsets of organizations that are assignable to different levels of integration, community level being among them. Can some organizations be said to operate primarily at the highest level – state or national – others primarily at the lowest level – perhaps "neighborhood" – and others operating in subsystems somewhere between – in what we might identify as the community levels in the sense that we have been using community in this paper?

I collected data on the relations among hundreds of organizations serving children and families in the several counties of the Tampa Bay area, administrative relations, relations based on common clientele, and fiscal relations. The analysis I will speak of here is based on one 577 X 577 adjacency matrix that summarized those complex data, recognizing only whether or not there was a relation between each pair, and ignoring both the type and strength of those relations. Geodesic distances were calculated for those 166,176 pairs, as were centralities, both closeness and betweenness for each of the 577 nodes. I am compelled to note here that that study – tagged by me "electronic ethnography" – was data-heavy for community studies of that period, 1995-1996, using data base management tools that were sophisticated for that time.

Regular equivalence coefficients were calculated for all pairs. Then, multi-dimensional scaling coefficients were calculated for the matrix of REGE coefficients. Applying hierarchical cluster analysis (HCA) to the MDS coefficients, the nodes were sorted into cluster/blocks, paying attention to the proportion of ties within each block and the proportion of ties between each pair of blocks, etc. Due to limitations of the equipment and programs available to me in 1995, I had to do each of these steps, I won't say "by hand," but, not as efficiently as it might be done today.

Application of HCA to the MDS coordinates produced a list of the 577 organizations, giving each node the cluster number with which it was associated. The distribution of those 577 nodes was then plotted with each node being labeled with its cluster number. Figure 1 shows that distribution. A first division into three sets is clearly visible with the naked eye. There is a top set (a cluster of nodes) all bearing the label 6, a middle set of clusters of nodes bearing the labels 1, 2, 3, and 4, and a bottom set of clusters of nodes bearing the labels 5, 7, and 8.

Before going on, I should mention that the one outlying node labeled 9 at the very bottom of the figure is the result of an error, my failure to remove that one organization when I removed others that, like this one, had only one tie to the rest of the network. Instead of dealing with 577 nodes, I should have been dealing with only 576.

The distribution of all the organizations shown in Figure 1 is based on the complex patterns of relations among them. The distribution is, it seems, indicative of differential participation in subsystems at different levels of integration. The organizations in Cluster 6 may operate predominantly in a wider-scale subsystem in terms of both area and function. The others, while still participating in the whole, may operate predominantly in subsystems that are narrower in range and lower on the scale of levels of integration. In Figure 1, one does not see all 577 nodes in this figure because 177 of them are "hidden" behind others in this two-dimensional representation of a multi-dimensional distribution.

Node labels represent membership in one of eight sets based on regular equivalence. [The node labeled 9 at -4.9 and -0.3 is an input error that node

*Figure 1. Distribution of 577 organizations based on regular equivalence coefficients*

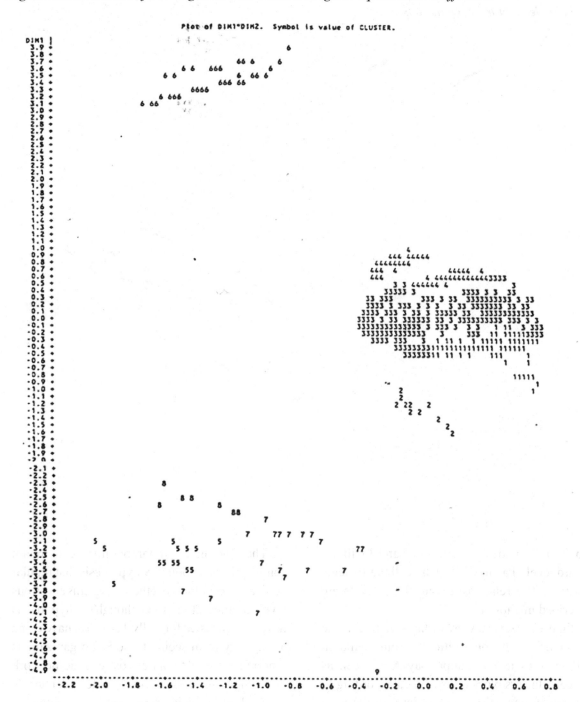

should have been removed prior to the analysis, and there should have been only 576 nodes.]

Hierarchical cluster analysis (HCA) permits one to identify clusters within clusters at dif-

ferent levels of hierarchy. Figure 1 reveals just two of those levels – one being the three-cluster "solution," that which is visually obvious, the other being the 8-level solution indicated by the

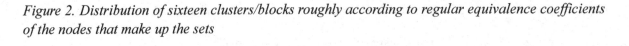

*Figure 2. Distribution of sixteen clusters/blocks roughly according to regular equivalence coefficients of the nodes that make up the sets*

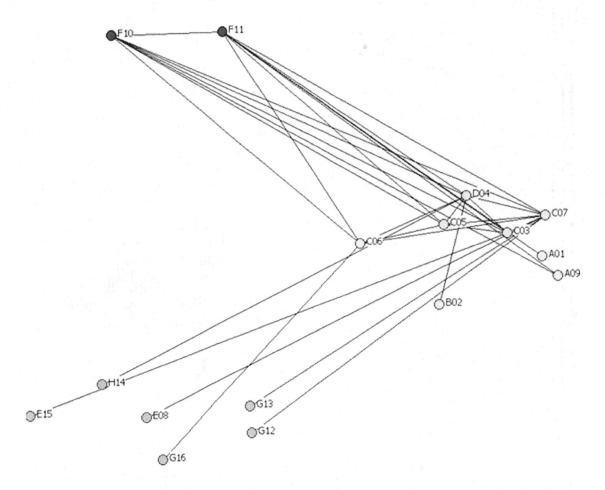

labels on the nodes, 1-8. Figures 2 and 3 will use a third level of analysis, which I call the 16-level solution. The relations among these levels are described in Table 1.

Figure 2 shows a view of the structure of the 577-node set of organizations serving children and families in the Tampa Bay Area, seen as sixteen clusters/blocks, distributed according to the regular equivalence coefficients of the individual nodes that are included in each of the regular equivalence sets. Remember that the clusters are based, not on cohesiveness, but on regular equivalence (having similar relations with others that are themselves equivalent).

The findings thus far permit me to retain some optimism about my hypothesis that regular equivalence will sort out the subsystems at various levels of integration. Even though the hypothesis has not been tested formally, I think we have come a long way from seeing these 577 organizations randomly related in an almost chaotic network of relations to seeing considerable order in 16, 8, or 3 blocks made up of clusters of somewhat equivalent nodes.

Looking at these figures as representing a view of the structure of communities from a network perspective, one must remember that the 577 organizations represented by these 16 nodes are

*Figure 3. Network of the 16 clusters/blocks of 576 agencies in the Tampa Bay area. The lines represent whether there are linkages between organizations in the different clusters.*

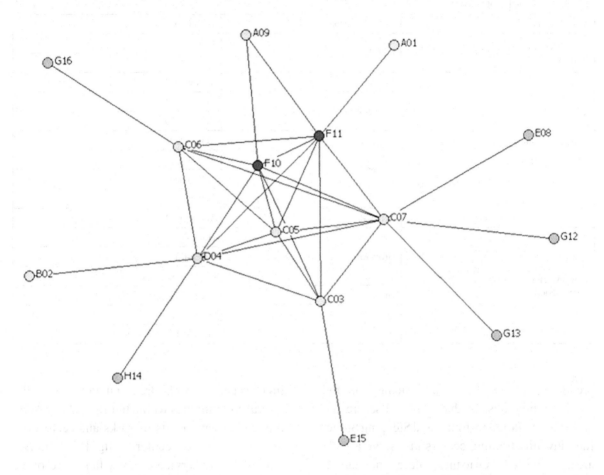

actually composed of thousands of persons carrying out the missions of the hundreds of organizations – and, of course, that each node itself represents a set of organizations. Within each cluster are many connections that are not shown as lines. The lines that do show represent the fact that there are some relations among organizations in clusters at the different levels.

How does this structural view relate to the real community? Think of the lower block or set of six green nodes in Figure 2 as representing the community-based organizations most directly serving the thousands of families living in the local communities of the Tampa Bay Area. Then the eight yellow nodes represent eight sets of organizations whose staff help to organize and

support the organizations that directly serve the communities. Finally the two red nodes at the top of Figure 2 represent the sets of agencies whose staff members represent the larger society, the State of Florida, national child welfare agencies, the "health system," and so forth. In terms of the "local versus cosmopolitan" dichotomy mentioned earlier, the organizations involved in the bottom blocks are like the locals, whereas those in the top blocks tend to be cosmopolitan, those in the middle blocks acting in their communities with connections both upward in the cosmopolitan direction and downward in the local direction.

Among the organizations in the top block are the several District Offices of the State Department of Health and Rehabilitative Services, the

*Table 1. Hierarchical nesting of clusters*

| Hierarchical Nesting of Clusters | | |
|---|---|---|
| 3-cluster perspective. | 8-cluster perspective | 16-cluster perspective |
| High level, wide coverage, red in figures 2 and 3. | Red-F | Red-F10 |
| | | Red-F11 |
| Mid level, medium coverage, yellow in figures 2 and 3. | Yellow-D | Yellow-D04 |
| | Yellow-A | Yellow-A01 |
| | | Yellow-A09 |
| | Yellow-C | Yellow-C03 |
| | | Yellow-C05 |
| | | Yellow-C06 |
| | | Yellow-C07 |
| | Yellow-B | Yellow-B02 |
| Low level, narrow coverage, green in figures 2 and 3. | Green-G | Green-G12 |
| | | Green-G13 |
| | | Green-G16 |
| | Green-H | Green-H14 |
| | Green-E | Green-E08 |
| | | Green-E15 |

predominant arms of the State reaching into the local communities. In that cluster also are the Associated Marine Institutes and Stepping Stone, Inc., juvenile training centers that serve a wide area, not limited even to this multi-county region, and All Children's Hospital, which, although located in St. Petersburg in Pinellas County, has a very broad service area as a regional hospital. Another is Florida Sheriffs Youth Ranch, which also serves a wide area, essentially the whole state. The Juvenile Welfare Board of Pinellas County is not so much a local service agency as it is a planning and evaluation institution, some of whose members are named by the Governor of the State, and its purview includes a wide range of planning for child welfare, not direct service. In a similar situation are Hillsborough County Head Start, Pinellas County Social Services, and Hillsborough County Department of Children's Services, and the YMCA.

In the middle range of clusters or blocks we find the large majority of agencies that provide direct services to children and families in the several communities within the Tampa Bay Area, municipal departments of parks and recreation, children's service centers, Big Brothers/Big Sisters, family service centers, family resource centers, family support centers, runaway centers, Women-Infants-Children (WIC) Office, Boy Scouts, Boys and Girls Clubs, Child and Family Developmental Services, Child Care Facilities Advisory Board, Children's Medical Services, Easter Seals Rehab Center, family group homes, family protection teams, Foster Parents Association, MacDonald Training Center, Mary Martha House, Parents Without Partners, developmental day care centers, women's resource centers, and many others.

In the bottom range of clusters or blocks we find organizations less focused on children, such as local hospitals – Horizon Hospital, Mease Hospital, Morton Plant Hospital, and Tampa Community Health Center – and such as adult institutions – AARP, Abilities Inc., Private Industry Council, American Cancer Society, Artists Unlimited, Deaf Service Center, Thomason Adult Centers, and Dunedin Community Center, Lowry Park Zoo, etc.

My interpretation of the results is that there are three reasonably recognizable regular equivalence sets that appear to represent roughly three different levels of integration. Figure 3, in which each node represents a set of "equivalent" organizations, shows that when you plot them according to the cohesive distances between blocks (rather than the coefficients of equivalence as in Figure 2) the network takes on the shape of roughly concentric circles around a "core."

Both of these visualizations are important to seeing "community" and its social environment in a network perspective.

More sophisticated approaches to the analysis of hierarchically nested sub-networks are being developed currently by other scholars also studying complex systems. I mention particularly three threads here.

One of those threads is expressed in the work of M. Girvan and E. J. Newman (2002). It is based on the idea that cohesive clusters with relatively strong ties within each are connected by weaker ties to form wider systems in a hierarchical structure, and that the identification of levels in such a system is facilitated by removing nodes successively to discover the structure.

Another thread of the kind of analysis I believe could serve to find the structures that help define effective human communities within wider social frameworks is represented in the work of an interdisciplinary group described well in Network science, Complexity in nature and technology edited by Ernesto Estrada et al. (2010). Using a measure of communicability they describe as a broad generalization of the concept of the shortest path, they identify communities within complex networks.

The other thread is expressed in the work of Douglas R. White and several colleagues using a graph theoretical basis with deeper roots but laid out clearly by White and Harary in 2001 under the title "The Cohesiveness of Blocks in Social Networks, Node Connectivity and Conditional Density" (White and Harary 2001). White and his associates, Moody, Owen-Smith and Powell, are developing and testing what they call Predictive Social Cohesion Theory (Moody and White 2003, White, Owen-Smith, Moody and Powell 2004).

While none of these three approaches has been demonstrated on any system quite so complex as the kinds of social systems that we have concerned ourselves with in this article – "whole" communities embedded in "whole" societies – there is no doubt that they are making enormous advances technically and theoretically. I will very briefly summarize Girvan and Newman first, then Estrada and Hatano, and finally, the approach of White and his colleagues in which I see more promise, perhaps because it is more rooted in my own discipline of anthropology.

Girvan and Newman clearly are thinking of these complex networks in both social and biological hierarchies, as I tend to do. "It is a matter of common experience," they say, "that such networks seem to have communities in them, subsets of vertices within which vertex-vertex connections are dense, but between which connections are less dense" (2002, 7821). They elaborate parenthetically, "Certainly it is possible that the communities themselves also join together to form metacommunities, and that those metacommunities are themselves joined together, and so on in a hierarchical fashion" (7821). They propose a method for detecting such community structure and then they apply it to the study of a number of different social and biological networks. They state their algorithm simply in four steps,

1. Calculate the betweenness for all edges in the network.
2. Remove the edge with the highest betweenness.
3. Recalculate the betweenness for all edges affected by the removal.
4. Repeat from step 2 until no edges remain.

Girvan and Newman are encouraged by the success of their method in identifying hierarchically ordered communities in relative simple data sets such as that in Zachary's (1977) Karate Club study and in the network formed by American college football competition. They admit, however, that it is not yet feasible to use on networks of greater scale. "Perhaps," they state, "the basic principles of our approach – focusing on the boundaries of communities rather than their cores, and making use of edge betweenness – can be incorporated into a modified method that scales more favorably with network size" (p. 7826).

Within a broad enterprise labeled the "science of connectivity," Estrada and Hatano (2008) propose a measure of communicability of a complex network they describe as a broad generalization of the concept of the shortest path. Recognizing that Community identification has been an active area of research in complex networks, they illustrate the identification of network communities by using their communicability function.

Estrada and Hatano (2008), investigating the structure-dynamics relationship in complex networks, use the correlation between the node degree and the "communicability function" that they have earlier defined (p. 3) to demonstrate several ways to classify a set of "real-world" complex systems into a small number of universality classes based on their structure-dynamic correlation (p. 11).

"In addition," they write in their abstract, "the new communicability measure is able to distinguish finer structures of networks, such as communities into which a network is divided. A community is unambiguously defined here as a set of nodes displaying larger communicability among them than to the rest of the nodes in the network"(p. 1). Like Girvan and Newman, Estrada and Hatano use Zachary's (1977) karate club data to illustrate their way of identifying communities within a network. Recognizing the limitations of their illustration, they say, "An interesting feature of this method is that it permits one to find overlapping communities in the network, which

is closer to the real-life situation than the definition of isolated communities"(p. 39). While I do respect the attempts at identifying communities on the part of Estrada and Hatano, as I do those of Girvan and Newman, for my own purposes of trying to identify real human communities within wider complex societies, the simple small clusters of members in Zachary's karate club are not very convincing models of real human communities.

The third thread, that of Douglas R. White and his coauthor James Moody, is, I believe, further along, and, as I said, more rooted in anthropology. In an article entitled "Structural Cohesion and Embeddedness, A Hierarchical Concept of Social Groups," White and Moody (2003) link social cohesion and social embeddedness "by developing a concept of structural cohesion based on network node connectivity" (2003). Then the structural dimension of embeddedness is defined through the hierarchical nesting of these cohesive structures.

This theoretical effort was built upon earlier ethnographic studies, notable among which are "Class, Property and Structural Endogamy, Visualizing Networked Histories" (Brudner and White 1997), and "Kinship, Property Transmission, and Stratification in Javanese Villages" (White and Schweizer 1998). The groundwork was thus laid for the next step by White and his colleagues that resulted in the publication entitled "Networks, Fields and Organizations, Micro-Dynamics, Scale and Cohesive Embeddings" (White, Owen-Smith, Moody and Powell 2004). Even more recently, White and Johansen present analyses of this kind in more detail in Network Analysis and Ethnographic Problems, Process Models of a Turkish Nomad Clan (2005). One brief quote suggests the relevance of this work for our concern of how any given community is a network embedded in a network of networks, "Networks are open systems in which boundedness is a relative phenomenon, not a matter of self-contained local systems" (White and Johansen 2005, 64).

Although White and his colleagues seldom use the term "community" precisely as I use it in this paper, their general approach fits well my own conception of community as being a subsystem identifiable at some level within a complex hierarchically structured network system.

These new techniques for network analysis open up new possibilities for us to better understand human communities.

A human community is certainly much more than a set of relations among individuals. In network perspective a community network is a set of levels including not only direct interpersonal relations but also relations among the clusters and groups and corporate entities making it up. At the same time, above a community in the hierarchy of a complex society, are the interacting components of wider systems, whether they be tribes, regions, states, and/or supranational systems. We may not yet be defining and describing human communities clearly in network terms, but we are beginning to see how it can be done.

## REFERENCES

Anderson, J. N., & Keyes, C. F. (1970). Perspectives on loosely organized social structures. *The Journal of Asian Studies, 9*(2), 415–419.

Arensberg, C. M. (1955). American communities. *American Anthropologist, 57*, 1143–1152. doi:10.1525/aa.1955.57.6.02a00060

Arensberg, C. M., & Kimball, S. T. (1940). *Family and community in Ireland*. Cambridge, MA.

Barnouw, V. (1961). Chippewa social atomism. *American Anthropologist, 63*, 1006–1013. doi:10.1525/aa.1961.63.5.02a00080

Barnouw, V. (1974). On Lieberman's use of the concept of atomism: Comment on *Atomism and mobility among underclass Chippewas and whites* by L Lieberman, with a reply by L Lieberman. *Human Organization, 33*, 418–421.

Borgatti, S. P., & Everett, M. G. (1992). Notions of position in social network analysis. In Marsden, P. (Ed.), *Sociological methodology* (pp. 1–35). doi:10.2307/270991

Borgatti, S. P., Everett, M. G., & Freeman, L. C. (2002). *UCINET for Windows: Software for social network analysis*. Harvard, MA: Analytic Technologies.

Brudner, L., & White, D. R. (1997). Class property and structural endogamy: Visualizing networked histories. *Theory and Society, 25*, 161–208. doi:10.1023/A:1006883119289

Burt, R. S. (1982). *Toward a structural theory of action: Network models of social structure perception and action*. New York, NY: Academic Press.

Burt, R. S. (1992). *Structural holes: The social structure of competition*. Cambridge, MA: Harvard University Press.

Burt, R. S. (2001). Structural holes versus network closure as social capital. In Lin, N., Cook, K., & Burt, R. S. (Eds.), *Social capital: Theory and research*. New York, NY: Aldine De Gruyter.

Christiansen, K., & Levinson, D. (Eds.). (2003). *Encyclopedia of community: From the village to the virtual world*. Thousand Oaks, CA: Sage Publications.

Commission on Children at Risk. (2003). *Hardwired to connect: The new scientific case for authoritative communities*. New York, NY: Institute for American Values.

Doreian, P. (1999). An intuitive introduction to blockmodeling with examples. *BMS Bulletin de Methodologie Sociologique, 61*, 5–34.

Driskell, R. B., & Lyon, L. (2002). Are virtual communities true communities? *City & Community, 1*, 373–390. doi:10.1111/1540-6040.00031

Embree, J. (1950). Thailand: A loosely structured social system. *American Anthropologist, 52,* 181–193. doi:10.1525/aa.1950.52.2.02a00030

Estrada, E. (Eds.). (2010). *Network science: Complexity in nature and technology.* London, UK: Springer-Verlag.

Estrada, E., & Hatano, N. (2008). Communicability in complex networks. *Physical Review E: Statistical, Nonlinear, and Soft Matter Physics, 77*(3), 036111. doi:10.1103/PhysRevE.77.036111

Evers, H. D. (Ed.). (1969). *Loosely structured social systems: Thailand in perspective.* Cultural Report Series No 17. New Haven, CT: Yale University (Southeast Asia Studies).

Fortes, M. (1953). The structure of unilineal descent groups. *American Anthropologist, 55,* 17–41. doi:10.1525/aa.1953.55.1.02a00030

Foster, B. L. (1980). Minority traders in Thai village social networks. *Ethnic Groups, 2*(3), 221–240.

Freeman, L. C. (1978). On measuring systematic integration. *Connections, 2*(1), 13–14.

Gallaher, A. (1961). *Plainville fifteen years later.* New York, NY: Columbia University Press.

Gans, H. J. (1962). Urbanism and suburbanism as ways of life. In Rose, A. M. (Ed.), *Human behavior and social processes: An interactionist approach.* Boston, MA: Houghton Mifflin.

Girvan, M., & Newman, M. E. J. (2002). Community structure in social and biological networks. *Proceedings of the National Academy of Sciences of the United States of America, 99*(12), 8271–8276. doi:10.1073/pnas.122653799

Goldschmidt, W. (1947). *As you sow.* New York, NY: Harcourt Brace.

Gouldner, A. (1957). Cosmopolitans and locals: Toward an analysis of latent social roles. *Administrative Science Quarterly, 2*(3), 281–306. doi:10.2307/2391000

Hickerson, H. (1967). The feast of the dead among the seventeenth century Algonkians of the upper Great Lakes. *American Anthropologist, 62,* 81–107. doi:10.1525/aa.1960.62.1.02a00050

Huang, Y. (2003). *Fishing-dependent communities on the Gulf Coast of Florida: Their identification, recent decline and present resilience.* Master's Thesis, University of South Florida.

Krackhard, D., Blythe, J., & McGrath, C. (1994). Krackplot 3.0: An improved network drawing program. *Connections, 17*(2), 53–55.

Laumann, E. O., Galaskiewicz, J., & Marsden, P. (1978). Community structure as interorganizational linkages. *Annual Review of Sociology, 4,* 455–484. doi:10.1146/annurev.so.04.080178.002323

Lin, N., Cook, K., & Burt, R. S. (Eds.). (2001). *Social capital: Theory and research.* New York, NY: Aldine de Gruyter.

Linton, R. (1936). *The study of man.* New York, NY: Appleton-Century-Crofts.

Lynch, O. M. (1984). *Culture and community in Europe: Essays in honor of Conrad M Arensberg.* Delhi, India: Hindustan Publication Corp.

Lynd, R. S., & Lynd, H. M. (1929). *Middletown: A study in American culture.* New York, NY: Harcourt Brace and Company.

Maine, H. (1866). *Ancient law.* London, UK: Oxford University Press.

Maslow, A. H., & Honigmann, J. J. (1970). Synergy: Some notes of Ruth Benedict. *American Anthropologist, 72,* 320–333. doi:10.1525/aa.1970.72.2.02a00060

Mayer, A. C. (1966). The significance of quasi-groups in the study of complex societies. In Banton, M. (Ed.), *The social anthropology of complex societies. ASA Monograph no 4*. New York, NY: Praeger.

Merton, R. K. (1957). *Social theory and social structure*. Glencoe, IL: Free Press.

Moody, J., & White, D. R. (2003). Structural cohesion and embeddedness: A hierarchical concept of social groups. *American Sociological Review*, *68*(1), 103–127. doi:10.2307/3088904

Putnam, R. (2000). *Bowling alone: The collapse and revival of American community*. New York, NY: Simon and Schuster.

Redfield, R. (1960). *The little community and peasant society and culture*. Chicago, IL: University of Chicago Press.

Reitz, K. P., & White, D. R. (1989). Rethinking the role concept: Homomorphisms in social networks. In Freeman, L. C., White, D. R., & Romney, A. K. (Eds.), *Research methods in social network analysis* (pp. 429–488). Fairfax, VA: George Mason University Press.

Romney, A. K., Weller, S. C., & Batchelder, W. H. (1986). Culture as consensus: A theory of culture and informant accuracy. *American Anthropologist*, *88*(2), 313–338. doi:10.1525/aa.1986.88.2.02a00020

Stone, J. V. (2000). *Public participation in environmental management: Seeking participatory equity through ethnographic inquiry*. Doctoral Dissertation, University of South Florida.

Taylor, C. (1945). Techniques of community study and analysis as applied to modern civilized societies. In Linton, R. (Ed.), *The science of man in the world crisis* (pp. 416–441). New York, NY: Columbia University Press.

Warner, W. L., & Lunt, P. S. (1941). *The social life of a modern community*. New Haven, CT: Yale University Press.

Warner, W. L., & Lunt, P. S. (1942). *The status system of a modern community*. New Haven, CT: Yale University Press.

Weber, M. (1947). *The theory of social and economic organisation*, (transl. by A. R. Hudson and Talcott Parsons).

Wellman, B. (Ed.). (1999). *Networks in the global village: Life in contemporary communities*. Boulder, CO: Westview Press.

Wellman, B., & Berkowitz, S. D. (Eds.). (1988). *Social structures: A network approach*. Greenwich, CT: JAI Press.

Wellman, B., Carrington, P. J., & Hall, A. (1988). Networks as personal communities. In Wellman, B., & Berkowitz, S. D. (Eds.), *Social structures: A network approach*. New York, NY: Cambridge University Press.

West, J. (1945). *Plainville, USA*. New York, NY: Columbia University Press.

White, D. R. (2003). Ties weak and strong. In Christensen, K., & Levinson, D. (Eds.), *Encyclopedia of community* (*Vol. 4*, pp. 1376–1379). Thousand Oaks, CA: Sage Reference.

White, D. R. (2005). Ring cohesion in marriage and social networks. In Degenne, A. (Ed.), *Social networks, Mathématiques informatique et sciences humaines. Journal of the Ecole des Hautes Etudes en Science Sociales Paris*. doi:10.4000/msh.2940

White, D. R., & Harary, F. (2001). The cohesiveness of blocks in social networks: Node connectivity and conditional density. *Sociological Methodology*, *31*, 305–359. doi:10.1111/0081-1750.00098

White, D. R., & Johansen, U. (2005). *Network analysis and ethnographic problems: Process models of a Turkish nomad clan*. Lanham, MD: Lexington Books.

White, D. R., Owen-Smith, J., Moody, J., & Powell, W. W. (2004). Networks fields and organizations: Micro-dynamics, scale and cohesive embeddings. *Computational & Mathematical Organization Theory, 10*(2), 95–117. doi:10.1023/B:CMOT.0000032581.34436.7b

White, D. R., & Reitz, K. (1983). Graph and semigroup homomorphisms on networks of relations. *Social Networks, 5*(2), 193–234. doi:10.1016/0378-8733(83)90025-4

Whitten, N. A., & Wolfe, A. W. (1973). Network analysis. In Honigmann, J. (Ed.), *Handbook of social and cultural anthropology* (pp. 717–746). Chicago, IL: Rand-McNally.

Wolf, E. R. (1955). Types of Latin American peasantry: A preliminary discussion. *American Anthropologist, 57*(3, Part 1), 452–471. doi:10.1525/aa.1955.57.3.02a00050

Wolf, E. R. (1957). Closed corporate communities in Mesoamerica and Java. *Southwestern Journal of Anthropology, 13*(1), 1–18.

Wolf, E. R. (1986). The vicissitudes of the closed corporate peasant community. *American Ethnologist, 13*(2), 325–329. doi:10.1525/ae.1986.13.2.02a00080

Wolfe, A. W. (1961). *In the Ngombe tradition: Continuity and change in the Congo*. Evanston, IL: Northwestern University Press.

Wolfe, A. W. (1963). The African mineral industry: Evolution of a supranational level of integration. *Social Problems, 11*(2), 153–164. doi:10.1525/sp.1963.11.2.03a00040

Wolfe, A. W. (1970). On structural comparisons of networks. *The Canadian Review of Sociology and Anthropology. La Revue Canadienne de Sociologie et d'Anthropologie, 7*(4), 226–244. doi:10.1111/j.1755-618X.1970.tb01296.x

Wolfe, A. W. (1977). The supranational organization of production. *Current Anthropology, 18*(4), 615–636. doi:10.1086/201973

Wolfe, A. W. (2005). Connecting the dots without forgetting the circles. *Connections, 26*(2), 107–119.

Wolfe, A. W., Lex, B. W., & Yancey, W. L. (1968). *The Soulard area: Adaptations by urban White families to poverty*. St Louis, MO: The Social Science Institute Washington University.

Zachary, W. W. (1977). An information flow model of conflict and fission in small groups. *Journal of Anthropological Research, 33*(4), 452–473.

## KEY TERMS AND DEFINITIONS

**Anthropology/Anthropological:** Scientific study of human form and behavior.

**Block:** In networks, a subset of nodes seen as occupying a position relative to others in a network.

**Cluster:** In networks, a subset of nodes that are relatively more connected with each other than with others in a network.

**Communicability:** In networks, measure of the degree to which a set of nodes communicate among themselves rather than with the rest of the nodes in the network.

**Corporate:** Having the character of a single entity, e.g. a set of nodes that behave as one in their relations with others.

**Embedded:** In hierarchical systems, the condition of a subsystem operating within a wider system or subsystem.

**Equivalence:** In networks, similarity measured in reference to relations among nodes (structural, automorphic, regular).

**Level (of integration):** In a hierarchical system, the position relative to the subsytems embedded within it and relative to the systems in which it is embedded.

**Node:** In networks, a point or vertex representing a component connected to others by arcs, lines, or edges.

**Structural:** Pertaining to and emphasizing the relations among elements.

# Chapter 3
# Civic Engagement and Communication Technology Networks

**Philip J. Salem**
*Texas State University, USA*

## ABSTRACT

*Individuals address public issues by becoming involved with civic groups and performing civic activities such as charity and political work. Changes in communication technology have led to changes in civic engagement, and it is now possible to perform civic activities digitally. Actors develop social networks as they use various communication technologies, and the resultant networks act as passive constraints on individual activities. This chapter reports the results and implications of one study exploring the relationships between civic engagement and communication technology networks.*

*The researcher investigated face-to-face, telephone, email, private electronic, and public electronic communication networks. Private electronic communication networks develop through text messaging, instant messaging, and private chat, and public electronic communication networks emerge through the exchange of messages over blogs, social network sites, and Twitter. Results indicate individuals used different technology to develop different networks to assist them in different ways. Public electronic communication was unrelated to civic engagement.*

DOI: 10.4018/978-1-61350-444-4.ch003

# CIVIC ENGAGEMENT AND COMMUNICATION TECHNOLOGY NETWORKS

Civic engagement (CE) involves those individual and collective actions designed to identify and address issues of public concern (APA, 2010). CE includes participation in social groups, charitable groups, and political groups. The construct involves all forms of service learning and community service, and public figures often call for greater involvement of the public in common concerns (The White House, 2010). The Journal of Civic Commitment is a biannual publication devoted to research in this area.

Putnam (1995, 2000) is one source of the current scholarly interest in CE. Individuals obtain various resources through their connections to others, and social capital refers to those resources that would otherwise not be available outside a social network. Putnam argues that there was another type of social capital - resources shared by all by virtue of being connected in the same community. He contended that Americans are connected less to each other and are losing that common social capital. Individuals are more socially isolated and less involved with each other for a common good. There is less social engagement. Others echo these concerns (McPherson, Smith-Lovin, & Brashears, 2006; Pew Research Center, 2010).

Three factors challenge these arguments. First, the nature of community is changing. Wellman and his colleagues argue that individuals construct their own communities, and personal networks are the locus of CE (Chua, Madej, & Wellman, 2011). Communities are changing from places such as neighborhoods or collections of people with shared interests, to the set of people connected to a person – a personal community. This argument suggests the next challenge by noting that communication has evolved from door-to-door, to place-to-place, to person-to-person. Technology leads to the blending of local and global.

A second factor is the nature of communication technology. Communication is a social process in which individuals in a relationship construct messages as part of ongoing episodes (Salem, 2009). Communication technology refers to the way people communicate with each other. Contemporary technologies include e-mail, private electronic technology such as text messaging or instant messaging, and public electronic communication such as exchanging messages on a blog or through social networking sites, as well as telephone and face-to-face methods. The nature of this technology means that individuals may engage in CE in many ways. People may discuss issues, exchange opinions, and contribute actual civic behavior and funds electronically as well as in traditional ways. A recent report suggests that greater Internet involvement related strongly to greater overall CE (Smith, Lehman Scholzman, Verba, & Brady, 2009).

Finally, the emerging structures of networks act as passive constraints to individual action (Salem, 2008, 2009). As individuals communicate with each other, they develop a pattern of interactions forming a network. A network constrains the interactions of an individual, making some interactions more likely than others and some resources easier to obtain than others. Although an individual has direct control over his or her own messages and some control over the interactions with direct contacts - alters, individuals have less and less influence on the interactions between alters or between the alters of alters. No one individual or group of individuals controls a network, but a network emerges through the accumulation of individual local actions. A network is a passive constraint on local actions, including CE. People communicate in different ways, developing separate communication technology networks and different passive constraints.

The purpose of this chapter is to report on an investigation of the relationships between communication technology personal networks and civic engagement. I review current research on civic engagement and communication networks, and I report the preliminary results of a study involving American young people. Throughout this essay I will note the application of this material to the international community.

## THE CHANGING NATURE OF CIVIC ENGAGEMENT AND COMMUNICATION

### Culture, Community, Network

Culture is a set of communicative practices distinguishing one group from another (Salem, 2009). One identifies a set of practices because actors repeat episodes with variation. Individuals discard, add, or amplify some behaviors as they develop mental scripts for the later performance of the episodes. Instrumental social routines are practices accomplishing some task function, and rituals are communication practices defining, reinforcing, or changing relationships between actors (Rothenbuhler, 1998). Rituals may involve formal rites and ceremonies, but most rituals are sequences actors eventually may enact mindlessly as part of making sense of each other and each other together. The tendency to reenact functional episodes is a constraint, and the constraint is passive since the actor loses agency with each successive reenactment. Furthermore, no one person or persons have agency over the set of group communicative practices, and the practices do not have agency in and of themselves. The natural movement from loose coupled behaviors, reflection, and mindfulness to tightly coupled sequences, reflex, and mindlessness explains the emergence of the constraint. Culture is a passive constraint.

The tension between similarity and difference is part of the emergence of culture. As actors become proficient at performing some communication practices, the actors limit those performances to those behaviors most rewarding with others. There is the danger that actors would

treat variety as disruption, and a larger danger that even small differences could jeopardize a pattern that has become efficient only in a limited stable environment. Such structures are brittle (Marion, 1999). Alternatively, performances can be so varied that actors must reestablish a pattern with each encounter, and this continual re-negotiation of relational expectations prevents the actors from accomplishing other functional outcomes. Family systems researchers have characterized the first pattern as rigid and the second one as chaotic (Olson, Sprenkle, & Russell, 1979).

In some cultures, differences are bad. Any involvement with public issues is not likely, citizens suspect the public process and public officials, and the members of these societies tend to rely on many precise and often unwritten rules to maintain social order (Hofstede & Hofstede, 2005). The members of these conservative cultures tend to be more anxious and may share a general fear of anyone different from themselves. When the members from one uncertainty avoidance culture migrate into regions with a different uncertainty avoidance culture, conflict and violence are likely.

When Alexis de Tocqueville wrote about democracy in America (2002/1835, 1840), he noted Americans proclivity to join groups and form civic organizations. The formation of groups reflected the basic tension between similarity and difference as pressures to conform but remain an individual. In organizations, the tension has been between socialization and individualization. The American ideal has been for newer members of the society, immigrants, to provide a continuing supply of differences while community groups provide acculturation as the society continues to form itself.

For many urban sociologists, community was synonymous with neighborhood. Beginning in the late 1970s, Wellman sought to bring a social network perspective to the understanding communities. First, he argued that communities were not bound by space, but that communities consisted of varied links between social actors enabling them to deal with the various challenges of life (Wellman & Leighton, 1979). Neighborhood relations were part of community, part of a larger network.

Second, Wellman (2001) argued the locus of community was with the individual actor and personal networks and not with groups. He noted that contemporary life involves managing many specialized relationships with others at a great distance besides managing nearby family and neighborhood relationships. Organizational relationships often involved working with distant others, and friends lived in the same metropolitan area or far away. Ultimately, people gained social resources from those who were not in the same neighborhood. Analyzing personal networks provided a more realistic description of community than understanding groups.

## Communication and Communication Technologies

Human communication is a process in which individuals cue each other as they make sense of the world they are constructing (Salem, 2009). The process involves individual communicators, messages, relationships, and episodes. The entire process is an emergent one in which actors develop rules for dealing with each other in relationships to enact episodes. The process is analogous to the complexity of all living systems in that small differences may accumulate to reinforce, disrupt, or transform the communication practices and the relationships between people (Salem, 2009).

Several features of the process act as passive constraints. A constraint is anything that limits the complete range of actions. When actors attempt to persuade each other, they are engaged in active constraint. Each actor attempts to shape the choices of the other such that the other is more likely to select one set of beliefs, attitudes, values, or behaviors over others. A constraint is passive when the constraint has no immediate agency. For example, actors may mindfully choose a given message, but they become constrained by the set of past decisions, messages, and interactions that constitute the circumstances of their current decision and behavior. Passive constraints also include a host of biological, chemical, physical, and environmental factors as well as stable personality characteristics and culture that predispose communicators to act in some fashion.

One set of constraints is inherent in the use of communication technologies. Face-to-face communication (FtF) has greater variety than telephone (TEL) because FtF can contain more nonverbal signals. Email (EML) was originally a text only technology between two individuals, but advances allow for the inclusion of sound and visual displays and broadcast to all on a mailing list. Private electronic communication (PEC) such as text messaging, instant messaging, and private chat began as one-to-one shorter versions of EML, but real time exchanges increase the synchronicity beyond most EML communication. The recent development of blogs, social network sites, and Twitter expand the possibilities for public electronic communication (BEC) in which one person can exchange messages with others, but in the presence of an audience. Although one might still argue that FtF is the most rich and least constraining of technologies (Fulk & Steinfeld, 1990; Lengel & Daft, 1988), it is difficult to array the remaining technologies across a continuum from most constraining to least constraining.

Social network sites are one type of BEC. These sites allow individuals to (1) create a public or semipublic profile, (2) develop a list of users with whom they share a connection, and (3) view and traverse their list of connections and those made by others within the system (Boyd & Ellison, 2007). The primary feature of these sites is that they allow users to make visible their list of connections, and this visibility may allow others to communicate with each other. There may be communication through a social network site, but the site may stimulate communication using some other technology. This is similar to a blog in that a posting may lead to an exchange of postings between people on a blog, but a posting may stimulate some other form of communication between bloggers.

There are a variety of positions about the social or cultural factors associated with the use of technology. One position holds that the new technology is associated with positive factors, another position associates contemporary technology with negative factors, and yet another claims there are no associations. Often, communication technology has paradoxical impacts – both positive and negative simultaneously, and so there is the possibility that technology acts as a catalyst amplifying already existing conditions (Salem, 1998). One report suggests that greater Internet involvement correlates to greater overall CE, but the increases were also among the most affluent and educated citizens (Smith et al, 2009).

**RQ1:** *How does the use of technology correlate with CE?*

## Communication Technology Networks

Individuals can communicate in many ways, and they can engage with various communities in many ways. Communication technologies contain their own constraints on interaction, and some technologies may enhance CE while others may limit CE. The emerging communication patterns form networks, and these networks have their own constraint. The recurring use of a given technology leads to the development its own unique communication technology network (CTN). I studied how the face-to-face (FtF), telephone (TEL), email (EML), private electronic communication (PEC) and public electronic communication (BEC) networks related to CE.

Wellman notes the influence of technology to extend a network and to weaken ties. He argues that contemporary technology has moved communities from groups to glocalization to networked indi-

vidualism (Wellman, 2002). Glocalization refers to the combination of global and local influences in personal networks. People can communicate with many other people in many different places. They may still form groups, but the groups are of actors sharing interests and little else. There is less social control. Networked individualism refers to the current situation in which actors can communicate with each other directly regardless of place. Although a wireless world might mean less group identity and more role fragmentation, it also means each person can operate his or her networks to obtain a unique mix of information, collaboration, orders, support, sociability, and a sense of belonging (Wellman, 2002. p. 3). Wellman and his colleagues identify several network characteristics and view this situation as an opportunity for personal growth (Chua et al, 2011). They do not compare various CTNs to each other.

Burt (2005) contrasted the network characteristics of brokerage and closure. Brokers were actors who were members of a group filling the gaps between groups in a network. The gap, a structural hole, provided the adept broker with information and rewards unavailable to others. A broker must have sufficient within-group ties to maintain the trust of those in the home group, and so the number of weak ties between groups should be great, but not too great. Other actors had the advantage of closure. They may have had weak ties, but many had links between the same groups. For those with closure, within group ties were generally stronger allowing them to develop greater depth of shared group knowledge. Social identity had greater salience for those with closure, but personal identity was more important for brokers. Most important for this paper is that brokers were likely to explore or influence in an attempt to improve current practices, but others would act out of fear and to avoid falling behind. Brokers would be more likely to have greater CE than others.

Burt (2005) does not compare various CTNs to each other, but the network features he discovered seem to apply to this investigation of CE. Brokers have more heterogeneous and diverse contacts. Heterogeneity refers to the extent to which an actor's direct ties are diverse in some way. I explored the extent to which direct ties were diverse about education, ethnicity, age, and sex. I assumed heterogeneity was advantageous to CE believing that greater diversity would provide greater opportunities for collective action.

**H1:** *Greater education, ethnic, age, and sex heterogeneity will be positively correlated with CE across all CTNs.*

Brokers have networks likely to contain more ties than others (Burt, 2005). Degree is the size of a personal network, the number of alters in the network (Monge & Contractor, 2003). I assumed greater degree was advantageous to CE believing more contacts gave greater opportunity.

**H2:** *Greater degree will be positively correlated with CE across all CTNs.*

The alters in a broker's networks would not connect to each other very much (Burt, 2005). Network density is the number of ties between actors compared to the number possible (Monge & Contractor, 2003). I assumed less density was advantageous to CE, believing more diverse contacts gave greater opportunity.

**H3:** *Greater density will be negatively correlated with CE across all CTNs.*

Because the density is low, a broker's network would contain many components. A component is an independent and disconnected part of a network (Monge & Contractor, 2003). In a personal network, components may be isolates or cliques and groups that connect to each other only through the ego. The maximum number of components in a personal network is equal to the number of alters in the network, a zero density situation. Ef-

ficiency is the number of components compared to the actual number of components (Burt, 2005). I assumed greater efficiency provides more diverse opportunities for CE.

**H4:** *Greater efficiency will be positively correlated with CE across all CTNs.*

Brokers would distribute their energy across the entire network avoiding the possibility that they might devote too many resources to a few links. Constraint increases as an actor develops a network to fewer alters with many connections to each other or connections to one central alter (Burt, 2005). Brokers personal networks have less constraint than others. I assumed that higher constraint would limit CE to fewer civic groups involved in fewer civic activities.

**H5:** *Greater constraint will be negatively correlated with CE across all CTNs.*

The strength of a tie refers to (a) the extent to which actors regard their relationship as close or intimate or (b) the frequency, duration, or intensity of their communication (Granovetter, 1973). Strong ties occur routinely and between family, friends and coworkers, but weak ties are important for obtaining information and support, especially for exceptional circumstances or events (Blau & Fingerman, 2009). Weak ties are more important to brokers (Burt, 2005) and are more likely with the development of network individualism (Wellman, 2002). I assumed the weak tie networks would be more related to CE than the strong tie networks.

**H6:** *There will be more significant correlations in the weak tie networks than the strong tie networks when comparing FtF, TEL, EML, PEC, and BEC CTNs.*

Finally, differences in technology should manifest themselves when comparing CTNs. I assume the direct use of a technology has less association to CE than the network that emerges as a function of that use. However, actors might use some technologies to develop smaller networks of strong ties for some forms of CE but use other technologies to develop the predicted larger networks of weak ties for other forms of CE. Some declare that the Internet encourages tribalization and polarization on public issues (Mandel & Van der Luen, 1996; Shenk, 1998), and public Internet discourse confirms these patterns (Ellis & Maoz, 2007; Oegma, Kleinnijenhuis, Anderson, & von Hoof, 2008). Although I am assuming the development of CTNs related to CE is analogous to the development of broker networks, it is just possible that different CTNs may relate to different forms of CE in different ways. The FtF CTN may be more associated with group involvement in the predicted manner than with traditional or digital civic activities, but the PEC CTN may be more related to digital civic activities in an unpredicted way, and unrelated to other forms of CE, for example.

**RQ2:** *How will specific CTNs relate to CE differently than others when comparing FtF, TEL, EML, PEC, and BEC CTNs?*

# METHODS

## Sample

The sample for this study consisted of the students in an undergraduate section of a Communication and Technology senior level class and the instructors and student assistants associated with that class and this project. Although 41 subjects began the project, most results come from the responses of 34 communication studies seniors who completed all parts of the project, three graduate assistants, and two instructors (N=39). This is a convenience sample, and students participated as part of the class requirements.

## Measures and Procedures

I was attempting to test procedures to improve those used in the East York studies in Canada (Hogan, Carrasco, & Wellman, 2007; Wellman et al, 2006). In that project, the researchers distributed a 32-page survey packet to 621 people, and 350 took 1-2 hours to complete the survey. In a second wave of the process, 84 subjects agreed to a two-four hour follow-up interview about the specifics of their personal networks. I believed breaking the process into four smaller parts would improve the processing time. In this project, the entire four-part process averaged 120 minutes, and so, my approach cut the administration time in half. However, there were a few subjects who took three hours.

Students completed a four-part data gathering process. Part 1 involved several standard scales including a 16-item CE scale. Part 2 began with a scale unrelated to this study, but the remainder of Part 2 involved a name generator, alter data, and estimates of communication episodes using various technologies with those alters. Part 3 involved an interview where researchers obtained alter-alter ties for the five separate CTNs. Part 4 was a survey unrelated to this study, and I will not explain it in any detail.

The CE scale contained items from the Pew study (Smith, et al, 2009). Subjects indicated their group involvement (GI) with six groups on a scale ranging from "0 = not a member" to "1 = a member but not active," to "2 = an active member." The maximum, score on the GI scale was 12. Subjects indicated their participation in five traditional civic activities (TCA) and five digital civic activities (DCA) by simply checking the space next to each to each activity. One TCA item was "Contacted a government official in person, by phone or by letter," and a comparable DCA item was "Contacted a government official by electronic communication technology (email, text, etc.)." The maximum score on either scale was 5.

Part 2 of the survey included a request for subjects to list the names of people with whom they communicate. The survey explained communication as follows:

*Communication means more than just reading a post or a comment. Communication means the exchange of messages. When we use the term "communication" or "communicates," we mean that you exchange messages – face-to-face, telephone, email messages, text messages, posts on a blog or Facebook wall, etc. How you exchange messages is not important. That you exchange messages is the minimum condition for communication.*

Then, researchers asked subjects to list the names of people with whom they communicate at least several times per month. The author chose this minimum condition because it is the condition used in the social support literature (Cohen, Doyle, Skoner, Rabin, & Gwaltney, J. 1997; Cohen, Doyle, Turner, Alper, & Skoner, 2003). This research regarded ties that involved communication of any sort of at least several times per month as strong ties.

Research team members then prompted subjects to reconsider their list. Researchers asked subjects to add anyone with whom they communicated less than several times per month but was someone with whom they discussed important matters "such as personal matters, work or school matters, financial matters, whatever topics you regard as important." Researchers then asked subjects to think of people not already on the list, people with whom they communicated less than several times per month, but were people "you can count on if you need them." These last two prompts were attempts to generate the names of weak ties. Subjects described the ethnicity, education, level, age, sex, and other tie characteristics.

Subjects completed forms indicating how often they communicated with each person using one of five technologies: FtF, TEL, EML, PEC, and BEC. Subjects completed one form per technol-

ogy. They estimated their frequency using the following choices: (D) several times a day, (W) several times a week, (M) several times a month, (Y) several times a year, and (0) less than yearly or never. Research team members coded their answers as 500, 80, 20, 2, and 0 to reflect the relative frequency of episodes. The process produced frequency scores for each tie per technology, and the researchers added the frequencies over all the technologies to obtain estimates of technology use (overall episodes per technology) and per alter. Any tie less than 20 was a weak tie in a given network. It was possible for one alter to be a weak tie in one CTN, but a strong tie in another.

In Part 3 researchers obtained alter-alter ties for the five separate CTNs. I anticipated using the circle and strips of paper interview method employed by the Toronto group, and research team members drew such circles and supplied paper tabs with instructions for subjects. However, I asked student researchers to record the ties directly onto a matrix. Researchers eventually developed a procedure of asking subjects to tell them directly about the ties between alters, and if subjects had difficulty, then researchers asked them to use paper strips to model the configurations. Most subjects competed the task averaging 30 minutes. One subject did take over two hours.

Summarily, after subjects completed the process, we had indicators of technology use, GI, TCA, and DCA. We also had data to describe four different types of tie heterogeneity (education, ethnicity, sex, and age), the degree, density, efficiency, and constraints on five CTNs – FtF, TEL, EML, PEC, BEC. Furthermore, we could limit our analyses to separate investigations of strong tie or weak tie networks.

This study used SPSS and Enet to analyze the data. When subjects reported degree of 0 or 1, the author set efficiency at 0 and density and constraint at 1, as recommended by theory (Burt, 2010, p. 300). In the end, the researcher performed 240 correlations (3 types of CE * 8 variables *

*Table 1. The relative number of episodes per technology*

| Technology | Mean | SD | 33rd | 66th |
|---|---|---|---|---|
| FtF | 1607 | 1128 | 954 | 1744 |
| TEL | 1287 | 863 | 904 | 1443 |
| EML | 343 | 559 | 64 | 200 |
| PEC | 1543 | 1215 | 1000 | 1591 |
| BEC | 651 | 1049 | 84 | 561 |
| OCE | 5430 | 3469 | 3291 | 6243 |

5 technology networks * 2 levels of ties) to test hypotheses.

## RESULTS

## Descriptive Results

Table 1 displays the relative number of episodes per technology. Most episodes occur using FtF, PEC, and TEL. Note the smaller numbers for EML and BEC. Several subjects do not use EML or BEC such as social networking sites or Twitter. The men and women in our study did not report significant differences on four types of technologies. However, women had significantly more BEC episodes (M = 930) than men (M = 232) (t = 2.15, df = 38, p < .04).

Table 2 reports CE data. The percentages of subjects involved in various forms of CE were comparable to the Pew study (Smith, et al, 2009). Approximately 35% of the individuals in both groups were involved with a civic or political group in the last three years, and both groups reported comparable civic and political activities

over the last year. Thirty-nine percent of subjects were not involved in any TCA, and 56% were not involved in any DCA. The data from my group were most similar to the Pew descriptions of younger adults, who engaged in more DCA than older adults. Men and women in my study were not significantly different in their CE.

Table 3 displays the means for various heterogeneities in the CTNs. Subjects constructed CTNs with little ethnic heterogeneity. The EML and BEC CTNs have the lowest heterogeneity in strong tie networks, and PEC and BEC CTNs have the least heterogeneity in weak tie CTNs. Notice that heterogeneity is considerably less in weak tie networks than in strong tie networks, an unexpected finding.

Table 4 displays the mean structural variables for CTNs. Degree was highest in FtF, TEL, and BEC strong tie CTNs. EML and BEC networks were the simplest - suggesting small, dense, inefficient, and constrained CTNs. Weak tie networks were more dense, less efficient, and more constrained than most of strong tie CTNs.

Subjects communicated in strong tie CTNs resembling more brokerage than closure, and their

*Table 2. The extent of subject civic engagement*

| CE | Items | Mean | SD |
|---|---|---|---|
| GI (0-12) | 6 | 4.51 | 2.53 |
| TCA (0-5) | 5 | 1.00 | 1.10 |
| DCA (0-5) | 5 | .93 | 1.27 |

*Table 3. A comparison of the mean heterogeneity of communication technology networks*

| Networks | Heterogeneity | | | |
| --- | --- | --- | --- | --- |
| | Education | Ethnicity | Sex | Age |
| Strong Ties | | | | |
| FtF | .47 | .21 | .40 | .39 |
| TEL | .52 | .21 | .42 | .49 |
| EML | .33 | .11 | .22 | .34 |
| PEC | .46 | .19 | .38 | .39 |
| BEC | .28 | .13 | .22 | .21 |
| Weak Ties | | | | |
| FtF | .32 | .09 | .24 | .35 |
| TEL | .26 | .11 | .20 | .19 |
| EML | .20 | .08 | .16 | .15 |
| PEC | .18 | .08 | .14 | .17 |
| BEC | .12 | .04 | .11 | .10 |

weak tie networks were more about closure than brokerage. Strong tie CTNs generally had more heterogeneity, greater degree, less density, more efficiency, and less constraint than weak tie networks. These findings were counter to the literature.

## Inferential Results

Although technology use was somewhat related to CE, correlations suggested the relationships were more nuanced and conditional than one might suspect. Those with more GI used more FtF ($r = .49$, $df = 38$, $p < .01$), more TEL ($r = .37$, $df = 38$, $p < .02$), and more PEC ($r = .41$, $df = 38$, $p <$

*Table 4. A comparison of the mean structural variables of communication technology networks*

| Networks | Structural Variable | | | |
| --- | --- | --- | --- | --- |
| | Degree | Density | Efficiency | Constraint |
| Strong Ties | | | | |
| FtF | 13.33 | .38 | .77 | .46 |
| TEL | 12.08 | .23 | .85 | .43 |
| EML | 5.13 | .49 | .59 | .67 |
| PEC | 11.74 | .21 | .87 | .39 |
| BEC | 7.93 | .49 | .60 | .51 |
| Weak Ties | | | | |
| FtF | 5.26 | .52 | .54 | .61 |
| TEL | 4.18 | .49 | .53 | .63 |
| EML | 2.00 | .63 | .40 | .79 |
| PEC | 3.00 | .60 | .44 | .72 |
| BEC | 1.88 | .70 | .32 | .82 |

*Table 5. Heterogeneity patterns related to CE*

| Heterogeneity | CE | | |
|---|---|---|---|
| | GI | TCA | DCA |
| Education | | | |
| Ethnicity | | | |
| Sex | S | | W |
| Age | S | | W |

*Table 6. Network structural patterns related to CE*

| Structure | CE | | |
|---|---|---|---|
| | GI | TCA | DCA |
| Degree | S | | |
| Density | | | |
| Efficiency | | | |
| Constraint | | S | |

*Table 7. CTN patterns related to CE*

| CTN | CE | | |
|---|---|---|---|
| | GI | TCA | DCA |
| FtF | | | W |
| TEL | S | | |
| EML | | S, W | S |
| PEC | | | W |
| BEC | | | |

.01). There were no other significant two-tailed correlations. However, TCA was correlated with DCA (r = .32, df = 38, p < .05). The answer to RQ1 is that some technology use was positively associated with GI, but it was not associated with TCA or DCA, and TCA had a direct association with DCA. There was a catalytic effect – those who were engaged used technology to become more engaged.

Tables 5-7 summarize patterns across the correlations. An S means the majority of correlations in strong tie network were related to a particular form of CE, and a W means the majority of correlations in weak tie networks were related to a particular form of CE. "Majority" means that there were significant correlations in at least three of five CTNs. For example, in Table 5 sex and age heterogeneity in most strong tie CTNs were correlated with GI, but sex and age heterogeneity in most weak tie CTNs were correlated with DCA.

Table 5 displays patterns between heterogeneity in CTNs and CE. Only age and sex heterogeneity were related to CE and not all forms of CE. Furthermore, there were no patterns of relationships across both strong and weak tie networks. The data did not support Hypothesis 1

Table 6 displays patterns about network structural variables and CE. Greater degree in most CTNs was associated with GI, and more constraint in most CTNs was associated with TCA. The bold format indicates this relationship was not in the hypothesized direction. Furthermore, there were no patterns of relationships across both strong

and weak tie networks. The data did not support Hypotheses 2-5.

Table 7 displays the overall patterns across CTNs. Notice that the number of S patterns is equal to the number of W patterns. Strong tie CTNs were as important as weak tie CTNs. The data did not support Hypothesis 6.

Which CTNs were most strongly related to CE? Characteristics of BEC networks had little or no relationship to any facet of CE. Subjects who used BEC did not use it for CE

Characteristics of the TEL strong tie networks demonstrated a clear pattern of association to GI, but no pattern emerged with TCA or DCA. Those with greater GI used TEL to develop a strong tie CTN with significantly greater sex and age heterogeneity, more alters, and less constraint than those with less GI.

Most characteristics of FtF and PEC weak tie networks were associated with DCA, but there was no pattern between characteristics of FtF and PEC strong or weak tie networks and GI or TPA. The CTN patterns are similar to the ones in the last paragraph. Those with greater DCA used FtF and PEC to develop a weak tie CTNs with significantly greater sex and age heterogeneity, more alters, and less constraint than those with less DCA.

Most characteristics of EML strong and weak tie networks were associated with TCA, and most characteristics of the EML strong tie networks were associated with DCA. These relationships have considerable nuance. Those with greater TCA used EML to develop both the strong and weak tie networks that exhibited some greater age or sex heterogeneity, but exhibited significantly more degree, less density, more efficiency, and less constraint than those with less TCA. By contrast, those with more DCA used EML to develop strong tie CTNs with significantly more education, sex, and age heterogeneity, and significantly more alters than those with less DCA.

Summarily, data did not confirm a direct extension of Burt's brokerage-closure model to CE. However, data did support modeling networks as CTNs. There were significant differences between the various CTNs related to CE.

## CONCLUSION

Individuals address issues of public concern by becoming involved with civic groups and performing civic activities such as charity and political work. Changes in communication technology have led to changes in civic engagement, and it is now possible to perform civic activities digitally. Actors develop social networks as they use various communication technologies, and the resultant communication technology networks act as passive constraints on an individual's activities. This chapter reports the results and implications of one study about civic engagement and communication technology networks.

Individuals communicate using face-to-face methods, telephone, email, private electronic communication, and public electronic communication.

The results suggest using any one technology has little association with traditional or digital civic activities, and actors mix face-to-face methods and telephone use with private electronic technologies as they increase group involvement. Those who are more involved with civic activities in traditional ways use newer technologies to perform more digital civic activities, a conclusion confirmed in earlier studies.

Different types of civic engagement are related to different aspects of communication technology networks. Actors more involved with groups do so using technology to develop a network of strong ties containing more people and more people of greater sex and age diversity than those who are less involved. The strong tie telephone network appears to be particularly important to greater group involvement.

The development of strong and weak tie email networks corresponds with actors performing more traditional civic activities. However, when actors increase their traditional civic activities, they also do so within strong tie networks that constrain and limit their communication activities. This kind of result suggests a tactical team structure rather than a problem-solving or creative team pattern (Larson & LaFasto, 1989). Actors use technology to form implementation networks that efficiently increase activities.

Actors who perform more digital civic activities use technology to form weak tie networks with more sex and age diversity than those who are less engaged. The formation of face-to-face and private electronic communication weak tie networks appears to be important to increasing digital civic activity, but the development of email strong tie networks also corresponds to more of this type of engagement. Actors may be using the different technology networks for different functions associated with digital engagement. For example, the face-to-face and private electronic communication weak tie networks may be part of recruitment, and the email network may consist of a portion of the other two that assist in the actual performance of the digital activities.

When examining personal network data, there has been the challenge of determining the best methods to test hypotheses or display results (Carrington, Scott & Wasserman, 2006; Schensul, LeCompte, Trotter, Cromley, & Singer, 1999; Scott, 2000). These challenges are common to studying phenomena with a small percentage of participants, such as civic engagement. By trying to rigorously avoid a Type I Error, falsely rejecting the null, there is a possibility of Type II Error, falsely accepting the null. Researchers should replicate network and civic engagement studies, and there is a greater need to replicate this study, one investigating both social networks and civic engagement.

This project explored civic engagement and communication technology networks with American subjects, and this is a limitation. One striking finding was the lack of relationships between public electronic communication and public electronic communication networks to any form of civic engagement. Do the members of other cultures prefer the anonymity of blogs and discussion sites to make sense of public issues? Would the members of more conservative societies endorse the dramatic and ritualistic display of behaviors that is common on personal social network sites to the more intimate and nuanced exchanges of messages in other ways? The members of some cultures may prefer the dramatic display of opinion common to American political and commercial social network sites as a method of recruitment, and the use of other communication as a way to organize civic engagement. Future research should investigate multiple cultures.

## REFERENCES

American Psychological Association. (2010). *Civic engagement*. Retrieved May 18, 2010, from http://www.apa.org/education/undergrad/civic-engagement.aspx

Blau, M., & Fingerman, K. L. (2009). *Consequential strangers: The power of people who don't matter, but really do*. New York, NY: W. W. Norton.

Boyd, D. M., & Ellison, N. B. (2007). Social network sites: Definition, history, and scholarship. *Journal of Computer-Mediated Communication*, *13*(1), 210–230. doi:10.1111/j.1083-6101.2007.00393.x

Burt, R. E. (2005). *Brokerage and closure. An introduction to social capital*. Oxford, UK: Oxford University Press.

Burt, R. E. (2010). *Neighbor networks: Competitive advantage local and personal*. Oxford, UK: Oxford University Press.

Carrington, P. J., Scott, J., & Wasserman, S. (Eds.). (2006). *Models and methods of social network analysis*. Cambridge, UK: Cambridge University Press.

Chua, V., Madej, J., & Wellman, B. (2011 forthcoming). Personal communities: The world according to me. In Carrington, P., & Scott, J. (Eds.), *Handbook of social network analysis*. London, UK: Sage.

Cohen, S., Doyle, W. J., Skoner, D. P., Rabin, B. S., & Gwaltney, J. M. Jr. (1997). Social ties and susceptibility to the common cold. *Journal of the American Medical Association*, *277*, 1940–1944. doi:10.1001/jama.277.24.1940

Cohen, S., Doyle, W. J., Turner, R., Alper, C. M., & Skoner, D. P. (2003). Sociability and susceptibility to the common cold. *Psychological Science*, *14*(5), 389–395. doi:10.1111/1467-9280.01452 de Tocqueville, A. (2002). *Democracy in America* (Mansfield, H. C., & Winthrop, D., Trans.). Chicago, IL: University of Chicago Press. (Original work published 1835)

Ellis, D., & Maoz, I. (2007). Online argument between Palestinians and Jews. *Human Communication Research, 33*(3), 291–309. doi:10.1111/j.1468-2958.2007.00300.x

Fulk, J., & Steinfeld, C. (1990). *Organizations and communication technology*. Newbury Park, CA: Sage.

Granovetter, M. (1973). The strength of weak ties. *American Journal of Sociology, 78*, 1360–1380. doi:10.1086/225469

Hofstede, G., & Hofstede, G. J. (2005). *Cultures and organizations: Software for the mind* (rev. 2nd ed.). New York, NY: McGraw-Hill.

Hogan, B., Carrasco, J.-A., & Wellman, B. (2007). Visualizing personal networks: Working with participant-aided sociograms. *Field Methods, 19*(2), 116–144. doi:10.1177/1525822X06298589

Larson, C. E., & LaFasto, F. (1989). *Teamwork. What must go right/What can go wrong*. Newbury Park, CA: Sage.

Lengel, R. H., & Daft, R. L. (1988). The selection of communication media as an executive skill. *The Academy of Management Executive, 2*, 225–232. doi:10.5465/AME.1988.4277259

Mandel, T., & Van der Luen, G. (1996). *Rules of the net: Online operating instructions for human beings*. New York, NY: Hyperion.

Marion, R. (1999). *The edge of organization*. Thousand Oaks, CA: Sage.

McPherson, M., Smith-Lovin, L., & Brashears, M. (2006). Social isolation in America: Changes in core discussion networks over two decades. *American Sociological Review, 71*, 353–375. doi:10.1177/000312240607100301

Monge, P. R., & Contractor, N. S. (2003). *Theories of communication networks*. Oxford, UK: Oxford University Press.

Oegma, D., Kleinnijenhuis, J., Anderson, K., & von Hoof, A. (2008). Flaming and blaming: The influence of mass media content on interactions in online discussions. In Konijin, E. A., Utz, S., Tanis, M., & Barnes, S. B. (Eds.), *Mediated interpersonal communication* (pp. 331–358). New York, NY: Routledge.

Olson, D. H. L., Sprenkle, D. H., & Russell, C. S. (1979). Circumplex model of marital and family systems: Cohesion and adaptability dimensions, family types, and clinical applications. *Family Process, 18*, 3–28. doi:10.1111/j.1545-5300.1979.00003.x

Pew Research Center. (2010, April). *The people and their government: Distrust, discontent, anger, and partisan rancor*. Washington, DC: Author.

Putnam, R. D. (1995). Bowling alone. *Journal of Democracy, 6*(1), 65–78. doi:10.1353/jod.1995.0002

Putnam, R. D. (2000). *Bowling alone: The collapse and revival of American community*. New York, NY: Simon & Schuster.

Rothenbuhler, E. W. (1998). *Ritual communication: From everyday conversation to mediated ceremony*. Thousand Oaks, CA: Sage.

Salem, P. J. (1998, July). *Paradoxical impacts of electronic communication technology*. Paper presented to the National Research Center of the University of Siena, International Communication Association and National Communication Association Conference on Communication: Organizing for the Future, Rome Italy. (ERIC No. ED 420-891, 24p)

Salem, P. J. (2008). *Preliminary observations on the notion of passive constraint*. Paper presented at the Annual Meeting of the Russian Communication Association meeting in Moscow, Russia.

Salem, P. J. (2009). *The complexity of human communication*. Cresskill, NJ: Hampton Press.

Schensul, J. J., LeCompte, M. D., Trotter, R. T. II, Cromley, E. K., & Singer, M. (1999). *Mapping social networks, spatial data, and hidden populations*. Walnut Creek, CA: Altimira Press.

Scott, J. (2000). *Social network analysis: A handbook* (2nd ed.). Los Angeles, CA: Sage.

Shenk, D. (1998). *Data smog: Surviving the information glut (rev.)*. San Francisco, CA: Harper Edge.

Smith, A., Lehman Scholzman, K., Verba, S., & Brady, H. (2009, September). *The Internet and civic engagement*. Report for the Pew Internet and American Life Project, Washington, DC. Retrieved from http://www.pewinternet.org/Reports/2009/15--The-Internet-and-Civic-Engagement.aspx

The White House. (2010). *Service*. Retrieved May 18, 2010, from http://www.whitehouse.gov/issues/service

Wellman, B. (2001, October). *The persistence and transformation of community: From neighbourhood groups to social networks*. Report to the Law Commission of Canada.

Wellman, B. (2002). Little boxes, glocalization, and networked individualism. In Tanabe, M., van den Besselaar, P., & Ishida, T. (Eds.), *Digital cities II: Computational and sociological approaches* (pp. 11–25). Berlin, Germany: Springer-Verlag. doi:10.1007/3-540-45636-8_2

Wellman, B., Hogan, B., Berg, K., Boase, J., Carrasco, J. A., & Coté, R. ... Tran, P. (2006). Connected Lives: The project. In P. Purcell (Ed.), *The networked neighbourhood* (pp. 161-216). Berlin, Germany: Springer.

Wellman, B., & Leighton, B. (1979, March). Networks, neighborhoods and communities. *Urban Affairs Quarterly*, *14*, 363–390. doi:10.1177/107808747901400305

## KEY TERMS AND DEFINITIONS

**Civic Engagement:** Involves those individual and collective actions designed to identify and address issues of public concern. It includes participation in social groups, charitable groups, and political groups. The construct also involves all forms of service learning and community service.

**Communication Technology Network:** Refers to a social network in which how actors communicate is an attribute for defining nodes or the links between them. This essay investigated face-to-face, telephone, email, personal electronic, and public electronic communication technology networks.

**Ego or Personal Network:** A social network for an individual node. Ego is the term for the central node, and alter is the term for those nodes connected to the ego. Relational variables refer to characteristics of an actor's direct ties, and structural variables refer to characteristics of the configuration of ties including alter-alter ties.

**Network Constraint:** A structural variable referring to the extent to which an actor's network limits the actor's social behavior or the actor's opportunities to obtain social resources. Constraint increases as an actor develops a network to fewer alters with many connections to each other or with connections to one central alter. In this chapter, network constraint refers to the extent to which the configuration of alters in communication technology personal networks limits an actor's civic engagement.

**Network Degree:** A structural variable meaning the number of nodes in a network. In this chapter, degree refers to the number of alters in communication technology personal networks.

**Network Density:** A structural variable referring to the interconnectedness among nodes. A common indicator of density is the ratio of the actual number of links between nodes compared to the number possible. In this chapter, density refers to the interconnectedness among alters in communication technology personal networks.

**Network Efficiency:** A structural variable meaning the extent to which an actor can obtain unique resources from each contact. A common measure is one minus the ratio of the number of components in a network compared to the number possible. A component is an independent unit in a network such as an isolate, dyad, or group. In this chapter, efficiency refers to the ability of

egos to obtain unique resources from alters in communication technology personal networks.

**Network Heterogeneity:** A relational variable indicating the extent to which alters are diverse with respect to some characteristic. This chapter reports on the education, ethnic, age, and sex heterogeneity of alters in communication technology personal networks.

**Strength of a Tie or Link:** A variable denoting (a) the extent to which actors regard their relationship as close or intimate or (b) the frequency, duration, or intensity of their communication. In this chapter, tie strength is a relational variable referring to the frequency of communication between an actor and alters in communication technology personal networks. I defined a strong tie as communication occurring at least several times per month, and a weak tie as occurring less frequently. I analyzed the strong tie and weak tie networks separately for each communication technology.

# Section 2
# Modeling and Developing Social Networks and Online Communities

*This section outlines some models of social networks that describe how online social networks and communities are formed, developed and analyzed. Analytical tools are used to provide an adequate interpretation of these newly created social networks such as the famous friendship network in Second Life. In addition, the section concludes with key success factors for the development for social networking websites.*

# Chapter 4

# The Social Construction of New Cultural Models through Information and Communication Technologies

**Almudena Moreno**
*Universidad de Valladolid, Spain*

## ABSTRACT

*This chapter presents an approach to sociological and anthropological theories as to the meaning of the new cultural formats resulting from the application of today's communications technologies. This introductory theoretical chapter aims to contextualize social networking and community behaviour within an analytical framework, which allows us to understand the significance of these new realities. Thus, this chapter analyzes the cultural significance of the new concept of cyberculture and the new socio-cultural constructs such as authority, identity, and socialization that arise from the use of new technologies as a basic source of knowledge and information. In summary, this chapter contains a theoretical reflection on the meaning of the new forms of social relations in this ICT-based culture, as well as on the need to define new analytical tools to enable an adequate interpretation of this new cultural context within the framework of globalization and digitalization.*

DOI: 10.4018/978-1-61350-444-4.ch004

## INTRODUCTION

In this chapter technology is conceptualized as a tool for the creation of a new cultural space, a hyperreal, symbolic space emerging as a consequence of the technological implosion of the human world, a space that is free from the power of formal organizations, a space that lies outside normalization, a pioneering space, in a word cyberspace. The term used in the scientific literature, which best describes these new styles of life and culture[1] is "cyberculture"[2].

The work presented in this chapter examines the concept of *cyberculture* in order to theoretically analyze how far the explosion of new information technologies has transformed social relations, and thus the traditional meaning of cultural concepts such as socialization, identity and authority.

The traditional model of *socialization* and learning based on the intergenerational reproduction of knowledge based on the principles of authority and *identity* (Durkheim, 1984) has led to a new interpretive paradigm (e-learning) in which knowledge is transmitted vertically has led to a new culture in which knowledge is also obtained horizontally from the ICTs[3] due to the weakening of the authority structures from which knowledge has traditionally been obtained, such as the family and school. It means that young people socially construct their *identity* on a parameter of authority based on new technologies. This means that they attach more importance and authority to the information they get from the Internet that the information provided in the traditional agencies of *socialization* such as family, school, university or the labour market. This is revolutionizing not only the cultural models of social relations but also the basis of *socialization* leading to a new cultural model based on horizontal transmission of knowledge and a new meaning of authority, *socialization* and *identity*, all traditional concepts integrated in the definition of socio-cultural formation[4] (Castells, 2003; Wessels, 2010; Terranova, 2004).

This chapter is intended to provide a general introduction to key issues surrounding the significance of information technology and the new models of culture in the context of globalization and digitalization. In the classical conception, the term Globalization is restricted to the trade deregulation and proliferation of new information technology, which have transformed the world into a global village. According to this definition I consider that the Internet makes it technologically possible to have access to global knowledge and has strengthened the ability to communicate more effectively across the world.

The work presented here involves an exclusively theoretical approach, and is in no way an attempt to contribute empirical data on the significance of the new framework of social relations resulting from cyberculture. The ultimate aim of this research is to present a theoretical reflection from a sociological and anthropological standpoint which enables us to adequately contextualise the analysis of social networking and community behaviour.

The first half of the chapter concentrates on review of sociological theories of the information society and postmodernism, the increasing significance of information and communication technology in contemporary capitalism, and the emerging disparities and conflicts which result. The second half of the chapter examines 'digital culture' and the model of *"cyberculture"* through themes of *identity*, community, sociality, authority and virtuality[5]. This last part also contains a reflection on the significance of the online communities that coexist with regular communities as an example of the cultural duality which affects today's citizens all over the world as a result of the globalization of technology.

In synthesis, the main contribution of this theoretical research is to reflect, in the light of sociological and anthropological theories, on the meaning of the social relations emerging around the concept of *cyberculture*, which requires re-examining the meaning of traditional concepts such as identity, authority and socialization.

## CULTURE AND ICT IN SOCIOLOGICAL THINKING

It is generally accepted by most sociologists that technological revolutions do not create new societies around the basic pillars, which underpin civilisation, but they do change the terms in which individuals develop their social, political and economic relationships.

While the industrial revolution represented a new way of relating to work and acquiring a new *identity* through paid work, the technological revolution of the last century ushered in a different way of acquiring *identity* through consumption and saw the creation of new *social networks*, thus revolutionising the classical parameters of sociability. These parameters involved the underlying foundations, which structured societies around gender, social class, etc. In the modern age, however the determination of social position has been replaced with a flexible self-determination, based on our way of relating to other people through the new communications technologies.

Several exponents of classical sociology uphold the primacy of social structures over individuals, and maintain that these determine practically all of people's actions. For example, Durkheim (1984) believes that the reality of the individual is subordinated to the collective; people are obliged to take into account collective ways of behaving and thinking, and find it extremely difficult to change them. For Durkheim, individual *identity* is based on learning the norms and values which structure the collective consciousness through institutions such as the family and the educational system, which act as channels for the transmission of values. This society was solidly structured around the concept of vertical learning, in which authority was represented by the established orders at the political and com-

munity level. This new digital context involves the development of new instruments and tools for learning and knowledge, such as e-learning and what is known as *Instructional Systems Design* (ISD), which coexist with traditional ones.

From a totally different theoretical perspective, Louis Althusser (2003) applies the same logic when he maintains that far from individuals being the ones who produce the ideology, it is the ideology, which constitutes or transforms individuals in order to confine them to a Subject (with a capital S), which is the social structure (capitalism, in his analysis). According to this viewpoint, the new communications technologies such as the Internet have been instrumental in creating a new communications "ideology" in the form of a social structure, which determines the way individuals relate to one another.

According to Weber's theory of methodological individualism (1978) (MI)[6], society is the product of a large number of individual actions and decisions and of competences between people. To explain a social phenomenon, MI uses a twofold technique: it reconstructs the meaning given by the actors involved in this phenomenon, and explains the objectives pursued by these actors in the course of the action. This leads to an examination of the relationship between individuals and institutions or structures. In this approach, structures are known as "social formations" (the State, cooperatives, private companies, foundations, etc.), which exist only as products of the actions of individuals. This school of thought is based on recognition of structural limits, but conceives them not as absolute prohibitions, nor as social structures endowed with independent life, which control individuals, but rather as the boundaries defining a space in whose interior the individuals move. Within this framework of interpretation, the new communications technologies constitute a new social formation, which is the product of the actions of individuals, at the same time transforming the behaviours of the individuals from within, blurring traditional boundaries and the elements, which define sociability, and personal and social *identity*.

Post-modern thinkers interpret social change within a framework of analysis, which recognises the fragility of the traditional outlines of sociability (Giddens, 1991Bauman, 1990). There is no doubt that today's communications technologies are giving a new meaning to the notions of privacy, the individual, authority, socialisation and culture. Whereas the traditional concept of culture refers to behaviour patterns formed by customs, traditions, sets of habits and control mechanisms (Geertz, 1987; Harris, 2001 this concept is nowadays being superseded by the notion of *cyberculture* as a new cultural model based on Internet technology. Lévy (2000) argues that the spread of the Internet has led to the emergence of new forms of knowledge and new forms of knowledge distribution. These new forms transform not only the ways we manipulate information, but society itself. *Cyberculture* is synonymous with this change, and refers to the "set of techniques (material and intellectual), practical habits, attitudes, ways of thinking and values that develop mutually with cyberspace" (Lévy 2000: 15), as well as embodying "a new form of universality: universality without totality" (ibid: 105). According to Lévy, this new universality symbolizes the peak of the Enlightenment project of humanity – the humanity of free, empowered subjects oppressed neither by the power of the unity of language and meaning nor by unified and binding forms of social being. For Lévy, *cyberculture* proves the fact that we are close to this humanistic paradise, and points to the possibility of "creating a virtual participation in your own self (universality) in a way that is different from the identity of meaning (totality)" (ibid: 107).

Thus, *cyberculture* was at the core of social studies about Internet, most of them assuming that a new cultural model was emerging from Internet use that would change patterns of social relation, self *identity* and community (Bell, 2001; 2007; Turkle, 1995; Terranova, 2004). Some research-ers also thought that Internet would bring a new way of political practice and economic exchange (Castells, 1996; 2002 Moreno and Suárez, 2009; thus, Internet was seen as a new technology that will affect all spheres of our life. Internet has been seen as a technology that will bring a new era or that it is the maximum exponent of a new cultural order called *Informational and Knowledge Society, Network Society* according to Manuel Castells (2000-2003)

The use of today's information technologies such as the Internet is originating new cultural forms in which individuals relate with others and with their own environment in a novel way, thus requiring the definition of new analytical and conceptual instruments. Although in analytical terms social scientists have made distinctions between social and cultural forms, this is questioned in anthropological terms. Clifford Geertz in particular addresses the interlacing of the social and the cultural. He argues that cultural and social phenomena are symbiotic and that culture is deeply embedded in the realities of social and economic structures (Geertz, 1973). This understanding of the interweaving of the economic, social and cultural aspects of the social world reaches into the richness of communication systems and socio-cultural life, as these systems are at once shaped by economic, social and political imperatives and made meaningful through culture. In the book written by Wessels (2010), the term 'cultural forms' is used to address both the cultural meaningfulness of social forms as well as cultural forms within the genres of entertainment and other culturally defined activities.

According to Wessels (2010:4) "Internet is embedded in contemporary socio- cultural forms and by understanding the relations of production, the narratives and participation in these forms one can analyse the Internet's characteristics, meaning and significance to contemporary society"… "Its characteristics such as interactive networked communication, virtual worlds and cyber cultures are understood as they materialize through social and cultural processes into specific social and cultural forms such as mobile work, e- citizenship, diasporic hubs and social networking sites"

David Porter in his introduction to *Internet Culture*, points out that communication through Internet can be understood from the perspective of culture since in virtual spaces one can found shared systems of believes, values and norms, specific ways of doing, a common understanding of symbols as emoticons, a netiquette and other signs that can perform a collective sense of belonging and create community. We can find here theoretical background linked to a holistic perspective of culture, such as the structural-functionalist approach, in the sense that a social group can be studied in isolation, as a complete cultural system. According to Margaret Mead (2000), culture and personality model was used to some extent to develop ethnographic oriented studies to describe virtual communities as if they were a new "tribe". In fact, Elisabeth Reid - 1994- ethnography takes Geertz perspective to show how people involved in virtual communities called multi-user domains MUDs develops specific cultural forms as they create places, objects, subjects and actions, laws and social order, but over all, from these interactions emerge a sense of community and belonging of similar characteristics of offline social life.

Given the importance of culture as a map of meanings in social relationships, numerous researchers have proposed integrating culture into the design of ICTs, both in the area of *Human Computer Interaction (HCI)* (Aykin, 2005) and instructional design (ID) (Subramony, 2004). Integrating culture into ICT design would enable us to shed light on the relationships we maintain with others through tools such as the Internet. According to Young (2008:14), the literature has examined some of the design specifications for HCI and ID and revealed the limited scope of culture in the design process.

## CYBERCULTURE THEORISTS: TOWARDS AN ANALYTICAL FRAMEWORK

In his discussion of the three stages of *cyberculture* studies outlined earlier, David Silver (2000) names Sherry Turkle's (1995) "Life on the Screen: *Identity* in the Age of the Internet" as one of the main pillars of the second stage, in which virtual communities and online identities become the main focus of discussion, and where the tone of that discussion is largely optimistic, highlighting the possibilities offered by cyberspace to rethink and recreate *identity* and community.

Her work combines sociological and psychotherapeutic analysis – she is also a licensed clinical psychologist – and draws on a range of theoretical approaches and a huge amount of empirical material collected over many years. "Life on the Screen", her third and best-known book, centres on what she calls the 'nascent culture of simulation', a culture she aligns with postmodernism, understood as people interacting with computers. As she comments, computers are 'bringing postmodernism down to earth' (Turkle 1995: 268), providing many 'objects-to-think-with'.

Thus, the analysis of the cultural forms of the Internet encompasses the research strategies, which focus on cultural aspects and refer to a new form of social interaction and sociability, which is instrumentalised through the computer. From this standpoint, the concept of *cyberculture* and socialisation implies the cultural traits that characterise virtual communities and the diverse cultural forms of interaction, which emerge through online communication. Culture as the product of social evolution and as an adaptive strategy of our species points to a generalised idea of individuals' transformation of their environment through the use of technology (Ardevol, 2003; Núñez et. al, 2004). In this case the new information technologies such as the Internet have revolutionised the classical parameters within which social change can be interpreted from a cultural point of view. As indicated by Lévy (1997), *cyberculture* represents a major mutation in the very essence of culture.

According to Lévy (1997: 203-204): "Far from being a subculture of Net fanatics, *cyberculture* expresses an important change in the very essence of culture [...] Thus *cyberculture* invents another way of bringing about humanity's virtual presence to itself, other than by imposing a unity of meaning". This reflection by Lévy raises a question, which we will attempt to answer in this chapter, namely: what are the key elements of this cultural change? Here we find several theoretical viewpoints, which use a macrosocial and holistic perspective to refer to the cultural and social change produced by the Internet as one more stage in the evolution of the capitalist system, in the same way that the introduction of the telephone led to a change in the way that individuals relate to one another. For the purposes of our analysis we will consider mainly the microsocial perspective, which refers to the new cultural form introduced by the Internet (*cyberculture*) and includes the lifestyles and the construction of self and the other within the new and elusive scenario known as cyberspace (Figuerora Sarriera, 2006). A considerable number of social and cultural studies have focused on the analysis of the cultural forms, which arise from online interaction. From this point of view and according to Ardevol (2005: 8), *cyberculture* is a new cultural form which is produced and reproduced through the Internet in social relationships on the web, and is linked to the concept of virtual communities and to the new "fields"[7] of social interaction which emerge through the computer, such as role-playing games, chat rooms in real time, discussion forums and distribution lists.

This leads to the view that social relations originating from the Internet constitute a particular lifestyle in which Internet-mediated communication represents a new form of learning and sociability, in what can be termed new lifestyles belonging to virtual communities and online communications. These new lifestyles have been a source of interest for a line of investigation that focuses on a cultural analysis of social learning and social life in virtual communities. In this analytical framework, culture refers to the various ways of life learned by the individual in diverse social contexts and which mould his or her *identity* and personality –particularly during infancy– in the process of socialisation and enculturation. This outlook explains cultural adaptation as based on social interaction and learned behaviour, that is to say, it proposes the study of culture as the analysis of the complex and interrelated patterns of interaction that the individual learns throughout his life in society. According to Margaret Mead (2000), for example, cultures constitute systems of behaviour learned and shared by the members of a group. Following this line of investigation, the first studies on cultural aspects of the Internet sought to find evidence of the presence of cultural elements online in order to decide whether we can speak of the emergence of an independent culture of communities arising from and maintained by computer-mediated communication. Using various theoretical viewpoints and definitions of culture, this research strategy addresses themes such as online *identity* and sociability, the establishment of social categories online, rules of behaviour, conflict resolution, jargon, the sense of group belonging, etc. (see Miller and Slater, 2000; Morely and Robin, 1996; Shields 1996; Ardèvol, 2003).

Although it is true that this analytical outlook has met with considerable criticism due to its failure to take into account the mixed social learning which takes place both outside and inside the Internet, it is also true that it has opened up new avenues for interpreting and analysing traditional concepts of sociability, such as the role of authority in shaping *identity*, and learning based on the transmission of knowledge between generations, essentially in young people.

Thus a study of the Internet from the viewpoint of the emergence of new cultural forms can be approached in two ways: one which focuses on a study of virtual communities as "complete communities", and another which proposes the study of the interdependence and interrelation between the different structural levels of society, and in this respect goes beyond the limits of *cyberculture* understood as an exclusively online phenomenon.

Online communication creates a new online *identity*, which is liberated from the sociocultural and biological restrictions inherent in traditional sociability (Dery, 1994). This means that in many cases the sources of learning and knowledge transmission are de-hierarchised and devertebrated into multiple and plural virtual communities of learning where the individual is the protagonist of his own learning (*e-learning*) and where the communications and learning networks are transmitted horizontally (the importance of peers) as opposed to the traditional vertical learning between generations. Lévy (2007: 226) expresses this very well when he says: "Far from uprooting the pattern of *tradition*, cyberculture turns it at a forty-five degree angle, in perfect synchrony with cyberspace. Cyberculture embodies the horizontal, simultaneous, purely spatial form of transmission. Its ability to provide temporal connections is an afterthought. Its principal activity is connecting in space, constructing and extending rhizomes of meaning".

According to Ardevol (2003) the design of our online *identity* is constructed from the decisions we take in relation with the available sociotechnical resources. The objectives we set ourselves, the meaning we give our action, depend on our imaginaries about the Internet and on what we know it to mean socially, for example, when taking part in a forum or in a chat room. Each one of us has our own expectations as to what the Internet is and what it can do for us. These expectations are generated from the common meaning we elaborate with regard to the Internet and its promises (Vayreda et al., 2003). The subjective perception of person feeds a series of utopias relating to the possibility of being "other", of inhabiting different identities (San Cornelio, 2004). These expectations and promises intervene creatively

in the appropriation made by the users of sociotechnical resources for social interaction and to present themselves in cyberspace. As in real life, defining one or another strategy depends on how the user defines the contexts of interaction based on the objectives of his or her participation. Thus it is not so much a question of interacting based on multiple identities in a range of contexts, but rather of acting the *identity* based on different strategies, thereby configuring different contexts (Durante and Goodwin, 1997). It is therefore not necessary to speak of multiple, distributed and fragmented identities in cyberspace, nor is it a case of experiencing ubiquity or a loss of the cohesion that we never previously had. It is simply that we act socially in cyberspace as we do outside it, with real consequences both inside and outside the Net. What really changes in this way of relating socially in cyberspace is the new way of learning, communicating and transmitting knowledge in favour of multiple forms of knowledge online through the Net, essentially among young people (Murakami, 2008). This could explain the disaffectation towards forms of traditional authority, which many young people do not recognise in their parents, although they do, for example, in the peer group, which they have formed online through a virtual community.

In summary, these cultural interpretations of the features, which constitute online *identity* (online cultures) and their coexistence with traditional *identity* (off-line cultures) underline the difficulty of analysing the mixed learning and communications flows that occur jointly in online and off-line communication. The research conducted so far indicates precisely the "subculture" condition of "cybercultures", and highlights the existence of interconnections between online life (virtual communities) and off-line life (traditional communities). Indeed it is essential from a methodological standpoint to widen the conceptual frameworks of cyberculture in order to consider the reconfiguration of the entire social space wrought by the Internet, and the fact that it structures behaviours both on and off the Net, thereby giving rise to the new cultural form we call cyberculture.

The solution to the theoretical controversy revolving around the cultural analysis of the new technologies may lie in defining culture as a process and not as something static. Of particular interest within this array of possible research strategies is the approach, which examines the problematisation of the concept of *cyberculture* itself (Ardevol, 2003).

## SOCIALIZATION AND IDENTITIES IN THE CYBERCULTURE: SOCIOLOGICAL AND ANTHROPOLOGICAL INTERPRETATIONS

The social context in which individuals use the new information technologies is characterised by diversity versus globalisation. In this new contradictory and ambivalent scenario of risks and uncertainties, cultural changes must necessarily be interpreted in the context of the production of new identities and transformations occasioned by the use of new technologies such as the Internet (Bauman, 1990; 2007; Castells, 1996; 2002; Giddens, 1991; Beck and Beck_Gernsheim, 2002).

The post-modern sociological critique offers an excellent theoretical framework for exposing and overcoming the contradictions of modernity. The specialists see *cyberculture* as their realisation of the post-modern era, and with it the (partial) surmounting of the contradictions of modernity. Thus they assume that *cyberculture*, in essence post-modern, encourages a new way of understanding socialisation and *identity*, not from the authoritarian and schematic aspect of vertical learning, but from the deconstructed, individualised, horizontal and relativist form of horizontal learning.

Several decades ago, our conceputalisation of *identity* drew on the psychological concept of *identity* (Erikson 1963). Other sibling sociological

terms such as self-concept, self-efficacy (Mead, 2000; Bandura 1997), or self-esteem have constituted orthodoxy and are largely focused on the individual as a centre of investigation. Within the last few decades, this view has been challenged as it tends to view *identity* as socially constructed, fluid, multiple, relational, and dialogic and open for re-description (Brubaker and Cooper 2000).

The platforms of *social networks* thus become a catalyzing example of how individuals interact in a liquid society –to use Bauman's term– in which the norms, which defined the pillars of communication and sociability in the solid society, are intertwined with the elements. This defines online communication, outside the boundaries of time, space and the self. This condition is a key factor because it fundamentally challenges the diverse locality and traditional values, reduces the sense of social and cultural distance between communities, and affects our relationship to time and space, the fundamental coordinates of experiential reality (Giddens 1991). Communication through social networks is changing the meaning of authority and the perception of one's self in keeping with the fragility of the new social relationships. These relationships are forged in a society which is behaving more and more like a vast shopping mall, in which individuals define their *identity* primarily through the exchange of information than through actual production arising through reflection. In this game of online social relationships, the concept of privacy becomes devirtualised and the meanings of our *identity* become public through Facebook, Tuenti, etc. This is just one more paradox of the online society, in which individuals strive to reinforce security and privacy in their homes and computers, while they publicise their lives on *social networks*.

In addition, the concept of authority also changes its meaning, and becomes a sphere which is now the competence of the peer group, in substitution of the figures of the "schoolmaster", "father" and "mother". There is little research which examines how far *social networks* affect the authority relationships between parents and children and in schools (Green & Hannon, 2007; Attwell, et al, 2009; Riley, 2008), and this investigation is indeed far from conclusive. The lack of research on this topic indicates the need for studies to investigate the mechanisms whereby people on the network affect personal decisions: through family-related norms, resources, role models or social learning.

Thus, the proliferation of the use of ICTs has combined with other factors (like changes in family structure and decline in manufacturing industries) to bring about profound shifts in how young people make sense of themselves. For example, the traditional move from identifying with the family to a single peer group has now been replaced by identifying with family to multiple peer groups, many of which are virtual. ICT also ensures that young people now have access to an instant, international, dynamically shifting and vast range of stories and forms of knowledge that can inform their *identity* management. These identities are rarely unified, but rather multiple in nature and increasingly fragmented (Murakami, 2008).

These new processes of social and cultural change which affect individuals' ways of communicating and socialising, and particularly in the younger generations, must be analysed within a global context of social change, which is characterised by an increasing information flow, uncertainty, individualisation, the fragility of social norms and thus the devirtualisation of normative references, in which ICTs emerge as a partial solution to the problems of individualisation through what has been termed "connected individualism" (Moreno Mínguez and Suárez, 2009). This new social framework requires new instruments of analysis, which enable us to deconstruct the parameters of the new sociability, in which individuals construct their *identity* both through ICTs and through traditional elements of socialisation. In order to achieve this objective it is crucial to include cultural analysis both in research into ICTs and in the design of new

technologies, by using what has been termed the "cultural based model" (*CBM*).

According to Young (2008) there is a need for models of culture that meet the globalization of technologically advanced societies. The inclusion of culture in all researches about ICTs must emanate throughout the cooperation between sociology, anthropology and the design process. The cultural based model (*CBM*) is just one example of a model of new culture to understand the late modernity. *CBM* is an intercultural, instructional design framework that guides designers through the management, design development, and assessment process while taking account explicit culture-based considerations (Young, 2008:107)

According to Murakami (2008) with the rapid innovations in information and communication technology (ICT) we go through in the global, postmodern and information era, it is important to examine how *identity* construction has become increasingly complicated. Appadurai (1996) and Castells (1996) propose that we look at the modern network society dynamically, in terms of disjunctive, networks of flow of things, people, ideas and finance that get transformed and organized. These features of the society seem to have bearing on the late-modern meaninglessness with which young people find difficult in coping when it comes to *identity* formation.

Post-modern thinkers such as Bauman (2007) have equated online social relationships with the typical form of consumption of the capitalist society. Bauman considers that this consumer lifestyle transforms people themselves into objects of consumption:

*"In the society of consumers no one can become a subject without first turning into a commodity, and no one can keep his or her character of subject secure without perpetually resuscitating, resurrecting and replenishing the capacities expected and required of a sellable commodity (Bauman, 2007: 25).*

According to this interpretation there could be said to be a social dynamic in online communication, which revolves around "the presentation of the person" on the Internet, and this dynamic is very close to a consumer relationship (for example, the consumption of the body, of personality, of *identity*, of comments, etc.). In this same line of interpretation, Ardévol (2005) has carried out an ethnographic analysis in order to study how people represent themselves in cyberspace through the Internet in order to determine to what extent online personal relations are represented as a market relationship.

## CONCLUSION

In the reflection presented in this article we have shown how the new communications technologies such as the Internet introduce a new cultural system of communication and sociability between humans, which coexists with the traditional model of social relationship based on the transfer of knowledge from one generation to another. This new cultural model, characteristic of the post-modern society, is characterised by the instantaneity and horizontality of the communication. The new instantaneity of time and space in *cyberculture* is transforming the meanings of authority, power, privacy, and of culture itself, but always within a particular historic context which changes in relation to the uses and advances of the new communications technologies.

The modern Internet society is changing the modality of human relationships through *social networks* and what are known as virtual communities, as well as the way in which humans socialise, learn and relate collectively. The new cultural interpretations of the effects of online social relationships require culture to be conceptualised as a process rather than as something static, in which the meanings which give significance to this social relationship change according to the

actual parameters of the communication which are defined through *social networks* (cyberculture).

Thus, I understand *cyberculture* within the conceptual framework that I have outlined in this chapter, as a wide social and cultural movement that is closely linked to advanced information and communication technologies. The theoretical discussion proposed in this work around the concept of *cyberculture* based on the review of the scientific literature leads to the conclusion that this new cultural format is playing a significant role in reshaping the traditional mechanisms of transmission and reproduction of information and communication. This is part of a feedback process in which technology conditions society and where individuals themselves are a factor in the creation of new technological artefacts (Bakardjieva, 2001; 2005: Haraway, 2003; Bell et al., 2004; 2007; Silver and Massanari, 2006)

The social context for interpreting this new form of social relationship is the individualised, liquid and risk-laden society described by authors such as Giddens, Beck or Bauman. Social relationships are characterised by immediacy, the fragility of human bonds, a change in the meaning of authority from vertical to horizontal, and in the very notion of privacy which is becoming more and more public in *social networks*, in stark contrast with the demands for security and privacy in our computers and our homes.

The new lines of analysis and investigation into ICTs will need to include cultural analysis both for designing communication tools and for interpreting the effects of their application and use in social relationships. The processes of social construction of *identity* are being transformed at great speed in the new *social networks*, giving rise to new ways of relating to education, politics, the family, friends and the community, essentially among the younger generations. This is contributing to modifications in the classical parameters of culture within which sociologists used to interpret the meanings of social relationships.

To conclude we quote a phrase from Bauman (2007:14) which neatly expresses and summarises the significance of culture and the new contradictions which emerge in the new Internet society:

"The teenagers equipped with portable electronic confessionals are simply apprentices training and trained in the art of living in a confessional society – a society notorious for effacing the boundary which once separated the private from the public, for making it a public virtue and obligation to publicly expose the private, and for wiping away from public communication anything that resists being reduced to private confidences, together with those who refuse to confide them".

# REFERENCES

Althusser, L. (2003). *Ideología y aparatos ideológicos de estado*. Buenos Aires, Argentina: Nueva Visión.

Appadurai, A. (1996). *Modernity at large: Cultural dimensions of globalization*. Minneapolis, MN: University of Minnesota Press.

Ardèvol, E. (2003). *Cibercultura / ciberculturas: La cultura de Internet o el análisis cultural de los usos sociales de Internet*. IX Congreso de Antropología, Barcelona, septiembre.

Ardèvol, E. (2005). *Dream gallery: Online dating as a commodity*. Paper for Media Anthropology e-seminar. Retrieved from http://www.media-anthropology.net/workingpapers.htm.

Attwell, G., Cook, J., & Ravenscroft, A. (2009). *Appropriating technologies for contextual knowledge: Mobile Personal Learning Environments*. Paper presented at the Second World Congress on the Information Society.

Aykin, N. (2005). Overview: Where to start and what to consider. In Aykin, N. (Ed.), *Usability and internationalization of Information Technology* (pp. 3–20). Mahwah, NJ: Lawrence Erlbaum Associates Publishers.

Bakardjieva, M. (2005). *Internet society: The Internet in everyday life*. London, UK: Sage.

Bakardjieva, M., & Smith, R. (2001). 'The internet in everyday life: Computer networking from the standpoint of the domestic user. *New Media & Society, 3*, 67–83.

Bandura, A. (1997). *Self-efficacy: The exercise of control*. New York, NY: Freeman.

Bauman, Z. (1990). *Thinking sociologically*. Oxford, UK: Blackwell.

Bauman, Z. (2007). *Consuming life*. Cambridge, UK: Polity Press.

Beck, U., & Beck-Gernsheim, E. (2002). *Individualization: Institutionalized individualism and its social and political consequences*. London, UK: Sage Publication.

Bell, D. (2001). *Introduction to cyberculture*. London, UK: Routledge.

Bell, D. (2007). *Cyberculture theorists: Manuel Castells and Donna Haraway*. New York, NY: Routledge.

Bell, D., Loader, B., Pleace, N., & Schuler, D. (2004). *Cyberculture: The key concepts*. London, UK: Routledge.

Bourdieu, P. (1988). *Cosas dichas*. Barcelona, Spain: Gedisa.

Brubaker, R., & Cooper, F. (2000). Beyond identity. *Theory and Society, 29*, 1–47. doi:10.1023/A:1007068714468

Castells, M. (1996). *The rise of network the society*. Oxford, UK: Blackwell Publishing.

Castells, M. (2002). *La galàxia Internet*. Barcelona, Spain: Rosa dels Vents.

Castells, M. (2003). The power of identity: The information age: *Vol. II. Economy, society, and culture*. Oxford, UK: Wiley-Blackwell.

Castells M. (2000-2003). *The information age*, vols. 1-3. London, UK: Routledge

Dery, M. (Ed.). (1994). *Flame wars: The discourse of cyberculture*. Durham, NC: Duke University Press.

Durante, A., & Goodwin, Ch. (1997). *Rethinking context*. Cambridge, UK: Cambridge University Press.

Durkheim, E. (1984). *The division of labour in society*. London, UK: Macmillan. (Original work published 1893)

Escobar, A. (2000). Welcome to Cyberia, notes on the anthropology of cyberculture. In Bell, D., & Kennedy, B. (Eds.), *The cybercultures reader*. London, UK: Routledge. doi:10.1086/204266

Figueroa Sarriera, H. J. (2006). Connecting the selves: Computer mediated identification processes. In Silver, D., & Massanari, A. (Eds.), *Critical cyberculture studies: Current terrains, future directions*. New York, NY: NYU Press.

Flew, T. (2004). New media: An introduction. In Shields, R. (Ed.), *Cultures of Internet*. London, UK: Oxford University Press.

Geertz, C. (1987). *La interpretación de las culturas*. Barcelona, Spain: Gedisa.

Giddens, A. (1991). *Modernity and self-identity: Self and society in the late modern age*. Cambridge, UK: Polity Press.

Green, H., & Hannon, C. (2007). *Their space: Education for a digital generation*. London, UK: Demos. Retrieved 3 August, 2009, from http://www.demos.co.uk/files/Their%20 space%20-%20web.pdf

Gross, B. (2000). *De la cibernética clásica a la cibercultura: Herramientas conceptuales desde donde mirar el mundo cambiante*. Salamanca, Spain: Ediciones Universidad de Salamanca.

Hakken, D. (1999). *Cyborgs@Cyberspace?: An ethnographer looks at the future*. New York, NY: Routledge.

Haraway, D. (2003). Cyborgs to companion species: Reconfiguring kinship in technoscience. In Idhe, D., & Selinger, E. (Eds.), *Chasing technoscience: Matrix for materiality*. Bloomington, IN: Indiana University Press.

Harris, M. (2001). *The rise of anthropological theory: A history of theories of culture*. London, UK: AltaMira Press.

Latour, B. (2001). *La esperanza de Pandora: Ensayos sobre la realidad de los estudios de la ciencia*. Barcelona, Spain: Gedisa.

Layder, D. (2009). *Intimacy and power. The dynamics of personal relationship in modern society*. Basingstoke, UK: Palgrave Macmillan.

Lévy, P. (1997). *La cibercultura, el segon diluvi?* Barcelona, Spain: Edicions UOC-Proa.

Mead, M. (2000). *The study of culture at a distance*. New York, NY: Bregan.

Miller, D., & Slater, D. (2000). *The Internet: An ethnographic approach*. Oxford, UK: Berg.

Morely, D., & Robin, K. (1995). *Spaces of identity*. London, UK: Routledge. doi:10.4324/9780203422977

Moreno Mínguez, A., & Crespo Ballesteros, E. (2007). Critical issue: Ensuring equitable use of education technology. In Cruz-Cunha, M. M., & Putnik, G. D. (Eds.), *Encyclopedia of networked and virtual organizations*. Hershey, PA: Idea Group Reference.

Moreno Mínguez, A., & Suárez Hernan, C. (2009). Online virtual communities as a new form of social relations: Elements for the analysis. In Cunha, M., Oliveira, E. F., Talavera, A. J., & Ferreira, L. G. (Eds.), *Handbook of research on social dimensions of semantic technologies and Web services.* Hershey, PA: Idea Group Reference. doi:10.4018/978-1-60566-650-1.ch022

Murakami, K. (2008). *Re-imagining the future: Young people's construction of identities through digital storytelling.* London, UK: DCSF/Futurelab. Retrieved 4 August, 2009, from http://www.beyondcurrenthorizons.org.uk/wp-content/uploads/final_murakami_youngpeoplesdigital-storytelling_20081201_jb2.pdf

Newman, D. (2005). *Sociology: Exploring the architecture of everyday life.* Pine Forge Press.

Núñez, F., Ardèvol, E., & Vayreda, A. (2004). *La actuación de la identidad online: Estrategias de representación y simulación en el ciberespacio.* Bilbao, Spain: Ciberart.

Porter, D. (Ed.). (1996). *Internet culture.* New York, NY: Routledge.

Reid, E. M. (1994). *Cultural formations in text-based virtual realities.* M. A. Thesis, University of Melbourne. Retrieved from http://www.ee.mu.oz.au/papers/emr/work.html

Riley, S. (2008). *Identity, community and selfhood: understanding the self in relation to contemporary youth cultures.* London, UK: Futurelab/DCSF. Retrieved 4 August 2009, from http://www.beyondcurrenthorizons.org.uk/wp-content/uploads/final_riley_identitycommunityself-hood_20081201_jb.pdf

San Cornelio, G. (2004). Art i identitat: una relació utòpica amb la tecnologia. *Arnodes,* 1-8. Retrieved from http://www.uoc.edu/artnodes/cat/art/pdf/sancornelio0604.pdf

Schields, R. (1996). *Cultures of internet: Virtual spaces, real histories, living bodies.* London, UK: Sage Publications.

Schumpeter, J. (1909). On the concept of social value. *The Quarterly Journal of Economics, 23*(2), 213–232. doi:10.2307/1882798

Silver, D., & Massanari, A. (2006). *Critical cyberculture studies.* New York, NY: New York University Press.

Subramony, D. P. (2004). Instructional technologists' inattention to issues of cultural diversity among learners. *Educational Technology,* 19–24.

Terranova, T. (2004). *Network culture: Politics for the information age.* Basingstoke, UK: Palgrave Macmillan.

Tönnies, F. (1957). *Community and society.* East Lansing, MI: Michigan University Press.

Turkle, S. (1995). *Life on the screen: Identity in the age of the Internet. London, UK: Weidenfeld & Nicolson. Shepard, J., & Greene, R. W. (2003). Sociology and you. Ohio.*Glencoe: McGraw-Hill.

Tylor, E. (1958). *Primitive culture.* New York, NY: Harper & Row.

Vayreda, A., Nuéz, F., & Miralles, L. (2001). La interacción mediatizada por ordenador: Análisis del Fòrum d'Humanitats i de Filologia de la Universitat Oberta de Catalunya. *Apuntes de Psicología, 19*(1), 101–122.

Wandrip-Fruin, N., & Montefort, N. (Eds.). (2003). *The new media reader.* MIT Press. Webster, F., & Puoskari, E. (Eds.). (2003). *The information society reader.* London, UK: Routledge.

Weber, M. (1978). *Economy and society: An outline of interpretive sociology.* Berkeley, CA: University of California Press.

Wessels, B. (2010). *Understanding Internet: A socio-cultural perspective.* Basingstoke, UK: Palgrave Macmillan.

Young, P. A. (2008). The culture based model: constructing a model of culture. *Journal of Educational Technology & Society, 11*(2), 107–118.

Young, P. A. (2008a). Integrating culture in designs of ICTs. *British Journal of Educational Technology, 39*(1), 6–17.

## KEY TERMS AND DEFINITIONS

**Culture-Based Model (CBM):** This approach makes it possible to adapt the new technologies to the range of cultural environments in order to achieve greater efficiency in the design and development of IT processes. According to Young (2008: 107) CBM is an intercultural, instructional design framework that guides designers through the management, design, development, and assessment process while taking into account explicit culture-based considerations. The model is intercultural because it operates inside, outside, and across cultures. This approach makes it possible to adapt the new technologies to the diversity of cultural environments in order to achieve greater efficiency in the design and development of the IT processes.

**Cyberculture:** The culture that has emerged from the use of computer networks for communication, entertainment and business. It is also the study of various social phenomena associated with the Internet and other new forms of network communication, such as online communities, online multi-player gaming, and email usage. Cyberculture is a wide social and cultural movement closely linked to advanced information science and information technology, their emergence, development and rise to social and cultural prominence between the 1960s and the 1990s. Manifestations of Cyberculture include various human interactions mediated by computer networks. Examples include, but are not limited to, blogs, *social networks*, games, chat, e- commerce, etc.

**E- Learning:** The name given to distance education or with a combination of virtual and classroom-based learning (this last is also known as "blended learning") through the new electronic channels (new communications networks, and particularly the Internet), using tools or hypertext applications (e-mail, web pages, discussion forums, chat rooms, platforms). With these communications technologies (ICTs), online students can communicate with their classmates and teachers (teachers, tutors, mentors, etc.) synchronously or asynchronously without limitations of space and time. *E-learning* is primarily a mode of distance or virtual learning, which enables students to interact with the teachers through the Internet, and manage their learning process autonomously.

**Human Computer Interaction (HCI):** The study of social interaction between people (users) and computers. It is often regarded as the intersection of computer science, behavioural sciences, design and several other fields of study. Interaction between users and computers occurs at the user interface (or simply interface), which includes both software and hardware; for example, characters or objects displayed by software on a personal computer's monitor, input received from users via hardware peripherals such as keyboards and mice, and other user interactions with large-scale computerized systems such as aircraft and power plants. The Association for Computing Machinery defines human-computer interaction as "a discipline concerned with the design, evaluation and implementation of interactive computing systems for human use and with the study of major phenomena surrounding them. An important facet of HCI is the securing of user satisfaction.

**Instructional Design (also called Instructional Systems Design (ISD)):** The practice of maximizing the effectiveness, efficiency and appeal of instruction and other learning experiences. The process consists broadly of determining the current state and needs of the learner, defining the end goal of instruction, and creating some "intervention" to assist in the transition. Ideally the process is informed by pedagogically and andragogically (adult learning) tested theories of learning and may take place in student-only, teacher-led or community-based settings. The outcome of this instruction may be directly observable and scientifically measured or completely hidden and assumed. There are many instructional design models but many are based on the ADDIE model, which includes analysis, design, development, implementation, and evaluation phases. As a field, instructional design is historically and traditionally rooted in cognitive and behavioural psychology.

**Identity/Online Identity:** An online identity, Internet identity, or Internet persona is a social identity that an Internet user establishes in online communities and websites. Although some people prefer to use their real names online, some Internet users prefer to be anonymous, identifying themselves by means of pseudonyms, which reveal varying amounts of personally identifiable information. In some online contexts, including Internet forums, MUDs, instant messaging, and massively multiplayer online games, users can represent themselves visually by choosing an avatar, an icon-sized graphic image. As other users interact with an established online identity, it acquires a reputation, which enables them to decide whether the identity is worthy of trust. Some websites also use the user's IP address to track their online identities using methods such as tracking cookies. The concept of the personal self, and how emerging technologies influences this, is a subject of research in fields such as psychology and sociology. The Online disinhibition effect is a notable example, referring to a concept of unwise and uninhibited behaviour on the Internet, arising as a result of anonymity and audience gratification.

**Social Networks:** A social network is a social structure formed by people connected by one or various types of relationships, such as friendship, family ties, common interests, economic exchanges, sexual relationships; or who share beliefs, knowledge or prestige. In the case of online social networks the social structure is based

on digital communication through the Internet on platforms such as Facebook or Tuenti, where individuals express and share their interests, tastes and demands. A social network service is an online service, platform, or site that focuses on building and reflecting of social networks or social relations among people, e.g., who share interests and/or activities. A social network service essentially consists of a representation of each user (often a profile), his/her social links, and a variety of additional services. Most social network services are web based and provide means for users to interact over the Internet, such as e-mail and instant messaging. Although online community services are sometimes considered as a social network service in a broader sense, social network service usually means an individual-centred service whereas online community services are group-centred.

**Socialization/Digital Socialization:** In the field of sociology research, socialization means to convert individual into group tacit knowledge. Face-to-face meetings and phone calls undoubtedly facilitate socialization. Further, both media are not good at supporting asynchronous socialization. Digital socialization refers to the extent Internet-based media can promote cross-firm socialization and enhance collaborative work. Digital socialisation coexists with traditional socialisation, contributing new elements for learning and interiorising norms through the use of new technologies, and promoting collaborative learning through the multiple platforms of *social networks* designed for this purpose.

## ENDNOTES

[1]    For Tylor, the term "culture" is used to denote the totality (see holism) of the humanly created world, from material culture and cultivated landscapes, via social institutions (political, religious, economic etc.), to knowledge and meaning. Tylor's definition is still widely cited: "Culture, or civilization,

taken in its broad, ethnographic sense, is that complex whole which includes knowledge, belief, art, morals, law, custom, and any other capabilities and habits acquired by man as a member of society." (Tylor 1958: 1)

2    For more on the meaning of this concept see Moreno and Suárez (2009).

3    ICTs – Information and Communication Technologies; also new technologies, digital technologies, information technologies or advanced technologies.

4    The term social formation (respectively socio-cultural formation) originally refers to Marx's concept of socio-economic formation, but its meaning is different. Hakken (1999: 45) defines social formation as the "abstraction of preference in contemporary social thought with which we refer to social entities. This term does not give unwarranted priority to any one level, as is the case, for example, in standard uses of the term 'society', which privilege the national level. From a 'social formation' perspective, the basic questions are how social entities are reproduced from one period to the next, whether more or less the same, modified somewhat, or fundamentally different."

5    **Authority**: Weber defined domination (authority) as the chance of commands being obeyed by a specifiable group of people. Legitimate authority is that which is recognized as legitimate and justified by both the ruler and the ruled. According to Shepard et al. (2003), authority is defined as the legitimate or socially approved use of power. **Socialization**: According to Newman (2005), socialization is the process of learning to adopt the behavior patterns of the community. The most fertile time of socialization is usually the early stages of life, during which individuals develop the skills and knowledge and learn the roles necessary to function within their culture and social environment. **Community and identity**: German sociologist Ferdinand Tönnies (1957) distinguished between two types of human association: Gemeinschaft (usually translated as "community") and Gesellschaft ("society" or "association"). In his 1887 work, Gemeinschaft and Gesellschaft, Tönnies argued that Gemeinschaft is perceived to be a tighter and more cohesive social entity, due to the presence of a "unity of will". He added that family and kinship were the perfect expressions of Gemeinschaft, but that other shared characteristics, such as place or belief, could also result in Gemeinschaft. This paradigm of communal networks and shared social understanding has been applied to multiple cultures in many places throughout history. Gesellschaft, on the other hand, is a group in which the individuals who make up that group are motivated to take part in the group purely by self-interest. He also proposed that in the real world, no group was either pure Gemeinschaft or pure Gesellschaft, but, rather, a mixture of the two. In some contexts, "community" indicates a group of people with a common identity other than location. Members often interact regularly in this community. A virtual community is a group of people primarily or initially communicating or interacting with each other by means of information technologies, typically over the Internet, rather than in person. These may be either communities of interest, practice or communion. Research interest is evolving into the motivations for contributing to online communities

6    Methodological individualism is a widely used term in the social sciences. Its advocates see it as a philosophical method aimed at explaining and understanding broad, society-wide developments as the aggregation of decisions by individuals. The term was originally coined by Joseph Schumpeter (1909).

[7]  Term used by P. Bourdieu (1988: p.127-142) to refer to a system of positions and objective relationships in a temporal and cultural context, which involves introducing the historic dimension. In fact the application of the concept of culture –together with the historical concept– to the analysis of ICTs allows us to relativise the new, as both concepts are the coordinates from which we trace the map of the world in transit" (Ardevol, 2005: 22).

# Chapter 5
# From Virtual to the Simulated World:
## An Agent-Based Model of Friendship Network in Second Life

**Sadaf Alvi**
*University of Karachi, Pakistan*

**Shah Jamal Alam**
*University of Michigan, USA*

## ABSTRACT

*Second Life is a virtual world that allows users to engage in various social activities, meet friends, form communities, attend events of interests, and trade online with other users represented through their virtual 3D avatars. For social and behavioral scientists, this provides an opportunity to investigate the dynamics of social interaction and formation of interpersonal and group affiliation ties. We present a prototype agent-based model that takes into account a number of qualitative and quantitative studies of social networking in Second Life. Initial results concerning friendships and acquaintance ties are reported.*

## INTRODUCTION

Understanding social systems and the dynamics of empirical social networks has always been a challenge for social ethnographers (Schensul et al., 1999). For ethnographers and social networks researchers, acquiring relational data about actors and their ties (such as friends, advice networks or social clubs) could be challenging. While gathering such data is both time consuming and expensive in many situations, relevant issues such as the 'boundary-specification' problem can affect the conclusions drawn from the analysis of such networks (Degenne and Forsé, 2003). The boundary-specification problem as posed by Niklas Luhmann refers to the task of specifying inclu-

DOI: 10.4018/978-1-61350-444-4.ch005

sion rules for actor or relations in a network study (Kossinets, 2006). In practice, inferences drawn from the analysis of such empirical networks are not taken back to the original respondents or validated against the target system.

Recent technological advances coupled with the availability of faster and cheaper internet services have opened new research frontiers and challenges for social and behavioral scientists in understanding human social interaction in the cyberspace. The tremendous increase in the use of social networking sites in the last few years has not only linked millions of people around the global but have also accelerated the advancements in the development of communication devices such as 'smart phones'. On the other hand, having millions of subscribers imply that the social networking sites have to make relentless efforts in scaling up their servers and back-end databases in order to minimize risks such as outage or system unavailability. Managing 3D virtual sites is a further challenge in terms of fast and interactive rendering of the virtual world as well as requiring fast internet and powerful computers at the client side. The enormity of demographic, social networking data of the users has also tremendously increased the challenges for computer scientists developing tools of knowledge discovery and data mining techniques. It is also challenging for the social and behavioral scientists to analyze similarities and differences in social networks of online communities and the 'traditional' social networks (e.g. friendship networks) from the real world (Pfeil et al., 2009; Pollet et al., 2010; Subrahmanyam et al., 2008; Wellman, 2004).

In contrast to online social networking communities, (3D) virtual worlds provide the environment where real actors participate through their 'alter-egos' or *avatars.* Individuals may wish to keep their identity hidden and/or interact with other avatars similar to the real world. For example, in the massively multiplayer role-playing game *World of Warcraft*[1] *(WoW)*, people can make alliances, join hands on common objectives, have friends and foes

and build ties that may change in the passage of time. Linden labs™' virtual world Second Life[2], provides a much more general environment for individuals to socialize, trade and build their own spaces inside the virtual world. Whereas in the real world, there is a dearth of offline social networks data, in particular, longitudinal data, logs of all activities of avatars and events in these virtual worlds open up the opportunities for social and behavioral scientists to test theories concerning generalized exchange, norms, friendship ties, trust and reputation (c.f. Bainbridge, 2007; Krotoski, 2007). As we discuss in the following section, Linden Labs have shared users' interaction data to researchers interested in studying social interaction in online communities and virtual worlds. This allows researchers to conduct ethnographic and social network studies within Second Life as well as to study users' behavior by analyzing data over a given time period using data mining techniques and statistical methods (c.f. Bakshy et al., 2010).

Social systems are sources of complexity in themselves in the sense that interactions between individuals can give rise to unexpected and unpredictable behavior at the macro level. One way of understanding the interplay of such interactions is through simulating some aspects of the target system, whether it is from real or a virtual world. Agent-based social simulation is a modeling technique that is suitable for analyzing such systems, by capturing individual behavior and observing the generated behavior at the macro level (Gilbert & Troitzsch, 2005; Epstein & Axtell, 1996). In contrast to traditional 'top-down' modeling, agent-based modeling is developed in a 'bottom-up' fashion, i.e. the behavior and the processes are specified at the entities' level (Davidsson, 2001). While agent-based models have had a long history of application to real world social systems, simulating and understanding social dynamics in virtual world using agent-based models is scarce. There has been a growing interest, however, in the agent-based modeling and simulation of preferences for friends in social networking, e.g. Abbas (2010) who study segregation in online friendship network of college students on Facebook. Crooks et al. (2009) demonstrated how agent-based simulation models could be embedded in Second Life so that simulated agent and real users represented by their avatar in Second Life may influence simulation outcomes in the same environment.

In this chapter, we take the idea of simulating dynamical social networks in Second Life and present a prototype agent-based simulation model of friendship network formed 'in world' of Second Life. The aim of this modeling exercise is to devise behavioral rules for the agents in the model and to analyze the generated friendship network. These rules are abstracted from observations and literature discussing various mechanisms for making acquaintances and community memberships in Second Life.

## BACKGROUND AND RELATED WORK[3]

Second Life is a '3D online digital virtual world, created, and owned by its residents' (Rymaszewski et al., 2007). Launched in 2003, the numbers of current user accounts exceed 22 million[4]. Users represented by their avatars in the virtual world can explore the world, interact with other avatars', build social and economic ties and create their own virtual objects such as places, apparel and/ or social groups and communities.

An interest in research in the evolution of social and normative behavior of users in Second Life dates back to its early days when it was launched by Linden labs, the company that created and manages the virtual world. Krotoski (2005), for example, discusses the potential of studying the evolution of trust among friends in Second Life and its sociological implications. Later, through performing snowballing sampling of users 'in world' and acquiring the users' social networks data from Linden labs, Krotoski (2007; 2009) stud-

ied network and psychological drivers that predict social influence in the avatars' social networks.

More recently, social networks researchers have analyzed data about social and transactional exchange among users in Second Life, acquired from Linden labs. For instance, two articles by Bakshy et al. (2010) study the 'social dynamics' of trade and economic activities within the users' social circles and among strangers. A companion study by Chun-Yuen & Adamic (2010) used logistic regression to identify key predictors of users retention based on their economic activities, if any, interaction (such as instant messaging) with friends and strangers, and groups affiliations. In another relevant work in progress, Welles et al. (2010) investigate 'structural signatures' of the friendship networks in Second Life and compared them with studies of offline friendship networks – they investigated social networking behavior of users belonging to three different age groups: adolescents, adults and seniors. Yee & Bailenson (2008) and Harris et al. (2009) focus on methods for analyzing the temporal evolution of social networks in Second Life. Qualitative studies such as Case et al. (2009) and Nood et al. (2006) provide anecdotal accounts of users' activities and preferences for friends in Second Life. Such qualitative accounts and/or domain experts' opinion inform agents' behavior at the micro-level in agent-based models introduced in the next section (Moss & Edmonds, 2005).

Teleporting in Second Life allows the users in the virtual world to move to any place immediately. In contrast to the real world, there is no cost of maintaining social ties in Second Life when it comes to spatial proximity. Users are able to look for their friends' online status and may give access to their whereabouts in Second Life to 'closer' friends. La & Michiardi (2008), for instance, studied avatars' mobility in Second Life and observed spatial clustering of avatars similar to the real world; i.e. preference for places of interests. Another interesting aspect studied in Second Life is the role of spatial proximity in triggering social interaction among users (see e.g. Friedman et al., 2007). Huffaker et al. (2010) provides a descriptive study of 'successful sellers' activities in Second Life. One of their interesting findings is the periodic fluctuations in transactions that occur at the hourly scale, while the authors did not cyclic patterns at the daily level. They also find geographic concentration and groups' membership to be important factors in economic transactions and the role social networks play in the economic activities in Second Life. Another relevant work is by Pedica & Vilhjálmsson (2008) who study group dynamics in shared virtual environments, allowing avatars to generate an act based on a set of reactive behaviors under various social situations.

## AGENT-BASED MODELING OF SOCIAL PHENOMENA

Social Simulation according to Gilbert & Troitzsch (2005) "is the idea that one can build a computer program that models the behaviour of some social phenomena". It aims at an abstract representation of a real-world phenomenon, which in the case of computer simulation requires model development in a programming language or a simulation platform. According to Gilbert (2002), most social science research begins with either a classical theory or a model conceptualizing social phenomena. Simulation provides the third way where it is possible in many areas to carry out computer-generated experiments and test hypotheses where it is impossible or very costly to conduct the same experiments in real social systems. Through a simulation model, as argued by Barthélémy (2006), one develops a formal representation of the system that could be helpful in understanding the target system. ABSS models simulate social behavior of autonomous individuals and the interaction among them (Gilbert & Troitzsch, 2005). As Moss (2008) argues, the real strength of agent-based simulation is that it

allows incorporating both quantitative and qualitative evidence that may represent stakeholders' perspectives.

From the social sciences perspective, the concept of agent may follow some or all of the nine characteristics as outlined by Ferber (1999). An important distinction in explaining an agent's choice of actions is between omniscience and bounded-rationality (Russell & Norvig, 2005). Omniscience implies that an agent has complete knowledge of the outcome of its action. In the latter case, however, an agent's actions depend upon its partial knowledge of the system and its experiences only. The term "bounded rationality" was originated by Herbert Simon (Simon, 1957), which according to Edmonds (1998) implies that the agent possesses the following characteristics: an agent,

- does not have a perfect knowledge about the "dynamically changing environment" that is acquired through interaction,
- does not have a perfect model of their environment,
- is bounded by computational power which limits the agent's ability to fully optimize its actions
- has limited resources including memory and both exogenous and endogenous constraints

Developing agent-based models involves identifying social entities from the target system as agents in the model. Agents are encapsulated with their attributes and a set of actions through which they can change their states and the environment. Agents may interact with the model's environment, e.g. harvesting crops over land parcels (c.f. Bharwani et al., 2006), or interact with other agents, in friendship and advice networks (c.f. Ernst et al., 2007) allowing to explore different sets of agent interaction rules without having to change the model's environment. This is useful in cases where micro-level rules are intuitively derived or are based from limited observation. Outcomes from such different rule sets raise further questions that can then be asked from the stakeholders. Environment design is also an important step in developing agent-based social simulation models (Gilbert, 2004). Agents may be situated in a spatially explicit environment or may be socially embedded. Social embeddedness means that an agent's behavior may be influenced by a network of social relations that the agent is part of (Granovetter, 1985; Edmonds, 2006). As explained by Edmonds (1998, p. 2), "An agent is socially embedded in a collection of other agents to the extent that it its more appropriate to model that agent as part of the total system of agents and their interactions as opposed to modeling it as a single agent that is interacting with an essentially unitary environment."

Some of the references for an introduction to agent-based modeling and their use in social sciences include Gilbert & Troitzsch (2005), Axtell & Epstein (1996), Edmonds & Moss (2011, forthcoming) and Miller & Page (2007). Axelrod & Testfatsion (2006, appendix A) provides some starting pointers for agent-based modeling. Currently, several modeling frameworks and libraries are available for developing agent-based models. Some of these include Repast, Mason, NetLogo, Swarm, Ascape, AnyLogic, Brahms and Cormas. Cynthia & Madey (2009) provide a list and comparison of some of the more widely used agent-based modeling frameworks.

## THE PROTOTYPE MODEL[5]

In this section, we introduce a prototype model for simulating social interactions among avatars in Second Life. The abstracted Second Life's virtual world (known as the 'Second Life grid') is currently represented in the model as a 2D toroid grid, where each cell on the grid represents a place (or a land parcel) in the virtual world. Time is represented in the model as tick counts (or time steps) on an hourly scale. The prototype model is developed in Java and uses the Repast Simphony[6] modeling toolkit.

## Agents as Avatars

Agents in our model represent *avatars* in Second Life, i.e. the virtual persona of real-world individuals. In the prototype model reported in this chapter, social interactions and identifying characteristics, described below, remain within the scope of users' interaction in Second Life. Subsequent extensions of the model will include individuals' behavioral rule based on both their real world (offline) and virtual world (online) identities and activities.

Avatar appearance is one of the key predictors of an avatar's social activities in the Second Life Boellstorff (2008). Individuals, especially those investing money in Second Life are likely to invest on their appearances and the outlook of their land parcels. In our model, we represent *appearance* in the form of an abstract tag, which is a finite sized array of integers assigned to each avatar object at the time of its creation (c.f. Moss, 2008). Each index in the tag array may represent a particular aspect of avatars' appearance in Second Life. An avatar agent's 'acceptance' of another avatar's physical appearance depends upon the number of entries in their tag arrays that are similar. In our model, each avatar agent is assigned an acceptance threshold (percentage), which is drawn from the Uniform distribution a model assumption. An avatar agent endorses another avatar agent as 'attractive' if the percentages of identical entries in their tags exceed the former avatar agent's threshold (a model parameter). Being 'attractive' in our model is used as a proxy for acceptance of another avatar's appearance. For instance, Asif (2009) in a limited survey of Second Life users' report 47% of the respondents consider other avatars' appearance to be 'very important', while only 7% find it as 'not important'.

Endorsements are labels that are used by agents to 'endorse' other agents for making acquaintances and subsequently making the best-endorsed acquaintances as friends. These include 'is-similar-tag', 'is-same-ethnicity', 'is-same-gender', is-opposite-gender', 'shared-interests', 'shared-communities-affiliation'. The concept of endorsements originated from Cohen (1985), were incorporated into agent-based social simulation models by Moss (1998). Our model's implementation follows from the concept that was previously described in Alam et al. (2010). By default, the weights are assigned randomly to all agents for the endorsements. These are used by the avatar agents, e.g. to rank their acquaintances as 'close friends' or to have a preferential ordering of events and communities when determining their next action, as described later in this section.

Agents are defined with respect to their profiles, assigned at the start of the simulation. Avatar agents' basic characteristics include avatar appearance (tags), gender in Second Life, and users' ethnicity. Avatar agents are assigned 'some' (a parameter) interests drawn randomly from the pool of interest categories. The following interest types in the model are taken from Second Life events and communities categories: *arts & culture, commercial, discussion, education, contests, music, night entertainment* and *sports*. An important characteristic of agents is their *usage type per week*; each agent is assigned a usage type at the time of its entry into the simulation. These are, on average, *between 7 and 14 hours, between 15 and 28 hours, between 29 and 49 hours* per week. In our model, agents are assigned their daily schedule based on the average number of hours that they would spend in a week. By default, we assume agents are assigned either of the above three usage types randomly.

The number of communities/groups memberships for agents is a fixed upper limit that is assigned uniform randomly from a range of 5 to 15 communities to each agent. Agents maintain a list of favorite places/location ('picks') that they

had previously visited during simulation and had found them 'interesting'. Each agent may choose, currently with equal probability, to either visit a place (random or from the 'picks'), attend an event of interest, or visit friends. Currently, we assume that all online agents are aware of the online status and locations of their friends.

## Communities, Events and Places

In Second Life, users can join communities that comprise of groups, blogs and forums. Communities in Second Life are identified with interest categories. Users may join these communities given their respective interests and expect to find other users with similar interests and activities. At the start, we assign agents a starting location representing the 'welcome' location in Second Life. In our model, we assume a global calendar, as in Second Life, for all public events. Here, we do not assume any private or restricted events. Furthermore, we assume that each event has a category (event type) and a specific location on the simulated grid, and has a fixed duration. The events' calendar in the model is updated every 24th hour – and enlists the events whose start time falls within a whole day in the simulation. At every time step (hour) in a simulation run, each agent updates its next 'login' time depending upon its usage type. Each community in the model decides whether they would convene an event depending upon the time since the last event by that community.

Agents may prefer to roam around or be 'teleported' to specific fixed locations of interests on the simulated grid. They have a visibility range, currently the entire place in the model (i.e. a cell on the grid), and if they find another agent, they can check that agent's basic characteristic and can invite them to be their acquaintance. Being co-located and online at the same time is a requisite in our model for the avatar agents to meet and make acquaintances. This includes meeting strangers, friends, and friends of friends. Two agents are identified as 'co-located', if they are both 'online' and are present at the same place. This may be because of one or both agents may find the place as interesting or if they happen to be attending the same event.

## Representation of Acquaintance and Friendship Networks

In our model, an agent's acquaintances are those avatar agents at a land parcel or a location to which the agent is most likely to interact. This is implemented in the model as follows: agents may add other agents as their acquaintances given they are attracted based on the avatar agents' physical appearance (tag), shared interest (i.e. an avatar's profile in Second Life) and a bias for same or opposite gender (a model parameter). That is, two acquaintance avatar agents who meet each other more frequently than otherwise are likely to share similar interests and preferences for locations. The acquaintance relation in our model is mutual, i.e. both the invitee and the invited agents must add each other as acquaintances. This may correspond to initiating and having chat with avatars that are found online at same location, by chance, or attending an event. Moreover, an avatar agent may introduce, with a small chance, two of its acquaintances who are 'online' and are present at the same location. We assume that having a mutual acquaintance relaxes the criteria for accepting an agent as acquaintance. That is, the chance for two agents to have a tie in the acquaintance network is higher when they share a mutual friend or acquaintance.

The 'friendship' network in the model is an asymmetric relation where an agent chooses its friends from its acquaintance network. Acquaintances, who meet frequently, are likely to build a stronger friendship tie between each other. After every two to three weeks, avatar agents in the model determine whether any of their acquaintances is endorsed as a friend. This decision depends upon the similarity between their tags,

*Table 1. Outline of the simulation schedule in the model*

**Initialization Phase:**
  I. Create the 2D grid representing the Second Life virtual world.
  II. Create locations and assign them categories.
  III. Create communities with specific categories and randomly assign them locations.
  IV. Create initial avatar agents and assign them the 'starting location'.
**Main Schedule: Runs for *n* time steps (hours)**
  1. Update events calendar for the next 24 hours (every $24^{th}$ step).
  2. Remove all expired events (each step).
  3. call create-new-avatar-agents (every $24^{th}$ step).
  4. For each agent ∈ Avatar_Agents
       call set-next-login-schedule
  5. For each community ∈ Communities
       If should-create-event(community)
         Then call create-new-event (community)
  6. For each agent ∈ Avatar_Agents
       If agent is online
         Then call set-new-activity(agent)
  7. For each agent ∈ Avatar_Agents s.t. is-online(agent)
       call update-acquaintance-network (agent)
       If agent is mutual-acquaintance (agent-A, agent-B)
           Then introduce-acquaintances(agent-A, agent-B)
  8. For each agent ∈ Avatar_Agents
       call update-friendship-network(agent)
       call update-communities-affiliation-network (agent)
  9. call remove-avatar-agents
**End**

frequency of their interaction, co-location, and having overlapping community memberships. A likely consequence of this implementation is an asymmetric friendship relation, i.e. an agent *A* identifying an agent *B* as a friend, while for agent *B* might only merely remain an acquaintances. Both the acquaintance and friendship ties are dynamic and are updated by agents regularly.

## The Simulation Schedule

Table 1 gives an outline of the main simulation schedule of the model, whereas Table 2 gives a summary of the model parameters used in running simulations. A UML class diagram of the key classes in the model is shown in Figure 1.

At every time step, 'online' avatar agents decide their next activity, which spans for one

*Table 2. Model parameters' values for the reported simulation results*

| Parameter | Description | Default value |
|---|---|---|
| *communityEventPreference* | Chance for attending an event organized by one's community | 65% |
| *membershipSize* | Maximum number of communities that an agent is allowed to join | 15 |
| *acquaintanceRecall* | Recall period for recognizing another avatar agent as an acquaintance based on meeting at a place (location) during that period. | 14 * 24h |
| *communityWeightThreshold* | Preference for recognizing an avatar agent as acquaintance based on 'same community' membership only (chance) | 15% |
| *ethinicityRanges* | Distribution of ethnicity of users in the simulation | {W (0.65), B (0.25), O (0.1)} |
| *friendsLimit* | Range from which the max. friends for an avatar agent is drawn | U (7, 11) |

hour (a time step in the model). An agent may choose to stay at the same place as it were previously or continue to attend an ongoing event at its present location. Alternatively, it may choose a new activity, i.e. visit some location on the grid (new or from a list of favorite locations) or choose an event from calendar. It may also choose to meet friends. By default, an agent chooses from these above activities with equal probabilities. Different sets of probabilities may be assigned to agents to represent heterogeneous preferences in the model.

## SIMULATION RESULTS

In this section, we report initial results from three simulation configurations for the prototype agent-based model. Simulations were run for 2500 time steps (~3.5 months), where each step corresponds to one hour of activity in the simulated Second Life world. Figure 2 shows a snapshot of the simulated world representing the Second Life grid during a simulation run. Colored cells on the grid represent places that either may be public or may be owned by a particular community. Two places shown with same colors denote that they have same categories. In our model, agents may stay at the same place or teleport elsewhere. Places that belong to a particular community are venues for the community events; we assume all

events are open for everyone. White cells on the grid represent vacant locations. Currently, we assume that agents move only to places, i.e. to the colored cells. In the next step, places will be dynamically created on vacant locations on the model grid. Circles on the grid cells depict avatar agents: the darker a circle is shown, the greater is the agents' density at a place.

One of the issues being addressed by network researchers such as Chun-Yuen & Adamic (2010) is finding reliable predictors for user retention in Second Life. From the methodological perspective, investigating the effect of changing population structure on the temporal evolution of social networks is a research area. Here, we consider three cases concerning the exit rates of agents over the course of a simulation run (see Table 1). In Case I, we use a uniform exit rate for all agents independent of their duration of stay in the simulation. This we update every day, i.e. every 24th hour. In the second case (Case II), we take into account three factors in determining an agent's chances of exiting the simulation, viz. the time since entry in simulation, number of friends made by an avatar, and total number of memberships of an avatar. We use logistic regression to determine probability where we give the highest weights to the number of friends, followed by community memberships and finally the 'resident period' of an avatar agent in hours. We adapted these three factors as some of the important predictors for

*Figure 1. UML Class diagram of the agent-based model of friendship network in Second Life*

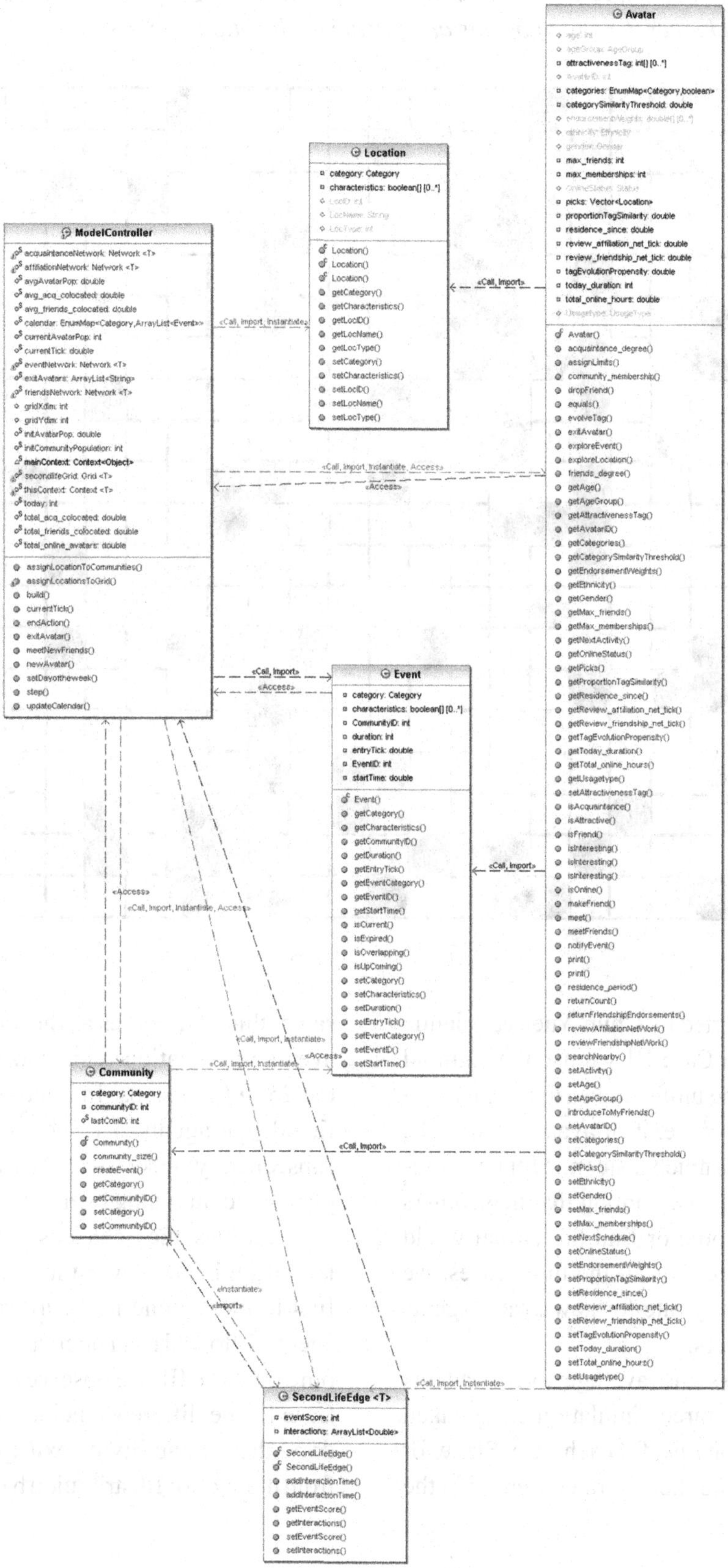

*Figure 2. A snapshot of the simulated grid representing the Second Life virtual world, where each cell represents a vacant location or a place. Circles represent avatar agents at a location on the grid Dark circles represent a higher density of agents at a particular location on the grid.*

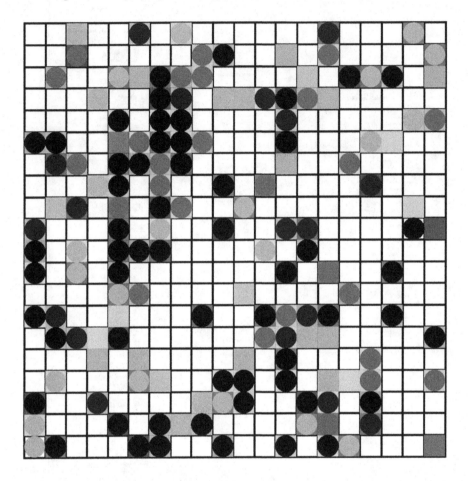

user retention reported by Chun-Yuen & Adamic (2010). Finally, in Case III we use the sigmoid curve instead of the uniform distribution used in Case I applied for the exit of avatar agents: the idea being to have a much faster rate for newcomers to leave the world assuming that newcomers are likely to get bored or find the virtual world difficult to navigate. For all the three cases, we assume that the entry rate for new avatar agents is 1/365 per 24 hours.

Figure 3 shows the average avatar agents population for the three simulation cases taken over five simulation runs for each case. Since for Case I, the entry and the exit rates were kept the

same, this case serves as the base case where the average population remained stable throughout the 2500 time steps. In contrast, for case II, we find that as agents make new acquaintances (and subsequently, make friends) by visiting interesting places and attending events of interests, and join communities, their chances for exiting the simulation diminishes over time. Thus, we observe, first in the decline in the average population of agents followed by an increasing trend after some time. In Case III, we observe a similar trend as in Case II; the difference being that, in Case III we draw the probability of exit for an avatar agent from the sigmoid distribution based on the resident

*Table 3. Summary of preliminary simulation configurations for the three cases concerning exit of avatar agents from simulation*

| Configuration | Description |
|---|---|
| Case I | Uniform random probability for exiting avatars (1/365)<br>– called every 24th hour |
| Case II | Exit probability determined by logistic regression for variables:<br>(i) time since entry in simulation;<br>(ii) # of friends;<br>(iii) # of community memberships |
| Case III | Exit probability based on the sigmoid curve only. |

period only, whereas in Case II, agents' degrees in the friendship and the community affiliation network as well. As we may observe, the retention rate of the avatar agents in Case II is highest; the reason being that chances for exit for those who entered the simulation at the start went negligible as they spent time in the simulated world. This is why one sees a drop in the population for Case II during the first half, whereas in the later period of the simulation runs, agent population increased due to retention of the old agents and a constant entry rate for the new ones.

Figure 4 shows histograms for degree distributions of the avatar agents' acquaintance network at the 2500th time step for Cases I, II and II respectively. For Cases I and II, we find similar shape of the degree distribution of the agents' acquaintance networks in the respective simulation runs. However, the frequency in the latter case was higher due to a higher agent population. One distinguishing factor in the histogram for Case II is that some agents stay for longer periods as compared to agents in Case I and Case III. This is because the more contextualized exit mechanism for the agents, which takes into account their

*Figure 3. Average population of five simulation runs for the three cases concerning exit of avatar agents from simulation*

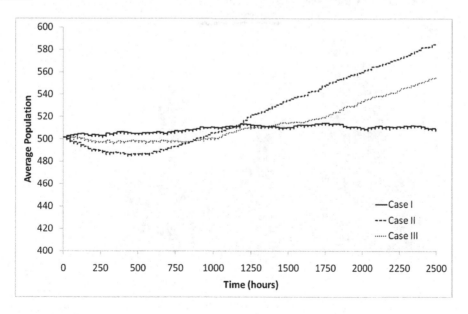

*Figure 4. Acquaintance network degree distribution for the three cases concerning exit of avatar agents from simulation: Case I (a), Case II (b) and Case III (c).*

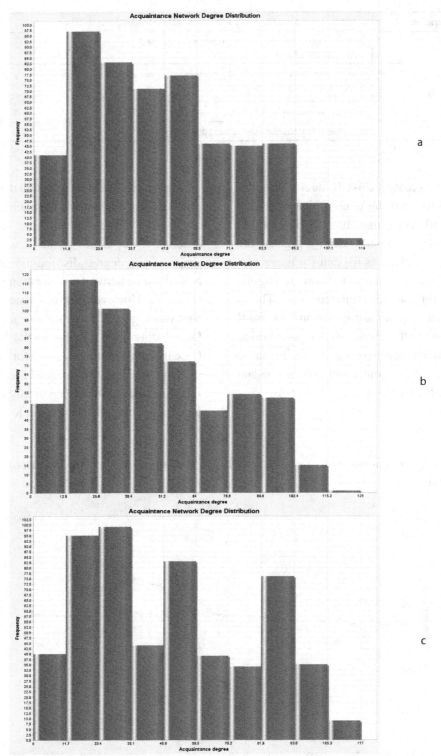

*Figure 5. Average friends by usage type for the four cases with, 'no entry and no exit' (top-left) and the three cases concerning the exit of avatar agents from the simulation with Case I (top-right); Case II (bottom-left); Case III (bottom-right).*

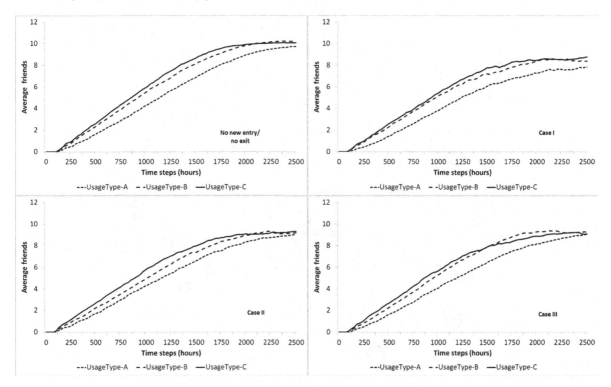

social interaction with their friends and their community memberships during simulation. Nevertheless, the same entry rate for all the three cases implies that new agents are introduced into the simulation at a constant rate. Thus, we find a proportion of agents who have fewer acquaintances.

For the friendship network in the model, we assume a given range from which a maximum limit of friends is assigned to each agent. Agents choose their friends from among their acquaintances. As discussed before, we assume that the friendship network in the model is asymmetric in contrast to the acquaintance network. As shown in Figure 5, when there is no entry or exit in a simulation, agents are able to identify friends from their pool of acquaintances for the maximum allowed limit (see Table 2). The usage type categories are based on the average number of 'online'

hours per week. That is, those who spend between 7 and 14 hours ('A'), between 15 and 28 hours ('B') and between 29 and 49 hours ('C') per week. For the other three panels concerning Cases I, II and III, we find the average friends to be lower since new agents enter the system and existing agents leave the system over the course of a simulation run. In all the four panels in Figure 5, agents with the usage type 'A' were the slowest in getting the stable average friends as compared to types 'B' and 'C'. Agents who spend more time online are likely to have more acquaintances and thus a bigger pool from which they choose friends. The relation of agents' usage types and friendship networks is given in Figure 6. We show the graph for a simulation run with 50 agents for the purpose of illustration. Agents' usage types are depicted with different colors, green correspond to the usage type 'A', blue for type 'B' and red for type

*Figure 6. Agents' friendship network with agents in the nodes having colors and sizes with respect to their 'usage types' and in-degree respectively.*

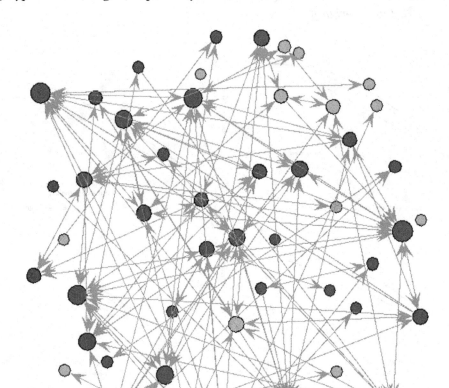

'C'. The size of the nodes in Figure 6 corresponds to the in-degree of the agents, i.e. which agents were identified as 'friends' by other avatar agents. Those who spend more time online are more likely to be included in other agents' acquaintances list. This is because two acquaintances agents would endorse each other as friends depending upon the time spent together while 'online'.

## OUTLOOK

One of the objectives of this book is to identify methods and case studies that address modeling and analysis of complex social networks. Maintaining social ties in the real world can be costly in many ways. Spatial proximity, availability of time and other resources and frequency of contacts are important aspects in understanding the structure and dynamics of social networks for a real world case study. Size of social networks is therefore limited (c.f. Dunbar, 1992). The increasing use of internet worldwide and the availability of faster and cheaper communication devices makes online social networking as 'cost-free' on one hand, while becoming excellent sources of data on social networking ties among organizations and individuals.

Virtual worlds, in particular, Second Life is different to online social networking sites: it allows users to hide their real world identities, create their avatar(s) or a virtual alter ego and have commercial and social interactions 'in world'. Unlike social networking sites such as Facebook or Hi5, users of Second Life require fast internet connections, better hardware and a steeper learning curve in being acquainted with the virtual world. This may explain why some users would leave Second Life very early if they find it difficult to navigate. Nevertheless, it opens up new opportunities for understanding how individuals perform social and economical exchange, studying emotions such as intimacy or fear, and study temporal evolution of social networks[7].

In this chapter, we present a prototype agent-based model for friendship networks in Second Life. Agent-based models are testbeds, which help in understanding individual-level processes that generate macro level properties in a system, e.g. social network structures. Some of the papers cited in this chapter, use statistical analysis of the Second Life data provided by Linden labs. Others conducted experiments in Second Life about social and psychological behavior of the enrolled users. Ours is perhaps the first attempt in developing an agent-based simulation model for Second Life, aiming at incorporating various types and sources of data concerning individuals' characteristics and social interaction to the observed social network data in the Second Life. This is a work in progress and we are currently exploring and tuning various processes and schedule of the model.

The prototype model may be extended in a number of ways. One such extension of this work is investigating the evolution of trust among the agents based on the findings reported from the virtual world. The simulated networks and their statistical characteristics could then be validated against the empirical research about friendship ties and trust in Second Life (Krotoski, 2009).

## ACKNOWLEDGMENT

We are thankful to the editors and the reviewers for their comments and feedback. SJA likes to thank Bruce Edmonds for the motivation to study social and normative behavior in Second Life using simulation.

## REFERENCES

Abbas, S. M. A. (2010). *A segregation model of Facebook*. Paper presented at the Sixth UK Social Networks Conference, London, UK.

Alam, S. J., Geller, A., Meyer, R., & Werth, B. (2010). Modelling contextualized reasoning in complex societies with "endorsement". *Journal of Artificial Societies and Social Simulation*, *13*(4). Retrieved from http://jasss.soc.surrey.ac.uk/13/4/6.html.

Asif, S. (2009). *Exploring e-commerce in an online virtual world: Second Life*. Unpublished B.Sc. (Hons.) dissertation, University of Manchester, Manchester, UK.

Axelrod, R., & Testfatsion, L. (2006). A guide for newcomers to agent-based modeling in the social sciences. In Ammon, H. M., & Kendrick, D. A. (Eds.), *Handbook of computational economics*. Amsterdam, The Netherlands: Elsevier. doi:10.1016/S1574-0021(05)02044-7

Bainbridge, W. S. (2007). The scientific research potential of virtual worlds. *Science*, *317*, 472–476. doi:10.1126/science.1146930

Bakshy, E., Karrer, B., & Adamic, L. A. (2009). Social influence and the diffusions of user-created content. In *Proceedings of the ACM Conference on Electronic Commerce* (pp. 325-334). The ACM Press.

Barthélémy, O. T. (2006). *Untangling scenario components with agent based modelling: An example of social simulations of water demand forecasts.* Unpublished doctoral dissertation, Centre for Policy Modelling, Manchester Metropolitan University, Manchester, UK.

Bharwani, S., Bithell, M., Downing, T. E., New, M., Washington, R., & Ziervogel, G. (2005). Multiagent modelling of climate outlooks and food security on a community garden scheme in Limpopo, South Africa. *Philosophical Transactions of the Royal Society B., 360,* 2183–2194. doi:10.1098/rstb.2005.1742

Boellstorf, T. (2008). *Coming of age in Second Life: An anthropologist explores the virtually human.* Princeton University Press.

Case, C. J., King, D. L., & DeSimone, K. (2009). Virtual worlds: An exploratory study of undergraduate behavior. *Proceedings of the Academy for Studies in Business.*

Chun-Yuen, T., & Adamic, L. A. (2010). Longevity in Second Life. In *Proceedings of the Fourth International AAAI Conference on Weblogs and Social Media.* AAAI Press.

Cohen, P. R. (1985). *Heuristic reasoning about uncertainty: An artificial intelligence approach.* Boston, MA: Pitman Advanced Publishing Program.

Crooks, A., Hudson-Smith, A., & Dearden, J. (2009). Agent Street: An environment for exploring agent-based models in Second Life. *Journal of Artificial Societies and Social Simulation, 12*(4), 10. Retrieved from http://jasss.soc.surrey.ac.uk/12/4/10.html.

Davidsson, P. (2002). Agent based social simulation: A computer science view. *Journal of Artificial Societies and Social Simulation, 5*(1). Retrieved from http://jasss.soc.surrey.ac.uk/5/1/7.html.

Degenne, A., & Forsé, M. (2003). *Introducing social networks* (Borges, A., Trans.). London, UK: Sage Publications.

Edmonds, B. (1998). Modelling bounded rationality in agent-based simulations using the evolution of mental models. In Brenner, T. (Ed.), *Computational techniques for modelling learning in economics* (pp. 305–332). Kluwer. doi:10.1007/978-1-4615-5029-7_13

Edmonds, B. (2006). How are physical and social spaces related? Cognitive agents as the necessary glue. In Billari, F. (Eds.), *Agent-based computational modelling: Applications in demography, social, economic and environmental sciences* (pp. 195–214). Berlin, Germany: Springer-Verlag. doi:10.1007/3-7908-1721-X_10

Edmonds, B., & Moss, S. (2011). *Simulation social complexity: A handbook.* Springer.

Epstein, J., & Axtell, R. (1996). *Growing artificial societies: Social science from the bottom up.* Boston, MA: The MIT Press.

Ernst, A., Krebs, F., & Zehnpfund, C. (2007). Dynamics of task oriented agent behaviour in multiple layer social networks. In Takahashi, S., Sallach, D., & Rouchier, R. (Eds.), *Advancing social simulation* (pp. 319–330). Berlin, Germany: Springer-Verlag. doi:10.1007/978-4-431-73167-2_29

Ferber, J. (1999). *Multi-agent systems: An introduction to distributed artificial intelligence.* Addison Wesley.

Gilbert, N. (2002). Varieties of emergence. In *Proceedings of the Agent 2002 Conference: Social agents: Ecology, Exchange, and Evolution,* Chicago, USA.

Gilbert, N. (2004). The art of simulation. In *Proceedings of the Second European Social Simulation Conference (ESSA'04),* Groningen, The Netherlands.

Gilbert, N., & Troitzsch, K. (2005). *Simulation for the social scientist*. Open University Press.

Granovetter, M. (1985). Economic action and social structure: The problem of embeddedness. *American Journal of Sociology, 91*, 481–510. doi:10.1086/228311

Harris, H., Bailenson, J. N., Nielson, A., & Yee, N. (2009). The evolution of social behavior over time in Second Life. *Presence (Cambridge, Mass.), 18*(6), 434–448. doi:10.1162/pres.18.6.434

Huffaker, D. A., Simmons, M., Bakshy, E., & Adamic, L. A. (2010). Seller activity in a virtual marketplace. *First Monday, 15*(7).

Kossinets, G. (2006). Effects of missing data in social networks. *Social Networks, 28*, 247–268. doi:10.1016/j.socnet.2005.07.002

Krotoski, A. K. (2007). *Making e-friends and influencing people: Assessing the perceptions of opinion leaders in a virtual world*. Paper presented at the International Sunbelt Social Network Conference, Corfu, Greece.

Krotoski, A. K. (2009). *Social influence in Second Life: Social network and social psychological processes in the diffusion of belief and behaviour on the Web*. Unpublished doctoral dissertation, University of Surrey, Department of Psychology, School of Human Sciences.

Macy, M. W., & Willer, R. (2002). From factors to actors: Computational sociology and agent-based modeling. *Annual Review of Sociology, 28*, 143–167. doi:10.1146/annurev.soc.28.110601.141117

Miller, J. H., & Page, S. E. (2007). *Complex adaptive systems: An introduction to computational models of social life*. Princeton University Press.

Moss, S. (1998). Critical incident management: An empirically derived computational model. *Journal of Artificial Societies and Social Simulation, 1*(4). Retrieved from http://jasss.soc.surrey.ac.uk/1/4/1.html.

Moss, S. (2008). Simplicity, generality and truth in social modeling. In *Proceedings of the Second World Congress on Social Simulation (WCSS'08)*, Fairfax VA, USA.

Moss, S., & Edmonds, B. (2005). Sociology and simulation: Statistical and qualitative cross-validation. *American Journal of Sociology, 110*(4), 1095–1131. doi:10.1086/427320

Nikolai, C., & Madey, G. (2009). Tools of the trade: A survey of various agent based modeling platforms. *Journal of Artificial Societies and Social Simulation, 12*(2). Retrieved from http://jasss.soc.surrey.ac.uk/12/2/2.html.

Nood, D., & Attema, J. (2006). *Second Life, the second life of virtual reality*. The Hague, The Netherlands: EPN Electronic Highway Platform.

Pedica, C., & Vilhjálmsson, H. (2009). Lecture Notes in Computer Science: *Vol. 5773. Spontaneous avatar behavior for human territoriality* (pp. 344–357). Berlin, Germany: Springer Verlag.

Pfeil, U., Arjan, R., & Zaphiris, P. (2009). Age differences in online social networking – A study of user profiles and the social capital divide among teenagers and older users in MySpace. *Computers in Human Behavior, 25*(3), 643–654. doi:10.1016/j.chb.2008.08.015

Pollet, T. V., Roberts, S. G. B., & Dunbar, R. I. M. (2010). Use of social network sites and instant messaging does not lead to increased offline social network size, or to emotionally closer relationships with offline network members. *Cyberpsychology. Behavior and Social Networking, 14*(4). doi:10.1089/cyber.2010.0161

Russell, S., & Norvig, P. (2003). *Artificial intelligence: A modern approach* (2nd ed.). Prentice Hall.

Schensul, J. J., Lecompte, M. D., Trotter, R. T. II, Cromley, E. K., & Singer, M. (1999). *Mapping social networks, spatial data, and hidden populations*. London, UK: Altamira Press.

Simon, H. (1957). *Administrative behaviour: A study of decision-making processes in administrative organization*. New York, NY: Macmillan Press.

Subrahmanyam, K., Reich, S. M., Waechter, N., & Espinoza, G. (2008). Online and offline social networks: Use of social networking sites by emerging adults. *Journal of Applied Developmental Psychology*, *29*(6), 420–433. doi:10.1016/j.appdev.2008.07.003

Tobias, R., & Hoffman, C. (2004). Evaluation of free Java-libraries for social-scientific agent based simulation. *Journal of Artificial Societies and Social Simulation*, *7*(1). Retrieved from http://jasss.soc.surrey.ac.uk/7/1/6.html.

Welles, F. B., Van Devender, A., & Contractor, N. (2010). *Is a "friend" a friend? Investigating the structure of friendship networks in virtual worlds*. Paper presented at the 28th International Conference on Human Factors in Computing Systems (CHI), Atlanta, GA, USA.

Wellman, B. (2004). Connecting community: On- and off-line. *Contexts*, *3*(4), 22–28. doi:10.1525/ctx.2004.3.4.22

Yee, N., & Bailenson, J. N. (2008). A method for longitudinal behavioral data collection in Second Life. *Presence (Cambridge, Mass.)*, *17*(6), 594–596. doi:10.1162/pres.17.6.594

## KEY TERMS AND DEFINITIONS

**Agent-Based Modeling:** Computer simulation modeling concerned with the representation of a target system at the individual level and observing the phenomena at the macro-level.

**Community Affiliations:** Individuals memberships of communities in the simulation model of Second Life based on the individuals' own interests and the interests of the communities they join.

**Endorsements:** In the context of this chapter, endorsements 'tags' or labels (e.g. is-similar, is-same-gender etc.) that agents assign to other agents. They describe an endorsing agent's perspective of the endorsed agent.

**In-Degree:** The in-degree of an avatar agent (ego) in the friendship networks gives the number of other avatar agents that endorse ego as their friend, at a given time step.

**Second Life:** A 3D online virtual world where individuals may socially interact, reside and/or trade through their avatars.

**Social Simulation:** An interdisciplinary field understanding aspects of social complexity through computational modeling and simulation

**Social Networks:** In the context of this chapter, individuals' social (acquaintances and friendship) ties in the simulation.

## ENDNOTES

[1] http://www.wow-europe.com/en/index.xml (last accessed: Jan 30, 2011)

[2] http://secondlife.com/ (last accessed: Jan 30, 2011)

[3] The literature cited in this section is by no means exhaustive.

[4] http://secondlife.com/xmlhttp/secondlife.php (last accessed: Jan 30, 2011)

[5] The source code and further details on the model are available from the corresponding author.

[6] http://repast.sourceforge.net/ (last accessed: Jan 30, 2011)

[7] See, e.g. the *NormWatch initiative* -http://cfpm.org/sl/normwatch.html (last accessed Jan 30, 2011)

# Chapter 6
# Analysis of Success Factors in Social Networking Website Development

**Zanita Zahari**
*La Trobe University, Australia*

**Eric Pardede**
*La Trobe University, Australia*

## ABSTRACT

*The popularity and rapid growth of social networking sites is undeniable. However, it is hard to guarantee the success and sustainability of these sites. This study will focus on identifying the key success factors for each phase in agile iteration development for social networks. A qualitative and quantitative analysis was adopted using web analytical tools to gather and measure these success factors. A comparative study between popular and unpopular social networking was undertaken to gather realistic data. Results reveal that determinants of success for agile development phases include: goal setting, developing brand image, quality content, trust building, user-centered design, technology and client server platform, service quality, user satisfaction and stability. The successful implementation of these factors will benefit developers and users in order to achieve the success and survival of the social networking website development.*

DOI: 10.4018/978-1-61350-444-4.ch006

## INTRODUCTION

Research into online communities is abundant and they have been studied from the various perspectives of many academic disciplines such as psychology, sociology, information systems, communication, management, health, education and economics. However, only a small amount of research proposes and verifies the success factors of online communities. In order to develop long lasting social networking sites, there are different factors in different phases of development that determine the success. This paper will benefit website designers and developers by suggesting the success factors for each phase in agile iteration development. Most social networking sites fail because several important factors are missing in the development phases, for example the goal and purpose are not defined clearly, too much attention is focused on technology rather than usability and social design, they lack appeal which results in user inactivity and low quality content. With the goal of identifying the success factors of social networking website development, we survey the social networking and agile software development process model. We review metrics of success and integrate the findings of success factors with the six phases in social networking website development. Finally, we conclude this paper and provide recommendations for future research.

## BACKGROUND

People of all ages and backgrounds use social networking to enrich their lives through the contacts they make on social networking sites. Three of the most popular social websites are Facebook, Youtube and Wikipedia (The Nielsen Company, 2010). In addition, different social networking sites emphasize different aspects of human interaction (Weaver and Morrison 2008). Social networking sites allow users to set up online profiles and develop their online social network. The profile page contains personal information, such as interests, activities and contact information. Moreover, some social network sites allow users to design the appearance of their page and upload photos and videos. When users sign up for social network sites, they are able to socialize and build a network of connections to friends. Being affiliated with a network also allows the users connect to each other, share content and disseminate information. There are many applications and types of content that can be used on social networking sites.

The history of social networking began with the launch of Six Degrees in 1997 with basic features such as being able to create profiles, list and search for friends and send messages (Boyd and Ellison, 2010). Several other major social networking sites, namely Live Journal, Asia Avenue, Black Planet, LunarStorm, MiGente and Cyworld, followed this, which supported various combinations of profiles and friends from 1997 to 2001. Social networking sites expanded from personal to business networks when Ryze.com was launched in 2001. In 2002, the launch of Friendster resulted in social networking hitting its stride, boasting more than three million users a year later. LinkedIn, networking resources for business people and MySpace were introduced a year later in 2003. Facebook was launched in 2004 as a Harvard project for two years before opening to the public in 2006, and now leads all other social networking sites.

## Software Development Process Model

Social networking sites evolve in stages and have a life span as a software development process model. The basic popular models used for software development are *System Development Life Cycle (SDLC), Rapid Application Development (RAD), Prototyping* and *Agile Development*. See Figure 1 for the agile iteration life cycle.

We have chosen Agile Development for this study as it is quite similar to the waterfall model

*Figure 1. Agile iteration life cycle*

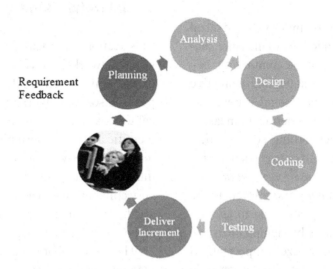

and has the ability to revisit the phases that dramatically enhanced the efficiency of software. In agile development, software is developed progressively with each new release adding more capabilities based on the highest priority to satisfy customers. The aims are of good design and technical excellence is met by breaking projects into small iterations in a time box. The project's priorities and direction are re-evaluated at the end of the iteration so that the software can be delivered faster and can be of higher quality.

The simple rules to develop a long lasting social networking community are based on three principles, namely *start off small, create and maintain a feedback loop* and *empower members over time* (Kim, 2000). Simple and focused social networking communities are easy to maintain and grow over time to meet user's needs and changes in the environment. This rule is similar to the agile concept where the entire application is distributed in incremental units called iterations. Each iteration will deliver an increment of functionality based on customer requirements. As a result, the community will evolve, gain some efficiency and survive in the long term. The principle *creates and maintains a feedback loop*

highlights the ongoing communication between management and users to satisfy the needs of the social networking community. Active customer involvement, especially face-to-face interaction, is also one of the key features in agile development. Once the iteration is tested, users will approve it and give feedback. The iteration is then repeated, based on the feedback to ensure a high level of customer satisfaction. Finally, the *empower members over time* principle means that users play a role in providing content and maintaining the community when the online community is mature enough and has a clear and well-stated purpose. Users are willing to participate when they believe the community is secure and they have achieved a certain level of trust. This feature is also important in agile development, as it emphasizes the user's satisfaction by involving them in software development. The three principles that have been discussed are practical for application to social networking website development with the agile iteration approach, in order to help designers and developers improve the value and quality of social networking sites.

## Metrics of Success

Every social networking community should set up its own indicators or guidelines to measure success, as all developers want the community they build to be successful. Quantitative and qualitative metrics can be used as success measurements. There are many quantitative metrics to measure the success of social networking communities. However, the most important ones chosen for this study were *community size, user participation* and *user contributions. Community size* refers to the number of people that pay attention to and are interested in the community by signing up to join the community as a member. Size is important and is often cited as a measurement of the success of a social networking community. One may consider communities as successful based on the size of active members rather than total members. For instance, *Facebook* had more than 500 million active users as of September 2010 (Facebook, 2010). *User participation* is based on user activities such as number of visits, login activity and page views. Uniqueness and similarity of group members will influence member participation in online communities (Ludford, Cosley et al., 2004). *User contributions* are the content that members actively contribute to the communities. The volume of threads, messages and comments posted by the members indicates stronger interactions between members. These strong contributions will lead to communities' stability and vitality as more contact between members shows the development of relationships. The qualitative metrics include *user satisfaction* and *quality of member's relationships* (Iriberri and Leroy, 2009). It is important to fulfill the user's needs by giving what they want because the success of social networking communities depends on how satisfied and loyal users are. *The quality of member's relationships* is also commonly quoted as a success metric for social networking communities where it reflects customer perceptions by fulfilling their expectation and objectives.

## Success Factors of Social Networking

This section will identify the success factors of social networking development in the six phases of the agile iteration life cycle. The planning phase in social networking development is critical to its success. Effective planning allows the identification of opportunities in the future. The differences between agile planning and other traditional project planning is that agile planning is very collaborative, where the whole team including the project manager, developers and users are responsible for planning.

The factors that contribute to success in the planning phase are establishing the *goal setting* and *developing brand image. Goal setting* is important in the early planning phase of social networking development where by establishing clearly defined goals, the developers can stay focused on what to achieve and concentrate on the actions to be taken to reach the goals by organizing the development of social networking in short iterations. The goals will depend on the specific needs of the social networking site such as social searching, developing new connections or marketing the business. For instance, the purposes of Facebook are social searching and social browsing (Lampe, Ellison et al., 2006). Social searching refers to the practice of people who use Facebook to find out information about people they have met offline whereas social browsing refers to the use of the site to develop new social connections. Social network sites are also a creative and affordable way for companies to reach their potential customers. The goal setting theory shows that specific goals will stimulate higher performance in business and influence members to contribute more actively than non-specific goals (Beenen, Ling et al., 2004). *Developing brand image* and trademarks help differentiate social networking communities from each another and rapidly generate word-of-mouth for most brands (Jansen, Zhang et al., 2009). The content can be created and spread via social networking sites and as a result, increases brand awareness and familiarity, especially for new businesses. The brand image factor can affect member participation in social networking (Rood and Bruckman, 2009). Famous branding platforms such as Facebook, Youtube, Twitter and LinkedIn can be used to market the business. Once people are devoted to a brand, they will participate in the community which leads to consumer brand loyalty (Sha, Wen et al., 2009). It is important in the planning phase, that the company manager uses social networking sites as a marketing method and constructs a brand community where members can share their experience and knowledge with others.

The analysis phase is where the developers analyse the user's requirements and engage the communication with users as the sustainability of social networks is highly dependent on user participation. It is important to note that agile analysis should be communication rich, iterative and incremental. The success factors in the analysis phase include *quality content* and *trust building*. *Quality content* refers to updated content by the moderator that meets the users' needs, allows customization and has quality questions and answers(Agichtein, Castillo et al., 2008). *Trust building* and loyalty are the critical factors in the analysis phase in order to develop a social network that satisfies member needs. It is vital that developers understand the user group that will use the service, the goals and the context of use (Brandtzaeq and Heim, 2007). Interaction from an engaged user can be anything from leaving comments or taking part in a support forum to customer reviews and ratings. Moreover, the motivational issues should be analysed in order to manage trust among the users. In order to gain user loyalty, the online community must provide benefits and experiences that members seek (Brandtzaeq and Heim, 2007).

The design phase is where the choice is made concerning the type of architecture which will be used in building the social networking website.

The success factor for this phase is the usability of a *user-centered design*. The *user-centered design* is an important principle that should be applied in designing long-lasting social network sites. It is necessary to understand the underlying psychology of human behaviour to deliver an effective social networking site that supports interaction between users. The activities and content of social networks are mostly driven by the users who are expected to interact and post messages. In order to achieve this, the best approach in agile development is to improve the look and feel of social network websites through users' involvement in the design phase obtained through comments and feedback.

The coding phase of social networking website development involves hundreds of thousands of lines of code. The success factors for this phase are making the right choice in terms of *technology* and the *client server platform*. It is important that the *technology* and *client server platform* that are chosen provide features that support the requirements and design in the previous phases (Dwyer, Hiltz et al., 2008). In agile development, the coding is done by building customizable social network sites and allowing these to evolve with the customer's new requirements.

The testing phase is to identify any problems or bugs in the social network software application. The success factors for this phase are *service quality* and *user satisfaction*. *Service quality* means that the social network built is tangible, reliable, responsive, assured and promotes empathy (In, Hye et al., 2009). On the other hand, *user satisfaction* depends on service quality and ensuring that it meets the user's needs. In agile development, a few tests such as the unit test, integration test and acceptance test, are done for each iteration. Agile testers are required to test the social network sites from the customer's perspective rather than doing ad-hoc testing by testing iteratively the newly developed code of functionality.

The deliver increment phase refers to the continuous release of new functionalities of social

*Table 1. Top 10 ranking for Facebook pages*

| Rank | Pages | Category | Fans |
|------|-------|----------|------|
| 1. | Texas Hold'em Poker | Games | 23,185,881 |
| 2. | Michael Jackson | Musicians | 19,028,455 |
| 3. | Facebook | Brands-Technology | 17,175,859 |
| 4. | Lady Gaga | Musicians | 16,484,627 |
| 5. | Family Guy | TV Shows | 16,037,963 |
| 6. | Vin Diesel | Actors | 14,611,488 |
| 7. | Mafia Wars | Games | 13,631,819 |
| 8. | Starbucks | Brands - Food/Beverage | 12,888,628 |
| 9. | House | TV Shows | 12,874,420 |
| 10. | Barack Obama | Politicians | 12,827,194 |

network sites in each iteration. *Stability* (Leimeister, Sidiras et al., 2004) is the success factor for this phase. The *stability* will push the social network to evolve and motivate high participation from users. It is important to note that the agile iteration life cycle continuously improves and refines the processes to deliver better and higher quality social networking sites.

## METHODS

This section analyses all the proposed success factors for the six phases of agile iteration in the development of social networking website by using analytical web tools and a comparison study of popular and unpopular social networking websites such as Facebook and Friendster.

## Planning Phase

The important success factors for this phase are *goal setting* and *developing brand image. Goal setting* is the critical factor in the planning phase in order to achieve success in social networking as discussed in the previous chapter. Goals for social networking sites are varied such as to increase visitor traffic, achieve popularity and a higher rank, building consumer awareness, increase

consumer loyalty and establish relationships with the customer. Facebook is chosen for a case study to evaluate these factors as it is listed as the second top site on the web after Google by the web analytical applications (Alexa, 2010). For this quantitative analysis, we measure the success of goal setting for visitor traffic and the most popular social networking page on the Facebook site by using traffic tracking services. In addition, size is often cited as a significant factor when measuring the success of social networking website. The data is gathered and analysed using various independent traffic tracking services for the Facebook platform such as PageData (PageData, 2010) and FanPageList (Fan Page List, 2010). The results show that the *Texas Hold'em Poker* Page is the top ranked page, having the highest numbers of visitors and traffic on the Facebook site. Therefore, this social networking site is considered a successful community based on its goals to increase visitor traffic and to be ranked in the top ten most popular internet sites.

Alternatively, qualitative analysis can also be done to evaluate the success of *goal setting* by identifying who is in the network, what motivates people to join the network and the interactions in the network. Fan Counts for each Facebook page show how many people 'like' the page, pay attention to the content and interact with the page.

*Table 2. Interactions for Top 10 Facebook Pages (Vitrue, 2010)*

| Rank | Facebook Page | Fans | Page Posts | Interactions |
|------|---------------|------|------------|--------------|
| 1. | Texas Hold'em Poker | 23,185,881 | 104 | 1,123,653 |
| 7. | Mafia Wars | 13,631,819 | 30 | 803,796 |
| 10. | Barack Obama | 12,827,194 | 62 | 792,196 |
| 4. | Lady Gaga | 16,484,627 | 30 | 643, 460 |
| 2. | Michael Jackson | 19,028,455 | 12 | 287, 251 |
| 3. | Facebook | 17,175,859 | 26 | 144,327 |
| 6. | Vin Diesel | 14,611,488 | 3 | 134,735 |
| 8. | Starbucks | 12,888,628 | 12 | 74,167 |
| 9. | House | 12,874,420 | 9 | 65,125 |
| 5. | Family Guy | 16,037,963 | 3 | 27,632 |

Based on the goal to maximize visitor interactions in Facebook, it will involve a balance between the frequency of interaction and increasing the number of people who see and engage with the content. Web analytical tools such as Vitrue help to show the interaction of the users. These interactions measure how interested the users are in the content of a Facebook page. However, the number of interactions could increase or decrease depending on the type of content offered by the page.

The results indicate that the interactions on each page vary and do not depend on the community size (number of fans). For instance, *Mafia Wars* has the second highest number of interactions although it is ranked 7th, based on the number of fans. In conclusion, one may consider social networking communities as successful based on the size of the total membership, whereas others stated that the number of active participating members as the indicator of success. Furthermore, the participation and interactions of users is a valuable indicator in terms of the success of social networking website over a longer period of time.

Another important factor to highlight in the planning phase is *developing brand image*. Quantitative analysis can be done to evaluate *brand* as an influencing factor in successful social networking website development. For the purpose of this analysis, we will concentrate on the food and beverage category, as there are various other categories in Facebook. Starbucks is the most popular brand on Facebook when ranked by the number of people who 'like' a brand. Over 12 million people on Facebook 'like' this coffee chain, which is almost 2 million more than the second most popular brand, Coca-Cola (Fan Page List, 2010). This data can be used in order to understand user behaviour as it shows which brands users are more likely to click on to say that they 'like' it. However, from the viewpoint of qualitative analysis for the brand, the number of people who 'like' a page on Facebook is not the most important measurement because actual engagement is more important. For instance, Coca-Cola is ranked number two, based on the number of fans, but it falls to number four based on the number of interactions (Vitrue, 2010).The number of people or fans who engage with the brand is a more valid measurement of a brand. The engagement number is used more for brands where it means that people or fans actively contribute more than just 'liking' the brand.

## Analysis Phase

The important factors for this phase are *quality content* and *trust building*. The research from Forrester which analyses consumer social behaviour shows that content creation for social networking sites decreased from 2009 to 2010 (Forrester, 2010). Social networking sites in agile development rely on moderators and users to contribute content. Therefore, it is important that the content is of high quality and not spam. Low quality content is defined as too few content updates, too much focus on topics in which the user is not interested, restricted activities in the communities and nothing new happening in the community ((Brandtzaeq and Heim, 2007).

*Quality content* is an important ingredient in achieving a successful social networking site. Informative content satisfies the goal setting and brand images in the previous planning phase. In agile iteration, content is produced and updated regularly, based on the feedback and testimonials from the users. On the other hand, *trust building* is a factor that interacts with *quality content* as users normally show their trust and loyalty if they find that the content is of high quality. For instance, the increased number of brand interactions in Facebook shows the increased trust from the users (fans). For social networking, the engagement that leads to trust can be classified into two categories, namely application engagement and social engagement. Application engagement refers to how users interact with the application such as game action, whereas social engagement relates to the number of active users of that application. The developers of social networking sites can measure quality content and trust building factors by using Facebook Insights (Figure 2) for Facebook pages and Google Analytics. Facebook Insights enable the administrators and developers to analyse how well their posts and content are engaging people by measuring user exposure, actions and user behaviour to a Facebook Page. The data is straight-forward and easy for people who do not have an analytical background to understand and analyse the trends of their Facebook Page. With the new Insights tool, the developers can track total interaction per post, including the number of active users, likes, counts of wall posts and feedback on any content such as photos, links, videos or notes. Developers who post engaging and high quality content will generate a higher number of interactions. In addition, the Insights Dashboard provides more analysis in the dashboard, including a graph showing different types of fan interactions with the page over time, interactions per post, page views and reviews. Also useful, the developers have the ability to view their fan demographic information such as age and gender or geographic data such as country, city and language.

Google Analytics also offers information about the health of social networking sites by providing a top content report for quality content and a trust building factor measurement. Top content, for new visitors and returning visitors is shown to the developers in order to compare the content that drives repeat visitors and as a result, increases trust building and loyalty to the community.

## Design Phase

The *user-centered design* factor plays an important role in the design phase of social networking development. This factor places users at the center of the design process and is a continuous process from the planning and analysis phases. Agile development in social networking is well-suited to this approach as developers design the social networking sites in small iterations and add to the design based on feedback from users. The application comparison study between the top social networking site, Facebook and the largest social networking site before Facebook, Friendster is examined in order to evaluate this factor. The researchers of social networking sites have noted the rise of Facebook over Friendster in recent years. Statistics from the Facebook site show that there are 500 million active users as of

*Figure 2. Screenshot of Facebook Insights (Facebook Insights, 2010)*

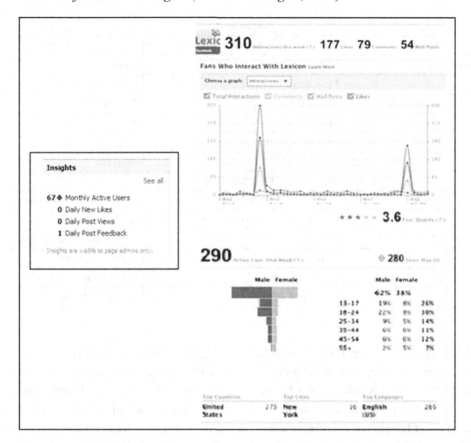

August 11, 2010 (Facebook, 2010). On the other hand, the Friendster site shows that there are only 115 million registered users worldwide. When Friendster first debuted in 2002, it grew tremendously, especially in Asia. However, its growth has since slowed, while Facebook, established in 2004, took competitive moves such as being more inclusive in membership, being the first to open the platform to allow co-development with third-party vendors, actively pursuing alliances and continuously creating and improving services.

Based on an observation of similarities and differences, Facebook has applied and added a more user- centered design in comparison with Friendster. The neat user interface in Facebook integrates more social elements and several different designs have been tested to improve the navigation of commonly used features. The top

menu provides the newest notifications, requests and messages whereas the left menu has been organized for communication and friends. On the other hand, Friendster has the least user-friendly interface and flashy graphics. As a result, a number of users switched to newer social networking sites, particularly Facebook. Facebook provides a Photo dashboard where users can browse recent photos of their friends and an Events dashboard which lists upcoming events. In contrast, Friendster's photos menu only shows photos of the user and if the user wants to browse their friend's photos, they have to click that particular friend's page. The Bulletin board on Friendster limits users to compose messages to friends compared to the Events dashboard on Facebook which has the event invitations with a "Respond" button. More-

*Table 3. Design comparison of Facebook and Friendster*

| The Similarities | | |
|---|---|---|
| **Features** | **Facebook** | **Friendster** |
| 1. Shouts on profile | What's on your mind | Shoutout |
| 2. Comments | Post comments on the Wall | Post a comment |
| 3. Notifications of friends update | Email notifications | Email notifications |
| 4. Search bar | Profile page | Profile page |
| 5. Photos | Tagging and privacy | Tagging and privacy |
| 6. Group | Available | Available |
| **The Differences** | | |
| **Features** | **Facebook** | **Friendster** |
| 1. Events | Create, invite and confirmation | Not Available |
| 2. Customizable profile | Not Available | Allow users to change layout |
| 3. Blog | External link | Its own blog builder |
| 4. Chat | Available | Not Available |
| 5. Applications | 3$^{rd}$ party developers | Closed development |

over, most of the applications are built by outside developers compared to Facebook developers.

The design of social networking sites has to be user-friendly, intuitive to navigate and look professional in order to achieve success. It is undisputed that Facebook is constantly changing its site, making it more attractive to users and providing a good user experience. The design changes occur iteratively and involve users' participation by including a form for users' feedback on the new design.

## Coding Phase

The success factors in the coding phase of social networking development are *technology* and *client server platform*. The Content Management System (CMS) is a popular feature used in the development of social networking websites. A lot of successful social networking sites have been created using CMS. It is easy to use and allows users of all knowledge levels to participate in the updating and maintenance of social networking sites. There are hundreds of available open source CMS all over the world, the most popular being EzPub-

lish, Joomla and Drupal (CMS Reviews, 2010). The advantage of using open source CMS is that there is no cost associated with using the software to set up the social networking sites. However, only some templates provided by CMS are free and the rest require payment. It is important that when choosing a social networking platform, the developers consider the flexibility, the ease of use, sophistication of design and whether it is feature rich. Another feature to consider is the popularity of the social networking platform. The developers of social networking must provides features that support the user's requirements (Dwyer, Hiltz et al., 2008). Therefore, in agile development, it is often necessary for developers to do additional coding and make changes to the code in order to satisfy the user's needs. The agile code is also extensible where it depends on the previous design phase in the iteration cycle.

## Testing Phase

The success factors for this phase are *service quality* and *user satisfaction,* as any deliverable piece of a social networking site produced within an agile iteration cycle will be tested. A case study on the giant social gaming company Zynga, which developed Zynga Poker (Texas Hold'em Poker), the number one Facebook game based on the number fans and interactions, is chosen to measure the success factors in this phase. Other popular games on Facebook that were also developed by Zynga are Farmville, Yoville, FishVille, PetVille, Cafe World, Mafia Wars and Vampires.

There are various types of tests to improve the *service quality,* namely unit test, functional test, integration test, load or performance test and accessibility test. To ensure that the delivered games meet the end user's requirements Zynga, undertook a wide range of testing of all scenarios and features. Several beta testers test various aspects of the games every week with the users in order to achieve the goal of bringing social gaming to the world. Mark Pincus, the founder of Zynga, describes the Zynga process as constant iteration, design and testing with a starting stage of what he calls the "ghetto test". Instead of surveys asking people their opinion, a "ghetto test" creates a suggestion and posts the idea on the web. If sufficient audience interest is measured, then the first version of the game is created. The feedback received from the first version will be considered in order to add more features in the future based on the user's requirements. *User satisfaction* depends on the service quality offered by social networking sites. The approach taken by Zynga is similar to the early tests in agile development as the key to agile development is the iteration of six phases. This means that the testing is done at each cycle of development. In addition, frequent testing and testing from the customer's point of view is a good agile process to detect defects in the code. Another important approach is to have good communication between testers, developers and users so that they can work closely together to obtain the most from testing.

## Deliver Increment Phase

In the deliver increment phase, through agile iterative development, a new added functionality of social networking sites is released. The development cycle builds system increments to deliver the highest priority requirements from previous phases. *Stability* (Leimeister, Sidiras et al., 2004) is the success factor for this phase. The constructed cycles of six phases iteratively emerge during iterations. It is important to measure the stability of each delivered increment to validate that the developers deliver working functionality quickly. The checklist metric can be used to measure products or processes delivered per iteration. For instance, if the development of social networking sites is for business purposes, the key metric "business value delivered" can be applied. The basic measurement would be net cash flow per iteration. Regular assessment and feedback per iteration review provides visibility throughout the social network development timeline and reduces the risks of failure.

All the success factors mentioned in this section can be measured by using web analytical tools. These powerful, flexible and easy to use analytical tools give the designers and developers of social networking rich insights into the health of their sites.

## RESULTS

## Success Factors of Social Networking Development

There is no easy way to measure the success of social networking development. Qualitative measurement is normally based on the user's interactions whereas quantitative measurement concentrates on measuring the quantitative effects of social networking such as site traffic, ranking or popularity of the social networking site. Recently, various web analytical tools have become

*Figure 3. Success factors in social networking development*

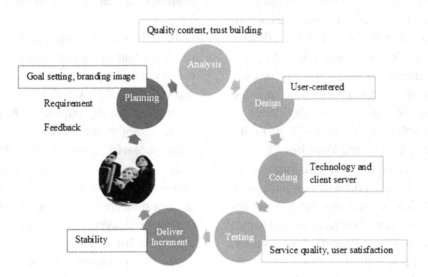

available such as Google Analytics, Google Trends, Facebook Insights and Vitrue to name a few, for developers to measure the health of their social networking sites. These analytical tools help developers gain additional insight into how well their planning phase contributes to overall social networking achievement. All factors are important and measurable using qualitative or quantitative analysis to promote success in agile social networking development as discussed in the previous section. The listed factors interact with each other and are continuously related to all six phases in order to contribute to the success of social networking website development (see Figure 3). All the phases have to be up-to-date and adaptive to meet the new requirements per iteration in agile development.

*Goal setting* in the planning phase is the most important factor, as different goals require different approaches to measure it. For instance, the goals for most commercial social networking sites are tracking sales revenue and increasing user engagement. The measurement of this goal can be achieved using traffic tracking sites such as PageData and FanPageList. Meanwhile, user engagement or the depth of visitor interaction on the website can be measured with web analytical

tools such as Vitrue. It is important to note that an engaged customer is a highly valuable one compared to the number of customers who visit the sites. Customer engagement also influences the *brand image* factor because an engaged customer will recommend the brand to others and purchase more often. Social networking developers should plan how to attract customers as there are a variety of brand choices and customers can switch from one brand to another with great ease.

The factors in the analysis phase determine the *quality content* and *trust building*. Google Analytics and Facebook Insights provide content analysis features to measure the quality of content on social networking sites. The results of this analysis enable developers to identify what kind of content drives more visitors and improves the trust building or loyalty rates of the sites. The concept of *create and maintain a feedback loop* (Kim, 2000) satisfies agile development by providing the flexibility to developers to keep improving the quality of content, based on the feedback from users. Ensuring consistency in the quality of the content and the trustworthiness of the system helps developers achieve the targeted goal setting in analysis phase.

The design phase applies the *user-centered design* and based on the analysis in the previous section, this can be measured by identifying the design features that are more user-friendly and user-oriented. For instance, Facebook integrates more social elements when compared to Friendster, as discussed in the previous section. The concept of *empower members over time* (Kim, 2000) gives users the opportunity to play a role in agile iteration development. The design input comes from the analysis phase and content that has been previously identified.

The coding phase is related to the *technology* and *client server platform*. Developers should research the available resources in order to apply the latest technology to develop a site which is feature rich and cost effective in terms of social networking website development. For example, a Content Management System (CMS) such as EzPublish, Joomla or Drupal, is widely used in social network development, offers a sophisticated design, is flexible and offers several templates which are ready to use for free. Although, the coder in agile development does more coding when compared to a coder using a traditional approach to development, the results from the continuous process of coding per iteration ensure the long term success of the social networking site. The right choice of technology attracts more users and offers better *service quality*.

The testing phase involves *service quality* and *user satisfaction* towards social networking sites. Sufficient test cases for any deliverable piece of social networking are tested in order to ensure the application meets the user's needs and is of high quality. The success of Zynga, the giant social gaming company has shown that the success of social community sites depends on the constant process of testing of all features. The *service quality* factor will have a significant effect on *user satisfaction* and will influence the users in deciding whether to switch to another social networking site or not.

The success of the final phase in social networking development depends on the stability of added functionality per iteration in the agile development life cycle. The stability of each delivered increment can be measured by using a checklist agreed to by the users and developers. The *start of a small community,* such as a social networking site (Kim, 2000), will evolve as each iteration delivers an incremental functionality in social networking development.

## Guidelines for Social Network Developers

Based on the success factors in the previous section, we provide guidelines for social networking developers in order to maximize the success of social networking sites.

It is important that in the planning phase, the developers are focused on reaching the goals and assigning a specific period of time to accomplish each prioritized task. Once the developers have assigned times to the task, they should execute the task. In agile development, the developers share the goal in the *transparent manner,* based on feedback from the users. Each planning iteration in social networking development reviews whether the goals that have been set are achievable or not. On the other hand, some social networking sites also have business goals rather than simply social interaction. Therefore, a *unique* brand image helps to establish reputable and respected brand. Maintaining the social networking brand image in agile iteration helps the evolution of the site.

The quality of content in the analysis phase depends on the *content sources* and *continuous content*. The content sources include the internal sources from the developers and users, and external sources such as the media. It is important that both sources provide interesting and *continuous content* that attracts more users to participate on the site. In addition, quality content is the number one way to build trust with potential users and fans of social networking. *Consistency* of developers'

*Table 4. Characteristics for success factors*

| Phases | Success Factors | Characteristics |
|---|---|---|
| Planning | Goal setting | • Focus<br>• Transparency of goals |
| | Brand image | • Unique |
| Analysis | Quality content | • Content sources<br>• Continuous content |
| | Trust building | • Consistency |
| Design | User-centered design | • User experience<br>• Ease of use |
| Coding | Technology and client server platform | • Scalable |
| Testing | Service quality | • Involvement of testers |
| | User satisfaction | • Incremental quality |
| Deliver Increment | Stability | • Users assess the version |

actions helps to build trust and ensure that users feel safe and secure in the community.

Good designers aim to ensure positive user experiences such as enjoyment, self expression and curiosity when designing a social networking site (Hart, Ridley et al., 2008). The ease of use feature enables users to navigate pages easily. The technology and client server platform chosen by developers in the coding phase must be practical and *scalable* in the future so that the social network can integrate with other collaboration tools in the future.

Testing is an activity that is intended to produce quality social networking sites. The *involvement of testers* is important in agile iteration development, as testers need to find the bugs in each new functionality early in each iteration cycle. The skill of a tester should lie in writing good and efficient test cases and being able to prioritize the order in which test cases should be executed. Agile testing also increases users' satisfaction where testing closely interacts with other phases and is done in parallel when a piece of code or functionality is developed. It is important to note that in every cycle of the development phase the testing will produce *incremental quality*.

In agile iteration development, the deliver increment phase is essentially a release of an updated version of a social networking site. The delivery is not just about the functionality built during the completion of the iteration; rather it is about demonstrating its completion. The stability of the functionality which is released can be evaluated by allowing users to use and *access the running version*. Thus, every iteration gives the opportunity for developers to obtain feedback and guidance from users about how to make the system more valuable in the future.

We have also designed a questionnaire survey as a guideline for researchers in the future to conduct an empirical study (see Figure 4 and Figure 5). This will identify which factors should be more implemented or less implemented for all development phases based on the user's characteristics that may influence the success factors of social networking development.

The questionnaire contains questions on general demographic information and the nature of social networking usage of the respondent to understand the behaviour of different types of users. Respondents are asked to express their agreement or disagreement with statements relating to all the possible success factors in the six phases of social networking development, including goal setting, brand image, quality content, trust building, user-centered design, technology

*Figure 4. Success factors in social network development questionnaire, part A*

| Instructions |
|---|
| This questionnaire should take about 10 minutes to complete. Please answer each statement by selecting the option that best reflects your degree of agreement or disagreement with the statement. Please be assured that your response will be treated confidentially and with anonymity as the data obtained will be used for the purpose of this thesis only. The outcome of this study is to devise a list of success factors that are important as a guideline in the development of social networks. Many thanks for your time and interest. |

**Part A: Demographic profile**

This section seeks information about the respondent characteristics (e.g. gender, age) that might influence the success factors of social networking development. Please complete the following details about yourself.

1. What is your gender?
   ☐ Male
   ☐ Female

2. What is your age?
   ☐ 21-40
   ☐ 41-60
   ☐ 61 and above

3. What is your nationality?
   _____

4. What is your occupation?

   _____

5. Do you have a profile on any of the following social networks? (You can choose more than one)
   ☐ Facebook
   ☐ MySpace
   ☐ Twitter
   ☐ Friendster
   ☐ LinkedIn

6. Please state how many hours you spend each day on social network site(s)?
   ☐ 1 - 3 hours     ☐ 9 – 12 hours
   ☐ 5 - 8 hours     ☐ 13 hours and above

and client server platform, service quality, user satisfaction and stability. If this survey is conducted, we will be able to identify the significance of each success factor based on correlation analysis and rank them according to their importance to agile iteration development.

## CONCLUSION AND FUTURE WORK

The aim of the work in this paper is to identify the success factors for each phase in social networking development. Although there are numerous social networking sites available, it is hard to guarantee their success and stability.

We have discussed various available software development process models and we have chosen the agile iteration life cycle approach for social networking development. The advantage of the agile concept is it has the ability to revisit all of the six development phases. In addition, the agile concept delivers increments of functionality per iteration and involves users who give feedback based on the small release or new version of the social networking site. As a result, the social networking site will evolve and the quality will be maximized in the long term. Quantitative and qualitative metrics of success are used to measure the identified factors in each phase by using web analytical tools and a comparative study between

*Figure 5. Success factors in social network development questionnaire, part B*

| Part B: Success Factors in Social Network Development | | | | | | | | | |
|---|---|---|---|---|---|---|---|---|---|
| The following are factors that influence the development of social network sites. Please indicate on the scale below the level that best reflects your degree of agreement or disagreement with the statement. | | | | | | | | | |
| Strongly Disagree  1  2  3  4  5  6  7  Strongly Agree | | | | | | | | | |
| 1. | Social networking websites enable people to communicate globally | 1 | 2 | 3 | 4 | 5 | 6 | 7 | Goal Setting |
| 2. | Social networking websites are an effective means of business promotion | 1 | 2 | 3 | 4 | 5 | 6 | 7 | Goal Setting |
| 3. | Social networking websites are the best way to improve people's opinion of a brand | 1 | 2 | 3 | 4 | 5 | 6 | 7 | Branding image |
| 4. | Social networking websites build trust among their members | 1 | 2 | 3 | 4 | 5 | 6 | 7 | Trust building |
| 5. | The success of a social networking website can be measured by the number of its members | 1 | 2 | 3 | 4 | 5 | 6 | 7 | Branding image |
| 6. | The success of a social networking website can be measured by the degree of participation of active members | 1 | 2 | 3 | 4 | 5 | 6 | 7 | Branding image |
| 7. | Offering rewards encourages member loyalty | 1 | 2 | 3 | 4 | 5 | 6 | 7 | Trust building |
| 8. | Social networking websites offer quality content | 1 | 2 | 3 | 4 | 5 | 6 | 7 | Quality content |
| 9. | Social networking websites offer up-to-date content | 1 | 2 | 3 | 4 | 5 | 6 | 7 | Quality content |
| 10. | The stability of social networking sites is important | 1 | 2 | 3 | 4 | 5 | 6 | 7 | Stability |
| 11. | Fast reaction time is important when using a social networking website | 1 | 2 | 3 | 4 | 5 | 6 | 7 | User satisfaction |
| 12. | The design of a social networking website is based on members' preferences | 1 | 2 | 3 | 4 | 5 | 6 | 7 | User-centered design |
| 13. | The technology used allows the social networking website to evolve | 1 | 2 | 3 | 4 | 5 | 6 | 7 | Technology |
| 14. | It is difficult to conform to social rules and regulations when using a social networking website | 1 | 2 | 3 | 4 | 5 | 6 | 7 | Goal Setting |
| 15. | New members need assistance and support from experienced members | 1 | 2 | 3 | 4 | 5 | 6 | 7 | Service quality |
| 16. | Social networking websites satisfy the user's needs | 1 | 2 | 3 | 4 | 5 | 6 | 7 | User-centered design |
| 17. | The member's ideas influence the evolution of a social networking website | 1 | 2 | 3 | 4 | 5 | 6 | 7 | User-centered design |
| **General comments:** | | | | | | | | | |
| Do you have any other thoughts or comments you would like to share about your experiences with social networking websites? | | | | | | | | | |

popular and unpopular social networking sites. Results reveal nine determinants of success for agile development phases: goal setting, brand image, quality content, trust building, user-centered design, technology and client server platform, service quality, user satisfaction and stability.

This study will benefit designers and developers by suggesting the success factors for each phase in the agile iteration development cycle. The benefits are:

- It promotes the stability and success in achieving the goals of social networking sites in the long term.
- Agile development and all success factors for each phase will accelerate the delivery of various functions for social networking sites through a process of continuous loop phases and feedback from users.

- The developers are able to align the delivered social networking site with desired users and business needs.

- It provides an opportunity to build a good relationship between the developer and users through the trust building and user-centered factors.

- By delivering a functional networking site that is working and tested on an incremental basis, agile development delivers increased value, visibility and adaptability per iteration. As a result, the developers significantly reduce project risks.

- The developers do not have to invest as much time and effort because agile iteration gives the users opportunity verify their requirements per iteration.

Our study highlights the need for further investigation to identify other possible factors that promote success in social networking development. In addition, we should extend the scope of the study to identify success factors for diverse types of online communities. Finally, a comparative study can be done in order to see the interaction of all factors with the community types.

# REFERENCES

Agichtein, E., Castillo, C., Donato, D., Gionis, A., & Mishne, G. (2008). Finding high-quality content in social media. *Proceedings of the Int'l Conf. on Web Search and Data Mining* (pp. 183-194). ACM.

Alexa. (2010). *Alexa*. Retrieved August 19, 2010, from http://www.alexa.com

Beenen, G., Ling, K. S., Wang, X., Chang, K., Frankowski, D., Resnick, P., & Kraut, R. E. (2004). Using social psychology to motivate contributions to online communities. *Proceedings of the 2004 ACM Conf. on Computer Supported Cooperative Work* (pp. 212-221). ACM.

Boyd, D. M., & Ellison, N. B. (2007). Social network sites: Definition, history and scholarship. *Journal of Computer-Mediated Communication, 13*(1). Retrieved July 13, 2010, from http://jjmc.indiana.edu/vol13/issue1/boyd.ellison.html

Brandtzaeq, P. B., & Heim, J. (2007). User loyalty and online communities: Why members of online communities are not faithful. *Proceedings of the 2nd Int'l Conf. on INtelligent TEchnologies for Interactive EnterTAINment* (p. 11). ICST.

Dwyer, C., Hiltz, S. R., & Widmeyer, G. (2008). Understanding development and usage of social networking sites: The social software performance model. *Proceedings of the 41st Hawaii Int'l Conf. on System Sciences* (p. 212). IEEE CS.

Facebook. (2010). *Facebook statistics*. Retrieved August 11, 2010, from http://www.facebook.com/press/info.php

Facebook Insights. (2010). *Facebook upgrading "Insights" metrics dashboard for page managers tonight*. Retrieved August 22, 2010, from http://www.insidefacebook.com/2009/05/05/facebook-upgrading-insights-metrics-dashboard-for-page-managers-tonight/

Fan Page List. (2010). *Top Facebook fan pages*. Retrieved June 29, 2010, from http://fanpagelist.com/category/top_pages/

Forrester. (2010). *Forrester research*. Retrieved September 29, 2010, from http://www.forrester.com/rb/research

Hart, J., Ridley, C., Taher, F., Sas, C., & Dix, A. (2008). Exploring the Facebook experience: A new approach to usability. *Proceedings of the 5th Nordic Conf. on Human-Computer Interaction: Building Bridges* (pp. 471-474). ACM.

In, K. J., Hye, A. S., & Lee, C. C. (2009). A study on service quality determinants that influence continued success of portal online community services. *Proceedings of the 2nd IEEE Int'l Conf. on Computer Science and Information Technology* (pp. 171-175). IEEE CS.

Iriberri, A., & Leroy, G. (2009). A life-cycle perspective on online community success. *ACM Computing Surveys, 41*(2), 1–29. doi:10.1145/1459352.1459356

Jansen, B. J., Zhang, M., Sobel, K., & Chowdury, A. (2009). Micro-blogging as online word of mouth branding. *Proceedings of the 27th Int'l Conf. on Human Factors in Computing Systems.* (pp. 3859-3864). ACM.

Kim, A. J. (2000). *Community building on the Web: Secret strategies for successful online communities.* Berkeley, CA: Peachpit Press.

Lampe, C., Ellison, N., & Steinfield, C. (2006). A Face(book) in the crowd: Social searching vs. social browsing. *Proceedings of the 20th Conf. on Computer Supported Cooperative Work* (pp. 167-170). ACM.

Leimeister, J. M., Sidiras, P., & Krcmar, H. (2004). Success factors of virtual communities from the perspective of members and operators: An empirical study. *Proceedings of the 37th Annual Hawaii International Conference on System Sciences* (pp. 70194a). IEEE CS.

Ludford, P. J., Cosley, D., Frankowski, D., & Terveen, L. (2004). Think different: Increasing online community participation using uniqueness and group dissimilarity. *Proceedings of the SIGCHI Conf. on Human Factors in Computing Systems* (pp. 631-638). ACM.

PageData. (2010). *Page leaderboards.* Retrieved June 29, 2010, from http://pagedata.insideface-book.com

Reviews, C. M. S. (2010). *Content management software review.* Retrieved September 21, 2010, from http://cms-software-review.toptenreviews.com

Rood, V., & Bruckman, A. (2009). Member behavior in company online communities. *Proceedings of the ACM 2009 Int'l Conf. on Supporting Group Work* (pp. 209-218). ACM.

Sha, Z., Wen, F., Gao, G., & Wang, X. (2009). Antecedents and consequences of flow experience in virtual brand community. *Proceedings of the Int'l Conf. on e-Business and Information System Security* (pp. 1-5). IEEE CS.

The Nielsen Company. (2010). *Social networks.* Retrieved June 19, 2010, from http://blog.nielsen.com/nielsenwire/online mobile/nielsen-provides-topline-u-s-web-data-for-march-2010

Vitrue. (2010). *Virtrue social page evaluator.* Retrieved June 29, 2010, from http://evaluator.vitrue.com/

Weaver, A. C., & Morrison, B. B. (2008). Social networking. *Computer, 41*(2), 97–100. doi:10.1109/MC.2008.61

## KEY TERMS AND DEFINITIONS

**Agile Software Development:** A methodology that has the ability to revisit any phases in software development. It focuses on keeping the code simple and testing often by breaking projects into small iterations in a time box for a quality delivery.

**Social Networking Website:** Websites that allow users to share content, interact and develop communities around similar interests.

**Software Design:** A process of planning for a software solution where the choice is made concerning the type of architecture which will be used in building the social networking website. The software design refers to the software requirements analysis by the developers based on the user needs.

**Software Development:** The development of software in a planned and structured process for a variety purposes to meet the specific needs of users. The basic popular models used for software development are System Development Life Cycle (SDLC), Rapid Application Development (RAD), Prototyping and Agile Development.

**Success Factors:** Factors that are necessary condition for achieving an objective.

**Success Measurement:** Quantitative and qualitative metrics used as the indicators or dimensions to measure of a success factor.

# Section 3
# Information–Knowledge Discovery and Diffusion in Social Networks and Online Communities

*The growth of the Internet and online communities has led to an increasing importance for understanding the social network structure of communities, the relationships between members, and how information is discovered and diffused in such virtual networks. This section overviews the gathering of network data by means of both qualitative and quantitative methodologies. It describes the state-of-the-art data mining algorithms and tools oriented to knowledge discovery, collective decision-making, information diffusion, and identifying relationships from online communities.*

# Chapter 7
# Knowledge Discovery from Online Communities

**Luca Cagliero**
*Politecnico di Torino, Italy*

**Alessandro Fiori**
*Politecnico di Torino, Italy*

## ABSTRACT

*During recent years, the outstanding growth of social network communities has caught the attention of the research community. A huge amount of user-generated content is shared among community users and gives researchers the unique opportunity to thoroughly investigate social community behavior. Many studies have been focused on both developing models to investigate user and collective behavior and building applications tailored to the most common community user activities.*

*This chapter presents an overview of social network features such as user behavior, social models, and user-generated content to highlight the most notable research trends and application systems built over such appealing models and online media data. It first describes the most popular social networks by analyzing the growth trend, the user behaviors, the evolution of social groups and models, and the most relevant types of data continuously generated and updated by the users. Next, the most recent and valuable applications of data mining techniques to social network models and user-generated content are presented. Discussed works address both social model extractions tailored to semantic knowledge inference and automatic understanding of the user-generated content. Finally, prospects of data mining research on social networks are provided as well.*

DOI: 10.4018/978-1-61350-444-4.ch007

## INTRODUCTION

In the last years, social network communities such as Facebook, Flickr, and Twitter have shown a steady growth. Since their introduction, social network sites (SNSs) have attracted millions of users, many of who have integrated these sites into their daily practices. These sites provide the basis for maintaining social relationships, for finding users with similar interests, for improving the content of web documents as well as sharing multimedia content. While their key technological features are fairly consistent, the cultures that emerge around SNSs are varied. Most sites support the maintenance of pre-existing social networks, but others help strangers connect based on shared interests. Some sites cater to diverse audiences, while others attract people based on common social characteristics. Sites also vary in the extent to which they incorporate new information and communication tools, such as mobile connectivity, blogging, and photo/video-sharing.

Many studies have been devoted to developing models for supporting the investigation of user behavior in online communities. For example, understanding the structure of online social networks is very useful for developing systems tailored to real user interests. Moreover, due to the nature of these Web services, the common user social behavior in online communities significantly differs from typical real-life social interactions. Indeed, online social models are worth being thoroughly investigated.

Recent works have investigated social correlations among user behaviors in social network sites and applied their models to emergent real life cases of study, such as conflict of interest detection and social hierarchy detection in household corporations. The well-founded analysis of social correlation in user actions enables the investigation of user behavior at large. Collective behavior modeling is focused on discovering recurrences in groups of users. A wide range of scientific paper on this topic is presented in this chapter

(Backstrom et al., 2006; Tang & Liu, 2009; Tang & Liu, 2010). A general-purpose categorization, first proposed in Backstrom et al. (2006), is adapted to well discriminate between analysis focused on group membership and formation and group model evolution. Other approaches tried to figure out discriminative behaviors in specific communities, compare behavioral recurrences in different social networks as well as apply traditional analytical models to mostly used online communities (Mislove, 2008).

Nevertheless, online communities are the new main resource of human knowledge. For example, the effort of thousand of Wikipedia users has produced the biggest and most complete online encyclopedia. All the information provided by the tags on media content is a powerful and huge resource suitable for knowledge inference. Thus, combining network analysis, social networks models, and information extraction algorithms are a challenging and interesting task focused on developing new systems able to improve the human knowledge. Information provided by online community users can be employed for different purposes. For example, the information stored in Wikipedia pages can be extracted to infer ontologies (Suchanek et al., 2008). Moreover, the social tagging is fundamental to classify videos and photos in order to improve search results (Yin et al., 2009).

The main purpose of this chapter is to investigate how the user-generated content (UGC) and the social network models can be employed to build systems based on social network data. The chapter is organized as follows. The first part of the chapter will provide a brief overview of most representative online communities such as Digg, Flickr, Twitter, and Wikipedia. The goal of this section is to introduce the reader to the most notable features of online communities over which outstanding models and applications have been recently developed. Secondly, we will investigate the user behavior in these web communities and the most relevant social models tailored to common community user activities. To this aim, some techniques to extract social network models from web content, such as emails and blogs, will be presented. Furthermore, the semantic social knowledge representation of user-generated content provided by online media data and social tags will be introduced. Since knowledge representation enables the exploitation of well-founded Semantic Web technologies in social network analysis, main efforts in semantic knowledge retrieval from online communities will be outlined as well. The last section of this chapter will focus on presenting most relevant applications built over social network data. We will present some examples of systems that effectively integrate social network models and media data. We focus our investigation on recommendation systems and efficient querying engines based on social tagging to improve data retrieval by means of query expansion techniques and user profile analysis. Finally, new trends on social network analysis will be outlined.

## ONLINE COMMUNITIES

The past few years have witnessed the rapid proliferation of web-based communities such as social networking sites, wikis, blogs, and media sharing communities. Different web services have been developed to satisfy the need of web users of sharing data, feelings, thoughts, and any other kind of information. Every day millions of people access online web services generating a huge amount of data and, thus, becoming self-publishing consumers. This has resulted in User-Generated Content (UGC) becoming a popular and everyday part of the Internet culture, thus establishing new viewing patterns and novel forms of social behavior. The Web services can be classified in different categories according to both their purpose and the characteristics of the shared content. In the rest of the paper, we followed the theoretically based analysis proposed by De

*Figure 1. Social network sites*

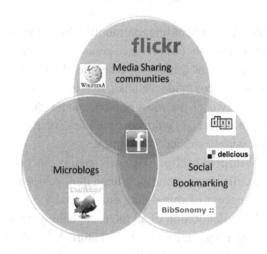

Souza & Preece (2004). It proposed an analytical framework, which addresses computer-mediated communications between community members and also communications from interactive software designers to users. As shown in Figure 1, we identified three main categories:

- Media sharing communities, which are focused on media content (i.e., documents or photos)
- Social bookmarking, which provide services to share and categorize bookmarks (i.e., web links)
- Microblogs, in which users post short, messages to express their feelings and thoughts.

In the following, for each category, a selection of most popular web services with their main characteristics is presented. However, many other online communities exist and integrate different features. Since, as shown in Figure 1, Facebook belongs to all the above categories, it will be separately analyzed.

## Media Sharing Communities

In the last years, online communities have greatly contributed to collect user-generated content. Media content can be, for example, documents, photos, videos, and web links. In this section, we present two of the most popular media sharing communities (i.e., Wikipedia and Flickr) that have been widely studied in literature.

**Wikipedia** (http://www.wikipedia.com/) is a free, collaborative, and multilingual encyclopedia. The success of this online encyclopedia is due to the collaboration of all the users belonging to the web community. Due to its nature, Wikipedia is one of the most dynamic and fastest-growing resources over the Web. This effort has produced over 15 million articles in different languages. The English version, which is the most developed, contains over 3.5 million articles at February 2011. Thus, the content of Wikipedia is really huge and covers many different topics, as reported by the study of Gabrilovich & Markovitch (2007).

Since any Web user can edit every article, except for few pages, the content may be exposed to errors. However, the community itself has improved the control of the content by reducing the number of mistakes and small typos.

Wikipedia encyclopedia is composed of articles (or pages). Each article defines and describes a concept or an event by means of a hypertext document including hyperlinks to other Web pages. The role of the hyperlinks is to guide the reader to Web pages that provide additional information about concepts or events mentioned within an article. All the articles are uniquely identified by one or more words separated by spaces, underscores, and, occasionally, by a parenthetical explanation. Since concepts can be identified by different names, "Redirect" pages are exploited to point readers to the identifier preferred by Wikipedia.

**Flickr** (http://www.flickr.com/) is a photo sharing website that allows users to store, search, and share their photos. Unlike other photo-sharing websites, Flickr allows both private and public image storage. In such a way, a large collection of photos has become quickly available to Web community in the last years. Furthermore, Flickr users can socially interact with the community. For example, a user can define a list of friends with which share his photos, comments, and tag pictures of his friend networks, send messages, and participate to groups about common interests.

Browsing techniques and search functionalities are rather limited because they are mainly based on metadata and tag information. Tags associated with each photo are taking a primary role in this community for finding similar resources and people having common interests. Flickr users are used to tag for their own retrievals, but, due to the abundance of communication mechanisms, the system design encourages gaming and exploration of tag use.

## Social Bookmarking

Social bookmarking services allow organizing, storing, managing, and searching for bookmarks of online resources. Differently to the media content sharing, only the references to the resources are shared.

Like in photo-sharing website, users can attach additional information to the bookmarks as comments, tags and votes. The tags provided by the community can be exploited to build a folksonomy and are useful for navigating the shared resources. In the following, some popular social bookmarking sites are presented.

**Del.icio.us**. (http://delicious.com/) is a popular social bookmarking Web service for storing, sharing, and discovering Web bookmarks. All the bookmarks posted on del.icio.us. site can be tagged by registered users. The tags are exploited by the system to group resources that share similar topics, perform user queries, and navigate the bookmarks. When a user submits a query, the list of bookmarks with the associated tag is shown. Moreover, statistics on the number of bookmarks posted with the same tag and a list of related tags are provided as well. The most recent bookmarks with the associated information (e.g., tags, the number of users that share the resource) are shown in the front page. The Web service also allows exploring the folksonomy provided by the tags.

The main advantage of del.icio.us. is the public availability of all the bookmarks. In fact, the site is not focused on storing private bookmark collections. Thus, a lot of research activities have been developed on the information stored on del.icio.us.

**BibSonomy** (http://www.bibsonomy.org/) is a social bookmarking and publication-sharing system proposed and developed by Hotho et al. (2006). It integrates features of both bookmarking systems and publication management environments. It allows submitting bookmarks and/or publication references. Users can tag the resources to provide additional information. As the descriptive terms can be freely chosen, the assignment of tags from different users creates a spontaneous, uncontrolled vocabulary, called folksonomy. In BibSonomy, the folksonomy evolves from the participation of users organizing their information needs. Algorithms to manage and analyze the folkosonomy are integrated in the system. A detailed description of all the system features can be founded in Hotho et al. (2006).

**Digg** (http://digg.com/) is one of the most successful social news bookmarking sites. Users can submit links to news published on online websites and the other members of the community can assign votes, named digs, on these stories. When a news become popular, it may get many positive digs and be promoted in the home page. Less popular news is instead stored in the "Upcoming" story pages.

The graphical interface is very simple. A Digg page contains a list of about 20 stories. The stories are in reverse chronological order with respect to the submission/promotion order, thus most recent stories appear at the top of the page. The title of each story is the link to the online resource, while the icon with the number of diggs is the link to the history of the bookmark. This allows browsing

all discussions about news and the list of people that assigned a digg.

Like other online community websites, Digg allows creating a list of friends in order to track their recent activities (e.g., the number of news submitted, commented or voted). The friends interface acts upon a social filtering system, recommending to the user stories that his friends has found interesting. As pointed out by Lerman (2007), this mechanism tends to promote the stories published by users having a large network. Moreover, the users are encouraged to submit and promote more news.

## MicroBlogs

Compared with regular blogs, microblogs fulfills the need of an even faster Web communication tool. By encouraging shorter posts, it definitely reduces user time spent in content generation. Another important difference is the frequency of updates. On average, a prolific blogger may update his blog once every few days. Oppositely, a microblogger may post several updates per day. Many social networks are based on the idea of microblogs. For example, Facebook is usually exploited by its members to post short messages on their own profile page to share their thoughts with other people. In the following, we present Twitter that may be considered as the first microblog Web service.

**Twitter** (http://twitter.com/) is one of the most popular microblogging services. It is mainly based on the messages, named tweets, posted by users. Tweets are posts of at most 140 characters that are publicly visible by default. Nevertheless, the user can restrict the delivery of a tweet to his network. Due to the limited length of the messages, many external applications have been developed to submit posts by means of smartphones or Short Message Service (SMS). Unlike other social network sites, Twitter users can subscribe (follow) to other user profiles. Users who perform this action are named followers. All the tweets posted on the page of the followed author are notified on the follower page. Similarly to social bookmarking services, users can assign tags to all the posts. This feature is useful for browsing all the posts that share the same topic. Since Twitter has become very popular, a lot of research studies have been focused on both the structure of its network and the social aspects of this online community. For instance, Java et al. (2007) studied the microblogging phenomena by analyzing the topological and geographical properties of Twitter. They figure out interesting observations about the social aspects of the Twitter community and the more general influence of social networks in giving more relevance to some specific topics.

## Facebook

Facebook (http://www.facebook.com/) is one of the most popular social websites that integrates different features of other social network services. It has been launched in February 2004 and at July 2010; it has more than 500 million active users. The users can create a personal profile, add other users as friends and exchange messages, including automatic notifications of updated information. Moreover, they can share and tag media content and publish private and/or public posts of any length. Similarly to Twitter, Facebook is usually exploited by its members to share their thoughts with other people. Additionally, users may join common interest user groups, organized by workplace, school, college, or other characteristics. The set of provided services is hard to be fully categorized at a single stroke. For example, the scope of media sharing communities significantly differs from Facebook's one as they are mainly focused on content sharing (e.g., photos) while Facebook just provides this as an additional feature to enable users with similar interests to get in touch. Moreover, unlike del.icio.us., Facebook allows users to choose whether a resource is publicly available or not. A number of other provided services are based on ideas coming from other popular web services. For example, Facebook suggests to a user new possible friendships based upon their common friends or interests.

## SOCIAL NETWORK MODELS

Different social and data models have been studied and extracted from social networks. They have been well adopted in shaping the behavior of the users. User behavior in a social network can include a broad range of actions, such as joining a group or connecting to a friend. The increasing amount of online communities, in which users interact with their acquaintances, allows analyzing user actions at the individual level in order to understand user behavior at large. Collective behavior refers to behaviors of groups of individuals who are exposed in a social network environment. In a social network environment, behaviors of individuals tend to be inter-dependent. This naturally leads to behavior correlation among connected people.

According to the analyzed features and the models retrieved, we propose an insight overview of most recent and appealing research works as follows. Social correlations among individuals acting in the social network environment are first detected, categorized and measured based on strong theoretical foundations (Anagnostopoulos et al., 2008). Two real-life application scenarios of advanced analysis on social correlations are also presented (Aleman-Meza et al., 2006; Rowe & Creamer, 2007). Secondly, with the aim at generalizing singular user interactions to collective behavior modeling, most relevant works on collective behavior analysis are thoroughly discussed (Backstrom, 2006; Macskassy & Provost, 2007; Tang & Liu, 2009; Tang & Liu, 2010). Classical collective behavior analysis discriminates between group formation and membership, and group evolution over time. Each of these social model aspects is discussed by addressing most relevant analytical and sociological issues. Finally, we address the problem of social knowledge representation as well. The semantics-based representation of knowledge extracted from the user-generated content may be employed to effectively categorize concepts and relationships between social network users. Moreover, it enables the usage of Semantic Web techniques to access and reason about the represented social knowledge.

## Social Correlation Analysis

User profiling in a social network requires the meaningful categorization of user interactions. Social correlation among user behaviors in social networks may be classified in:

1. *Homophily*, which is the tendency of individuals to choose friends with similar characteristics
2. *Environmental influences* (confounding factors), which are factors that are more likely to affect individuals that are located close each other in the social network
3. *Social influences*, that refer to the phenomenon that the action of individuals can produce their friends to act in a similar way.

Different kinds of social correlations may differently affect social model features. Social models are typically exploited to discriminate between correlation and causality.

Social influence discovery is an important branch of study in social correlation analysis. In Anagnostopoulos et al. (2008), a statistical analysis on data collected from large social systems is performed. The aim of this work is to identify and measure social influence as a source of correlation between the actions of individuals having social ties. A relevant research issue is how to measure social correlations and to test whether influence is a source of such correlation. The basic idea is to exploit the availability of data about the timestamp of each user action to study the problem. Two different statistical analyses have been

applied: the shuffle and the edge-traversal tests. The *shuffle test* is based on the simple idea that in a non-influence model, even though an agent's probability of activation can depend on his friends, his timing of activation is independent. Indeed, it first computes the social correlation coefficient among users; next it shuffles the time stamps of all actions and re-estimate the coefficient. If the former and the latter coefficients are similar, social influence could be ruled out, otherwise it does not. The *edge-traversal test* has been proposed by Christakis & Fowler (2007) in the context of medical investigations on the spread of obesity in real-world social networks. It distinguishes between influence and other social correlations by reversing edges connecting people in social graphs and performing logic regression on data using this new graph. This approach is based on the intuition that other forms of correlation are roughly independent of which of two correlated individuals has named the other as a friend. By applying both shuffle and edge-reversal tests on the real Flickr social network, the user tagging behavior in the image sharing context turns out to be weakly affected by social influence, even if the impact of social correlation on Flickr appears relevant.

The problem of social influence analysis in social networks has been investigated from a wide range of different perspectives. An interesting application scenario concerns the problem of conflict of interest detection. In Aleman-Meza et al. (2006) a Semantic Web application that detects Conflicts Of Interest (COI) relationships between potential reviewers and authors of scientific papers has been presented. They applied Semantic Web techniques to discover semantic associations between reviewers and authors in an ad-hoc ontology. Integrating entities and relationships coming from two different social networks populates the ontology: the FOAF (Friend-Of-A-Friend) social network and the DBLP co-authorship network. The proposed framework heavily relies on the quality of the extracted metadata. Some online social networking sites provide machine-readable personal information using RDF/XML and FOAF vocabularies. The entity *Person* is a fundamental concept in the considered online communities. It is identified by one or several properties. Different sources might have different set of properties. Links among entities, such as *FOAF: knows* and *DBLP: co-author* respectively in the FOAF and the DBLP namespaces, directly provide information about social ties. Finally, COI detection is mainly focused on the analysis of the two most valuable relationships, *FOAF: knows* and *DBLP:co-author*, which enables the system to systematically evaluate their correlation grade through semantic association discovery (Anyanwu & Sheth, 2003).

The identification of social correlations inside a corporate household is another appealing research field. Corporate entity charts sometimes exist on paper, but they do not reflect the day-to-day reality of large and dynamic corporations. Corporate insiders are aware of these private relationships, but they can be hard to come by. In Rowe & Creamer (2007) this information is automatically extracted by analyzing the e-mail communication data within the Enron Corporation. Corporation e-mail collection is publicly available set of private corporate data released during the judicial proceedings against the Enron Corporation. For each e-mail user, several statistics are exploited in a probabilistic framework to rank and group corporate members within the organization or across organizational departments. An overall social normalized score is computed by weighting two different statistics: (i) volumetric and temporal statistics about the number of emails that each user has sent and the average response time per email, and (ii) the nature of connections formed in the communication network (i.e., the number and the characteristics of the maximal complete subgraphs involving each user). The statistical analysis is based on the assumption that users involved in larger flows of information exchange are more likely to play an important role in the corporation entity. In such a way, it is

possible to judge the strength of communication links between users based on their overall communication pattern. The proposed approach is able to automatically (i) rank the major officers of an organization, (ii) group similarly ranked and connected users in order to accurately reproduce the organizational structure in question, and (iii) understand relationship strengths between specific sets of users.

Nowadays social networks provide plenty of opportunities to perform semantics-based analytics on user behavior. However, the lack of integration among web services as well as privacy concerns still significantly limit the possibility and the effectiveness of metadata extraction addressed to conflict of interest or social hierarchy detection.

## Collective Behavior Modeling

The main objective of social network analysis is to profile users to better understand the behavior of groups of real users. The step beyond the analysis of different kinds of social user interactions is the discovery and the analysis of the most relevant social groups. According to the general-purpose categorization proposed by Backstrom et al. (2006), two main aspects concerning collective behavior analysis have been addressed: (i) *group formation and membership* and (ii) *group evolution*. The first aspect regards the influence of structural model features on individuals joining communities. On the other hand, the second aspect is focused on the main factors affecting individual group growing over time and the time-dependent correlation between individual group membership and common topics of interest. In the following, the above issues are separately analyzed.

## Group Formation and Membership

The influence of both social model features and already existent groups significantly affects singular user actions in online communities. Many works address group formation and user membership to restricted communities inside a larger online social environment.

For the sake of uniformity, we adopt the following widespread notation used by Backstrom et al. (2006). Given a collection of individuals linked in an underlying social network, the groups and communities are represented as subgraphs of this network, growing and overlapping one another in a potentially complex fashion. A group that grows mainly through the aggressive recruitment of friends by other friends would appear as a subgraph branching out rapidly over time along links in the network. On the other hand, a group in which the decision to join depends relatively little on the influence of friends might appear instead as a collection of small disconnected components that rows in a "speckled" fashion.

To model interesting collective behaviors, one classical model well studied in social science and behavioral study is the threshold model (Granovetter & Soong, 1983), in which an actor adopts one action when the number of his friends taking an action exceeds a certain threshold. Based on a similar idea, collective inference (Macskassy & Provost, 2007) is adopted in machine teaching community to make predictions about collective behavior. It assumes that the behavior of one actor is dependent upon that of his friends. For prediction, collective inference is required to find an equilibrium status such that the inconsistency between connected actors is minimized. The above interdependency models suffer from multidimensionality of social media connections. An actor can connect to another one due to different factors (e.g., living in the same city or sharing similar interest). Collective inference normally does not differentiate these kinds of connections. To address this issue, Tang & Liu (2009) proposed to extract latent social dimensions based on network information firstly, and then exploit them as features to perform discriminative learning. Social dimensions are introduced to represent relations associated with actors of the social environment (i.e., users), in which each dimension denotes

one relation (e.g., the University affiliation of a researcher). Social dimensions capture prominent interaction patterns presented in a network.

As already mentioned above, connections in social media are often not homogeneous. The heterogeneity presented in network connections can negatively affect the process of collective inference. Users usually connect to their family, colleagues, college classmates, or simple acquaintances. Only some of these relations are helpful for determining their targeted behavior. Moreover, online social networks tend to be noisier than those in the physical world, as it is much easier for users to get connected online. Among a large set of contacts, it might be the case that only a small portion of them can influence the actor's behavior. Some web sites, such as LinkedIn (http://www.linkedin.com/) and Facebook, ask people how they know each other when they become connected. However, most of the time people decline to share such detailed information. Indeed, neither explicit knowledge about pair wise relation types nor their relevance in predicting the behavior of the users are available. In summary, people are involved in different relations and it is helpful for differentiating these relations for behavior prediction. Tang & Liu (2010) presented the *SocioDim* framework that addresses the relation heterogeneity presented in social networks. They proposed to apply a hybrid node-view and edge-view approach to help locate those cross-community nodes and edges in order to extract a meaningful social dimension representation. When a network becomes more and more heterogeneous, it becomes difficult to learn a clean social dimension representation, thus, some weak ties may bridge two different communities. Filtering out those irrelevant dimensions during extraction may yield a more accurate model.

## Group Evolution

A parallel research effort has been devoted to modeling the temporal evolution of social models. The problem of collecting and analyzing large-scale time-evolving data on social groups and communities has been largely investigated.

Backstrom et al. (2006) analyzed friendship link evolution on both LiveJournal and DBLP communities. It performed an insight analysis on group evolution within online communities by exploring principles by which groups develop and evolve in large-scale social networks. The authors found that a reasonable performance estimation can be obtained based purely on the structural properties of the group as a subgraph in the social network. As with group membership, relatively subtle structural features are crucial in distinguishing between groups likely to grow rapidly and those not likely to. For example, groups with a very large number of triangles (i.e., consisting of three mutual friends) grow significantly less quickly overall than groups with relatively few triangles. Thus, the framework is able to identify the most "informative" group of features that can be interpreted in terms of the underlying sociological considerations.

Assuming that social networks are shaped by a set of common growth processes, a significant research effort has been devoted to explaining the similarity in the high-level structural properties. For example, the power-law degree distribution, often found in these networks, can be produced through preferential attachments, where new links tend to attach to already popular nodes. One class of growth models uses global processes to determine the source and destination of new links. The well-known Barabasi-Albert (BA) model (Barabasi & Albert, 1999) has been shown to result in networks with power-law degree distributions. In the BA model, new links are attached to nodes using a probability distribution weighted by node degree. Many extensions to the BA model have been proposed, for example by adding a tunable level of clustering (Holme & Kim, 2002). A more detailed description of these and other similar analytical models is given by Mitzenmacher (2004).

Mislove et al. (2008) followed a hybrid approach with respect to previously mentioned ones. It studied the link formation process that drives the growth of Flickr online social networks by comparing empirical observations with the predictions of previously proposed models. The authors collected data covering three months of growth from Flickr, encompassing 950,143 new users and over 9.7 million new links. The analysis was focused on the ways in which new links are formed. The results highlighted that links tend to be created by users who already have a large neighborhood and users usually create a connection with other users already close in the network. Moreover, users tend to respond to incoming links by creating links back to the source. The overall links formation process followed the well-known preferential attachment model, but that global mechanisms (such as the BA model) alone are insufficient to explain the observed proximity between link sources and destinations.

## Social Knowledge Representation

Knowledge extracted from the UGC should be effectively organized in order to identify key concepts and relationships between them. A semantics-based representation needs the "understanding" the meaning of a resource and the related domain. Key concepts are: (i) disambiguation of terms, (ii) shared agreement on meanings, and (iii) description of the domain, with concepts and relations among concepts. Data extracted from UGC often does not say much about "how related" a resource is to a given subject. Semantic Web provides the instruments to semantically enrich social knowledge representation through subject-based classification.

*Subject-based classification* is any content classification that groups objects based on their subjects. It allows distinguishing between the objects to be classified and the subject used to classify them. Several subject-based techniques have been proposed. According to Smith & Welty (2001), they may be classified based upon an increasing semantic clarity index, which scales linearly

*Figure 2. Subject-based classification techniques and their applications*

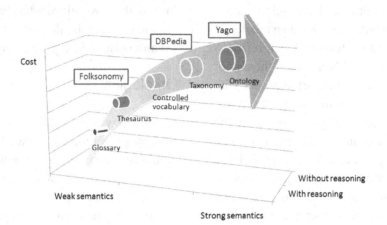

with their construction and maintenance costs (see Figure 2). Ranging from simple controlled vocabularies, in which a closed list of named subjects is provided as topic map for classification, to a complete ontology, which formally represents knowledge by a set of concepts within a domain and the relationships between those concepts, Semantic Web provides a full technological stack to access semantics-based resources.

Advanced semantic knowledge (e.g., taxonomies and ontologies) enables the usage of semantic reasoning engines. In the following, we present three among the most relevant works that address social knowledge collection and semantic-based representation in the social network context. To better highlight the semantic level at which different analysis has been performed, selected approaches are presented in increasing semantic clarity order, according to the classification presented in Figure 2.

## Folksonomy

Folksonomy (from folk and taxonomy) is a neologism for a practice of collaborative categorization using freely chosen keywords. Folksonomies, also called social tagging mechanisms, have been implemented in a number of online knowledge sharing environments since the idea was first

adopted by social bookmarking site del.icio.us in 2004. The idea behind a folksonomy is to allow the users to describe a set of shared objects with a set of keywords of their own choice. What the objects are depends on the goal of the site. For instance, the object of the classification process is bookmarks in del.icio.us, photos in Flickr, scientific publications in *CiteULike* (www.citeulike.com), and goals and plans (e.g., trips, lose weight) in *43Things* (www.43things.com). Since the number of keywords is not fixed and there is not unique correspondence between terms and concepts, the set of selected keywords cannot be formally considered as well-formed vocabularies, according to the subject-based classification on the continuous scale of Smith and Welty (2001). Specia & Motta (2007) suggested using folksonomies to automatically populate ontologies. They proposed an approach to make explicit the semantics behind the tag space in social annotation systems. This is achieved by a pipeline of processes, including the cleaning up of tags, the analysis of tag co-occurrence, the clustering of tags based on co-occurrence measures, the mapping of tags in a cluster into ontological elements (e.g., concepts, relations and/or properties) and the discovery of semantic relationships between them by using already existent ontologies available on the Semantic Web. Mika (2005) proposed a three-layered view of the Semantic Web, namely the layer of communities and their relations, the layer of semantics (ontologies and their relations), and the layer of content items and their relations (the hypertext web). In Mika (2007) the author formalized this view as a tripartite model with three different classes of nodes (actors, concepts, and instances) and hyperedges representing the commitment of a user in terms of classifying an instance belonging to a certain concept. Folding ternary relations into binary relations, it yielded concept relations based on instance overlaps, and concept relations based on actor overlap. The proposed approach has shown its usefulness for modeling networks of large-scale folksonomies at an abstract level.

## Structured Knowledge

With the steady growth of web resources many research efforts have been devoted to linking heterogeneous web data and making this structured knowledge freely available. The W3C SWEO Linking Open Data community project aims at extending the Web with a data commons by publishing various open data sets as RDF and by setting RDF links between data items from different data sources. One of the most popular dataset produced by this project is DBPedia. DBpedia (http://dbpedia.org/) is a research project that focuses on converting the Wikipedia content into structured knowledge. Since most of the article metadatas are included into the text by means of special syntactic constructs, structured knowledge can be obtained by simply parsing article texts. The baseline extraction framework proposed in Auer et al. (2007) converted Wikipedia content into the machine-readable RDF dataset. Moreover, they proposed a graph pattern builder for efficiently querying the extracted Wikipedia content. Indeed, DBpedia content mining may effectively drive both ontology construction and sophisticate query processes. Since the querying process has to deal with large datasets, schema users can hardly know

which properties are used in the knowledge base. Indeed, they are guided when building queries. A look-ahead search allows the system to propose suitable options during the user query form filling.

## Ontologies

An ontology can formally model social knowledge by generating a set of well defined concepts within a domain and the relationships between those concepts. Semantic Web architectures are enabled to fully access the social domain representations by reasoning about properties inferred from these domains. An important project that focuses on extracting structured ontological information from Wikipedia and WordNet (http://wordnet.princeton.edu/) is YAGO (Suchanek et al., 2008). It builds on entities and relations and currently contains more than 1 million entities and 5 million facts. This includes the Is-A hierarchy (i.e., a taxonomy) as well as non-taxonomic relations between entities (such as *hasWonPrize*). The facts have been automatically extracted from Wikipedia and unified with WordNet, an ontological well-defined taxonomy of synsets (i.e., sets of one or more synonyms), using a carefully designed combination of rule-based and heuristic methods. Each synset of WordNet becomes a class of YAGO, excluding proper nouns known to WordNet, which, in fact, would be individuals. The resulting knowledge base is a major step beyond WordNet. It improves both knowledge qualities, by adding information about individuals like persons, organizations, products, etc. with their semantic relationships, and knowledge quantity, by increasing the number of facts by more than one order of magnitude.

## APPLICATIONS

Online communities are a powerful resource suitable for discovering hidden social knowledge and developing new approaches tailored to user interests. In the last years, many research efforts have been devoted to developing new ideas that take advantages of the huge amount of the UGC provided by online social networks. For example, many commercial websites exploit recommender systems to either suggest new products to their customers (e.g., books, CDs, movies) or enhance the quality of the offered services. These recommender systems are usually targeted on the customer behavior and preferences of the customer. The user-generated media content, shared and tagged by community members, can be also useful for improving the understanding of online resources (e.g., photos, videos) by exploiting data mining techniques (e.g., classification). Furthermore, query engines can take advantage of folksonomies and ontologies extracted from UGC. In this section, a survey on the most interesting works focused on these issues is proposed. The goal is to provide an overview on recent algorithms and applications from which readers may figure out most appealing state-of-the-art research topics.

## Recommender Systems

Recommender systems are one of the mostly used technologies, especially in the context of e-commerce. They are focused on presenting information on items that are likely to be of customer interest. To determine the most interesting items, the recommender systems usually exploit detailed user profile knowledge and other correlated pieces of information provided by the online community. Other online applications also exploit these recommendation systems. News Web services is starting employing recommender systems to provide the last news to their users according to their interests. In the last years, recommender systems have been also employed to improve the data quality of user-generated content. Since the users can express the same concept with different tags according to their own interests, recommender systems can be effectively used to suggest smart tags for a new resource.

Two main strategies can be employed to discover user-item associations: (i) content-based and (ii) collaborative filtering approaches. The *content filtering* approaches create a profile for each user and product. Profiles allow algorithms to associate users with matching items. Moreover, these techniques are based on matching the personal user knowledge with related data of similar users. For example, some of these approaches rely only on past user behavior without requiring the creation of explicit profiles. In Herlocker et al. (2004) an interesting overview on popular algorithms is discussed.

However, all these methods are exclusively based on similarity measures without regarding to the trust rating associated with users within the social network. One of the first works addressed to incorporate the trust rating in the computation of the similarity among user profiles and recommended items was presented in Golbeck & Hendler (2006). The system required users to provide a trust rating for each friend of their network. Moreover, the website allowed users to assign rating to films and provide comments. Consider a movie $m$ and a set of raters $R$, where each rater $r$ has an associated trust rate $t_r$. The recommended movie rating is computed by considering all the ratings for the movie $m$ weighted by the trust value $t_r$ assigned by the user to each rater $r$. The results obtained by this approach show a significant improvement in terms of accuracy with respect to simple recommendation approaches based on ratings assigned to movies and Pearson similarity measure between user profiles. DuBois et al. (2009) adopted a clustering approach on a trust network of users to improve recommendation accuracy. It defined a metric space based on a trust function over which a variant of correlation clustering algorithm is applied. The users that belong to the same cluster show a high level of agreement for recommended items. This approach has been integrated into two basic recommendation algorithms. Experimental evaluation showed a statistically significant accuracy increase.

Unfortunately, some critical issues affect these approaches. The collaborative filtering techniques suffer from the *cold start* problem, due to their inability to draw any inferences for users or items about which they have not gathered sufficient information yet. On the contrary, they are, on average, more accurate than content filtering approaches because they could address a broader range of different aspects. Moreover, the power law distribution in user rating could negatively affect the recommendation system performance. Indeed, few users rate for most of available resources while the large part of users do not apply any rating. Recent technologies address the data sparseness. For instance, Koren et al. (2009) presented a matrix factorization technique to map both users and items to a joint latent factor space.

According to data information employed in selecting most relevant items, we categorize the recommender systems in two main categories: (i) news recommendation and (ii) tag recommendation. In the following, for each category, some of the most relevant recently proposed solutions are presented.

## News Recommendation

Unlike the basic systems, recommending news introduces new challenges in data analysis. In fact, the systems should suggest the last news of user interest. Thus, a collaborative filtering based only on similarity measures between user profile and the news content in many cases is not enough. In literature, some systems have been developed to improve the quality of recommended news.

Xue et al. (2008) proposed systems that also take into account the opinion of readers. For each news discussion thread posted on a social bookmarking site, a topic profile is built. The computation of the topic profile is based on the considerations that (i) a comment with a high number of votes is more interesting for the reader and (ii) a more recent comment indicates with a higher accuracy the trend of the topic. Using such

profile, the system can retrieve the most relevant news by evaluating. For each news, its relevance according to the topic profile, the popularity, and the timeliness.

An evolution of the previous approach was presented in Wang et al. (2010). The authors incorporated a graph representation to model the content similarity between comments and logic relationships among them. Thus, the relevance of comments and their relationships are used to compute the topic profile. Moreover, the authors introduced a novel approach to suggest to the reader the relationships between the recommended news. The approach is based on the analysis of the set of keywords that represent the news topic. Manual evaluation of a pool of judgers has been performed. The proposed system achieved better performance in terms of precision and novelty with respect to basic recommendation approaches (e.g., Okapi method).

Buzzer system proposed by Phelan et al. (2009) is instead focused on the identification of the current trend in a social community. The recommendation system gathered public and private posts published on Twitter to build a Lucene index. This index is then employed to compare the content of the news provided by the RSS (Really Simple Syndication) sources selected by the user. Analyzing the behavior and the preferences of a pool of ten participants tested the systems.

## Tag Recommendation

In many online communities it is possible to assign tags to shared resources (e.g., photos). Tags, that also highlight the user interest, represent a useful knowledge about the UGC for building efficient query engines. However, they are typically very noisy because the same concept can be described by means of different keywords and the same keyword can be associated with different resources covering different contexts. Recommendation systems can be exploited to enhance the quality of tags by analyzing the interest of a single user and the trend of the social community. For example, Basile et al. (2007) proposed to apply a classification approach for the purpose of identifying the documents and the associated tags that are more likely to be of user interest. De Meo et al. (2010) recently proposed a query expansion method to build and maintain a user profile. When a user submits a query, the system automatically enriches the query with further "authoritative" tags matching with user needs and desires.

Shepitsen et al. (2008) focused its attention on the problem of tag redundancy and ambiguity. To overcome this issue, it employed a hierarchical clustering algorithm to identify the correlation among groups of tags. The system was tested on two popular bookmarking systems, delicious and Last.fm, by evaluating the position of a resource in the ranks computed by a baseline method based on tf-idf and the proposed approach with different parameters settings. The results showed a significant improvement by using the hierarchical clustering approach.

Other approaches simulated the generation process of social annotations to model the interaction among different objects in social tagging systems. This allows effectively facing the problems of tag noise and sparseness. For instance, Wu et al. (2006) proposed a probabilistic generative model in which the three entities in social tagging systems are mapped to a common multi-dimensional vector. Each dimension corresponds to a knowledge category. Besides, Latent Semantical Analysis (LSA) and Latent Dirichlet Allocation (LDA) have been also proposed to model the social tagging process. Kashoob et al. (2009) discovered latent structures in large-scale social annotations collected from Flickr and Delicious, while Krestel et al. (2009) proposed an approach based on Latent Dirichlet Allocation (LDA). Latent topics are elicited from resources equipped with a fairly stable and complete tag set to recommend topics for new resources with only a few tags. Symeonidis et al. (2008) proposed to exploit a 3-order tensor to represent the three main entities

of social tagging systems. On the tensor-based representation, a latent semantic analysis and dimensionality reduction is performed by using the Higher Order Singular Value Decomposition (HOSVD) technique.

To improve the quality of suggested tags for photo annotation, Sigurbjörnsson & van Zwol (2008) proposed a method based on two steps. Given a photo with user-defined tags, an ordered list of candidate tags is first provided for each photo, based on co-occurrence measure. The co-occurrence between two tags is computed as the number of photos in which both tags are used in the annotation. Both symmetric and asymmetric measures were exploited. Then, the lists of candidate tags are aggregated to generate a ranked list of recommended tags according to two different ranking strategies. Experimental results show that, for almost 70% of the photos, the system suggested a good descriptive tag at the first position of the ranked list, and, for 94%, a good tag is provided among the top 5 ranked tags.

Instead, Garg & Weber (2008) evaluated different approaches to improve Flickr tag recommendation system. An approach that considered the history of tags selected by both the single user and the community has been proposed. In particular, analyzing both the user and the group profiles first identifies a set of promising groups. Then, for each of these groups, a ranked list of suggested tags is generated according to the tag frequency and the previously inserted tags. Experimental results showed that the proposed hybrid approach achieved good accuracy performance. Pictures characterized by a higher number of tags achieved the best results.

## Data Classification

Social tags and user-generated media content can be employed to improve the representation of resources like documents, Web pages, photos, and videos. Classification methods can take advantages of these new representations. For example, in Schőnhofen (2009) a new classification model based on Wikipedia was proposed. The algorithm identified and ranked all Wikipedia categories related to the analyzed document by matching Wikipedia articles titles with the words present in the document. The retrieved categories are then ranked according to their relevance statistics. Experimental results on Wikipedia article body and the well-known news corpora, showed that the best performance were achieved by combining Wikipedia categorization with the top terms identified by tf-idf statistics (Tan et al, 2006).

Wikipedia can be also employed to augment the bag-of-word (BOW) representation of a document. Wang et al. (2009) proposed to enrich the BOW representation by means of a thesaurus automatically extracted using redirect and disambiguation pages and the hyperlink graph of Wikipedia. The thesaurus is employed to identify synonyms, hyponyms, and correlations among entities cited in the document. In such a way, documents related to the same topic that involve few co-occurred terms are shifted closer to each other in the new representation. The effectiveness of BOW representation enriched with Wikipedia related terms was empirically demonstrated on different document collections by means of a linear Support Vector Machine (SVM) (Tan et al. 2006). The micro-average and the macro-average of the precision-recall break-even point (BEP) were used to compare classification performance with respect to the baseline approach (i.e., the bag-of-word representation without enrichment). Against the baseline method, the proposed approach yielded an average improvement of 2-5%.

In Mihalcea & Csomai (2007) the Wikify! System, based on keyword extraction and word sense disambiguation, was proposed. The keyword extraction algorithm followed a two-step approach: (i) candidate extraction, which extracts all possible n-grams that are present in a controlled dictionary and (ii) keyword ranking, which is based on tf-idf statistics, $\chi^2$ independence test, or Keyphraseness (i.e., the probability of a term to be

selected as a keyword for a document) (Tan et al, 2006). Three different disambiguation algorithms have been integrated in the system. The first one is based on the overlap between the terms in the document and a set of ambiguous terms stored in a dictionary. The second one is based on a Naïve Bayes classifier whose model is built on feature vectors of correlated Wikipedia articles. Finally, a voting system, which takes care of disambiguation results obtained by previous techniques, has been exploited as well. Independent evaluations carried out for each of the two tasks showed that both system components produce accurate annotations. The best were achieved by the Keyphraseness statistics. Which yields an accuracy, recall, and F-measures results of, respectively, 53.37%, 55.90% and 54.63%. The disambiguation procedure reached an accuracy of 94% at best.

Unlike the information provided by the Wikipedia articles, social tags associated by the users with Web sources can be employed to categorize Web objects (e.g., Web pages, products). The work presented in Yin et al. (2009) showed the effectiveness of this approach. By modeling the relations between Web objects and social tags provided by del.icio.us as graphs, an optimization framework has been proposed to assign the correct category associated with tags. A comparison with SVM and harmonic Gaussian classifiers, which used the title and the tags associated with each web resource as feature space, was performed. The proposed approach outperformed the other classifiers in terms of F-measure (Tan et al., 2006). Thus, the authors concluded that social tags are effective features in the Web object classification as they allow propagating the category information of training samples from one domain to another.

## Query Engines

As pointed out by the analysis on del.icio.us performed by Heymann et al. (2008), information provided by online social networks can be useful for improving the quality of search results.

Moreover, tags provided by the users can be exploited to personalize the online searches. Some works that address the above issues are presented in the following.

Bender et al. (2008) proposed a framework to improve query results according with the user interest. The social relationships between users and the correlation among tags associated with media resources (e.g., photos, bookmarks) are represented into a unified graph model. The resulting graph is composed of different types of nodes, which represent different elements of the online community, and links, whose weights depend on the type of relationships between nodes. For example, the weight associated with a link between two users can reflect the mutual interest overlap or can be in inverse proportion with the total number of friends of the user. A scoring model is introduced to evaluate the correlation between the keywords query and the relations in the graph model. Different search strategies are exploited to take into account different relationships between query terms, users, and documents. Experiments performed on dumps of the social communities del.icio.us and Flickr showed good precision results according to the interest of the user that performed the query.

In Schenkel et al (2008) the same graph model is exploited to build an efficient query engine. The proposed approach, named ContextMerge, combines a top-k algorithm with dynamic tag expansion, by considering the semantic relationships between tags and dynamic social expansions according to the strength of the relations among users. The effectiveness of the method is evaluated by computing the precision and the normalized discounted cumulative gain (NDCG) on two out of three different datasets crawled from del.icio.us, Flickr and LibraryThing. On average, the precision achieved by different experimental settings is around 36% on del.icio.us and 55% on LibraryThing. Instead, the NDCG score is on average 0.41 and 0.66 for, respectively, Flickr and LibraryThing. Interesting results are also the ef-

ficiency performance in term of the cost measure, wall-clock runtimes and abstract cost in terms of the disk accesses. ContextMerge is up to an order of magnitude faster than the standard baseline method of processing inverted list.

The information provided by online communities can be also employed to improve the online search of news. For example, Abrol & Khan (2010) exploited Twitter messages to retrieve keywords that are highly correlated with the user query. In particular they focused their analysis on the geographical content of Twitter message, to determine which messages are more relevant according to the user query. From the retrieved messages a set of keywords are extracted also considering the semantic relatedness among them. The system has been tested on three different news events and compared with the document retrieved by original query. An improvement in terms of accuracy has been achieved for all the considered events.

## FUTURE RESEARCH DIRECTIONS

The user-generated content provided by social network sites has been studied under different perspectives with the aim at inferring previously undisclosed knowledge. However, most of the works presented in this chapter are focused on a specific application field or peculiar data characteristics. For example, tag recommendation systems are focused on improving the accuracy and the quality of recommended tags. A more limited attention has been paid to the integration of heterogeneous data on different online social networking sites to infer new knowledge and improve the web service personalization. Media sharing communities (e.g., Wikipedia) and news recommendation systems may be both employed to improve the classification of news topics. Moreover, the opinions posted on microblogs may be exploited to both build reliable user profiles and filter news according to their geographical location, the main user interests, and/or the widespread community opinion.

An open issue concerning social network applications is the validation of the achieved results. According to the context of usage, different performance measures have been employed. For instance, accuracy is used in the classification of Web objects or documents, execution time measures the speedup of query engines, and user opinions retrieved by questionnaires are focused on assessing the quality of recommendation systems. Indeed, both benchmarks on which authors can test new recommendation systems and well-define strategies to compare existing applications are still missing.

Finally, we believe that the contribution of new data mining approaches, mathematical social models, and natural language methods could definitely improve knowledge discovery from the user-generated content, by enabling the creation of new and interesting applications.

## CONCLUSION

Social network analysis provides powerful tools to understand user and group behavior in an online environment. Many research efforts have been devoted to discovering relevant knowledge from UGC. This chapter reviews main contributions of recent works regarding social network analysis and its most appealing data mining applications oriented to knowledge discovery from online communities.

Analytical social models enable researchers to shape their own applications to the expected user behavior, analyze social tagging, and predict social group formation and evolution. To introduce the reader to the problem of knowledge discovery from online communities, we first described most commonly used social network analytical models. Since Semantic Web applications are usually exploited to enrich media content with their semantic

meanings, collection and modeling of online media data tailored to semantic knowledge inference are also discussed. Next, the most appealing data mining approaches to social network mining are thoroughly described. The exploitation of well-known data mining techniques, such as clustering and classification, allows discovering hidden correlations in social data. Since the process of data mining and knowledge discovery may effectively support both the creation and the evaluation of social network models we expect that, in the next years, web-oriented domain applications even more rely on social models and machine learning algorithms. Thanks of community shared content; they will gain leverage in web services.

## REFERENCES

Abrol, S., & Khan, L. (2010). TWinner: Understanding news queries with geo-content using Twitter. *Proceedings of the 6th Workshop on Geographic Information Retrieval,* (pp. 1-8).

Aleman-Meza, B., Nagarajan, M., Ramakrishnan, C., Ding, L., Kolari, P., & Sheth, A. P. … Finin, T. (2006). Semantic analytics on social networks: Experiences in addressing the problem of conflict of interest detection. *Proceedings of the 15th International Conference on World Wide Web,* (pp. 407-416).

Anagnostopoulos, A., Kumar, R., & Mahdian, M. (2008). Influence and correlation in social networks. *Proceeding of the 14th ACM SIGKDD International Conference on Knowledge Discovery and Data Mining,* (pp. 7-15).

Anyanwu, K., & Sheth, A. P. (2003). P-Queries: Enabling querying for semantic associations on the Semantic Web. *Proceedings of the 12th International Conference on World Wide Web,* (pp. 690-699).

Auer, S., Bizer, C., Kobilarov, G., Lehmann, J., Cyganiak, R., & Ives, Z. (2007). Dbpedia: A nucleus for a web of open data. *The Semantic Web, 4825,* 722–735. doi:10.1007/978-3-540-76298-0_52

Backstrom, L., Huttenlocher, D., Kleinberg, J., & Lan, X. (2006). Group formation in large social networks: Membership, growth, and evolution. *Proceedings of the 12th ACM SIGKDD International Conference on Knowledge Discovery and Data Mining,* (pp. 44-54).

Barabasi, A. L., & Albert, R. (1999). Emergence of scaling in random networks. *Science, 286*(5439), 509–512. doi:10.1126/science.286.5439.509

Basile, P., Gendarmi, D., Lanubile, F., & Semeraro, G. (2007). Recommending smart tags in a social bookmarking system. *Bridging the Gap between Semantic Web and Web, 2,* 22-29.

Bender, M., Crecelius, T., Kacimi, M., Michel, S., Neumann, T., & Parreira, J. X. … Weikum, G. (2008). Exploiting social relations for query expansion and result ranking. *IEEE 24th International Conference on Data Engineering Workshop, 2,* (pp. 501-506).

Christakis, N. A., & Fowler, J. H. (2007). The spread of obesity in a large social network over 32 years. *The New England Journal of Medicine, 357*(4), 370–379. doi:10.1056/NEJMsa066082

De Meo, P., Quattrone, G., & Ursino, D. (2010). A query expansion and user profile enrichment approach to improve the performance of recommender systems operating on a folksonomy. *User Modeling and User-Adapted Interaction, 20*(1), 41–86. doi:10.1007/s11257-010-9072-6

De Souza, C. S., & Preece, J. (2004). A framework for analyzing and understanding online communities. *Interacting with Computers, 16*(3), 579–610. doi:10.1016/j.intcom.2003.12.006

DuBois, T., Golbeck, J., Kleint, J., & Srinivasan, A. (2009). *Improving recommendation accuracy by clustering social networks with trust.* ACM Workshop on Recommender Systems & the Social Web.

Gabrilovich, E., & Markovitch, S. (2007). Computing semantic relatedness using Wikipedia-based explicit semantic analysis. *Proceedings of the 20th International Joint Conference on Artificial Intelligence,* (pp. 6-12).

Garg, N., & Weber, I. (2008). Personalized tag suggestion for flickr. *Proceeding of the 17th International Conference on World Wide Web,* (pp. 1063-1064).

Golbeck, J., & Hendler, J. (2006). Filmtrust: Movie recommendations using trust in web-based social networks. *Proceedings of the IEEE Consumer Communications and Networking Conference, 42,* (pp. 43-44).

Granovetter, M., & Soong, R. (1983). Threshold models of diffusion and collective behavior. *The Journal of Mathematical Sociology, 9*(3), 165–179. doi:10.1080/0022250X.1983.9989941

Herlocker, J. L., Konstan, J. A., Terveen, L. G., & Riedl, J. T. (2004). Evaluating collaborative filtering recommender systems. [TOIS]. *ACM Transactions on Information Systems, 22*(1), 5–53. doi:10.1145/963770.963772

Heymann, P., Ramage, D., & Garcia-Molina, H. (2008). Social tag prediction. *Proceedings of the 31st Annual International ACM SIGIR Conference on Research and Development in Information Retrieval,* (pp. 531-538).

Holme, P., & Kim, B. J. (2002). Growing scale-free networks with tunable clustering. *Physical Review E: Statistical, Nonlinear, and Soft Matter Physics, 65*(2), 26107. doi:10.1103/PhysRevE.65.026107

Hotho, A., Jäschke, R., Schmitz, C., & Stumme, G. (2006). BibSonomy: A social bookmark and publication sharing system. *Proceedings of the Conceptual Structures Tool Interoperability Workshop at the 14th International Conference on Conceptual Structures*, (pp. 87-102).

Java, A., Song, X., Finin, T., & Tseng, B. (2007). Why we Twitter: Understanding microblogging usage and communities. *Proceedings of the 9th WebKDD and 1st SNA-KDD 2007 Workshop on Web Mining and Social Network Analysis* (pp. 56-65).

Kashoob, S., Caverlee, J., & Ding, Y. (2009). A categorical model for discovering latent structure in social annotations. *Proceedings of the International AAAI Conference on Weblogs and Social Media* (pp. 27-35).

Koren, Y., Bell, R., & Volinsky, C. (2009). Matrix factorization techniques for recommender systems. *Computer*, *42*(8), 30–37. doi:10.1109/MC.2009.263

Krestel, R., Fankhauser, P., & Nejdl, W. (2009). Latent Dirichlet allocation for tag recommendation. *Proceedings of the 3rd Conference on Recommender Systems,* (pp. 61-68).

Lam, H. Y., & Yeung, D. Y. (2007). *A learning approach to spam detection based on social networks.* 4th Conference on Email and Anti-Spam (CEAS).

Lerman, K. (2007). Social networks and social information filtering on Digg. *Proceedings of International Conference on Weblogs and Social Media.*

Macskassy, S.A., & Provost, F. (2007). Classification in networked data: A toolkit and a univariate case study. *Journal of Machine Learning Research, 8*, 935–983.

Mihalcea, R., & Csomai, A. (2007). Wikify!: Linking documents to encyclopedic knowledge. *Proceedings of the Sixteenth ACM Conference on Information and Knowledge Management, 7,* (pp. 233-242).

Mika, P. (2005). Social networks and the Semantic Web: The next challenge. *IEEE Intelligent Systems, 20*(1), 82–85.

Mika, P. (2007). Ontologies are us: A unified model of social networks and semantics. *Web Semantics: Science. Services and Agents on the World Wide Web, 5*(1), 5–15. doi:10.1016/j.websem.2006.11.002

Mislove, A., Koppula, H. S., Gummadi, K. P., Druschel, P., & Bhattacharjee, B. (2008). Growth of the Flickr social network. *Proceedings of the First Workshop on Online Social Networks,* (pp. 25-30).

Mitzenmacher, M. (2004). A brief history of generative models for power law and lognormal distributions. *Internet Mathematics, 1*(2), 226–251. doi:10.1080/15427951.2004.10129088

Phelan, O., McCarthy, K., & Smyth, B. (2009). Using twitter to recommend real-time topical news. *Proceedings of the Third ACM Conference on Recommender Systems*, (pp. 385-388).

Rowe, R., & Creamer, G. (2007). Automated social hierarchy detection through email network analysis. *Proceedings of the Joint 9th WEB-KDD and 1st SNA-KDD Conference,* (pp. 109-117).

Schenkel, R., Crecelius, T., Kacimi, M., Michel, S., Neumann, T., Parreira, J. X., & Weikum, G. (2008). Efficient top-k querying over social-tagging networks. *Proceedings of the 31st Annual International ACM SIGIR Conference on Research and Development in Information Retrieval,* (pp. 523-530).

Schönhofen, P. (2009). Identifying document topics using the Wikipedia category network. *Web Intelligence and Agent Systems, 7*(2), 195–207.

Shepitsen, A., Gemmell, J., Mobasher, B., & Burke, R. (2008). Personalized recommendation in social tagging systems using hierarchical clustering. *Proceedings of the 2008 ACM Conference on Recommender Systems,* (pp. 259-266).

Sigurbjörnsson, B., & van Zwol, R. (2008). Flickr tag recommendation based on collective knowledge. *Proceeding of the 17th International Conference on World Wide Web,* (pp. 327-336).

Smith, B., & Welty, C. (2001). Towards a new synthesis. In *Formal ontology in Information Systems* (pp. iii–x). Ontology.

Specia, L., & Motta, E. (2007). Integrating folksonomies in the Semantic Web. In *The Semantic Web: research and applications,* (pp. 624-639).

Suchanek, F. M., Kasneci, G., & Weikum, G. (2008). Yago: A large ontology from Wikipedia and Wordnet. *Web Semantics: Science. Services and Agents on the World Wide Web, 6*(3), 203–217. doi:10.1016/j.websem.2008.06.001

Symeonidis, P., Nanopoulos, A., & Manolopoulos, Y. (2008). Tag recommendations based on tensor dimensionality reduction. *Proceedings of the ACM Conference on Recommender Systems,* (pp. 43-50).

Tan, P., Steinbach, M., & Kumar, V. (2006). *Introduction to data mining.* Pearson Addison Wesley.

Tang, L., & Liu, H. (2009). Relation learning via latent social dimensions. *Proceedings of the 15th ACM SIGKDD International Conference on Knowledge Discovery and Data Mining,* (pp. 817-826).

Tang, L., & Liu, H. (2010). Toward predicting collective behavior via social dimension extraction. *IEEE Intelligent Systems, 25*(4), 19–25. doi:10.1109/MIS.2010.36

Wang, J., Li, Q., Chen, Y. P., Liu, J., Zhang, C., & Lin, Z. (2010). News recommendation in forum-based social media. *Proceedings of the Twenty-Fourth AAAI Conference on Artificial Intelligence,* (pp. 1449-1454).

Wang, P., Hu, J., Zeng, H. J., & Chen, Z. (2009). Using Wikipedia knowledge to improve text classification. *Knowledge and Information Systems, 19*(3), 265–281. doi:10.1007/s10115-008-0152-4

Wu, X., Zhang, L., & Yu, Y. (2006). Exploring social annotations for the Semantic Web. *Proceedings of the 15th International Conference on the World Wide Web,* (pp. 417-426).

Xue, Y., Zhang, C., Zhou, C., Lin, X., & Li, Q. (2008). An effective news recommendation in social media based on users' preference. *Proceedings of the 2008 International Workshop on Education Technology and Training & 2008 International Workshop on Geoscience and Remote Sensing, 1,* (pp. 627-631).

Yin, Z., Li, R., Mei, Q., & Han, J. (2009). Exploring social tagging graph for web object classification. *Proceedings of the 15th ACM SIGKDD International Conference on Knowledge Discovery and Data Mining,* (pp. 957-966).

## ADDITIONAL READING

Agrawal, R., & Srikant, R. (1994). Fast algorithms for mining association rules in large data-bases. *Proceedings of the 20th International Conference on Very Large Data Base,* 487-499.

Bonhard, P., & Sasse, M. A. (2006). 'Knowing me, knowing you' - Using profiles and social networking to improve recommender systems. *BT Technology Journal, 24*(3), 84–98. doi:10.1007/s10550-006-0080-3

Cha, M., Mislove, A., & Gummadi, K. P. (2009). A measurement-driven analysis of information propagation in the flickr social network. *Proceedings of the 18th international conference on World Wide Web*, 721-730.

Crandall, D., Cosley, D., Huttenlocher, D., Kleinberg, J., & Suri, S. (2008). Feedback effects between similarity and social influence in online communities. *Proceedings of the 14th ACM SIGKDD international conference on Knowledge discovery and data mining*, 160-168.

Ereteo, G., Buffa, M., Gandon, F., Grohan, P., Leitzelman, L., & Sander, P. (2008). State of the Art on Social Network Analysis and its Applications on a Semantic Web. *Proceedings of the 7th International Semantic Web Conference.*

Ghita, S., Nejdl, W., & Paiu, R. (2005). Semantically Rich Recommendations in Social Networks for Sharing, Exchanging and Ranking Semantic Context. *The Semantic Web - ISWC*. 293-307.

Guo, L., Tan, E., Chen, S., Zhang, X., & Zhao, Y. E. (2009). Analyzing patterns of user content generation in online social networks. *Proceedings of the 15th ACM SIGKDD international conference on Knowledge discovery and data mining*, 369-378.

Hu, X., Zhang, X., Lu, C., Park, E. M., & Zhou, X. (2009). Exploiting Wikipedia as external knowledge for document clustering. *Proceedings of the 15th ACM SIGKDD international conference on Knowledge discovery and data mining*, 16(7), 389-396.

Jung, J. J. (2008). Query transformation based on semantic centrality in Semantic Social Network. *Journal of Universal Computer Science*, 14(7), 1031-1047.

Jung, J. J., & Euzenat, J. (2007). Towards semantic social networks. *Proceedings of the 4th European conference on The Semantic Web*. 267-280.

Kumar, R., Novak, J., & Tomkins, A. (2010). Structure and evolution of online social networks. *Link Mining: Models, Algorithms, and Applications*, 337-357.

Kuramochi, M., & Karypis, G. (2004). An Efficient Algorithm for Discovering Frequent Subgraphs. *IEEE Transactions on Knowledge and Data Engineering*, 16(9), 1038–1051. doi:10.1109/TKDE.2004.33

Lau, R. Y. K., Song, D., Li, Y., Cheung, T. C. H., & Hao, J. (2009). Toward a Fuzzy Domain Ontology Extraction Method for Adaptive e-Learning. *IEEE Transactions on Knowledge and Data Engineering*, 21(6), 800–813. doi:10.1109/TKDE.2008.137

Liu, B. (2007). *Web data mining*. Springer.

Lu, C., Hu, X., Chen, X., Park, J. R., He, T., & Li, Z. (2010). The topic-perspective model for social tagging systems. *Proceedings of the 16th ACM SIGKDD international conference on Knowledge discovery and data mining*, 683-692.

Matsuo, Y., Mori, J., & Hamasaki, M. (2006). POLYPHONET: An Advanced Social Network Extraction System from the Web structure and evolution of online social networks. *Proceedings of the World Wide Web Conference*, 262-278.

Michalski, R.S., & Stepp, R. (2009). Automated Construction Of Classifications Conceptual Clustering Versus Numerical Taxonomy. *IEEE Transactions on pattern analysis and machine learning, 4,* 396-410.

Mislove, A., Marcon, M., Gummadi, K. P., Druschel, P., & Bhattacharjee, B. (2007). Measurement and analysis of online social networks. *Proceedings of the 7th ACM SIGCOMM conference on Internet measurement*, 29-42.

Passant, A., Hastrup, T., Bojars, U., & Breslin, J. (2008). Microblogging: A semantic and distributed approach. *Proceedings of the 4th Workshop on Scripting for the Semantic Web.*

Shen, H. T., Shu, Y., & Yu, B. (2004). Efficient semantics-based content search in P2P network. *IEEE Transactions on Knowledge and Data Engineering*, *16*(7), 813–826. doi:10.1109/TKDE.2004.1318564

Szomszor, M., Cattuto, C., Alani, H., O'Hara, K., Baldassarri, A., Loreto, V., & Servedio, V.D.P. (2007). Folksonomies, the semantic web, and movie recommendation. *4th European semantic web conference, bridging the gap between semantic web and web, 2*.

Tang, J., Sun, J., Wang, C., & Yang, Z. (2009). Social influence analysis in large-scale networks. *Proceedings of the 15th ACM SIGKDD international conference on Knowledge discovery and data mining, 807-816*.

Tang, J., Zhang, J., Yao, L., Li, J., Zhang, L., & Zhoung, S. (2008). ArnetMiner: Extraction and Mining of Academic Social Networks. *International conference on Knowledge discovery and data mining, 990-998*.

Tao, L., & Sarabjot, S. A. (2009). Exploiting Domain Knowledge by Automated Taxonomy Generation in Recommender Systems. *Proceedings of 10th International Conference on E-comemerce and Web Technologies, 120-131*.

Walter, F. E., Battiston, S., & Schweitzer, F. (2008). A model of a trust-based recommendation system on a social network. *Autonomous Agents and Multi-Agent Systems*, *16*(1), 57–74. doi:10.1007/s10458-007-9021-x

Yu, L. (2011). OWL: Web Ontology Language. *A Developer's Guide to the Semantic Web*, 155-239.

## KEY TERMS AND DEFINITIONS

**Collective Behavior:** Behaviors of groups of individuals who are exposed in a social network environment.

**Folksonomy:** A folksonomy is a classification system derived from the practice and method of collaboratively creating and managing tags to annotate and categorize content.

**Knowledge Discovery in Data (KDD):** The process of extract hidden information from data. It includes the tasks of data selection, preprocessing, transformation, mining, and evaluation.

**Media Online Communities:** Media online communities are all the online communities that share user-generated media content like photos, videos, and text.

**Microblog:** Microblogging is a form of blogging where the users post short messages (few hundreds of characters).

**Ontology:** An ontology is a formal representation of the knowledge by a set of concepts within a domain and the relationships between those concepts. It is used to describe a domain and reason about its properties.

**Social Bookmarking:** Social bookmarking web services allow users to share, organize, search, and manage bookmarks of web resources.

**Social Influence:** The phenomenon that the action of individuals can produce their friends to act in a similar way.

**Social Network Services:** Social network services allow users to define a profile, build a network with other users (friends) and share information or user-generated media content with their friends.

**User-Generated Content:** User-generated content (UGC) refers to various kinds of publicly available media content that are produced by end-users, such as document, photos, and videos.

# Chapter 8
# Information Diffusion in Social Networks

**Dmitry Zinoviev**
*Suffolk University, USA*

## ABSTRACT

*The issue of information diffusion in small-world social networks was first systematically brought to light by Mark Granovetter in his seminal paper "The Strength of Weak Ties" in 1973 and has been an area of active academic studies in the past three decades. This chapter discusses information prolifieration mechanisms in massive online social networks (MOSN). In particular, the following aspects of information diffusion processes are addressed: the role and the strategic position of influential spreaders of information; the pathways in the social networks that serve as conduits for communication and information flow; mathematical models describing proliferation processes; short-term and long-term dynamics of information diffusion, and secrecy of information diffusion.*

## BACKGROUND

Social networks as abstract means of representing relations and communications within and between social groups of arbitrary size, and information dissemination in them, have been an object of active studies for the greater part of the XXth century—see, e.g. Davis (1969) and especially Rogers (1995) who reviewed 506 diffusion studies,

DOI: 10.4018/978-1-61350-444-4.ch008

though without proper sociometric information. In what follows I present a brief overview of key ideas and key authors. Readers interested in the subject are advised to consult additional literature listed at the end of the chapter.

The issue of information diffusion in small-world social networks was first seriously studied by Mark Granovetter in his seminal paper "The Strength of Weak Ties" (1973) and the follow-up paper "The strength of weak ties: a network theory revisited" (1983). Granovetter suggested that the main information exchange takes place along the so-called weak ties—loose, "acquaintance-style" connections between social network members, while strong ("friendship-style") ties are responsible for decision-making and knowledge generation and preservation. The theory of weak and strong ties serves as a basis for contemporary information diffusion theories.

Information in social networks spreads in the form of messages, wall posts, and even so-called one-bit pokes researched by Kaye *et al.* (2005) and Xiao *et al.* (2007). Golder *et al.* (2007) published the first massive study of message dynamics in Facebook and discovered that the messages follow regular temporal patterns based on time of day, day of week, and season. The origins and the destinations of the messages are not random, suggesting that the dissemination processes are homophily driven. The findings of Golder *et al.* (2007) were corroborated by Singla & Richardson (2008) and Leskovec & Horwitz (2008) who explored homophily and planetary-scale message traffic in Microsoft™ Instant Messenger, respectively. Gruhl *et al.* (2004) observed similar temporal message patterns. In addition, Leskovec & Horwitz have shown that there is a dependency of communication patterns on geographical proximity of the correspondents at the session-level (rather than message-level): longer distances yield fewer and shorter conversations.

Navigability in complex networks —i.e., efficient mechanisms for finding intended communication targets—was modeled by Boguña *et al.* (2008). The authors proposed a concept of a hidden metric space underlying a complex network, with its own coordinates and distances that serve as guidelines for making routing decisions. At the observable level, navigability translates into scale-free node degree distributions and strong clustering, both properties being common in social networks—which are, thus, navigable.

Kossinets *et al.* (2008), based on the work of Gibson (2005), noticed that the members of a social network do not continuously participate in communications with their neighbors. Information only spreads as a result of discrete communication events and the frequencies of these events make strong influence on the preferred communication pathways. These pathways form a communication backbone that dynamically changes to reflect the momentary fluctuations of the event frequencies.

Wilson *et al.* (2009) further elaborated the concept of the communication backbone by correlating social and interaction degrees of network members and discovering that they do not scale uniformly.

Viswanath *et al.* (2009) traced the mechanisms that trigger communications in online social networks and discovered that 54% of the interactions are attributed to site mechanisms (such as birthday reminders) and that most links in a communication backbone rapidly die out.

Chwe (2000), Pastor-Satorras & Vespignani (2001), and Kitsak *et al.* (2010) studied dissemination protocols and information origins. Chwe (2000) and Kitsak *et al.* (2010) applied gossiping protocols described by Kermack & McKendrick (1927) and Bailey (1975) and widely used by mathematicians and computer system theoreticians, to social network systems. They emphasized the role of cliques as the "containers" of community knowledge and singled out the role of "insurgent network members" as influential spreaders.

For some special cases of social networks—e.g., one-shot networks commonly found in online commerce, —it is possible to apply mathematical game theory to decide whether or not the next round of communications between any two network members takes place. Emanuelson & Willer (2009) argue that the interactions in one-shot networks differ from "continuous" networks, where the connections between members are relatively stable. Zinoviev & Duong (2010) and Zinoviev *et al.* (2010) also used mathematical game theory to study information flow along a communication link, based on the psychological traits of the participants.

Security and secrecy in social networks recently became an important research topic. Albert *et al.* (2000) demonstrated that scale-free networks are robust to random node-level attacks. Farley (2003), Enders & Su (2007), and other authors studied security and secrecy in small al-Kaeda-style social networks. However, the first attempt to find quantitative connections between informational performance and secrecy in arbitrary networks through their topology was made by Lindelauf *et al.* (2009).

The purpose of this chapter is to give an overview of information and innovation diffusion in social networks. (I will use the words "information" and "innovation" interchangeably, unless different mechanisms are involved in the dissemination of information and innovations).

The rest of the chapter is organized as follows. I will start by defining several taxonomies of informational messages, followed by the introduction to social network topology (strong and weak links) and homophily analysis in social networks. Then, I will discuss the mechanisms of information adoption by network members. I will continue by exploring the sources of dissemination. Next, message dynamics will be added to the static model. The origin of diffusion patterns will be related to the navigability of the networks. I will conclude by describing theoretical and actual information pathways and influence of secrecy on diffusion.

## DIFFUSION: SOURCES, PATHS, AND MECHANISMS

Gruhl (2004) reminds that until recently, the cost of technical infrastructure required to reach a large number of people was the major barrier for someone who wanted to spread information, innovation or influence through a community. Today, with the proliferation of Internet-based massive online social networks (MOSNs), this technical bottleneck has been largely removed. As more and more individuals join MOSNs and become

information sources, the problem of understanding diffusion of information or innovations through population is attracting a lot of researchers and practitioners' attention.

The problem has been studied in a number of communities, ranging from thermodynamics to epidemiology to marketing. Yet, up to date there is no single, mutually agreed upon understanding of the mechanisms involved in and controlling the diffusion processes. For the rest of this section, I will summarize the current state of the diffusion theory.

## Message Taxonomies

I will start by elaborating on the nature and content of the objects of communications—disseminated messages. I will purposefully avoid the discussion of the message content, only mentioning that the content, in general, is subject to distortions along the proliferation paths, as shown by Harary *et al.* (1965).

Messages as information/innovation containers can be categorized, based on their content type, physical representation, and intended audience.

The content type describes messages from the sender's/recipient's perceptional point of view. The classification discriminates audio/voice messages (face-to-face voice conversations and phone calls), text messages (letters, telegrams, Internet instant messages, text chats), still images (drawings, postcards), motion images (television, videoconferencing, sign language communications), and even tactile messages (handshakes). Different content types can be mixed to form multipart messages (e.g., a letter with a photograph or a voice chat with gestures). Since the content type *per se* does not influence dissemination mechanisms, I present this taxonomy only for the sake of completeness.

Based on the physical phenomena involved in the content distribution, messages can be subdivided into acoustical (face-to-face voice communications, public speeches), optical (face-to-face visual communications, gestures, mechanical telegraph), mechanical (letters), and electronic (telephone, electric telegraph, radio, TV, and computer-based communications). Note that seemingly acoustical telephone conversations and seemingly optical TV programs are carried over wires in the form of electrical signals and, as such, belong to the electronic group.

Because of spacial attenuation, messages that are represented acoustically or optically have a limited diffusion range (on the order of 1 km). They are suitable only for local communications. Yet, until the end of the XIXth century they dominated the informational landscape in social networks.

Finally, disseminated messages can be intended for individuals (private/personal messages), limited groups of individuals (newsletters, conference calls) or unlimited groups (public messages: broadcasts, newspapers, public speeches).

Online social networks offer a wide variety of electronic communication mechanisms, supported both directly and through social networking Web sites. Direct communications include electronic mail (with or without multimedia attachments; addressed to a single recipient or to a mailing list) and instant messages (Skype, Google Talk, AOL™ and Microsoft™ instant messengers). Indirect communications use built-in social network messaging mechanisms (private messages) and community- and world-addressed posts. Some social networking sites allow network members control the intended audience of their groupcast posts (e.g., "friends-only", "friends and friends-of-friends", "friends and networks", and "everyone" in Facebook or "selected friends", "all friends", "community", and "everyone" in LiveJournal). Groupcast and especially broadcast messages improve the dissemination speed—provided that the intended recipients do not ignore them.

An interesting class of messages that seem to exist solely in massive online social networks is pokes, also known as contentless messages, or pings. Pokes were first studied by Kaye *et al.* (2005) with respect to a Virtual Intimate Object

computer application that allowed two people to stay literally in touch online by clicking a button on the computer desktop toolbar. Pressing the button causes a similar button at the remote computer to blink or change color, thus letting the other individual know that he or she is being thought of. Despite a common belief, expressed, e.g., by Golder *et al.* (2007), a poke does not always carry one bit of information. The amount of information in a poke is $M=1-\log_2(1-L)$, where $L$ is the loss rate of the end-to-end communication channel between the involved computers—that is, the fraction of all sent messages that have not been received. Consequently, $M=1$ bit only if the connection is lossless ($L=0$).

For the material presented in this chapter, the most important properties of all messages mentioned above are their propagation speed and whether or not they can be used for groupcast. For the rest of the chapter I assume that messages propagate virtually instantly and exclusively from the sender to the recipient, unless stated otherwise.

## Strong and Weak Links

Knoke & Yang (2008) define a social network as a "structure composed of a set of actors, some of whose members are connected by a set of one or more relations." Wikipedia (2010) further clarifies that the actors can be "individuals (or organizations) called nodes," and that they are "tied (connected) by one or more specific types of interdependency, such as friendship, kinship, common interest, financial exchange, dislike, sexual relationship or relationships of beliefs, knowledge or prestige." The social connections in a network serve dual purpose: they indicate the level of proximity between the nodes and provide communication channels.

Social networks are the field of study of social network analysis, which, according to Wikipedia (2010), "emerged as a key technique in modern sociology. It has also gained a significant following in anthropology, biology, communication studies, economics, geography, information science, organizational studies, social psychology, and sociolinguistics, and has become a popular topic of speculation and study."

An analysis of a social network begins with the construction of its formal graph G(V,E). The graph G consists of vertices V (nodes) and edges E (links or ties). A node in a social graph represents a member (an individual or an organization) and a link represent a relationship or interdependency between any two members (see Figure 1).

Granovetter (1973) proposed a classification of links, based on the strength of the represented relationships. The classification includes weak ties ("acquaintanceship"), strong ties ("friendship"), and bridges, where a bridge is a link in a network that provides the only direct path between some two nodes (link **i** in Figure 1 is a bridge). The strength of a link is determined by a multitude of factors, such as persistence, reciprocity, frequency and duration of communications, and duration of existence. Strong ties in massive online social networks indicate the presence of a strong off-line relationship between the peers, while weak ties do not necessarily correspond to any off-line relationships at all.

It has been suggested by Granovetter (1973) that if two nodes (say, 1 and 2 in Figure 1) are strongly linked to another node (3), then with very high probability they are also strongly linked together: "a friend of my friend is my friend." This mechanism is called a triadic closure. Moreover: the stronger is the tie between two network members, the greater is the extent of the overlap of their friendship circles, and the greater is the probability of the closure. Note that triadic closure does not work for weak ties ("an acquaintance of my acquaintance is not necessarily my acquaintance").

Because of the triadic closure, a group of nodes that have some strong ties tends to progressively form more and more strong ties and eventually becomes a fully and strongly tied clique (groups A and B in Figure 1).

*Figure 1. A small social network consisting of 20 nodes, 25 strong ties, 4 weak ties, and two cliques (A and B)*

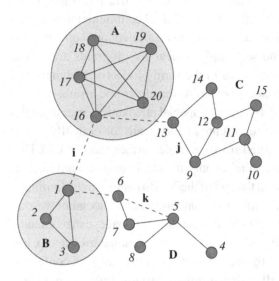

In a clique, everyone is everyone's "friend": every *ego* has only one circle of *alteri* who belong to the same clique. As shown by Lewis (1969), this dense social proximity makes a clique a perfect common knowledge pool: frequent communications between clique members ensure that the clique rapidly knows a new fact. If the fact is forgotten or distorted by a clique member, it can be rapidly and robustly recovered.

The limitation of strong ties is their short diffusion range: unless the whole social network is one single clique, there inevitably will be regions not affected by the dissemination. The relative number of cliques in a network is characterized by the clustering coefficient C—the average number of triadic closures in the immediate neighborhood of an *ego* node that do not include the *ego* node itself. C is a number in the range from 0 to 1: C equals 1 for a network that forms a single clique and C equals 0 for a tree (a network with no chords). For most real social networks, C is less than 0.5, which means that more than one clique forms these networks and the strong ties do not act as efficient conduits.

Weak ties that bridge the "gaps" between the cliques are essential for information dissemination in real social networks. The weak ties create more and shorter paths between the knowledge pools and let the information diffuse. The weak ties empower network members adjacent to them: individuals with many weak ties are best placed to diffuse information. This in turn improves the social status of these individuals.

To summarize, there is a division of labor in a social network (Figure 2): the strong ties are responsible for clique formation, which in turn serve as common knowledge pools, as well as credibility and influence sources ("brains"); the weak ties act as information and innovation conduits ("nerves").

## Homophily Improves Diffusion

Homophily is the tendency of individuals to associate and bond with similar others. The structure of dissemination pathways in social networks strongly depends on the homophily among users: people have more conversations and converse for longer duration with people who are similar to themselves. If there is a link in a social network graph representing a connection between two individuals, there is a strong reason to believe that the individuals have something in common. Additionally, the more treats they have in common, the stronger is the tie between them.

Homophily in modern massive online social networks has been studied by Golder *et al.* (2007) and Leskovec & Horvitz (2008).

Instead of observing individual messages, which can be random and often triggered by social networking site mechanisms (such as birthday reminders, which reportedly initiate more than half of all interactions), one can group consequent and reciprocal messages into sessions (conversations). A conversation is a better indication of homophily: the session's duration (either in the number of messages or in the ordinal time) can be used as a quantitative measure of homophily.

*Figure 2. Strong ties and cliques as "brains" and weak ties as "nerves"*

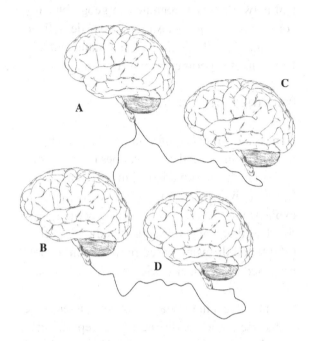

The strongest homophily among the users of major online social networks exists for the language used, school co-attendance (on Facebook), followed by the parties' geographic locations, and then age (but not gender: people tend to converse more frequently and with longer durations with the opposite sex).

From the age perspective, younger individuals (in the age group from 14 to 35 years old) mainly communicate with the individuals of approximately the same age (as a side note, they also talk faster, while the older network members talk for longer times and send more messages per session).

The homophily based on geographical locations (or, rather, on the geographical distance between the locations of the connected individuals) follows the reciprocal law: the number of conversations decreases with distance $d$ as roughly $1/d$. Conversation duration also decreases with distance; however, the number of exchanged messages remains constant before decreasing slowly.

Combined, these observations imply that the majority of traffic in modern massive online social networks is concentrated in geographically compact areas—probably in the strong tie-defined communities (although the latter statement still lacks direct experimental confirmation).

## Information Adoption

A message with new information received by an individual in a social network does not necessarily lead to this information's immediate adoption by the individual. At least two classes of models explain the adoption mechanisms: staged propagation based on collective action studied by Chwe (2000) and diffusion based on infection models proposed by Kermack & McKendrick (1927) and other authors.

Individuals in the staged models disseminate and sense others' willingness to accept the new knowledge. Their motto is "I'll go [for something] if you go [for it]." If a critical mass of adopters is formed, they together accept the knowledge (and possibly become new information sources). Otherwise, the new knowledge is collectively rejected.

To form the critical mass, it is important for the individuals to have sufficient information about the intention of other network members: do they plan to "rebel" and accept the new knowledge or to "withdraw"? A member can collect this information only by exchanging messages with the immediate neighbors. Note that the neighbors are in a similar position: before they "rebel" or "withdraw," they better learn the intentions of their neighbors, too (or use their intuition, which can be modeled using mathematical game theory but is beyond the scope of this chapter). This recursive problem has at least one good solution: a clique that has been already mentioned above.

Indeed, in a clique all members have immediate direct access to all other members and are in the best position to learn their intentions—thus forming a common metaknowledge about whether or not to accept the new knowledge.

*Figure 3. Staged information dissemination in a social network. Arrows show dissemination along weak ties. Dashed lines show the frontiers of the new knowledge at times T0, T1, and T2 (T0<T1<T2)*

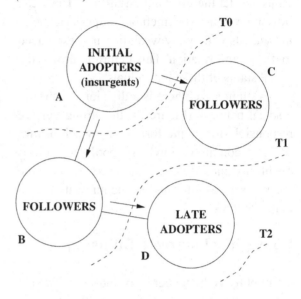

The common (meta) knowledge is a result of a gradual and heterogeneous process. It starts, according to Chwe (2000), from initial adopters: "maverick" social network members who lock in the intention to accept the new knowledge. These initial adopters, or "insurgents," are not special, dedicated network members: they simply assume this role for this particular dissemination process, even though the same individuals may be psychologically predisposed to initiate knowledge dissemination over and over again. The initial adopters typically form a clique of their own—a "leading clique."

The information "flows along" the weak ties from the leading clique through a chain of cliques: from the initial adopters to the followers and then from the followers to the late adopters (Figure 3). The staged model shows that weak ties are more important for information dissemination, and strong ties—for trust, knowledge, and collective action building.

The staged model gives some insight about the dynamics of information dissemination. However, it fails to account for social network members' forgetfulness: according to Chwe (2000), once a community or an individual learns a fact, it is never forgotten and cannot be relearned. The infectious diffusion models partially reviewed by Kitsak *et al.* (2010) take care of these phenomena.

There are two basic groups of infectious (or gossiping) models dating back to Kermack & McKendrick (1927): Susceptible-Infectious-Recovered (SIR) and Susceptible-Infectious-Susceptible (SIS). The models use epidemiological terminology and metaphors to describe information dissemination.

In the SIR model, each network node can be in one of the following states: Susceptible (S), Infected (I) or Recovered (R). Initially, all nodes are susceptible—the corresponding individuals do not know the fact that is being disseminated, and therefore can become "infected" by learning it. (Note that, unlike in epidemiology, there are no nodes immune to information in either SIR or SIS models. This is a constraint that can be easily removed by adding another state—Immune.) At each time step, the infectious nodes try to infect the susceptible nodes in their network neighborhood (pass new information to them) with probability $\beta$ and then enter the Recovered state. Recovering means becoming immune *post factum*. The recovered nodes do not remain infectious (they cannot further disseminate the information).

In a SIS model, an infected node at each time step either remains infectious with the probability of $(1-\lambda)$ or becomes susceptible again with the probability of $\lambda$. The latter situation corresponds to forgetting information: after an implicit recovery, a susceptible node can be "infected" with the same information again.

Boguñá *et al.* (2003) proved that SIS models have an essential weakness: they have a zero epidemic threshold. This means that a fact injected in a network described using a SIS model eventually becomes known to everyone, which in general is false in real social networks.

Neither infectious nor staged models fully and accurately describe information adoption process in social networks. A new model that is free of their limitations remains to be proposed.

## Locating Influential Spreaders

Efficient dissemination in social networks is not possible in the absence of influential spreaders (that is, the "insurgents" or the "early adopters" of the new knowledge) in strategical positions around the network. For example, the node 4 in Figure 1 hardly can be an influential spreader: all messages from 4 have to be received and then retransmitted to the neighbors by the node 5; if the individual represented by the node 5 is unresponsive, busy or simply in a bad mood, then the dissemination will stop before it even starts.

A question arises: how can we tell that the node 4 is a bad spreader and can we identify true influential spreaders? (Preferably simply by looking at the social network graph.)

Chwe (2000) observed that the influential spreaders at least should not be too closely connected and should be optimally dispersed: if the spreaders are dispersed too finely, they may be "atomized"; if they are not dispersed enough, they are "ghettoized."

As we have already seen, communication along long paths is infeasible, because information can be distorted and there is a growing probability of a message being discarded by an "immune"— non-cooperating—node. A spreader node acts as a lantern: it casts an "informational light cone" on its network neighborhood; if the cones cast by different spreaders do not intersect, no global dissemination is possible. This limitation leads to the "atomization." The cause of the "ghettoization" is similar: if two spreaders are packed together, their "light cones" overlap almost entirely, leaving the rest of the network "unlit."

In other words, a node at the periphery alone has minimal effect, and so do densely packed or loosely dispersed nodes.

To quantify the relative importance of an individual in a social network, the concept of centrality has been proposed (see Knoke & Yang (2008)). The centrality is a number (typically from 0 to 1) that shows to what extent the *ego* node representing an individual is "central" (in some sense). Different types of centrality are in use: degree centrality (the number of *ego*'s neighbors), closeness centrality (the mean distance from the *ego* node to all other nodes in the network), betweenness centrality (the fraction of all shortest paths in the network passing through the *ego* node), etc. All flavors of centrality can be formally calculated from the network graph (although the computation may be very expensive, depending on the network size).

According to Freeman (1979) and other researchers, it is the high centrality that makes a node an efficient spreader. Indeed, high degree centrality means that an individual has many neighbors and can make information available at once to his or her entire inner circle of friends. High closeness centrality implies that the paths from the individual to the rest of the network are short, making the dissemination process less subject to distortions and attenuation. Finally, high betweenness is believed to determine who has more "interpersonal influence" on others.

However, Kitzak *et al.* (2010) suggest that the centrality criteria of the efficiency are valid only to some extent, and propose another quantitative approach to the problem of identifying influential spreaders, based on k-cores.

A k-core (or a k-shell) of a network is a set of vertices K, where each vertex in K has at least *k* links to other vertices in K (Figure 4 shows 1-shell, 2-shell, 3-shell, and 4-shell of the same network). The number *k* is called the index of the core. The size of a k-core drastically diminishes for larger values of *k*.

Kitzak *et al.* (2010) show that neither degree nor betweenness centrality play an important role

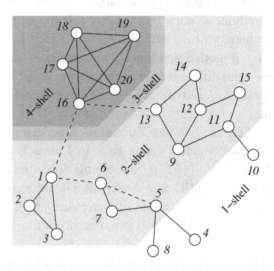

*Figure 4. 1-shell, 2-shell, 3-shell, and 4-shell in a social network. The entire network is a 1-shell. The 3-shell and the 4-shell coincide*

in predicting the efficiency of a node as a spreader. In the case of a single spreader, the size of the "infected" population is affected mainly by $k_S$—the index of the smallest core that still contains the spreading node. The nodes with the largest value of $k_S$ will probably be the best spreader. Whether $k_S$ is correlated with the closeness centrality, is unknown as yet.

The situation changes if there is more than one spreader, all spreaders disseminating the same information in a correlated (synchronous) way. In this case, a better spreading strategy is to choose either the nodes with the highest degree—or the nodes with the highest shell index $k_S$ with the requirement that no two of them are directly linked to each other (to avoid "ghettoization").

There is an interesting connection between the SIS gossiping models described above and the k-shells: if there is a self-reproducing "virus" in a SIS social network (such as a rumor, an urban myth or a horror story), then, according to Kitzak *et al.* (2010), it persists mainly in high-index cores. A practical consequence of this observation is that in order to suppress the circulation of unwanted information, one has to pay special attention to the inner k-shells of the network.

## Message Dynamics

The models that represent a social network as a graph assume that all nodes and all links are equal: in particular, the communication channels represented by the links have the same (or similar) properties and only the topological properties of the graph as a whole (e.g., centrality measures and geodesic path length) matter. However: at the very least we know that the links can be strong and weak, and this difference, while essential from the dissemination point of view, is not usually reflected in a network graph.

At a close view, a link between two hypothetical network members, Alice and Bob, is a complex object that has some properties of its own (physical implementation, transmission speed or delay, maximum message capacity, reliability or message loss rate, data distortion rate, etc.) and implicitly shares some properties of Alice and Bob. We have seen that either member can be in one of the information acceptance modes, depending on the spreading model (e.g., Bob may be "recovered" from the fact **F**—that is, not accepting any new messages related to **F**; in this case, the link connecting Alice and Bob carries information only selectively: everything but **F**).

A more important property of links in real social networks is that they are not continuous. Kossinets *et al.* (2008) remind that information only spreads "as a result of discrete communication events—such as e-mail or text messages, conversations, meetings or phone calls—that are distributed non-uniformly over time." The non-uniform distribution of messages makes dissemination virtually unpredictable: one simply cannot tell ahead of time when a particular link will be used for communication and even if it will be used at all.

There is an interesting corollary from the non-uniformity of message distribution: If a link is heavily used for communications, then it is likely a strong tie. Therefore, it is unlikely to be on an active information dissemination pathway. The converse is true about a lightly used (weak) link. In other words, more [messages] is less [information], and the other way around.

Gruhl *et al.* (2004) and Golder *et al.* (2007) studied message dynamics in aggregated Internet blogs and Facebook—the largest to date massive online social network. They found out that messaging in MOSNs, though subject to non-uniform patterns, is not totally random. It exhibits temporal rhythms that are robust and consistent—at least across university campuses used for analysis and across seasons. Thousands of individual choices made by the network members collectively look as if having been choreographed by an invisible director. Interestingly, not only "classical" messages with text and possibly multimedia attachments behave synchronously, but also the contentless messages—pokes—follow the same temporal patterns.

The message frequencies (and volumes) in a MOSN follow three major cycles: the daily cycle, the weekly cycle, and the yearly (seasonal) cycle. This is not nearly surprising, since messaging and poking activities are proxies for online social activity, and if network members live similar lifestyles (as would high school and college students on Facebook in 2007), their communication patterns are similar, too.

The daily social network cycle has a minimum at 3–8AM, followed by a steep raise by noon and a flat "plateau" between noon and midnight. (Compare this to the daily messaging cycle in a corporate e-mail network—not a social network!—that has two maximums at 11AM and 5PM and a flat minimum from 7PM to 7AM). Both the social network and the corporate network demonstrated high members' activity during the first few days of the week and the minimum at the weekend. Finally, the individuals in both types of networks were much more active in June–August and December–January than in the remaining seasons.

In addition to the periodic fluctuations, the message frequencies are subject to temporal exponential attenuation: due to social fatigue, the activity level of user pairs tends to decrease markedly over time (for example, up to 70% active connections in Facebook die over the course of one month). Only a small fraction of links matures and persists for a substantial time.

An extreme case of periodic message frequency fluctuations is messaging in relatively poorly studied one-shot networks. In one-shot networks, exchanges occur once between individuals who do not anticipate exchanging again in the future. Examples of one-shot networks are Ebay™ (2010)—an online auction Web site—and other Web-based marketplaces. It is not known in the one-shot networks whether two individuals will be connected in the future and if so, then when. Likewise, the presence of a link between two nodes in a one-shot network graph does not mean much: it indicates that there was an interaction between the nodes in the past, but it is not clear if the nodes will ever interact in the future again.

Studying one-shot networks involves using mathematical game theory that quantifies individuals' intentions and expected benefits from communications and tries to predict if an interaction between two network members is possible in the future (but it won't say, when). It has been proposed by Emanuelson (2009) that one-shot and iterated exchange structures differ, and the diffusion structures differ as well. However, as of now there is no systematic theory that explains diffusion in one-shot networks.

To summarize, the relative unpredictability of communication frequencies leads to the unpredictability of the member-to-member message delay. With the median geodesic path length in a typical social network being close to six links (the "six degrees of separation" phenomenon), the median communication latency between node pairs can be as high as eight days. This latency slows down information diffusion and strongly affects the configuration of the preferred communication channels.

## Navigability

From the practical point of view, one of the most important problems associated with dissemination in social networks is message routing: How does one calculate the most efficient pathway (route) from the message source to an arbitrary destination or to all network destinations at once? In many real networks, introducing either a hierarchical addressing scheme or a metric coordinate system has solved the problem.

The Internet uses hierarchical addressing. A four-byte (Internet Protocol version 4) or 16-byte (Internet Protocol version 6) IP address is a unique identifier assigned to a networking object; it is a combination of the network address and the host address of the object. A host is usually an individual computer and a "network" is a collection of hosts directly connected to one another. In the social network terminology, a host is a node representing an individual and a network is something like a clique. Navigation (routing) happens by first locating the destination network (using so-called routing tables) and then contacting the host in that network.

Social networking sites like Facebook and Twitter indeed assign numerical identifiers to network nodes. However, these identifiers are simply random numbers. They are related neither to the positions of nodes in the network nor to their demographics and cannot be used for navigation.

A metric coordinate system associates in a systematic way a collection of coordinates with every node in the network. Well-known optimization techniques (such as gradient descent) can be used then to find the shortest path through the network from the source to the destination. An example of an efficiently implemented metric space in a network is Manhattan-style street and avenue naming scheme.

The hypothetical metric coordinate system would be a part of the hidden metric space—a metric space not visible to the majority of the network members and even to external observers but essential for making routing decisions. That such hidden metric space may exist, implicitly follows from the famous Milgram's (1967) small world experiment, where random people were asked to mail a postcard to an unknown addressee by first forwarding it to one of their immediate friends or acquaintances. Evidently, the participants used some guidance (which we can call either intuition or the sense of the hidden metric space) to decide, which of their immediate social network peers is the most suitable next destination.

A hidden metric space is expected to have at least one property: the smaller is the distance between any two nodes in the hidden space, the more likely they are connected in the observable (real) topology of the social network graph. The likelihood of two nodes being connected depends on the similarities between the nodes, which in turn depend on the demographics and other intrinsic psychological characteristics of the nodes.

Currently, there is no systematic way of constructing a hidden metric space for an arbitrary massive online social network. What we know from the work by Boguña *et al.* (2007) is that good navigability in general depends on the crisp scale-free (power-law) node degree distribution and high clustering. If the distance between two arbitrary nodes is defined as $(kk')^\alpha$, where $k$ and $k'$ are the degrees of both nodes and $\alpha$ is the clustering coefficient, then a zoom-out/zoom-in (ZOZI) routing scheme can be used: a message is first sent from the source node A to some high-degree node (a "hub") in the immediate neighborhood of A, then from this "hub" to another "hub" in the neighborhood of the destination node B, and from there down to B. For the ZOZI principle to work, the network must have sufficiently many "hubs," which is typically not the case in real MOSNs.

## Actual Information Pathways

In general, the links in a social network graph are not valid indicators of real user interaction. They are often displayed publicly to reflect status and identity of the network members represented by the adjacent nodes. They do not necessarily show the level of mutual trust, shared interests or anything shared at all—even information (for example, Wilson (2009) writes that only 50% of Facebook links have been ever used for interaction).

As such, the network graph links can be used for information dissemination prediction only with caution. A better alternative to the network graph is an interaction graph (also known as an activity network). It is a graph G'(V,E') that consists of the same vertices V as the original network graph, and edges E'. A social link between two nodes A and B exists in G' if and only if the users represented by the nodes have interacted directly through communication or an application. (It is not required for the corresponding link between A and B to exist in the original network graph.) Some researchers propose that only the most recent interactions are considered for the construction of the interaction graph—a graph that reflects the actual interactions between the individuals. Its links are actual communication channels (as opposed to the links in the network graph that are potential channels, whose potential may not be realized).

Since many links in a real network graph are lightly or never used, the corresponding interaction graph typically has fewer links. This means that the interaction degree $D_I$—the number of interaction links per node—is typically lower than the social degree $D_S$ of the same node. Wilson (2009) graphically presents an experimental dependency between the two degrees, from which it follows that $D_I \sim D_S^\pi$, where $\pi \ll 1$. In addition, the interaction graph exhibits more precise power-law scaling, has longer path lengths, fewer "supernodes" ("hubs"), and lower clustering. The latter two properties suppress efficient navigability in particular and dissemination in general.

Kossinets (2008) demonstrates that the structure of the interaction graph is not random: the graph is a self-sustained structure that both is built around high-efficiency links in the original network graph and contributes to the high efficiency of the links.

Consider the network in Figure 1 again. If the nodes 5 and 6 are not communicating actively and the nodes 6/7 and 5/7 are active pairwise, then the link between the two nodes is relatively inefficient: it takes more time for 5 to learn the news directly from 6 than indirectly from 6 through from 7 (who in turn would learn it from 6). The information pathways in real social networks with unideal links are not always direct. Furthermore, a message that takes a direct path may be out-of-date. This phenomenon violates the triangle inequality and the structure of communication in real social networks is dominated by such violations.

To distinguish the interaction graph that shows what interactions took place in the recent past from the actual and current message pathways, we call the latter "the network backbone." The social network backbone at time T is the subset of links in the interaction graph that are not bypassed by a faster alternative path—in other words, the links that are not in violation of the triangle inequality. The backbone represents a very sparse subgraph consisting both of highly embedded links and long-range bridges.

Because of the dynamic nature of message patterns in a social network, the backbone will not always be the same: some links may slow down, while other may accelerate; in a social network that spans across several time zones, this scenario is not just possible, but also very likely. The network backbone at time T+ΔT may look very different from the backbone at time T. Yet, surprisingly, each instantaneous backbone uses on average 75% links of the aggregate backbone—the union of all instantaneous backbones over some reasonable time.

Predicting the structure of the aggregate backbone in a MOSN is crucial for efficient dissemination. The locations of the influential spreaders rely on the network topology, but bringing the link dynamics into the picture may drastically change their influence: think of a "fat hub" that has thousands connections on the list and resides in the innermost k-shell—but the links are used only once a month!

## Secrecy

While it is true that most massive online social networks have not been designed with secrecy in mind, some real world social networks are extremely sensitive to it—terrorist and intelligence networks, to name a few. In the secrecy-aware networks, it is important to maintain a balance between information performance (dissemination speed and reach) and secrecy *per se*. To quantify secrecy, one can estimate link detection probability and node exposure probability (which in turn are monotonic functions of the number of links: more links mean higher detection and exposure probabilities). Unfortunately, fewer links means fewer dissemination pathways, which hurts the information performance. The secrecy problem may have an optimal solution that improves secrecy but maintains reasonable performance and the other way around, but in general it this solution is not perfect.

Implications of secrecy on diffusion in social networks is a relatively new research topic, brought to life by the events of 9/11 in the USA. Enders & Su (2007) studied the relationship between network density (defined as the the proportion of ties in a network relative to the total number possible) and communication efficiency and concluded that denser networks provide for better communications but are easier to infiltrate. Lindenlauf *et al.* (2009) developed a more elaborate model by applying mathematical game theory to find a strong dependency of the optimal solution on the

*Figure 5. Optimal structures of covert networks: (A) star graph, (B) complete graph, and (C) reinforced ring*

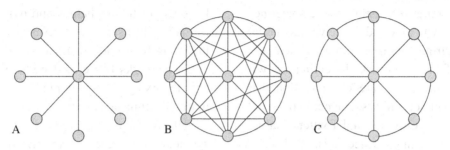

network topology (however, without looking into the link dynamics).

According to Lindenlauf *et al.* (2009), an important decisive factor in the "security vs efficiency" trade-off is the stage of the covert operation executed by the network. In the initial stage of a covert operation, when the network hierarchy has not been cast in stone yet, the optimal communication structure corresponds to either a star graph (a network with one central "fat hub") or a complete graph (an all-to-all network), depending on the link detection probability: a star for a less secure network and a complete network for a more secure network. In the intermediate stage of the operation, the optimal communication structure corresponds to a reinforced ring (a "wheel" with the "fat hub," radial links, and chord links; Figure 5). Additional studies in this direction are needed.

## FUTURE RESEARCH DIRECTIONS

Despite having been researched for almost a half of a century, social networks still present numerous academic and practical challenges, some of which are partially due to the enormous computational resources required to process social graphs of typical real-life MOSNs.

Surprisingly, two "future research" directions have been set forth by Granovetter (1973) himself and have not been exhaustively or even sufficiently studied.

One of them is the study of information transition velocity, measured in ordinal time. In particular, the following questions still lack proper answers: How fast the information spread in a social network, depending on the physical properties of the network? Does the transmission velocity differ at the beginning and at the end of the diffusion process? How does the velocity depend on the time of day, day of the week, season, etc.? (I am not referring to the temporal activity patterns studied by Golder *et al*. (2007).) Do information and innovation propagate at the same speed or not?

The second possible direction of research is the study of information distortion. As messages diffuse through a social network, they are subject to multiple forms of distortion, both unintentional (noises, typographical errors, misinterpretation, and forgetfulness) and intentional (partial or full disinformation). The distortions make communications along long paths infeasible, as mentioned by Harary *et al*. (1965). If the nature, character, and speed of these distortions are understood, it may become possible to construct distortion-prone messages and improve the overall quality of dissemination.

To improve navigability, it is very tempting to follow the approach proposed by Boguñá *et al.* (2007) and introduce a somewhat easily computable hidden metric space for social networks. In that metric space, every node will be associated with a unique combination of metric coordinates, which will be used to calculate directions of the most efficient information dissemination.

As the number of existing active social networks grows with time and the networks overlap further and further by sharing common members, the topic of cross-network dissemination will inevitably come to researchers' attention. Recently, many major online social networks (such as Facebook, LiveJournal, and Twitter) enabled cross-network posting—a mechanism that allows one message to be submitted to multiple networks. Since the neighbors of the submitting individuals in one network are likely (to some extent) to be his or her neighbors in other networks and the dissemination speed in different networks may differ, the cross posting may lead to interesting interference.

Another virtually unexplored area deals with one-shot networks. As I mentioned above, the one-shot networks that are based on one-shot exchanges, have been all but excluded from the social network analysis due to their unusual nature. It is still unclear to what extent diffusion structures differ in one-shot and "traditional" (repetitive) social networks.

Finally, more research is expected to take place in the area of human motivation behind dissemination. At the end of the day, information in social networks is "owned" by member individuals, and it is up to them whether to release it to their neighbors, their communities or the general audience. Several subjective factors controls the information release, such as trust in the peers, confidence in the information, lust for popularity, and thirst for enlightenment, all of which are hard to quantify and calculate. Building a credible numerical model describing these and other relevant parameters would allow researchers to better understand the driving forces of dissemination.

## CONCLUSION

I discussed the mechanics and dynamics of information diffusion processes in social networks, including both traditional (offline) and massive online networks. I described the "strength of weak ties" theory by Granovetter (1973), the organization of disseminated information, several diffusion models, role and strategic position of influential spreaders, message flow dynamics and pathways, and dissemination secrecy.

The issue of diffusion is of paramount importance both to academia and industry. Some practical industrial application of a diffusion theory would be efficiently targeted advertising, fast and up-to-date news delivery, rumor control, tracking infectious diseases, and counter-terrorism operations. Researchers in the "Ivory Tower" of academia, on the other hand, are in the anticipation of the intellectual feast that a comprehensive diffusion theory would offer.

However, while the topic has been studied for almost half a century by researchers from such diverse fields as social sciences, marketing, epidemiology, and physics, I have to conclude that there is no single coherent theory so far that would explain every aspect of information, innovation, and influence diffusion in social networks. The two major obstacles to its creation seem to be an unpredictable and hardly quantifiable nature of the individuals involved in the diffusion process, and the mind-blowing magnitudes of the modern social networks that require enormous computational resources for processing and model verification and testing.

Yet, as the field of social network studies (which naturally includes diffusion studies) is becoming more and more popular among researchers in social sciences, natural sciences, computing sciences, and mathematics, I optimistically expect that a comprehensive theory of diffusion in social networks will be developed in the nearest future—perhaps even earlier than the Great Unification Theory in physics.

## REFERENCES

Albert, R., Jeong, H., & Barabasi, A.-L. (2000). Error and attack tolerance of complex networks. *Nature, 406*(378).

Boguña, M., Krioukov, D., & Claffy, K. C. (2007). Navigability of complex networks. *Nature Physics, 5*(1).

Boguña, M., Pastor-Satorras, R., & Vespignani, A. (2003). Absence of epidemic threshold in scale-free networks with connectivity correlations. *Physical Review Letters, 90*(02), 8701–8704. doi:10.1103/PhysRevLett.90.028701

Chwe, M. S.-Y. (2000). Communication and coordination in social networks. *The Review of Economic Studies, 67*, 1–16. doi:10.1111/1467-937X.00118

Davis, J. (1969). Social structures and cognitive structures. In Abelson, R. (Ed.), *Theories of cognitive consistency*. Chicago, IL: Rand McNally.

eBay. (2010). *Online auction website*. Retrieved September 15, 2010, from http://ebay.com

Emanuelson, P., & Willer, D. (2009). One-shot exchange networks and the shadow of the future. *Social Networks, 31*(2), 147–154. doi:10.1016/j.socnet.2009.02.001

Enders, W., & Su, X. (2007). Rational terrorists and optimal network structure. *The Journal of Conflict Resolution, 51*(1), 33–57. doi:10.1177/0022002706296155

Farley, J. (2003). Breaking Al-Qaeda cells: A mathematical analysis of counterterrorism (a guide for risk management and decision making). *Studies in Conflict and Terrorism, 26*, 399–411. doi:10.1080/10576100390242857

Freeman, L. (1979). Centrality in social networks: Conceptual clarification. *Social Networks, 1*, 215–239. doi:10.1016/0378-8733(78)90021-7

Gibson, D. (2005). Concurrency and commitment: Network scheduling and its consequences for diffusion. *The Journal of Mathematical Sociology, 29*(4), 295–325. doi:10.1080/00222500590957491

Golder, S., Wilkinson, D., & Huberman, B. (2007). Rhythms of social interaction: Messaging within a massive online network. In *Proc. 3rd International Conference on Communities and Technologies (CT2007)*, East Lansing, MI.

Granovetter, M. (1973). The strength of weak ties. *American Journal of Sociology, 78*(6), 1360–1380. doi:10.1086/225469

Granovetter, M. (1983). The strength of weak ties: A network theory revisited. *Sociological Theory, 1*, 201–233. doi:10.2307/202051

Gruhl, D., Liben-Nowell, D., Guha, R., & Tomkins, A. (2004). Information diffusion through blogosphere. In *Proc. 13th International World Wide Web Conference*.

Harary, F., Norman, R., & Cartwright, D. (1965). *Structural models*. New York, NY: Wiley.

Kaye, J., Levitt, M., Nevins, J., Golden, J., & Schmitt, V. (2005). Communication intimacy one bit at a time. In *CHI Extended Abstracts on Human Factors in Computing Systems*.

Kermack, W., & McKendrick, A. (1927). A contribution to the mathematical theory of epidemics. *Proceedings of the Royal Society of London. Series A, Containing Papers of a Mathematical and Physical Character, 115*, 700–721. doi:10.1098/rspa.1927.0118

Kitsak, M., Gallos, L., Havlin, S., Liljeros, F., Muchnik, L., Stanley, H., & Makse, H. (2010). Identifying influential spreaders in complex networks. *Nature Physics, 6*(888).

Knoke, D., & Yang, S. (2008). *Social network analysis*. Los Angeles, CA: Sage Publications.

Kossinets, G., Kleinberg, J., & Watts, D. (2008). The structure of information pathways in a social communication network. In *Proc. KDD'08* (pp. 24–27). Las Vegas, Nevada, USA.

Leskovec, J., & Horvitz, E. (2008). Planetary-scale views on a large instant-messaging network. In *Proc. 17th International Conference on World Wide Web* (pp. 915–924). New York.

Lewis, D. (1969). *Convention: A philosophical study.* Cambridge, MA: Harvard University Press.

Lindelauf, R., Borm, P., & Hamers, H. (2009). The influence of secrecy on the communication structure of covert networks. *Social Networks, 31*(2), 126–137. doi:10.1016/j.socnet.2008.12.003

Milgram, S. (1967). The small world problem. *Psychology Today, 1*(1), 60–67.

Pastor-Satorras, R., & Vespignani, A. (2001). Epidemic spreading in scale-free networks. *Physical Review Letters, 86*(14), 3200–3203. doi:10.1103/PhysRevLett.86.3200

Singla, P., & Richardson, M. (2008). Yes, there is a correlation from social networks to personal behavior on the Web. In *Proc. WWW'08*.

Spinuzzi, C. (2003). Knowledge circulation in a telecommunications company: A preliminary survey. In *Proc. the 21st Annual International Conference on Documentation* (pp. 178–183). New York.

Viswanath, B., Mislove, A., Cha, M., & Gummadi, K. (2009). On the evolution of user interaction in Facebook. In *Proc. 2nd ACM Workshop on Online Social Networks* (pp. 37–42). New York.

Wikipedia. (2010). *Social network.* Wikipedia, the Free Encyclopedia. Retrieved September 4, 2010, from http://en.wikipedia.org/wiki/Social_network

Wilson, C., Boe, B., Sala, A., Puttaswamy, K., & Zhao, B. (2009). User interactions in social networks and their implications. In *Proc. 4th ACM European Conference on Computer Systems* (pp. 205–218). New York.

Xiao, Z., Guo, L., & Tracey, J. (2007). Understanding instant messaging traffic characteristics. In *Proc. ICDCS'07*.

Zinoviev, D., & Duong, V. (2010). A game theoretical approach to modeling full-duplex information dissemination. In *Proc. SCMC'10* (pp. 358–363). Ottawa, Canada.

Zinoviev, D., Duong, V., & Zhang, H. (2010). A game theoretical approach to modeling information dissemination in social networks. In *Proc. IMCIC 2010, volume I* (pp. 407–412). Florida: IIIS.

## ADDITIONAL READING

Bailey, N. (1975). *The Mathematical Theory of Infectious Diseases and Its Applications* (2nd ed.). London: Griffin.

Brown, J., & Duguid, P. (2000). *The Social Life of Information.* Boston: Harvard Business School Press.

Hedetniemi, S., Hedetniemi, S., & Liestman, A. (1988). A survey of gossiping and broadcasting in communication networks. *Networks, 18*, 319–349. doi:10.1002/net.3230180406

Kempe, D., Kleinberg, J., & Tardos, E. (2003). Maximizing the spread of influence through a social network. In *Proc. KDD'03*.

Moore, A., & Newman, M. (2000). Epidemics and percolation in small-world networks. *Physical Review E: Statistical Physics, Plasmas, Fluids, and Related Interdisciplinary Topics, 61*, 5678–5682. doi:10.1103/PhysRevE.61.5678

Rogers, E. (1995). *Diffusion of Innovations* (4th ed.). New York: Free Press.

Schelling, T. (1978). *Micromotives and Macrobehavior*. New York: Norton.

Weimann, G. (1980). *Conversation Networks as Communication Networks*. PhD thesis, University of Haifa, Israel.

Young, H. (2002). The diffusion of innovation in social networks. *Santa Fe Institute working paper* 02-04-018.

## KEY TERMS AND DEFINITIONS

**Diffusion:** A theory that seeks to explain how, why, and at what rate information and innovations spread through social networks.

**Homophily:** The tendency of individuals to associate and bond with similar others.

**Information:** A collection of one or more facts, processed, organized, structured and presented in a given context.

**Innovation:** An idea, practice or object that is perceived as new by an individual or group of individuals.

**Message:** An object of communication, a vessel that provides information.

**Navigability:** Easiness of moving around in a search for a particular destination.

**Pathway:** A sequence of social network links that a message traverses while propagating through the network.

**Secrecy:** The practice of hiding information from certain individuals or groups, while sharing it with other individuals.

**Social Network:** A structure composed of a set of actors, some of whose members are connected by a set of one or more relations.

# Chapter 9
# Social Network, Information Flow and Decision-Making Efficiency:
## A Comparison of Humans and Animals

**Cédric Sueur**
*Free University of Brussels, Belgium & Kyoto University, Japan*

## ABSTRACT

*Every day, millions of humans make decisions about issues of interest for the group they represent. Equivalent processes have already been well described for animal societies. Many animal species live in groups and have to take collective decisions to synchronize their activities. However, group members not only have to take decisions satisfying the majority of individuals (i.e. decision accuracy) but also have a relatively short period to do so (i.e. decision speed). In decision-making, speed and accuracy are often opposed. The decision efficiency will vary according to the way individuals are inter-connected, namely according to the social network. However, the traditional approach used in management and decision sciences has been revealed to be insufficient to fully explain decision-making efficiency. This chapter addresses the question of how social network may enhance collective decision-making by increasing both the accuracy and the speed of decisions. Studies within different animal species are discussed. These studies include human beings, and combine field experiments, social network analysis, and modelling to illustrate how the study of animals may contribute to our understanding of decision-making in humans.*

DOI: 10.4018/978-1-61350-444-4.ch009

## INTRODUCTION

Humans take decisions several times per day. The general public elects a President, workers decide on the best project for their firm, family members choose which film they will watch on TV, friends decide where to go for dinner... The decision made by an individual varies according to the relationships he or she has with the surrounding people (such as in a hierarchy, family, or friendship) as well as the number of individuals involved in the decision-making. For instance, the head of a firm or the parents of a family may have a great influence on the decision-making. For a presidential election, people do not generally know the opinions of other citizens and decide individually which candidate they will vote for (Acemoglu and Robinson, 2006; van Vugt *et al.*, 2008). In firms, the information flow, distribution of decisions and experience of individuals will have an impact on decision efficiency, that is to say not only on its productivity but also on the well-being of its workers. The efficiency of a decision is often defined as the ratio between two parameters: the time taken to make the decision and the accuracy of the decision. Accuracy means the quality of the decision, or whether almost all the individuals in the group or the community will be entirely satisfied by the decision. On the other hand, a shorter time taken to make the decision will also enhance productivity within the firm.

Equivalent processes in animal societies have already been well described by several authors (Conradt and Roper, 2003, 2005; Franks *et al.*, 2003; Langridge *et al.*, 2004; Marshall *et al.*, 2006; Pratt and Sumpter, 2006). Many animal species live in groups and have to take collective decisions. Group living decreases the risk of predation (Wrangham, 1980) and increases foraging efficiency (Alexander, 1974). However, this strategy requires group members to remain cohesive and to synchronize their activities in order to avoid group fission (Conradt and Roper, 2005; Krause and Ruxton, 2002). In many species, the different

activities cannot be carried out in the same area. Animals often have a specific resting area: for example, a cliff in the case of some primates or birds (Danchin *et al.*, 1998; Kummer, 1968), a burrow for many social carnivores or rodents (Fox, 1972; Rasa, 1986), or a collective building for social insects (Camazine *et al.*, 2001). However, individuals have to move collectively to another spot in order to forage or drink (Boinski and Garber, 2000; Fischhoff *et al.*, 2007; Kummer, 1968). Individuals have to decide when and where they will move collectively. However, animal groups are often composed of individuals with different needs. Males often have a higher body weight than females and therefore need more energy. Lactating females need more water than their conspecifics. This individual heterogeneity will have an impact on the decision-making process. Group members must take decisions that satisfy the majority of individuals (i.e. decision accuracy) but in a relatively short period (i.e. decision speed). In decision-making, speed and accuracy are often opposed. A substantial amount of time may be required to make an accurate decision between alternatives, because weighing up information may be a long process. This compromise between speed and accuracy is very common and has been termed "the speed–accuracy trade-off paradigm" (Busemeyer and Townsend, 1993; Osman *et al.*, 2000; Nikolic and Gronlund, 2002). Nevertheless, empirical studies demonstrating the conflict between speed and accuracy in decision-making are mostly investigations in the field of human performance and psychology. In many cases, people can actively choose their own compromise between accuracy and speed (Osman *et al.*, 2000; Vitevitch, 2002).

A speed–accuracy trade-off is not a desirable feature of a decision-making process in itself. Commonly, only one of these two factors can be controlled, but not both of them. It would, of course, be preferable to be able to make highly accurate decisions in the minimum time possible, but the individual or the group environment could fix one of these two parameters. In this case, the problem can be understood as exhibiting a Pareto-front: a region in the performance space in which the performance according to one parameter (speed or accuracy) cannot be improved without a decrease in the performance of the other parameter (accuracy or speed) (Figure 1).

This Pareto-front depends on environmental and individual/group conditions at any given moment. Nevertheless, there are several factors that may change this Pareto-front positively, that is, that may increase the accuracy and the speed of the decision. Several factors can affect this trade-off between speed and accuracy. Better information can enhance the efficiency of the decision. This may be measured as a quantity (number of individuals having information about a foraging site or a nest site, for instance) or as a quality (the right information about a good quality foraging site). However, the decision efficiency also depends on how the information will be transmitted between group members. This information flow will vary according to the way individuals are connected, that is to say, according to the social network. For instance, information has a greater probability to be transmitted between two individuals if both individuals spend more time together. The more spatially or socially distant individuals are, the more probable it becomes that the information will either not be transmitted at all, or will be distorted. Globally, that is at a group level, specific connections between group members may increase the decision speed. Here, I will develop how information quality and social network may enhance collective decision-making by increasing both the accuracy and the speed of the decision. Increasing numbers of studies show that decision-making processes are similar between different animal species. However, few studies directly compare humans with animals in the way that they decide. I will try to explain in this chapter how this comparison between human beings and animals might help in the understanding of decision efficiency and thus might help in

*Figure 1. The performance of a decision-making system can move along the Pareto-front (interface between grey and black regions) depending on the decision problem. The characteristics of the decision problem mean that it is impossible to go beyond the Pareto-front into the grey region. Only combinations of decision time and decision accuracy in the black region are possible.*

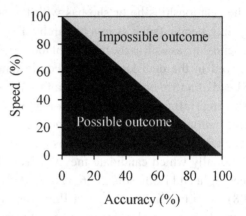

cases such as enhancing productivity in firms. Few studies to date have made this direct comparison.

## INFORMATION

Whether they are animal or human, group decisions can be shared or unshared between individuals. For instance, when moving together, all group members can propose a movement or a direction or only some specific group members can do so, such a dominant individual or old individuals (King et al., 2009). Some individuals have more weight in decision-making, depending on their internal or social traits. The decision to move seems to be taken by those with the highest needs in fish, zebra, and primate species (King *et al.*, 2009). Using a modelling approach, Rands *et al.* (2003) and recently Conradt *et al.* (2009) showed that individuals with the highest motivation are more prone to lead the group. However, individuals cannot satisfy their needs if they do not know where to find the nutrients. Information about the environment is therefore probably the most important factor influencing decision-making and leadership. Studies of elephants, ravens and fish have shown that some individuals may have a greater knowledge of their environment – namely concerning the best sites for eating or drinking – and these individuals have been observed leading their groups more often than their conspecifics (King *et al.*, 2009).

In a wide variety of biological taxa, individual organisms have been shown to improve their performance with experience, that is, better knowledge (Schneirla, 1943; Thorpe, 1963). The matriarch in elephants, who is the oldest female, is the one who decides for the entire group where and when to move because she is the only individual to know where some rare and distant waterholes are. In human beings, literature shows the clear relationship of knowledge with organisational productivity (Argote, 1999; Levitt and March, 1988). In the work of Pisano *et al.* (2001), differences in productivity across firms are linked to cumulative experience and the initial competences of individual actors. In the short term, improved performance as a result of experience generally involves a modification of the behaviour of individuals and can be an adaptation to dynamic environments. In ants, foragers (ants leaving the nest and searching for food) suffer high mortality, even in the absence of predation, compared to ants of the same age which stay inside (Schmid-Hempel and Schmid-Hempel, 1984; Tripet and Nonacs, 2004). Robinson *et al.* (2009) tried to assess which factors make individuals take the risky decision to leave the nest and showed that social information influences when an ant leaves the nest. When the colony needs a change of nest, the ant *Leptothorax albipennis* makes collective decisions using a quorum response process in their selection between the different alternatives of the best available nest site. If an ant has only found a low-quality nest site, a lag is built into the

emigration process that may enable the colony to find a better alternative nest site. Time-lags are used in this decision-making process in ants in order to favour accuracy (Franks *et al.*, 2002). Franks *et al.* (2003) tried to understand how these speed–accuracy trade-offs occur when ants have the information to make the appropriate choice but make errors because they cannot take the time to use the information correctly, or because environmental conditions constrain their actions, for instance. They demonstrated that in harsh conditions, the ants have lower quorum thresholds, and thus decide to accept a nest of lower quality. This is a classic trade-off between speed and accuracy in decision-making. Similar results were found in primates: in spontaneous collective movements, individuals seem to join a movement according to the social relationships they have with their conspecifics (Sueur et al., 2009), but in risky conditions the mechanisms underlying the decision-making are different. Actually, an event such as the presence of a predator leads individuals to join the movement according to an allelomimetism process, whatever the identities of their congeners: they all run away from the predator (Meunier et al., 2006; Sueur et al., 2009). The decision –making process and the influence of social relationships therefore seem to be different according to the situation, and specifically according to the risk of the situations. However, more studies are needed to understand how concurrent information about mutually exclusive alternatives or information in risky situations is transmitted in a group and how this transmission allows, or does not allow, the best collective decision to be taken at the colony level. We need to understand how animals and human beings behave individually or collectively, with and without risks or uncertainties.

## SOCIAL NETWORK

In most animal and human populations, individuals interact in different ways with their partners and we see a highly structured social organization reflecting the differences between individuals in the number of social interactions, the degree to which some individuals are central or peripheral to the population network, and the tendency to interconnect different communities or clusters (Krause and Ruxton, 2002; Krause *et al.*, 2007; Croft *et al.*, 2008). More recent "evolutionary graph theory" models (for example Ohtsuki *et al.*, 2006; Santos *et al.*, 2008) use networks to quantify social heterogeneity and study their impact on the evolution and the maintenance of cooperation.

An animal group can be defined as a network in which each dyad of individuals is characterized by one or several specific bonds (Newman and Girvan, 2004; Wasserman and Faust, 1994; Whitehead, 1997) that can be of a hierarchical, kin, or affiliative nature. Social network analyses are a powerful tool used to assess associations between individuals, in situations ranging from the group to an entire population (Croft *et al.*, 2005; Krause *et al.*, 2007; Sueur and Petit, 2008; Wey *et al.*, 2008; Whitehead, 1997; Wittemeyer *et al.*, 2005). The strength of the network approach is that many types of interaction (sexual, aggressive, cooperative, prey–predator interaction, and so on) in different species can be treated within the same conceptual framework and using the same analytic tools. Recent research in social networks has defined different kinds of social patterns. Some of these may be comparable to networks of animal or human groups. Others are strictly artificial; they have not been described in the wild (Amblard, 2002; Voelkl and Noë, 2008; Wang and Chen, 2003).

In biology, social network analysis has contributed to our understanding of gene, protein and cell relationships (Laughlin and Sejnowski, 2003; Barabasi and Oltvai, 2004), and over the past ten years, this methodology has been increasingly applied to the study of animal behaviour (Borgatti et al., 2002; Lusseau, 2003; Whitehead, 1997; Krause et al., 2009). For instance, Lusseau (2007) used the betweenness coefficient to determine the centrality of individuals in a bottlenose dolphin population living in fission-fusion societies. They found that some individuals had a significantly higher betweenness coefficient than others, and suggested that these central individuals were key elements mediating the fusion of the whole population. Such social roles can then be linked to other individual traits. In the case of dolphins, Lusseau and Conradt (2009) showed that central individuals appear to have greater knowledge of their environment, and as a consequence precipitate shifts in behaviour of their conspecifics. Sueur and Petit (2008) studied collective movement in rhesus macaques (*Macaca mulatta*) and Tonkean macaques (*M. tonkeana*). They created matrices describing the frequency with which individuals followed one another when moving following a resting period. Calculating an eigenvector centrality coefficient for the resulting networks, they found that some individuals were more central than others. When these individuals departed, whatever their position in the movement (i.e., initiator, first joiner, second joiner, etc.), they were followed by a great number of individuals. These "determinant individuals" were the dominant individuals or the individuals linking different matrilines in rhesus macaques, while they were the most affiliated ones in Tonkean macaques (Sueur and Petit, 2008; Sueur *et al.*, 2009). Finally, in the case of group cohesion, Ramos-Fernandez *et al.* (2009) used the same eigenvector centrality coefficient to understand spatial association in spider monkeys (*Ateles geoffroyi*). They showed that females had a higher eigenvector than males, but reported young adult males playing the roles of "brokers" between the female and the male clusters, similar to that seen in a dolphin population (Lusseau, 2007). These different examples show that certain phenomena seen in humans, such as group cohesion, leadership and information flow, can also be found and measured in animals. Studying animals helps us to understand the origins of leadership and collective decision-making in humans and, by comparing animals to humans, to enhance

*Figure 2. Schematic relationship between individual behaviour and group or population social network*

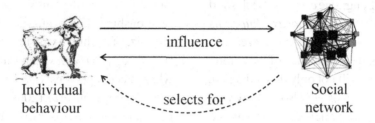

productivity in firms. These studies also showed that social network within a group seems to have a great impact and influence on everyday collective processes in animals, such as group movements, information diffusion or cohesion maintenance (Sueur *et al.,* 2011).

A major question in current network science is how to best understand the relationship between the structure and functioning of real networks (Sueur *et al.*, 2011). Indeed, network architecture depends more on the functioning of the particular community than on taxonomic differences (Bhadra *et al.*, 2009). Using social network analyses, we can determine how individual behaviour influences the group or population social network and we can likewise study the implications of these social networks for the individual fitness (Figure 2). This kind of feedback loop is essential for understanding the role of local interactions in social systems (Camazine *et al.*, 2001; Couzin and Krause, 2003). The social structure of the population can have important repercussions on the fitness of individuals.

In baboons, Silk et al. (2009) showed that females with greater centrality have more offspring than females with fewer relationships. Social interactions are critical to the organization of worker activities in insect colonies and their consequent ecological success (Naug, 2009). The social network structure is therefore crucial for understanding organization and functioning within colonies and groups. The dominant view of colony organization in social insects is that it is self-organized, with numerous individuals in-

teracting locally to produce global attributes that are far greater than the mere sum of local interactions (Camazine *et al.*, 2001). This explains how social insects with their relatively simple, individual cognitive capacities are able to display amazingly complex, colony-level behaviours. Network theory, which deals with quantifying the local and global properties characterizing the structure and behaviour of a set of interconnected units (Newman, 2003; Krause *et al.*, 2007, 2009; James *et al.*, 2009), is therefore an ideal tool to gain new insights into some of the long-standing issues in animal group organization.

Several studies have shown that social networks constrain many social phenomena such as information or disease transmission; such networks also influence a range of social behaviours such as grooming, coalitions, and group fission (Chepko-Sade *et al.*, 1989; Dow et de Waal, 1989; Silk *et al.*, 2004; Van Horn *et al.*, 2007; Voelkl and Noë, 2008; Whitmeyer and Yeingst, 2006). For instance, some key individuals may favour the diffusion of information or disease by their position in the network. Recent work by Ahuja *et al.* (2003) shows that individual centrality is a strong predictor of individual performance in firms. However, few studies have reported how social networks may enhance the efficiency of decisions in animal groups. Whilst some authors consider that individuals in insect colonies all have the same weight in the decision-making process, other authors have speculated that the connectivity within an insect colony is likely to be non-random, with a few key individuals playing major roles in organizing colony activity (Fewell, 2003; Naug, 2009). Langridge *et al.* (2009) showed that colonies of the ant *Leptothorax albipennis* are able to improve their performance over successive emigrations. The efficiency of the colony during an emigration will not only depend on the performance of individuals but also on how well the behaviour of the individuals can be integrated into coordinated, collective behaviour at the colony level, or in other words, on how well individuals are connected together. How individuals are connected together in insect societies, as well as in other species, and also how these connections may favour information flow and enhance decision efficiency, are still unknown. Studying decision processes in animal groups will of course lead to a better understanding of how social network influences decision efficiency in animals, but also in human beings. This knowledge will permit a better control of decision efficiency by controlling interactions and relationships between the different components of the social network.

## COMPARISON BETWEEN ANIMALS AND HUMANS

In order to better understand the rules underlying decision-making in humans and therefore enhance decision efficiency in firms, we need to compare social networks in firms to those in animals. Indeed, more and more studies show similarities in the way individuals decide collectively and reach a consensus between humans and animals and between animals, whatever the order concerned.

Whilst some studies on primates suggest that individuals display complex negotiation behaviours during the decision-making process (with intentions, insight, and so on; Tomasello and Call, 1997), and take decisions together (Boinski and Campbell, 1995; Conradt and Roper, 2005; Prins, 1996), similarities have also been observed in the patterns of collective motion between insects and mammals (Buhl *et al.*, 2006). Recent studies

have demonstrated that self-organized processes can exist in small groups with highly structured relationships. For example, allelomimetic synchronization, shown first in insects, exists in Merino sheep (*Ovis aries*, Gautrais *et al.*, 2007) and white-faced capuchins (*Cebus capucinus*; Meunier *et al.*, 2006). Sueur *et al.* (2009) showed in Tonkean macaques (*Macaca tonkeana*) that processes used for joining a movement and the organization of group members at departure depend on selective mimetism, where individuals decide to follow only highly affiliated conspecifics. In the same way, authors have applied this theory to explain behaviour in human crowds (Dyer *et al.*, 2007; Helbing *et al.*, 2000). These results suggest that the same general principles underlie collective decisions whatever the study species (Detrain and Deneubourg, 2006; Sumpter, 2006) and that comparative studies need to be done in order to understand these general principles. Similarly, whilst some studies have suggested that all processes in insects are anonymous, others showed that individual characteristics and network structure play a role in the efficiency of the collective decision (Fewell, 2003; Naug, 2009).

Some studies show striking parallels between decision-making in primate (human and non-human) brains and collective decision-making in social insect colonies: in both systems, separate populations accumulate evidence for alternative choices. Sueur *et al.* (2010) showed that macaques are able to vote between several alternatives. They used a quorum response similar to that used in human beings voting, for instance, to elect their President. However, this quorum rule was also found in ants and bees when they have to choose a new nest site or new foraging site from several different alternatives. Marshall *et al.* (2009) showed that social insect colonies may also be able to achieve statistically optimal collective decision-making in a very similar way to primate brains, via direct competition between evidence-accumulating populations. Their approach is also the first attempt to identify a common theoretical framework for the study of decision-making in diverse biological systems. However, other comparative studies need to be done, specifically at the group level.

The main species identified in these previous lines (humans, non-human primates and eusocial insects) need to be studied in more detail, but more importantly also be compared using a similar methodology.

The leader's management style has an impact on the productivity of the firm. Two indices measured from the manager allow us to qualify the social network: consideration and participation (Sarin and Dermott, 2003). Consideration is how the leader considers his or her workers, how he or she is attentive to what they say and how their comments will be taken into consideration. Participation is how far the firm manager allows his or her workers to participate in meetings, and life within the firm. If the manager does not take workers into consideration or let them participate in everyday life in the firm, a despotic social network will result from the interactions between people, with the leader holding a very central position within the network. On the other hand, if the leader has a great index of consideration and participation, then the network will be egalitarian, with all individuals having almost the same influence and the same centrality. A democratic and participatory style of leadership makes communication among team members more efficient. Thus, the higher the levels of consideration and participation are, the better the workers' well-being will be. The level of innovation is also higher when the leader is egalitarian. Here again, similar findings can be described in animals. Different and contrasted social networks exist within a single animal order or genus. Thierry and colleagues showed that, at least in the genus *Macaca*, some behavioural features such as aggression intensity, level of reconciliation or nepotism co-vary from one species to another (Petit et al., 1997; Thierry, 2007; Thierry et al., 2007). Some behaviours constrain the presence and intensity of others.

These constraints and co-variations are not due to current ecological pressures (Ménard, 2004) but to a phylogenetic inertia (Thierry, 2004). Based on these interspecies variations in social traits, Thierry (2000) proposed a 4-grade scale of social styles. Grade 1 includes rhesus macaques (*M. mulatta),* Japanese macaques (*M. fuscata*) and Taiwan macaques (*M. Cyclopis*). These species display the highest degree of nepotism and asymmetry in aggression. In this grade, a subordinate attacked by a dominant individual will display a low probability of counter-attack because of a high injury risk. This highly strict hierarchy leads to a high nepotism because individuals limit their interactions to less risky individuals, i.e., their relatives. Contacts and grooming are mainly observed between related individuals. In contrast to the grade 1 species, grade 4 includes the Sulawesi species (*M. maura, M. nigra, M. ochreata* and *M. tonkeana*) which display the least nepotism and the most symmetrical aggressive interactions. Because of a low injury risk, grade 4 species show a high tendency to retaliate and less submissive behaviours. Individuals in these tolerant species can thus develop affiliative relationships with most of their conspecifics and not only with their relatives. This inertia affects how individuals are associated and, as a feedback loop, affiliative relationships will constrain behaviours of group members (Thierry, 2004, 2007). Bhadra *et al.* (2009) suggested that *R. marginata* wasp colonies and communities of children in classrooms are similar from the viewpoint of being more homogeneous (more democratic and egalitarian), while *R. cyathiformis* wasp colonies are governed by one or a few key individuals, i.e., the system is despotic.

These results show that it would be very interesting to compare humans to primates and insects, especially those displaying different social networks, such as macaques and hymenoptera (bees, wasps and ants).

## MODELLING COLLECTIVE DECISIONS

Collective decisions have been successfully simulated in a multi-agents system (Bryson et al., 2007; Sellers et al., 2007; Wilensky, 1999). First and foremost, the use of modelling allows us to understand the emergence of a global structure or collective phenomenon by the dynamic of all individual interactions. The study of the link between global and local can be made either by using a top-down approach: by modelling the global patterns, we try to explain the local mechanisms; or by using a bottom-up one: by suggesting hypotheses about local and individual behaviours and their interactions, we try to assess the rules underlying the global phenomenon. This last method is mainly used in the understanding of collective phenomena. The observed data are then compared to the simulated data resulting from the hypothesis implemented in the model (Epstein & Axtell, 1996). We try to understand how the social behaviour of each individual or agent allows the emergence of a global and complex system. These kinds of model allow us to understand, for instance, how ants manage to exploit their environment in an optimal way – to choose the best foraging site or the best nest – even though ants do not have a global view of their ecological and social environment, but only have access to local information. Wood and Ackland (2007) also carried out a model to assess whether a decreased predation risk or better food research efficiency could drive animals to live in a group. Sueur et al. (2009) built a model of decision-making during the joining of collective movement. In this model, one individual initiates a movement and the other members follow it according to different social networks: dominance, kinship, affiliative relationships. They scored simulated data such as latencies of departure, order and organization of individuals. These simulated data were then compared to the observed one. The results showed that all observed variables are better explained

by affiliative relationships. The rule used in the primary model originates from models used to explain interactions and emergence of collective patterns in eusocial insects (Camazine et al., 2001).

In the same way, Hemelrijk (2000, 2002) explained some aspects of social and spatial behaviours of macaques with the use of an agent-based model that did not implement their developed cognitive abilities (Hemelrijk 2002). Using simple rules based on who won and who lost after a fight, Hemelrijk could explain why dominant individuals are more often observed in the middle of the group whilst subordinate individuals are peripheral. Several models were also developed to explain how individual characteristics such as nutrient requirements or knowledge of individuals influence the emergence of leadership in animals (Rands et al. 2004; Couzin et al. 2005; Conradt et al. 2009).

## CONCLUSION

Both the study of social networks and the comparison of different species contribute to literature on strategic human resource management and social networks. This allows us to understand the process of information flow in humans and animals, but also other phenomena such as disease transfer. However, further studies are necessary in order to understand the mechanisms underlying collective phenomena such as social learning or collective movements. The mechanisms by which animals divide labour, partition tasks, and exchange information have attracted a great deal of interest not only from students of social insects but also from scientists hoping to apply such principles to engineering and computational problems (Bonabeau *et al.*, 2000). Many scientists working on artificial intelligence or robotics use results on collective decision-making processes in animals to enhance communication between agents or robots (Halloy *et al.*, 2007; Wang and Chen, 2003). This comparison of social networks between animals and human beings will allow an adequate and optimal social network to be found, improving not only productivity and the well-being of workers in firms, but also the management of endangered or domestically animal species.

# REFERENCES

Acemoglu, D., & Robinson, J. A. (2008). Persistence of power, elites, and institutions. *The American Economic Review*, *98*, 267–293. doi:10.1257/aer.98.1.267

Ahuja, M., Galletta, D., & Carley, K. (2003). Individual centrality and performance in virtual RandD groups: An empirical study. *Management Science*, *49*, 21–38. doi:10.1287/mnsc.49.1.21.12756

Alexander, R. D. (1974). The evolution of social behavior. *Annual Review of Ecology and Systematics*, *5*, 326–383. doi:10.1146/annurev.es.05.110174.001545

Amblard, F. (2002). Which ties to choose? A survey of social networks models for agent-based social simulations. *Proceedings of the 2002 SCS International Conference on Artificial Intelligence, Simulation and Planning in High Autonomy Systems,* (pp. 253-258).

Argote, L. (1999). *Organizational learning: Creating, retaining and transferring knowledge*. Norwell, MA: Kluwer.

Ashworth, M. J., & Carley, K. M. (2006). Who you know vs. what you know: The impact of social position and knowledge on team performance. *The Journal of Mathematical Sociology*, *30*, 43–75. doi:10.1080/00222500500323101

Bhadra, A., Jordan, F., Sumana, A., Deshpande, S. A., & Gadagkar, R. (2009). A comparative social network analysis of wasp colonies and classrooms: Linking network structure to functioning. *Ecological Complexity*, *6*, 48–55. doi:10.1016/j.ecocom.2008.10.004

Boinski, S., & Campbell, A. F. (1995). Use of trill vocalisations to coordinate troop movement among white-faced capuchins: A second field test. *Behaviour*, *132*, 875–901. doi:10.1163/156853995X00054

Boinski, S., & Garber, P. A. (2000). *On the move*. Chicago, IL: University of Chicago Press.

Bonabeau, E., Theraulaz, G., Deneubourg, J.-L., Aron, S., & Camazine, S. (1997). Self-organization in social insects. *Trends in Ecology & Evolution*, *12*, 188–192. doi:10.1016/S0169-5347(97)01048-3

Borgatti, S. P., Everett, M. G., & Freeman, L. C. (2002). *Ucinet for Windows: Software for social network analysis*. Harvard Analytic Technologies.

Borgatti, S. P., Mehra, A., Brass, D. J., & Labianca, G. (2009). Network analysis in the social sciences. *Science*, *323*, 892–895. doi:10.1126/science.1165821

Buhl, J., Sumpter, D. J. T., Couzin, I. D., Hake, J. J., Despland, E., Miller, E. R., & Simpson, S. J. (2006). From disorder to order in marching locusts. *Science*, *312*, 1402–1406. doi:10.1126/science.1125142

Busemeyer, J. R., & Townsend, J. T. (1993). Decision field theory: A dynamic cognitive approach to decision-making in an uncertain environment. *Psychological Review*, *100*, 432–459. doi:10.1037/0033-295X.100.3.432

Camazine, S., Deneubourg, J. L., Findividuals, N. R., Sneyd, J., Theraulaz, G., & Bonabeau, E. (2001). *Self-organization in biological systems*. Princeton, NJ: Princeton University Press.

Chepko-Sade, B. D., Reitz, P. R., & Sade, D. S. (1989). Sociometrics of Macaca mulatta IV: Network analysis of social structure of a pre-fission group. *Social Networks*, *11*, 293–314. doi:10.1016/0378-8733(89)90007-5

Conradt, L., & Roper, T. J. (2003). Group decision-making in animals. *Nature, 421*, 155–158. doi:10.1038/nature01294

Conradt, L., & Roper, T. J. (2005). Consensus decision making in animals. *Trends in Ecology & Evolution, 20*, 449–456. doi:10.1016/j.tree.2005.05.008

Couzin, I. D., & Krause, J. (2003). Self-organization and collective behaviors in vertebrates. *Advances in the Study of Animal Behavior, 32*, 1–75. doi:10.1016/S0065-3454(03)01001-5

Croft, D. P., James, R., & Krause, J. (2008). *Exploring animal social networks*. Princeton, NJ: Princeton University Press.

Croft, D. P., James, R., Ward, A. J. W., Botham, M. S., Mawdsley, D., & Krause, J. (2005). Assortative interactions and social networks in fish. *Oecologia, 143*, 211–219. doi:10.1007/s00442-004-1796-8

Danchin, E., Boulinier, T., & Massot, M. (1998). Conspecific reproductive success and breeding habitat selection: Implications for the study of coloniality. *Ecology, 79*, 2415–2428. doi:10.1890/0012-9658(1998)079[2415:CRSABH]2.0.CO;2

Detrain, C., & Deneubourg, J. L. (2006). Self-organized structures in a superorganism: Do ants "behave" like molecules? *Physics of Life Reviews, 3*, 162–187. doi:10.1016/j.plrev.2006.07.001

Dow, M. M., & de Waal, F. B. M. (1989). Assignment methods for the analysis of network subgroup interactions. *Social Networks, 11*, 237–255. doi:10.1016/0378-8733(89)90004-X

Dyer, J. R. G., Ioannou, C. C., Morrell, L. J., Croft, D. P., Couzin, I. D., Waters, D. A., & Krause, J. (2007). Consensus decisions making in human crowds. *Animal Behaviour, 75*, 461–470. doi:10.1016/j.anbehav.2007.05.010

Fewell, J. H. (2003). Social insect networks. *Science, 301*, 1867–1870. doi:10.1126/science.1088945

Fischhoff, I. R., Sundaresan, S. R., Cordingley, J., Larkin, H. M., Sellier, M. J., & Rubenstein, D. I. (2007). Social relationships and reproductive state influence leadership roles in movements of plains zebra, *Equus burchellii*. *Animal Behaviour, 73*, 825–831. doi:10.1016/j.anbehav.2006.10.012

Fox, M. W. (1972). *Behavior of wolves, dogs and related canids*. New York, NY: Harper and Row.

Franks, N. R., Dornhaus, A., Fitzsimmons, J. P., & Stevens, M. (2003). Speed versus accuracy in collective decision making. *Proceedings of the Royal Society, Series B, 270*, 2457–2463. doi:10.1098/rspb.2003.2527

Franks, N. R., Pratt, S. C., Mallon, E. B., Britton, N. F., & Sumpter, D. J. T. (2002). Information flow, opinion polling and collective intelligence in house-hunting social insects. *Philosophical Transactions of the Royal Society of London, Series B, 357*, 1567–1583. doi:10.1098/rstb.2002.1066

Gautrais, J., Michelena, P., Sibbald, A., Bon, R., & Deneubourg, J. L. (2007). Allelomimetic synchronization in Merino sheep. *Animal Behaviour, 74*, 1443–1454. doi:10.1016/j.anbehav.2007.02.020

Helbing, D., Farkas, I., & Vicsek, T. (2000). Simulating dynamical features of escape panic. *Nature, 407*, 487–490. doi:10.1038/35035023

James, R., Croft, D. P., & Krause, J. (2009). Potential banana skins in animal social network analysis. *Behavioral Ecology and Sociobiology, 63*, 989–997. doi:10.1007/s00265-009-0742-5

King, A. J., Johnson, D. D. P., & van Vugt, M. (2009). The origins and evolution of leadership. *Current Biology, 19*, R911–R916. doi:10.1016/j.cub.2009.07.027

Krause, J., Croft, D. P., & James, R. (2007). Social network theory in the behavioural sciences: Potential applications. *Behavioral Ecology and Sociobiology, 62*, 15–27. doi:10.1007/s00265-007-0445-8

Krause, J., Lusseau, D., & James, R. (2009). Animal social networks: An introduction. *Behavioral Ecology and Sociobiology, 63*, 967–973. doi:10.1007/s00265-009-0747-0

Krause, J., & Ruxton, G. D. (2002). *Living in groups*. Oxford, UK: Oxford University Press.

Kummer, H. (1968). *Social organization of Hamadryas baboons*. Chicago, IL: University of Chicago Press.

Langridge, E. A., Franks, N. R., & Sendova-Franks, A. B. (2004). Improvement in collective performance with experience in ants. *Behavioral Ecology and Sociobiology, 56*, 523–529. doi:10.1007/s00265-004-0824-3

Langridge, E. A., Sendova-Franks, A. B., & Franks, N. R. (2009). How experienced individuals contribute to an improvement in collective performance in ants. *Behavioral Ecology and Sociobiology, 62*, 447–456. doi:10.1007/s00265-007-0472-5

Levitt, B., & March, J. (1988). Organizational learning. *Annual Review of Sociology, 14*, 319–340. doi:10.1146/annurev.so.14.080188.001535

Lusseau, D. (2007). Evidence for social role in a dolphin social network. *Evolutionary Ecology, 21*, 357–366. doi:10.1007/s10682-006-9105-0

Lusseau, D., Wilson, B., Hammond, P. S., Grellier, K., Durban, J. W., & Parsons, K. M. (2006). Quantifying the influence of sociality on population structure in bottlenose dolphins. *Journal of Animal Ecology, 75*, 14–24. doi:10.1111/j.1365-2656.2005.01013.x

Marshall, J. A. R., Bogacz, R., Dornhaus, A., Planqué, R., Kovacs, T., & Franks, N. R. (2009). On optimal decision-making in brains and social insect colonies. *Journal of the Royal Society, Interface, 6*, 1065–1074. doi:10.1098/rsif.2008.0511

Marshall, J. A. R., Dornhaus, A., Franks, N. R., & Kovacs, T. (2006). Noise, cost and speed–accuracy trade-offs: Decision making in a decentralized system. *Journal of the Royal Society, Interface, 3*, 243–254. doi:10.1098/rsif.2005.0075

Meunier, H., Leca, J. B., Deneubourg, J. L., & Petit, O. (2006). Group movement decisions in capuchin monkeys: The utility of an experimental study and a mathematical model to explore the relationship between individual and collective behaviours. *Behaviour, 143*, 1511–1527. doi:10.1163/156853906779366982

Naug, D. (2009). Structure and resilience of the social network in an insect colony as a function of colony size. *Behavioral Ecology and Sociobiology, 63*, 1023–1028. doi:10.1007/s00265-009-0721-x

Newman, M. E. J. (2003). The structure and function of complex networks. *SIAM Review, 45*, 167–256. doi:10.1137/S003614450342480

Newman, M. E. J., & Girvan, M. (2004). Finding and evaluating community structure in networks. *Physical Review E: Statistical, Nonlinear, and Soft Matter Physics, 69*, 026113. doi:10.1103/PhysRevE.69.026113

Nikolic, D., & Gronlund, S. D. (2002). A tandem random walk model of the SAT paradigm: Response times and accumulation of evidence. *The British Journal of Mathematical and Statistical Psychology, 55*, 263–288. doi:10.1348/000711002760554589

Ohtsuki, H., Hauert, C., Lieberman, E., & Nowak, M. A. (2006). A simple rule for the evolution of cooperation on graphs and social networks. *Nature, 441*, 502–505. doi:10.1038/nature04605

Osman, A., Lou, L. G., Muller-Gethmann, H., Rinkenauer, G., Mattes, S., & Ulrich, R. (2000). Mechanisms of speed– accuracy trade-off: Evidence from covert motor processes. *Biological Psychology, 51*, 173–199. doi:10.1016/S0301-0511(99)00045-9

Pisano, G., Bohmer, M., & Edmondson, A. (2001). Organizational differences in rates of learning: Evidence from the adoption of minimally invasive surgery. *Management Science, 47*, 752–768. doi:10.1287/mnsc.47.6.752.9811

Pratt, S. C., & Sumpter, D. J. T. (2006). A tunable algorithm for collective decision-making. *Proceedings of the National Academy of Sciences of U.S.A., 103*, 906–15 910. doi:10.1073/pnas.0604801103

Prins, H. H. T. (1989). Buffalo herd structure and its repercussions for condition of individual African buffalo cows. *Ethology, 81*, 47–71. doi:10.1111/j.1439-0310.1989.tb00757.x

Rasa, O. A. E. (1986). *Mongoose watch: A family observed*. New-York, NY: Anchor Press.

Robinson, E. J. H., Richardson, T. O., Sendova-Franks, A. B., Feinerman, O., & Franks, N. R. (2009). Radio tagging reveals the roles of corpulence, experience and social information in ant decision making. *Behavioral Ecology and Sociobiology, 63*, 627–636. doi:10.1007/s00265-008-0696-z

Santos, F. C., Santos, M. D., & Pacheco, J. M. (2008). Social diversity promotes the emergence of cooperation in public goods games. *Nature, 454*, 213–216. doi:10.1038/nature06940

Schmid-Hempel, P., & Schmid-Hempel, R. (1984). Life duration and turnover of foragers in the ant Cataglyphis bicolor (Hymenoptera, Formicidae). *Insectes Sociaux, 31*, 345–360. doi:10.1007/BF02223652

Schneirla, T. C. (1953). Modifiability in insect behaviour. In Roeder, K. D. (Ed.), *Insect physiology* (pp. 23–747). New York, NY: Wiley.

Silk, J. B., Alberts, S. C., & Altmann, J. (2004). Patterns of coalition formation by adult female baboons in Amboseli, Kenya. *Animal Behaviour, 67*, 573–582. doi:10.1016/j.anbehav.2003.07.001

Sueur, C., Deneubourg, J. L., & Petit, O. (2010). Sequence of quorums during collective decision-making in macaques. *Behavioral Ecology and Sociobiology, 64*, 1885–1895. doi:10.1007/s00265-010-0999-8

Sueur, C., Jacobs, A., Petit, O., Amblard, F., & King, A. J. (2011). How can social network analysis improve the study of primate behaviour? *American Journal of Primatology, 73*, 703–709. doi:10.1002/ajp.20915

Sueur, C., & Petit, O. (2008). Organization of group members at departure of joint movements is driven by social structure in macaques. *International Journal of Primatology, 29*, 1085–1098. doi:10.1007/s10764-008-9262-9

Sueur, C., Petit, O., & Deneubourg, J.-L. (2009). Selective mimetism at departure in collective movements of Macaca tonkeana: An experimental and theoretical approach. *Animal Behaviour, 78*, 1087–1095. doi:10.1016/j.anbehav.2009.07.029

Sumpter, D. J. T. (2006). The principles of collective animal behavior. *Philosophical transactions of the Royal Society of London, Series B, 361*, 5-22.

Thorpe, W. H. (1963). *Learning and instinct in animals* (2nd ed.). London, UK: Methuen.

Tomasello, M., & Call, J. (1997). *Primate cognition*. New York, NY: Oxford University Press.

Tripet, F., & Nonacs, P. (2004). Foraging for work and age-based polyethism: The roles of age and experience on task choice in ants. *Ethology, 110*, 863–877. doi:10.1111/j.1439-0310.2004.01023.x

Van Horn, R. C., Buchan, J. C., Altmann, J., & Alberts, S. C. (2007). Divided destinies: Group choice by female chacma baboons during social group fission. *Behavioral Ecology and Sociobiology, 61*, 1823–1837. doi:10.1007/s00265-007-0415-1 van Vugt, M., Hogan, R., & Kaiser, R. B. (2008). Leadership, followership, and evolution, some lessons from the past. *The American Psychologist, 63*, 182–196. doi:10.1037/0003-066X.63.3.182

Vitevitch, M. S. (2002). Influence of onset density on spoken word recognition. *Journal of Experimental Psychology. Human Perception and Performance, 28*, 270–278. doi:10.1037/0096-1523.28.2.270

Voelkl, B., & Noë, R. (2008). The influence of social structure on the propagation of social information in artificial primate groups: A graph-based simulation approach. *Journal of Theoretical Biology, 252*, 77–86. doi:10.1016/j.jtbi.2008.02.002

Wang, F. W., & Chen, W. (2003). Complex networks: Small-world, scale-free and beyond. *IEEE Circuits and Systems Magazine,* first quarter 2003.

Wasserman, S., & Faust, K. (1994). *Social network analysis*. Cambridge, UK: Cambridge University Press.

Wey, T., Blumstein, D. T., Shen, W., & Jordan, F. (2007). Social network analysis of animal behavior: A promising tool for the study of sociality. *Animal Behaviour, 75*, 333–344. doi:10.1016/j.anbehav.2007.06.020

Whitehead, H. (1997). Analysing animal social structure. *Animal Behaviour, 53*, 1053–1067. doi:10.1006/anbe.1996.0358

Whitehead, H. (2007). *Programs for analyzing social structure*. Retrieved from http://myweb.dal.ca/hwhitehe/MANUAL.htm

Whitmeyer, J. M., & Yeingst, C. N. (2006). A dynamic model of friendly association networks. *Social Science Research, 35*, 642–667. doi:10.1016/j.ssresearch.2005.05.001

Wittemeyer, G., Douglas-Hamilton, I., & Getz, W. M. (2005). The socioecology of elephants: Analysis of the processes creating multitiered social structures. *Animal Behaviour, 69*, 1357–1371. doi:10.1016/j.anbehav.2004.08.018

Wrangham, R. W. (1980). An ecological model of female-bonded primate groups. *Behaviour, 75*, 262–300. doi:10.1163/156853980X00447

## KEY TERMS AND DEFINITIONS

**Decision Accuracy:** Quality of the decision that is to say the level of satisfaction of all group members.

**Decision Efficiency:** The extent to which time or effort is well used for choosing the best alternative between several ones; often defined as the ratio between the speed and the accuracy of a decision.

**Decision Speed:** Time to take a decision.

**Decision-Making:** Process in which individuals or groups of individuals can adopt one of two or more alternative behaviours.

**Information:** Property of a source resulting in a reaction of a receiver in a biologically functional manner and leading to a reduction of uncertainty (see Scrott-Phillips, 2008 and Fichtel and Manser, 2010).

**Self-Organisation:** Process in which patterns at the global level of a system emerge solely from numerous interactions among the lower level components of the system, without a global referent or central authority; parsimonious way to explain the complexity of animal societies (see Camazine et al., 2001).

**Social Network:** The whole of relationships between members of a group, a relationship being the sum of interactions between two individuals (see Hinde, 1976 and Sueur et al. 2011).

# Chapter 10
# Extracting and Measuring Relationship Strength in Social Networks

**Steven Gustafson**
*GE Global Research, USA*

**Abha Moitra**
*GE Global Research, USA*

## ABSTRACT

*This study examines how extracting relationships from data can lead to very different social networks. The chapter uses online message board data to define a relationship between two authors. After applying a threshold on the number of communications between members, the authors further constrain relationships to be supported by each member in the relationship also having a relationship to the same third member: the triangle constraint. By increasing the number of communications required to have a valid relationships between members, they see very different social networks being constructed. Authors find that the subtle design choices that are made when extracting relationships can lead to different networks, and that the variation itself could be useful for classifying and segmenting nodes in the network. For example, if a node is 'central' across different approaches to extracting relationships, one could assume with more confidence that the node is indeed 'central'. Lastly, the chapter studies how future communication occurs between members and their ego-networks from prior data. By increasing the communication requirements to extract valid relationships, it is seen how future communication prediction is impacted and how social network design choices could be better informed by understanding these variations.*

DOI: 10.4018/978-1-61350-444-4.ch010

# INTRODUCTION

Studies on real-world complex social networks have not typically considered the existence of erroneous links in the observed social network. Most prior work assumes that with a large enough sample size, the true, or accurate, relationships will out-weigh the false ones. However, as demonstrated in two recent publications (Gustafson et al., 2009, Choudhury et al., 2010a), this is not always the case for real-world social network data. As more data becomes available, and more societal and cultural benefits of analyzing social networks are identified (Lazer et al., 2009), it will be critical to fully understand social network data issues. In this paper, we build upon recent work (Gustafson et al., 2009, Choudhury et al., 2010a) that shows how a simple threshold condition on the number of ties between nodes can lead to dramatic effects in the network structure as well as the types of information one could infer about the network and individual nodes in the network.

# BACKGROUND

Recently, Latapy and Magnien (2008) validate the sample size assumption and show that it is possible to distinguish between cases where this assumption is reasonable, those large enough data sets overcome issues of noise within the data, and they also find cases where the assumption must be discarded. Latapy and Magnien (2008) conclude that the qualitative properties of some statistics do not depend on the sample size, as long as it is not trivially small. They find that some statistics, like average degree, can be used to infer other statistics, whereas other statistics like transitivity are generally unstable as sample sizes grow. These more 'structural' statistics are somehow more related to other measures like maximal degree. While qualitative estimations of the more stable statistics, for example average degree, are possible, obtaining accurate estimations of these statistics

remains difficult. Lin and Zhao (2005) present a study on the impact of erroneous links on degree distribution estimation and show that the degree distributions of power-law networks still have power-law degree distributions for the middle range degrees, but can be greatly distorted for low and high degrees. Borgatti et al. (2006) show that centrality measures are surprisingly similar with respect to pattern and level of robustness to data errors and different types of errors have relatively similar effects on centrality robustness. The limitation of this last study is that they consider only random errors on random networks. As we are primarily interested in real-world data and the impact of design choices when extracting social network relationships, we will not address prior work that has examined this topic within simulated data. In Costenbader and Valente (2003), several centrality measures are studied for stability across several different social network data sets. Using various degrees of sampling, the authors find that some measures are more stable than others, and some, like Bonacich's Eigenvector measure, are very unstable when comparing the correlation between the centrality measurements of the sampled populations to the centrality measurement of the original un-sampled population. Recently, in Choudhury et al. (2010b), sampling is studied on very large-scale data to estimate information diffusion. The authors find that sampling can be improved by using contextual information, like physical location, to direct future samples toward other actors that may share similar interests or attributes and be important for the sample to estimate information diffusion.

While some statistics and social network measurements are more stable across sampling or collection strategies, we still face a lot of uncertainty when considering the future, where data is collected for other purposes and then leveraged in a social network analysis setting. Marsden (1990) discusses several issues with social network data collection that are very relevant today, including: the fact that some relationships are persistent while others are more episodic, and the concept that some social tie measurements are 'indicators' for ties rather than precise 'descriptions' of the ties. If measurements are indicators, than like other measurement systems, they should be tested for reliability and robustness. Golder et al. (2007) analyze a large-scale online social network and highlights the strong episodic nature of the data across different scales. Rothenberg (1995) provides an overview of sampling and data collection in social networks and the challenges faced when the assumptions used for analysis and measurements are not supported by the data collection approach. In Bernard et al. (1984), the topic of accuracy, particularly from retrospective data, is studied. The authors find that many factors contribute to the typically low accuracy of retrospective data. Among many approaches to improve accuracy, two that are related to our study are: approaches targeted at identifying concepts capture the data better than asking people to recall the data directly, and leveraging a group of actors to identify data can be more accurate than what the same group can do individually. Coming back to the recent growth of social network data, Adar and Re (2007) discuss the challenges in leveraging such data across a variety of applications. The authors propose a framework for collecting and analyzing data that is based on probabilistic databases to better deal with the increasing uncertainty of data quality and precision found in such systems.

In Gustafson et al. (2009), a real-world online social network is analyzed to understand the impact of requiring supporting evidence to corroborate friend relationships. By counting the number of communications between members, a friend relationship is validated by having both a greater number of communications than the threshold as well as by having friendships to a third member. That is, two members are friends if they firstly elect to become friends (the typical 'friending' in online social networks), they secondly validate their friendship with some number of communications, and lastly, they both share a

validated friendship to another member. These requirements are not explicit in the social network; they are data requirements imposed during the analysis. The results indicate that while some stability in network measurements were found, the presence of key nodes and edges lead to a significant amount of variation that make inferences about the network less robust across friend threshold values. One may reach very different conclusions about individuals in these networks due to these variations. The authors in Gustafson et al. (2009) propose to use the variation itself to understand the appropriate grouping of members or communities that are more stable and better represent real and significant relationships. In Choudhury et al. (2010a), two other real-world social networks are analyzed, this time in the form of electronic email between users. The authors define a threshold on the number of emails received between two people that constitute a relationship. The results show how different threshold values lead to different network structures. Interestingly, for these specific data sets, the authors find some consistencies in terms of the threshold values for several prediction tasks: requiring friendships to have 5-10 reciprocated emails per year.

The primary conclusions in these last two last studies on inferring relationships in social networks are not surprising in that different threshold values lead to different networks. However, both studies suggest that (1) we can use the variation across threshold values to identify the "attainable" level of robustness or stability for a given network (Gustafson et al., 2009), and (2) identifying the appropriate threshold values can lead to upward of a 30% accuracy improvement in prediction tasks on those relationships (Choudhury et al., 2010a). Like in previous work with centrality measures (Costenbader and Valente, 2003), the variation across measurements and sampling approaches could suggest which measures or approaches are appropriate. However, the variation may also identify groups or communities that are stable as compared to other groups: as in Bernard et al.

(1984) where groups were found to identify the data better than the individual, under imprecise and uncertain data, studying the variation across threshold values may identify groups that are always higher in some measurement than other groups, even though the measurement of the individuals in the group may not be stable. In these studies, robustness refers to the ability to analyze the networks and have confidence that the results capture meaningful properties. If two slight variations in the method of identifying relationships lead to different conclusions, then the results are not robust. In the age of analyzing digital social networks, which are increasing more based upon online communications and behaviors than traditional self-report or surveys, it is of vital importance to understand how one can process this data into meaningful relationships.

In this chapter, we build upon recent work (Gustafson et al., 2009) to analyze a different form of social network relationship. We show that the assumptions and conclusions hold and identify some interesting subtleties. Lastly, we extend recent work (Choudhury et al., 2010a) and study the ability of the social networks to predict future communications between members–and highlight that by using the proposed method to identify social relationships that represent a meaningful bond or connection between members; we can improve the chance of identifying which member is likely to respond to other members.

## DATA AND METHODS

We analyze data from an online message board site. The data consists of conversation 'threads' focused on different topics. Each thread is a collection of messages sent from members via email accounts. Each message is assigned to a thread and refers to a previous message that it 'replies to'. If we construct a network of messages and the messages that they reply to, we can have linked lists as well as tree structures as conversations

branch into sub-topics within a thread. The specific message board data comes from a site dedicated to discussing cybersecurity, and for the privacy of the participants, we will leave the specific details hidden as well as mask user names. As described below, the message board is very similar in terms of its posting and thread statistics to previously studied message board and newsgroup data, and thus, we expect the results to be quite general. Next, we describe how to extract a relationship between members.

To define a relationship between members within a message board, it is typical to consider the reply-network as defining a relationship. For example, if a member A replies to B, we would say that A and B are 'friends' or that there is a relationship between them. Many different definitions are possible, but we will build upon the work by Fisher et al. (2006) that recently analyzes very similar data to understand the distribution of member types within different message boards for a classification task. And like in our prior work (Gustafson et al., 2009); we will define a threshold value $K$ that ranges from 1 to 4, that defines whether a relationship is 'validated'. A value of $K=1$ means that any 'reply-to' relationship constitutes a potential relationship. A value of $K=2$ means that only relationships between members that share 2 or more replies are considered. Note that while the edges are directed, coming from the 'reply-to' concept, after constructing the larger member network, we will consider all the edges to be undirected. Finally, and like in Gustafson et al. (2009), we will require that two members A and B have a valid relationship if and only if their edge meets the $K$ threshold criteria as well as each A and B also having a valid relationship with a third member C. Thus, one can imagine that as $K$ increases and more edges are removed, the ability to maintain triangles will become harder and the resulting network will be formed by more and stronger relationships. Like in Choudhury et al. (2010a), we could have simply used the number of links between members. Alternatively, we could define edges based upon shared language or based upon the timing of replies. Our choice of using triangles is based on two considerations: we want to represent the fact that members naturally form groups based on shared interests and location, and we also want a slightly more conservative measure of relationship while also highlighting the structural impact of increasing the value of $K$. That is, even if members only share one communication in our data, if both members also communicate with the same third member, under the lowest value of $K$, we still want to consider their relationship. Next, we describe some key statistics about our data set.

As mentioned, the data set comes from a message board dedicated to discussing cybersecurity. Most likely due to the complexity of the topic, the message board is primarily a place for discussion (as evident by the statistics below) and not a forum or question and answering, as some message boards on simple and straightforward topics often are. The specific forum was chosen due to its lack of spam, the dedication of its members, and the high amount of consistent activity across many years. Our subset of data comes from October 2008 until May 2010. We split our data into two sets: (1) messages received prior to 2010, and (2) message received in 2010. The first data is used for studying the value of $K$ and how the networks vary. The first data set is also used to generate member ego-networks, which will then be used to predict member communications in the 2010 dataset, which we will describe in more detail later. First, let us view some statistics about our data, mirroring those reported in Fisher et al. (2006).

Table 1 shows the message board statistics for our data, as well as those reported in Fisher et al. (2006). The cybersecurity data is most similar to the Social Support Newsgroups (divorce, autism) and to the Political Newsgroup. The cybersecurity data is clearly different than the Flame Newsgroups, the Technical Newsgroups, and the General Discussion Newsgroup. This comparison of the cybersecurity data with those newsgroups in

Fisher et al. (2006) demonstrates that indeed the cybersecurity members appear to be engaged in a more social conversation – like those we would expect to find on topics like divorce, autism and politics. The comparison also supports the quality of data in that it is different from those in flame and technical question/answer type newsgroups. The cybersecurity data has a decent number of authors with only one message, but there are just as many with > 10 links to other authors. Also, there are twice as many threads that have 5 or more messages as there are with just 2 messages. In summary, we are comfortable that, along with manual inspection and consultation with an active message board member, the cybersecurity message board data is appropriate for our study of extracting and measuring social networks. Next, we will describe the process of extracting the social network between members of the message board.

## EXTRACTING AND MEASURING SOCIAL NETWORKS

Like in Fisher et al. (2006), we will create our social network based on the reply structure of the messages in the thread. As in Choudhury et al. (2010a), we will label the edge between two members with the number of times the two members communicated (replies) with each other directly. Note that each message, if not the initial start message, is 'in-reply-to' another message, not necessarily the one immediately preceding it in the discussion thread. That is, someone can reply directly to an earlier message. Therefore, our thread networks are tree structures that can branch at any node. Many thread structures are linked lists with no branching. So, we create a relationship between author A and author B if author A replies to a message from author B, or vice versa. While the direction of the relationship is based on the 'reply-to' direction, the edges in our network will be undirected. That is, if author A replies to author B, there is an edge from A to

*Table 1. Basic statistics about the cybersecurity message board, similar to those reported in Fisher et al. (2006)*

| Network | Authors | Posts | Replies | Threads | % threads with 2 messages | % threads with 5+ messages | % authors with degree > 10 | % authors with 1 message |
|---------|---------|-------|---------|---------|---------------------------|----------------------------|----------------------------|--------------------------|
| **Newsgroup data published in Fisher et al. (2006)** | | | | | | | | |
| Technical 1 | 437 | | 712 | | 28% | 20% | 3% | 41% |
| Technical 2 | 855 | | 1489 | | 33% | 10% | 3% | 51% |
| Discussion 1 | 276 | | 924 | | 19% | 32% | 12% | 32% |
| Discussion 2 | 1263 | | 6105 | | 23% | 22% | 20% | 26% |
| Political 1 | 2187 | | 16059 | | 17% | 40% | 20% | 26% |
| Flame 1 | 618 | | 3802 | | 16% | 34% | 13% | 32% |
| Flame 2 | 755 | | 6494 | | 17% | 50% | 16% | 33% |
| Social Support 1 (divorce) | 339 | | 2937 | | 14% | 53% | 21% | 23% |
| Social Support 2 (autism) | 188 | | 3095 | | 17% | 60% | 32% | 20% |
| **Cybersecurity data analyzed in this study** | | | | | | | | |
| Pre-2010 | 328 | 3558 | 3106 | 452 | 20% | 46% | 33% | 30% |
| 2010 | 247 | 1546 | 1339 | 207 | 20% | 52% | 32% | 26% |

B with an initial edge weight of 1. If B replies to A, the edge weight will increase by 1. Note that we could define relationships between other authors who posted 'further up' the thread chain, or earlier in time. We could even create a weight that decayed based on distance between messages or time. However, in this study, we will keep the network definition simple, as we are interested in demonstrating the impact of extracting the relationships.

Whereas in Gustafson et al. (2009), we considered the network of explicit communities from an online social network, in this work, we will consider the ego-network of individual members like in Fisher et al. (2006). We have recently found good results for using ego-networks constructed from similar types of data to over-come noise and estimate global network metrics well (Ma et al., 2009, 2010). In this study, we build degree-two networks from each node, or the members' friend-of-a-friend network. So, each ego-network will consist of all those other members who have direct relationship to the ego, as well as the friends' relationships. For a value of $K=1$, only the triangle constraint is enforced. For values of $K>1$, first any edge with a weight less than $K$ is removed, and any nodes that no longer connect into the ego-network are dropped. Then, the triangle constraint is enforced, removing any nodes that do not participate in a triangle in the ego-network, and any of their edges.

As in our prior work, we will look at the following metrics to understand the impact of $K$ on extracting social networks: ego-network transitivity (or clustering coefficient), ego-network size or number of nodes, and ego-network transitivity/ density. For each value of $K$, we extract all the ego-networks, calculate the ego-network metrics, and define for each metric the rank of each ego-network. Lastly, we will then compare the value of the metrics as $K$ increases. In Gustafson et al. (2009), we studied the largest 10 communities. In

*Figure 1. Network size (left-hand graph) and the Rank of Network Size (right-hand graph) for the 25 ego-networks that persist across cutoff values of* **K** *from* **1** *to* **4**. *Network size is measured by the number of nodes in each ego-network.*

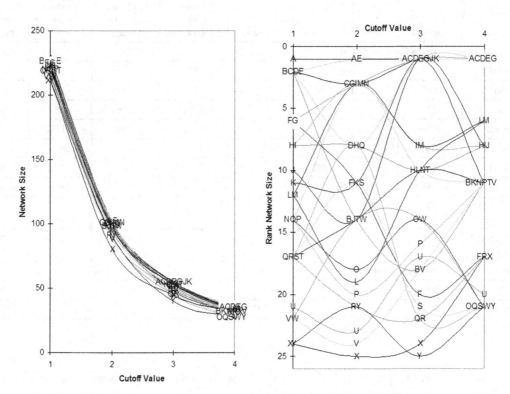

this work, we will identify the top 25 ego-networks that persist across all values of *K*, and then study their metric values and rank across the values of *K*. Each ego-network will be arbitrarily labeled from A to Y to maintain member privacy.

In Figure 1, we can see how the number of nodes (network size) decreases uniformly across the 25 ego-networks. Each ego-network begins at close to 200 nodes for *K=1*, and then decreases to around a size of 40 nodes at *K=4*. This behavior is expected as we increase the edge weight requirement with increasing values of *K*, while maintaining the triangle constraint. It is surprising, however, that all the ego-networks behave a little similarly. Intuitively, the uniform decrease in network size could be linked to the friend-of-a-friend ego-networks and the fact that the cybersecurity network appears to be very

social and thus members engage with many other members over the long period of time in our study. Also, by examining the right-hand of Figure 1, where the ranks of the 25 member ego-networks are shown for the network size, we can see that when *K=4*, several members are tied at rank values of 1, 6, 8, 11, 17 and 21. Lastly, the rank graph for network size shows how the different ego-networks do vary in size reductions across the values of *K* – all networks do not decrease by the same, and some networks actually behave relatively differently than others. Remember that this variation, as demonstrated by the rank chart in Figure 1 is precisely the point we are driving at here, in Gustafson et al. (2009), and one of the key results in Choudhury et al. (2010a): small design choices in extracting relationships from which to build social networks can lead to big impacts in the

*Figure 2. Ego-network transitivity (left-hand graph) and the Rank of ego-network transitivity (right-hand graph) for the 25 ego-networks that persist across cutoff values of **K** from **1** to **4**. The line representing member X is shown in BOLD in both graphs.*

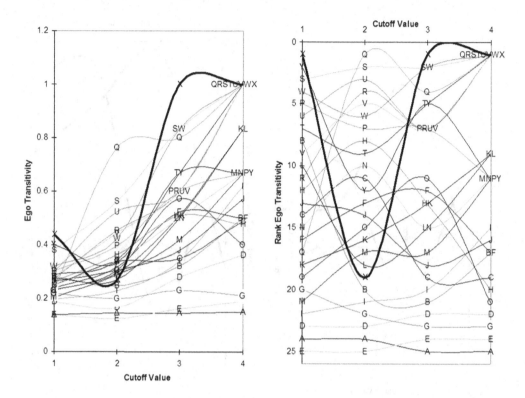

network structure and any subsequent inferences we might draw from the networks.

In Figure 2, we measure the transitivity of the ego-networks for each of the same 25 members. Note that the member numbers A to Y persist for the same members from Figure 1 to Figure 2. As transitivity is a measure that tells us how 'community' oriented a network is (it actually measure the chance that two nodes are connected if they both connect to the same third node), and as we enforce the triangle constraint on our ego-networks, we see relatively high values for transitivity. In the left-hand plot of Figure 2, we can see how dramatic the change in transitivity can be when $K$ is increased. In general, as $K$ increases, most ego-networks also increase their value of transitivity. However, some ego-networks appear to hit a critical point in their connectedness and

transitivity suddenly jumps or falls off. For example see the ego-network for member X, which in the left-hand plot of Figure 2 reaches a value slightly over 1 for transitivity for $K=3$. In the right-hand graph of Figure 2, which shows the ranks of transitivity for the network members, we see that member X goes from being a top-ranked member (according to transitivity) when $K=1$, drops to a rank of 19 for $K=2$, and then raises back to the top with a rank of 1 for $K=3$ and $K=4$. Imagine the data came from a different domain like health, and that we were using transitivity to score how much community support each member had. For those members with the lowest amount of support we recommend them for some sort of intervention. Now, if we used a $K=2$, we would recommend member X. However, for all other values of $K$ (*1, 3* or *4*), X is actually a top-ranked

*Figure 3. Ego-network transitivity / density (left-hand graph) and the Rank of ego-network transitivity / density (right-hand graph) for the 25 ego-networks that persist across cutoff values of* **K** *from* **1** *to* **4**. *The line representing members Q and X are shown in BOLD in both graphs.*

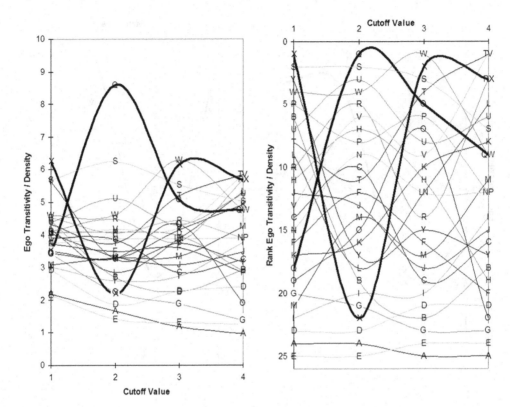

socially supported member. Clearly, we would need to take care when using this data and making decisions like intervention recommendations.

In Figure 3, we show the ego-networks measured and then ranked according to transitivity over network density. Network density measures the number of existing ties between members divided by the possible number of ties, which tells us how dense or sparse the network is. We 'normalize' transitivity with network density to understand the strength of transitivity better. For example, it would be possible to assign the same number of ties between members that achieved a very low transitivity as well as a very high transitivity. Also, between two ego-networks that had a few edges and one that had a lot of edges, we could achieve a similar transitivity score.

In the left-hand graph of Figure 3, we can see how the values of transitivity over density tend to decrease with increasing values of **K**. We can see from Figure 2 that transitivity tends to increase, as expected, with increasing values of **K**. By looking at the rate at which density and transitivity change with **K**, we can conclude that density is increasing at a faster rate than transitivity with increasing values of **K**. For some ego-networks, the value of transitivity over density remains quite stable while **K** increases, while for others, like members Q and X, the values vary significantly. The right-hand graph Figure 3 demonstrates this behavior more clearly with the ranks of the members. As in Gustafson et al. (2009), what is even more interesting from the rank graph is how some members tend to be similar to each other in how they vary across increasing values of $K$. We can see members that tend to decrease in rank at the same time together, increase with subsequent increases in $K$, and then decrease again. And it is those variations that could be potentially interesting to capture and use to segment members and further classify them.

Consider a hypothetical member that maintains a strong social network with only a few members – and each of their ego-network members behave similarly in this regard. However, this member also works harder to reach out to other members in an attempt to network and meet new people. When we consider all the ties that this member establishes with other members, we might find them to have a very high transitivity score: many ties are maintained but some only at a superficial level with infrequent communications. However, when we require that ties are supported by at least two messages or interactions, we might see many members become disconnected and our hypothetical members' transitivity score to dramatically drop off. Increasing the tie-requirement even more could now reduce our members' network down to their 'core' friends, and we would then expect to see their transitivity increase once again. This example is one way we might expect to see the behavior of member X in Figure 3: transitivity starts high for $K=1$, takes a strong dip for $K=2$, and then increases again for $K=3$ and $4$. A similar story might be constructed for member W, which behaves like member X in Figure 2 (transitivity), but critically different in Figure 3 (transitivity/density) for $K=4$, where W's rank drops from 1 to 9 suddenly.

## PREDICTING MEMBER COMMUNICATIONS

In Choudhury et al. (2010a), the authors construct several prediction tasks using their email data sets. A non-trivial classifier is constructed using a rich feature vector for each network node and a Support Vector Machine over a k-fold cross-validation of the training data for parameter tuning. The results showed that there was a range of network thresholds that yielded better prediction accuracies, and that the range was somehow consistent across prediction tasks and data sets. While it is intriguing to speculate that a general network property could be inferred from one type of network and applied to another one, once we start looking at richer and more complex data sets, it is highly likely that specialized and one-off type data analysis and processing will still be necessary. Therefore, in the task and data at hand, we will not attempt to learn the most accurate model of predicting future member communication. Rather, we investigate how much of the future member communications is covered by our rather simple social network construction process.

As mentioned earlier, we held out data from 2010 that came from the same online cybersecurity message boards. As can be seen in Table 1, the pre-2010 data and 2010 are very similar, and based upon inspecting various network diagrams, we are comfortable that it is reasonable to ask whether our pre-2010 ego-networks can somehow infer something about 2010 communication between members. Before describing the details of the experiment, first let us remember that our ego-networks for each member are friend-of-a-friend networks constructed from undirected communications between members within the message board, where a communication event is when either member replies directly to the other. That is, our ego-network construction method is not optimized for predicting future member communications, nor is it even comprehensive in identifying all the potential social relationships that might exist between members who never or rarely reply directly to each other.

Given a member A's ego-networks (across the different values of $K$), we will look into the 2010 data and determine how often A is replied to by someone from their ego-network. We will limit the analysis to those 2010 posts that come from a

*Table 2. Statistics from determining how many future communications between members were covered by member ego-networks. Results from the test data set from 2010 are reported at the top, and results from the training (pre-2010) data are reported at the bottom.*

| K | Replies | Replies from Ego-Network | % Replies from Ego-Network | Chance of Selecting Replier | Number of Times Replier was Most Frequent Replier |
|---|---|---|---|---|---|
| **Evaluated on Testing (2010)Data** | | | | | |
| 1 | 608 | 555 | 91.3% | 0.5% | 1.3% |
| 2 | 490 | 352 | 71.8% | 1.2% | 1.6% |
| 3 | 405 | 237 | 58.5% | 2.0% | 1.7% |
| 4 | 340 | 163 | 47.9% | 3.2% | 1.2% |
| **Evaluated on Training (pre-2010) Data** | | | | | |
| 1 | 2,084 | 1,953 | 93.7% | 0.6% | 10.3% |
| 2 | 1,704 | 1,278 | 75.0% | 1.2% | 5.9% |
| 3 | 1,302 | 726 | 55.85 | 2.1% | 4.1% |
| 4 | 1,005 | 433 | 43.1% | 3.3% | 3.4% |

member for which an ego-network exists and for which a reply comes from someone who existed in the pre-2010 data. That is, we will ignore 2010 posts and replies that come from new members. Also, if our pre-2010 data was unable to construct an ego-network for a member, for example when *K=4*, then we will also not include these posts by these members – although they may participate in the *K=3* statistics if their ego-network was possible there.

Table 2 reports the statistics for the test data set (2010), as well as for the training data set (pre-2010) as a sanity check. As the number of replies "testable" in the data is reduced when *K* is increased, due to fewer ego-networks being feasible from the pre-2010 data, the number of replies contained in the ego-networks also decreases from 91.3% to 47.9% (in the 2010 data). We know from earlier analysis that as *K* increases from *1* to *4*, the size of the ego-networks drops from around 200 to around 40. So, by generating pre-2010 ego-networks for each member, for some subset of members that have ego-networks, nearly half of all their future communication comes from their ego-network when *K=4*. This is even higher when *K<4*. Also, it is interesting to note that as

the size of the ego-networks decreases when *K* increases, the chance of randomly picking one of the ego-network members as the replier increases by a factor of nearly 6 from 0.5% to 3.2%. As we make the ego-networks smaller while increasing *K*, there are indeed fewer future repliers contained in them, as well as fewer ego-networks, but the ego-networks appear to be of more quality in terms of having less noise and more useful relationships contained in them. We also include the number of times the most frequent replier to an ego-network member was the future replier (very rarely), as well as the same results from when we test the ego-networks on the same training (pre-2010) data from which they were generated (not surprising, results are improved). It is highly likely that we could cover more future communications by a member's ego-network with slightly more intelligent ego-network construction that was geared toward that task, as well as by introducing some simple heuristics to obtain smaller ego-networks that make it more likely to identify who would be the future repliers (for example, a member who recently replied is probably more likely to be another replier within the same thread as the conversations go back and forth between mem-

*Figure 4. The average percent of communications that occur within member ego-networks, compared to the average fraction of total members within the ego-network, for cutoff values of* **K** *from* **1** *to* **4**.

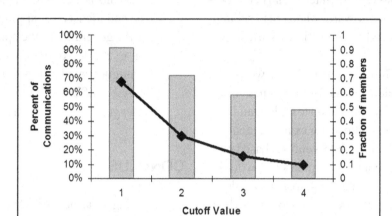

bers). However, it is out of the scope of this study to look for such optimizations.

The results presented in Table 2 do suggest, as we found earlier in the study, that the variation across network designs could be used to determine appropriate social network constructions. For example, the rate of future ego-network communications decreases at a slower rate than the size of the ego-networks. That is, as *K* is increased from *1* to *4*, the average size of the ego-networks drops by 56%, then by 47%, and then 38% for *K=4*. However, the number of future replies to ego-network members that come from their ego-networks decreases, as *K* goes from *1* to *4*, by 21%, then by 19%, then by 18%. This point is illustrated nicely by Figure 4, which plots the average percent of communications in 2010 that occur within the member ego-networks from pre-2010 data, compared to the average size of the ego-networks, relative to the total members. It would seem then, that our ego-networks contain a lot of unnecessary nodes in terms of identifying where future communications might come from – since we can significantly decrease the size of the ego-networks while maintaining a similar

percentage of future communications that come from them. This result could suggest another approach to construct ego-networks. As studied by Choudhury et al. (2010b), using contextual information like the types of words, geo-graphic location, or frequency of communications, could establish ego-networks that contained fewer unnecessary nodes and better predicted future communications.

## FUTURE RESEARCH DIRECTIONS

This study, and previous ones referenced, all highlight the challenges of creating social networks from data, either data collected actively or passively, as in the case of message board relationships. There are many interesting avenues of research in this area, and we list just a few here:

1.  As in Choudhury et al. (2010a), look for common processing and thresholds techniques that span data sets, communication modalities and demographics. Just as many real-world networks have power-law degree

distributions, we might find a property embedded in passively collected social network data that points toward where real social relationships end and superficial or artificial ones begin.

2.  Here and in Gustafson et al. (2009), we have suggested that the variation across network designs becomes important to understand in the light of applications, for example identifying individuals for interventions based on their social or community metrics. It would be interesting to study real-world examples of such social network uses. It would also be beneficial to analyze the outcomes of such applications on social network data that was collected using more traditional and rigorous methods. For example, how accurate was the identification of network members in terms of selecting people who should be selected for an intervention? What were the sources of noise?

3.  Earlier in this study, we suggested that the variation across network designs could be useful for segmenting and further classifying individuals in the social network. For example, members could be classified by various ego-network sizes and network metrics. We could also classify ego-networks by their robustness to edge-weight thresholds and to structural constraints like the triangle constraint used in this study that become harder to understand with individual network measurements.

4.  Lastly, there are many other attributes of the data that could be used in creating the social networks. Our method was simple to illustrate the main points. The method in Choudhury et al. (2010a) is more complex. Additionally, we could take into account the topics of communication, the timing between message and response, and the overall relationships length from first communication to most recent, the trend of communications over time, etc. The danger, however, is that

different people behave differently with each other, and as methods become more specialized and focused for applications, we could see the generality of the approach diminish. For example, one network construction technique that identifies ones friends would likely be different than one for identifying colleagues and family members.

## CONCLUSION

Constructing social networks from data, where that data is often collected passively and perhaps for other purposes than to record the social network, presents scientists with new data challenges and opportunities. The challenges are highlighted here, in Gustafson et al. (2009) and in Choudhury et al. (2010a), where slight variations in the data processing steps can lead to very different networks. These variations are magnified in networks where one network change can percolate throughout the network creating cascades of effects – often the "network effect". We expect to see network effects in real-world networks where the degree distribution often follows a power-law: many nodes have a few ties while a few nodes have many ties. And we can learn and improve our network processing choice to take into account these variations by experimenting with several design choices, understanding the variation, and look for stable design choices that are amenable to generating quality and sound inferences. The opportunities of constructing social networks from data are also reported here, in Gustafson et al. (2009) and in Choudhury et al. (2010a). For example, design choices can lead to significantly better performance for subsequent prediction tasks. Also, the variations between design choices can themselves become segmenting opportunities from which hard to measure member characteristics can be extracted. As the field of computational social sciences becomes adopted throughout more industries and applications, it is of critical importance that our understanding of data collection and processing of passive, active, and massive data sets keeps pace.

# REFERENCES

Adar, E., & Ré, C. (2007). Managing uncertainty in social networks. *Data Engineering Bulletin*, *30*(2), 23–31.

Bernard, H. R., Killworth, P., Kronenfeld, D., & Sailer, L. (1984). The problem of informant accuracy: The validity of retrospective data. *Annual Review of Anthropology*, *13*, 495–517. doi:10.1146/annurev.an.13.100184.002431

Borgatti, S. P., Carley, K. M., & Krackhardt, D. (2006). On the robustness of centrality measures under conditions of imperfect data. *Social Networks*, *28*(2), 124–136. doi:10.1016/j.socnet.2005.05.001

Choudhury, M. D., Lin, Y.-R., Sundaram, H., Candan, K. S., Xie, L., & Kelliher, A. (2010b). How does the data sampling strategy impact the discovery of information diffusion in social media? In *Proceedings of the Fourth International AAAI Conference on Weblogs and Social Media*, (pp. 34-41).

Choudhury, M. D., Mason, W. A., Hofman, J. M., & Watts, D. J. (2010a). Inferring relevant social networks from interpersonal communication. In *Proceedings of the Nineteenth World Wide Web Conference*, (pp. 301-310).

Costenbader, E., & Valente, T. W. (2003). The stability of centrality measures when networks are sampled. *Social Networks*, *25*(4), 283–307. doi:10.1016/S0378-8733(03)00012-1

Fisher, D., Smith, M., & Welser, H. T. (2006). You are who you talk to: Detecting roles in Usenet newsgroups. *Proceedings of the 39th Hawaii International Conference on System Sciences*.

Golder, S., Wilkinson, D., & Huberman, B. (2007). Rhythms of social interaction: Messaging within a massive online network. In *Proceedings of the Third Communities and Technologies Conference*, (pp. 41-66).

Gustafson, S., Ma, H., & Moitra, A. (2009). A note on creating networks from social network data. *Connections*, *29*(2), 77–84.

Latapy, M., & Magnien, C. (2008). Complex network measurements: Estimating the relevance of observed properties. *IEEE Conference on Computer Communications*, (pp. 1660-1668).

Lazer, D., Pentland, A., Adamic, L., Aral, S., Barabasi, A. L., & Brewer, D. (2009). Computational social science. *Science*, *323*(5915), 721–723. doi:10.1126/science.1167742

Lin, N., & Zhao, H. (2005). Are scale-free networks robust to measurement errors? *BMC Bioinformatics*, *6*(1), 119. doi:10.1186/1471-2105-6-119

Ma, H., Gustafson, S., Moitra, A., & Bracewell, D. (2009). Ego-centric network sampling in viral marketing applications. In *IEEE International Conference on Computational Science and Engineering*, (pp. 777-782).

Ma, H., Gustafson, S., Moitra, A., & Bracewell, D. (2010). Ego-centric network sampling in viral marketing applications. In Ting, I.-H., Wu, H.-J., & Ho, T.-H. (Eds.), *Mining and analyzing social networks. Studies in Computational Intelligence* (p. 288). Springer-Verlag. doi:10.1007/978-3-642-13422-7_3

Marsden, P. V. (1990). Network data and measurement. *Annual Review of Sociology*, *16*, 435–463. doi:10.1146/annurev.so.16.080190.002251

Rothenberg, R. B. (1995). Commentary: Sampling in social networks. *Connections*, *18*(1), 104–110.

## KEY TERMS AND DEFINITIONS

**Cybersecurity:** Security of the communication network and other infrastructure networks against electronic attacks.

**Ego-Network:** A network that is 'focused' on one network node, or ego, which usually represents a single person, actor or entity. Ego-networks are useful for studying the relationships focused only around one actor at a time.

**Network Robustness:** A measure of how stable the properties of a network are in the face of incomplete or inaccurate data.

**Online Communities:** A community where members interact with each other through the Internet.

**Relationship:** Interactions between people, which may include various forms of communications.

**Transitivity:** A measure that counts the number of triangles found in a graph, where a triangle consists of three nodes, each connected with an edge to one another. The measure is normalized by dividing it by all possible triangles that could be formed.

# Chapter 11
# Bringing Qualitative and Quantitative Data Together:
## Collecting Network Data with the Help of the Software Tool VennMaker

**Markus Gamper**
*University Trier, Germany*

**Michael Schönhuth**
*University Trier, Germany*

**Michael Kronenwett**
*University Trier, Germany*

## ABSTRACT

*In this chapter, the authors investigate the issue of gathering network-related social data by means of both qualitative and quantitative methodology. An overview of the most relevant visual approaches such as network pictures and different kinds of network maps ("paper and pencil", "paper, pen, and tokens," and "digital network maps") will be given, including an example of a migration study in which a network survey was carried out with the aid of the software program VennMaker. Finally, the authors discuss the advantages and disadvantages of data collection based on digital network maps and make suggestions for future research.*

## INTRODUCTION

Being part of a "social network" is in vogue. It seems as if being embedded in social structures and relationships (Granovetter, 1973) has virtually become the key for the individual to gain access to postmodern forms of sociation in an era where institutional ties are becoming more and more diversified. For example, the numbers of users of social networking sites like Facebook or Twitter has increased from about 770 million (July 2009) to 945 million (July 2010) all over the world (Comscore, 2010).

DOI: 10.4018/978-1-61350-444-4.ch011

There is no denying that networks provide ample scope for action by paving the way to information, emotional support or material resources. On the other hand, networks constrain one's room for manoeuvre, entailing obligations or conflict with others in the network (Kapferer, 1969; Emirbayer & Goodwin, 1994). For studying structures and social relations, two different approaches have been developed in the field. Collecting and analyzing network data (density, centrality measures) has so far been predominantly carried out by means of a highly standardized methodology requiring considerable effort and qualified research staff (Wasserman & Faust, 1994). Qualitative network analysis, on the other hand, has its roots in psychology (Moreno, 1934; Bott, 1957; Kahn & Antonucci, 1980) as well as in cultural anthropology (Davis et al., 1941; Barnes, 1954). In contrast to the quantitative approach, this methodology is more open, descriptive and flexible.

Despite the rapid development of mathematical and user-friendly computer programs for calculating and visualizing large data files (Freeman, 2004; Gamper & Reschke, 2010), the quantitative method suffers from limitations in terms of analysis and heuristic value. Fowler and Christakis (2008), for example, emphasize in their large-scale medical longitudinal "Framingham Heart Study", that people who know each other are equally happy. At the same time, they notice that they do not have a significant explanation for the relationship between these two factors. In their own words the "[...] data do not allow us to identify the actual causal mechanisms of the spread of happiness, but [that] various mechanisms are possible" (Fowler & Christakis, 2008, p. 8). One reason is that there is no qualitative data that might give a deeper and qualitative explanation about the correlation between the two factors. Conversely, Padgett and Ansell in their famous network study would not have found any substantial evidence for the rise of the Medici in Florence after the failed weaver-revolt in the 15th century, if their study had only

focussed on the description of relation and not on the structure as a whole (Padgett & Ansell 1993). Because of their simple structure and the selective way in which the data are collected, the models of qualitative data collection are limited in terms of informative value and empirical validity and are therefore not without controversy (Diaz-Bone, 2007). Against this background, there is a growing methodological debate about triangulation (Denzin, 1970) in social network analysis (Coviello, 2005; Edwards, 2010). New studies are trying to take advantage of combining qualitative and quantitative approaches. So far, most researchers have combined the two approaches in succession (Crossley, 2008; Bidart & Lavenu, 2005).

In addition to the trend of triangulation, there is also a tendency to digitally collect data. Much of the data in social network analysis, qualitative and quantitative, is still collected by "traditional methods" such as participant observation (Moreno, 1934; Roethlisberger & Dickson, 1939; Davis et al., 1941; Barnes, 1954), qualitative interviews (Bott, 1957; Kahn & Antonucci, 1980) and standardized questionnaires (Laumann, 1973; Fischer et al., 1977; Wellmann, 1979), but for both methods, a trend towards computer-assisted data collection can be observed (Vehovar & Manfreda, 2008; Vehovar et al., 2008; Herz & Gamper, 2011).

In a joint interdisciplinary project, the authors of this study together with a team of historians, sociologists, anthropologists and software specialists have tried to bridge this gap by combining qualitative and quantitative approaches with the help of the new developed Software VennMaker.[1] This software enables the user to interactively collect network relationship data from an actor's point of view and render them comparable and quantitatively analyzable by means of a graphical user interface that can be operated intuitively.[2] Where complex questionnaire procedures or intense employment of staff have dominated so far, VennMaker allows users to draw actors and their relationships in an intuitive way on the computer. It is the act of drawing and commenting itself which creates data. Collecting data in this way has become more prominent since the 1980s (Kahn & Antonucci, 1980) – at that time still haptically. The test person either draws the relationships maintained with the most important persons he or she feels attached to on paper by way of free drawing (network picture) or a network map is provided, often based on a pattern with concentric circles, in which contacts are placed depending on emotional closeness as felt by Ego. After conducting non-standardised interviews, these network maps/network pictures are communicatively assessed or narratively interpreted to obtain qualitative information, which is created from the stories behind nodes and edges.

Our goal was to develop a tool that may prove efficiently applicable for practical purposes and at the same time be in keeping with academic standards in generating and processing social network data flexibly. Not only is the entire process of generating the network map documented digitally – as the choice, positioning, moving and spatial distribution of actors (nodes) and the drawing of different relation categories (ties) – also statements regarding content and importance of social relationships can be audio–recorded during the interview and evaluated later via content analysis methods. From the vantage point of the social sciences, the gap between quantitative and qualitative network research might be narrowed down this way. There have been many developments in the area of "mixed methods methodology", as it has recently been termed (Coviello, 2005; Hollstein & Straus, 2006), but to our knowledge, however, there is no project, which has solved the complexity problem in qualitative network maps and the issue of interlacing qualitative and quantitative data so far in a satisfying way. What makes VennMaker different combine to other software tools?

First, VennMaker allows two forms of data collection. It is possible to perform participatory, process-oriented interviews, where the client/interviewee and researcher/coach develop and discuss the network map together in a commu-

nicative process. But it also allows standardized interviews. Moreover, it is possible to combine these different kinds of research approaches. Second, VennMaker is suitable for jointly generating strategic network maps of organizational branches or projects ("strategic actor mapping") in a group process. This form of application is suitable in situations where the elicitation and merging of different actor views for joint action is a goal. Finally, the software with its various already implemented features and the possibility of user defined amplification of graphical representations can also be applied as a user friendly drawing instrument to visualize network data that have been already surveyed with other analytical methods beforehand.

In this chapter we want to follow up recent developments by embedding this new digital tool in a broader discussion on the role of network maps in the quantative/qualitative network analysis nexus. Following a brief outline of network forms (ego-networks/whole networks) and a section where a distinction is drawn between quantitative and qualitative network analysis, we shall discuss different types of network maps and their advantages and disadvantages respectively. A selected example from current research on migration will provide us with an opportunity to demonstrate a digital network survey with the help of VennMaker. We shall conclude with a discussion of the advantages and disadvantages of digital network maps.

## Forms of Network Analysis

Social networks can be defined "[…] as a specific set of linkages among a defined set of persons [actors], with the additional property that the characteristics of these linkages as a whole may be used to interpret the social behaviour of the persons [actors] involved" (Mitchell, 1969, p. 2). Historically, two ideal types of network analysis have developed, whole networks and egocentric ones (Burt, 1980). The analysis of whole networks seeks to establish all existing interior relations of a set of actors. These form part of a delimited system. The focus of inquiry lies on whether and in what way the members within the defined boundary are linked up. Relations to actors outside are not accounted for. So the focus of interest lies on the global structure of the network and the interactive patterns it contains (Wasserman & Faust, 1994). The focus of egocentric network analysis lies on the relations of an actor (ego) and the social environment. Through this method, ego's personal network is established from his or her subjective point of view. Questions touching on ego's partners ("actor/name generators") in everyday life are posed to identify ego's contacts (alteri) to whom a defined relation is maintained which is then shown using connecting lines (edges). Further personal and socio-demographic data such as age, sex, contact frequency, and level of education are subsequently gathered using so-called "actor/ name interpreters". Ego-networks represent an individual's overall pattern of relationships. The focus lies on the embeddedness of single actors in their social environment. Egocentric network analysis is put to work in cases where the group under investigation is hard to delineate or the sheer size of the whole suggests the study of individual cases (Fischer et al., 1977; Wellman, 1979; Mc-Carty et al., 2011).

Networks can be established quantitatively or qualitatively (Coviello, 2005; Schnegg, 2010). Quantitative network analysis focuses on calculating formal aspects of network structure, i.e. standardised data on the basis of which structural units of measurement like centrality or actors' prestige, cutpoints between sub-networks (cliques) and density can be calculated (Wasserman & Faust, 1994). The advantages of quantitative data collection lie in fact that they are comparable and representative in every case. The formal, quantitative analysis has dominated the field in recent decades despite qualitative aspects having been touched upon among the founding generation.[3] A trend to include qualitative methods in network analysis

in entirely different areas has emerged since the 1980s. "These seek to incorporate particularly the actor's point of view in network analysis, to explore networks, as well as comprehend and analyse their dynamics", argues Diaz-Bone in his review of an anthology devoted to qualitative network analysis in 2007 (Diaz-Bone, 2007).[4]

Qualitative network analysis has had a long-standing tradition, especially in and psychology (e.g. Moreno, 1934) and cultural anthropology (e.g. Roethlisberger & Dickson, 1939; Davis et al., 1941; Barnes, 1954), nevertheless, it has only been since the 1980s (Kahn & Antonucci, 1980; Antonucci & Akiyama, 1995; Trotter, 1999) that formal network analysis has been slowly following up this tradition. Particularly White (1992, 2002), Emirbayer and Goodwin (1994) and Schweitzer (1996) have embraced cultural symbols, scope for action and subjective perception of social actors in their works both theoretically and empirically.[5] The focus no longer lies solely on the mere existence of relations in a social network but their quality too.[6] According to White, it is the stories actors tell about themselves or alteri which constitute relations and dynamics in a network. "Stories express perceptions of social process and structure [...]" (White, 1992, p. 13). Ties between actors can be "[...] regarded as phenomenological constructs which come into being through the narration of stories" (Haas & Mützel, 2007, p. 60). At the same time, these stories construct "[...] the identities of the actors involved in their respective contexts" (Haas & Mützel, 2007, p. 60)1. One has to learn about people's stories and their scope for action in their respective contexts to fully grasp the emergence of networks and their dynamics (White, 1992; Schweitzer, 1996).

## Forms of Visualised Network Surveys

Ever since the 1980s (Kahn & Antonucci, 1980; Schönhuth & Kievelitz, 1995; Straus, 2002; Hollstein & Pfeffer, 2010), network pictures and network maps have been put to use for gathering data on the basis of egocentric network analysis as carried out by Elisabeth Bott during the 1950s (Bott, 1957). They can be read as maps of social relations in which individuals graphically represent their social networks. The main interest rests on the stories and subjective meanings of the network actors and making sense of their relationships (White, 1992, 2002; Emirbayer & Goodwin, 1994).

Network pictures come into being as free drawings by the test person without any specifications (Straus, 2002). Network maps are more or less pre-structured through given coordinates (e.g. concentric circles, sectors). As a rule, they are set up with the help of face-to-face interviews as ego-centred (the respondent being the point of reference) but also as non-ego-centred networks (ego being a node in the network) (e.g. Kolip, 1993; Krumbein, 1995; Hollstein & Pfeffer, 2010). Within the framework of organisation and project counselling or village development, they are also gathered as whole networks featuring selected (or all) agents of the system under investigation (Schönhuth, 2007; Schiffer, 2007). They yield the jointly established point of view of those concerned on the respective system (depending on the focus of investigation with or without external relations). The advantages of collecting data by means of visualisation are multifaceted. A comprehensive depiction of complex structures is rendered feasible and helps respondent and interviewer alike. Subject matters, which are elusive and difficult to memorize, are illustrated and visibly retained for the whole duration of the interview. This creates common ground for the interlocutors, an objectified medium of communication enabling them to exchange views, talk and make reference to it time and again. Using network maps for visually arranging ties is preferable in many ways to classic computer-based or paper-based alternatives. Hogan et al. assert: "it is more dependable, pleases respondents, looks visually compelling, and can be seen at once (making it a useful prop in ad-

dition to a data-gathering technique)" (Hogan et al., 2005, p. 140).

The mnemonic pitfall, which crops up in verbal interviews, i.e. the tendency of actors and relations named earlier to fade into the background compared to newer information, can be avoided. Referring to these pieces of information is possible thanks to visualisation.[7] Thus diachronic narratives are transformed into synchronically analysable and navigable maps. These are useful advantages in situations where the resulting network is less crucial than the circumstances surrounding its formation or its potential for future development. That is why this kind of network has spread in the fields of psychology, education (Straus, 2002), and development counselling (Chambers, 1985). Not only are they an invaluable asset for generating narrations or focussed points of inquiry, but for research from a purely epistemic perspective too.

As is the case with all methods of data collection, there are advantages and disadvantages for applying them. It depends on the focus and epistemic interest, which one has in mind. Below, we would like to compare in table form (based on Straus, 2002, p. 239) advantages and disadvantages of network pictures and network maps (see Table 1). Depending on their degree of structuring, methodologically network maps; do have more in common with the quantitative tradition of network analysis, network pictures lying on the open/qualitative end of the continuum. Accordingly, explorative settings requiring some amount of intrinsic logic generally lend themselves to network pictures, whereas settings, which are already known or aim at comparability, are better suited for prearranged maps.

Three ideal types of maps can be distinguished: 1. paper and pencil (e.g. Kahn & Antonucci, 1980): two space dimensions, only few specifications visualisable, 2. paper, pen and tokens (paper and toolkit (e.g. Rambaldi & Callosa-Tarr, 2000; Schiffer, 2007), adding a third dimension, and 3. digital network maps (two space dimensions, process of data collection can be traced, reversible,

*Table 1. Advantages and drawbacks of network pictures/network maps (based on Straus, 2002, p. 239)*

| Methods | Advantages | Drawbacks |
|---|---|---|
| Network pictures | 1 creative freedom: different dimensons can be combined (topics, places, individuals)<br>2 heavily imbued with metaphor<br>3 idiographic elements (individual/cultural)<br>4 explorative | 5 little comparability (more geared to Gestalt-psychology)<br>6 as of yet little empirical variance (currently changing!)<br>7 possible inhibitions against free drawing/modelling |
| Network maps | 8 comparability<br>9 replicability<br>10 empirically tested<br>11 oriented towards analysis<br>12 quantifiable<br>13 guidable | 14 little freedom of choice due to standardisation<br>15 culture-specific<br>16 cognitively "clamped" (preliminary decisions of the interviewer) |

more specifications visualized, filtering and analysis function).

The "paper-and-pencil" approach is the most commonly used type of network map. In its most popular form, it has recourse to the egocentric circular model of Kahn and Antonucci (1980).[8] Ego is placed in the centre while interaction partners are put around ego within concentric circles depending on emotional importance. A more complex variant is featured in Straus's et al. (2002) EGONET-QF maps, but also in several contributions in Hollstein and Straus (2006), including the division of concentric circles into sectors pertinent to different areas of life (e.g. work, family, friends) or the creation of multiple maps containing different dimensions of relations (importance, closeness, support). EGONET-QF additionally works with marker pins and labels, which make it possible to move around actors who have already been placed (see Figure 1).

Venn-diagrams (Chambers, 1985), which have been used in development cooperation and management consultancy in line with rapid appraisal methods (Schönhuth & Kievelitz, 1995) since the 1980s, have followed a similar path. Names and symbols of the generated actors are written on paper circles of different size according to the importance ascribed to them for maintaining the system or its future perspectives and then placed closer to or farther from the centre (village/project) according to their accessibility or performance

*Figure 1. Graphic rendering of a cork tile and marker pins of an EGONET QF map (Höfer et al., 2006, p. 283) (translated)*

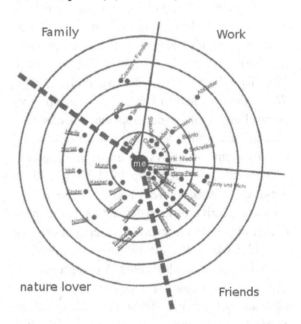

for the system. Big-sized (i.e. important) actors remote from the centre are critical actors because they are, on the one hand, relevant to the system, but they can, on the other hand, only be contacted with some difficulty or provide their resources merely in a suboptimal fashion (see Figure 2 and 3).

In 2007, social scientist Eva Schiffer (2007) developed a method to visualise networks for the International Food Policy Research Institute

*Figure 2. Chapati/VennDiagramm, relevant actors in an Indian village from the local men's point of view (Mascarenhas, 1991)*

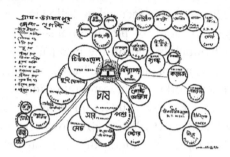

*Figure 3. Actors placed according to importance and accessibility in an African-German development project; containing a future scenario (indicated by arrows) and suggestions for improvement for "excluded" actors (Schönhuth, 2005)*

*Figure 4. Paper and toolkit: (Net-map) "Influence Mapping of Social Networks" (Schiffer, 2007)*

(IFPRI) independently of the tools mentioned so far. She introduced a third dimension to the map aided by tokens, so the perceived influence of actors is no longer indicated through their size as in VennMaker but rather through the height of the stacked tokens (see Figure 4).[9]

The advantages of paper-and-pencil variants are apparent. Their simple, intuitive handling and the haptic components make them easily amenable to respondents. Applied with cultural sensitivity, they can be employed in the context of foreign cultures and with people with various levels of education. They are largely independent from sources of energy and as a consequence nearly universally applicable in any field situation. Cost of materials is low. Doing network interviews is therefore also an option for studies working on a low budget (e.g. Schiffer & Hauck, 2011).

Alongside the advantages, there are some drawbacks as well. Firstly, the data collected have to be entered into statistical software prior to a quantitative analysis (e.g. density, centrality). This transmission is time-consuming and prone to errors. A visual representation of data, too, on the basis of mathematical calculations (e.g. representation by a *spring-embedder* which reassigns positions to actors according to their centrality) can only be conducted afterwards by manually transmitting the data with software such as UCINET (e.g. Borgatti et al., 1999), VISONE (Brandes et al., 2001) or SIENA (Snijders, 2001),

for instance. Other than that, inaccuracies occur during software-aided post-visualisation since a completely accurate transmission of the test person's visual depiction is impossible. These inaccuracies are later reflected in the statistical analysis. Thirdly, qualitative information in the shape of oral statements made during the process of drawing cannot be linked up with the respective representation of relations and actors. This leads to a high expenditure of time for transcription because statements made in the interview have to be crosschecked with the visualised information. In other words, a precise coupling of visualised and spoken data does not take place. Finally, once network maps have been fixed, they cannot be modified anymore without having to create them anew. Also, circulating network maps and post-processing by others (e.g. other researchers) is both time-consuming and labour-intensive.

## DIGITAL NETWORK MAPS: AN ACTUAL CASE STUDY

The advantages and disadvantages of digital network maps will be looked at referencing a current research project on integration and network relations of ethnic German repatriates from the former Soviet Union in the Trier area in Germany as an example. The study aimed at depicting the network structure as well as social support of the target group (Fenicia et al., 2010). A previously conducted quantitative survey with a paper questionnaire (n=71) had found that repatriates' networks are strongly family-centred and exhibit a high degree of ethnic homophily.[10] Nonetheless, it became clear that the number of family members or relatives might vary depending on the kind of social support. For instance, emotional support or support in case of illness are mainly provided by family members whereas native Germans are generally relied on most when looking for employment (Fenicia et al., 2010).

In a second step, digital network maps were used to look more closely into the reasons given by repatriates as to why they count on certain social relations and, conversely, why certain social relations do not exist at all. It is particularly in the case of such missing links where the problem-centred, scripted interview (Witzel, 1982, 2000), which was used together with a digital network map, comes into its own. Already in the process of visualising the network diagram, the interviewer can discern certain missing links or special struc-

tures differing from the quantitative survey. The reasons for this can be addressed specifically and almost simultaneously during the conversation.

In this study we focused on following major categories: Family centrality, transnationality, ethnic homophily and on the occupational and private patterns of integration. Based on evidence in pertinent works on ethnic migration to Western Europe (e.g. Bastians, 2004; Lubbers et al., 2007; Lubbers et al., 2010). We set up following hypotheses, looking at the patterns of social integration of ethnic German repatriates:

H1:  Family centrality should be expected to be high

H2:  Transnationality should be low

H3:  Ethnic homophily should be high

H4:  Occupational and private patterns of integration in Germany should be low

A digital actor generator ("Please name the people you think of and you personally know"), which was exactly the same for all test persons, was employed for the survey. The network map was partly standardised and structured for ease of comparability and quantitative analysis of data. In this way, the survey, by means of a digital network map, resembled the quantitative one with the paper questionnaire. However, certain attributes were drawn straight on the network map. These could be further processed with additional software right after the interviews in contrast to the paper-and-pencil approach where data has to be entered into a computer. In order to ensure that the digital network maps can be operated as easily as the ones made of paper, an electronic whiteboard (see Figure 5) was put into operation. The latter is akin to a conventional blackboard or whiteboard, the difference being that a projector is used to display the content while sensors keep track of any movement from fingers or pens on the surface of the board. The sensors report any input to a computer, which in turn processes the information obtained. Then, the results are again

*Figure 5. Digital network map on an electronic whiteboard with touchscreen*

projected onto the board. An electronic whiteboard bestows upon the interviewer the advantage of being able to fully concentrate on the interview. He or she can work directly on the digital network map; taking a detour by using the mouse is no longer necessary. Negative side effects of an interview caused by problems with input devices like mouse or keyboard are minimised.

The network survey was carried out with the aid of the tool VennMaker.[11] VennMaker is a software program that allows data to be jointly gathered both qualitatively and quantitatively at the same time during an interview. In addition, the interview is recorded on an audio track. While the respondent is visualising and describing the personal network in conversation, qualitative data can be collected visually and/or by way of audio recording and adding comments. Quantitative data can be directly established on the digital network map or with an optional electronic questionnaire. The interviewer is able to configure the digital questionnaire prior to the survey, making adjustments according to the focus in question. For non-standardised surveys, e.g. narrative interviews, it is possible to adjust all settings of the network map during the course of the interview as well.

The governing principle in visual data collection with the aid of digital network maps describes the way from graphics to data, which means that everything drawn on the network map can be used for further qualitative and quantitative assessment. The software keeps records of every action on the digital network map and can be accessed afterwards and played synchronically along with the audio files. It is possible to represent relational and non-relational attributes as graphics or texts. Other than that, the representations of nodes and edges can be configured freely. Visual variables such as size, shape, colour, and texture can be linked to attribute values and shown on nodes and edges. Additional graphical elements, e.g. concentric circles, sectors, pie charts, and geographical maps can be added alongside nodes and edges (Kronenwett, 2010). VennMaker expands conventional network maps and written or oral surveys in combining both of these methods.

Using the following actor generator has assembled the ego-centred networks: Please name the people you think of and you personally know. After that, an enquiry followed concerning alteri from which she could borrow money or obtain support in case of emotional problems. The actor generator had been set up in the shape of an input mask.

Hypothesis 1 "Family centrality should be expected to be high" were tested with the non-relational attribute role (e.g. family, boyfriend) and additionally socio-demographic variables like sex or age were also evaluated. These non-relational attributes were collected via a digital questionnaire. Some of these attributes, e.g. alter's role (family, boyfriend) were automatically displayed on the network map with corresponding colour coded and shape coded icons.

Moving onward from the input mask to the map at the right time is crucial. If done too late, the benefit of joint visualisation is lost. For this reason, only three attributes had been chosen for collection via the questionnaire, enabling researchers to switch to the network map immediately.

For testing hypothesis 2 "Transnationality should be low" we use concentric circles, which were employed to establish the spatial distance between alteri and ego. At this point, we consciously deviated from the classical pattern, in which the spatial distance to ego stands for emotional distance, because geopolitical space or spatial closeness are essential for explaining network relations in the context of migration. Concentric circles are well suited for grasping distances as the spatial layout of the digital network map corresponds to the spatial distance felt. Moreover, the interviewer can perceive while the respondent is drawing how spatial distances are distributed and ask again more precisely if the need should arise (McCarty et al., 2007). The farther alter was placed from ego, the longer the actual distance, having been divided into the following categories: "same household", "same neighbourhood", "same town", or "other German town". Alteri whose whereabouts are beyond the German border were put outside the outermost circle.

For testing hypothesis 3 "Ethnic homophily should be high" and hypothesis 4 "Occupational and private patterns of integration in Germany should be low" the alteri were assigned to different sectors according to the following three categories: "native German", "ethnic German repatriate", or "other migrant". The sectors swiftly show potential tendencies for ethnic homophily or heterophily that can in turn be qualitatively examined.

Unidirectional relations between ego and alteri were evaluated by means of a five-tier scale, ranging from conflict-laden to positive relationship, and plotted as colour-coded lines. Financial support was defined as a yellow line, emotional support as a purple one. In the course of a network survey with the aid of network maps the number of alteri increases together with the number of plotted relationships. This effect may lead to faulty input or a rise in missing relations. The issue of increasing complexity was tackled with filters which can be switched on and off dynamically while collecting data. In order to avoid haphazard selection of alter-alter relations in the process of drawing which might cause some of them to be forgotten, the respondent was asked to proceed clockwise, commencing with the outer alteri, when drawing in relations between pairs of alteri. After all alteri had been plotted on the digital network map together with the relevant relations by means of the actor generator, the two forms of social assistance were enquired afterwards orally with the aim of obtaining more profound information by way of more open oral expression.

The interview lasted 90 minutes in total. The names were rendered anonymous with VennMaker and given an identity (ID) number afterwards. The respondent is female, comes from Kazakhstan, studied economics, and was 29 years old at the time of the survey. The respondent (ego) is located in the middle of the digital network map; the other circular symbols represent alteri. The respondent named 36 alteri altogether. The number of alteri thus came out higher than compared to the average of the 71 repatriates from the quantitative survey carried out in advance. On average, 10.3 alteri were given there.

The respondent maintains the majority of her relationships with other repatriates. Yet contacts to other migrants and native Germans exist as well. This is in line with the findings of the quantitative survey by questionnaire. The proportion of repatriates amounted to 74.4 percent here. Conversely, locals make up merely 17.2 percent and other immigrants 8.3 percent of the repatriates' network that was investigated.

Ties between members of different ethnic groups became apparent too among the interviewed. This is due to the fact that most of her female friends have a significant other from Germany or from an area abroad where Russian is spoken and that her best friend (alter no. 36) is linked up with almost all her repatriate friends. All in all, the friend mentioned above maintains most relationships (nine relations) compared to other German alteri (four relations at most)

The Germans represented in the network include her best friend, her flat mate, older neighbours and the work colleagues the respondent got to know during a period of work experience. She is on particularly good terms with her older neighbours, who are aged between 50 and 70 (see Figure 8: alteri no. 32-35). She stated in the interview that especially the latter found it easy to be sympathetic to her situation as a repatriate in Germany. On the other hand, she has only little contact to fellow students of her age. She indicated that it was difficult for her to form relationships to her fellow students because those were generally rather superficial and did not relate to her situation as an immigrant.

The average age of the alteri discussed so far is 38 years, hence nine years older than the respondent, with a high spread (standard deviation = 18 years). The higher average age of the alteri is based on the high age of the family members, neighbours and little contact with fellow students of the same age. The spread suggests a heterogeneous age composition. Even though the respondent knows many older persons, these do not exhibit homogeneous age composition. Considering the composition of alteri according to their social roles, it is quite striking that compared to the total number of alteri (n=35) only relatively few family members appear in the network. When this was pointed out, it was argued that the father was already 80 years old and the better part of the paternal relatives deceased.

What does the structure of the network look like if only the relations between alteri are considered? Into which subgroups would the network split if ego were not there? The normalised density value is used to answer the first question. The repatriates' network has a normalised density value of 0.10. This density value takes only relations between alteri into account; all alter-ego relations are left out. Normalised means that the size of the network has no influence on the calculation. As a consequence, the density value can be compared with those of other networks. A density value of 1 would mean that all alteri are connected amongst each other. The lower the value, the fewer relations exist between the alteri. A density value of 0.10 suggests a low level of interconnectedness between the individuals. If ego were excluded from the network, a network of low density would remain.

If the structure of the network is represented with a spring embedder layout (see Figure 6), connected actors are arranged closer to each other, while actors without any relations or only a few are placed farther away from others. In addition, once ego has been removed from the network, subgroups and isolated individuals can be graphically represented within the network.

Figure 6 shows existing relations, subgroups and isolated individuals. The edge size represents the betweenness of the actor. The higher the betweennes value the bigger the edge. Betweennes is useful as an index of the potential of an actor for control of communication and information flow (Freeman, 1979). The betweenness index can be between 0 and 1. Zero (0) means that the actor falls on no geodesics and 1 means that the actor falls on all geodesics. The edge colour represents the ethnic group.

Just based on the relational-data the German friend (actor no. 36) takes a central position within the largest subgroup (standardized betweenness value of 0.07). When asked once more about that friend, the respondent replied that she had introduced the German friend into the clique of her repatriate friends on purpose in case something should happen to herself. This individual is thus a stable and essential link between alteri in Trier and Hamburg.

*Figure 6. Relational network without ego, representation by Spring Embedder Layout*

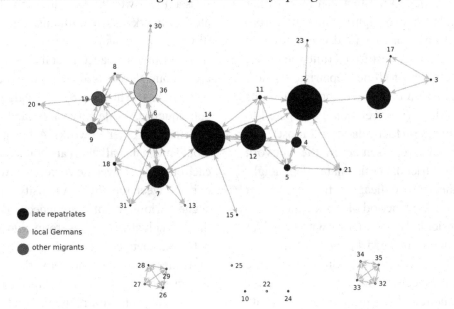

If one compares this emerging picture with the digital network map showing the two kinds of social support (Diewald, 1991, p. 71), covering the two factors of emotional and financial support here, it can be seen that actor no. 2 and no. 23 are mentioned regarding financial support. This seems surprising at first sight since both individuals and actor no. 23 in particular are only little embedded in the social network (see Figures 6 and 7).

There are only two alteri from which the respondent would borrow money if she were in financial straits: her mother and a female friend. She would not borrow any money from her father because he lives abroad and receives only a moderate pension. When asked why she thought that actor no. 23 would lend her some money, she answered: *"I've known her for ages, since I was five. [...] Her granddad and grandma were friends of my dad's. And they only came here to see us in summer. And we're still friends. That's why I know the family is very strong and very big. They all know me anyway and it's no great deal if I ask for money[...]"*

The length of their relationship, trust, and her acquaintance's strong embeddedness in the family network are given as the reason why the respondent would turn to alter no. 23 if she were in financial straits. In other words, the network behind actor 23 is the decisive factor and not the attributes or financial means of actor 23 themselves. From the vantage point of a purely quantitative analysis of the network structure this would not have become clear why this friend had been chosen for financial support since she does not hold a central position in ego's network.

The group of alteri (n=7) providing emotional support largely comprises friends from the same ethnic group (n=4) and only to a small extent Germans (a German friend and a German neighbour and a friend from Kazakhstan) and hypothesis 3 "Ethnic homophily should be high" can be verified and also hypothesis 4 "Occupational and private patterns of integration in Germany should be low" must be verified. Here too, parallels to the quantitative survey, which included the paper questionnaire, emerge. There, 75.5 percent of repatriates provided emotional support (not counting family members). Hypothesis 2 "Transnationality should be low" can be verified because there were just 3 from Kazakhstan and additionally only one of

*Figure 7. Digital network map*

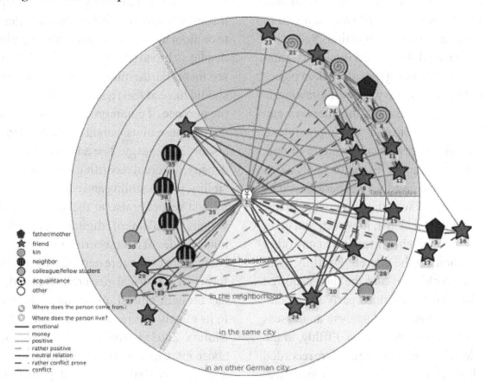

them provides support. Also hypothesis 1 "Family centrality should be expected to be high" must be falsified. The lack of emotional support from family members was justified by ego in saying that the number of family members was low and that she did not want to put a strain on her sickly father because of emotional problems. Furthermore, she falls specifically back on persons residing at different places and being only weakly linked or not linked at all. The respondent benefits from third parties being incapable of receiving information, which she passes on. In doing so, the repatriate creates social spaces in which parts of her network are at her disposal without information or secrets being passed on without her knowledge.

## Assets and Drawbacks of Digital Network Maps

As has been shown previously, there are different possibilities of gathering network-related data.

Qualitative research with the aid of network maps in particular has proved hugely popular in recent years. Data is collected in this process using paper-and-pencil tools, tool kits, and, for quite some time, software. All these data collection approaches have their own advantages and drawbacks. While the methods first touched upon have been investigated rather extensively, there are as of yet only few reliable results on the applicability of digital network maps. Citing a concrete example, this article has pointed out a way of collecting data with the help of the VennMaker software. The assets and drawbacks of this kind of survey are discussed below.

One asset of digital network maps, like the VennMaker software, lies in the range of possibilities for representing and storing network maps. Compared to paper-and-pencil tools and tool kits, for instance, size, colours, and shapes of alteri can be assigned almost without limit. Even relations between ego and alter or between alter and alter are almost infinitely modifiable. Because of this, digital network maps can be flexibly adjusted to the respective interview in question. Secondly, audio files are created along with visual representations. The advantage being that all spoken pieces of conversation are saved while the drawing is in process. During assessment, the interview can be played like a film clip and so it is possible to follow the whole process once more one-to-one. This allows for a further in-depth analysis of particular situations. Thirdly, time periods can be collected more easily with digital network maps. The data is not hard and fast, however, and is retrievable again for another interview at any other point in time and can be altered. Fourthly, both the digital network maps and the data acquired can be easily sent to any third party by e-mail. Thus it becomes possible to analyse and assess the data record at different places. Fifthly, in the process of drawing, quantitative data are recorded as well. These can be subjected to a statistical analysis after the interview. It is also possible to follow a standardised procedure in order to ensure comparability of results, provided the sample is sufficiently sized.[12]

Not every person interviewed is able to cope with digital network maps to the same extent. The latter are not quite suitable for individuals from less-educated strata of society, elderly people, and the computer-illiterates. The same holds true for research in development co-operation projects in the South. Here too, one has not only to consider for which group of people operating a computer might be an obstacle (usually rural dwellers, elderly people), but equally where its employment is particularly well suited (e.g. urban young people, communication between project management and collaborators, when dealing with handovers, evaluations and political events/ rallies). Secondly, one or more computers or laptops are needed with the right hardware. This technical gear requires that the financial means available have to be kept in mind when planning research. Thirdly, the physical environment has

to lend itself to collecting data with a laptop. For instance, digital network maps are rather ill suited to outdoor applications since the reflections of the display in broad sunlight make it rather difficult to see them. Furthermore, carrying a laptop, which should have at least a screen size of 15 inches for the purpose of communicative work, is a burden, be it because of its weight or the constant need for a source of energy. The advantages of recording density, different recording layers and easy accessibility, processability and electronic transmission of data records raise at the same time the more serious problem of digitally created network maps. Issues of data security and the protection of sources are even more pertinent here than to other forms of empirical research. Network analysis has brought ethical questions to the fore owing to its mostly informal subject matter (Borgatti & Molina, 2003; Kadushin, 2005). The liability to abuse increases yet further in the case of digitally and audio-visually collected participatory and qualitative data. Informed consent, anonymisation and data protection are at the very core of new developments in digital networking tools.

## PROSPECTS

What are the prospects for visualizing and analyzing tools at the intersections between quantitative/ qualitative, and between paper-pencil and digital? At Trier University, we are currently working on a technical solution to transfer hand drawn network maps into VennMaker automatically. The idea is to take pictures of paper-drawn-networks, which then can be digitally copied, to VennMaker for further analysis. This should merge the advantages of digital network maps and paper and pencil network maps discussed above. Secondly, we try to implement more analyzing tools like that of the spring embedder to automatize the calculation of network measures. This should save time for the researcher, as copying the data to other programs is no longer necessary. In a further step, we want to move from CAPI (Computer Assisted Personal Interview), where the network map is drawn by the interviewee with the help of an interviewer (Baker, 1992), to CASI (Computer Assisted Self Interview), where the respondent with the help of wizards will be guided by VennMaker itself (Couper & Nicholls, 1998).

It will also be important to show, how to come from the processing of only a few data sets to data sets of a large number of respondents. Pre-studies like that of von der Lippe & Gaede 2011, with 92 students being interviewed using VennMaker, can help to prove the capacity of instruments gathering quantitative and qualitative data with big samples. Another critical field will be the testing of the convergent validity of name generators in the different network collecting approaches. Against this background, it should be analyzed whether standardized digital network maps, digital questionnaires and paper questionnaires, with comparable sets of respondents produce comparable results. Moreover, in usability studies it would be useful to test, for which group which of these approaches is more user friendly. The main challenge however lies in the consolidation and merging of different strands at the intersection between digital and non-digital participatory network mapping currently springing up at various research places all over the world, a field, which is innovative, fascinating yet growing, and where we still are in an initial state, methodologically, theoretically and practically.

## REFERENCES

Antonucci, T. C., & Akiyama, H. (1995). Convoys of social relations: Family and friendships within a life span context. In Blieszner, R., & Bedford, V. H. (Eds.), *Handbook of aging and the family* (pp. 355–371). Westport, CT: Greenwood Press.

Baker, R. P. (1992). New technology in survey research: Computer assisted personal interviewing (CAPI). *Social Science Computer Review*, *10*, 145–157.

Barnes, J. A. (1954). Class and committees in a Norwegian island parish. *Human Relations*, *39*, 39–58. doi:10.1177/001872675400700102

Bastians, F. (2004). *Die Bedeutung soziaer Netzwerke für die Integration russlanddeutscher Spätaussiedler in der Bundesrepublik Deutschland*. Bissendorf, Germany: Methodos.

Bidart, C., & Lavenu, D. (2005). Evolutions of personal networks and life events. *Social Networks*, 359–376. doi:10.1016/j.socnet.2004.11.003

Borgatti, S. P., Everett, M., & Freeman, L. C. (Eds.). (1999). *UCINET 5.0 version 1.00*. Natick, MA: Analytic Technologies.

Borgatti, S. P., & Molina, J. L. (2003). Ethical and strategic issues in organizational social network analysis. *The Journal of Applied Behavioral Science*, *39*(3), 337–349. doi:10.1177/0021886303258111

Bott, E. (1957). *Family and social network*. London, UK: Tavistock.

Brandes, U., Raab, J., & Wagner, D. (2001). Exploratory network visualization: Simultaneous display of actor status and connections. *Journal of Social Structure*, *2*(4). Retrieved August 24, 2010, from http://www.library.cmu.edu:7850/JoSS/brandes/index.html

Burt, R. S. (1980). Models of network structure. *Annual Review of Sociology*, *6*, 79–141. doi:10.1146/annurev.so.06.080180.000455

Chambers, R. (1985). Shortcut methods of gathering social information for rural development projects. In Cernea, M. (Ed.), *Putting people first: Sociological variables in rural development* (pp. 515–537). New York, NY: Oxford University Press.

Comscore. (2010). *Facebook captures top spot among social networking sites in India.* Retrieved December 20, 2010, from http://www.comscore.com/Press_Events/Press_Releases/2010/8/Facebook_Captures_Top_Spot_among_Social_Networking_Sites_in_India

Couper, M. P., & Nicholls, W. L. (1998). The history and development of computer assisted survey information collection. In Couper, M. (Ed.), *Computer assisted survey information collection* (pp. 1–23). New York, NY: Wiley.

Coviello, N. (2005). Integrating qualitative and quantitative techniques in network analysis. *Qualitative Market Research, 8*(1), 39–60. doi:10.1108/13522750510575435

Crossley, N. (2008). Pretty connected: The social network of the early UK punk movement. *Theory, Culture & Society, 25,* 89–116. doi:10.1177/0263276408095546

Davis, A., Gardner, B. B., & Gardner, M. R. (1941). *Deep south. A social anthropological study of caste and class.* Chicago, IL: University of Chicago Press.

Denzin, N. K. (1970). *The research act.* Chicago, IL: Aldaline.

Diaz-Bone, R. (2007). *Does qualitative network analysis exist?* Retrieved November 21, 2010, from http://www.qualitative-research.net/index.php/fqs/article/viewArticle/224/493

Diewald, M. (1991). *Soziale Beziehungen, Verlust oder Liberalisierung?: Soziale Unterstützung in informellen Netzwerken.* Berlin, Germany: Edition Sigma.

Edwards, G. (2010). *Mixed-method approaches to social network analysis.* Retrieved December 21, 2010, from http://eprints.ncrm.ac.uk/842/1/Social_Network_analysis_Edwards.pdf

Emirbayer, M., & Goodwin, J. (1994). Network analysis, culture, and the problem of agency. *American Journal of Sociology, 99,* 1411–1451. doi:10.1086/230450

Fenicia, T., Gamper, M., & Schönhuth, M. (2010). Integration, Sozialkapital und soziale Netzwerke. Egozentrierte Netzwerke von (Spät-)Aussiedlern. In M. Gamper & L. Reschke (Eds.), *Knoten und Kanten. Soziale Netzwerkanalyse in Wirtschafts- und Migrationsforschung* (pp. 305–332). Bielefeld, Germany: transcript-Verl.

Fielding, N., Lee, R. M., & Blank, G. (Eds.). (2008). *The Sage handbook of online research methods.* Los Angeles, CA: SAGE.

Fischer, C. S., Jackson, R. M., Steuve, A. C., Gerson, K., Jones, L. M., & Baldassare, M. (1977). *Networks and places: Social relations in the urban setting.* New York, NY: Free Press.

Fowler, J. H., & Christakis, N. A. (2008). Dynamic spread of happiness in a large social network: longitudinal analysis over 20 years in the Framingham heart study. *British Medical Journal, 337,* 1–9. doi:10.1136/bmj.a2338

Freeman, L. C. (2004). *The development of social network analysis: A study in the sociology of science.* Vancouver, Canada: Empirical Press.

Gamper, M., & Reschke, L. (2010). Soziale Netzwerkanalyse. Eine interdisziplinäre Erfolgsgeschichte. In M. Gamper & L. Rechke (Eds.), *Sozialtheorie. Knoten und Kanten. Soziale Netzwerkanalyse in Wirtschafts- und Migrationsforschung* (pp. 13–51). Bielefeld, Germany: transcript.

Granovetter, M. (1973). The strength of weak ties. *American Journal of Sociology, 78,* 1360–1380. doi:10.1086/225469

Haas, J., & Mützel, S. (2010). Netzwerkanalyse und Netzwerktheorie in Deutschland. Eine empirische Übersicht und theoretische Entwicklungspotentiale. In Stegbauer, C. (Ed.), *Netzwerkanalyse und Netzwerktheorie. Ein neues Paradigma in den Sozialwissenschaften* (pp. 49–64). Wiesbaden, Germany: VS Verlag für Sozialwissenschaften.

Herz, A., & Gamper, M. (2011). Möglichkeiten und Grenzen der Erhebung ego-zentrierter Netzwerke via Computer und Internet. In M. Gamper, L. Reschke, & M. Schönhuth (Eds.), *Knoten und Kanten 2.0: Soziale Netzwerkanalyse in Medien- und Kulturforschung*. Bielfeld, Germany: transcript. (forthcoming)

Höfer, R., Keupp, H., & Straus, F. (2006). Prozesse sozialer Verortung in Szenen und Organisationen – Ein netzwerkorientierter Blick auf traditionale und reflexive moderne Engagementformen. In Hollstein, B., & Straus, F. (Eds.), *Qualitative Netzwerkanalyse. Konzepte, Methoden, Anwendungen* (pp. 267–294). Wiesbaden, Germany: VS Verlag für Sozialwissenschaften.

Hogan, J., Carrasco, A., & Wellman, B. (2007). Visualizing personal networks: Working with participant-aided sociograms. *Field Methods, 19*, 116–144. doi:10.1177/1525822X06298589

Hollstein, B., & Pfeffer, J. (2010). *Netzwerkkarten als Instrument zur Erhebung egozentrierter Netzwerke*. Retrieved November 14, 2010, from http://www.wiso.uni-hamburg.de/fileadmin/ sozialoekonomie/hollstein/Literatur_Betina/ Netzwerkkarten_Hollstein_Pfeffer_2010.pdf

Hollstein, B., & Straus, F. (Eds.). (2006). *Qualitative Netzwerkanalyse: Konzepte, Methoden, Anwendungen*. Wiesbaden, Germany: VS Verlag für Sozialwissenschaften.

Kahn, R. L., & Antonucci, T. C. (1980). Convoys of life course: Attachment, roles, and social support. In Featherman, D. L., Lerner, R. M., & Perlmutter, M. (Eds.), *Life-span development and behaviour* (pp. 253–286). Hillsdale, NJ: Lawrence Erlbaum.

Kapferer, B. (1969). Norms and the manipulation of relationships in a work context. In J. C. Mitchell (Ed.), *Social networks in urban situations. Analyses of personal relationships in Central African towns* (pp. 181–244). Manchester, UK: Published for the Institute for Social Research, University of Zambia, by Manchester U.P.

Kolip, P. (1993). *Freundschaften im Jugendalter: Der Beitrag sozialer Netzwerke zur Problembewältigung*. Weinheim, Germany: Juventa.

Kronenwett, M. (2010). *VennMaker 1.0 Anwenderhandbuch*. Retrieved October 21, 2010, from http://www.vennmaker.com

Krumbein, S. (1995). *Selbstbild und Männlichkeit. Rekonstruktion männlicher Selbst- und Idealbilder und deren Veränderung im Laufe der individuellen Entwicklung*. München, Germany: Opladen.

Laumann, E. O. (1973). *Bonds of pluralism: The form and substance of urban social networks*. New York, NY: J. Wiley.

Lubbers, M. J., Molina, J. L., & McCarty, C. (2007). Personal networks and ethnic identifications. *International Sociology, 22*, 721–741. doi:10.1177/0268580907082255

Lubbers, M. J., Mollina, J. L., Brandes, U., Ávila, J., & McCarty, C. (2010). Longitudinal analysis of personal networks. The case of Argentinean migrants in Spain. *Social Networks, 32*, 91–104. doi:10.1016/j.socnet.2009.05.001

Mascarenhas, J. (1991). Participatory rural appraisal and participatory learning methods: Recent experiences from Myrada and South India. *RRA Note, 13*, 26–32.

McCarty, C., Molina, J. L., Aguilar, C., & Rota, L. (2007). A comparison of social network mapping and personal network visualization. *Field Methods, 19*, 145–162. doi:10.1177/1525822X06298592

McCarty, C., Molina, J. L., Lubbers, M. J., & Gamper, M. (2011forthcoming). Personal networks analysis. In Barnett, G. (Ed.), *Encyclopedia of social networks*. Thousand Oaks, CA: SAGE.

McPherson, M., Smith-Lovin Lynn, & Cook James. (2001). Birds of feather: Homophily in social networks. *Annual Review of Sociology*, *27*, 415–444. doi:10.1146/annurev.soc.27.1.415

Mitchell, J. C. (Ed.). (1969). *Social networks in urban situations: Analyses of personal relationships in Central African towns*. Manchester, UK: Published for the Institute for Social Research, Manchester U.P.

Moreno, J. L. (1934). *Who shall survive?* Washington, DC: Nervous and Mental Disease Publishing Company.

Nadel, S. F. (1957). *The theory of social structure*. London, UK: Cohen & West.

Northway, M. L. A. (1940). Method for depicting social relations by sociometric testing. *Sociometry*, *3*, 144–150. doi:10.2307/2785439

Padgett, J., & Ansell, C. (1993). Robust action and the rise of the Medici, 1400-1434. *American Journal of Sociology*, *98*, 1259–1319. doi:10.1086/230190

Rambaldi, G., & Callosa-Tarr, J. (2000). *Manual on participatory 3-D modeling for natural resource management. Essentials of protected area management in the Philippines*. Retrieved June 05, 2010, from http://www.iapad.org/publications/ppgis/p3dm_nipap.pdf

Roethlisberger, F. J., & Dickson, W. J. (1939). *Management and the worker*. Cambridge, MA: Harvard University Press.

Schiffer, E. (2007). *Net-map toolbox. influence mapping of social networks*. Retrieved September 05, 2010, from http://www.ifad.org/english/water/innowat/tool/Tool_2web.pdf

Schiffer, E., & Hauck, J. (2011). (forthcoming). Net-map: Collecting social network data and facilitating network learning through participatory influence network mapping. *Field Methods*.

Schnegg, M. (2010). Strategien und Strukturen. Herausforderungen der qualitativen und quantitativen Netzwerkforschung. In M. Gamper & L. Rechke (Eds.), *Sozialtheorie. Knoten und Kanten. Soziale Netzwerkanalyse in Wirtschafts- und Migrationsforschung* (pp. 55–75). Bielefeld, Germany: transcript.

Schönhuth, M. (2005). *Entwicklung, Partizipation und Ethnologie. Implikationen der Begegnung von ethnologischen und partizipativen Forschungsansätzen*. Retrieved from http://ubttest.opus.hbz-nrw.de/volltexte/2005/300/pdf/habil_schoenhuth.pdf

Schönhuth, M. (2007). Diversity in der Werkstatt – Eine Feldstudie zum Thema Vielfalt und Behinderung. In Jent, N. H., & Steinmetz, B. (Eds.), *Diversity Management und Antidiskriminierung* (pp. 95–114). Weimar, Germany: Bertuch.

Schönhuth, M., & Kievelitz, U. (1995). *Participatory learning approaches: Rapid rural appraisal, participatory appraisal: An introductory guide*. Rossdorf, Germany: TZ-Verlagsgesellschaft.

Schweitzer, T. (1996). *Muster sozialer Ordnung*. Berlin, Germany: Reimer.

Snijders, T. A. B. (2001). The statistical evaluation of social network dynamics. In Sobel, M. E., & Becker, M. P. (Eds.), *Sociological methodology* (pp. 361–395). Boston, MA: John Wiley & Sons. doi:10.1111/0081-1750.00099

Straus, F. (2002). *Netzwerkanalysen: Gemeinde-psychologische Perspektiven für Forschung und Praxis*. Wiesbaden, Germany: Dt. Univ.-Verl.

Trotter, R. T. (1999). Friends, relatives and relevant others: Conducting ethnographic network studies. In Schensul, J. J., LeCompte, M. D., Trotter, R. T., Cromley, E. K., & Singer, M. (Eds.), *Mapping social networks, spatial data, and hidden populations*. Thousand Oaks, CA: AltaMira Press.

Vehovar, V., & Manfreda, K. L. (2008). Overview: Online surveys. In Fielding, N., Lee, R. M., & Blank, G. (Eds.), *The Sage handbook of online research methods* (pp. 177–194). Los Angeles, CA: SAGE.

Vehovar, V., Manfreda, K. L., Koren, G., & Hlebec, V. (2008). Measuring ego-centered social networks on the web: Questionnaire design issues. *Social Networks*, *30*, 213–222. doi:10.1016/j.socnet.2008.03.002

Von der Lippe. Holger & Gaede, Nina-S (2011). Die Konstitution personaler Netzwerke: ein psycho-logisches Studienprojekt mit VennMaker 0.9.5 VIP. In M. Schönhuth, M. Gamper, M. Kronenwett & M. Stark (Eds.), *Vom Papier zum Laptop – Perspektiven elektronischer Tools zur partizi-pativen Visualisierung und Analyse sozialer Netzwerke*. Bielfeld, Germany: transcript. (forthcoming).

Wasserman, S., & Faust, K. (1994). *Social network analysis: Methods and applications*. New York, NY: Cambridge University Press.

Wellman, B. (1979). The community question: The intimate networks of East Yorkers. *American Journal of Sociology*, *84*, 1201–1233. doi:10.1086/226906

White, H. C. (1992). *Identity and control: How social formations emerge*. Princeton, NJ: Princeton University Press.

White, H. C. (2005). *Markets from networks: Socioeconomic models of production*. Princeton, NJ: Princeton Univ. Press.

Witzel, A. (1982). *Verfahren der qualitativen Sozialforschung: Überblick und Alternativen*. Frankfurt, Germany: Campus Verlag.

Witzel, A. (2000). *The problem-centered interview*. Retrieved September 21, 2010, from http://www.qualitative-research.net/index.php/fqs/article/viewArticle/1132/2521

## ADDITIONAL READING

Coviello, N. (2005). Integrating Qualitative and Quantitative Techniques in Network Analysis Qualitative Market Research 8(1): 39-60. *Qualitative Market Research*, *8*, 39–60. doi:10.1108/13522750510575435

Edwards, G. (2010). *Mixed-Method Approaches to Social Network Analysis*. Retrieved December 21, 2010, from http://eprints.ncrm.ac.uk/842/1/Social_Network_analysis_Edwards.pdf

Hogan, J., Carrasco, A., & Wellman, B. (2007). Visualizing Personal Networks: Working with Participant-aided Sociograms. *Field Methods*, *19*, 116–144. doi:10.1177/1525822X06298589

Lubbers, M. J., Molina, J. L., & McCarty, C. (2007). Personal Networks and Ethnic Identifications. *International Sociology*, *22*, 721–741. doi:10.1177/0268580907082255

Lubbers, M. J., Mollina, J. L., Brandes, U., Ávila, J., & McCarty, C. (2010). Longitudinal analysis of personal networks. The case of Argentinean migrants in Spain. *Social Networks*, *32*, 91–104. doi:10.1016/j.socnet.2009.05.001

McCarty, C., Molina, J. L., Aguilar, C., & Rota, L. (2007). A Comparison of Social Network Mapping and Personal Network Visualization. *Field Methods*, *19*, 145–162. doi:10.1177/1525822X06298592

Vehovar, V., Manfreda, K. L., Koren, G., & Hlebec, V. (2008). Measuring egocen-tered social networks on the web: Questionnaire design issues. *Social Networks*, *30*, 213–222. doi:10.1016/j.socnet.2008.03.002

Wasserman, S., & Faust, K. (1994). *Social network analysis: Methods and applications*. New York: Cambridge University Press.

## KEY TERMS AND DEFINITIONS

**Digital Network Map:** A digital network map is a space where the interviewer or interviewee with the aid of a computer can paint social networks. A digital network map is more or less pre-structured through given coordinates (e.g. concentric circles, sectors).

**Egocentric Network Analysis:** The focus of egocentric network analysis lies on the relations of an actor (ego) and the social environment (alteri). Through this method, ego's personal network is established from his or her subjective point of view.

**Network Map:** A network map ("paper and pencil", "paper, pen and tokens" and "digital network maps"), is a space where social networks can be painted by the interviewer or interviewee. Test person can draw their personal network, which will be analyzed by the researcher. Depending on their degree of structuring, methodologically network maps; do have more in common with the quantitative network analysis.

**Network Picture:** Test person draw the relationships maintained with the most important persons they feels attached to. Network pictures come into being as free drawings by the test person without any specifications. Network pictures have more in common with the qualitative network analysis.

**Qualitative Network Analysis:** Qualitative network analysis asks about the meanings and processes (e. g. "the stories behind the relations").

**Quantitative Network Analysis:** Quantitative network analysis calculates the causal relationship between network elements.

**Triangulation (Methodological):** Using two or more methods (e.g. questionnaires, problem-centered interviews, observations, network map) to gather data.

## ENDNOTES

[1] What does the name "VennMaker" stand for? "Venn", first of all acts as a reverence for "Venn Diagram", a tool, used with much success in the participatory appraisal of stakeholders in development contexts for the last 20 years (Schönhuth & Kievelitz, 1995). Its name giver was the English mathematician and philosopher John Venn (1834-1923).

[2] The first presentation of VennMaker (beta-Version) took place at the Sunbelt Conference in Florida in 2008. Since then, we have been in contact with e.g. Christopher McCarty and other researchers in the field of egocentric network analysis. From this point on, we have been engineering the software simultaneously with researchers, non-academic users, and computer engineers (simultaneous Engineering). Therefore, we presented our first pre-study in the year of 2009. In the same year, the software was handed over to beta testers all around the world. In January 2010, the version 1.0 was released at the University of Trier. We held a workshop and some beta testers presented their first results at the Sunbelt XXX in Italy.

[3] The first qualitative methods of data collection are found in the work of Moreno (1934). Despite his research being exceedingly formal, he used qualitative methods to be able to better describe and understand particular relations. Even though Moreno relies on summaries of conducted interviews

in his description, he falls short of a qualitative analysis and structured synthesis. For an outline on the history of social network research see Schnegg (2010).

[4]  Translated from the German.

[5]  Siegfried Nadel had made allowances for these aspects in his theory but could not flesh them out in detail before his death. His ideas, however, laid the foundations (directly or indirectly) for later ethnological work (Nadel, 1957).

[6]  According to Granovetter, relations within the network can be arranged in at least four dimensions: the time two people have spent together, emotional intensity, intimacy connecting them, and reciprocal services that characterise the relationship (Granovetter, 1973).

[7]  The following fictitious exchange may serve as an illustration: "I'd quite like to go back to the conflict between your colleague up there on the left and with Ms X from the export department over there and the new manager you've only" just placed, who actually might be able to mediate from her position instead of "half an hour ago you told me about some conflict between…"

[8]  Using concentric circulars is not a new method for structuring network data (Northway, 1940).

[9]  Using the third dimension in maps created with the respondent's participation is, however, nothing new (e.g. Rambaldi & Callosa-Tarr, 2000).

[10]  "Homophily is the principle that a contact between similar people occurs at a higher rate than among dissimilar people" (McPherson et al., 2001, p. 416).

[11]  http://www.vennmaker.com

[12]  For example, von der Lippe and Gaede interviewed 92 students of the psychology department at the Otto-von-Guericke-University of Magdeburg with the help of VennMaker. Their goal was to analyse the subjectively perceived importance of familial and non-familial-relations of young adults as well as the subjective perception of the relationship between the individuals (i.e. the cognitive relational network structure) quantitatively.

# Section 4
# Evolution of Social Networks and Online Communities

*This section introduces two case studies of actual social networks with an objective to analyze their formation and evolution in time. Dynamic social network analysis was applied to a learning community built around a Master's Program in an Italian University, and some international terror networks to help in detecting, or modifying the created/evolved networks.*

# Chapter 12
# Observing the Evolution of a Learning Community Using Social Network Analysis

**Francesca Grippa**
*University of Salento, Italy*

**Marco De Maggio**
*University of Salento, Italy*

**Angelo Corallo**
*University of Salento, Italy*

## ABSTRACT

*During the last decades, social and computer scientists have been focusing their efforts to study the effectiveness of collaboration in both working and learning environments. The main contributions clearly identify the importance of interactivity as the determinant of positive performances in learning communities where the supportive dimension of exchanges is balanced by the interactive one. In this chapter, authors describe a method based on social network metrics to recognize the stages of development of learning communities. The authors found that the evolution of social network metrics - such as density, betweenness centrality, contribution index, core/periphery structure – matched the formal stages of community development, with a clear identification of the forming, norming, and storming phases.*

## INTRODUCTION

In this contribution we propose an empirical correlation between the stages of development of a learning community and a set of social network metrics. We applied Social Network Analysis (SNA), defined as set of methods and tools to dynamically assess the growth of value derived by social interactions. We used SNA metrics to observe a learning community built around a Master's Program launched by the e-Business Management Section of Scuola Superiore ISUFI, University of Salento, Italy. The program was designed to train talented young students to become "e-Business Solutions Engineers". The program adopted a project-based learning strategy that

DOI: 10.4018/978-1-61350-444-4.ch012

required a constant interaction and collaboration between students and tutors, as well as between students and industrial/academic partners. Students were located partly on campus and partly at the partner companies' locations, interacting with their colleagues and tutors via email and via an institutional blog.

This community has the characteristics of a hybrid community in terms of *mode of communication*: its members use both asynchronous and synchronous channels. They also work on individual projects and, at the same time, on team activities sharing tasks and deliverables. The community acted as a team throughout its life, as students where involved every day in research activities in collaboration with internal tutors and external/industrial supervisors. The goal of this study is to observe how the structure of a learning community that is digitally connected changes over time starting from the simple observation of social network metrics. Because of the hybrid nature of the observed community, the literature background covers the main research findings in the area of communities of practice and team structure/development as well as of online learning communities.

After describing the literature background, we introduce the research setting and we present the findings of the data analysis based on email exchanges. Besides studying the level of interaction within and across the community, we monitored the community evolution looking at the level of *satisfaction, knowledge acquisition, and perception of individual growth*. In this contribution we use a Social Network approach to address the following research question: *How to detect the stages of development of a learning community based on the application of SNA metrics?*

Most of the traditional methods used to measure the evolution of communities have been criticized for their static nature. They have the limitations to be made ex-post, as they offer a photograph of the knowledge assets based on three dimensions (Bontis, 2001): human capital (know-how, capa-

bilities, skills); structural capital (organizational capabilities, patents, routines, databases); social capital (network of relationships inside and outside the organization). Despite the reference to the network of relationships, these strategic frameworks do not offer a dynamic perspective able to tell how a community is creating and sharing knowledge *over time*. There is a need to build a monitoring system in order to observe communities' evolution in a more dynamic way. The interdisciplinary field of Social Network Analysis represents a valuable contribution to reduce this gap. SNA has been defined as "*the disciplined inquiry into the patterning of relations among social actors, as well as the patterning of relationships among actors at different levels of analysis*" (Breiger, 2004, p. 506).

## LITERATURE BACKGROUND

The literature background is focused on the areas of community structure, team dynamics, and online community development. The reason for this broad perspective is the hybrid role of many learning communities today, where students connect to each other with the goal of acquiring new knowledge, skills and competencies through their involvement in real projects. The members of these learning communities work in teams, collaborating with other students and reaching out to external actors. The case discussed in this chapter is an example of learning community working as an extended team. Their approach to learning is project-based as it focuses mostly on a *production model*: students start by defining end-product, identify their audience, research the topic, design the product, do the project management, solve the problems that arise and finish the product followed by a self-evaluation and critical reflection. As students work on projects, they interact through digital media such as email, forums, wiki and blogs. By doing so, these learning communities configure themselves as online communities.

Because of this hybrid nature of many learning communities where members works on projects having real goals, in this study we look at the literature on learning communities adopting at the same time different models of team development.

People who interact for a variety of social and professional reasons, interacting via the Internet, form virtual or online communities. Online communities have become another form of communication between people who know each other primarily in real life. Brown (2001) studied archived online course records and interviewed students and teachers with the goal of monitoring the stages of development of a community in an online environment. In his study, Brown discovered that community building seems to follow a three-stage process: 1) students become comfortable with responding to their classmates; 2) students become more involved by participating in common discussions and 3) students achieve *camaraderie* by adding personal communication. The study conducted by Brown has the merit to propose some basic stages of community development.

In this chapter we offer a complementary method based on social network indicators that can be used to *automatically* monitor community development, without conducting time consuming interviews, which might only give an idea of what people, *perceive*. We use a real case study of a learning community, whose members interact both online and offline. We observe a learning community using social network indicators, by parsing email archives and recording wiki participation. The main contribution of this study is to provide further empirical evidence of the benefits of SNA methods and techniques to automatically visualize the rise of connectivity and the shift from one stage to another.

## The Role of Communities in Today's Organizations

Building organizational communities by encouraging people to share ideas and work towards the same goal helps to build an integrated network of interdependencies with clients, employees and other stakeholders. Organizations have recognized informal communities as an important new engine of innovation, as their most dynamic "knowledge resource".

Scholars found that less dynamic companies initiate new projects within a rigid *mechanistic*, framework, and suffered accordingly while flexible and dynamically responsive organizations adopt an *organic* style of management (Chesbrough, 2003). The concept of "community" is the organizational form most typical of the *organic* organization: instead of little individual freedom of action, long decision chains and slow decision making, the organic organization promotes interdisciplinary teams and supports informal communities.

The most famous conceptualization of communities has been provided by Wenger (1998) using the concept of Communities of Practice (CoPs), that are formed by people who share a concern, a set of problems or a passion about a topic and connect to each other to deepen their knowledge in a common area. CoPs' members regularly engage in sharing and learning, based on their common interests. According to Etienne Wenger, social participation is not merely the participation to the events of engagement in certain activities within a group, but a more encompassing process, including the involvement in the practices of social communities, and the building of identities as related to those communities (Wenger, 1998).

Many examples of successful companies such as 3M and GE have demonstrated that the synergic integration of multiple units in cross-functional teams or communities is a key element to provide the company with that level of flexibility and responsiveness required to continuously reinvent the business (Bartlett and Mohammed, 1995). Combining knowledge from several companies, business units or departments is facilitated by the identification of informal communities that share common interests, are willing to learn and collaborate towards common goals.

Scholars have been using different labels to define these new organizational forms: community of practice, community of interests, virtual teams, work groups, project teams, and informal networks. Despite differences in terms of goals, use of volunteer participation or not, the common characteristic of these emergent social networks is the facilitation of learning and knowledge sharing between people conducting practice-related tasks. Each member brings his or her special knowledge and capabilities, but also interpersonal relationships with the rest of the community, as well as with external members.

Recent contributions propose that communities can be productive even when they are self-organized and self-sustaining. Peter Gloor (2006) introduced the concept of Collaborative Knowledge Networks, a virtual instance of Communities of Practice, defined as *groups of self-motivated individuals driven by the idea of something new and exciting, a way to greatly improve an existing business practice, or a new product or service for which they see a real need.* A new concept introduced to focus the attention on the real objective of such communities is Collaborative Innovation Networks (COIN). A COIN is a group of individuals working together using various communication technologies to achieve a common vision (Gloor, 2006). It can be formed when like-minded, self-motivated peers become interested in a new idea and "swarm" around it, working together to informally develop the new concept. Companies who come together to create an innovative product when their talented developers happen to be living and working in different physical locations can also form it intentionally.

## Online Learning Communities

Since the community is recognized as an effective setting to improve individual and collective knowledge, higher education programs and corporate training initiatives are today supporting the development of communities as part of the strategic process of competencies development. An important aspect of higher education programs offered either online or in a hybrid format (i.e. partly online and partly on ground) is the degree to which the programs are successful in building a community of learners (Brown, 2001; Hiltz, et al., 2000; Rogers, 2000). Online communities of practice and online learning communities are becoming widespread within higher education institutions thanks to enabling factors such as technological development and the incorporation of collaborative pedagogical models. As Hiltz and colleagues demonstrated (2000), when online students work in a collaborative group, the length, the student perception of learning and the quality of assignments improve.

Communities of Practice were initially considered to be mainly co-located (Brown et al., 1989). Thanks to the spread of information and communication technology we observe today the emergence and development of virtual Communities of Practice. There are many examples of these in both the educational and corporate environment (Rogers, 2000). Web 2.0 technologies increase and accelerate learners' ability to work in-group for project purpose. They place learners at the centre of online activities and enable new types of collaboration and consumption, new ways of interacting with web-based applications. Blogs, wikis, RSS feeds represent "social software" able to support users to develop web content in a cooperative way.

If the strategic importance of the learning community finds confirmation in literature, the shift from a traditional "closed" classroom context to an "open" community setting still needs to be fully investigated (Moore, 1996, Rheingold, 2000).

The emergence of Internet-based technologies represents an important step in the evolution of the teaching and learning experience. Collaboration among learners and between learners and tutors seems to increase significantly the learning potential of learners in an online environment (Aplin, 2008). The most suitable setting for a fruitful learning experience seems to be an *open, networked learning community* where students establish and nurture relations within and across the communities' boundaries, involving internal and external stakeholders in their process of knowledge acquisition and personal growth.

Despite the strong trend towards the creation of collaborative learning community, little is known about how they work, how they develop, what the success factors are, and how to support them with technology. Brown (2001) describes a process of community-building in distance learning classes based on a three-stage process: *"The first stage was making friends on-line with whom students felt comfortable communicating. The second stage was community conferment (acceptance) which occurred when students were part of a long, thoughtful, threaded discussion on a subject of importance after which participants felt both personal satisfaction and kinship. The third stage was camaraderie which was achieved after long-term or intense association with others involving personal communication. Each of these stages involved a greater degree of engagement in both the class and the dialogue"* (Brown, 2001, p.18).

The main challenge is to identify the phases followed by communities whose members meet not only online, but also in person and through digital media. Our contribution intends to provide empirical evidence to address the previous point, adopting and applying a methodology based on Social Network Analysis to study community evolution.

## Team and Community Development

In this paragraph we rely on the main contributions within the area of community and team development. Kim (2000) proposed a life cycle for online communities suggesting that members of virtual communities begin their life in a community as *lurkers*, by simply visiting the online environment without an active participation. After a period of familiarization, people become *novices* and participate in the community's activities more intensely. After a constant period of contribution, members might become *regulars*. As Kim (2000) proposed, if they "break through another barrier" members might become *leaders*, and after some time they become *elders*. This model of community's life cycle is general and might be applied to many virtual communities. Lave and Wenger (1991) proposed a cycle of how community members become integrated into online communities using the principles of *legitimate peripheral participation*. The authors suggest five types of paths in a community: 1) Peripheral - i.e. lurker with an outside, unstructured participation; 2) Inbound - i.e. Novice, progressively invested in the community; 3) Insider - i.e. Regular, fully committed in the community development; 4) Boundary - i.e. Leader, who supports members and pushes towards a greater participation; 5) Outbound - i.e. Elder, who starts a process of leaving the community due to new relationships or new positions.

Lave and Wenger's model still remains a general framework that does not explain how to exactly recognize when members shift from one phase to another and from one role to another. How to recognize the main steps of community development? In this chapter we propose to use SNA and the network metrics to observe community life cycle and the emergence of informal roles such as leader, contributor or lurker. To better study the characteristics of the phases of community development, we use the contribution of theories developed in the team research area, which fits our unit of analysis represented by a hybrid learning community.

A formalization that we use in this chapter is the model proposed by Tuckman in 1956 and then revised by Tuckman and Jensen in 1977. These models are focused on studying the evolution of teams through the recognition of different stages of development. The initial model was based on four sequential phases: 1) forming, characterized by initial enthusiasm and relationships establishing; 2) storming, when roles and responsibilities are defined and conflicts may emerge; 3) norming, when rules and codes of behavior are established; 4) performing, characterized by successful team interactions with interdependent team members who act as knowledgeable decision makers. These phases are all necessary to allow the team to grow, deal with internal and external challenges, tackle problems, find solutions, plan work, and produce results. In his revised model, Tuckman added a fifth stage to the Forming, Storming, Norming and Performing model which he called Adjourning, also referred to as Deforming and Mourning.

The Forming Stage is characterized by high dependence on the leader for guidance and direction; by little agreement on teams' aims other than received from leader and by unclear individual roles and responsibilities. The team is formed, but its member's expectations are yet to be defined. In the Storming Stage decisions don't come easily within the team. Cliques and factions form and there may be power struggles and internal conflicts. The team needs to be focused on its goals to avoid distraction by relationships and emotional issues. The Norming Stage is characterized by an increasing agreement among members, who respond more positively to facilitation by the leader. Roles and responsibilities become more accepted and clear and the whole team makes important decisions. In the Performing Stage there is an increasing focus on over-achieving goals, and the team makes most of the decisions against criteria agreed with the leader. In this "trade-off phase", the team experiences a higher degree of

autonomy, while leaders delegate and oversee. The fifth stage, Adjourning, is more about completion and disengagement from the tasks.

Building on this important recognition of formal and informal communities and teams, other authors (Ancona and Bresman, 2007) have recently proposed key principles that represent a pattern for successful communities. These principles are: *extensive ties, exchangeable membership and expandable tiers*. Effective groups, defined by the authors "extended communities" or "X-teams", go beyond their boundaries, adapting their structure over time to enable useful outsiders to contribute on common projects (principle of the *extensive ties*). With their flexible membership and leadership structure, X-teams reach outward to foster the innovation process. *Exchangeable membership* means the inclusion in the community of people who come in and out and rotate leadership. The third principle of the extended community is *expandable tiers*. This means adopting a flexible structure with a core that coordinates the community, a group of other members who carry out the activities and others who drop in and out for short periods. Table 1 presents the classification proposed by Ancona and Bresman to define the tools for building extended communities (2007, pp. 165-193).

As part of the Selection phase, the members self-organize their activity in focus groups according to the individual skills and competencies. In this initial period, people need to know each other and to define the role within the community. Another important ingredient to complete the kick-off phase is looking at the social networks or ties that each member may bring to the future development of the community.

In the Exploration phase, members "*need to suspend their prior views of the situation and look at the world with new eyes – to explore their new terrain so that they're able to describe it, to find hidden opportunities*" (Ancona and Bresman, 2007, p. 170). In this phase it is vital to strengthen the collaboration with other organizational units

*Table 1. Phases of community development*

| Phases | Description |
|---|---|
| *Selection (Forming)* | Select the members and set the stage. The initial phase goes from selecting and motivating members to encouraging knowledge sharing. |
| *Exploration (Storming)* | Explore internal and external possibilities. This is the time of intense sense making, task coordination and relating. |
| *Exploitation (Norming)* | In this phase members must shift from brainstorming on different ideas to actually creating one reality. |
| *Exportation (Performing)* | This is the time to bring the community's work to other parts of the extended organization. |

that might have been engaged in similar tasks and to learn from other experiences.

In the Exploitation phase, the team must shift the focus from the brainstorming of ideas and possibilities to a stage of implementation and execution. This is the phase when product prototypes are made and roles are re-allocated and re-defined to meet new stakeholders' expectations. The communities test their ideas by scanning continuously the environment and facing the dilemma of building external relations with the need of being internally focused and respect the coordination mechanisms.

The final phase is called Exportation. Communities turn outward exporting the project to the rest of the organization and to the external stakeholders such as other units, end users, and partners. The goal of exportation is to transfer the excitement, the motivation, the know-how and the tacit knowledge of the community. The focus of the community is mainly external and the effort is in transforming the output in something that is recognized as "value creating" for the organization and not just something that the only community is excited about.

Each team member brings his or her special knowledge and capabilities, but also interpersonal relationships with the rest of the community as well as with external members (Wenger and Snyder, 2000). To measure the ability of a community to connect with internal and external stakeholders, we propose to use tools and metrics of Social Network Analysis to quantitatively assess the evolution of learning communities.

## Adopting a Social Network Perspective to Observe Community Evolution

As described by Penuel et al. (2006) many teachers consider the process of collecting social network data to be problematic though still feasible. Others are concerned about privacy issues and the impact on the educational goals when data is shared with the learning community. Nevertheless, they all recognize the value of the information provided by visual maps of social interactions within and across classes, in order to better plan activities in support of peripheral students and to identify possible sources of conflict.

As Iyer, Lee and Venkatraman (2006) stated: *"We urge managers to view their company's network scorecard as the blueprint for navigation in complex dynamic settings that call for intense degree of competition and cooperation. It is a scorecard that allows for multiple managers involved in different types of relationships to know how their actions and interactions are constrained or facilitated by other existing and potential ties in the network"* (p.18). In this perspective, the application of Social Network Analysis might help to recognize when and how different phases of a community emerge, following the evolution of key social network indicators and combining

*Table 2, Social network indicators (Wasserman and Faust, 1994; Borgatti and Everett, 2006; Gloor, 2006)*

| Social Network Indicators | Description | Main Benefits |
|---|---|---|
| Actor Between-ness Centrality | It is the number of times an actor connects pairs of other actors, who otherwise would not be able to reach one another. It measures the extent to which a particular point lies "between" the various other points in the graph. | • To identify gatekeepers and boundary spanners<br>• To quickly diffuse strategic information such as best practices or organizational changes. |
| Actor Degree Centrality | It is the total number of other points to which a point is adjacent. It is also defined as the total number of a point's neighborhood. A point is central if it has a high degree, defined in the interval (0.00-1.00). | • To recognize individual prominence<br>• To help overly burdened community members |
| Contribution Index | CI is a number that ranges from "-1" to "+1". A +1 value indicates that somebody only sends messages and does not receive any messages. A −1 value indicates that somebody only receives messages and never sends any messages. A 0 value indicates that somebody sends and receives the same number of messages | • To evaluate actor's interactivity level<br>• To recognize coordinators, ambassadors |
| Group Between-ness Centrality | The proportion of geodesics (shortest path between actors) connecting pairs of non-groups actors that pass through the group. GBC of the entire group is 1 for a perfect star structure, where one central person, the star, dominates the communication. GBC is 0 in a totally democratic structure where everybody displays an identical communication pattern. | • To identify innovative phases within a community life cycle<br>• To avoid centralized, star structures that might impede free knowledge flows |
| Group Degree Centrality | The number of actors outside the group that are connected to members of the group | • To recognize similarity in the communication patterns among different group members |
| Density | The total number of relational ties (connections) divided by the total number of possible relational ties. | • To evaluate the network's compactness and the presence of sub-groups |

the social network insights with interviews and observation. Table 2 presents some of the most used social network indicators and their benefits.

By looking at the most central actors within a network or discovering the phases in which the communication is more intense, frameworks based on SNA may provide managerial recommendations at individual, group, organizational and inter-organizational level. Managerial insights can derive from the static representation of the network (sociogram), from the dynamic evolution of network indicators or from the visualization of the intra and inter-community interactions.

Our analysis is based on the main findings of research conducted by Burt (2000), Gloor (2006) and Cummings and Cross (2003), describing the organizational benefits of social network indicators to recognize community dynamics. Peter Gloor (2006) has introduced an interesting concept, Collaborative Innovation Network (COIN). He found a correlation between performing virtual

communities and social network metrics. COINs are composed of self-motivated individuals who share the same vision, who gather around an innovative idea, which is pushed forward by charismatic leaders, who are able to assemble a group of highly motivated collaborators. As stated by Gloor (2006): "*The COIN core team has comparatively high density, but low group betweenness centrality (GBC)*, while Collaborative Learning Network or a Collaborative Innovation Network have lower density, but higher GBC, "*as external members are only connected to core team members, but not among themselves*".

Social Network Metrics such as network density and GBC describe the network as a whole and can be used to track macro-level dynamics. Metrics like degree centrality and betweenness centrality can be used at meso-level to understand the evolution of a community or an organization within an extended network of stakeholders. Applied to the single organization, the same metrics can identify relative positions with reference to partners or competitors. At individual level, the most used metrics for obtaining "point centrality" are degree centrality, betweenness centrality and closeness centrality. This derives from the assumption that the power of individual actors is not an individual attribute, but arises from their relations with others. Centralization and density are important complementary measures, since the concept of density describes the general level of cohesion in a graph, while centralization describes the extent to which this cohesion is organized around particular focal points. In terms of the benefits of these metrics for organizational studies, the use of a metric like individual betweenness centrality allows to identify brokers and boundary spanners. These actors are located on the shortest path between many others in the network, thus they are ideal people to work through when trying to diffuse strategic information.

The use of a metric like betweenness centrality helps to identify the information brokers that are able to span the organization's boundaries, helping strategic knowledge to flow from one department to the other. As Cross et al. said (2002): "*Network analysis can also help reveal loosely connected or isolated members that often represent under-utilized resources of a community as their skills, expertise, and unique perspectives are not leveraged effectively*" (Cross et al., 2002, p.39).

## OBSERVING A LEARNING COMMUNITY THROUGH SNA METRICS

### Study Methodology

To observe the structural properties of the community over time, we used the case of a Master's Program jointly organized by the e-Business Management Section (University of Salento, Italy) and industrial partners in the software and aerospace industry. The Master's program involved young students who were studying and researching at the same time, in a context of learning and applying the practical knowledge to real projects. Based on a public-private partnership, the Master's program was characterized by a combination of several factors: a) inward and outward orientation; b) strong integration between curricular and extracurricular activities (students acted as researchers working directly with industrial partners); c) combination of virtual collaboration and face-to-face interaction during the phases in which students worked at the industrial partners' facilities.

Collaboration within the community was facilitated by the use of a technological platform that enabled the creation of personal and community blogs, a forum and a wiki around the topics of new product development in the aerospace and software industry.

The main goal of the team was to define two wikis: a first wiki described new product development in the aerospace industry and the other discussed the software industry.

To build our case study, we used a triangulation of data to collect information on the individual and community development. In particular, we gathered e-mail archives sent and received by the whole population of students (10) during the observation period (10 months). We collected the e-mail archives from the University servers, while we could not collect any of the industrial partners' e-mail archives. We then interviewed the Director of the Master's Program and the Program Manager who acted as liaison between students, internal tutors and external supervisors. Finally, we administered five web questionnaires every month in order to monitor variables such as students' satisfaction and personal involvement in the Program's activities. Based on a set of 14 questions, we identified their satisfaction in areas such as: knowledge and skills acquired; level of interactivity within and across the community; and personal involvement in the activities.

Personal development was observed using indicators such as self-esteem, emotional development, communication skills, goal setting. Student satisfaction has been mainly translated in the assessment of mentors and tutors' effectiveness, and through the evaluation of learning modules' consistency and quality.

We validated the results of the analysis through the interviews to key informants and through the involvement of academic and industrial partners in the formal assessment of the students' performance.

To visualize the maps of the team's social networks we used Condor, a software suite that can take email archives and translate them into data on the sender, recipient(s), and date/time of each message. With this data, Condor can generate sociograms (i.e. visual maps), adjacency matrices and interactive movies of communication flows over time. In the visual maps each line represents an email relation. The shorter the distance between two people, the higher their frequency of communication. The closer two nodes to each other, the most frequent the exchange of emails between them (Gloor, 2006).

The analysis was articulated as a three step-process. The *first* step was to look at the evolution over time in terms of social interactions, to identify peaks and trough in the community's evolution and observe the emergence of informal roles. The *second* step consisted of comparing the insights emerging from the network analysis with the data collected through the web-questionnaire. The *third* step was to match this data with the stages of community development based on the interviews with key informants.

Given the limitations provided by analyzing only e-mail archives, we used web questionnaires to recognize different types of social networks. We asked students to describe their technical support network (i.e. Who do you contact for technical support?); friendship network (i.e. With whom do you spend your free time and share your personal interest?); preference for communication media (i.e. Whom do you communicate with by chat/phone/e-meeting?).

To recognize the extent of individual growth, we used the Life Effectiveness Questionnaire (LEQ) tool designed by Neill, Marsh and Richards (Neill et al., 2003). The LEQ tool was used to analyze the psychological and behavioral factors that accompany the learners' developmental change due to experiential education initiatives. Based on a Likert Scale (1= very low and 8=very high), the LEQ questionnaire allows to track the path of improvement at different stages of personal and community development during the program. The dimensions monitored in the questionnaire are: Time Management, Social Competence, Motivation, Intellectual Flexibility, Task Leadership, Emotional Control, Active Initiative, Self Confidence, Locus of Control, Community Involvement.

## Stages of Community Development and Social Network Indicators

The results show that the density of the communication network increased by more than 80% over 10 months. We observed 31 connections between 18 members during the initial phase of community creation, and we noticed that after ten months these connections were 227 and the active members were 64. The sociograms showing the email communication indicate a gradual extension of the community's boundaries to progressively include other researchers, faculty members, tutors and industrial partners.

The main results of this research are the observation that the path that the community followed reflects the four stages of the model defined by Tuckman (1965): forming, storming, norming and performing.

In the first month of activities students were involved in team building activities and general workshops. This phase was the typical phase defined *forming* by Tuckman. During the following three months students built an aerospace wiki, which was considered a learning tool for organizing and creating knowledge in a collective way. As reported by a student, and confirmed by the Program Manager: *"during the first months our team experienced many internal conflicts as we looked for the right coordination mechanisms. We just didn't know how to work together"*. After knowing each other, the community of students had to develop spontaneously methods to increase efficiency and effectiveness. They had to learn by themselves how to collaborate and deliver the main learning outcome represented by the collective editing of a wiki section. In the monthly interview, they reported, *"spending a lot of time defining their individual roles"* within the group. In this three-month period the community seems to be in a *storming* phase, characterized by conflicts and polarization around interpersonal issues, with continuous discussions on how to perform a task.

When students started to co-develop the second wiki describing the software industry a *norming* phase seemed to emerge: resistance to collaborate was overcome and in-group feeling and cohesiveness developed. Discussions were more on technical rather than personal level, while clear roles were assigned.

During this shift to a norming phase, we observed increasing values of the Satisfaction factor (from 6 to 7.2 out of 8) and Personal Development (from 6.5 to 7.3 out of 8). Before the end of the norming phase, students had consolidated a set of collaboration rules to operate within and across their boundaries. They built stable interactions with internal and external tutors and reported an increased level of personal development (27% higher than the previous month). After presenting the wiki to industrial partners, students experienced a period of increased group and self-esteem, higher awareness of their competencies and an increase of satisfaction (+0.05%). We interpreted this positive trend as an expression of their maturation process.

In the final month of observation, the community increased their density by 40%, increasing from 25 actors exchanging 83 emails, to 37 actors linked through 148 c-mails. In this period, students

opened the boundaries of their group by asking the Program Coordinator and tutors to organize specific workshops on specific topics. These patterns of behaviors and interactions seem to reflect the beginning of a *performing* stage.

Based on the interviews to managers of the companies involved in the projects, all the indicators of performance increased over time. During the first period, when learners had to build the aerospace wiki, they experienced internal conflicts in interacting and finding the right coordination mechanisms. The need to collaborate to define a common deliverable, exploring a completely new industry and defining their individual roles within the group, required them to develop - in an emergent manner – methods to increase efficiency and effectiveness of their work.

Figure 1 indicates that the software wiki was evaluated as a better product of the community, as it was the result of a more mature stage of community development. The second wiki was assessed as a better deliverable in terms of several factors: content consistency; level of depth, accuracy of the editing; ability to use interdisciplinary concepts and ability to work as a team.

To observe how social network structure changed over time, we analyzed the interactions within the community and we plotted the trends in terms of *degree centrality*, *betweenness centrality* and *contribution index*. The network increased in 10 months from 30 connections among 17 nodes to 316 connections among 103 nodes, indicating a progressive extension of the community's boundaries to include faculty members, mentors, tutors and industrial partners.

Looking on a weekly base at the evolution of social network indicators (Figure 2) we noticed a shift in the period October-November, in terms of *Group Betweenness Centrality (GBC)*, together with an increase in the number of actors within the network. The value of *GBC* is 1 for a perfect star structure, where one person dominates the communication, and is equal to 0 when the information flows more freely.

*Figure 1. Evaluation of the wiki following five criteria*

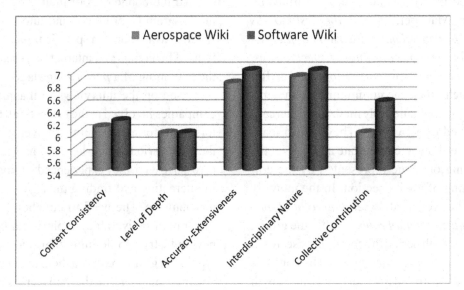

We observed a growth in the *Satisfaction* index (Figure 3) from September to October (0.3 average increased value). The trend changed in the next month when no increase was recorded. At the beginning of November students expressed a decreased satisfaction for the activities they were involved on and reported a lower motivation.

Then, we observed a second trend in terms of decreased *personal development* (Figure 4): for the first two months there was no improvement in the reported values of personal development, which then increased at an average rate of 0.27 at the beginning of the third month, when the

aerospace wiki was presented to external managers.

At the beginning of November the community started to develop an internal organization, with central actors performing the role of coordinators and gatekeepers (Figure 5); at the same time the community was reporting an improvement in terms of personal growth. We interpret this trend as an expression of the maturation process of the community.

The third trend is visible by matching the above-described results with the assessment of the ability to create knowledge in a collaborative

*Figure 2. Group level indicators over time*

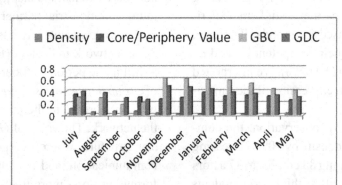

*Figure 3. Overall satisfaction over time (each line represents the evolution of an individual student identified by an acronym)*

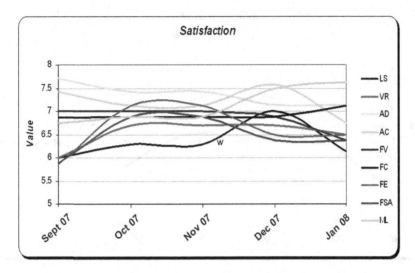

way. Until October 2007 students had the goal to finalize and present the *aerospace wiki* to the managers of the partner companies. In this phase, the community had been inwardly oriented, only focused on this specific task. After presenting their work to the companies' managers, the students experienced a period of increased self-esteem, higher awareness of their competencies, and the need to deepen their knowledge in the aerospace and software industry.

We shared these insights with the Program Coordinator who made the decision to promote a new *software wiki* project. In the same period, the increase in Group Betweenness Centrality

*Figure 4. Personal satisfaction over time (each line represents the evolution of an individual student identified by an acronym)*

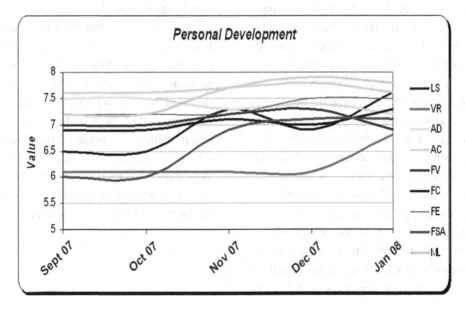

*Figure 5. Individual growth: Average values of satisfaction and personal development*

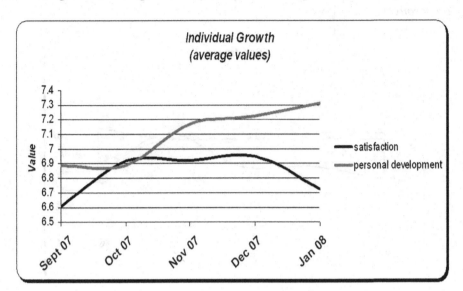

(+27%) was associated to a higher involvement of the software companies' managers as speakers in the Master's, in order to better contextualize the wiki content. The result of this action was a better satisfaction reported by students in terms of what they were doing (with a further increase of the average value of about 0.05), a higher pride and a social network structure more centralized around the mentors.

The decision to use a software tool, Condor, that creates movies of the communication patterns over time was motivated by the necessity to observe not only the structural characteristics of the community, but also the peaks and the trough in terms of collaboration and openness.

Looking at the evolution of the social networks from the first day until the end of the Program helped to identify the main informal roles (e.g., gatekeeper, boundary spanner, ambassador) and the phases in which the team communicated more freely. During the first week of February a master's student started to act as a boundary spanner, opening the boundaries of the community to new, external stakeholders (three partners from the aerospace industry). Looking at the evolution of three network metrics (density, group degree

centrality, group betweenness centrality) we noticed how group betweenness centrality decreased from 0.6 to 0.5, indicating how the team started to interact in a less centralized way (Gloor, 2006).

A final consideration emerges by looking at the static map of the communication flows within the learning community. Figure 6 shows the communication via email that community's members exchanged for the whole observation period. After ten months, about 180 actors were exchanging more than 700 emails.

As shown in Figure 6, students, tutors and mentors are strongly connected with each other, while managers and tutors of the partnering companies are slightly more peripheral, with the exception of the three actors represented by triangles who were part of the core team. These members were in charge of working closely with students to increase the effectiveness of their learning. Their duty was to help students learn how to transfer their knowledge and competencies from the classroom to the working environment.

*Figure 6. Visual map of 10 months of emails*

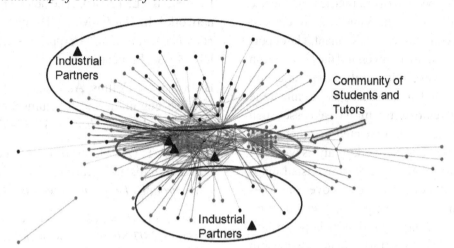

## DISCUSSION AND CONCLUSION

The application of Social Network Analysis allowed recognizing important phases during which the number of connections and actors involved in the community increased in a significant way. In November students became more connected to internal tutors and mentors, while in March they started communicating with external company's tutors. These phases are important periods as they represent the creation of more extensive ties between internal and external members.

Other key periods of transition for the community are represented by October - when the second wiki was started - and February, when the companies communicated the projects to the students. From those months on, we observed increased values of density, GBC and number of connections. We also noticed an increase in learners' satisfaction and perception of individual growth. Based on these results, the Program Manager defined specific actions to better support the students.

As the Program Manager said: *"At the end of October, we decided to increase the level of support for our students. We provided them with a better technical support, guidelines on how to better collaborate and how to extract content from* technical documents and use it for the software wiki. During the design of the first wiki, students asked for more face-to-face interactions with tutors and mentors; to complete the second wiki, students seemed more independent as community and used written guidelines and less interaction with tutors. It seemed like students required a less hierarchical structure to coordinate their activities".

Looking at the sociograms, the School's Direction identified the tutors and mentors who seemed to be more connected and could more easily act as facilitators of connection in the community. In order to boost collaboration, students were asked to increase the frequency of formal presentations of their results: more frequent discussions, more deadlines and more self-organized meetings helped the students create a wiki whose content was appreciated by the partner companies (the software wiki).

The adoption of the SNA method allowed the Program Manager to react immediately to negative signals in terms of community development. These interventions energized learners during the most critical phases and permitted *ad-hoc* activities such as the organization of focused seminars, meetings with industrial partners and community facilitators, and one-to-one coaching.

The use of social network metrics and the use of surveys allowed identifying gaps in terms of personal and community development. The opportunity to mine email archives and the observation of the dynamic evolution of the communication flows represented an important tool to intervene real-time and remove structural weaknesses such as the presence of disconnected members. The application of Social Network Analysis provided tangible managerial input, such as visual maps of members and evolution of ties over time. Peripheral students have helped to become better integrated; curricula were refined to improve their effectiveness; and mentor-student relationship was intensified.

As a practical recommendation, it is important to remember that Social Network Analysis provides only the basis for a structural analysis of communities, either online of hybrid communities. Focused interviews and other archive data are required to confirm the evidences from the social network maps.

# REFERENCES

Ancona, D., & Bresman, H. (2007). *X-Teams. How to build teams that lead, innovate, and succeed.* Boston, MA: HBS Press.

Aplin, C. T. (2008). Innovative trends in learning tools. *Journal of Cognitive Affective Learning, 4*(2), 26–28.

Bartlett, C. A., & Mohammed, A. (1995). 3M: Profile of an innovating company. *Harvard Business School Case,* 395-016.

Bontis, N. (2001). Assessing knowledge assets: A review of the models used to measure intellectual capital. *International Journal of Management Reviews, 3*(1), 41–60. doi:10.1111/1468-2370.00053

Borgatti, S. P., & Everett, M. G. (1999). Models of core/periphery structures. *Social Networks, 21,* 375–395. doi:10.1016/S0378-8733(99)00019-2

Breiger, R. L. (2004). The analysis of social networks. In Hardy, M., & Bryman, A. (Eds.), *Handbook of data analysis* (pp. 505–526). London, UK: SAGE Publications.

Brown, J. S., Collins, A., & Duguid, P. (1989). Situated cognition and the culture of learning. *Educational Researcher, 18*(1), 32–42.

Brown, R. E. (2001). The process of community-building in distance learning classes. *Journal of Asynchronous Learning Networks, 5*(2), 18–35.

Chesbrough, H. W. (2003). The era of open innovation. *MIT Sloan Management Review, 4*(3), 74–81.

Cross, R., Borgatti, S. P., & Parker, A. (2002). Making invisible work visible: Using social network analysis to support strategic collaboration. *California Management Review, 44*(2).

Gloor, P. A. (2006). *Swarm creativity. Competitive advantage through collaborative innovation networks.* New York, NY: Oxford University Press.

Hiltz, S. R., Coppola, N., Rotter, N., Turoff, M., & Benbunan-Fich, R. (2000). Measuring the importance of collaborative learning for the effectiveness of ALN: A multi-measure, multimethod approach. *Journal of Asynchronous Learning Networks, 4*(2), 103–125.

Iyer, B., Lee, C., & Venkatraman, N. (2006). Managing in a small world ecosystem: Lessons from the software sector. *California Management Review, 48*(3), 27–47.

Kim, A. J. (2000). *Community building on the Web: Secret strategies for successful online communities.* London, UK: Addison Wesley.

Lave, J., & Wenger, E. (1991). *Situated learning: Legitimate peripheral participation.* Cambridge, UK: Cambridge University Press.

Moore, M. G., & Greg, K. (1996). *Distance education: A systems view*. Belmont, CA: Wadsworth Publishing Company.

Neill, J. T., Marsh, H. W., & Richards, G. E. (2003). The life effectiveness questionnaire: Development and psychometrics. Sydney, Australia: University of Western Sydney. Retrieved September 16, 2010, from http://wilderdom.com/tools/leq/leqreferences.html

Penuel, W. R., Sussex, W., Korbak, C., & Hoadley, C. (2006). Investigating the potential of using social network analysis in educational evaluation. *The American Journal of Evaluation*, *27*(4), 437–451. doi:10.1177/1098214006294307

Rheingold, H. (2000). *The virtual community homesteading on the electronic frontier*. Cambridge, MA: The MIT Press.

Rogers, J. (2000). Communities of practice: A framework for fostering coherence in virtual learning communities. *Journal of Educational Technology & Society*, *3*(3), 384–392.

Tuckman, B. (1965). Developmental sequence in small groups. *Psychological Bulletin*, *63*(6), 384–399. doi:10.1037/h0022100

Tuckman, B., & Jensen, M. (1977). Stages of small-group development revisited. *Group and Organizational Studies*, *2*, 419–427. doi:10.1177/105960117700200404

Wassermann, S., & Faust, K. (1994). *Social network analysis: Methods and applications*. Cambridge, UK: Cambridge University Press.

Wenger, E. (1998). *Communities of practice: Learning, meaning, identity*. Cambridge, MA: Cambridge University Press.

Wenger, E. C., & Snyder, W. M. (2000). Communities of practice: The organizational frontier. *Harvard Business Review*, *78*(1), 139–145.

## KEY TERMS AND DEFINITIONS

**Community of Practice:** A group of people who share an interest and/or a profession and that evolve because of the members' common interest in a particular domain or area. It can also be created with the intention of improving knowledge and expertise related to the individuals' field.

**Learning Community:** A group of people who share a common interest towards a specific knowledge domain, and who are actively engaged in learning together from each other.

**Online Community:** A group of people who share a domain of interest about which they communicate online.

**Social Network Analysis (SNA):** The interdisciplinary study of the relations between social entities - such individuals and organizations - and the implications of these connections through the application of network metrics.

**Team:** A group of people associated in some joint actions and tasks and working together toward a common goal.

# Chapter 13
# Social Networks and Terrorism

David Knoke
*University of Minnesota, USA*

## ABSTRACT

*This chapter explains how international terror networks, consisting of individuals and organizations spanning countries and continents, form and evolve. It describes tools and methods used by social network analysts to study such networks; their applications by counterterrorist organizations; their limitations and problems in data collection and analysis; and directions for future research. It also discusses a few recent case studies by prominent researchers.*

## INTRODUCTION

The historical antecedents of terrorism can be traced from Antiquity through the Middle Ages (Chaliand & Blin, 2007). As early instances of asymmetric warfare, Jewish Zealots revolted against the Roman Empire, while Hassan-i-Sabah sent his Iranian followers on suicide missions to kill Sunni Caliphate leaders in the 11th century (from whence the word *assassin* might have originated). The French word *terrorisme* (from the Latin *terrere,* "to frighten") originated in 1793-94 during the French Revolution's Reign of Terror (*la Terreur*) when the Committee on Public Safety killed

DOI: 10.4018/978-1-61350-444-4.ch013

between 15,000 and 40,000 citizens. Despite its initial application to states terrorizing their own citizens, the concept was subsequently broadened to include actions by nonstate actors. Historians identify several global waves of terrorism: social revolutionaries and anarchists in the 19th century; anti-colonial rebellions and nationalist independence struggles in the mid-20th century; leftist revolts of the late-20th century (Rapoport, 2001; Sedgwick, 2007). The most recent wave – international Islamist militancy – emerged during the 1979 Iranian Revolution and Soviet invasion of Afghanistan and continues today. But, periodization is never neat: far-left and anarchist attacks have resurged in Europe recently (Winfield & Gatopoulos 2010).

Analysts have proposed more than a hundred definitions and measures of terrorism, suggesting that no consensus will soon be reached (e.g., Ruby, 2000; Butko, 2006; Halwani, 2006). Actions may be variously characterized as terrorism according to legal, moral, religious, political, or behavioral criteria. However, among features common to many definitions is violence committed by groups with political goals, targeted against civilians, and intended to create fear among a larger population. Following U.S. law, the Department of State defines international terrorism as "premeditated, politically motivated violence perpetrated against non-combatant targets by subnational groups or clandestine agents." The State Department publishes an annual list of about 40 Foreign Terrorist Organizations, and a comparable number of Groups of Concern, considered threatening U.S. national security. Critics charge that the State Department's methodology is politically biased and its reports are inaccurate (e.g., Kreuger & Laitin, 2004). The European Union and other nations use varying criteria to construct their terrorist organizations lists. In this chapter, terrorist organization refers to a group using violence against civilian targets for political purposes.

Terrorism overlaps with two related forms of asymmetric warfare waged by less-powerful groups against nation states: guerilla wars and insurgencies. Guerillas are small-group formations that fight in uniform using mobile military tactics, such as ambushes, raids, and sabotage, targeted on military and police forces rather than civilians. Insurgencies are armed uprisings, often by groups neither wearing uniforms nor fighting in military formations, with the political aim of overthrowing a constituted national government and replacing it with another regime. Some insurgents and guerillas carry out terror acts against civilians to undermine a populace's confidence that the central government can ensure its security. But, whereas an insurgency typically uses violence to advance revolutionary goals, for many terrorists "violence replaces rather than complements a

political program" (Morris, 2005, p. 2). Applying the distinctions among these ideal types to actual historical cases is often difficult. Thus, the Iraq and Afghanistan conflicts of the early 21st century could be construed as terrorism, insurgency, or guerilla war at differing times and places: Sunni and Shiite militias, Taliban insurgents in Afghanistan (Smith, 2008), and Al-Qaida terrorists in both nations as well as in Pakistan's tribal areas. Given these ambiguities, the social network principles discussed below are pertinent to all three forms of asymmetric warfare.

## TERROR NETWORKS

Some theorists seek the origins of terrorism in macro-level socioeconomic grievances and repressive political conditions (e.g., Tilly, 2004; Tosini, 2007; Intriligator, 2010). For example, Donald Black's theory of "pure terrorism" examined its social geometry (Black, 2004). Terrorists strike more often across greater social distances; for example, indigenous people rise up against their colonial masters or members of one religion assault adherents of another. Violent acts less frequently occur downwardly or laterally, against social inferiors or members of one's ethnic group or community. A necessary condition for terrorism across large social distances is geophysical propinquity, which modern technologies have greatly increased. Airplanes, cell phones, satellite maps, and high-rise offices facilitate perpetration of mass violence against civilians in arenas far from militants' homelands. Robert Pape (2003, 2005) analyzed 315 suicide bombings from 1980 through 2003. Almost all those suicide terror campaigns aimed to coerce liberal democracies into withdrawing their military forces occupying the militants' homelands.

*For example, spectacular suicide terrorist attacks have recently been employed by Palestinian groups in attempts to force Israel to abandon the*

*West Bank and Gaza, by the Liberation Tigers of Tamil Eelam to compel the Sri Lankan government to accept an independent Tamil homeland, and by Al Qaeda to pressure the United States to withdraw from the Saudi Arabian Peninsula. (Pape, 2003, p. 343)*

A later campaign by Iraqis sought to expel American and British occupying armies from Iraq (Pape, 2005, pp. 255-259). However, suicide bombing against occupiers is only a small portion of the violence by hundreds of militant groups between 1968 and 2006 (Jones & Libicki, 2008). Many other analysts emphasize micro-level dynamics – including personality factors, psychological stress, and altruistic motivations – that dispose individuals to become terrorists (e.g., Sageman, 2004; Victoroff, 2005; Bird, Blomberg, & Hess, 2008). Absent from most macro- and micro-level accounts are explanations of the meso-level processes through which people are recruited, trained in violent skills, organized into effective clandestine teams, provided with financial resources and weaponry, and plan and carry out attacks. Social network analysis provides conceptual, theoretical, and methodological tools that can help to fill this gap.

Two core elements of a social network are a set of actors (natural persons, groups, or organizations) and a set of social relations, or type of tie, that connect them. Ties may be directed (e.g., giving money) or nondirected (communicating), vary in magnitude from weak to strong, and differ in frequency and duration. Multiple types of ties can occur, such as friendship and advising, and each type comprises a distinct network. The smallest unit of network analysis is a dyad, a pair of actors and its relation (which may be absent or present to varying extent). If a person (*ego*) is taken as focal unit of analysis, his egocentric network consists of all others (*alters*) with whom he has direct dyadic ties and all the dyadic connections among those altars. In a small social system (e.g., a few dozen actors, probably no more than

a few hundred), a complete network consisting of one type of relational tie among all its members can be graphed (diagrammed) as a two- or three-dimensional map in which labeled points represent actors and lines represent their dyadic ties. Additional analyses using matrix algebra techniques can identify such features as density, reachability (number of indirect steps, or paths, between dyads), central actors, brokers, cohesive subgroups, and competitive positions (see Knoke and Yang [2008]). These methods can uncover network patterns, revealing who has direct and indirect connections to whom, and disclosing the network's strengths and vulnerabilities to counterterror disruptions.

A terrorist network is typically composed of a small number of militants who have dense, strong-tie relations that are often based on kinship. The social homophily principle (preference for affiliation with similar others), coupled with the necessity to maintain secrecy about covert operations, explains how networks recruit members as revealed by their multiple social attributes. Networks in general tend to be homogeneous across many social dimensions, such as ethnicity, gender, age, education, and class. Because persons located at greater distances in social space are less likely to interact, the social distances between network members typically remain small. Geographic propinquity further constrains the possibilities for recruiting participants for violent actions. New recruits often live in the same village or urban neighborhood, go to the same school or religious organization, and attend the same training camp as current network members. More socially dissimilar persons tend to be regarded as suspicious and untrustworthy, particularly when they initiate efforts to join a network. By restricting their social bases, networks better evade penetration by agents connected to counterterror organizations.

A handful of researchers have conducted formal social network analyses of relations among members of actual terrorist groups. Data collection is hampered by necessary reliance on public sources, such as news reports and court records, because police and military records from surveillance and interrogation are unavailable. Valdis Krebs (2001) created the seminal graph, based on newspaper articles published shortly after Al-Qaida's 9/11 attacks, which reconstructed connections among the 19 hijackers and 43 accomplices who provided money, skills, and information. Not only was the head of field operations, Mohammed Atta, at the center of the network, but also the four pilots formed a tight clique. Moreover, every hijacker was just two or fewer steps (path distance) from two other hijackers, Nawaf Alhazmi and Khalid Almihdhar. The CIA knew that both men had participated in a January 2000 meeting in Malaysia attended by several Al-Qaida top leaders. But, the CIA failed to put their names on a watch list and the FBI later claimed that the CIA never shared its information about Almihdhar's multiple-entry visa (National Commission, 2004). The intelligence community's failure to follow those two suspects upon their return to the U.S. was a missed opportunity to detect and possibly apprehend the 9/11 network before it struck. Krebs (2001) concluded that a "dense under-layer of prior trusted relationships made the hijacker network both stealth and resilient," but "concentrating both unique skills and connectivity in the same [persons] makes the network easier to disrupt - once it is discovered."

Among the prominent researchers who have diagrammed networks: (1) Marc Sageman (2004, p. 138) analyzed the kinship, friendship, religious, and work relations among 366 militants to identify four global hubs: Al-Qaida Central Staff, Southeast Asians (from Indonesia and Malaysia), Maghreb Arabs (North Africa), and Core Arabs (Saudi Arabia, Egypt, Yemen, Kuwait). For a longitudinal analysis of that network's evolution, see Xu, Hu and Chen (2009). (2) Javier Jordán and Nicola Horsburgh (2005) depicted a schematic map of networks in Spain and Algeria involved in the 2004 Madrid train bombings. (3) Steven Koschade (2006) graphed 17 members of the Jemaah Islamiyah (JI) cell that bombed a Bali,

Indonesia, and nightclub in 2002. (4) Magouirk, Atran, & Sageman (2008) displayed several diagrams of the larger Jemaah Islamiyah leadership network involved in numerous 2000-05 attacks across Southeast Asia. (5) Ami Pedahzur and Arie Perliger (2006) diagrammed four Palestinian networks that dispatched 42 suicide bombers during the al-Aqsa Intifada. (6) Pedahzur and Perliger (2009) mapped Jewish networks inside Israel – Jewish Underground, Kahane Network, and Amir Brothers Network – that targeted Palestinians and assassinated Prime Minister Yitzhak Rabin. (7) Other analysts took less-formal approaches in describing militant networks; for example, the Sunni and Shiite insurgencies in Iraq (Reed, 2007); the Bakri-Hamza network emanating from Finsbury Park Mosque in England (Pantucci, 2010); and the Haqanni network operating between Pakistan and Afghanistan (Rashid, 2010).

Koschade's in-depth study of Jemaah Islamiyah's Bali cell (2006), and his comparisons of JI to three other terrorist cells (2007), illuminated the relevance of social network analysis for developing knowledge useful to counterterror efforts. He found a high density of ties (.43) among the 17 JI cell members, indicating "a mix between efficiency and covertness" (2006, p. 570). Two members had exceptionally high scores on three centrality measures, and the whole network was quite centralized. These indicators and a related graph revealed that

*Samudra and Idris were the most important individuals in the cell, specifically due to their high centrality scores. ... Samudra was the weakest point in the cell, and his capture would possibly have led to the isolation of Team Lima (which included the suicide bomber and contingency [actors]) and the loss of the most active and centralized member of the network. (p. 571)*

Given the high degree of connections within the cell, detection of any member by the authorities could have exposed the entire cell. Koschade's

(2007) comparative network study concluded that cells focusing on efficiency rather than covertness were more successful in completing their objectives, and that betweenness centrality (control of information flow) is crucial for identifying cell leaders.

## EVOLVING CELL STRUCTURES

Many "dark networks," such as mafias and espionage rings, use a cell structure to avoid detection and decapitation (Raab & Milward, 2003). In formal network terms, a cell is a subgroup of actors within a larger cellular network, such that all actors within a cell are fully connected but connections between subgroups are minimal (Frantz & Carley, 2005; Carley, 2009). Cell sizes are typically very small, on the order of three to six members, most of who know only their cell members' identities. The cell leader communicates via a single contact to the larger network. This low-density structure minimizes the risk that law enforcement agents could roll up the entire organization by capturing and interrogating any cell member. A sleeper cell is designed to infiltrate a community and remain dormant for months or years, awaiting a signal to launch an attack. Osama bin Laden, in videotape found in Afghanistan, described the 9/11 operations as a classic cell structure: "Those who were trained to fly didn't know the others. One group of people did not know the other group" (ABC News, 2001).

Cell durability comes from the strong, direct ties among members, which build trust and reinforce the reciprocity norm of responding in-kind to one another's actions. These self-regulatory mechanisms explain how cells can achieve sufficient cohesion and commitment to undertake effective militant actions without requiring hierarchical coordination. Self-managed cells validate members' belief in an altruistic, even sacrificial, ideology; inspire fanatical loyalty to comrades; reward exceptional performances with communal esteem; punish deviations from the group's norms; and pressure irresolute members to conform to the cell's mission. Despite these beneficial dynamics, cell members are susceptible to obsessive suspicions of penetration or betrayal. Law enforcement organizations can intensify this intrinsic paranoia, by picking up and detaining suspected militants incommunicado before releasing them, thus nudging a cell toward self-destructive purges. But, militants can likewise infiltrate counterterror organizations, as occurred in 2009 when an Al-Qaida double agent killed seven CIA operatives by suicide bomb at an Afghanistan base.

Some analysts speculate that, reacting to counterterror activities, international terrorist organizations innovate at the tactical, operational, and strategic levels (Jackson, 2006; Sageman, 2008). Pressured by police and military forces, they must adopt new structures to survive in a radically changing environment. In formal network analysis terms, "rational terrorists will attempt to counter increased efforts at infiltration and restructure themselves to be less penetrable," by finding an optimal trade-off between security and intra-group communication (Enders and Su, 2007, p. 54; Enders and Jindapon, 2010). Groups will reduce the density of ties among members and conduct fewer logistically complicated operations, such as assaults on embassies and coordinated plane hijackings. Brian Jackson (2006) argued that authority evolves from initially tightly coupled organizations, to coupled networks, and then to loosely coupled movements. An organization might originally use a more centralized hierarchical form, where functional committees coordinate and provide material support to specialists in policy, planning, financing, recruiting, and training activities. Al-Qaida's earlier field operations, including the *USS Cole* bombing and 9/11 were conducted by "a carefully selected clandestine cell, headed by a senior Al-Qaeda operative who reported personally to Bin Laden" (National Commission, 2004). But, as it evolves toward leaderless and decentralized network forms, top leadership only loosely coordinates the tactical cells. Loose coupling hampers counterterror organizations' detection of cells and "what actions should be taken to identify and exploit any vulnerabilities found there" (Jackson, 2006, p. 242). To secure secrecy and resilience from counterterror actions, the organization sacrifices control and efficiency.

When counterterror efforts seriously damage an organization, as happened to Al-Qaida and the Taliban after 9/11, remnant cells can eventually regroup and launch new operations. In a fragmented network structure, cells acquire greater autonomy to select targets and manage their own logistics. But, self-sufficiency carries some risk of cells "going rogue," abandoning the organization's original mission and undertaking spectacular but futile gestures. Some analysts argue that shifting from hierarchies toward loosely structured networks reduces success because of poor security, as evidenced by numerous foiled Al-Qaida plots (Eilstrup-Sangiovanni & Jones, 2008). Others speculate that forced decentralization pushes mid-level militants to cooperate with criminal gangs to raise revenues and obtain weapons (Dishman, 2005; Mullins, 2009). Evidence points to an emerging narco-terror hybrid network form that combines expertise from both types of dark organizations.

## FINANCIAL NETWORKS

Financial networks are crucial to raise and move the funds necessary for routine organizational maintenance and to run field operations. Organizations must pay staff salaries and cover media expenses. Cells must obtain sufficient revenues to purchase munitions and pay for travel, lodging, and false documents. Among the primary income streams flowing to such organizations as Al-Qaida, Hamas, Hezbollah, Lashkar-e-Taiba, and Jemaah Islamiyah, are contributions by group members and outsiders, including such state sponsors as Iran and Syria (Winer, 2008); sales by legitimate front businesses including diamond, honey, and import-export trades (Basile, 2004); donations skimmed from charities and nongovernmental organizations; "petty crime, racketeering, extortion, gun-running and kidnapping" (Abuza, 2003, p. 170); and "an 'inverse triangle model' in which a broad network of social services supports a smaller jihadist core" (Abuza, 2009). U.S. government reports alleged that individuals and charities based in Saudi Arabia provide major financial support for militants, with other donations from Persian Gulf emirates, Iran, and Syria (e.g., Blanchard & Prados, 2007). The Irish Republican Army and Tamil Tigers raised funds from their migrant diasporas, while the Revolutionary Armed Forces of Columbia (FARC), Peru's Shining Path, and Basque Homeland and Freedom (ETA) resorted to diverse criminal rackets.

Organizations must move money from financiers to cells despite unrelenting efforts by counterterror organizations to thwart them. The solutions they devise closely resemble many practices by criminal syndicates involved in narcotics smuggling, gun-running, extortion, bank robberies, and human trafficking (Jacobson & Levitt, 2010). Both groups are embedded in loosely integrated systems of legitimate banks, front businesses, courier services, and underground affiliates to transfer and launder money. Key nodes in some networks are *hawala* ("bill of exchange" or "promissory note") bankers, largely unregistered and unregulated in many jurisdictions, who transfer both legal and illicit remittances. Hawaladars in one country accept cash, checks, and other valuable goods. After contacting counterparts in a destination country, they arrange for payment of a corresponding cash sum, thus bypassing record-keeping requirements of official financial institutions (Razavy & Haggerty, 2009). Other money-laundering techniques include: bulk-transport of currency and high-value commodities such as diamonds and precious metals; multilayered investment companies, trusts, and shell corporations; fraudulent prepaid gift- and phone-cards; and false invoices over- and understating merchandise prices in international trade to transfer money between colluding importers and exporters (Zdanowicz, 2009).

Internet and mobile communication technologies expand financial options. Although Internet penetration in developing nations lags behind the West, Hamas, Hezbollah, Lashkar-e-Taiba, and Chechen *mujahidin* effectively use it to raise and transfer funds electronically (Jacobson, 2010). Savvy operators adopt fake identities on Web sites to steal credit-card numbers, solicit humanitarian and charitable donations, and sell counterfeit goods. Internet gambling sites make online money laundering easy. Internet security and anonymity, for example email encryption, even emboldened some militants to link their Websites to host companies inside the U.S. (Jacobson, 2010, p. 358). Terrorist exploitation of the Internet creates both dilemmas and opportunities for disruptive counterterror action.

## DARK SIDE OF THE WEB

Social networking Websites are fast becoming low-cost mechanisms for political radicalization, fostering militant collective identities and virtual communities, recruiting footsoldiers, planning attacks, and propagandizing results. Innovative communication devices abet indoctrination and training functions that previously required face-to-face contacts. Websites and chatrooms propagate an online knowledge base of audio sermons, martyrdom testimonials, bomb-construction manuals, hostage-beheading videos, and car-bomb montages set to music (Hafez, 2007). Well-educated but disaffected young European and American men (and increasingly women), trolling the Web in search of validation and social support for their angry alienation from Western liberal culture, are easy prey for radical recruiters. For example, in 2009, Pakistan authorities caught five young Muslim men from Washington, DC, suburbs traveling to North Waziristan to train with the Taliban

and eventually fight against American troops in Afghanistan. They had watched militant YouTube videos and shared an email account, which brought them to the attention of a Pakistani recruiter with ties to Al-Qaida. An American citizen hiding in Yemen, Anwar al-Awlaki, used Internet and personal contacts to inspire the Fort Hood shooter, the Christmas-Day underwear bomber, and the Times-Square van bomber. Internet activities by U.S., Italian, and German right wing and violent organizations are also growing (Caiani & Wagemann, 2009).

A rising phenomenon is "homegrown terrorism," acts by persons born or raised in Western countries that are "executed without significant assistance from overseas networks" (Kirchick, 2010, p. 16). Wannabe terrorists are self-mobilized via Websites, chatrooms, and email exchanges with inspirational preachers. For example, the four men from Leeds who carried out the 2005 London subway and bus bombings, which killed 52 and injured 700, had no direct connections to Al-Qaida. They were a "self-starter" clique (Kirby, 2007), radicalized by watching militant videos, who obtained online instruction in suicide bombing missions. Similarly, the network behind the 2004 Madrid train bombings, which killed 191 and injured 2,000, involved no direct connections to Al-Qaida, but were extremists inspired through the Internet (Jordán & Horsburgh, 2005). Recent attacks and plots inside the U.S., Europe, and Australia suggest rising trends in homegrown terror (Kohlmann, 2008; Wilner & Dubouloz, 2010). Although self-recruited militants often lack professional skills and sophisticated training, their costs are minimal, while the potential payoff from an occasional success can be huge.

## COUNTERTERROR NETWORK ANALYSIS

Applying the notion, "It takes a network to fight a network" (Jones, 2007), counterterror organizations seek to detect the connections among militants and organizations. To connect-the-dots, counterterror agencies construct their own communication and intelligence-sharing networks. Public policies can be enacted to offer stronger incentives for law enforcement, military, and security organizations to collaborate in exchanging and evaluating raw field reports. The 9/11 National Commission urged stronger central control over the U.S. Intelligence Community (IC) to overcome interagency fragmentation and rivalry. The Director of National Intelligence (DNI) was created to supervise 16 civilian and military agencies and report directly to the President. The DNI also oversees the National Counterterrorism Center, charged with analyzing IC intelligence and supporting counterterror ops with information technology. But, critics charge that centralization under the DNI, instead of rationalizing counterterror actions, produces new information overload without adequate means for sifting through enormous volumes of daily data (de Bruijn, 2006). Similar inefficiencies of information flow plague counterterror networks in the UK (Field, 2009) and the transnational intelligence community (den Boer, Hillebrand & Nolke, 2008; Pawlak, 2009). A major intelligence disconnect occurred in 2009 when a Nigerian on board a U.S. airliner tried to detonate an explosive device concealed in his underwear. He was allowed to board despite several IC agencies knowing that the British had denied him a visa renewal; his father reported the son's radicalization to the U.S. Embassy in Nigeria; his name appeared on a watch list but not on a no-fly list; and he paid cash for a ticket without checking baggage. Although some intelligence gaps were closed after the incident, others will likely emerge as international terrorists continually probe for security weaknesses.

Law enforcement agencies have acquired enhanced capabilities to surveil Internet and Web users for criminal activity, including suspected terrorists. "They can use active and passive attacks, (e.g., viruses and surveillance/traffic analysis) on terrorist computers to gather address books, cookies, passwords and similar information. Counter-terrorist operations include the use of black propaganda to destroy trust" (Brown & Korff, 2009:122). Network analysis techniques enable counterterror experts to track money flows via connections from charities and foundations, through multiple transfers across financial institutions and front organizations, to terrorist organizations (Abuza, 2009; Zdanowicz, 2009). After 9/11, the U.S. federal government identified and shut down many domestic charities channeling contributions overseas. In a prominent legal case, the Holy Land Foundation and its leaders were tried and convicted in 2009 of providing "material support to a foreign terrorist organization." Five leaders were given life sentences for sending $12 million to Hamas, which supported schools to encourage "children to become suicide bombers and to recruit suicide bombers by offering support to their families" (U.S. Department of Treasury, 2007). The creation of new legal and financial tools to promote more transparent transactions – such as the U.S. Financial Crimes Enforcement Network (FinCEN) and the E.U. Financial Action Task Force on Money Laundering – have strengthened the capacity of the international community to disrupt dark networks. However, substantial portions of the global financial system, such as *hawala* networks, remain untouched by international authorities, enabling militants to continue collecting and disbursing funds.

U.S. military counterinsurgency doctrine belatedly realized that social network analysis could be a valuable tool. (The Israeli Defense Forces had much earlier adopted a "networked warfare" strategy to fighting insurgents in the West Bank [Jones, 2007].) At the start of the Iraq War in 2003, most U.S. combat troops lived in large bases and patrolled contested ground outside. Attacks by Shiite militias, Sunni insurgents, and Al-Qaida-in-Mesopotamia inflicted increasing casualties and wore down American public support. After the Democrats gained congressional seats in the

2006 election, President George Bush changed strategy, assigning General David Petraeus to deploy a "surge" of 20,000 troops. Petraeus had coauthored Army Field Manual 3-24 *Counterinsurgency*, which advocated "a mix of familiar combat tasks and skills more often associated with nonmilitary agencies" depending on the local situation (Petraeus and Amos, 2006, p. 2). Appendix B discussed social network diagrams as one such skill:

*SNA can help commanders understand how an insurgent organization operates. Insurgent networks often do not behave like normal social networks. However, SNA can help commanders determine what kind of social network an insurgent organization is. That knowledge helps commanders understand what the network looks like, how it is connected, and how best to defeat it. (p. B-17)*

Network analysts incrementally constructed "link diagrams" showing everyone related to Saddam Hussein by blood and tribe, eventually leading to his capture in 2003 (see also Reed and Segal, 2006). In implementing the 2007 surge, Petraeus based small patrol units in neighborhoods and villages, where troops could better forge ties to residents and gain their trust. Those connections gave troops access to timely intelligence on the whereabouts of insurgents, their arms caches, and planned assaults. Iraqi violence fell dramatically following the surge, although some analysts argued that a major factor was the Sunni Awakening, in which tribal militias with funding from the U.S. revolted against the excesses of Al-Qaida-in-Mesopotamia (Jones & Libicki, 2008, p. 83). Whether Petraeus could replicate this strategy in Afghanistan remained to be seen, as the Taliban resurgence involved quite different social and political dynamics.

## FUTURE RESEARCH DIRECTIONS

Better applications of social network analysis to counterterrorism necessitate steady improvements in empirical data collection and formal modeling. Academic researchers and counterterror practitioners must forge stronger collaborative ties, with increased funding of both basic and applied projects. Empirical data collectors and computer modelers, who tend to operate under disparate assumptions, should learn more about one another's advantages and limitations. Empirical researchers cope with restricted access to information about ties inside terror cells; inaccurate and incomplete relational data; simplifying conjectures, such as assuming no relation exists if data are missing; post-attack reconstructions instead of real-time analysis to anticipate impending actions. By contrast, formal modelers work in largely data-free environments that are minimally informed by historical and social science knowledge. They use computer science methods to construct complex models and run simulations to assess dynamic interactions between militants and counterterrorists (e.g., Carpenter, Karakostas, & Shellcross, 2004; Memon et al., 2009; Arce & Sandler, 2010). A promising perspective is computational organization theory, a multidisciplinary combination of artificial intelligence, organization studies, bargaining theory, and simulation methods (Carley, 2009). Researchers try to identify the strengths and vulnerabilities of covert network structures to destabilization by designing agent-based models and varying the parameters in computer simulations or online multi-person role-playing games. For example, Lindelauf, Borm & Hamers (2009) showed that the optimal communication structure – balancing tradeoffs between secrecy and operational efficiency – does not exhibit the small-world structures (short path distances and high clustering around a few central hubs) characteristic of many noncriminal networks. Instead, covert networks combine short paths for maintaining communication with low clustering for avoiding detection. One implication for designing effective counterterror strategies is that targeting and removing numerous highly connected members would not disintegrate a sparsely connected network, but, ironically, may increase its secrecy.

Several research centers comprise a solid foundation for future development of network approaches to terrorism and counterterror strategies (see Additional Readings for links). The University of Arizona's Artificial Intelligence Laboratory gives online access to its Dark Web Forum Portal containing almost 13 million messages culled from 28 jihadist forums, and provides statistical analyses and network visualizations. At Carnegie Mellon University, the Center for Computational Analysis of Social and Organizational Systems (CASOS) has developed several toolkits for network data collection and analysis, and has validated multi-agent network models for application to such real-world problems as bio-terrorism, covert networks, and organizational adaptation. The National Consortium for the Study of Terrorism and Responses to Terrorism (START), housed at the University of Maryland, supports research and educational programs at more than 50 institutions. Although the EU's European Security Research and Innovation Forum (ESRIF) mainly boosts security industry competitiveness, it has sponsored some research on artificial intelligence technologies for text-mining.

Another important direction is greater inclusion of social network analysis in the education and training curricula for terror researchers, counterterror experts, and intelligence analysts. In 2006, Steve Ressler, then a Department of Homeland Security Fellow, remarked, "I would like social network analysis to be taught as one of the tools available in a number of these areas, including risk management and analysis, intelligence, terrorism prevention, and the sociology of homeland security" (2006, p. 8). His recommendation remains relevant for the success of future counterterror efforts.

## CONCLUSION

The social network analysis of terrorism is still in its infancy nearly a decade after the 9/11 attacks. The slow accumulation of case studies by prominent network researchers demonstrates the feasibility of applying these methods to uncover structural relations among individual militants and terrorist organizations. Network tools have great potential to complement more conventional approaches to understanding and explaining political violence aimed at civilian populations. Yet, as the preceding sections revealed, academic researchers and intelligence analysts face numerous obstacles to realizing the full potential of network analysis for detecting, disrupting, and dismantling terrorist operations. Promising developments by empirical researchers and formal modelers imply optimism that social network analysis will ultimately throw much light onto the shadowy regions where international terrorism prowls.

## REFERENCES

Abuza, Z. (2003). Funding terrorism in Southeast Asia: The financial network of Al Qaeda and Jemaah Islamiya. *Contemporary Southeast Asia, 25*, 169–199. doi:10.1355/CS25-2A

Abuza, Z. (2009). Jemaah Islamiyah adopts the Hezbollah model. *Middle East Quarterly, 16*, 15–26.

Arce, D. G., & Sandler, T. (2010). Terrorist spectaculars: Backlash attacks and the focus of intelligence. *The Journal of Conflict Resolution, 54*, 354–373. doi:10.1177/0022002709355414

Basile, M. (2004). Going to the source: Why Al Qaeda's financial network is likely to withstand the current war on terrorist financing. *Studies in Conflict and Terrorism, 27*, 169–185. doi:10.1080/10576100490438237

Bird, G., Blomberg, S. B., & Hess, G. D. (2008). International terrorism: Causes, consequences and cures. *World Economy, 31*, 255–274. doi:10.1111/j.1467-9701.2007.01089.x

Black, D. (2004). The geometry of terrorism. *Sociological Theory, 22*, 14–25. doi:10.1111/j.1467-9558.2004.00201.x

Blanchard, C. M., & Prados, A. B. (2007). *Saudi Arabia: Terrorist financing issues*. Washington, DC: Congressional Research Service.

Brown, I., & Korff, D. (2009). Terrorism and the proportionality of internet surveillance. *European Journal of Criminology, 6*, 119–134. doi:10.1177/1477370808100541

Butko, T. (2006). Terrorism redefined. *Peace Review, 18*, 145–151. doi:10.1080/10402650500510933

Caiani, M., & Wagemann, C. (2009). Online networks of the Italian and German extreme right: An explorative study with social network analysis. *Information Communication and Society, 12*, 66–109. doi:10.1080/13691180802158482

Carley, K. M. (2009). *Dynamic network analysis for counter-terrorism*. Unpublished manuscript, Carnegie Mellon University, Pittsburgh, PA.

Carpenter, T., Karakostas, G., & Shallcross, D. (2004). *Practical issues and algorithms for analyzing terrorist networks*. Morristown, NJ: Telcordia Technologies.

Chaliand, G., & Blin, A. (Eds.). (2007). *The history of terrorism: From antiquity to Al Qaeda*Schneider, E., Pulver, K., & Browner, J., Trans.). Berkeley, CA: University of California Press.

De Bruijn, H. (2006). One fight, one team: The 9/11 commission report on intelligence, fragmentation and information. *Public Administration, 84*, 267–287. doi:10.1111/j.1467-9299.2006.00002.x

den Boer, M., Hillebrand, C., & Nolke, A. (2008). Legitimacy under pressure: The European web of counter-terrorism networks. *Journal of Common Market Studies, 46*, 101–124. doi:10.1111/j.1468-5965.2007.00769.x

Dishman, C. (2005). The leaderless nexus: When crime and terror converge. *Studies in Conflict and Terrorism, 28*, 237–252. doi:10.1080/10576100590928124

Eilstrup-Sangiovanni, M., & Jones, C. (2008). Assessing the dangers of illicit networks: Why Al-Qaida may be less dangerous than many think. *International Security, 33*, 7–44. doi:10.1162/isec.2008.33.2.7

Enders, W., & Jindapon, P. (2010). Network externalities and the structure of terror networks. *The Journal of Conflict Resolution, 54*, 262–280. doi:10.1177/0022002709355439

Enders, W., & Su, X. (2007). Rational terrorists and optimal network structure. *The Journal of Conflict Resolution, 51*, 33–57. doi:10.1177/0022002706296155

Field, A. (2009). Tracking terrorist networks: Problems of intelligence sharing within the UK intelligence community. *Review of International Studies, 35*, 997–1009. doi:10.1017/S0260210509990416

Frantz, T. L., & Carley, K. M. (2005). *A formal characterization of cellular networks*. Unpublished manuscript, Carnegie Mellon University, Pittsburgh, PA.

Hafez, M. M. (2007). Martyrdom mythology in Iraq: How jihadists frame suicide terrorism in videos and biographies. *Terrorism and Political Violence, 19*, 95–115. doi:10.1080/09546550601054873

Halwani, R. (2006). Terrorism: Definition, justification, and applications. *Social Theory and Practice, 32*, 289–310.

Intriligator, M. D. (2010). The economics of terrorism. *Economic Inquiry, 48*, 1–13. doi:10.1111/j.1465-7295.2009.00287.x

Jackson, B. A. (2006). Groups, networks, or movements: A command-and-control-driven approach to classifying terrorist organizations and its application to Al Qaeda. *Studies in Conflict and Terrorism, 29*, 241–262. doi:10.1080/10576100600564042

Jacobson, M. (2010). Terrorist financing and the internet. *Studies in Conflict and Terrorism, 33*, 353–363. doi:10.1080/10576101003587184

Jacobson, M., & Levitt, M. (2010). Tracking narco-terrorist networks: The money trail. *The Fletcher Forum of World Affairs, 34*, 117–124.

Jones, S. G. (2007). Fighting networked terrorist groups: Lessons from Israel. *Studies in Conflict and Terrorism, 30*, 281–302. doi:10.1080/10576100701200157

Jones, S. G., & Libicki, M. C. (2008). *How terrorist groups end: Lessons for countering Al Qa'ida*. Santa Monica, CA: Rand Corporation.

Jordán, J., & Horsburgh, N. (2005). Mapping jihadist terrorism in Spain. *Studies in Conflict and Terrorism, 28*, 169–191. doi:10.1080/10576100590928089

Kirby, A. (2007). The London bombers as self-starters: A case study in indigenous radicalization and the emergence of autonomous cliques. *Studies in Conflict and Terrorism, 30*, 415–428. doi:10.1080/10576100701258619

Kirchick, J. (2010). The homegrown-terrorist threat: It can happen here, and it is happening here. *Commentary (New York, N.Y.), 129*, 16–20.

Knoke, D., & Yang, S. (2008). *Social network analysis* (2nd ed.). Thousand Oaks, CA: Sage Publications.

Kohlmann, E. F. (2008). 'Homegrown' terrorists: Theory and cases in the war on terror's newest front. *The Annals of the American Academy of Political and Social Science, 618*, 95–109. doi:10.1177/0002716208317203

Koschade, S. (2006). A social network analysis of Jemaah Islamiyah: The applications to counterterrorism and intelligence. *Studies in Conflict and Terrorism, 29*, 559–575. doi:10.1080/10576100600798418

Koschade, S. (2007). *The internal dynamics of terrorist cells: A social network analysis of terrorist cells in an Australian context*. Unpublished doctoral dissertation, Queensland University of Technology, Brisbane, Australia.

Krebs, V. (2001). Mapping networks of terrorist cells. *Connections, 24*, 43–52.

Krueger, A. B., & Laitin, D. D. (2004). Misunderestimating terrorism: The State Department's big mistake. *Foreign Affairs (Council on Foreign Relations), 83*, 8–13. doi:10.2307/20034063

Lindelauf, R., Borm, P., & Hamers, H. (2009). The influence of secrecy on the communication structure of covert networks. *Social Networks, 31*, 126–137. doi:10.1016/j.socnet.2008.12.003

Magouirk, J., Atran, S., & Sageman, M. (2008). Connecting terrorist networks. *Studies in Conflict and Terrorism, 31*, 1–16. doi:10.1080/10576100701759988

Memon, N., Farley, J. D., Hicks, D. L., & Rosenorn, T. (Eds.). (2009). *Mathematical methods in counterterrorism. Vienna, Austria*. Wien: Springer-Verlag. doi:10.1007/978-3-211-09442-6

Morris, M. F. (2005). *Al-Qaeda as insurgency*. Master's thesis. Carlisle Barracks, PA: U.S. Army War College. Retrieved July 31, 2010 from http://www.strategicstudiesinstitute.army.mil/pdffiles/ksil234.pdf

Mullins, S. (2009). Parallels between crime and terrorism: A social psychological perspective. *Studies in Conflict and Terrorism, 32*, 811–830. doi:10.1080/10576100903109776

National Commission on Terrorist Attacks Upon the United States. (2004). *The 9/11 commission report*. Washington, DC: U.S. Government Printing Office.

News, A. B. C. (2001,December 13). *Transcript of Osama bin Laden video*. Retrieved December 24, 2009, from http://www.globalresearch.ca/articles/BIN112A.html

Pantucci, R. (2010). The Tottenham Ayatollah and the hook-handed cleric: An examination of all their jihadi children. *Studies in Conflict and Terrorism, 33*, 226–245. doi:10.1080/10576100903555770

Pape, R. A. (2003). The strategic logic of suicide terrorism. *The American Political Science Review, 97*, 343–361. doi:10.1017/S000305540300073X

Pape, R. A. (2005). *Dying to win: The strategic logic of suicide terrorism*. New York, NY: Random House.

Pawlak, P. (2009). Network politics in transatlantic homeland security cooperation. *Perspectives on European Politics and Society, 10*, 560–581. doi:10.1080/15705850903314833

Pedahzur, A., & Perliger, A. (2006). The changing nature of suicide attacks: A social network perspective. *Social Forces, 84*, 1987–2008. doi:10.1353/sof.2006.0104

Pedahzur, A., & Perliger, A. (2009). *Jewish terrorism in Israel*. New York, NY: Columbia University Press.

Petraeus, D. H., & Amos, J. F. (2006). *Counterinsurgency*. Field manual 3-24. Washington, DC: Headquarters Department of the Army.

Raab, J., & Milward, H. B. (2003). Dark networks as problems. *Journal of Public Administration: Research and Theory, 13*, 413–439. doi:10.1093/jopart/mug029

Rapoport, D. C. (2001). The fourth wave: September 11 in the history of world terrorism. *Current History (New York, N.Y.)*, (December): 419–424.

Rashid, A. (2008). *Descent into chaos: The United States and the failure of nation building in Pakistan, Afghanistan and Central Asia*. New York, NY: Viking.

Razavy, M., & Haggerty, K. D. (2009). Hawala under scrutiny: Documentation, surveillance and trust. *International Political Sociology, 3*, 139–155. doi:10.1111/j.1749-5687.2009.00068.x

Reed, B. (2007). A social network approach to understanding an insurgency. *Parameters*, (Summer): 19–30.

Reed, B. J., & Segal, D. R. (2006). Social network analysis and counterinsurgency analysis: The capture of Saddam Hussein. *Sociological Focus, 39*, 251–264.

Ressler, S. (2006). Social network analysis as an approach to combat terrorism: Past, present, and future research. *Homeland Security Affairs, 2*, 1-10. Retrieved January 9, 2010, from http://www.hsaj.org

Ruby, C. L. (2002). The definition of terrorism. *Analyses of Social Issues and Public Policy (ASAP), 2*, 9–14. doi:10.1111/j.1530-2415.2002.00021.x

Sageman, M. (2004). *Understanding terror networks*. Philadelphia, PA: University of Pennsylvania Press.

Sageman, M. (2008). *Leaderless jihad: Terror networks in the twenty-first century*. Philadelphia, PA: University of Pennsylvania Press.

Sedgwick, M. (2007). Inspiration and the origins of global waves of terrorism. *Studies in Conflict and Terrorism, 30*, 97–112. doi:10.1080/10576100601101042

Smith, H. (2008). Defining terrorism: It shouldn't be confused with insurgency. *American Diplomacy*. Retrieved July 26, 2010, from http://www.unc.edu/depts/diplomat/item/2010/0103/comm/smith_hurtorhelp.html

Tilly, C. (2004). Terror, terrorism, terrorists. *Sociological Theory, 22*, 5–13. doi:10.1111/j.1467-9558.2004.00200.x

Tosini, D. (2007). Sociology of terrorism and counterterrorism: A social science understanding of terrorist threat. *Social Compass, 1*, 664–681. doi:10.1111/j.1751-9020.2007.00035.x

U.S. Department of Treasury. (2007). *The Holy Land Foundation for Relief and Development.* Washington, DC: Office of Terrorism and Financial Intelligence. Retrieved August 23, 2010, from www.ustreas.gov/offices/enforcement/key-issues/protecting/charities_execorder_13224e.shtml#h

Victoroff, J. (2005). The mind of the terrorist: A review and critique of psychological approaches. *The Journal of Conflict Resolution, 49*, 3–42. doi:10.1177/0022002704272040

Wilner, A. S., & Dubouloz, C. (2010). Homegrown terrorism and transformative learning: An interdisciplinary approach to understanding radicalization. *Global Change, Peace & Security, 22*, 33–51. doi:10.1080/14781150903487956

Winer, J. M. (2008). Countering terrorist finance: A work, mostly in progress. *The Annals of the American Academy of Political and Social Science, 618*, 112–132. doi:10.1177/0002716208317696

Winfield, N., & Gatopoulos, D. (2010). European anarchists grow more violent, coordinated. *Yahoo! News.* Retrieved December 28, 2010, from http://news.yahoo.com/s/ap/20101228/ap_on_re_eu/eu_italy_embassy_blasts

Xu, J., Hu, D., & Chen, H. (2009). The dynamics of terrorist networks: Understanding the survival mechanisms of global Salafi jihad. *Journal of Homeland Security and Emergency Management, 6.* Retrieved July 26, 2010, from http://www.bepress.com/jhsem/all.

Zdanowicz, J. S. (2009). Trade-based money laundering and terrorist financing. *Review of Law & Economics, 5*, 1–24. doi:10.2202/1555-5879.1419

## ADDITIONAL READING

Asal, V., & Rethemeyer, R. K. (2006). Researching terrorist networks. *Journal of Security Education, 1*, 65–74. doi:10.1300/J460v01n04_06

Asal, V., & Rethemeyer, R. K. (2008). The nature of the beast: Terrorist organizational characteristics and organizational lethality. *The Journal of Politics, 70*, 437–449. doi:10.1017/S0022381608080419

Center for Computational Analysis of Social and Organizational Systems (CASOS) <http://www.casos.cs.cmu.edu/>

European Security Research and Innovation Forum (ESRIF) <http://www.esrif.eu/>

Farooqi, M. N. (2010). Curbing the use of hawala for money laundering and terrorist financing: Global regulatory response and future challenges. *International Journal of Business Governance and Ethics, 5*, 64–75. doi:10.1504/IJBGE.2010.029556

Gray, D. H., & Stockham, E. (2008). Al-Qaeda in the Islamic Maghreb: The evolution from Algerian Islamism to transnational terror. *African Journal of Political Science and International Relations*, *2*, 91–97.

Horowitz, M. C. (2010). Nonstate actors and the diffusion of innovations: The case of suicide terrorism. *International Organization*, *64*, 33–64. doi:10.1017/S0020818309990233

Krueger, A. B. (2008). What makes a homegrown terrorist? Human capital and participation in domestic Islamic terrorist groups in the U.S.A. *Economics Letters*, *101*, 293–296. doi:10.1016/j.econlet.2008.09.008

LaFree, G., & Dugan, L. (2009). Research on terrorism and countering terrorism. *Crime and Justice*, *38*, 413–477.

Memon, N., Larsen, H. L., Hicks, D. L., & Harkiolakis, N. (2008). Detecting hidden hierarchy in terrorist networks: Some case studies. *ISI Workshops*. 477-489.

National Consortium for the Study of Terrorism and Responses to Terrorism (START) <http://www.start.umd.edu/start/>

Plumper, T., & Neumayer, E. (2010). The friend of my enemy is my enemy: International alliances and international terrorism. *European Journal of Political Research*, *49*, 75–96. doi:10.1111/j.1475-6765.2009.01885.x

Robins, G. (2009). Understanding individual behaviors within covert networks: The interplay of individual qualities, psychological predispositions, and network effects. *Trends in Organized Crime*, *12*, 166–187. doi:10.1007/s12117-008-9059-4

Sandler, T., & Enders, W. (2007). Applying analytical methods to study terrorism. *International Studies Perspectives*, *8*, 287–302. doi:10.1111/j.1528-3585.2007.00290.x

Tsvetovat, M., & Carley, K. M. (2007). On effectiveness of wiretap programs in mapping social networks. *Computational & Mathematical Organization Theory*, *13*, 63–87. doi:10.1007/s10588-006-9009-0

University of Arizona Artificial Intelligence Laboratory <http://ai.arizona.edu/research/terror/>

## KEY TERMS AND DEFINITIONS

**Cell:** A subgroup within a larger cellular network, where cell members are fully connected but connections between subgroups are minimal.

**Counterterror Organization:** A government agency that seeks to detect, disrupt, and suppress terrorism.

**Financial Network:** Loosely integrated systems of legitimate banks, front businesses, courier services, and underground affiliates to transfer and launder money.

**Homegrown Terrorism:** Acts by persons born or raised in a Western country that are undertaken without significant assistance from overseas networks.

**Social Network:** A set of actors and a set of social relations that connect them.

**Social Network Analysis:** Visual and matrix algebra methods for analyzing social networks.

**Terrorism:** Violence committed by groups with political goals, targeted against civilians, and intended to create fear in a population.

# Section 5
# Business Impact of Social Networks and Online Communities

*This section focuses on the methods, frameworks, and approaches that study the relationship between social network users/customers and businesses and analyses the important role that social network sites can play in market penetration. It identifies the mechanisms to extract useful information from the community structure, and how this information can be used to improve business efficiency and customer satisfaction. An overview of how the proposed frameworks and approaches can be used by others is given along with the wider context of its use.*

# Chapter 14
# Social Network Sites:
## Modeling the New Business–Customer Relationship

**Pedro Isaías**
*Universidade Aberta, Portugal*

**Sara Pífano**
*Information Society Research Lab, Portugal*

**Paula Miranda**
*Polytechnic Institute of Setubal, Portugal*

## ABSTRACT

*The internet and the emergence of social technologies and platforms are at the origin of new consumer trends. The growing empowerment of customers is having a restructuring impact in business-consumer relationships and it is pressing businesses to uncover new strategies to engage their clients. This chapter argues that the presence of the corporate sector in Social Network Sites (SNSs) presents a successful method of building proficient relationships with customers that are more compliant with the new facets of consumers' profile and behaviour. This research crosses classical academic literature with case studies available in social media to gather a compilation of challenges and potential solutions to the application of SNSs to business-consumer relationships. This compilation is preceded by an introductory section, which explores the definition and possible applications of SNSs in business, and a section dedicated to an overview of the novel consumer trends.*

DOI: 10.4018/978-1-61350-444-4.ch014

## INTRODUCTION

The consumer behaviour and profile has been changing in light of the innovations brought initially by the Internet and more recently by its new, more interactive and user-centred, version Web 2.0. Besides the rising demand of online delivery and offer of products and services, in online contexts, contact is not only with marketers or the companies advertising, but with online communities and users (Constantinides & Fountain, 2008). Web 2.0, also known as Social Web, introduces numerous interactive tools that revolutionise the way people navigate and perceive the internet. Social Network Sites (SNSs) are one of the most admired productions of the Social Web. Studies have showed that participating in SNSs is only second to email on the ranking of the most popular activities on the internet (Beresford Research, 2009). SNSs are powerful because they mimic real life situations such as cooperation, competitiveness and alliances (Maamar & Badr, 2009). The immediacy and extent of online social networks allied with their diversity in terms of interactive features have earned them the loyalty of millions of internet users.

The successful proliferation of online social networking has important repercussions at a corporate level. The adoption of SNSs by businesses began hesitantly, but it has evolved into an almost obligatory practice, deeply connected with the term Enterprise 2.0, which relates to the adoption of Web 2.0 tools by enterprises (Bughin, 2008). Some SNSs are already specifically directed at professionals (DiMicco, Millen, Geyer, Dugan, Brownholtz & Muller, 2008). Companies use social networks for multiple reasons: marketing, public relations, to provide information and to relate with customers. The exposition that the age of internet collaboration offers to businesses has immense potential, but it equally presents many challenges. The openness and publicity that give companies the opportunity to present their products and services to a wider audience are also increasing their vulnerability. Online environments are fundamentally different from traditional business venues, mainly because there are many aspects that corporations cannot control. Moreover, employing social technology in the corporate sector may sometimes require dismissing part of the traditional principles that reign business.

Notwithstanding the questions SNSs raise, this chapter aims to argue that they can be viable solutions for addressing the new demands of business-customer relationship building created by transformations in consumers' profile and behaviour. The analysis of business-customer relationships and the specificities of having to maintain these relationships outside the moulds of classical business venues, are central to understanding how they can be successfully transposed to an online, interactive and user-centred environment. This ensures that these changes do not compromise a core aspect of corporate proficiency, a good liaison with customers. Hence, this chapter begins by examining the definition of SNSs and their several applications to the corporate sector and moves on to explore the new facets of customers and their behaviours. The final section provides an insight on the implications of having a business presence in SNSs, using several case studies available in social media. It approaches the advantages and the disadvantages of having a corporate account on platforms designed for social interaction and assembles a compilation of best practices deriving from classical business theory and current case studies.

## BACKGROUND

SNSs are a widespread phenomenon, presently integrated in the day to day of many internet users (Boyd & Ellison 2008). There are approximately 900 platforms of tools classified for the purpose of social networking and this number grows every day (Wilson, 2009). These online social networks allow people the opportunity to communicate in a variety of ways. Users can set up online profiles and create networks of contacts. They offer possibilities of community building, where users exchange knowledge and have the opportunity to easily contact with their peers (Constantinides & Fountain, 2008). SNSs are also being used for information search, efficiency enhancement and business networking (Morris, Teevan & Panovich, 2010).

## ONLINE SOCIAL NETWORKING

SNSs share the same principle, but vary in terms of nature and classification. Some are specific and join people with common interests, nationality or religion and others encompass diverse populations with a variety of characteristics and believes; some aim to appeal to a niche and others to the widest population possible (Boyd & Ellison 2008).

Social network websites and services can be defined as platforms or applications that allow the user to create a personal profile online and upload content (Hosio, Kukka & Riekki, 2008). Boyd and Ellison (2008) defined social network sites as online services that enable the users to:

*(1) Construct a public or semi-public profile within a bounded system, (2) articulate a list of other users with whom they share a connection, and (3) view and traverse their list of connections and those made by others within the system. (p. 2)*

Although SNSs tend to offer different features, in general, users will have a public personal profile and a publicly displayed list of contacts with whom they interact through comments and private messages. In most cases, users will have the possibility to share with others a variety of content formats such as video, pictures, incorporated blogging, chat and the opportunity to interact using mobile technologies (Boyd & Ellison 2008). SNSs are believed to have acquired the important status of

mainstream communication tools (Ofcom, 2008), having become commonplaces (Wu, Majedi, Ghazinour & Barker, 2010).

Authors from various fields have tried to explain and transmit the magnitude of the success that SNSs are experiencing. Their descriptions intend to be illustrative of the phenomenon by using evocative expressions such as "recent boom of social applications" (Maamar & Badr, p.1: 2009) or proliferation "to the point of explosive use" (Fortino & Nayak, p1: 2010). However, as expressive as these descriptions might be, they cannot equal the enlightenment of the numbers. The recent results of an online poll (based on 1050 responses) created by PC Advisor (Price, 2010) revealed that 6 in every 10 people using the internet used social networks online. A Beresford Research (2009) study conducted in the United States revealed that Facebook members have an average of 138 friends and MySpace users an average of 178 and that SNSs members are using 22 hours per week (on average) on these sites. Furthermore, their results unveiled that using SNSs, in the ranking of the most popular online activities, is second after email and when compared with offline activities, engaging in SNSs was only overrun by going out with friends. Activities such as watching television, reading and playing sports all followed SNSs in significance (Beresford Research, 2009). Although different metrics and statistics are being used to rank SNSs, overall, Facebook, MySpace, Twitter, Linked In and Ning are some of the most popular SNSs (Alexa Internet, Inc., 2010; eBizMBA Inc., 2010). Facebook, for example, is not only the most popular SNS with the highest number of users it is also the second most visited website in the world (Alexa Internet, Inc., 2010).

## USING SOCIAL NETWORK SITES IN THE CORPORATE ARENA

The proliferation of web based social networks has led companies to think of them as potential tools of business. Brands have been reflecting on the best methods to extract value from SNSs (Microsoft Corporation, 2009). One could even go as far as to say that organisations are being *pushed* to employ SNSs to make improvements in their business procedures, productivity and competitiveness (Fortino & Nayak, 2010).

In addition to their success, there is a multiplicity of factors that compelled the business sector to adopt SNSs. Many large and prestigious companies have embraced Web 2.0 technologies and tools in a variety of forms (Borzo, 2007), motivating other organisations to follow. Once a company starts using SNSs it is almost compulsory for its competitors to also adhere. Moreover, SNSs are not only allowing people the possibility to interact, but to find people of like mind. The ability to create networks of contacts and communities means SNSs have become powerful communication mediums and information providers. Before their existence, brands could, to some extent, control what information to associate with their services and products, but with the growth and multidisciplinarity of SNSs, this power has shifted and these communities can influence consumers' perception of services and products (Microsoft Corporation, 2009). Only by using these channels they have access to this information and a certain amount of control over it. It is important to consider demographic reasons, since changes in the workforce and in clients have equally propelled this presence in online social networks. The denominated Y generation is entering the workplace and assuming managerial roles and clients use technology very comfortably and frequently (Buytendijk, Cripe, Henson, & Pulverman, 2008).

The applications of SNSs to the corporate area are countless. Many executive see Web 2.0 as a valuable resource that will increase revenue and reduce costs, with a positive impact on all business areas (Borzo, 2007). They are a problem solving resource (Infosecurity, 2010) that can be used for recruitment, browsing for suppliers and as a source of information (Skeels & Grudin, 2009). Using the internet as a collaborative platform will have important repercussions in a company's business model, the interaction with its employees and customers and the information available about a company's services and products. Additionally, it increases the power clients have over organizations and changes the connections they establish with each other (Borzo, 2007). Through SNSs, it is possible to provide better customer service, to create a more profound engagement with the brand, to increase cooperation with consumers and to improve services and/or products by resorting to co-creation with the customers (Borzo, 2007). Furthermore, they can drive sales, many companies, such as Dell have reported to have made large profits from their SNSs engagement, showing that investing time, money and human resources on SNSs can have real and measurable profits (Bradford, & Milstein, n.d.). SNSs have also started to be used internally. Companies like Deloitte, Microsoft and IBM are developing customised internal social SNSs (Wu, DiMicco & Millen, 2010).

On the other hand as SNSs make their way into the business arena, management teams become concerned (Fortino & Nayak, 2010). A Nucleus Research (2009) study has revealed that the use of Facebook in the workplace may result in a 1,5% productivity loss, with 1 in every 33 employees creating the entirety of their personal profile during working hours. Also, SNSs raise issues deriving from hierarchy boundaries, disclosure of confidential information and they dim the separation between the private and the public (Skeels & Grudin, 2009). The existence of different work practices between baby boomers and Gen Y-ers constitutes a source of generational divergence with regard to the use of social networking inside the workplace (Infosecurity, 2010). Privacy is one of the main concerns when using SNSs mainly because users have personal information displayed online and it may be misused to obtain even more private and confidential information such as social security numbers (Boyd & Ellison 2008). SNSs have the potential to strengthen relationships among the organisation's team, but the combination of professional and private aspects in the same platform can constitute a problem (Skeels & Grudin, 2009). They often merge professional and social aspects (Skeels & Grudin, 2009) reducing the periphery between the private and the public spheres. Finally, the fact that more services and products are being delivered online and more companies are investing in their online presence increases the discrepancy between those customers who use online tools and those who don't. Customers not resorting to technology, for whatever reason, may feel destitute and abandoned by their brands (Bollen & Emes, 2008).

## TRENDS IN CUSTOMER PROFILE AND BEHAVIOUR

Web 2.0's user-centricity represents a shift in internet use. The internet has always been directed at the users and its content made for them, but the primordial difference in the Social Web is that the internet is also made by the users. This power of being able to decide on content and the possibility of creating it is empowering users at many levels of society. The business sector is feeling the repercussions of this new behaviour at their core: their customers.

### Customers as Business Reviewers

Social technology is widely available and easy to use, making it possible for anyone with an internet connection to voice an opinion. Online communities have evolved into powerful influential elements. They harbour discussions, foster interaction and encourage people to share

their viewpoints and experiences. The increase of communities dedicated to customer support is one of the main influences in the communication between customers and companies (Leary, 2010). The dynamic nature that communication online has assumed, translates into an amplification of customers' satisfaction or dissatisfaction. Consumers expressing their opinions and sharing their experiences can reach extensive audiences and this new power transforms the relationship between companies and their clients.

Social networks and social media in general give the customer the opportunity to share their experience with a company as soon as it happens. Moreover, these technologies allow users to reach infinite audiences. Each customer can mean very positive publicity with the potential to boost business or a negative feedback with real damaging impact. The power of the customer has arrived to a point where "no bad deed will go unpublished by a dissatisfied customer" (Moltz, 2009). There are already several reports of customers exposing negative experiences with certain companies that were then snowballed into social media platforms with significant consequences (Constantinides & Fountain, 2008).

Consumers search for their peers' input on products and services and while this can reduce the costs of customer service and also create committed advocates (Leary, 2010), it also consigns progressively more power to customer reviews.

### Searching Information and Decision Patterns

Consumers have changed the way they search for information and also their purchasing patterns (Constantinides & Fountain, 2008). Morris et al. (2010) conducted a study which aimed to determine what exactly people were asking their online social networks. The research the authors conducted aimed to see how users were taking their information needs to social networks and how they were using their status update tools to make enquiries to fellow users. Half of the participants confirmed that they used SNSs to ask questions and obtain information. Also, the authors' findings demonstrated that the question types more frequently asked were recommendations and opinions. Consumers have changed the way they search for information. They frequently obtain information on products and services through social channels that businesses do not control, such as blogs or social networks (Constantinides & Fountain, 2008). Many users will consult other people's opinions about a certain product or service before purchasing it, in order to minimise the risk of becoming unsatisfied (Kim & Srivastava, 2007).

Clients buying patterns are greatly influenced by their fellow consumers, by other user's opinions (Constantinides & Fountain, 2008). Consumers tend to be more influenced by the opinions that other users have manifested online and it is believed that only word of mouth exerts more influence than online user-generated reviews and comments (Rubicon Consulting, 2008). In an increasingly social web, conventional influences are being overshadowed by online customers' reviews; many clients state the reviews they read online have had an impact on their buying decisions (Constantinides & Fountain, 2008). It is usual for people to resort to their close network of contacts, such as family, friends or co-workers when they have queries. SNSs have become fast and competent tools to do that (Morris et al., 2010).

## Customers as Co-Creators

Customers are aware of their power and demand equal participation and greater control (Constantinides & Fountain, 2008). As the relationship with customers deepens, some executives mention co-creation possibilities with clients (Bughin, 2008). Having customers as co-developers has consequences at a hierarchy level, since control is shared; power structures become more flexible (Bughin, 2008). As the growing power of the contemporary customer is recognised, businesses start to develop new strategies to engage customers in all processes of business. Sometimes this involvement is called for in the early stages of product or service creation (Bollen & Emes, 2008). Dell's IdeaStorm.com and MyStarbucksIdea.force.com from Starbucks Corporation are two examples of how customers are being called to participate in their brands and engage in a process of co-creation. The rising power of consumers is expected to lead businesses to a more customer-oriented service (Bollen & Emes, 2008).

Engaging with brands in the creation process gives customers a sense of collaboration and can increase loyalty. At the same time, involving clients will provide the company with more information on what their needs are, which will potentially increase consumer satisfaction.

## Concerns and Expectations

Consumers have a greater pallet of choice, access to more information and the power to express their opinions in a more authoritative manner. There is more choice on products and services on the internet than on traditional brick-and-mortar businesses. The internet provides information and access and, with some brands operating online on a 24/7 basis, consumers have developed higher expectations in terms of their relationship with businesses. As the balance of power leans progressively towards them, consumers have significantly increased their expectations (Bollen & Emes, 2008). Furthermore, there are resources on the internet that allow customers to compare goods and services. MoneySupermarket and uSwitch are examples of some of those resources. These sites supply varied information and comparison criteria to facilitate consumer's decisions. With the information supplied by them, customers can more easily compare and if needed switch brands (Bollen & Emes, 2008).

An international survey has demonstrated that consumers admit being influenced by companies' policies in terms of the environment. This influence extends not only to their trust in brands, but also to their decision of purchasing their products. The concerns of consumers equally include high standard working conditions for companies' employees and businesses contribution to the public good (Bonini, Hintz & Mendonca, 2008). The decisions people make as consumers have become an important part of their identity. Relationships with brands can mould or enhance customer's identity (Bollen & Emes, 2008). Social and environmental responsibilities have become important factors in purchasing behaviours as customers seem to be valuing companies which take these issues into consideration. Price is joined by environment and health as major areas of competition between brands (Bollen & Emes, 2008). Moreover companies are expected to consider not only the cost, but also the accessibility of their products and services and be open about their risks. Clients seem to appreciate more honest and transparent businesses practices (Bonini, McKillop, & Mendonca, 2007).

## RESHAPING THE BUSINESS-CUSTOMER RELATIONSHIP

Social networks are important facilitators of more direct and real human contact and aid the establishment of connections with existing and potential customers. Some believe that in SNSs the relationship between businesses and their clients becomes more genuine, because companies are portrayed by teams of people with faces and names that are there to help their clients, rather than dehumanised corporate entities (Ofcom, 2008). This creates a more authentic relationship, one that clients can rely on and trust more easily.

### Adapting to a New Business Order

The successful employment of SNSs has the potential to create business value, to find new customers, to maintain the allegiance of current ones (Constantinides & Fountain, 2008) and overall

improve the relationship between businesses and their customers (Microsoft Corporation, 2009). The internet setting introduces possibilities which would be unattainable in an offline context (Drury, 2008). Since SNSs are characterised by a general informality, businesses have the opportunity to relate to clients at a more personal degree. This type of involvement would be much more complex to reproduce through conventional media. Just as users can use SNSs to interact with each other, businesses can take advantage of that technology to engage with their most participative and social customers (Microsoft Corporation, 2009).

The corporate arena is then using social tools to provide more flexible customer service. Companies are using collaborative tools such as social networks to engage in more dynamic forms for cooperation with their customers. This cooperation varies in depth and can go as far as co-creation (Bughin, 2008). In order to use social media to successfully engage with customers it is central that companies: promote the integration of social media with conventional customer service; determine which social applications their customers are using; use a variety of mediums to engage with customers if necessary; allocate time from customer service teams (rather than public relations or marketing) to social media engagement; interact more, since it produces a more positive effect on the customer (Leary, 2010).

### Social Network Sites: Challenges and Best Practices

Despite their potential business value SNSs are composed of many actors that cannot be controlled by companies and that influence their relationship with customers. Businesses face many challenges posed by the new dynamics of their relationship with customers and must work to address them if they want to create real networks of consumer loyalty. The possibility that consumers have to provide feedback, due to the variety of social channels available, has become a powerful incentive for business owners to ensure their clientele is satisfied (Moltz, 2009). The process of interacting with customers in online, public social network platforms is intricate and poses many challenges to businesses. The most important of them is to learn how to avoid the hazards of SNSs and interact meaningfully with customers.

This section will conclude with the presentation and analysis of some of the most important aspects of using SNSs in Business. They represent the most mentioned advices and suggestion found on the literature and on companies own experience in SNSs.

## Using Mainstream Social Network Sites

Corporations need to be where people are. Facebook, MySpace, Twitter, Linked In and Ning are usually rated as the most popular SNSs (Alexa Internet, Inc., 2010; eBizMBA Inc., 2010). Brands have to invest on their visibility on the SNSs theirs customers are using. Community websites owned by companies seem to have fewer users than mainstream networks (Leary, 2010). An Ipsos (2010) study has revealed that consumers use companies' sites to search for information regarding brands and promotions, but they consider Facebook as a perfect resource for sharing information and interacting with other clients.

Before even considering having a presence in SNSs, it is vital to have an understanding of SNSs themselves: contextual particularities, language, special tools. It is crucial to read the terms and conditions of use of SNSs and to learn what practices are legitimate and which ones are interdicted. An important part of these terms and conditions are the delimitations of what is spam. Spam is highly condemned in these platforms. Facebook and Twitter, two of the most popular SNSs, have made resources available for users who aim to use them for business purposes (Twitter, n.d.; Facebook, 2007). Twitter has its own peculiar terms and symbols: users' contacts are called followers and it is possible to tweet (to publish

a post), to retweet (to repost a tweet authored by another user) and use hashtags to categorise the subject of a message. Private messages between users are called direct message. These are specially advised when dealing with customers' and companies' sensitive and private information (Milstein, n.d.a). Brands such as Chevrolet, Ford, Honda, Marriott International Hotels and Resorts, Hertz, The Travel Channel, Starbucks, Burger King, Dell, Kodak, Red Cross all have a Twitter account (Van Grove, 2009). Facebook's terminology is different. Facebook's page is an account for organisations, products or public figures. The people who join a company's Facebook page are called fans and from the moment fans connects with pages, they start receiving their posts on their News Feeds. Facebook pages have different tabs and the Wall is the tab where posts can be published. An important aspect of these pages is the Facebook Pages Insight feature that will show how fans have been interacting with the pages (Facebook, 2007). BMW, Disney, Fox News, Heinz, Intel, McDonalds, Nike Football, Nokia, Sony, and Windows are just some examples of brands with Facebook Pages (Hird, 2010).

A report shared by Burson-Marsteller (2010) which collected data from the leading 100 companies included on the *Fortune*'s Global 500 companies has concluded that 65% of the *Fortune* Globe 100 companies have an active account on Twitter and 54% of them have a Facebook Page.

## Listening

The initial stage of using SNSs is to listen to what the customer is saying, what conversations are taking place (Microsoft Corporation, 2009). Since clients buying patterns are greatly influenced by their fellow consumers and the social media, companies must listen to what is being said about them and their competitors (Constantinides & Fountain, 2008). Companies should take advantage of the search options to look for what is being said about them. If there is any negative feedback with regards to their products and services, that information should be used to invert the situation and leave those customers with a different opinion about the company. It is paramount to know where customers are in terms of social media and what they want (Ertell, 2010a). One afternoon an Empire State Building office tweeted about how much it wanted a Tasti D-lite dessert, but couldn't leave or order a delivery, since the building didn't permit food deliveries. Tasti D-lite, a dessert franchise, saw the tweet and quickly explained that since they had a store in the building those delivery limitations did not apply. Tasti D-lite soon noticed that other offices in the Empire State Building were not aware of this either and addressed the problem which then led to an increase of sales (Bradford & Milstein, n.d.) and left their clients satisfied. In this case, a reaction to a simple tweet was able to create a new group of clients.

## Honest Participation

Participation in SNSs needs to be transparent. If an initiative about a brand is being shared online by a user, that user has to be honest about the objectives and the sponsorship of that initiative (Bollen & Emes, 2008). Users are not very forgiving when brands are deceptive and it affects trust. Honda made a mistake when dealing with the highly negative feedback of their fans, when it decided to use Facebook to release new photos of its new model Crosstour. Many of the fans were not impressed by the design. Among the negative comments, the photos started to receive very positive feedback that was coming in fact from Honda's product manager, who failed to identify himself as such. It wasn't long until people discovered who he was and confronted him. It is crucial that a brand engaging in social media, knows that if they are promoting their products they should be prepared for negative feedback and when it happens it is important not to manipulate it. SNSs users are knowledgeable and they will expose these

cases. Frankness and authenticity are essential in social media settings (Barros, 2009). Trust is very important to participation and transparency is one of the key formulas to achieve it (Bughin, 2008). User engagement needs to be authentic, if user participation is somehow associated with a company, for example, through sponsorship, it will compromise the impartiality of that contribution and will very likely be uncovered and ricochet (Bollen & Emes, 2008). The focus of consumers has been greatly directed at openness and transparency. These values are essential contributors to the development of trust, which is vital for customer relationships (Bollen & Emes, 2008).

## Dealing with Complaints

Pepsi, states that most conversations on Twitter are positive, but sometimes, people use Twitter to complain. When it happens, they try to resolve those comments as quickly as possible. The tone and nature of the complaint is assessed and the process they use implies responding once in public and then if the complaint persists in direct messages. After that, email or telephonic contact is used to ensure the issues were resolved (Bradford & Milstein, n.d.). Michael Arrington, owner of the TechCrunch blog, (very popular and technology-oriented) was having problems with his internet connection and Comcast (his internet service supplier), was not very helpful in dealing with the situation. Michael Arrington decided to share this situation with his 12000 followers. Comcast called him 20 minutes after that to resolve the problem, successfully addressing a situation with the potential to disappoint 12000 people. This is one of the reasons why customer service is shifting to real customer engagement (Barros, 2009). Attention should be paid to all customers, particularly if the customer, like Michael Arrington, has the capacity to influence many customers.

These examples illustrated the importance of using SNSs wisely when addressing negative reactions. Depending on how companies use them, SNSs can either escalate negative feedback or provide a venue to show customers and other users how efficiently a certain company deals with clients concerns. Resolving complaints has always been a central aspect of business, but with a growing capacity to voice them, clients have acquire a power that places dealing with negative feedback high in the list of priorities of customer service.

## Informal Professionalism

The formality of business and the informality of social networking, poses the questions of what content can be shared with customers and where to place the barrier that separates what is appropriate from what crosses the line to an inappropriate personal and excessively familiar level? This is a very important balance to achieve. Using social media to engage customers has to be regarded as the responsibility of experts and not inexperienced professionals (Leary, 2010). Using SNSs to engage with clients must be regarded as an important customer service assignment to address this and other challenges that derive from using social technology in business.

Best practices for efficient customer service in SNSs include: placing trust in employee, while providing them with clear guidelines so they will know what their mission is and what are the boundaries to their contribution; finding a particularity that only that company can offer their clients and offer it for free; listening and actually using the information that has been gathered; humanising corporations, since brands are less trusted than people; developing user-friendly resources, to facilitate interaction (Bradford & Milstein, n.d.).

The fact that communication on Twitter is immediate implies that a swift reply to questions and ideas can be expected, but that means that if the client asks a question or posts a complaint he or she is expecting the same swiftness. Companies can use this immediacy to ask for feedback on recently launched products (Milstein, n.d.c). The expectation of a swift response applies also

for customers, so a regular monitoring of posts is advised.

## Encourage Participation

Facilitate and encourage participation is crucial to engage people in social contexts (Bughin, 2008). People have different reasons to participate, so it is important to facilitate and encourage contributions from clients and to fully engage with them in social contexts (Bughin, 2008). SNSs allow companies to determine who the most influential customers are (Microsoft Corporation, 2009). These customers are easier to interact with and play an important role in terms of influencing the other users. Also, it is important to know what they want from SNSs. Dell Outlet, for example, realised that their customers were interested in speaking with them and share their experiences independently of being positive or negative, so they invested in a more direct dialogue with customers my using Twitter (Bradford & Milstein, n.d.).

Customer feedback is even encouraged by web based businesses such as Amazon and eBay that have enhanced the dynamic between buyers and sellers by allowing users to leave feedback on the articles and the service itself (Bollen & Emes, 2008). This method is useful to define which products and suppliers have quality. In panoply of people selling their items it is important to have at least some information on what users are buying and on whom they are buying it from. The perceived usefulness of this service leads users to participate.

## Pertinent and Attractive Content

It is important to write posts that will appeal to the customers. There is a variety of aspects to account for: the tone of the posts should be casual and friendly; it is important to monitor for comments, concerns and praise and address each of them accordingly; the posts should present real advantages (ex. vouchers, promotions, previews of upcoming projects, photos of offices, stores, etc); and it crucial to remember that spamming users with persistent promotions is not acceptable. Brands must understand that the priority is to build relationships (Milstein, n.d.a). A company can start by learning what works best on a chosen SNS and test it on a smaller number of contacts and then when practice is perfected it can expand and gain more contacts. JetBlue started slowly and, over time, they concluded that "chatty posts and customer assistance tended to generate a lot of replies and new followers. Press releases announcements were met with silence." (Bradford & Milstein, n.d.: n.p.).

Dell states that the key is to provide people with information they are interested in, rather than submerging them with excessive amounts of information that does not remotely relate to them. When using SNSs, brands can offer more than just information about their services and products, they can offer information about pertinent matters that do not necessarily relate to their customers but are general to every client shopping in their brand, for example, when offering products online, a brand can offer information about tips on how to buy online, about e-commerce in general, which is a subject that will please all people buying online, even those buying in competitors websites, but that brand will be valued for sharing this information (Bradford & Milstein, n.d.). Participation in Social networks implies the exchange of personal details and privacy is one of the main concerns for SNSs' users. A user's privacy can be seen as the procedure to impose boundaries and decide what they want to share and with whom. Users are not always aware of the implications of their daily participation in terms of their privacy (Strater & Lipford, 2008). Information on privacy is an important resource for anyone using the internet. There is a general interest in keeping safe in an online environment, especially in SNSs that are so often the target of criticism for their vulnerability. Providing customers with best practices for online behaviour and security adds value to

the company. This type of content values customer care and it is appreciated by clients.

## Measurement

Despite their numerous advantages SNSs remain a problematic solution in terms of measurement. It is crucial to have data that businesses can use to obtain useful information (Microsoft Corporation, 2009). The introduction of SNSs in the business arena brings the need to search and adopt new metrics that can assess productivity in these new contexts (AT&T and Early Strategies Consulting, 2008).

Measurement is critical to determine if the interactions on these platforms are resulting in real advantages. Before considering more formal measurement tools, it is important to have an overview of the evolution of the interactions. Are the questions that customers pose being answered? What kind of feedback is being received? Are more people mentioning the name of that brand? Companies should try to keep a record of the interactions taking place and log the evolution of these exchanges. If a special promotion is being offered on Twitter, for example, setting up a specific code for Twitter users indicates how many people redeemed it. The existing offer of traffic and click-through metrics is diverse and useful to determine how successful Twitter business accounts are being (Bradford & Milstein, n.d.: n.p.).

Also, metrics are important, but SNSs are not mainly about revenue and this is a fact that should be kept in mind. JetBlue Airways say their success is based primarily in qualitative improvement and not so much quantitative. Being susceptible to so many uncontrollable factors, such as weather conditions, it is important to give people as much information as possible when delays occur or might occur. People appreciate this type of information because it makes their lives easier. Morgan Johnston, at JetBlue Airways believes that "Twitter really is about tearing down the artificial walls between customers and individuals who work at companies" (Bradford & Milstein, n.d.: n.p.).

## Beyond Sales

Dell does not focus exclusively in public relations and marketing, but in interacting with customers and they have come to realise that people appreciate this type of interaction and feel enthusiastic when Dell responds to them on Twitter. They also use it for special offers. They only do this a few times a week to avoid spamming the people who follow them and use a system to track URLs to assess what their followers show more interest in (Bradford & Milstein, n.d.). Social media, in general, are used by customers to search for technical support, special promotions and sales, to look for information on products and services and for customer support (Ertell, 2010b). So, the purpose of engaging in a relationship with a company online is not merely sales-based. Dave Brookes from the sales and marketing department of Teusnerwine, a small winery, says "it's not about trying to sell your products, but more building relationships with customers and potential customers (...) this is about building trust as well as relationships - and that comes from not selling" (Bradford & Milstein, n.d.: n.p.).

The fact that brands are able to focus on their relationships with their customers, rather than concentrating exclusively on sales, can sometimes be more beneficial to businesses. Companies should always be able to look beyond the sales aspect of their engagement in SNSs, as they are first and foremost social tools.

## FUTURE RESEARCH DIRECTIONS

The rising presence of businesses in Social Network Websites and in other Web 2.0 platforms is a subject of both enthusiasm and concern. As a rising number of disciplines become involved, research in this area benefits from an increasing multidisciplinarity.

This chapter explored the corporate implications of SNSs by focusing on the business-customer relationship. The subject of how social networks and online communities are moulding a new customer profile and consequently affecting the way they connect with brands is an important topic needing further development. Also, this chapter emphasised the qualitative aspects of embracing these changes and provided an overview of the contribution of various expert fields. Although an exhaustive list of best practices could never be created, research in this area could benefit from more real case studies with specific problem solving strategies that could guide businesses in this unfamiliar and intricate terrain. The topic discussed in this chapter, for its importance to businesses and customers is expected to raise the interest of different fields of research. Prospectively, it can be approached from the point of view of business disciplines such as marketing, public relations or sales or attract more behavioural and social subjects, for instance, psychology or sociology. Another possibility is a more technological approach suggesting formal metrics and specific technologies which can improve the success of business-customer relationships.

## CONCLUSION

The nature of the relationship between customers and businesses changes significantly when networks that are meant to be social are used also for professional reasons. Customers have always had power over brands, because business has always been around people and clients, but what has changed is the fact that customer satisfaction or dissatisfaction can reach more extensive audiences and this new power cannot be ignored.

Despite some resistance, the debate of corporate presence on SNSs has moved on to focus less on whether or not they should be there, to discuss how that presence should be shaped. The changes introduced by SNSs cessed to be previsions, they are real and they are happening in an increasingly palpable manner. Notwithstanding the challenges SNSs presented to businesses, those choosing to offer resistance risk losing competitiveness and their costumers' loyalty.

Given the nature of these platforms, businesses cannot expect their presence in SNSs to be a mere change of venue. The Social Web requires a different type of language, practice and, especially, mindset. It requires knowledge of customers' interest and attitudes and a deep understanding of this new business scenario. It demands experimenting and learning from other companies testimonials as they begin to experience with this environment.

Businesses need to have revenue and to increase sales and profits. Corporate presence on SNSs needs insightful metrics in order to ensure that the financial and human resources investment being done on these platforms is having a return, if it is beneficial and not detrimental. While it would be naive and negligent to overlook this factor, it was not the main concern of this chapter. This factor is at the heart of business and of many research projects. The real peril for businesses in SNSs is failing to realise the spirit behind the Social Web. Web 2.0's nature is social, interactive and collaborative, it is user-friendly and its essence is the connection of people, wherever and whenever. Social technology has provided the internet with multiple platforms so its users could communicate more easily and openly. This new version of the web has radically changed relationships. Anyone trying to be successful in social websites must first understand this primordial precept.

## REFERENCES

Alexa Internet, Inc. (2010, September 20). *Top sites - The top 500 sites on the Web*. Alexa Internet Inc. Retrieved September 20, 2010, from http://www.alexa.com/topsites/global

AT&T & Early Strategies Consulting. (2008). *The business impacts of social networking* [White Paper]. Retrieved January 27, 2011, from http://www.business.att.com/content/whitepaper/WP-soc_17172_v3_11-10-08.pdf

Barros, S. (2009, September 21). 5 social media disasters. *Penn Olson*. Retrieved September 28, 2010 from http://www.penn-olson.com/2009/09/21/5-social-media-disasters/

Beresford Research. (2009). *Use of online social networks results of US user survey* [White Paper]. Retrieved September 27, 2010, from http://beresfordresearch.com/_beresfordtest/pdf-documents/Use%20of%20Online%20Social%20Networks%20White%20Paper%20%20%28Beresford%20Research%29.pdf

Bollen, A., & Emes, C. (2008). *Understanding customer relationships - How important is the personal touch?* Ipsos MORI Loyalty, London. Retrieved September 20, 2010, from http://www.ipsos.com/loyalty/sites/ipsos. com.loyalty/files/IpsosLoyalty_UnderstandingCustomerRelationships.pdf

Bonini, S. M. J., Hintz, G., & Mendonca, L. T. (2008). Addressing consumer concerns about climate change. *McKinsey Quarterly (March)*. Retrieved September 25, 2010, from https://www.mckinseyquarterly.com/ PDFDownload.aspx?ar=2115

Bonini, S. M. J., McKillop, K., & Mendonca, L. T. (2007). What consumers expect from companies. *McKinsey Quarterly, 2007*(2). Retrieved September 25, 2010, from https://www.mckinseyquarterly.com/ PDFDownload.aspx?ar=1986

Borzo, J. (2007, February 8). *Serious business: Web 2.0 goes corporate: How Web 2.0 tools and trends are breaking out of the IT industry*. Economist Intelligent Unit. Retrieved July 15, 2010, from http://www.fastforwardblog.com/wp-content/uploads/2007/FASTSEconomist.pdf

Boyd, D. M., & Ellison, N. B. (2008). Social network sites: Definition, history, and scholarship. *Journal of Computer-Mediated Communication, 13*(1), 210–230. doi:10.1111/j.1083-6101.2007.00393.x

Bradford, R., & Milstein, S. (n.d.). Best practices. In Twitter (Ed.), *Twitter 101 for business — A special guide.* Retrieved July 15, 2010, from http://business.twitter.com/twitter101/

Bughin, J. (2008). The rise of enterprise 2.0. *Journal of Direct. Data and Digital Marketing Practice, 9*(3), 251–259. doi:10.1057/palgrave.dddmp.4350100

Burson-Marsteller. (2010). The global social media check-up (White Paper). *Burson-Marsteller.* Retrieved September 20, 2010, from http://www.burson-marsteller.com/Innovation_and_insights/blogs_and_podcasts/BM_Blog/Documents/Burson-Marsteller%202010%20Global%20Social%20Media%20Check-up%20white%20paper.pdf

Buytendijk, F., Cripe, B., Henson, R., & Pulverman, K. (2008). Business management in the age of Enterprise 2.0: Why business model 1.0 will obsolete you [White paper]. *Oracle.* Retrieved May 20, 2010, from http://www.oracle.com/solutions/business_intelligence/docs/epm-enterprise20-whitepaper.pdf

Constantinides, E., & Fountain, S. (2008). Web 2.0: Conceptual foundations and marketing issues. *Journal of Direct. Data and Digital Marketing Practice, 9*(3), 231–244. doi:10.1057/palgrave.dddmp.4350098

DiMicco, J., Millen, D. R., Geyer, W., Dugan, C., Brownholtz, B., & Muller, M. (2008). Motivations for social networking at work. In *CSCW '08: Proceedings of the 2008 ACM Conference on Computer Supported Cooperative Work,* (pp. 711-720).

Drury, G. (2008). Opinion piece: Social media: Should marketers engage and how can it be done effectively? *Journal of Direct. Data and Digital Marketing Practice, 9,* 274–277. doi:10.1057/palgrave.dddmp.4350096

eBizMBA Inc. (2010, September 15). Top 15 Most Popular Social Networking Websitess. *eBizMBA.* Retrieved September 21, 2010, from http://www.ebizmba.com/articles/social-networking-websites

Ertell, K. (2010a, February 9). The key to driving retail success in the UK with social media: Focus on Facebook [White Paper]. *ForeSee Results.* Retrieved January 20, 2011, from http://www.foreseeresults.com/research-white-papers/_downloads/foresee-results-how-to-drive-retail-success-social-media-uk-2010.pdf

Ertell, K. (2010b, February 9). The key to driving retail success with social media: Focus on Facebook [White Paper]. *ForeSee Results.* Retrieved January 20, 2011, from http://www.foreseeresults.com/research-white-papers/_downloads/foresee-results-how-to-drive-retail-success-social-media-us-2010.pdf

Facebook. (2007). Facebook Pages. *Facebook.* Retrieved June 20, 2010, from http://www.facebook.com/advertising/FacebookPagesProductGuide.pdf

Fortino, A., & Nayak, A. (2010). An architecture for applying social networking to business. *2010 Long Island Systems Applications and Technology Conference (LISAT),* (pp. 1-6).

Hird, J. (2010, August 18). 25 brilliant examples of Facebook brand pages. *eConsultancy.* Retrieved September 10, 2010, from http://econsultancy.com/uk/blog/6438-25-brilliant-examples-of-facebook-brand-pages

Hosio, S., Kukka, H., & Riekki, J. (2008). Leveraging social networking services to encourage interaction in public spaces. *Proceedings of the 7th International Conference on Mobile and Ubiquitous Multimedia*, (pp. 2-7).

Infosecurity. (2010 March/April). *RSA 2010 News Coverage: Pitfalls and promise of social networking*. Infosecurity. Retrieved August 30, 2010, from http://www.infosecurity-us.com/view/7761/hot-topic-at-rsa-the-pitfalls-and-promise-of-social-networking/

Ipsos. (2010, May 25). Engaging CPG consumers in the digital space Tuesday. *Ipsos*. Retrieved September 21, 2010, from http://www.ipsos-na.com/news-polls/pressrelease.aspx?id=4789

Kim, Y. A., & Srivastava, J. (2007). Impact of social influence in e-commerce decision making. In *ICEC '07: Proceedings of the Ninth International Conference on Electronic Commerce, 258*, (pp. 293-302).

Leary, B. (2010). The social customer engagement index (White Paper). *The Social Customer & The Society of Consumer Affairs Professionals*. Retrieved September 20, 2010, from http://thesocialcustomer.com/sites/default/docs/TSC-76KvzawuvVcXnLoCUUlk/TSC_Whitepaper_v10_083110.pdf

Maamar, Z., & Badr, Y. (2009). Social networks as a service in modern enterprises. *2009 International Conference on the Current Trends in Information Technology (CTIT)*, (pp. 1-5).

Microsoft Dynamics. (2009). *CRM and social networking: Engaging the social customer* [White Paper]. Retrieved June 15, 2010, from http://crm.dynamics.com/docs/CRM_and_Social_Networks.pdf

Milstein, S. (n.d.). Learn the lingo. In Twitter (Ed.), *Twitter 101 for business — A special guide*. Retrieved July 15, 2010, from http://business.twitter.com/twitter101/

Milstein, S. (n.d.). What is Twitter? In Twitter (Ed.), *Twitter 101 for business — A special guide*. Retrieved July 15, 2010, from http://business.twitter.com/twitter101/

Milstein, S. (n.d.). Getting started. In Twitter (Ed.), *Twitter 101 for business — A special guide*. Retrieved July 15, 2010, from http://business.twitter.com/twitter101/

Moltz, B. (2009, December 15). The 10 customer service trends for 2010. *Small Business Trends*. Retrieved July 30, 2010, from http://smallbiztrends.com/2009/12/customer-service-trends-2010.html

Morris, M. R., Teevan, J., & Panovich, K. (2010). What do people ask their social networks, and why?: A survey study of status message Q&A behavior. *Proceedings of the 28th International Conference on Human Factors in Computing Systems*, (pp. 1739-1748).

Nucleus Research. (2009). *Facebook: Measuring the cost to business of social notworking*. (Report No. J579). Retrieved July 15, 2010, from http://nucleusresearch.com/research/notes-and-reports/facebook-measuring-the-cost-to-business-of-social-notworking/

Ofcom. (2008). *Social networking: A quantitative and qualitative research report into attitudes, behaviours and use*. Retrieved September 6, 2010, from http://www.ofcom.org.uk/advice/media_literacy/medlitpub/medlitpubrss/socialnetworking/report.pdf

Price, D. (2010, September 8). Poll: 60 percent of web users visit social networks - Facebook by far the most popular site. *PC Advisor*. Retrieved September 20, 2010, from http://www.pcadvisor.co.uk/news/index.cfm?newsid=3238832

Rubicon Consulting, Inc. (2008). Online communities and their impact on business: Ignore at your peril (White paper). *Rubicon Consulting, Inc.* Retrieved June 30, 2010, from http://rubiconconsulting.com/downloads/whitepapers/Rubicon-web-community.pdf

Skeels, M. M., & Grudin, J. (2009). When social networks cross boundaries: A case study of workplace use of Facebook and Linkedin. *Proceedings of the ACM 2009 International Conference on Supporting Group Work*, (pp. 95-104).

Strater, K., & Lipford, H. R. (2008). Strategies and struggles with privacy in an online social networking community. *Proceedings of the 22nd British HCI Group Annual Conference on People and Computers: Culture, Creativity. Interaction*, *1*, 111–119.

Twitter. (n.d.) Twitter 101 for business — A special guide. *Twitter*. Retrieved July 15, 2010, from http://business.twitter.com/twitter101/

Van Grove, J. (2009, January 21). 40 of the best Twitter brands and the people behind them. *Mashable*. Retrieved September 10, 2010, from http://mashable.com/2009/01/21/best-twitter-brands/

Wilson, J. (2009, June 1) Social networking: The business case. *Engineering & Technology Magazine*. Retrieved August 14, 2010, from http://kn.theiet.org/magazine/issues/0910/social-networking-0910.cfm

Wu, A., DiMicco, J. M., & Millen, D. R. (2010). Detecting professional versus personal closeness using an enterprise social network site. *Proceedings of the 28th International Conference on Human Factors in Computing Systems*, (pp. 1955-1964).

## ADDITIONAL READING

Acquisti, A., & Ralph, G. (2006). Imagined Communities: Awareness, Information Sharing, and Privacy on the Facebook. In Golle, P. and Danezis, G. (Eds.), *Proceedings of 6th Workshop on Privacy Enhancing Technologies*, 36-58

Borges, B. (2009). *Marketing 2.0: Bridging the Gap between Seller and Buyer through Social Media Marketing*. Tucson, Arizona: Wheatmark.

Chan, K. W., Yim, C. K., Simon, S. K., & Lam, S. S. K. (2010). Is Customer Participation in Value Creation a Double-Edged Sword? Evidence from Professional Financial Services Across Cultures. *Journal of Marketing*, *74*(3). doi:10.1509/jmkg.74.3.48

DiMicco, J. M., Geyer, W., Millen, D. R., Dugan, C., & Brownholtz, B. (2009). People Sensemaking and Relationship Building on an Enterprise Social Network Site. *HICSS '09: 42nd Hawaii International Conference on System Sciences*, 1-10

Dwyer, C. (2007). Digital relationships in the 'MySpace' generation: Results from a qualitative study. *Proceedings of the 40th HICSS*

Edelman. (2010). 2010 Edelman Trust Barometer: an annual global opinion leaders study – executive summary. Retrieved September 18, 2010 from http://www.edelman.co.uk/trustbarometer/files/edelman-trust-barometer-2010.pdf

Ellison, N., Lampe, C. & Steinfield, C. (2009). Social Network Sites and Society: Current Trends and Future Possibilities. *Interactions Magazine*, 16 (1)

Fogg, B. J. (2008). Mass interpersonal persuasion: An early view of a new phenomenon. *Proceedings of the 3rd International Conference on Persuasive Technology*. Berlin: Springer

Girard, A., & Fallery, B. (2009). E-recruitment: new practices, new issues. An exploratory study. *3rd International Workshop on Human Resource Information Systems (HRIS 2009), in conjunction with ICEIS 2009.* Milan, Italy: INSTICC PRESS

Gwinner, K., Gremler, D., & Bitner, M. (1998). Relational Benefits in Services Industries: The Customer's Perspective. *Journal of the Academy of Marketing Science,* ▪▪▪, 101–114. doi:10.1177/0092070398262002

Lange, P. G. (2007). Publicly private and privately public: Social networking on YouTube. *Journal of Computer-Mediated Communication,* 13(1), article 18. Retrieved September 18, 2010 from http://jcmc.indiana.edu/vol13/issue1/lange.html

Li, C., & Bernoff, J. (2008). *Groundswell: Winning in a World Transformed by Social Technologies.* Boston, Massachusetts: Harvard Business Press.

Li, Y., Lin, C., & Lai, C. (2010). Identifying influential reviewers for word-of-mouth marketing. *Electron. Commer. Rec. App,* 9(4), 294–304. doi:10.1016/j.elerap.2010.02.004

Maia, M., Almeida, J., & Almeida, V. (2008). Identifying user behavior in online social networks. In SocialNets '08: *Proceedings of the 1st Workshop on Social Network Systems,* 1-6

Mislove, A., Marcon, M., Gummadi, K. P., Druschel, P., & Bhattacharjee, B. (2007). Measurement and analysis of online social networks. In IMC '07: *Proceedings of the 7th ACM SIGCOMM Conference on internet Measurement,* 29-42

Musiał, K., Kazienko, P., & Bródka, P. (2009). User position measures in social networks. *Proceedings of the 3rd Workshop on Social Network Mining and Analysis,* 1-9

Qualman, E. (2009). *Socialnomics: How Social Media Transforms the Way We Live and Do Business.* Hoboken, New Jersey: John Wiley & Sons, Inc.

Rowley, J., Teahan, B., & Leeming, E. (2007). Customer community and co-creation: A case study. *Marketing Intelligence & Planning,* 25(2), 136–146. doi:10.1108/02634500710737924

Scoble, R., & Israel, S. (2006). *Naked Conversations: How Blogs are Changing the Way Businesses Talk with Customers.* Hoboken, New Jersey: John Wiley & Sons, Inc.

Scott, D. M. (2010). *The New Rules of Marketing and PR: How to Use Social Media, Blogs, News Releases, Online Video, and Viral Marketing to Reach Buyers Directly* (2nd ed.). Hoboken, New Jersey: John Wiley & Sons, Inc.

Scullin, S. S., Fjermestad, J., & Romano, N. C. (2004). E-relationships marketing: Changes in traditional marketing as the outcome of eCRM. *Journal of Enterprise Information Management,* 17, 410–415. doi:10.1108/17410390410566698

Sigala, M. (2010). Special issue on web 2.0 in travel and tourism: Empowering and changing the role of travelers. *Computers in Human Behavior.*

Vascellaro, J. E. (2007, August 28). Social Networking Goes Professional: Doctors, Salesmen, Executives Turn to New Sites to Consult, Commiserate With Peers; Weeding Out Impostors. *Wall Street Journal,* Washington, D.C.

Wu, L., Majedi, M., Ghazinour, K., & Barker, K. (2010). Analysis of social networking privacy policies. *Proceedings of the 2010 EDBT/ICDT Workshops,* 1-5

Zhan, J., Loh, H. T., & Liu, Y. (2009). Gather customer concerns from online product reviews - A text summarization approach. *Expert Systems with Applications,* 36(2), 2107–2115. doi:10.1016/j.eswa.2007.12.039

## KEY TERMS AND DEFINITIONS

**Business-Consumer Relationship:** It is a central element of business and refers to the relationships that businesses develop with their clients and vice-versa.

**Customer Empowerment:** Refers to the growing power that customers have due to the existence of content creation and sharing tools.

**Enterprise 2.0:** Refers to the use of Web 2.0 technologies, tools and principles in enterprises.

**Online Communities:** Communities which are created and/or maintained on the internet with the assistance of social technologies and that usually are formed and gravitate around common subjects of interest.

**Social Network Sites:** Platforms that allow internet users the possibility of having individual pages displaying their personal profiles, their network of contacts and other information they may choose to share. Besides a venue, these sites also provide users with a multiplicity of means to interact with their contacts.

**Social Technologies:** Can also be referred to as collaborative technologies and include all the applications, features and tools that allow users to create, edit and share content online, usually in numerous formats.

**User-Generated:** Content that was created by internet users and that can assume a multiplicity of formats such as text, video or music.

**Web 2.0:** Also known as Social Web or Collaborative Web, consists in a set of revolutionary, user-centred principles of interaction, collaboration, user content and openness; and the entirety of technologies and tools that derive from and support them.

# Chapter 15
# Community Structure Extraction for Social Networks

**Helen Hadush**
*North Carolina Central University, USA*

**Gaolin Zheng**
*North Carolina Central University, USA*

**Chung-Hao Chen**
*North Carolina Central University, USA*

**E-Wen Huang**
*National Central University, Taiwan*

## ABSTRACT

*In this work, community structure extraction essentially resorts to its solution to graph partition problem. The authors explore two different approaches. The spectral approach is based on the minimization of balanced cut and its resulting solution comes from the spectral decomposition of the graph Laplacian. The modularity based approach is based on the maximization of modularity and implemented in a hierarchical fashion. In practice, the approach can extract useful information from the community structure, such as what is the most influential component in a given community. Being able to identify and group friends on social networks, the technique can provide a customized advertisement based on their interests. This can have a big return in terms of marketing efficiency. Community structure can also be used for network visualization and navigation. As a result, it can be seen which groups or which pages have more interaction, thus giving a clear image for navigation purposes.*

DOI: 10.4018/978-1-61350-444-4.ch015

## INTRODUCTION

The word "community" is a broad term for fellowship or organized society. Society offers a wide variety of possible group organizations: families, workspace and friendship circles, villages, towns, nations. The popularization of Internet has also led to the creation of virtual groups such as online communities. Indeed, social communities have been studied for a long time (Freeman 2004). Communities also occur in many networked systems from biology, computer science, engineering, economics, politics, etc. For example, in protein-protein interaction networks, communities are likely to group proteins of similar functions within the cell (Rives and Galitski 2003), in the World Wide Web they may correspond to groups of pages dealing with the same or related topics (Dourisboure, Geraci et al. 2007), in metabolic networks they may be related to functional modules such as cycles and pathways (Guimera and Nunes Amaral 2005), in food webs they may identify layers, and so on.

Communities can also have real applications. For example clustering web clients who have similar interests and are geographically close to each other may improve the performance of services provided on the World Wide Web, in that each cluster of clients could be served by a dedicated mirror server (Krishnamurthy and Wang 2000). Identifying clusters of customers with similar interests in the network of purchase relationships between customers and products of online retailers (e.g., www.amazon.com) enables us to set up efficient recommendation systems (Reddy, Kitsuregawa et al. 2002). Such a system increases the business opportunity by directing customers better through the list of items of the retailer. Clustering of large graphs can be used to create data structures for efficient storage and navigational queries, like path searches(Agrawal and Jagadish 1994). Graphs are used to represent networks due to their very relevant feature, namely community structure. The organization

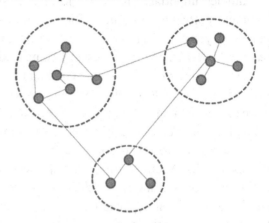

*Figure 1. Three communities, denoted by the dashed circles, which have dense intra-community links and sparse inter-community links*

of vertices in clusters is in such a way that edges joining vertices of the same cluster or community appear higher in number than the edges joining vertices of different clusters. Figure 1 illustrates this property. Grouping the nodes into clusters enables one to generate compact routing tables while the choice of the communication paths is still efficient (Steenstrup 2001).

In addition, community identification is useful for many more important reasons. Identifying clusters and their boundaries allows for a classification of vertices, according to their structural position in the clusters. Vertices with a central position in their clusters, i.e. sharing relatively many edges with the other group members, may have a key role of control and stability within the group; vertices lying at the boundaries between clusters play a key role of intercession and guide the relationships and exchanges between different communities(Csermely 2008). Finally, we can study the graph where vertices are the communities and edges are put between clusters if there are connections between some of their vertices in the original graph. As a result we can attain a clear description of the original graph, which reveals the relationships between clusters. Recent studies indicate that networks of communities have a different degree distribution with respect to the full graphs(Palla, Derenyi et al. 2005).

Another important characteristic related to community structure is the hierarchical organization displayed by most networked systems in the real world. Real networks are usually composed by communities including smaller communities, which in turn include smaller communities, etc. If we look at the human body we can see a model example of hierarchical organization: as it is composed of organs, organs are composed of tissues, tissues of cells. Another example is represented by business organizations, which are characterized by a pyramidal organization, starting from the workers to then the intermediate levels which include work groups, departments and management and finally to the president. Herbert A. Simon has emphasized the crucial role played by hierarchy in the structure and evolution of complex systems (Simon 1962). The generation and evolution of a system organized in interrelated stable subsystems are much quicker than if the system were unstructured, because it is much easier to gather the smallest subparts first and use them as building blocks to obtain larger structures, until the complete system is formed.

The goal of community identification in graphs is to identify the clusters by only using the information encoded in the graph topology. The problem has appeared in a range of forms in a number of disciplines. The first analysis of community structure was carried out by Weiss and Jacobson (Weiss and Jacobson 1955), who searched for work groups within a government agency. The authors studied the matrix of working relationships between members of the agency, which were identified by means of private interviews. Work groups were separated by removing the members working with people of different groups, which act as connectors between them. George Homans (Homans 1950) showed that social groups could be revealed by correctly rearranging the rows and the columns of matrices describing social ties,

until they take an approximate block-diagonal form. This procedure is now standard.

Identifying communities in graph is very useful in computer science too, for example, in parallel computing, it is crucial to know the best way to allocate tasks to processors so as to minimize the communications between tasks and attain a rapid performance of the calculation. This can be accomplished by splitting the computer cluster into groups with roughly the same number of processors, such that the number of physical connections between processors of different groups is minimal. The Mathematical formalization of this problem is called graph partitioning. The first algorithms for graph partitioning were proposed in the early 1970's (Kernighan and Lin 1970).

In this work, we propose to use spectral clustering based and modularity based methods to identify community structures in various types of social network models. We also use a power iteration based method to rank the importance of components within communities. The spectral clustering based approach is based on the minimization of balanced cut and its resulting solution comes from the spectral decomposition of the graph Laplacian. The modularity based approach is based on the maximization of modularity and implemented in a hierarchical fashion.

Community structure extraction essentially resorts to its solution to graph partition problem. Results show that community structures can be extracted from many different types of network models, which are represented in the form of graphs. In essence, our approaches can further extract useful information from the community structure, such as what is the most influential component in a given community. For example, on online social networks like FaceBook, we can extract information about the existing communities and also based on the relationships among friends we can see who plays the key role in a given community. Being able to identify and group friends on FaceBook we can provide a customized advertisement based on their interests. This can have a big return in terms of marketing efficiency. Community structure can also be used for network visualization and navigation. For example, in the experiments conducted on different websites we are able to see the structure of the overall site by grouping websites into different communities. As a result, we can see which groups or which pages have more interactions, thus giving a clear image for navigation purpose.

## LITERATURE REVIEW

### Introduction to Communities

Due to its applicability to the wide range of disciplines, community structure identification has been one of the most popular research areas in recent years. There have been many algorithms proposed so far. Communities are characterized by the tendency of vertices to divide into groups with dense connections within groups and only sparser connections between groups. To define communities on graph let us start with a subgraph $C$ of a graph g, with $|C| = n_c$ and $|g| = n$ vertices, respectively. We define the internal and external degree of vertex, $k_v^{int}$ and $k_v^{ext}$, as the number of edges connecting v to other vertices of $C$ or to the rest of the graph, respectively. If $k_v^{ext} = 0$, the vertex has neighbors only within $C$, which is likely to be a good cluster for v; if $k_v^{int} = 0$, instead, the vertex is disjoint from $C$ and it should be better assigned to a different cluster. The internal degree $k_{in}^c$ of $C$ is the sum of the internal degrees of its vertices. Likewise, the external degree $k_{ext}^c$ of $C$ is the sum of the external degrees of its vertices. The total degree $k^c$ is the sum of the degrees of the vertices of $C$ (Fortunato 2010). By definition, $k^c = k_{in}^c + k_{ext}^c$. We define the intra-cluster density $\delta_{int}(C)$ of the subgraph $C$ as the ratio between the number of internal edges of $C$ and the number of all possible internal edges, i.e.

$$\delta_{int}(C) = \frac{I_c}{\frac{n_c(n_c - 1)}{2}} \tag{1}$$

where $I_c$ represents the number of the internal edges of $C$. Similarly, the inter-cluster density $\delta_{ext}(C)$ is the ratio between the number of edges running from the vertices of $C$ to the rest of the graph and the maximum number of inter-cluster edges possible, i.e.

$$\delta_{ext}(C) = \frac{E_c}{n_c(n - n_c)} \tag{2}$$

where $E_c$ represents the number of the inter-cluster edges of $C$. For $C$ to be a community, we expect $\delta_{int}(C)$ to be significantly larger than the average link density of g, $\delta(g)$, which is given by the ratio between the number of edges of g and the maximum number of possible edges. On the other hand, $\delta_{ext}(C)$ has to be much smaller than $\delta(g)$. Searching for the best tradeoff between a large $\delta_{int}(C)$ and a small $\delta_{ext}(C)$ is the goal of most clustering algorithms. A simple way to do that is by maximizing the sum of the differences over all clusters of the partition.

Communities are parts of the graph with a few ties with the rest of the system. To some extent, they can be considered as separate entities with their own sovereignty. So, it makes sense to evaluate them independently of the graph as a whole. Local definitions focus on the subgraph under study, including possibly its immediate neighborhood, but neglecting the rest of the graph. There, four types of criterion were identified: complete mutuality, reachability, vertex degree and the comparison of internal versus external cohesion. The corresponding communities are mostly maximal subgraphs, which cannot be enlarged with the addition of new vertices and edges without losing the property which defines them.

Social communities can be defined as sub-groups whose members are all "friends" to each other (Luce and Perry 1949). In graph terms, this corresponds to a clique, i.e. a subset whose vertices are all connected to each other. In social network analysis, a clique is a maximal subgraph, whereas in graph theory it is commonly called nonmaximal subgraphs cliques. Triangles are the simplest cliques, and are frequent in real networks. But larger cliques are less frequent. Moreover, the condition is really too strict: a subgraph with all possible internal edges except one would be an extremely cohesive subgroup, but it would not be considered a community under this recipe. Another problem is that all vertices of a clique are absolutely symmetric, with no isolation between them. In many practical examples, instead, we expect that within a community there is a whole hierarchy of roles for the vertices, with central vertices coexisting with marginal ones.

## Graph Partitioning

Graph partitioning involves the dividing of the vertices in g groups of predefined size, such that the number of edges lying between the groups is minimal. The number of edges running between clusters is called cut size. Specifying the number of clusters of the partition is required. If we simply imposed a partition with the minimal cut size, and left the number of clusters free, the solution would be trivial, corresponding to all vertices ending up in the same cluster, as this would yield a vanishing cut size. Specifying the size is also required, as otherwise the most likely solution of the problem would consist of separating the lowest degree vertex from the rest of the graph, which is quite trivial. This problem can be actually avoided by choosing a different measure to optimize for the partitioning, which accounts for the size of the clusters (Fortunato 2010).

Graph partitioning is a fundamental issue in parallel computing, circuit partitioning and layout, and in the design of many serial algorithms, including techniques to solve partial differential equations and sparse linear systems of equations. But most graph partitioning problems are NP-hard. There are a number of good heuristic algorithms (Pothen 1997). Many algorithms perform a bisection of the graph. Partitions into more than two clusters are usually attained by iterative bisecting. Moreover, in most cases one imposes the constraint that the clusters have equal size. This problem is called minimum bisection and is NP-hard (Fortunato 2010).

## Divisive Algorithm

Divisive algorithm uses a simple way to identify communities in a graph, i.e. to detect and remove the edges that connect vertices of different communities, so that the clusters get disconnected from each other. This is the underlying technique of divisive algorithms. The important point is to find a property of intercommunity edges that could allow for their identification. Divisive methods do not introduce substantial conceptual advances with respect to traditional techniques, as they just perform hierarchical clustering on the graph. The main difference with divisive hierarchical clustering is that here we remove inter-cluster edges instead of edges between pairs of vertices with low similarity. But it is not guaranteed that inter-cluster edges connect vertices with low similarity. Even there could be cases where vertices (with all their adjacent edges) of whole subgraphs may be removed, instead of single edges. Being hierarchical clustering techniques, it is customary to represent the resulting partitions by means of dendrograms. Dendrograms are often used for displaying relationships among clusters. A dendrogram shows the multidimensional distances between objects in a tree-like structure. Objects which are closest to each other in the multidimensional data space are connected by a horizontal line, forming a cluster which can be regarded as a "new" object.

## K-Means Clustering

K-means is one of the simplest unsupervised learning techniques that can be used to solve the clustering problem. The method follows a simple and easy way to classify a given data set to a certain number of clusters (e.g. k clusters) fixed a priori. The main idea is to define k centroids, one for each cluster. These centroids should be placed in a wise way because of different location generate different results. The best choice is to place them as far away from each other as possible. It is an iterative procedure. At the beginning of each iteration, each point in the data set is assigned to its nearest cetriod. At the end of each iteration, recalculate the k new centriods to be used as centroids to be used as centers of the clusters for the next iteration. The iteration procedure terminates when the k centroids no longer move or a maximum number of iteration is reached. This algorithm aims at minimizing an objective *function*; in this case a squared error function.

Similar to other algorithm, K-means clustering has many weaknesses: (1) it is sensitive to the choice of initial grouping especially for small data sets and sensitive to initial condition. Different initial condition may produce different result of cluster. The algorithm may be trapped in the local optimum; (2) the number of clusters, $K$, must be determined beforehand. Determining the real cluster is impossible as the order of inputting the data may produce different clusters. This is true if the number of data is small; (3) we never know which attribute contributes more to the grouping process since we assume that each attribute has the same weight; (4) it is sensitive to outliers due to the use of arithmetic mean. A very far data from the centroid may pull the centroid away from the real one. One way to overcome those weaknesses is to use K-means clustering only if there are many data available. To overcome outliers problem, we can use median instead of mean. There are a lot of applications of the K-means clustering, ranging from unsupervised learning of neural network,

pattern recognitions, classification analysis, artificial intelligence, image processing, machine vision, etc. When we have several objects and each object has several attributes and we want to classify those objects based on their attributes, we can use this algorithm.

Thus, those algorithms we have observed during the literature reviews lack a reliable mechanism of control of their quality. If the research communities agree on a benchmark, the future development of the field will be more coherent and the progress proposed by new methods can be evaluated in an unbiased manner.

## METHODOLOGY

The focus of this work is to use Spectral clustering and Modularity method to detect communities on a graph. Once communities are identified, we apply page-ranking algorithm to rank pages with in each community.

## Spectral Clustering

Given a set of data points $A$, the similarity matrix may be defined as a matrix $S$ where $S_{ij}$ represents a measure of the similarity between points $i, j \in A$. Spectral clustering techniques make use of the spectrum of the similarity matrix of the data to perform dimensionality reduction for clustering in fewer dimensions. One such technique is the Shi-Malik algorithm, commonly used for image segmentation. It partitions points into two sets $(S_1, S_2)$ based on the eigenvector $v$ corresponding to the second-smallest eigenvalue of the Laplacian matrix, $L$:

$$L = 1 - D^{-1/2} S D^{-1/2} \qquad (3)$$

where $D$ is the diagonal matrix $\sum_j S_{ij}$. This partitioning may be done in various ways, such as by taking the median $m$ of the components in $v$, and placing all points whose component in $v$ is greater than $m$ in $S_1$, and the rest in $S_2$. The algorithm can be used for hierarchical clustering by repeatedly partitioning the subsets in this fashion. In recent years, spectral clustering has become one of the most popular modern clustering algorithms. Because it is simple to implement, and very often outperforms traditional clustering algorithms such as the k-means algorithm. On the first glance spectral clustering appears slightly mysterious, and it is not obvious to see why it works at all and what it really does. Results obtained by spectral clustering often outperform the traditional approaches. The main tools for spectral clustering are graphing Laplacian matrices. Let's define different graph Laplacians and point out their most important properties. We will see different variants of graph Laplacians. In this work, we always assume that $G$ is an undirected, weighted graph with weight matrix $W$, where $w_{ij} = w_{ji} \geq 0$ when we talk about eigenvectors of a matrix, we do not necessarily assume that they are normalized.

## Modularity Based Approach

Modularity is a recently introduced quality measure for graph clustering. It has immediately receives considerable attention in several disciplines, and in particular in the complex systems literature, although its properties are not well understood. In this work we deal with the problem of searching clusters with maximum modularity. Modularity is by far the most used and best-known quality function. It represented one of the first attempts to achieve a first principle understanding of the clustering problem, and it embeds in its compact form all essential ingredients and questions, from the definition of community, to the choice of a null model, to the expression of the "strength" of communities and partitions. Multi-Level Aggregation Method for optimizing modularity outperforms

other methods in terms of computation time, which allows us to analyze networks of unprecedented size (e.g. the analysis of a typical network of 2 million nodes only takes 2 minutes). The Louvain method has also shown to be very accurate by focusing on ad-hoc networks with known community structure. Moreover, it allows us to look at communities at different resolutions due to its hierarchical structure (Fortunato 2010).

The method consists of two phases. First, it looks for "small" communities by optimizing modularity in a local way. Second, it aggregates nodes of the same community and builds a new network whose nodes are the communities. These steps are repeated iteratively until a maximum of modularity is attained. The output of the program therefore gives several partitions. The partition found after the first step typically consists of many communities of small sizes. At subsequent steps, larger and larger communities are found due to the aggregation mechanism. This process naturally leads to hierarchical decomposition of the network. This is obviously an approximate method and nothing ensures that the global maximum of modularity is attained, but several tests have confirmed that our algorithm has an excellent accuracy and often provides a decomposition in communities that has a modularity that is close to optimality. Although modularity-based approach is greedy in nature, the solution it finds is very close to global maximum in most of the cases. We have not seen its performance being affected network size. But it might not be able to a good candidate for extremely overlapping community structures.

Modularity method focuses on maximizing the modularity value, or the quality function. And there is no need to specify the number of clusters we need, or in other words, we don't have to have a prior knowledge regarding the sizes and numbers of clusters in a given graph. As spectral clustering involves k-means, it suffers from the weaknesses of k-means. However, this weakness can be overcome by finding the eigen-gap between successive eigenvalues of the graph Laplacian. We can identify the proper value of k that will give the most stable clustering performance. Another issue with k-means is its instability. However, spectral clustering does not suffer from it because it works on the eigenspace of the graph Laplacian. Over all spectral clustering seems to be flexible and faster than the modularity technique.

## Ranking within Communities

In addition to getting hands on experience with different types of clustering techniques, in this work a new approach of page ranking is also introduced. The idea is to rank modules, the communities, rather than the entire website. By doing so, we can identify the most influential nodes in a given set of communities. This technique can make the ranking faster and gives a fairer rank for each page. The technique is similar to the idea of topic sensitive ranking. Given a website there could be hundreds of pages and each page with a unique information and content. For example let's consider news website, http://www.bbc.co.uk, some of the many topics the site has are news, sports, entertainments, weather and so on. By identifying the closely related pages as a community, and ranking within the communities we can make the searching space and the ranking more efficient. In the experiments, we can see that the technique is very useful.

PageRank is a topic much discussed by Search Engine Optimization (SEO) experts, webmasters, and geeks all over the world. At the heart of PageRank is a mathematical formula that seems scary to look at, but is actually fairly simple to understand. Any good web designer should take the time to fully understand how PageRank really works, so that he/she can design a highly search engine optimized website. A site that cannot be accessed through search engines is like a page that doesn't exist on the WWW. Within the past few years, Google has become by far the most utilized search engine worldwide. A decisive fac-

tor, besides high performance and ease of use, is the superior quality of search results compared to other search engines. This quality of search results is substantially based on a sophisticated method, called PageRank, to rank web documents. Google's founders, Larry Page and Sergey Brin, developed the PageRank algorithm when they were graduate students at Stanford University. PageRank is determined entirely by the link structure of the World Wide Web. It is recomputed about once a month and doesn't involve the actual content of any Web pages or individual queries. Then, for any particular query, Google finds the pages on the Web that match that query and lists those pages in the order of their PageRank.

One way to compute the stationary distribution of a Markov chain is by explicitly computing the distribution at successive time steps, using $x(k) = Ax(k-1)$, until the distribution converges. This leads us to the Power Method for computing the principal eigenvector of $A$. The Power Iteration Method is the oldest method for computing the principal eigen-vector of a matrix, and is at the heart of both the motivation and implementation of the original PageRank.

The power iteration is normally run to convergence in order to find the dominant eigenvector of a matrix. The intuition behind the convergence of the Power Iteration Method is as follows;

For simplicity, assume that the start vector $x(0)$ lies in the subspace spanned by the eigenvectors of $A$. Then $x(0)$ can be written as a linear combination of the eigenvectors of $A$:

$$x(0) = u_1 + a_2 u_2 + ... + a_m u_m \qquad (4)$$

Since we know that the first eigenvalue of a Markov matrix, $\lambda_1 = 1$,

$$x(1) = Ax(0) = u_1 + \alpha_2 \lambda_2 u_2 + ... + \alpha_m \lambda_m u_m \qquad (5)$$

*Figure 2. Communities in Zachary Karate club identified using spectral clustering method*

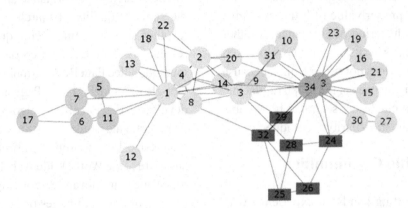

$$x(n) = A_n x(0) + \alpha_2 \lambda_{n2} u_2 + ... + \alpha_m \lambda_{nm} u_m \tag{6}$$

Since $\lambda_n \leq ... \leq \lambda_2 < 1$, $A_n x(0)$ approaches $u_1$ as n grows large. Therefore, the Power Iteration Method converges to the principal eigenvector of the matrix $A$.

## EXPERIMENTAL RESULTS

The experiment is conducted on different datasets including benchmark datasets and datasets generated by surfer function as part of the research. The datasets are of different sizes. Benchmark datasets used in this work include the Zachary Karate Club and dolphins datasets.

### Zachary Karate Club Dataset

The Zachary Karate Club data (Zachary 1977) is collected by Wayne Zachary from the karate club of a university. This dataset is widely used in testing of community identification algorithms. The vertices are the students and there is an edge between two vertices if these two students are good friends. The two communities represent two karate clubs, which are formed after a disagreement. This network includes 34 nodes and 78 edges. Figures

2 and 3 show the results by using spectral clustering and modularity-based approaches.

Modularity based method doesn't require a user defined number of clusters. The members in the club are divided into four groups. The instructor and his followers are labeled as pink, the members labeled as blue are loosely linked with the instructor faction (pink group). The administrator and his followers are labeled as red. The green group is loosely linked with the red group. If we merge the red and green group, we can obtain the administrator faction mentioned by Zachary (Zachary 1977). If we merge the pink and blue group, we can regenerate the instructor faction (Zachary 1977). Furthermore, this algorithm is able to identify some neutral groups (e.g. green group and blue group). The partitions found using spectral clustering are identical to the ones found using modularity based method although the coloring of the groups is different in the two figures.

### Dolphins Datasets

The network of bottlenose dolphins living in Doubtful Sound (New Zealand) were analyzed by Lusseau (Lusseau 2003). There are 62 dolphins and edges were set between animals that were seen together more often than expected by chance. The dolphins separated into two groups after a dolphin

*Figure 3. Communities in Zachary Karate club identified using modularity based method*

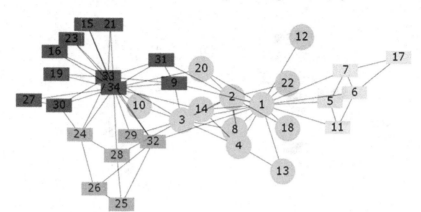

left the place for some time (squares and circles in the figure). Such groups are quite cohesive, with several internal cliques, and easily identifiable: only six edges join vertices of different groups. Due to this natural classification, Lusseau's dolphins network, as well as Zachary's karate club, are often used to test algorithms for community identification. Figure 4 and 5 show the results by using spectral clustering and modularity based approaches.

Spectral clustering found two groups that give the most stable clustering performance (Figure 4). The dolphin social network identified here was characterized by the presence of centers of associations, which shows that not all individuals have an equal role in the society. These hubs were mainly adult females and seemed to be older individuals (many scars and larger size) (Lusseau 2003). Modularity based approach stabilized until 5 clusters were found. Visualization of clusters in different colors help us identify those dolphins that play parts in maintaining short information flow between individuals in the population.

## Datasets Generated by Surfer Function

A surfer function was used to generate data for experiment. The function creates the adjacency graph for a given website. And this adjacency matrix is used as an input for the clustering algorithms, from

*Figure 4. Communities in bottle nosed dolphins identified using spectral clustering*

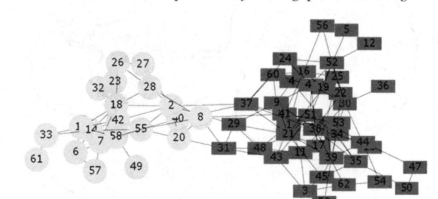

*Figure 5. Communities in bottle nosed dolphins identified using modularity based clustering*

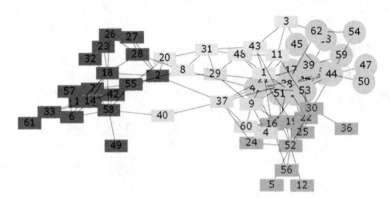

which we can generate the possible communities in the given web site. The surfer function takes to a root argument, which is the URL of the website we are interested in, and n, which is the number of nodes or the depth of the link we want to go. It starts at the root URL root and follows web links until it forms an adjacency graph with n nodes. The surfer function returns two values *U* and *G*, where *U* is a cell array of n strings, the URLs of the node, and G is an n-by-n sparse matrix with *G(i,j)=1* if node *j* is linked to node *i*.

Communities on the web represent pages of related topics. In the experiment done on differ-

ent websites, the communities detected displayed a common property, which is, pages from same directory are allocated to the same community. And pages, which have high ranks, seem to play a key role in the role of control and stability within the clusters identified; and most of the pages lying at the boundaries between clusters tend to be independent and don't play a role of intercession and guide the relationships and changes between the different clusters. Figure 6 shows the results for the website, www.bbc.co.uk, by using the modularity based approach. The partition found by spectral clustering generally agrees with that

*Figure 6. Communities identified in www.bbc.co.uk by modularity based approach, where 100 nodes (pages) were considered*

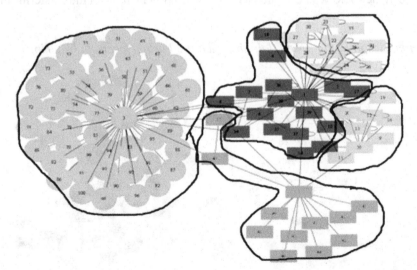

*Figure 7. Communities identified inwww.stanford.eduby modularity based approach, where 100 nodes (pages) were considered*

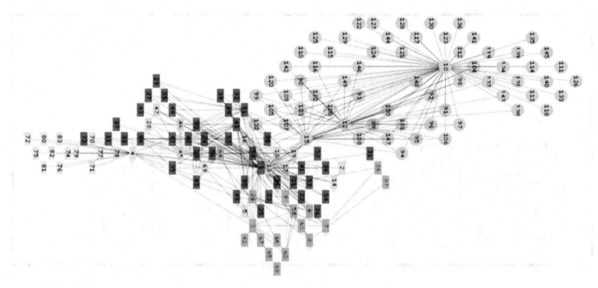

of modularity based method. Figure 7 shows the results for the website, www.stanford.edu, by modularity based approach. The partition found using spectral clustering is similar to Figure 7.

Figure 8 illustrates the performance differences between the modularity based and spectral clustering approaches. We can see that the performance of spectral clustering is better than the modularity based method in terms of running time.

## Ranking within Communities

The ranking of query results in a Web search-engine is an important problem and has attracted significant attention in the research community.

*Figure 8. Performance comparison between modularity based and spectral clustering approaches*

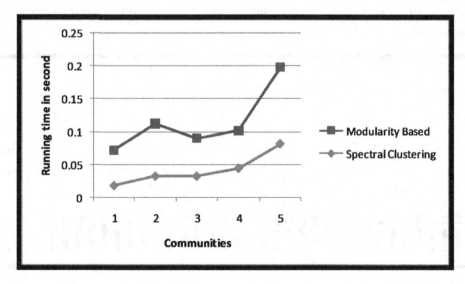

*Figure 9. Communities and in-community Rank of web pages from www.cs.nccu.edu using spectral clustering approach*

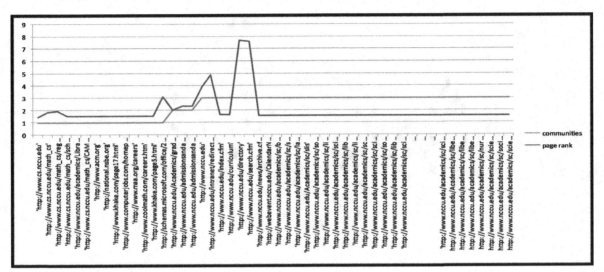

In order to maintain timely and accurate web pages ranking a huge crawling and indexing infrastructure is needed. On the other hand continuous crawling of the Web is almost impossible due to its dynamic nature, the large number of Web pages and bandwidth constraints. The same holds for the indexing and page ranking process, since the computations needed are very expensive.

The following figures illustrate the resulting relationship between the community structures and their corresponding ranks. A high rank in a community can be interpreted in several different ways: if a node or a page is ranked high in a given community that means the node/page plays a key role in the community. For example if we consider the case of Zachary's karate club, we can see that nodes 34 and 1 are ranked the highest. And from the given data it is possible to see that node 34 actually represents the president and node 1 is the instructor. This justifies the ground truth, which

*Figure 10. Communities and in-community rank of nodes from Zachary's karate club using spectral clustering approach*

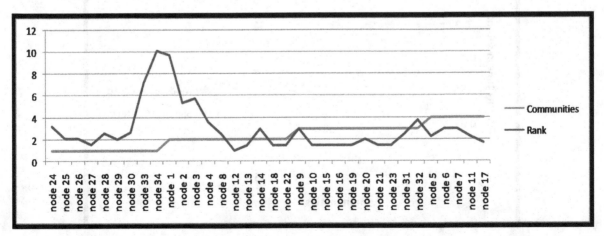

*Figure 11.Communities and in-community rank of nodes from bbc.co.uk using spectral clustering approach*

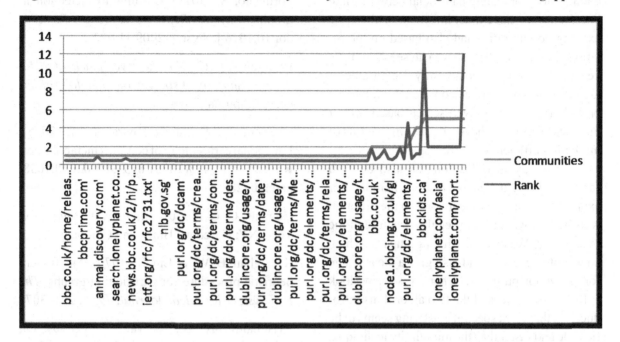

is the club was actually divided into two, those who are on the president's side and those who are on the instructor's side. Two concentrations were identified, one around vertices 33 and 34 (the president), another around vertex 1 (the instructor).

Figure 9 shows the communities and in-community Rank of web pages from www.cs.nccu.edu using spectral clustering. Generally the pages in the same community are ranked similarly except for those pages which have several linkages for example the index pages usually are ranked high. We can also observe on the figures that as we go from one community to the next one, the rank seems to get higher and reaches it maximum at the border between the different communities; this is a result of the high linkage both in incoming and outgoing links/edges that the specific page/node in the intersection has. The following list will show the top four highly ranked pages: (1) 'http://www. nccu.edu/directory'; (2) 'http://www.nccu.edu/ search.cfm'; (3) 'http://www.nccu.edu/intranet/ redirection.cfm'; (4) 'http://www.nccu.edu'

Figure 10 shows the communities and in-community Rank of web pages from Zachary's

karate club using spectral clustering. We can see that the rank line gets to its peaks on the nodes that have more connections with the rest of the nodes in their communities and among all these picks the nodes 34 and 1 are the highest, where node 34 corresponds to the administrator and 1 is the instructor. Similar properties can be observed in the case of bbc.co.uk too. Figure 11 shows the communities and in-community Rank of web pages from bbc.co.uk using spectral clustering.

## CONCLUSION

Our work showed that community structures can be identified from many different types of network structures. And these structures can be represented in the form of graphs, and by using the properties of graphs we can implement several different types of community identification algorithms. The output generated from the experiments can be interpreted in many ways and we can extract useful information from the structure, such as who is the most influential person in a given community. For example in social networks like FaceBook, we can extract information about the existing communities and also based on the relationships among friends we can see who plays key roles in a given community. Being able to identify and group friends on FaceBook we can provide a customized advertisement based on their interests. This could have a big return in terms of marketing efficiency.

Community identification can also be used for network visualization and navigation. For example, in the experiment done on the different websites we were able to see the structure of the overall site. We can see which groups or which pages interact more, and also give a clear image for navigation purposes. Generally when we look at the performances of the two algorithms introduced in this work spectral clustering seems to be flexible and faster than the modularity technique. And also we can see that the performance of spectral clustering is better than the modularity based method. Modularity method is better than spectral clustering by the fact that the user doesn't have to have a prior knowledge about the communities in the graph in question.

# REFERENCES

Agrawal, R., & Jagadish, H. V. (1994). Algorithms for searching massive graphs. *IEEE Transactions on Knowledge and Data Engineering, 6*(2), 225–238. doi:10.1109/69.277767

Csermely, P. (2008). Creative elements: Network-based predictions of active centres in proteins and cellular and social networks. *Trends in Biochemical Sciences, 33*(12), 569–576. doi:10.1016/j.tibs.2008.09.006

Dourisboure, Y., Geraci, F., et al. (2007). Extraction and classification of dense communities in the Web. *Proceedings of the 16th International Conference on World Wide Web*, (pp. 461-470). Banff, Canada: ACM.

Fortunato, S. (2010). Community detection in graphs. *Physics Reports, 486*(3-5), 75–174. doi:10.1016/j.physrep.2009.11.002

Freeman, L. C. (2004). *The development of social network analysis: A study in the sociology of science*. Empirical Press.

Guimera, R., & Nunes Amaral, L. A. (2005). Functional cartography of complex metabolic networks. *Nature, 433*(7028), 895–900. doi:10.1038/nature03288

Homans, G. C. (1950). *The human group*. New York, NY: Harcourt, Brace and Company.

Kernighan, B. W., & Lin, S. (1970). An efficient heuristic procedure for partitioning graphs. *The Bell System Technical Journal, 49*(1), 291–307.

Krishnamurthy, B., & Wang, J. (2000). On network-aware clustering of Web clients. *SIGCOMM Comput. Commun. Rev., 30*(4), 97–110. doi:10.1145/347057.347412

Luce, R., & Perry, A. (1949). A method of matrix analysis of group structure. *Psychometrika, 14*(2), 95–116. doi:10.1007/BF02289146

Lusseau, D. (2003). The emergent properties of a dolphin social network. *Proceedings. Biological Sciences, 270*(Suppl 2), S186–S188. doi:10.1098/rsbl.2003.0057

Palla, G., & Derenyi, I. (2005). Uncovering the overlapping community structure of complex networks in nature and society. *Nature, 435*(7043), 814–818. doi:10.1038/nature03607

Pothen, A. (1997). *Graph partitioning algorithms with applications to scientific computing*. Old Dominion University.

Reddy, P. K., Kitsuregawa, M., et al. (2002). A graph based approach to extract a neighborhood customer community for collaborative filtering. *Proceedings of the Second International Workshop on Databases in Networked Information Systems*, (pp. 188-200). Springer-Verlag.

Rives, A. W., & Galitski, T. (2003). Modular organization of cellular networks. *Proceedings of the National Academy of Sciences of the United States of America*, *100*(3), 1128–1133. doi:10.1073/pnas.0237338100

Simon, H. (1962). The architecture of complexity. *Proceedings of the American Philosophical Society*, *106*(6), 467–482.

Steenstrup, M. (2001). *Cluster-based networks. Ad hoc networking* (pp. 75–138). Addison-Wesley Longman Publishing Co., Inc.

Weiss, R. S., & Jacobson, E. (1955). A method for the analysis of the structure of complex organizations. *American Sociological Review*, *20*(6), 661–668. doi:10.2307/2088670

Zachary, W. W. (1977). An information flow model for conflict and fission in small groups. *Journal of Anthropological Research*, *33*(4), 452–473.

## ADDITIONAL READING

Chen, P., & Xie, H. (2007). Finding scientific gems with Google's PageRank algorithm. *Journal of Informatrics*, *1*(1), 8–15. doi:10.1016/j.joi.2006.06.001

Cicone, A., & Serra-Capizzano, S. (2010). Google PageRanking problem: The model and the analysis. *Journal of Computational and Applied Mathematics*, *234*(11), 3140–3169. doi:10.1016/j.cam.2010.02.005

Clark, L. H., & Shahrokhi, F. (1992). A linear time algorithm for graph partition problems. *Information Processing Letters*, *42*(1), 19–24. doi:10.1016/0020-0190(92)90126-G

Gori, M., & Numerico, T. (2003). Social networks and web minorities. *Cognitive Systems Research*, *4*(4), 355–364. doi:10.1016/S1389-0417(03)00016-0

Hagenbuchner, M., & Sperduti, A. (2009). Graph self-organizing maps for cyclic and unbounded graphs. *Neurocomputing*, *72*(7-9), 1419–1430. doi:10.1016/j.neucom.2008.12.021

Hsu, C.-C., & Wu, F. (2006). Topic-specific crawling on the Web with the measurements of the relevancy context graph. *Information Systems*, *31*(4-5), 232–246. doi:10.1016/j.is.2005.02.007

Knopfmacher, A., & Tichy, R. F. (2007). Graphs, partitions and Fibonacci numbers. *Discrete Applied Mathematics*, *155*(10), 1175–1187. doi:10.1016/j.dam.2006.10.010

Métivier, Y., & Robson, J. M. (2010). About randomised distributed graph colouring and graph partition algorithms. *Information and Computation*, *208*(11), 1296–1304. doi:10.1016/j.ic.2010.07.001

Nambiar, K. K. (2001). Theory of search engines. *Computers & Mathematics with Applications (Oxford, England)*, *42*(12), 1523–1526. doi:10.1016/S0898-1221(01)00259-0

Ning, H., & Xu, W. (2010). Incremental spectral clustering by efficiently updating the eigensystem. *Pattern Recognition*, *43*(1), 113–127. doi:10.1016/j.patcog.2009.06.001

Page, L., & Brin, S. (1999). *The PageRank Citation Ranking: Bringing Order to the Web*. Stanford University.

Qiu, H., & Hancock, E. R. (2006). Graph matching and clustering using spectral partitions. *Pattern Recognition*, *39*(1), 22–34. doi:10.1016/j.patcog.2005.06.014

Sarfraz, M., & Salah, K. (2003). Internet Computing. *Information Sciences*, *150*(3-4), 119–122. doi:10.1016/S0020-0255(02)00372-9

Sen, A., & Deng, H. (1992). On a graph partition problem with application to VLSI layout. *Information Processing Letters*, *43*(2), 87–94. doi:10.1016/0020-0190(92)90017-P

Shi, J., & Malik, J. (1997). Normalized Cuts and Image Segmentation. *Proceedings of the 1997 Conference on Computer Vision and Pattern Recognition (CVPR '97)*, IEEE Computer Society: 731-737.

Xia, T., & Cao, J. (2009). On defining affinity graph for spectral clustering through ranking on manifolds. *Neurocomputing, 72*(13-15), 3203–3211. doi:10.1016/j.neucom.2009.03.012

Xiang, T., & Gong, S. (2008). Spectral clustering with eigenvector selection. *Pattern Recognition, 41*(3), 1012–1029. doi:10.1016/j.patcog.2007.07.023

Zhao, F., & Jiao, L. (2010). Spectral clustering with eigenvector selection based on entropy ranking. *Neurocomputing, 73*(10-12), 1704–1717. doi:10.1016/j.neucom.2009.12.029

## KEY TERMS AND DEFINITIONS

**Cluster Volume:** The volume of a cluster A of vertices, denoted as vol(A), is the sum of the degrees of all the vertices belonging to cluster A.

**Clustering:** Assignment of a set of observations into subsets (called clusters) so that observations in the same cluster are similar in some sense.

**Graph Cut:** A graph G = (V, E) can be partitioned into two disjoint sets A and B by removing edges connecting the two parts. cut(A, B) is the total weight of the edges connecting A and B.

**Graph Partition:** A division of a graph vertex set into nonempty disjoint sets that completely cover the set.

**Modularity:** A benefit function used in the analysis of networks or graphs such as computer networks or social networks. It quantifies the quality of a division of a network into modules or communities.

**Normalized Cut:** When a graph G = (V, E) is partitioned into cluster A and B, its normalized cut, denoted as Ncut(A, B) is the sum of cut(A, B)/vol(A) and cut(A, B)/vol(B).

**Page Rank:** A link analysis algorithm, named after Larry Page, used by the Google Internet search engine that assigns a numerical weighting to each element of a hyperlinked set of documents, such as the World Wide Web, with the purpose of "measuring" its relative importance within the set.

**Spectral Clustering:** A clustering technique that makes use of the spectrum of the similarity matrix of the data to perform dimensionality reduction for clustering in fewer dimensions.

# Chapter 16
# Towards a Bespoke Framework for Eliciting Consumer Satisfaction in Second Life

**Mitul Shukla**
*University of Bedfordshire, UK*

**Marc Conrad**
*University of Bedfordshire, UK*

**Nik Bessis**
*University of Bedfordshire, UK and University of Derby, UK*

## ABSTRACT

*Second Life is a virtual world, a multi-user, 3D, immersive environment, which has its own internal economy. The aim of this chapter is to develop a framework that can be used to understand the complex and inter-related factors that affect the use of Second Life in terms of consumer satisfaction in a virtual world. Based on prior works, a framework has been developed which identifies seven interrelated components that provide a wider context to perceive the user experience of Second Life. The approach taken by the framework allows for it to be used as a means to consider Second Life both as a product and as a platform.*

*The approach taken to data gathering, analysis, and interpretation in the context of the framework is described; as well as refinements made to the framework as a consequence of emergent themes revealed through the analysis of the gathered data.*

DOI: 10.4018/978-1-61350-444-4.ch016

## INTRODUCTION

This chapter focuses on the development of a framework for eliciting consumer satisfaction perceptions in the context of the social virtual world Second Life. An introduction to Second Life is followed by an overview of the relevant literature. The framework and the inter-related component parts that it is made up from are then described in detail. This is followed by an evaluation of the framework through semi-structured in-world interviews as well as the refinement of the framework as a consequence of our evaluation. Finally an overview of how the framework can be used by others is given along with the wider context of its use.

Virtual worlds are multi-user, 3D, immersive environments which fall into two basic categories: game worlds such as World of Warcraft and social worlds such as Second Life. Both types of environment allow for computer mediated shared experiences where users can interact with one another, but social virtual worlds do not have an explicit storyline, plot or the necessity to achieve pre-determined goals.

## AN OVERVIEW OF SECOND LIFE

Released by Linden Lab in 2003, Second Life has operated a free-to-use model since 2005. Second Life has its own internal economy based on Linden dollars (L$); the economy has an approximate exchange rate of L$265 to $1(US). User-to-user transactions during the third quarter of 2009 reached $150 million (US), an increase of 54% from the same quarter in 2008 while resident-held Linden dollars rose by 19% for that same period (Linden, 2009). Although a full history of the development of Second Life is somewhat beyond the scope of this chapter, there are many sources for those interested. An excellent primer on Second Life and its evolution is available as a series of

online articles named 'The Virtual Whirl: A brief history of Second Life'[1], written by Tateru Nino.

Typical face-to-face communication relies on verbal and non-verbal cues (Moore et al. 2007). When the richness of multimodal communication, such as that in face-to-face (De Ruiter et al. 2003) is curbed through the use of mediating technology, the communicative process becomes leaner. Thus leaner communication capability in virtual worlds can be exemplified by the limitedness of non-verbal cues. Users are typically proxied 'in-world' by a character or 'avatar'. There is a limited translation capability from user to avatar in terms of body language and facial expressiveness; therefore, there is limited in-world communicative feedback (Gerhard et al. 2004; Moore et al. 2007). Expressing the context of a message through such leaner communications requires either extended communication about the original message or some form of in-channel adaptation such as the use of emoticons in text based communication (Walther & D'Addario 2001). The situation is made more complex when we take into account, that just because multimodal interaction is available, users may prefer not to use all of the modalities available (Oviatt, 1999).

## RELATED WORK

Here we consider the most relevant literature investigating the consumption process within virtual worlds. Second Life has received academic interest within a variety of academic disciplines. One reason for this, as Castranova (2006) points out about virtual world research in general, is that virtual worlds can be perceived to be social science research tools in the same manner that a supercollider is perceived among physicists. The literature on virtual worlds tends to be focussed on similar technologies, with standard definitions but with authors often using different names to identify them. Virtual worlds, virtual environments, immersive worlds, synthetic worlds, meta-verse, and meta-worlds are some of the terms in the literature. With this in mind, an overview of some of the most relevant works focussed on virtual worlds follows.

Guo and Barnes (2007) follow an Information Systems approach in their investigation of virtual worlds. Guo and Barnes have developed a model that takes the perspective of specifically investigating procurement and trust issues within virtual worlds and is made up of ten component parts. Their approach is mainly evolved from the Technology Acceptance Model (TAM), the Theory of Planned Behaviour (TPB) and the Unified Theory of Acceptance and Use of Technology model (UTAUT), amongst others. Seven of these components (trust, effort expectancy, perceived enjoyment, performance expectancy, social influence, perceived critical mass and behavioural intention) are from an amalgamation of the aforementioned models in the literature and the authors have added three new components (perceived quality, character competency and perceived information asymmetry).

Guo and Barnes do point out that "the likely outcome from testing the final model will be an extension to existing behavioural theories (e.g., TAM, TPB) via new constructs validated in the virtual game community domain" (Guo & Barnes, 2007, p. 74). Furthermore Guo and Barnes focus on investigating issues that relate to buying virtual goods and therefore do not investigate other concepts that can be part of the virtual world experience such as social networking, collaborative actions and so on.

Zhou et al. (2010) adopted a Uses and Gratification theory, from the mass media consumption domain, as a basis to survey and content analyse the approach to user acceptance factors in Second Life. Three key components were investigated as motivations for user acceptance, these were: utilitarian, hedonic and social motivations (see Hirschman & Holbrook, 1982). They concluded that "the uses and gratifications theory is robust and useful in the development of theoretical

dimensions representative of consumer motivations for social virtual world usage." (Zhou et al. 2010, p. 9).

The work by Lehdonvirta (2009) takes more of a sociological perspective and is focussed on what is involved in the buying of virtual goods and the revenue models required to make such purchases. Specifically, Lehdonvirta used functional, hedonic and social attributes with an "information-oriented sampling" (p. 104) approach to study 14 different online environments, including Second Life, where users can purchase virtual goods. The attributes were identified from the literature on the sociology of consumption and were sub-divided by Lehdonvirta under 9 further distinctions. Lehdonvirta posits these subsets as:

**Functional:** Performance, Functionality
**Hedonic:** Visual appearance and sounds, Background fiction, Provenance, Customisability, Cultural references, Branding
**Social:** Rarity

Further, Lehdonvirta asserts that the functional, hedonic and social attributes can co-exist in the same virtual item with the most prominent determined by the situation. Finally, Lehdonvirta points out that the level of abstraction used in his work could be developed to a finer granularity for investigating a specific virtual good or service.

An entirely different perspective is taken by Luz et al. (2008), who explore the idea of realism in digital gameplay. Luz et al. are highlighted here as they discuss the relationship between the real and virtual focus of a user, as well as what it means to be immersed in a virtual environment. Further they detail the implications of the physical interface being used in order to control and interact with the virtual environment.

Kaplan and Haenlein (2009), considered Second Life as a platform of consumer use and business potential. Their approach was to conduct interviews with Second Life users regarding their social networks, identities and commercial exchange preferences. The authors acknowledge a variety of motivations for Second Life usage, stating them as "the search for diversion, the desire to build personal relationships, the need to learn, and the wish to earn (real-life) money" (Kaplan & Haenlein, 2009, p. 94). Of note here is that their findings point out that "users consider SL less as a mere computer game and more as an extension of their real life, and that they tend to engage in activities that span beyond the single usage occasion".

In conclusion, we can see that when considering the virtual experience, the real-world experience of the user and their interaction with others must also be taken into account. Further, the application of factors from a differing domain when contextually executed can offer a valid approach when used to consider satisfaction as demonstrated by Lehdonvirta (2009). Finally,

## ELICITING CONSUMER SATISFACTION (ECSA), FRAMEWORK DESCRIPTION

As seen in the previous section the real world experience needs to be taken into account, along with social factors, when considering the virtual world experience. The following section of this chapter is a description of our conceptual framework and the components therein.

The framework described here has evolved from prior work by the authors on eliciting consumer satisfaction in the Second Life environment (Shukla et al. 2009 a/b) as well as from the literature. This previous work focussed on the elicitation of consumer satisfaction in arts and cultural exhibitions within Second Life. Exhibitions of this nature were chosen as these types of organisations encompass not-for-profit as well as profit-seeking ventures and the variety of organisational structures that underlie them. Further, the previous work predominantly took the perspective

*Figure 1. The eliciting consumer satisfaction (ECSA) in Second Life framework shows the inter-relation of factors related to the user experience of Second Life*

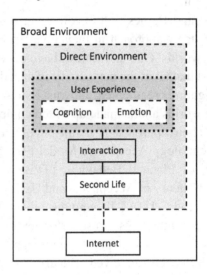

of elicitation, using self-report, in terms of total customer experience, as per Rowley (1999).

Accepting the conclusions by Giese and Cote (2002) consumer satisfaction is a mental state occurring in response to an expectation or experience and which has a distinct temporal aspect to its occurrence. What needs to be considered then is the nature of the factors that contribute to that state of mind, as well as how Second Life environments can best be tailored to encourage that state in a favourable sense. With this in mind a framework for this purpose has been developed, the initial conceptualisation of which is shown in Figure 1. This framework is the basis upon which testing will be undertaken with a view to further refinement as a consequence of the primary data gathered.

The conceptual starting point of the framework is the user along with the mental processes that affect their choice of, and experiences within, Second Life. The environment that the user is accessing Second Life from was then taken into consideration as being an influential factor upon the accessing and experiencing of Second Life.

Next, the functionality of Second Life needed to be taken into account as Second Life can only operate on an internet-connected computer. Finally, factors that impact upon, but are tangential to, the user were acknowledged. All of these factors are described by the seven essential interrelated components of our framework, which are:

1. The broad environment
2. The direct environment
3. The user experience
4. Cognition and emotion during the user experience
5. Interaction with and within Second Life
6. Second Life
7. The Internet

We now discuss these components in the context of Second Life both as a product and as a platform.

## The Broad Environment

The broad environment as shown in Figure 1 is indicative of the 'outside world' and is primarily to take into account the impact on the user of socio-economic, political, natural and geographic factors. An example here is that of legislation that applies to Intellectual Property Rights (IPR). Further, the broad environment is used here to also be indicative of influences such as religious, cultural, familial and peer bonds. These external factors impact on the state of mind of a user and can be perceived as the external world having a direct and indirect bearing on their satisfaction whilst operating within Second Life.

## The Direct Environment

The direct environment here can be understood as the environment that the user is in while operating a computer running Second Life. Essentially this is the user's location, which needs to be considered as this location impacts (Elliot, 2007 a/b) on the user's experience of Second Life.

The direct environment that the user is in while conducting their foray into Second Life needs also to be considered with regard to whether or not that environment is a public or private space. Further, consideration should be given to whether the space is one which is being shared with others and if so, for what purpose. For example, a friend sharing a bottle of wine while watching the user navigate an art exhibition will have an entirely different impact on the user and their state of mind and possibly their level of satisfaction of a given Second Life environment than if the same user was at their office desk during their lunch hour in a busy open plan office. Essentially then, the direct environment component of the framework encompasses not only the physical makeup of the location the user is situated but also the nature and purpose of the environment as well as who else is co-habiting it.

## The User Experience

The utilitarian and hedonic value or opportunities of using Second Life also needs to be considered. Here the utilitarian or functional value can be seen in aspects of Second Life such as the ability to create objects/structures using the in-world building tools as well as opportunities such as group meetings for those that are geographically dispersed or even the navigability through the 3D space of Second Life. Hirschman and Holbrook (1982, p. 92) define hedonic as "those facets of consumer behaviour that relate to the multi-sensory, fantasy and emotive aspects of one's experience". Second Life has many opportunities that allow the user to have such experiences which include issues around escapism, entertainment, identity, avatar creation and modification as well as gender and ethnicity roles, role-play and social masks – in so far as there are layers of separation between the user and any co-respondent.

## Cognition and Emotion

The framework shows how the user experience of consumer satisfaction within Second Life is perceived. Cognition here is the rational thought process, for example making a product choice based on price. However, matters become more complicated as product or service selection can be perceived not just as a matter of cost but rather of value, with value perceptions often being tied in with notions of quality and reputation that are often implicit with brand recognition. The dynamic link between cognition and emotion is well known, if not well understood (Gratch et al. 2009; Niedenthal, 2007; Clore, 2009; Jenkinson, 2007). The following hypothetical scenario exemplifies this: having just had a blazing row with their spouse, a user may be unlikely to report an excellent sense of satisfaction, as the user's general state of mind is likely to be still affected by the conflict. Alternatively, the user may, after said argument, have an overly positive sense of their experience, as immersion into Second Life is being used as an escapist or diversionary tactic.

Further there are physiological factors that can impact upon the level of perceived satisfaction of a user at any given time. These factors include chemical and hormonal imbalances that may be caused by illness, drug usage or poor diet amongst other reasons. Emotion, then, in this framework is the feeling state or affect (Cohen et al. 2008) that a user is experiencing whether or not they are aware of it.

Elicitation of emotional state with regards to consumer satisfaction preference is somewhat more problematic than the total customer experience approach taken previously. Autonomic measurements such as those gained via, for example, the Facial Action Coding System, Electroencephalography or Functional Magnetic Resonance Imaging (Sörensen, 2008) offer immediate measurement of the subject while they are experiencing an emotional state. However there are drawbacks to these approaches, such as interpretation of data, having an experienced tester on staff or the necessity for the subject to be in a laboratory environment during measurement.

Self-report of emotional states is often used in academic as well as marketing research (Sörensen, 2008). The issue here is that the actual emotional state is not being measured, rather it is the user's self-report of their perceived state that is reported. This consideration is deemed acceptable dependant on the reason behind a given research study (Sörensen, 2008) and models have been developed to pursue this type of investigation. Examples of this approach are Mehrabien and Russell's pleasure, arousal, dominance model (1974) or Richins' consumer emotions set (1997).

Also it should be recognised that typically consumer satisfaction in marketing is measured in terms of 'positive feelings'. This work, however, is more concerned with the impact of feelings (often referred to as arousal in the literature) both 'positive' and 'negative', as certain exhibitions may be highly impactful as an experience but have a 'negative' nature such as the 'Suicide Museum' or the 'Holocaust Memorial Museum' exhibitions within Second Life.

## Interaction

Social interaction plays an important part of the Second Life experience. Second Life has a group mechanism built into it that plays a central role in structuring the various social activities that can be performed by avatars in Second Life. A user can, join a group either by invitation, private application or public application. Groups can be joined in Second Life either for free or for a joining fee.

Groups in Second Life share characteristics with Communities of Practice (Lave & Wenger, 1991) which essentially relates to "groups of people who share a concern or a passion for something they do and learn how to do it better as they interact regularly" (Wenger, 2006). Bosua and Scheepers (2002, p. 4) point out that when Communities of Practice: "… are geographically dispersed and cannot communicate face-to-face, some infrastructure is needed to promote collaboration, communication and participation of its members". Further, there are similarities between groups in Second Life and those found in online social networking sites such as Orkut or Facebook. The study of social networks is not a new phenomenon and there is extant literature available in this subject area which now also includes the study of online social networking. The analysis of online social networks is typically focussed on the 'small world' effect, diffusion and clustering with regards to groups and group membership. Graph theory and network theory tend to dominate this area of research as the most applicable tools. The works of Backstrom et al. (2006) and Mislove et al. (2007) are recommended to the reader as a grounding in this field of investigation.

Available within Second Life is a number of in-world communications options. Predominantly these are: instant messaging, text and voice chat, note cards and some in-world objects such as opinion polls. All of these communications options can be accessed via the Second Life interface. This interface also allows for interaction with in-world objects as well as accessing profiles of other users.

Communications with other avatars can be conducted by any of the following:

- Instant messaging (IM) can be used for synchronous or asynchronous communication between avatars. With regard to synchronous communication, when avatars are in close proximity to one another, IM is a form of private messaging in so far as only the parties involved can see the dialogue. IM can also be used for communication with avatars that are online but not in the vicinity; again, only the parties involved are able to view the dialogue. IM can also be employed asynchronously in the event of messaging an avatar when their user is not online. When IM is used in this manner the Second Life interface displays an alert to the communication originator that the intended receiver is off-line. The system will then store the message for display to the receiver when they next login to Second Life, the system can also send a copy of the message to the user by e-mail.

- Second Life emulates open conversation through the use of 'chat'. This chat feature allows for synchronous, written communication between avatars within 20 meters of one another in-world. This is the default chat distance, however, chat can also be shouted or whispered with a change in distance of 100 meters and 10 meters respectively.

- Second Life also offers synchronous communication through the use of 'voice chat' which is an implementation of an in-world voice over IP (VoIP) technology. Voice chat is similar to the written chat of Second Life in that anyone within 60 to 110 meters in-world can hear the conversation dependent upon their user preference settings. The Second Life voice chat technology can also be used for synchronous private communication between avatars through the use of an interface feature known as 'private call', enabling only selected avatars to participate.

- Note cards are virtual objects within Second Life that emulate, as the name suggests, a written note. Used generally for asynchronous communication Note cards can contain written text and hyperlinks and can be transferred between avatars as an in-world object.

- Group communications tools are offered in Second Life that essentially allow for the IM feature to be applied to and across a whole group membership.

Therefore, interaction can occur in a number of different ways depending upon how the user is using the technologies available with Second

Life. Further, it is of interest here as to how users interact as well as why they choose to do so using this particular platform.

## Second Life

The internal economy of Second Life is based on a real-world equivalency rate and allows users to exchange their money into or out from Second Life. One important point here is that in-world monetary transactions can only be enacted using the supplied mechanism. Second Life then, as the name suggests, is a mediated reflection of our world to the extent that people interact with one another and go about pursuing their interests. For these reasons we can consider that the Second Life element of the framework to also have a direct and broad environment, in as far as the direct Second Life environment is the specific location of an avatar and the broad environment is composed of socio-economic factors and such like that can impact user experience but is not something necessarily in their control.

The idea of *place* is a difficult concept to define (Gration et al. 2008), however, a good starting point would be "Place = Space + Meaning" (Harrison as cited in Gration et al. 2008, p. 2). The distinction made here is that between the direct environment that the user is in and that of the virtual space that the user is navigating via their avatar. Harrison calls this a complex form of hybrid space and clarifies this concept as:

*A hybrid space is one which comprises both physical and virtual space, and in action is framed simultaneously by the physical space, the virtual space and the relationship between the two. (Harrison & Dourish, 1996, p. 6)*

This distinction between the real and virtual space becomes less clearly distinguished when we take into account that the mediated experience of immersive environments can have a strong psychological impact.

Waterworth and Waterworth explain it thus:

*When we experience strong mediated presence, our experience is that the technology has become part of the self, and the mediated reality part of the other. When this happens, there is no conscious effort of access to information, nor effort of action to overt responses. We can perceive and act directly, as if unmediated. (2008, p. 61)*

Within the Second Life environment an avatar can also interact with scripted objects, any virtual object within Second Life can have a script embedded. Almost all objects seen within Second Life have been user generated, this includes; buildings, plant life, vehicles and clothing. These objects are typically created in-world from the suite of 3D building tools available. Second Life uses 'prims', a primitive based approach to 3D construction, essentially the use of basic three dimensional geometric shapes that the user can alter and allocate a texture to as required. The scripting language used in Second Life is called Linden Scripting Language (LSL). Similar in syntax to C or Java, LSL is event-oriented rather than being object-oriented. Scripting is added to objects to either control that object in a specific way and/or allow for interaction with users. The most common ways interaction with scripted objects is achieved are:

- Within Second Life, web-based content can be accessed via the inbuilt web browser.
- The chat feature of Second Life can be used to interact with certain scripted objects through the use of text, for example, doors can be scripted to open or close if a user types the phrase "doors open" or "doors close".
- A dialogue menu is an independent script-generated interface that manifests when an avatar interacts with a given scripted object.

- Right-hand click context menus are represented within Second Life as pie menus which contain eight subdivisions, three of which can be used by a script to add further interactivity to a given scripted object.
- Head up displays, commonly referred to as HUDs, are virtual objects that can be worn in a similar way to clothing in Second Life. However, unlike clothing, head up displays can only be seen within the main Second Life interface of the user whose avatar is wearing it.
- Scripted objects can act as proximity sensors, for example emulating the sensors of automatic doors in the real world, since LSL is driven by events.

Therefore, the Second Life direct environment is important to consider due to the opportunities offered for the customisation of content. Further, the 'place' that the avatar is located in at any given time also needs to be taken into account as it can affect the user experience in terms of their cognition/emotion. Essentially this is the immersive component at work, here distinguishing between sensorial and psychological immersion. With Second Life sensory immersion is via the audio and visual modalities. The psychological immersive aspect of Second Life is similar to that experienced watching a film in so far as a certain level of suspension of disbelief is required. Moreover, communicating either synchronously or asynchronously with others elevates the experience to an involved interactivity that film cannot, as yet, achieve. Indeed, relationships are formed with other avatars and this has essentially the same impact, both positive and negative, that relationships have in the normal day-to-day world.

## The Internet

As Second Life uses a client server architecture which operates on internet technology, for example, the client server communication is achieved through the use of the User Datagram Protocol (UDP). As the client server architecture of Second Life operates as a layer upon existing Internet technologies, it is prone to similar failings, the prime example here being that of network lag. Network lag typically occurs when there is high usage or a technical failure on part of the Internet infrastructure between Second Life servers and the user client and is seen in-world as a slowdown or failure of in-world mechanics.

When using Second Life, the use of Internet technologies is not confined to client server data exchange. Scripted objects using LSL can operate outside of Second Life using HTTP, XML-RPC and even email. The Second Life modified Mozilla web browser allows access to web-based content from in-world although until Viewer 2 this was a fairly limited experience.

Second Life allows the use of 'QuickTime' supported streaming media in-world. All Second Life Viewers have streamed media playback preference settings. However, only the owner of a given area can enable this media to be streamed in. The Second Life interface, also known as a Viewer enables communication and interaction in-world, for example the capability for 'web on a prim'. The idea is that web-based media can be assigned as a texture onto a prim, which now makes it much easier for web-based content such as YouTube videos or SlideShare presentations to be made available in-world.

Finally, not only are web-based services often used to bring content into Second Life, there are numerous instances of Second Life created content being used as media on the web. For example, Linden Lab have a Second Life channel on YouTube, the content here is mostly either educational in the use of Second Life or promotional in terms of new features or functionality. However there is also a trend in what is known as machinima, which is the recording of in-world events in the form of an animation and many examples of this can be found on video sharing sites. Indeed Second Life produced machinima has been shown at film festivals and on television, the prime example here being 'Molotov Alva and His Search for the Creator: A Second Life Odyssey' by Douglas Gayeton[2].

Having discussed the various facets that make up the framework, consideration needs to be made of the approach taken to testing it. The next section is a discussion of the results gained from the in-world, semi-structured interviews that were conducted. The foci for the interviews were developed from the previous work on total customer experience and elaborated using the current framework.

## EVALUATING AND REFINING THE FRAMEWORK

This section describes how data was collected and interpreted. After a description of how in-world interviews were conducted, a synopsis is given of the results and an explanation of the interpretation of the data.

A series of semi-structured interviews were conducted in-world; either as one-to-one or group interviews. All interviewees freely volunteered their time to participate. Interviewees were recruited in-world at the 'University of Bedfordshire' and the 'London Hyde Park' locations. The latter location was chosen as it is a popular destination for a wide variety (age, geographic location, etc.) of Second Life users. Interviewees were made aware of the study being conducted and its purpose. Interviewees were also made aware of ethical and privacy issues and how they would be dealt with. It should be noted that real world identity/demographic questions were not pursued. The interviews were predominantly conducted in text chat although the use of the in-world voice chat system was used on occasion; when this was the case a transcription was made. It was felt that keeping to the mode of communication that was preferred by the interviewee would make the experience more comfortable for them to participate in.

Interviewees were asked a variety of questions about their Second Life usage, experiences and preferences. The interviews took a semi-structured approach in so far as a prompt sheet was used by the interviewer as a reference to keep conversations from straying too far off topic. These prompts were used not only as a basic structure for the interview but to also aid elaboration on a given point. The following shows our approach:

- How long have you been using SL?
- How many avatars do you have?
  - If you have more than one, do your avatars have different characters?
- Is your avatar like the real you?
- What kinds of things, both positive and negative, affect your experience of SL?
  - How do you deal with that?
  - How do you feel about that?
- What things are important to your use of SL?
- How do you see yourself in SL?
- Do you have friends in SL that you know in real life?
- Where is your favourite place in SL and what makes it so?
- Where do you normally access SL from?
- How much time do you think you spend in SL?
- How do you finance your Second Life purchases?
- Which viewer are you using?
- What was the last thing you bought in SL?
  - What made you buy that particularly?
  - Can you elaborate on why/where/what made you buy that?

Chat logs and transcriptions from the interviews were used as the basis for thematic/content analysis. This was undertaken by extracting the interviewee responses from the chat logs to construct response units. The response units were constructed either from a standalone response or from fragment responses. With fragmented responses,

*Table 1. Framework components, response rates and identified themes. Responses are shown as the number of response units that related to a framework component. Emergent themes are shown with the frequency with which they appeared.*

| Component | Responses | Themes (frequencies) |
|---|---|---|
| Broad | 52 (28%) | peers (15), geography (9), cultural (9), work/employment (4), family (3), finances (3), pastimes (3), infrastructure (2), technological (2), production (1), purchase (1) |
| Direct | 20 (11%) | accessories (6), natural (5), employment (3), comparative (2), finances (2), technology (2) |
| Hedonic | 28 (15%) | tastes (14), entertainment (4), exploration (4), aversion (2), desire (2), satisfaction (1), mask (1) |
| Utility | 14 (7%) | opportunity (4), functionality (3), rationalising (3), employment (1), knowledge (1), cost (1), finances (1) |
| Identity | 55 (29%) | perception (14), role-play (10), avatar (9), differentiation (8), personality (7), physical (4), social (2), taste (1) |
| Cognition | 36 (19%) | deduction (9), summation (8), identification (5), intent (4), query (3), timeframe (3), interpretation (3), self-determination (1) |
| Emotion | 15 (8%) | contempt (6), fear (3), pleasure (2), closeness (1), disappointment (1), humour (1), appreciative (1) |
| Interaction | 48 (25%) | meeting (9), judgement (6), pass-time (6), real-life (5), co-operation (4), frequency (4), lack (3), demands (3), undesired (2), gifting (2), network (2), trepidation (1), uncertainty (1) |
| Second Life | 115 (61%) | usage (23), distinction (21), interface (16), locations (14), financial (12), content (12), relations (8), searching (6), entertainment (3) |
| Internet | 16 (8%) | applications (6), streaming (6), availability (3), integration (1) |

where a response was separated over a number of chat lines, the response would be re-assembled into a single unit. In all, the 10 interviewees produced 189 response units each of which were aligned with the framework components. Adjustments were then made as necessary to the framework components in so far as the user experience component was sub-divided into hedonic, utilitarian and identity statement groups. All three of which were treated as an individual component. A process of inductive thematic analysis was then performed on each response unit in a given component area. The identified themes, their frequencies and the number of responses for each of the framework components can be seen in Table 1.

The percentages shown in Table 1 in the Responses column refer to the percentage of the 189 response units. Examples for each of the framework components follow, with selected extracts from the 189. The comments made by the interviewees are given here verbatim. Two abbreviations often used are *sl* for Second Life and *rl* for

real life. Further, the final example shown, towards the end of this section, is in relation to how interviewees adapted their communication to make use of the medium.

For the broad environment, 28% of all response units related to this component and 11 themes within this component were identified. The first two examples show how familial bonds have a bearing on Second Life usage. The third example is related to pastimes that are in competition with the use of Second Life. The fourth example here pertains to internet cafes in the country of the interviewee, this having implications for how and where Second Life can be accessed.

1. i have a friend that lives in ohio...we keep in touch in sl alot

2. things have been busy with family lately my sister got married and my other sister had a baby so that takes up time that i would rather spend in rl

3.   I like to camp and hike and read and travel go to live music
4.   they really dont have them here [internet cafes] like they do in Europe I went to France a few years ago, and they had tons.

For the direct environment component 11% of the response units were aligned to this component and here 6 themes were identified. The first two examples relate to equipment used to access Second Life as well as related items in the vicinity. The third example is about the weather, note the sad 'smiley' and the fourth example is about an accessory to hand for the interviewee.

1.   laptop, home and I recently bought a new Laptop in order to take it to my sons, if necessary as I am /was addicted to SL
2.   and in parallel I have a second computer - books - etc
3.   its raining:(
4.   Social Media Bible yes it is a good book

The hedonic user experience component relates to those factors that affect the user experience of Second Life. The component had 15% of response units align with it; 7 different themes were identified during analysis. The first example indicates the users' disposition to a given Second Life environment based on personal taste. The second example relates to aversion and disappointment felt by the interviewee based on their perception of certain occurrences during their experience of Second Life. The third example is the response given when asked about recent Second Life purchases.

1.   if i had to pick 1 shop it would be atomic plays great music as well =P its got my style of clothing... same as rl well... for the most part
2.   thats another thing i HATE about sl my fav sims being deleted or something along the lines i had a fav beach...noww its some free sex paradise or something had some good

memories in those places =P eh well... such is life
3.   a sexy kitty outfit

The utilitarian user experience component of the framework describes elements of the functional value in using Second Life. Here 11% of response units fell into this component description and 7 themes were identified. The first example is indicative of the interviewees' frustration using the tools available in Second Life. The second example is in response to being asked why the interviewee uses Second Life to run a virtual education business.

1.   skills I do not know how to do most of the scripting - and building what I still miss - is that someone tells you how to create .. I am kind of stuck in a wheel
2.   immersive no travel costs no office costs easier to learn not easier to teach lots of work

The identity user experience component had 29% of all response units align with it and 8 different themes were identified. The first three examples for the user experience (identity) describe facets of how the interviewees perceive themselves physically as well as in the virtual sense. The fourth and fifth examples relate to how the interviewees engage in role-play, shown here as taking different identities. The final example is the explanation by an interviewee in regard to not actively choosing role-play.

1.   i have red hair in rl...well now i do lol would youl ike to see a pic? yup that'sme
2.   its close i have bigger hips in rl lol... i dress about the same no lip peircing in rl though yeah I am not as slim lol
3.   as a matter of fact, I made an other shape looking like my own body .. in rl
4.   I have lots of accounts, all different they're all different parts of me

5.   yes, very different different ages and genders A few furry avatars, but not generally furry as is Dragon play... the role play gets old

6.   *its hard enough being myself, let alone pretending to be something that im not*

The cognition component of the framework relates to rational thought processes predominantly to do with choice. Here 19% of all response units related to this component and 8 themes were identified during analysis. The first example is one that expresses self-determination as well as aversion. The second example is deductive in nature while the third example is summative with regards to skill acquisition.

1.   i'm SO over being harassed for pixel sex. i should be allowed to have a 'sexy' avie without being sent dirty pics, etc lol

2.   I think SL will be unstable for a few months, as they transition to HTTP delivery of textures, while leaving everything else through the LL protocol

3.   still - I have to learn lots of thing

There were 8% of response units which related to the emotion component; from the 15 responses 7 themes were identified. The first example for the emotion component of the framework relates to the depth of friendship ties that this interviewee feels. The second example describes the pleasure felt by this interviewee for a certain style of accessorising their avatar and role-play; the term 'neko' is a Japanese word meaning cat, and in Second Life whole communities exist around the concept of being part person and part cat. The third example here refers to the aversion the interviewee felt towards unsolicited sexual advances whilst using Second Life. The fourth example refers to a sense of 'hurt feelings' after a comment made by another user as well as describing the interviewee's feeling towards the matter.

1.   my friends... i know it's sl, but i've become as close to some of them as some friends in rl silly i know =P

2.   i love nekos! it's cute, sexy, love nekos!

3.   old man creepers that want to get some (if ya know what i mean)

4.   *most of my lindens went for the skin which someone here just said my AV looks terrible and really new but I dont care I think it looks good*

The interaction component had 25% of response units relate to it; from these response units 13 themes were identified. The first two examples for the interaction component of the framework are descriptive of the preference by these interviewees in using Second Life as a medium to spend time with family or friends that are geographically distant from them. The third example is one faced by many new users of Second Life and that is a perceived lack of interaction by other users. The fourth, fifth and sixth examples are indicative of 'sense of community' be they entirely virtual or with an anchor to outside interests. The seventh and eighth examples are from the same interviewee and relate to how this person aspires to building up businesses that are entirely or partially based within Second Life.

1.   probably to my house =P hang out there with friends i have a friend that lives in ohio... we keep in touch in sl alot go to my little sl home and watch videos etc

2.   two but they live in france so its easier to talk in the game

3.   i have noticed that most people dont talk to each other they just dont talk. you are the 4th person besides my friends that has talked

4.   yes there is a buddhist sim that I enjoy ts very relaxing and the music is nice its a nice community

5.   well, i get to meet interesting people... and... get to help out with new residents arrive

6. I have also met some native americans because I translate in rl for native americans in an association
7. I have been using SL for 2 y and 9 month and only build up my network which is .. a long list of friends about 500 all over the world
8. yes and I have even made rl money because I sold one of my products to an american guy

The Second Life component of the framework had 61% of response units relate to it; from 115 responses that were applicable to this component 9 themes were identified. The first example given here for the Second Life component of the framework describes typical usage by this interviewee as well as an appreciation of their Second Life experiences. The second example has a somewhat contrasting perception as to what the Second Life experience can on occasion include. The third example relates to whether the interviewee would transfer real world funds into the Second Life economy. The fourth example is indicative of the amount of time spent in Second Life, while the fifth and sixth examples describe annoyances felt by these interviewees with regards to the functionality of Second Life. The seventh example is indicative of a positive aspect of Second Life functionality and the eighth example refers to in-world businesses operated by the interviewee in order to generate money to use for their own Second Life purchases. The final example refers to content available within Second Life. This example is of further interest due to how the interviewee mentions "*the shoes i have on*", referring to the shoes being worn by their avatar and is indicative of notions around identity and immersiveness.

1. i like to find the silliest/weirdest sims i can...and just check them out. some pretty entertaining stuff on here. amazing to think the time and thought that has been put into these places
2. this was the annoying side of SL you can not have a bf - and talk to someone, without having problems
3. I am not sure if I would it just depends on if I really wanted something
4. it's quite variable some days 6-8 hours, but i'll go days without
5. it seems like the destination guide only leads you to vampire areas or mazes
6. laggy ^_^
7. The main thing I like about Viewer 2 is the better support for outfits
8. I have earned my money on sl with classes - and shows I have had a model agency
9. ummmm i think the shoes i have on, like the style i suppose

The internet component of the framework had 8% of response units align with its description, from these responses 4 themes were identified. The first two examples of comments made by interviewees that relate to the Internet component of the framework relate to the use of streaming media being ported into Second Life. The third example relates to the use of other technologies used by this interviewee to communicate with friends made in Second Life. The final example relates to the use of a third party web site in order for this interviewee to transfer funds into the Second Life economy.

1. i like haning at Alt7 and hang at Hyde quite a bit...where i met my bf=P it's an Indie rock club yup...love finding new music!
2. go to my little sl home and watch videos etc
3. a few, I also have in skype but, I never met them live
4. I will have to buy lindens soon and will use Paysafe card because I do not have a credit card

Finally, it is relevant to note that there were 36 response units that contained abbreviations, these were predominantly the use of *rl*, *sl* or *lol* to indicate 'real life', Second Life and laugh out loud. There were 18 response units that contained some form of emoticon (Walther and D'Addario 2001) and two response units contained an in-channel adaptation to highlight either a comment or the user. These adaptations appeared as:

1.    *important*
2.    [14:19] Samanda XXX: <---- *will use emerald till it dies*

The second adaptation shown is a metalinguistic sign and is indicative of an in-channel adaptation that is using the layout and functionality of the interface to express meaning. This example shows how in the Second Life chat interface a timestamp and avatar identifier are given before the message content. Further, the example shows how this interface design feature has been used to highlight the message and differentiate this message content from others as well as replace the identifier 'I'. It should also be noted that the use of capitalisation and/or punctuation were often discarded by the interviewees, most likely in order to speed along their responses. In all 56 (30%) of the response units contained one or more in-channel adaptations.

## REFINED ECSA FRAMEWORK

What became apparent during the course of the interviews and the subsequent analysis was that the framework required further development. This was apparent especially with regards to some of the terminology used for the framework components. The main areas under consideration here were the terms 'broad' and 'direct'. The term direct environment was originally envisioned to encapsulate the current place the user was in both physically and mentally, the term broad environment was

an extrapolation of that concept to include those factors that were elsewhere or tangential.

The subdivision of the user experience component has already been described, through the inclusion of hedonic, utilitarian and identity components. Another difficulty that arose during the analysis was that there was no clear distinction available in the framework to differentiate responses in terms of understanding the user's experiences, current situation and future aspirations. Therefore the refined ECSA framework, Figure 2, has these adaptations incorporated into it.

## FUTURE RESEARCH DIRECTIONS

This section provides a description of how others can use the ECSA framework as well as the wider context in which the ECSA framework described can be used. The in-world Second Life environment is made up from a complex of unit parts having distinctive traits and therefore addressing different user needs, such as; role-play, shopping, socialising or education. The ECSA framework developed in this work is a means to understand the factors involved that affect the use of Second Life either as a consumer product from Linden Lab or as used by those who operate a virtual business in-world.

Through conducting interviews with the intended audience and categorising the responses in alignment with the ECSA framework (see Table 1), both platform and product developers can better understand their audience needs and motivations. Addressing those needs and motivations would be contextual to that audience. Therefore, any implementation of functionality, aesthetics, usability and so on based on this research would be customised or bespoke to the requirements of that audience. Specifically, any investigation along these lines should be particularly looking for patterns in the results.

When Second Life is perceived as a product, the ECSA framework given here can be used to

*Figure 2. The refined ECSA framework as a consequence of the primary data analysis. Temporal concepts as well as factors found during analysis have been incorporated.*

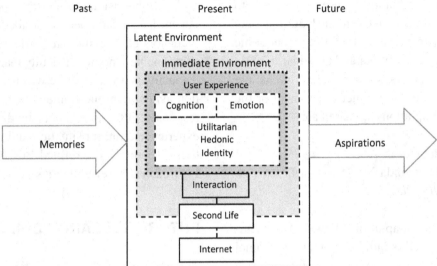

identify areas of attraction and factors that cause aversion amongst the user community. With these factors identified the usability and functionality of Second Life can be developed enabling users to better pursue their own objectives.

With regards to Second Life as a platform for operating an in-world business, the ECSA framework can be used similarly to identify attraction and aversion factors among the intended audience. With these factors identified the business operator could implement functional or process changes to increase attraction and/or decrease aversion as necessary. For example, a Second Life store owner could interview a number of store patrons as well as general Second Life users. Applying interview responses to the framework, see Table 1, can give the store owner vital business intelligence. It would be particularly useful for the store owner to compare and contrast the results from both sets of interviews, see Hood (1993). This approach of interviewing patrons as well as others is to gain a deeper understanding of why those patrons frequent that store and why others may not. Further this approach will identify how

to improve the store for those that do frequent it and to attract those who as yet do not.

Also, the identification of attraction and aversion factors through the use of the ECSA framework can be applied to in-world spaces. Here both Linden Lab and in-world business operators could engineer or adapt in-world spaces to further engender the mood of satisfaction amongst their users.

Finally, the aim in developing this framework was to understand the complex and inter-related factors that affect the use of Second Life, from the perspective of consumer satisfaction. One issue that has become apparent during the development of the framework is that it could in fact be used to consider a much wider variety of social interaction within online environments. Indeed with the growth in recent interest of virtual worlds by mainstream games console developers such as Microsoft (Xbox 360 Experience) and Sony (Play-Station Home) the ECSA framework described is flexible enough to be used for a variety of internet based platforms. Our framework can be adapted by replacing the Second Life component with a different component, for example, the browser based virtual environment ourWorld[3] which is aimed predominantly at the teenage market. However, the appropriateness of this type of adaption is yet to be tested. Here it should be noted that using the framework as guidance for investigating consumer satisfaction is particularly important to appropriately identify needs and motivations when an intended audience is deemed vulnerable.

## CONCLUSION

In this chapter we have described the development of a framework for eliciting consumer satisfaction perceptions in the context of the social virtual world Second Life. This was undertaken as the significance of virtual worlds is increasing, as can be seen in their uptake by leading consumer technology developers (Lehdonvirta, 2009). Moreover, social virtual worlds are now being employed to develop a sense of community among users (Lehdonvirta, 2009). Therefore the understanding of a key business concept such as consumer satisfaction among the user community is a necessity. With this in mind, a framework has been developed based on prior work such as that by Rowley (1999), Zhou et al. (2010), by Lehdonvirta (2009), Luz et al. (2008) as well as Giese and Cote (2002) amongst others.

Our initial ECSA framework identified seven components that are interrelated and provide the fuller context of the user experience of Second Life. The approach taken by the framework allows it to be used as a means to consider the user experience of Second Life both as a product and a platform.

Using this framework as a starting point, interviews have been conducted from among the user community. A semi-structured approach was taken for the interviews in order to explore the depth of experiences available for elicitation from the interviewees. The gathered data has been analysed in the context of the framework components. Emergent themes from the analysis revealed that further aspects of the user experience needed to

be considered. Therefore the framework has been refined as a consequence of these emergent themes and now incorporates a temporal aspect as well as a finer granularity to understanding the factors that affect the consumer satisfaction of Second Life.

## ACKNOWLEDGMENT

The authors would like to extend their thanks to Dr Peter Norrington from the University of Bedfordshire for his assistance during the completion of this chapter.

## REFERENCES

Bigné, J. E., Mattila, A. S., & Andreu, L. (2008). The impact of experiential consumption cognitions and emotions on behavioral intentions. *Journal of Services Marketing*, *22*(4), 303–315. doi:10.1108/08876040810881704

Blanchard, A., & Markus, M. L. (2004). The experienced sense of virtual community: Characteristics and processes. *ACM SIGMIS Database*, *35*(1), 64–79. doi:10.1145/968464.968470

Castronova, E. (2006). On the research value of large games: Natural experiments in Norrath and Camelot. *CESifo Working Paper Series No. 1621*. Retrieved from http://ssrn.com/abstract=87557

Chevalier, J. A., & Mayzlin, D. (2006). The effect of word of mouth on sales: Online book reviews. *JMR, Journal of Marketing Research*, *43*(3), 345–354. doi:10.1509/jmkr.43.3.345

Clore, G. L., & Palmer, J. (2009). Affective guidance of intelligent agents: How emotion controls cognition. *Cognitive Systems Research*, *10*(1), 21–30. doi:10.1016/j.cogsys.2008.03.002

Cohen, J. B., Pham, M. T., & Andrade, E. B. (2008). The nature and role of affect in consumer behavior. In Haugtvedt, C. P., Herr, P., & Kardes, F. (Eds.), *Handbook of consumer psychology* (pp. 297–348). Erlbaum.

De Ruiter, J. P., Rossignol, S., Vuurpijl, L., Cunningham, D. W., & Levelt, W. J. M. (2003). SLOT: A research platform for investigating multimodal communication. *Behavior Research Methods, Instruments, & Computers, 35*(3), 408–419. doi:10.3758/BF03195518

Ducheneaut, N., Wen, M., Yee, N., & Wadley, G. (2009). *Body and mind: A study of avatar personalization in three virtual worlds.* 27th Annual CHI Conference on Human Factors in Computing Systems (CHI 2009). Boston, USA.

Elliot, A. J., & Maier, M. A. (2007). Color and psychological functioning. *Current Directions in Psychological Science, 16*, 250–254. doi:10.1111/j.1467-8721.2007.00514.x

Elliot, A. J., Maier, M. A., Moller, A. C., Friedman, R., & Meinhardt, J. (2007). Color and psychological functioning: The effect of red on performance attainment. *Journal of Experimental Psychology. General, 136*, 154–168. doi:10.1037/0096-3445.136.1.154

Gerhard, M., Moore, D., & Hobbs, D. (2004). Embodiment and copresence in collaborative interfaces. *International Journal of Human-Computer Studies, 61*(4), 453–480. doi:10.1016/j.ijhcs.2003.12.014

Giese, J., & Cote, J. (2002). Defining consumer satisfaction. *Academy of Marketing Science Review, 1*, •••. Retrieved from http://www.amsreview.org/amsrev/theory /giese00-01.html.

Gratch, J., Marsella, S., & Petta, P. (2009). Modeling the antecedents and consequences of emotion. *Journal of Cognitive Systems Research, 10*(1), 1–5. doi:10.1016/j.cogsys.2008.06.001

Gration, D., Foster, D., & Raciti, M. (2008). *Emotion and place: A consumer perspective in the context of hallmark events.* Council for Australian University Tourism and Hospitality Education.

Guo, Y., & Barnes, S. (2007). Why people buy virtual items in Virtual Worlds with real money. *Advances in Information Systems, 38*(4), 69–75.

Harrison, S., & Dourish, P. (1996). Re-place-ing space: The roles of place and space in collaborative systems. In M. S. Ackerman, (Ed.), *Proceedings of the 1996 ACM Conference on Computer Supported Cooperative Work,* Boston, Massachusetts, United States, November 16 - 20, 1996, CSCW '96, (pp. 67-76). New York, NY: ACM.

Hemp, P. (2006). Avatar-based marketing. *Harvard Business Review, 84*(6), 48–56.

Hirschman, E. C., & Holbrook, M. B. (1982). Hedonic consumption: Emerging concepts, methods and propositions. *Journal of Marketing, 46*(3), 92–102. doi:10.2307/1251707

Hood, M. G. (1993). *After 70 years of audience research, what have we learned? Who comes to museums, who does not, and why? Visitor Studies: Theory, Research and Practice.* Visitor Studies Association.

Jenkinson, A. (2007). Evolutionary implications for touchpoint planning as a result of neuroscience: A practical fusion of database marketing and advertising. *Journal of Database Marketing & Customer Strategy Management, 14*, 164–185. doi:10.1057/palgrave.dbm.3250054

Kaplan, A. M., & Haenlein, M. (2009). Consumer use and business potential of virtual worlds: The Case of "Second Life". *International Journal on Media Management, 11*(3), 93–101. doi:10.1080/14241270903047008

Langerak, F., Verhoef, P. C., Verlegh, P., & de Valck, K. (2004). Satisfaction and participation in virtual communities. *Advances in Consumer Research. Association for Consumer Research (U. S.)*, *31*, 56–57.

Lehdonvirta, V. (2009). Virtual item sales as a revenue model: Identifying attributes that drive purchase decisions. *Electronic Commerce Research*, *9*, 97–113. doi:10.1007/s10660-009-9028-2

Linden, T. (2009). *The Second Life economy - First quarter 2009 in detail*. Retrieved 10th September, 2009, from https://blogs.secondlife.com/community/ features/blog/2009/04/16/the-second-life-economy--first-quarter-2009-in-detail

Luz, F., Damásio, M. J., & Gouveia, P. (2008). *Realism in gameplay: Digital fiction and embodiment*. In *Proceeding of the 2nd ACM International Workshop on Story Representation, Mechanism and Context*. SRMC '08, (pp. 1-8). New York, NY: ACM.

Meharabien, A., & Russell, J. A. (1974). *An approach to environmental psychology*. Cambridge, MA: MIT Press.

Moore, R. J., Gathman, C., Ducheneaut, N., & Nickell, E. (2007). *Coordinating joint activity in avatar-mediated interaction*. 25th Annual Conference on Human Factors in Computing Systems (CHI 2007). San Jose, USA.

Niedenthal, P. M. (2007). Embodying emotion. *Science*, *316*(5827), 1002. doi:10.1126/science.1136930

Oviatt, S. (1999). Ten myths of multimodal interaction. *Communications of the ACM*, *42*(11), 74–81. doi:10.1145/319382.319398

Parsons, C. (2007). Web-based surveys: Best practices based on the research literature. *Visitor Studies*, *10*(1), 13–33. doi:10.1080/10645570701263404

Preece, J. (2000). *Online communities: Designing usability, supporting sociability*. Chichester, UK: John Wiley & Sons.

Richins, M. L. (1997). Measuring emotions in consumption experience. *The Journal of Consumer Research*, 24.

Rowley, J. (1999). Measuring total customer experience in museums. *International Journal of Contemporary Hospitality Management*, *11*(6), 303–308. doi:10.1108/09596119910281801

Ryan, G., & Bernard, H. (2003). Techniques to identify themes. *Field Methods*, *15*(1), 85–109. doi:10.1177/1525822X02239569

Shukla, M., Bessis, N., Conrad, M., & Clapworthy, G. (2009a). *Development of a customer satisfaction model for enabling e-collaboration in Second Life*. IADIS International Conference on Computer Science and Information Systems, Web Based Communities. Algarve, Portugal.

Shukla, M., Bessis, N., Conrad, M., & Clapworthy, G. (2009b). *A dynamically adaptive, dimensionalised, experience feedback mechanism within second life*. IADIS International Conference on Computer Science and Information Systems, Web Based Communities. Rome, Italy.

Smith, A. (2002,24 October). Mind over matter. *The Guardian*.

Sörensen, J. (2008). *Measuring emotions in a consumer decision-making context – Approaching or avoiding*. Aalborg: Aalborg University, Department of Business Studies.

Strauss, A., & Corbin, J. (1998). *Basics of qualitative research: Grounded theory procedures and techniques*. Thousand Oaks, CA: Sage.

Walther, J., & D'Addario, K. (2001). The impacts of emoticons on message interpretation in computer-mediated communication. *Social Science Computer Review*, *19*(3), 324–347. doi:10.1177/089443930101900307

Waterworth, J. A., & Waterworth, E. L. (2008). Presence in the future. In A Spagnolli & L Gamberini (Eds.), *Proceedings of the 11th International Workshop on Presence* (pp. 61-65). University of Padova, Italy.

Zhou, Z., Jin, X. L., Vogel, D., Guo, X., & Chen, X. (2010). *Individual motivations for using social virtual worlds: An exploratory investigation in Second Life*. Hawaii International Conference on System Sciences.

## ADDITIONAL READING

Ardura, R., Lopez, M., Francisco, J., Huertas, L. (2010). Going with the consumer towards the social Web environment: a review of extant knowledge. *International Journal of Electronic Marketing and Retailing*. pp. 1741-1025.

Backstrom, L., Huttenlocher, D., Kleinberg, J., & Lan, X. (2006). Group formation in large social networks: membership, growth, and evolution. *Proceedings of the 12th ACM SIGKDD international conference on Knowledge discovery and data mining*. Philadelphia, United States of America, pp. 44-54.

Bitner, M. J., Zeithaml, V. A., & Gremler, D. D. (2010). Technology's Impact on the Gaps Model of Service Quality. *Handbook of Service Science*. pp. 197-218.

De Souza, C. S., & Preece, J. (2004). A framework for analyzing and understanding online communities. *Interacting with Computers. The Interdisciplinary Journal of Human-Computer Interaction, 16*(3), 579–610.

Gajendra, S., & Sun, W. (2010). Second Life: A Computer Mediated Environment for Communication and E-Business Management. *2010 International Conference on Challenges in Environmental Science and Computer Engineering*, pp. 431-434.

Lakoff, G., & Johnson, M. (1980). *Metaphors we live by*. Chicago: University of Chicago Press.

Mackenzie, K., Buckby, S., & Irvine, H. (2009). A framework for evaluating business lead users' virtual reality innovations in Second Life. *Electronic Commerce Research, 9*(3), 183–202. doi:10.1007/s10660-009-9035-3

Preece, J. (2000). *Online Communities: Designing Usability, Supporting Sociability*. New York: John Wiley & Sons.

Rheingold, H. (2000) The Virtual Community: Homesteading on the Electronic Frontier. The MIT Press; Rev Sub edition.

Wilson, M. (2002). Six Views of Embodied Cognition. *Psychonomic Bulletin & Review, 9*(4), 625–636. doi:10.3758/BF03196322

## KEY TERMS AND DEFINITIONS

**Avatar:** This is a general term used for the graphical in-world representation of the user. The original use of the word Avatar comes from Hindu mythology where it was used as the name for an incarnation of the Devine or an aspect of the Godhead.

**Bespoke:** Here we use the term to mean - customised for.

**Consumer Satisfaction:** There are a variety of definitions available in the literature for consumer satisfaction depending on the focus and discipline that the authors have come from. Giese & Cote (2002) analysed 20 definitions of consumer satisfaction from the literature. Based on their investigation Giese & Cote proposed that: consumer satisfaction is an emotional or cognitive response. That this response is due to their particular focus, expectation, or consumption experience and finally that the response occurs at a particular time, after consumption, after choice, based on previous experience. This 'meta-definition' is the one used for this chapter.

**Elicit:** Here the term is used to mean - to draw out. In this chapter we use semi-structured interviews to find out the views of our interviewees about different issues based on the framework we developed.

**Social Virtual World:** A social virtual world is distinct from Massive Multiplayer Online Role Playing Games such as World of Warcraft and Everquest, although both allow for computer mediated shared experiences where users can interact with one another. Within social virtual worlds the user, represented in world by an avatar, determines what they want to do without an explicit storyline, plot or the necessity to achieve pre-determined goals.

**Total Customer Experience:** This is a comprehensive approach to customer experience management. For example Rowley (1999) uses the Total Customer Experience approach to analyse the visitor experience at two different types of museum. This type of analysis considers as many of the issues as possible that make up the customer experience. These can include the first point of contact (reception/website/phone call/etc) through the rest of the customer visit; here car parking and washroom facilities are also included as well as lighting, seating capacity and so on.

**Viewer:** The Second Life interface, also known as a Viewer, enables communication and interaction in world. In late February 2010, Linden Lab released their Viewer 2, which took a new approach to the Second Life interface design compared to earlier versions. This new interface design has many similarities with web browsers in terms of navigation and although not mandatory as yet, older Viewer versions are getting less official support.

## ENDNOTES

1    See: http://massively.joystiq.com/2010/06/26/the-virtual-whirl-a-brief-history-of-second-life/

2    See: http://www.youtube.com/watch?v=-e716rQAdXw

3    See: http://ourworld.com

# Chapter 17
# Finding Similar Users in Facebook

**Pasquale De Meo**
*University of Messina, Italy*

**Emilio Ferrara**
*University of Messina, Italy*

**Giacomo Fiumara**
*University of Messina, Italy*

## ABSTRACT

*Online social networks are rapidly asserting themselves as popular services on the Web. A central point is to determine whether two distinct users can be considered similar, a crucial concept with interesting consequences on the possibility to accomplish targeted actions like, for example, political and social aggregations or commercial promotions. In this chapter, the authors propose an approach in order to estimate the similarity of two users based on the knowledge of social ties (i.e., common friends and groups of users) existing among users, and the analysis of activities (i.e., social events) in which users are involved. For each of these indicators, authors draw a local measure of user similarity, which takes into account only their joint behaviours. After this, the chapter considers the whole network of relationships among users along with local values of similarities and combine them to obtain a global measure of similarity. Applying the Katz coefficient, a popular parameter introduced in Social Science research, carries out such a computation. Finally, similarity values produced for each social activity are merged into a unique value of similarity by applying linear regression.*

DOI: 10.4018/978-1-61350-444-4.ch017

## INTRODUCTION

Online social networks like Facebook, My Space, YouTube or Linkedin are rapidly emerging as one of the most popular services on the Web. These systems are able to capture a significant portion of Web users: for instance as of January 2011, Facebook counts more than 500 millions active users and about 50% of active users log on to Facebook in any given day[1].

Facebook users are allowed to publish online profiles describing both *demographic data* (e.g., place and date of birth) as well as *interests*. In addition, users may be involved in a large number of social activities like getting in touch with other people and creating friendship relationships with them, create groups with the goal of raising public awareness on political or social themes, sponsoring an event or declaring to participate to it and so on.

A central problem in this scenario is to determine whether two users can be considered *similar*. A tool capable of correctly identifying similar users is advantageous for many purposes. We can, in fact, identify people who share the same political and social ideas and suggest them to form groups in such a way to better promote and plead their causes. We can suggest new possible friendships to users in some way connected by common interests, activities, etc. We can find out in a social crowd, people who can possibly form groups representing a threat for the society because sharing extremist views in particular contexts, such as terrorism, criminal behaviours, etc. We could predict the connections and the interactions, which are likely to occur in the near future among similar users (Liben-Nowell & Kleinberg, 2007). From a commercial standpoint, the identification of groups of users tied by shared interests would be beneficial to promote and diffuse new technologies as well as to advertise commercial products (Kleinberg, 2008).

The problem of identifying the similarity among users has received a strong attention in many fields of Computer Science (thinks of Recommender Systems (Resnick & Varian, 1997) or User Modelling (Kobsa, 2001)) but it is still largely unexplored in the context of very large social networks like Facebook.

We can put into evidence two research lines devoted to detect similarities between pairs of users. The first research line is based on social relationships (especially friendship relationships) existing among users in order to determine whether they are similar (Geyer, Dugan, Millen, Muller & Freyne, 2008, Spertus, Saham & Buyukkokten, 2005). Similarity derives from two different and competing factors (Crandall, Cosley, Huttenlocher, Kleinberg & Suri, 2008): social influence (Friedkin, 1998), according to which individuals adopt behaviors exhibited by those individuals they interact with, and homophily (Lazarsfeld & Merton, 1954, Mcpherson, Lovin & Cook, 2001), i.e., the tendency of individuals to create relationships with other individuals who are similar to them. Similarity can express along a broad range of dimensions like age, ethnicity, gender, religion and job. Extensive empirical research shows strong evidence of homophily in real contexts (Currarini, Jackson & Pin, 2009); for instance, a study on 12,067 people carried out between 1971 and 2003 indicated that a person has a high chance of being obese if her friends are obese too (Christakis & Fowler, 2007).

In online social networks like Facebook, friendship relationships are still a reliable indicator of similarity between two users but they are not enough. In fact, since the number of users of an online social network is typically huge, if we would select at random a pair of users, there would be a high chance they do not know each other. Selected users would be automatically recognized as not similar. Such a conclusion may be wrong because the two users may share, for instance, the same religious or political convictions and, then, a form of similarity between them could be envisaged.

A second category of approaches relies on the idea that, if two users participate/carry out to the same activities, then a form of similarity exists between them (de Gemmis, Lops, Semeraro & Basile, 2008, De Meo, Quattrone & Ursino, 2010). In particular, information associated with user activities contributes to form a *profile* capable of describing her preferences and needs. The similarity between two users is then computed as the similarity of their profiles. However, as pointed out in (Golder & Huberman, 2006), in online social networks user profiles are generally poor and sparse and, then, the process of computing user similarities may be not accurate (De Meo, Quattrone & Ursino, 2010, Zanardi & Capra, 2008).

In this chapter we propose a *hybrid* approach, i.e., an approach relying both on the knowledge of social ties existing between users and the analysis of the activities in which they are involved.

Our approach is structured in three stages:

- We first propose a range of parameters to compute similarities among Facebook users. We consider various types of activities that a user can carry out: like becoming friends, declaring to join a group, declaring to participate to an event and so on. Given a particular activity like the activity of creating a friendship relationship, we consider the sets $F(u_1)$ and $F(u_2)$ consisting of friends of $u_1$ and $u_2$ on Facebook and compare them to determine the degree of similarity between $u_1$ and $u_2$. In order to make such a comparison we could use appropriate tools like the *Jaccard similarity coefficient* (Sokal & Sneath, 1963, Han & Kamber, 2006). At the end of this stage, we are able to associate each pair of users with an array. Each of the components of the generated array represents the degree of similarity between $u_1$ and $u_2$ according to a specific user activity. As a consequence, our approach for computing similarity is *multi-dimensional* because we manage one

value of similarity for *each* activity we consider.

- The procedure outlined above to compute similarities makes only use of *local knowledge*, i.e., it considers only the joint behaviour of two users to decide to what extent they can be regarded as similar.

Local knowledge may produce rough and inaccurate similarity evaluations. To better clarify this concept, let us consider a simple example. In particular, let us focus only on friendship relationships and let us consider again the users $u_1$ and $u_2$ introduced above and assume they are University students enrolled in the same track but in *different* Universities. In such a case, a form of similarity between them can be envisaged even if they are not likely to share any friend and, then, the Jaccard similarity coefficient of $F(u_1)$ and $F(u_2)$ is zero.

Applying a more refined notion of similarity can solve this drawback. In particular, for any given user activity, we propose to map the space of Facebook users onto a *graph*. Vertices in the graph represent users while edges specify that the two users are somewhat tied according to the specific actions we are considering: for instance, if our reference action is friendship, an edge between two nodes may specify that the corresponding users share at least a particular number of friends. In our reference graph, a path joining two nodes specifies that there exists an indirect chain of relationships between the end-points of the path itself and, then, any path carries in a contribution useful to compute user similarity. We propose to use the *whole ensemble of paths* running between two nodes to compute the similarity of the corresponding users. To this purpose, we use a popular parameter introduced in Social Science called *Katz coefficient* (Katz, 1953).

- In the third stage we propose *some strategies* to merge all the similarity scores into a single and global value, which is then used to determine the final degree of similarity among users.

The plan of the chapter is as follows: we first cover the background about related problem providing a comparison of our approach with similar or related ones. After this we describe in the detail our approach for computing user similarities and we illustrate the experiments we carried out to validate it. Finally, we draw our conclusions.

## BACKGROUND AND RELATED WORK

In the context of online social networks, the problem of detecting whether two users are similar has received a limited attention until now.

Approaches for computing user similarities fall into three main categories, namely: *(i)* Approaches relying on social relationships, *(ii)* Approaches based on the analysis of social activities and *(iii)* Approaches to identifying potential customers.

Our approach is *hybrid*, in the sense that it combines both the features of approaches relying on social relationships and the features of approaches based on the analysis of social activities.

In the following subsections we shall illustrate the main features of each category and, for each category, we highlight the main similarities and differences with our approach.

## Approaches Relying on Social Relationships

A first category of approaches is based on social relationships existing among users. In many cases, this information is instrumental in producing suggestions (e.g., friendship relationships or affiliation to new communities).

In particular, the approach of (Spertus, Saham & Buyukkokten, 2005) analyzes the affiliation of users to multiple virtual communities and suggests them if it is worth or not joining new communities.

To this purpose, their approach considers *Orkut*, a big social network, as reference scenario and experimentally compares the effectiveness of a range of techniques to compute user similarities (e.g., *tf-idf* coefficient or parameters coming from Information Theory).

The *AboutMe* system (Geyer, Dugan, Millen, Muller & Freyne, 2008) is able to complete the profile a user *u* by examining the list of topics used by his acquaintances in a social network. Resulting profiles are more accurate and ultimately, they are relevant to enhance user participation in social activities.

The approach of (Groh & Ehmig, 2007) suggests to use the friendship lists to identify resources relevant to them. In particular, this approach handles the friendship list of a user *u* and the ratings of the users of these lists assigned with an object *o* to predict the rating that *u* would assign to *o*.

Approaches relying on social relationships are able to achieve a high level of accuracy in generating their suggestions (see (Geyer, Dugan, Millen, Muller & Freyne, 2008, Groh & Ehmig, 2007) for an experimental analysis). In addition, these approaches are less plagued by problems like *cold start*.

The effectiveness of these approaches, however, crucially depends on the number of social relationships created by users. In fact, if a user is involved in few friendship relationships, the information at disposal are poor and, then, the quality of suggestions will be inevitably poor.

Our approach merges the analysis of social relationship with *further* type of information (for instance, the affiliation to groups or the participation to events). This kind of information is a precious and reliable indicator to assess whether two users are similar or not even if they do not know directly: for instance, we can envisage a particular form of similarity between two users if they, driven by shared political or social motivations, decide to join an event even if no friendship relationship exists between them.

## Approaches Based on the Analysis of Social Activities

Approaches belonging to this category rely on the idea that if two users participate to the same activities, then a form of similarity exists between them. In particular, information associated with a user contributes to form a profile capable of describing her preferences and needs. The similarity between two users is then computed by taking into account the similarity of their profiles.

In (de Gemmis, Lops, Semeraro & Basile, 2008) the authors consider the tags applied by users to classify resources and provide a generative probabilistic model to build their profile. (Pazzani & Billsus, 1997) use a number of machine learning techniques (like Bayesian classifiers or decision trees) to analyze Web pages accessed by the user and build her profile. In (De Meo, Quattrone & Ursino, 2010) the authors propose to analyze semantic relationships between tags applied by users to classify folksonomy resources and use these tags to enrich user profiles.

Our approach, like those described in this section, considers the activities that the users of a social network can carry out and it mainly focuses on the affiliation to groups or the participation to events. By contrast, approaches illustrated in this section, rely on activities like *tagging* (de Gemmis, Lops, Semeraro & Basile, 2008, De Meo, Quattrone & Ursino, 2010) or *browsing* (Pazzani & Billsus, 1997). The analysis of user activities provides useful elements to generate accurate and complete profiles.

On the contrary, in Web 2.0 scenario, the so-called *power law* phenomenon emerges (Golder & Huberman, 2006). Due to the power law phenomenon, a low level of participation in community activities characterizes a large fraction of users. In such a case, the information about a user is in general poor and the process of computing user similarities may incur in some inaccuracies.

Our approach overcomes the drawbacks outlined above because it integrates information regarding user activities with information about social relationships created by a user.

## Approaches to Identify Potential Customers

The task of identifying potential customers plays a key role in marketing research and e-commerce (Romano, 2000; De Meo, Rosaci, Sarnè, Terracina & Ursino, 2003). In fact, enterprises may identify customers with similar needs and consuming behaviours and group them (*customer segmentation*). Customer segmentation is useful to better point out customer demands and to plan suitable commercial strategies to satisfy them. A product of interest to a given customer $c$ can be advertised and proposed to all the other customers of the same group of $c$; on the long run, the identification of potential customers enables enterprises to attract and keep valuable customers (Romano, 2000).

Our research efforts are strongly tied with those in the area of customer identification. In fact, the task of finding similar users is useful to augment the likelihood that a specific person is interested in a commercial product given that other customers similar to her have appreciated such a product. In this section we briefly review the main techniques to identify potential customers and discuss how they are related to our research.

Many of the existing approaches define a set of *features* able to describe the customer behaviour; for instance, relevant examples of features are the *customer profitability* (i.e., the difference between the revenues earned from and the costs associated with the customer relationship in a specified period) and the *customer loyalty* (i.e., the tendency of a customer to stay with a specific brand) (Wan, Xiaopeng, Liquan, 2010). The indices can be *equally relevant* or not; in the latest case, an *importance matrix IM* is defined. The generic entry $IM(i,j)$ specifies the relative importance of the feature $i$ against the feature $j$.

Once data about customers have been gathered and mapped onto a vector features, a clustering algorithm is usually applied; customers belonging to the same clusters are recognized as similar. A popular option is to use the *K-Means* algorithm (Han & Kamber, 2006). In (Wan, Xiaopeng, Liquan, 2010), the authors showed that the usage of genetic algorithms can lead to a meaningful improvement in clustering accuracy; however, approaches based on genetic algorithms are computationally more expensive and an analysis of their scalability on large datasets is still missing.

We address the reader to (Sotiropoulos, Tsihrintzis, Savvopoulos & Virvou, 2005) in which the authors experimentally compare the performance of three clustering algorithms (i.e., hierarchical clustering, fuzzy *k*-means and spectral clustering) on data about customers of an e-commerce Websites.

## COMPUTING SIMILARITY SCORES BETWEEN USERS

In this section we describe our approach for computing similarities among Facebook users. In the following we shall denote as $U = \{ u_1, u_2, ..., u_n \}$ the *space* of Facebook users and $u_x$ will indicate the generic user.

### Basic Similarity Measures

As pointed out in the Introduction, in online social networks like Facebook, friendship relationships are a reliable indicator of similarity between two users but they cannot be enough to produce satisfactory results.

Friendship relationships can be augmented with other sources of knowledge in order to detect user similarities in a more accurate fashion. Specifically, as for Facebook users, they are usually involved in a broad range of activities like: *(i)* to affiliate to groups, *(ii)* to declare to join events, *(iii)* to declare to be fan of a Web page, and so on. We propose to analyze some of these activities and use this knowledge to determine user similarities.

More formally, each user activity in Facebook will be denoted as $A_{type}$ where *type* specifies the kind of activity. For instance, possible activities are $A_F$ (indicating that two users become friends), $A_G$ (indicating that a user decides to join to a group), $A_E$ (specifying that a user has declared to participate to an event) and $A_P$ (specifying that a user has declared to be fan of a page). In the following we shall denote as $A_i$ a generic user activity.

For each activity $A_i$ and for a given pair of users $u_x$ and $u_y$ we can define a similarity measure (called $A_i$-similarity) $\sigma_{Ai}(u_x, u_y)$ between $u_x$ and $u_y$ according to the activity $A_i$: it takes a pair of users $u_x$ and $u_y$ and, depending on the nature of $A_i$, it returns a numerical value representing the degree of similarity between $u_x$ and $u_y$. Intuitively, $\sigma_{Ai}(\cdot, \cdot)$ must be *symmetric*, i.e., $\sigma_{Ai}(u_x, u_y) = \sigma_{Ai}(u_y, u_x)$.

Definitions 1 and 2 illustrate how to compute user similarity when the activities we consider are $A_F$, $A_G$, $A_E$ and $A_P$.

**Definition 1.** Let $u_x$ and $u_y$ be a pair of Facebook users. Let $F(u_x)$ (resp., $F(u_y)$) be the set of friends of $u_x$ (resp., $u_y$). The *F-similarity* between $u_x$ and $u_y$ is defined as:

$$\sigma_F(u_x, u_y) = J(F(u_x), F(u_y))$$

where $J(\cdot, \cdot)$ is the *Jaccard similarity coefficient* between $F(u_x)$ and $F(u_y)$, i.e.:

$$J(F(u_x), F(u_y)) = \frac{|F(ux) \cap F(uy)|}{|F(ux) \cup F(uy)|}$$

The Jaccard similarity coefficient is symmetric and it returns values in *(0,1)*. In particular, the higher the value of $J(F(u_x), F(u_y))$ is, the more similar $u_x$ and $u_y$ are.

In an analogous fashion we can consider different type of activities to define other similarity measures. This is encoded in Definition 2.

**Definition 2.** Let $u_x$ and $u_y$ be a pair of Facebook users. Let:

1.  *G (u_x)* (resp., *G (u_y)*) be the set of groups to which $u_x$ (resp., $u_y$) is affiliated to.
2.  *E (u_x)* (resp., *E (u_y)*) be the set of events to which $u_x$ (resp., $u_y$) has declared to participate.
3.  *P(u_x)* (resp., *P(u_y)*) be the set of pages to which $u_x$ (resp., $u_y$) has declared to be fan.

The *G-similarity,* the *E-similarity* and the *P-similarity* between $u_x$ and $u_y$ are defined as:

1.  $\sigma_G(u_x, u_y) = J(G(u_x), G(u_y))$
2.  $\sigma_E(u_x, u_y) = J(E(u_x), E(u_y))$
3.  $\sigma_P(u_x, u_y) = J(P(u_x), P(u_y))$

where *J(·,·)* is the *Jaccard similarity coefficient.*

## Similarities Based on Katz Coefficient

At the end of the previous step we were able to obtain information about user similarities by taking into account activities in which they were jointly involved. Such knowledge, as shown in the Introduction, could not be enough in real cases.

To overcome this drawback, we use some ideas successfully applied in the context of Social Network and Computer Science literature (Jeh & Widom, 2002, Leicht, Holme & Newman, 2006). In particular, some approaches represent objects and their relationships as graphs and introduce the notion of *regular equivalence* (White & Reitz, 1983, Borgatti & Everett, 1992, Doreian, 1999), which is largely accepted in the literature to detect the similarity of a pair of objects. According to regular equivalence theory, two objects are recognized as similar if they are connected to objects, which are similar themselves.

A popular example of regular equivalence is provided by the *Katz coefficient* (Katz, 1953).

In order to illustrate how the Katz coefficient works and how it can be adjusted to compute similarities among Facebook users, we need the following definition:

**Definition 3.** Let *U* be the space of Facebook users, let $A_i$ be a user activity and $\varphi_{Ai}$ a real parameter in (0,1). The $A_i$ - *induced graph* $G_{Ai} = <N_{Ai}, E_{Ai}>$ is an undirected graph such that: *(i)* there is a node $n_x^{Ai} \in N_{Ai}$ for each user $u_x \in U$ and *(ii)* there is an edge $e_{xy}^{Ai} = <n_x^{Ai}, n_y^{Ai}>$ linking $n_x^{Ai}$ and $n_y^{Ai}$ if $\sigma_{Ai} > \varphi_{Ai}$.

The graph $G_{Ai}$ stores the whole set of relationships among Facebook users according to the user activity $A_i$. The parameter $\varphi_{Ai}$ is necessary to cut off weak forms of correlation between users. Intuitively, it plays the same role of *minimum support* in association rule learning in the sense that $\varphi_{Ai}$ allows to filter out relationships among users which are not statistically significant.

For instance, if we would consider "friendship" as user activity, we would be able to build a graph $G_F$ which depicts friendship relationships among users and the nodes representing two users $u_x$ and $u_y$ will be linked if the number of friends that $u_x$ and $u_y$ share is large enough.

To introduce the Katz coefficient, we first consider only friendship relationships; we shall extend later our ideas to other type of user activities.

According to the definition of Katz coefficient, two users $u_x$ and $u_y$ are recognized as similar if there is a large number of users who, in their turn, are similar to both $u_x$ and $u_y$; in particular, given a user $u_x$, we consider the *neighborhoods* of $u_x$, i.e., the set of friends of $u_x$. For an arbitrary friend of $u_x$, say $u_y$ we consider his similarity with $u_x$; we repeat this operation for all friends of $u_x$ and sum all similarity values. More concretely, let $A_F$ be the adjacency matrix of $G_F$, i.e. the matrix such that $A_F(x,y) = 1$ if there is an edge between the nodes representing $u_x$ and $u_y$ and 0 otherwise; the *Katz similarity coefficient* $\sigma_F^K(u_x, u_y)$ of $u_x$ and $u_y$ is proportional to:

$$\sigma_F^K(u_x, u_y) \approx \Sigma A_F(x,i) \sigma_F^K(u_i, u_j) \qquad (1)$$

In addition, we consider a special case, known as *self-similarity,* in which users $u_x$ and $u_y$ may coincide. In such a case we increase $\sigma_F^K(u_x, u_y)$ by adding a *bonus*. In particular, the bonus is proportional to $\delta_{xy}$, being $\delta_{xy}$ the Kronecker symbol (i.e., $\delta_{xy} = 1$ if $u_x$ and $u_y$ coincide and 0 otherwise) and this allows to complete Equation (1) as follows:

$$\sigma_F^K(u_x, u_y) = \alpha \Sigma A_F(x,i) \sigma_F^K(u_i, u_j) + (1-\alpha)\delta_{xy} \tag{2}$$

Here $\alpha$ is a weighting coefficient ranging in (0;1). Equation (2) can be rewritten in a more interesting fashion by introducing matrix notation. In particular, let $S$ be the similarity matrix, i.e., $S(x,y) = \sigma_F^K(u_x, u_y)$ and let $I$ be the identity matrix. With this notation, Equation (2) can be rewritten as:

$$S = \alpha A_F S + (1-\alpha)I \tag{3}$$

With some simple manipulations, Equation (3) is equivalent to:

$$S - \alpha A_F S = (1-\alpha)I \rightarrow (I - \alpha A_F)S = (1-\alpha)I \rightarrow S = (1-\alpha)(I - \alpha A_F)^{-1}I \tag{4}$$

Finally, the term $(I - \alpha A_F)^{-1}$ can be developed by applying the so-called *Neumann series* (Stewart, 1998):

$$(I - \alpha A_F)^{-1} = I + \alpha A_F + \alpha^2 A_F^2 + \alpha^3 A_F^3 + \alpha^4 A_F^4 + \dots \tag{5}$$

Equation (5) is quite interesting. In fact, the element $A_F^i(x,y)$ represents the number of paths of length $i$ joining nodes $n_x$ and $n_y$ in $G_F$. As a consequence, the computation of the Katz coefficient of two nodes (and, then, of the corresponding users) requires computing all paths, of any arbitrary length joining the two nodes. Each path

carries in a contribution and the longer a path is, the weaker its contribution is. More formally, the Katz-similarity of $u_x$ and $u_y$ can be re-defined as follows:

$$\sigma_F^K(u_x, u_y) = \sum_{l=0}^{+\infty} \beta^l np(nx, ny, l) \tag{6}$$

where $\beta$ is a real parameter ranging in *(0,1)* and $np(n_x n_y, l)$ is a function returning the number of paths of length $l$ running from $n_x$ to $n_y$.

Efficient techniques (e.g., iterative algorithms) have been proposed to quickly compute the Katz coefficient (Leicht, Holme & Newman, 2006). In addition, experimental trials show that it usually provides more accurate results than simple Jaccard similarity coefficient.

The procedure we outlined above can be extended to all other user activities we want to consider. As a final result, a similarity measure between two users can be introduced for each activity we consider.

## Computing a Global Similarity Score

At the end of the previous stage we were able to associate each pair of users with $n$ coefficients $\sigma_{A1}^K, \sigma_{A2}^K, \dots, \sigma_{An}^K$, each of them representing the similarity between $u_x$ and $u_y$ according to the generic activity $A_i$. Each of these values represents a *partial* indicator of similarity between two users and they can be combined to obtain more accurate indications about the actual similarity of $u_x$ and $u_y$.

Therefore, we suggest to combine the values $\sigma_{A1}^K, \sigma_{A2}^K, \dots, \sigma_{An}^K$ to produce a global similarity value. In its general form, the global similarity $\sigma$ can be defined as a weighted mean of $\sigma_{A1}^K, \sigma_{A2}^K, \dots, \sigma_{An}^K$:

$$\sigma = a_1 \sigma_{A1}^K + a_2 \sigma_{A2}^K + \dots + a_K \sigma_{An}^K$$

Here $\alpha_1, \alpha_2, ..., \alpha_K$ are weighting coefficients which specify the relative importance of each similarity value. We used *two strategies* to define these coefficients.

In the former strategy, a user can decide, according to his personal needs, the values of weighting coefficients. Such an option is useful for expert users who can decide which factor influences in the most relevant fashion user similarity; for instance, in a specific application context, a user may decide that friendship actions are more relevant than other actions in defining global similarity; these users can, therefore, assign a large value to the weighting coefficient corresponding to the similarity value computed on the friendship graph and, at the same time, a low value for all remaining weighting coefficients.

By contrast, the latter strategy targets novice users and, in general, it is suitable in all cases in which no similarity value appears to dominate other ones. In such a case, we suggest to learn a *function f* which takes $\sigma_{A1}^K, \sigma_{A2}^K, ..., \sigma_{An}^K$ as input and returns a number in $(0,1)$ as output.

The problem of determining *f* can be regarded as a *binary classification problem*. In this chapter we used *linear regression* to determine *f* (Bishop, 2006). In particular, let $\sigma = (\sigma_{A1}^K, \sigma_{A2}^K, ..., \sigma_{An}^K)$ be an *n*-th dimensional array whose *i*-th component stores the *i*-th value of similarity $\sigma_{Ai}^K$, the function *f* can be written as:

$$f(\sigma) = w^T \sigma$$

Here $w = (w_1, w_2, ..., w_n)$ is an *n*-th dimensional array of weights which must be determined and $w^T$ is the transpose of *w*. The weights $w_1, w_2, ..., w_n$ are computed by applying the *least square error principle*. To this purpose, we assume that a set *y'* of similarity values provided by a human expert (*training set*) is available and we determine the weights *w* in such a way as to minimize:

$$|| y' - f(\sigma) || = || y' - w^T \sigma ||$$

being $|| \cdot ||$ the traditional Euclidean norm. Once we get the weights, we are able to compute the global similarity score of two users. If the obtained score exceeds a threshold, we may conclude that two users are similar.

## EXPERIMENTAL RESULTS

### Prototype Description

We built a Java prototype to experimentally validate the effectiveness of our system. The architecture of our system is graphically shown in Figure 1.

Our system consists of three layers:

- *Data Layer.*
- *Processing Layer.*
- *Interface Layer.*

The Data Layer is in charge of crawling Facebook, extracting publicly available data and persistently stores them. In particular, the Data Layer generates a *Sesame* repository[2]. Sesame is an open source framework for storage, inferencing and querying of RDF data. The Sesame repository is queried by applying SPARQL; retrieved data are used to populate a MySQL database.

The Data Layer has been implemented by using the public APIs offered by Facebook. Processing Layer interacts with Data Layer to extract data about Facebook users. In particular it first implements suitable Java methods to extract data about user contact list, affiliation to groups and so on. Extracted information are used to feed *JESS* engines, each of them capable of computing basic similarities as well as similarities based on the Katz coefficient. JESS[3] is a rule engine and scripting

*Figure 1. Software architecture of our system.*

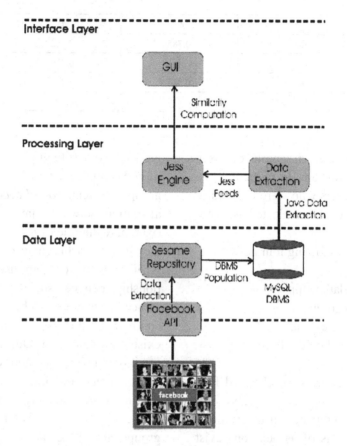

environment written entirely in Java. JESS allows to easily building software applications capable of "reasoning" by exploiting knowledge supplied in the form of declarative rules.

Finally, the interface layer implements a Java GUI enabling human users to interact with our system in a user-friendly fashion.

## Experimental Validation: A Case Study

In our experiments we crawled a large portion of Facebook users and retrieved about 25,000 user profiles. For each user we extracted her list of friends, the list of groups she is affiliated to, the list of groups she joined in the past and, finally, the list of pages she declared to be fan.

*Table 1. Some statistics about the dataset used in our experiments*

| Parameter | Value |
|---|---|
| Minimum / Average / Maximum Number of Friends | 4 / 110 / 2,540 |
| Minimum / Average / Maximum Number of Groups | 0 / 90 / 332 |
| Minimum / Average / Maximum Number of Events | 1 / 163 / 750 |
| Minimum / Average / Maximum Number of Fan | 1 / 103 / 250 |

*Table 2. Values of R2 for sF, sG, sE and sP*

| | $\sigma_F$ | $\sigma_G$ | $\sigma_E$ | $\sigma_P$ |
|---|---|---|---|---|
| $\sigma_F$ | 1 | 0.785 | 0.812 | 0.794 |
| $\sigma_G$ | 0.785 | 1 | 0.826 | 0.818 |
| $\sigma_E$ | 0.812 | 0.826 | 1 | 0.795 |
| $\sigma_P$ | 0.794 | 0.818 | 0.795 | 1 |

After this we extracted a sample of users referring to the same domain. In particular, we selected about 1,800 users who were University students. Some statistics about selected users are reported in Table 1.

We considered the following four activities:

1. $A_F$: friendship relationships.
2. $A_G$: affiliation to groups.
3. $A_E$: participation to events.
4. $A_P$: declarations to be fan of Web pages.

For each of these actions we obtained four similarity values, i.e., $\sigma_F$, $\sigma_G$, $\sigma_E$ and $\sigma_P$. As a preliminary test, we are interested in determining whether "positive" forms of associations exist between $\sigma_F$, $\sigma_G$, $\sigma_E$ and $\sigma_P$. For instance, we are interested in checking whether users who share a large number of friends also decide to affiliate to the same groups and whether users who joined the same groups also declared to participate to the same events. Such an analysis is quite interesting; in fact, if a positive correlation would emerge, we could conclude that multiple indicators agree on establishing a form of similarity between users. We applied *Ordinary Least Square* (OLS) regression to analyze the correlation of $\sigma_F$, $\sigma_G$, $\sigma_E$ and $\sigma_P$ and, we computed the $R^2$ coefficient. The corresponding results are shown in Table 2.

Reported results indicate a positive correlation between $\sigma_F$, $\sigma_G$, $\sigma_E$ and $\sigma_P$ variables. Such a result agrees with some fact already known in sociology and, in particular, in the research field of affiliation networks (Wasserman & Faust, 1994). An affiliation network can be essentially re-garded as bipartite graph such that a first group of nodes represents *real users* while the second group represents *social events*. For instance, an affiliation network may represent researchers (who play the role of *users*) and the conferences they attended (which play the role of *social events*). Affiliation networks are useful to disclose relationships between social network actors: for instance, if two researchers attended the same conferences, then we may hypothesize that a tie exists between them. Our analysis extends this intuition. In fact, data reported in Table 2 suggest us to *augment* the notion of social event and to give it a wider meaning; as a consequence, a tie between two users exists if they join the same groups, attend the same events or declare to be fan of the same Web page. If we would consider just one of these dimensions (e.g., if we would restrict our attention only to the participation to events), it could happen that the information at our disposal would be poor and, then, the process of deciding if two users are somewhat tied would be affected by inaccuracies. The power of our method is to consider *a range* of social facts to compensate the lack of knowledge in one of them.

As for the assessment of user similarity, it requires the validation of human expert (who is in charge of providing the "ground truth"). Due to the need of manually labelled data, we considered only a small fragment of our dataset which is however sufficient to show the effectiveness of our approach. In particular, we focused on a real use case in which five real users are considered. The users were student enrolled in a Computer

*Table 3. User-User similarity matrix provided by human expert*

| User / User | A | B | C | D | E |
|---|---|---|---|---|---|
| A | X | X | X | o | o |
| B | X | X | X | o | o |
| C | X | X | X | o | o |
| D | o | o | o | X | o |
| E | o | o | o | o | X |

Science track. Due to privacy reasons, we shall denote them as A, B, C, D and E.

Each student knew each other; in addition, in Table 3 we report the matrix of similarities between users reported by the expert. In particular, the entry at the $i$-th row and the $j$-th column reports a symbol "X" (resp, "o") if the expert recognized the $i$-th and $i$-th users are (resp., are not) similar. The matrix is clearly symmetric and all elements on the main diagonal are marked with X because each user is recognized as similar to himself.

## Performance Metrics

We defined two criteria in order to evaluate the performances of the system and to measure its reliability.

Given a generic similarity measure $\sigma^4$, its performance can be assessed by means of two metrics:

- *Misclassification error $E_1$*: it counts the percentage of times two users are recognized as similar by our system while they are actually not similar according to the expert opinion.
- *Misclassification error $E_2$*: it counts the percentage of times two users are recognized as not similar by our system while they are actually according to the expert opinion.

Clearly, both $E_1$ and $E_2$ range in (0,1) and the lower they are the better a similarity measure works.

*Table 4. User-user similarity matrix provided by $A_F$ activity*

| User / User | A | B | C | D | E |
|---|---|---|---|---|---|
| A | 1 | 1 | 1 | 1 | 1 |
| B | 1 | 1 | 1 | 1 | 1 |
| C | 1 | 1 | 1 | 1 | 1 |
| D | 1 | 1 | 1 | 1 | 1 |
| E | 1 | 1 | 1 | 1 | 1 |

## Performance Analysis of Basic Similarity Measure

We computed basic similarities between each pair of users. The obtained results were normalized to the real interval (0,1); if the normalized score exceeded a threshold, we classified the two users as similar. We first consider a default value for the threshold equal to 0.5 and, after this, we briefly show how its value impacted on system performance.

In the first experiment we apply the basic similarity measures $\sigma_F$, $\sigma_G$, $\sigma_E$ and $\sigma_P$. For each similarity measure $\sigma_t$ with $t \in \{F,G,E,P\}$, we fixed a threshold $\sigma_t$. If the similarity score $\sigma_t$ of a pair of users exceeded $\sigma_t$, we recognized the corresponding pair of users as similar. The value of $\sigma_t$ was initially set equal to $0.5 \times (M_t + m_t)$, being $M_t$ (resp., $m_t$) being the highest (resp., lowest) similarity score returned by $\sigma_t$. The scores achieved by each measure are reported in Tables 4, 5, 6 and 7.

From the analysis of these tables we can observe that:

*Table 5. User-user similarity matrix provided by AG activity*

| User / User | A | B | C | D | E |
|---|---|---|---|---|---|
| A | - | 0.120 | 0.131 | 0.034 | 0.035 |
| B | 0.120 | - | 0.096 | 0.053 | 0.063 |
| C | 0.131 | 0.096 | - | 0.037 | 0.045 |
| D | 0.034 | 0.053 | 0.037 | - | 0.050 |
| E | 0.035 | 0.063 | 0.045 | 0.050 | - |

*Table 6. User-User similarity matrix provided by AE activity*

| User / User | A | B | C | D | E |
|---|---|---|---|---|---|
| A | - | 0.182 | 0.182 | 0.014 | 0.020 |
| B | 0.182 | - | 0.113 | 0.054 | 0.058 |
| C | 0.182 | 0.113 | - | 0.015 | 0.015 |
| D | 0.014 | 0.054 | 0.015 | - | 0.105 |
| E | 0.020 | 0.058 | 0.015 | 0.105 | - |

*Table 7. User-user similarity matrix provided by AP activity*

| User / User | A | B | C | D | E |
|---|---|---|---|---|---|
| A | - | 0.051 | 0.075 | 0.075 | 0.006 |
| B | 0.051 | - | 0.058 | 0.014 | 0 |
| C | 0.075 | 0.058 | - | 0.014 | 0.015 |
| D | 0.075 | 0.014 | 0.014 | - | 0 |
| E | 0.006 | 0 | 0.015 | 0 | - |

1. The analysis of $A_F$ activity is not effective to compute similarities because all users are recognized as similar even if this is not actually true. This supports our initial claim about the fact that friendship relationships may not be enough to determine similarity.

2. As for $A_G$ activity, the similarity computation achieves the best performance. However, the similarity between $B$ and $E$ and $B$ and $D$ is quite large and close to the threshold we fixed to decide about user similarity. This demands a higher level of robustness in deciding about user similarities.

3. As for $A_E$ activity, users $D$ and $E$ are recognized as similar while the expert assumed they were not similar.

4. As for $A_P$ activity, we observe that similarity computation achieves results comparable with those of obtained in $A_G$ activity. However, the values it returns are quite low and close each other.

As a further experiment, we investigate how the threshold we use to decide about user similarity influences the performance of our system. Due to space limitations we considered just the $E$ activity because it presented the worst performance.

*Figure 2. Impact of threshold on E1 and E2 (E activity)*

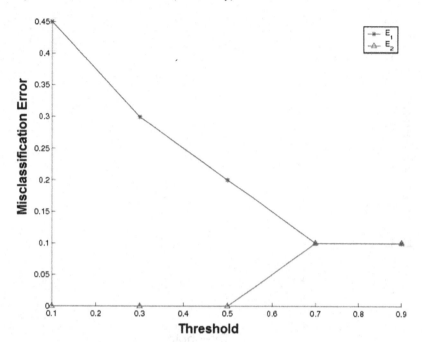

In Figure 2 we plot $E_1$ and $E_2$ when the threshold varied between 0.1 and 0.9.

Figure 2 show that the choice of threshold has a high impact on system performance. In particular, for low values of threshold (which implies that a large number of similarities are recognized) $E_1$ achieves its highest values (e.g., it equals 0.45 if the threshold equals 0.1). This means that our system tends to overestimate similarities. If the threshold increases, $E_1$ decreases while $E_2$ tend to be constant and equal to 0. When the threshold exceeds 0.5, $E_1$ continues decreasing while $E_2$ increases. In other words, if the threshold exceeds 0.5, our system gets more and more "restrictive" and the number of pairs of users recognized as similar decreases. On the one hand, this behaviour produces a decrease of $E_1$ (because some false similarities are no longer detected) but, on the other hand, it yields an increase of $E_2$ (because some pairs of users who are truly similar are not recognized as similar). We achieve a *break-even point* when the threshold is 0.7.

## Performance Analysis of Katz Coefficient

As a second experiment we are interested in determining if the *Katz coefficient* is able to provide better performances than basic similarities. To make an objective comparison, we fixed a threshold value ranging from 0.1 to 1 and, if the value of the Katz coefficient of two users exceeded this threshold, the users were recognized as similar.

In Figures 3, 4 and 5 we show the performance of the Katz coefficient when $A_G$, $A_E$ and $A_P$ activities are considered. The analysis of these figures shows that, even in presence of small networks, the Katz coefficient is able to significantly outperform basic similarity measures (for instance, the $E_1$ achieved by the Katz coefficient is up to 33% less than that achieved by basic similarity measures). In addition, both $E_1$ and $E_2$ are small until $\beta$ is less than 0.5. This depends on the fact that for large values of $\beta$ we would associate excessively large relevance to long paths. In addition, from Figures 3, 4 and 5, it emerges that if $\beta$ is *low*, then $E_2$ is

*Figure 3. Katz similarity for E1 and E2 (AG activity)*

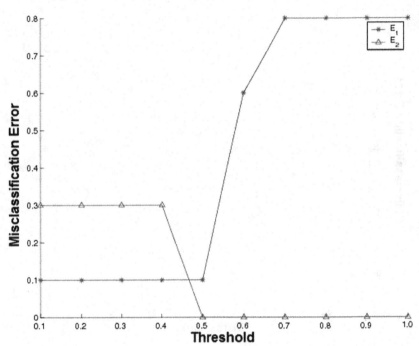

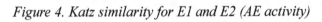

*Figure 4. Katz similarity for E1 and E2 (AE activity)*

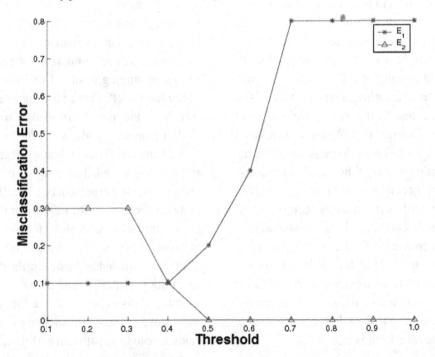

*Figure 5. Katz similarity for E1 and E2 (AP activity)*

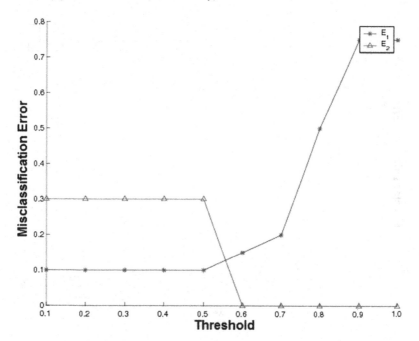

larger than $E_1$. In fact, if $\beta$ is low, our system essentially relies on local information and it discards information coming from paths containing more than one edge. As a consequence, some pairs of users are recognized as not similar even if they are actually similar.

An opposite behaviour emerges if $\beta$ is *high*: in such a case the contribution of long paths is relevant and some pairs of users are recognized by our system as similar even if they are actually not similar.

As a consequence, we get the best trade-off between $E_1$ and $E_2$ when $\beta \in (0.4, 0.5)$.

## Analysis of Regression Approach

A final experiment has been carried out to assess if our global similarity score produces better results than single similarity measures. To this purpose, we computed the value of $E_1$ and $E_2$ achieved by our system when the $\beta$ parameter ranges from 0 to 1. The corresponding results are shown in Figure 6.

From the analysis of this figure we can observe that the usage of a global score based on linear regression achieves results which are better than those achieved by each single action. In fact, the misclassification error $E_1$ is almost close to 0, i.e., users who are recognized as similar by our system are always similar according to user opinion. In addition, our system is also *robust* because variations in $\beta$ parameter do not affect the value of $E_1$. As for $E_2$, it ranges from 0.1 to 0.6 and the worst value achieved by $E_2$ when the global score is computed is about 25% lower than the worst value achieved by each single action. In such a case, weights used to compute global score are able to partially correct errors produced by each single activity. Finally, when $\beta \approx 0.2$, our system achieves the best performances in terms of both $E_1$ and $E_2$.

## Discussion of Experimental Results

In this section we briefly summarize the main findings of our experimental trials. In particular,

*Figure 6. E1 and E2 when global score is computed*

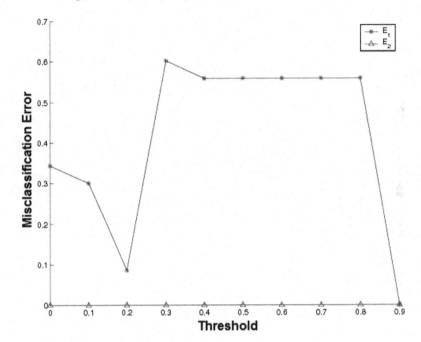

- The usage of a unique criterium (e.g. friendship) to compute user similarity may lead to wrong conclusions. To this purpose the usage of multiple criteria proved to be effective in correcting potential biases induced by a unique criterium.

- The usage of the Katz coefficient leads to a more accurate computation of similarity degree in comparison with the Jaccard coefficient. In fact, the Jaccard coefficient considers only the neighborhood of two users and compares them to define a similarity score. The Katz coefficient, by contrast, considers all potential paths linking two users to determine their similarity degree.

- The performance of the Katz coefficient depends on the value of the $\beta$ parameter. In particular, low values of $\beta$ imply that we neglect the contributions carried in by long paths joining two users; by contrast, high values of $\beta$ imply that long paths have a high impact in similarity computation.

Experiments show that the best trade-off is achieved when $\beta$ is around 0.4-0.5.

- The combination of multiple similarity scores by means of regression was able to yield accurate results. In other words, there are some similarity criteria, which lead to an overestimation of the similarity degree; by contrast, there are other criteria, which tend to underestimate the similarity degree. Linear regression is able to compensate these two effects and yields a more accurate computation of similarity.

## CONCLUSION

In this chapter we presented a novel approach to the problem of measuring the similarity among Facebook users. Our approach handles a variety of interactions carried out by users (e.g., the friends they share, the events they declared to participate, the groups they decided to join and so on). For each of these activities we analysed joint user behaviours and, by applying the Jaccard similarity coefficient, we computed a similarity value. After this, we suggested to map the space of Facebook users onto multiple weighted graphs and each graph corresponds to one of the social activity we considered: for instance, we built a graph to represent friendship relationship, a graph to model the co-participation to events and so on. We used each of these graphs to compute the level of similarity between two users. To this purpose, we applied the Katz coefficient, a popular parameter introduced in Social Science. Finally, applying linear regression to generate a unique similarity score merges the similarity values we obtained.

In the future we plan to extend our research by designing mechanisms capable of using similarities among users in order to suggest to a user other users with whom he can profitably interact or to discover to which a user can affiliate. A further research direction consists of extending the range of social activities currently considered in our approach. For instance, we could handle the textual comments the users post and apply on them text-mining techniques (like, for instance, techniques developed in the context of opinion or sentiment mining). This would be a precious tool to better detect user preferences and needs and, by aggregating these data on a large scale, we would be able to detect new trends. A final application scenario is to harness the power of social networks (and, in particular, of Facebook) to create novel applications in a range of domains like e-recruitment (De Meo, Quattrone, Terracina & Ursino, 2007) or e-learning (De Meo, Garro, Terracina & Ursino, 2003). For instance, in the case of e-recruitment, we could search the space of social network users to find the best candidates for a given position or, alternatively, to form teams working on a specific project. Analogously, in the case of e-learning, we could sift through a social network to find users with the same educational needs/goals or background and we could form well matched and homogeneous virtual classrooms in such a way as to enhance the outcomes of learning processes.

## ACKNOWLEDGMENT

The authors would heartily thank Santo Curreri for his invaluable contribution in implementing the prototype presented in this chapter.

## REFERENCES

Bishop, C. M. (2006). *Pattern recognition and machine learning (Information Science and Statistics)*. New York, NY: Springer-Verlag, Inc.

Borgatti, S. P., & Everett, M. G. (1992). Notions of position in social network analysis. *Sociological Methodology*, *22*(1), 1–35. doi:10.2307/270991

Christakis, N. A., & Fowler, J. H. (2007). The spread of obesity in a large social network over 32 years. *The New England Journal of Medicine*, *357*(4), 370–379. doi:10.1056/NEJMsa066082

Crandall, D., Cosley, D., Huttenlocher, D., Kleinberg, J., & Suri, S. (2008), Feedback effects between similarity and social influence in online communities. In *Proc. of the ACM SIGKDD International Conference on Knowledge Discovery and Data Mining (SIGKDD '08)*, (pp. 160-168). Las Vegas, NV, USA, ACM Press.

Currarini, S., Jackson, M., & Pin, P. (2009). An economic model of friendship: Homophily, minorities and segregation. *Econometrica: Journal of the Econometric Society*, *77*(4), 1003–1045. doi:10.3982/ECTA7528

de Gemmis, M., Lops, P., Semeraro, G., & Basile, P. (2008). Integrating tags in a semantic content-based recommender. In *Proc. of the ACM Conference on Recommender Systems (RecSys '08)*, (pp. 163-170). ACM Press.

De Meo, P., Garro, A., Terracina, G., & Ursino, D. (2003). X-Learn: An XML-based, multi-agent system for supporting "user-device" adaptive e-learning. In *Proc. of the International Conference on Ontologies, Databases and Applications of Semantics (ODBASE 2003)*, (pp. 739-756). Taormina, Italy. Lecture Notes in Computer Science, Springer.

De Meo, P., Quattrone, G., Terracina, G., & Ursino, D. (2007). An XML-based multi-agent system for supporting online recruitment services. *IEEE Transactions on Systems, Man ad Cybernetics - Part A, 37*(4), 467-480.

De Meo, P., Quattrone, G., & Ursino, D. (2010). A query expansion and user profile enrichment approach to improve the performance of recommender systems operating on a folksonomy. *Journal of User Modelling and User Adapted Interactions, 20*(1), 41–86. doi:10.1007/s11257-010-9072-6

De Meo, P., Rosaci, D., Sarnè, G., Terracina, G., & Ursino, D. (2003). An XML-based adaptive multi-agent system for handling e-commerce activities. *Proc. of the International Conference on Web Services (ICWS-Europe 2003)*, (pp. 152-166). Erfurt, Germany.

Doreian, P. (1999). An intuitive introduction to blockmodeling with examples. *Bulletin de Methodologie Sociologique, 61*(1), 5–34. doi:10.1177/075910639906100103

Friedkin, N. (1998). *A structural theory of social influence*. Cambridge University Press. doi:10.1017/CBO9780511527524

Geyer, W., Dugan, C., Millen, D. R., Muller, M., & Freyne, J. (2008). Recommending topics for self-descriptions in online user profiles. In *Proc. of the ACM Conference on Recommender Systems (RecSys '08)*, (pp. 59-66). Lausanne, Switzerland.

Golder, S. A., & Huberman, B. A. (2006). Usage patterns of collaborative tagging systems. *Journal of Information Science, 32*(2), 198–208. doi:10.1177/0165551506062337

Groh, G., & Ehmig, C. (2007). Recommendations in taste related domains: Collaborative filtering vs. social filtering. In *Proc. of the International ACM conference on Supporting Group Work (GROUP '07)*, (pp. 127-136).

Han, J., & Kamber, M. (2006). *Data mining: Concepts and techniques* (2nd ed.). Morgan Kaufmann Publishers.

Jeh, G., & Widom, J. (2002). SimRank: A measure of structural-context similarity. In *Proc. of the ACM SIGKDD International Conference on Knowledge Discovery and Data Mining (SIGKDD '02)*, (pp. 538-543). Edmonton, Alberta, Canada.

Katz, L. (1953). A new status index derived from sociometric analysis. *Psychometrika, 18*(1), 39–43. doi:10.1007/BF02289026

Kleinberg, J. (2008). The convergence of social and technological networks. *Communications of the ACM, 51*(11), 66–72. doi:10.1145/1400214.1400232

Kobsa, A. (2001). Generic user modeling systems. *User Modeling and User-Adapted Interaction, 11*, 49–63. doi:10.1023/A:1011187500863

Lazarsfeld, P., & Merton, R. K. (1954). Friendship as a social process: A substantive and methodological analysis. In Berger, M., Abel, T., & Page, C. H. (Eds.), *Freedom and control in modern society* (pp. 18–66). New York, NY: Van Nostrand.

Leicht, E. A., Holme, P., & Newman, M. E. J. (2006). Vertex similarity in networks. *Physical Review Part E, 73*(2), 026120. doi:10.1103/PhysRevE.73.026120

Liben-Nowell, D., & Kleinberg, J. (2007). The link-prediction problem for social networks. *Journal of the American Society for Information Science and Technology, 58*(7), 1019–1031. doi:10.1002/asi.20591

Mcpherson, M., Lovin, S. L., & Cook, J. M. (2001). Birds of a Feather: Homophily in social networks. *Annual Review of Sociology, 27*(1), 415–444. doi:10.1146/annurev.soc.27.1.415

Pazzani, M., & Billsus, D. (1997). Learning and revising user profiles: The identification of interesting web sites. *Machine Learning, 27*(3), 313–331. doi:10.1023/A:1007369909943

Resnick, P., & Varian, H. R. (1997). Recommender systems. *Communications of the ACM, 40*(3), 56–58. doi:10.1145/245108.245121

Sokal, R. R., & Sneath, P. H. A. (1963). *Principles of numerical taxonomy*. San Francisco, CA: W. H. Freeman and Co.

Spertus, E., Sahami, M., & Buyukkokten, O. (2005). Evaluating similarity measures: A large-scale study in the orkut social network. In *Proc. of the ACM SIGKDD International Conference on Knowledge Discovery in Data Mining (KDD '05)*, (pp. 678-684). ACM Press.

Stewart, G. W. (1998). *Matrix algorithms: Basic decompositions (Vol. 1)*. Society for Industrial Mathematics.

Wasserman, S., & Faust, K. (1994). *Social network analysis: Methods and applications*. Cambridge University Press.

White, D. R., & Reitz, K. P. (1983). Graph and semigroup homomorphisms on networks of relations. *Social Networks, 5*(2), 193–234. doi:10.1016/0378-8733(83)90025-4

Zanardi, V., & Capra, L. (2008). Social ranking: Uncovering relevant content using tag-based recommender systems. In *Proc. of the International Conference on Recommender Systems (RecSys 2008)*, (pp. 51-58). Lausanne, Switzerland. ACM Press.

## KEY TERMS AND DEFINITIONS

**Facebook:** A social networking Web site launched in February 2004. Facebook users can add people as friends and send them messages, and update their personal profiles to notify friends about themselves.

**Graph:** A data structure used to model a set $S$ of objects and relationships occurring between pairs of objects belonging to $S$.

**Homophily:** The tendency of individuals to associate and create personal relationships with similar individuals.

**Jaccard Coefficient:** A parameter used for comparing the similarity and diversity of sample sets. Given two sets $A$ and $B$, Jaccard coefficient is defined as the size of the intersection of $A$ and $B$ divided by the size of their union.

**Katz Coefficient:** A coefficient, introduced in sociology, to assess the degree of closeness of two nodes in a social network.

**Linear Regression:** A statistical approach to modeling the relationship between a variable $y$ and several variables $x_1, x_2, ..., x_n$.

**Social Network:** A structure consisting of individuals (or organizations) called "nodes" or "actors" which are connected by one or more specific types of relationships like friendships.

## ENDNOTES

[1] See http://www.facebook.com/press/info.php?statistics.

[2] http://www.openrdf.org/

[3] www.jessrules.com

[4] Here can denote both a basic similarity measure and a similarity measure relying on the Katz coefficient

# Compilation of References

Abbas, S. M. A. (2010). *A segregation model of Facebook.* Paper presented at the Sixth UK Social Networks Conference, London, UK.

Abrol, S., & Khan, L. (2010). TWinner: Understanding news queries with geo-content using Twitter. *Proceedings of the 6th Workshop on Geographic Information Retrieval,* (pp. 1-8).

Abuza, Z. (2003). Funding terrorism in Southeast Asia: The financial network of Al Qaeda and Jemaah Islamiya. *Contemporary Southeast Asia, 25,* 169–199. doi:10.1355/CS25-2A

Abuza, Z. (2009). Jemaah Islamiyah adopts the Hezbollah model. *Middle East Quarterly, 16,* 15–26.

Acemoglu, D., & Robinson, J. A. (2008). Persistence of power, elites, and institutions. *The American Economic Review, 98,* 267–293. doi:10.1257/aer.98.1.267

Acquisti, A., & Ralph, G. (2006). Imagined Communities: Awareness, Information Sharing, and Privacy on the Facebook. In Golle, P. and Danezis, G. (Eds.), *Proceedings of 6th Workshop on Privacy Enhancing Technologies,* 36-58

Acquisti, A., & Gross, R. (2006). Imagined communities: Awareness, information sharing, and privacy on the Facebook. *Privacy Enhancing Technologies, 4258,* 36–58. doi:10.1007/11957454_3

Adamic, L., & Adar, E. (2005). How to search a social network. *Social Networks, 27,* 187–203. doi:10.1016/j.socnet.2005.01.007

Adar, E., & Ré, C. (2007). Managing uncertainty in social networks. *Data Engineering Bulletin, 30*(2), 23–31.

Adler Lomnitz, L. (1988). Informal exchange networks in formal systems: A theoretical model. *American Anthropologist, 90*(1), 42–55. doi:10.1525/aa.1988.90.1.02a00030

Agichtein, E., Castillo, C., Donato, D., Gionis, A., & Mishne, G. (2008). Finding high-quality content in social media. *Proceedings of the Int'l Conf. on Web Search and Data Mining* (pp. 183-194). ACM.

Agrawal, R., & Srikant, R. (1994). Fast algorithms for mining association rules in large data-bases. *Proceedings of the 20th International Conference on Very Large Data Base,* 487-499.

Agrawal, R., & Jagadish, H. V. (1994). Algorithms for searching massive graphs. *IEEE Transactions on Knowledge and Data Engineering, 6*(2), 225–238. doi:10.1109/69.277767

Ahuja, M., Galletta, D., & Carley, K. (2003). Individual centrality and performance in virtual RandD groups: An empirical study. *Management Science, 49,* 21–38. doi:10.1287/mnsc.49.1.21.12756

Alam, S. J., Geller, A., Meyer, R., & Werth, B. (2010). Modelling contextualized reasoning in complex societies with "endorsement". *Journal of Artificial Societies and Social Simulation, 13*(4). Retrieved from http://jasss.soc.surrey.ac.uk/13/4/6.html.

Alba, R. D. (1981). From small groups to social networks. Mathematical approaches to the study of group structure. *The American Behavioral Scientist, 24*(5), 681–694. doi:10.1177/000276428102400506

Albert, R., Jeong, H., & Barabasi, A.-L. (2000). Error and attack tolerance of complex networks. *Nature, 406*(378).

Aleman-Meza, B., Nagarajan, M., Ramakrishnan, C., Ding, L., Kolari, P., & Sheth, A. P. ... Finin, T. (2006). Semantic analytics on social networks: Experiences in addressing the problem of conflict of interest detection. *Proceedings of the 15th International Conference on World Wide Web*, (pp. 407-416).

Alexa Internet, Inc. (2010, September 20). *Top sites - The top 500 sites on the Web*. Alexa Internet Inc. Retrieved September 20, 2010, from http://www.alexa.com/topsites/global

Alexa. (2010). *Alexa*. Retrieved August 19, 2010, from http://www.alexa.com

Alexander, R. D. (1974). The evolution of social behavior. *Annual Review of Ecology and Systematics, 5*, 326–383. doi:10.1146/annurev.es.05.110174.001545

Althusser, L. (2003). *Ideología y aparatos ideológicos de estado*. Buenos Aires, Argentina: Nueva Visión.

Amblard, F. (2002). Which ties to choose? A survey of social networks models for agent-based social simulations. *Proceedings of the 2002 SCS International Conference on Artificial Intelligence, Simulation and Planning in High Autonomy Systems*, (pp. 253-258).

American Psychological Association. (2010). *Civic engagement*. Retrieved May 18, 2010, from http://www.apa.org/education/undergrad/civic-engagement.aspx

Anagnostopoulos, A., Kumar, R., & Mahdian, M. (2008). Influence and correlation in social networks. *Proceeding of the 14th ACM SIGKDD International Conference on Knowledge Discovery and Data Mining*, (pp. 7-15).

Ancona, D., & Bresman, H. (2007). *X-Teams. How to build teams that lead, innovate, and succeed*. Boston, MA: HBS Press.

Anderson, J. N., & Keyes, C. F. (1970). Perspectives on loosely organized social structures. *The Journal of Asian Studies, 9*(2), 415–419.

Antonucci, T. C., & Akiyama, H. (1995). Convoys of social relations: Family and friendships within a life span context. In Blieszner, R., & Bedford, V. H. (Eds.), *Handbook of aging and the family* (pp. 355–371). Westport, CT: Greenwood Press.

Anyanwu, K., & Sheth, A. P. (2003). P-Queries: Enabling querying for semantic associations on the Semantic Web. *Proceedings of the 12th International Conference on World Wide Web*, (pp. 690-699).

Aplin, C. T. (2008). Innovative trends in learning tools. *Journal of Cognitive Affective Learning, 4*(2), 26–28.

Appadurai, A. (1996). *Modernity at large: Cultural dimensions of globalization*. Minneapolis, MN: University of Minnesota Press.

Arce, D. G., & Sandler, T. (2010). Terrorist spectaculars: Backlash attacks and the focus of intelligence. *The Journal of Conflict Resolution, 54*, 354–373. doi:10.1177/0022002709355414

Ardèvol, E. (2003). *Cibercultura / ciberculturas: La cultura de Internet o el análisis cultural de los usos sociales de Internet*. IX Congreso de Antropología, Barcelona, septiembre.

Ardèvol, E. (2005). *Dream gallery: Online dating as a commodity*. Paper for Media Anthropology e-seminar. Retrieved from http://www.media-anthropology.net/workingpapers.htm.

Ardura, R., Lopez, M., Francisco, J., Huertas, L. (2010). Going with the consumer towards the social Web environment: a review of extant knowledge. *International Journal of Electronic Marketing and Retailing*. pp. 1741-1025.

Arenas, A., Danon, L., Dıaz-Guilera, A., Gleiser, P. M., & Guimer, R. (2004). Community analysis in social networks. *European Physical Journal, 38*, 373–380.

Arensberg, C. M. (1955). American communities. *American Anthropologist, 57*, 1143–1152. doi:10.1525/aa.1955.57.6.02a00060

Arensberg, C. M., & Kimball, S. T. (1940). *Family and community in Ireland*. Cambridge, MA.

Argote, L. (1999). *Organizational learning: Creating, retaining and transferring knowledge*. Norwell, MA: Kluwer.

Asal, V., & Rethemeyer, R. K. (2006). Researching terrorist networks. *Journal of Security Education, 1*, 65–74. doi:10.1300/J460v01n04_06

Asal, V., & Rethemeyer, R. K. (2008). The nature of the beast: Terrorist organizational characteristics and organizational lethality. *The Journal of Politics, 70*, 437–449. doi:10.1017/S0022381608080419

Ashworth, M. J., & Carley, K. M. (2006). Who you know vs. what you know: The impact of social position and knowledge on team performance. *The Journal of Mathematical Sociology, 30*, 43–75. doi:10.1080/00222500500323101

Asif, S. (2009). *Exploring e-commerce in an online virtual world: Second Life*. Unpublished B.Sc. (Hons.) dissertation, University of Manchester, Manchester, UK.

AT&T & Early Strategies Consulting. (2008). *The business impacts of social networking* [White Paper]. Retrieved January 27, 2011, from

Attwell, G., Cook, J., & Ravenscroft, A. (2009). *Appropriating technologies for contextual knowledge: Mobile Personal Learning Environments*. Paper presented at the Second World Congress on the Information Society.

Auer, S., Bizer, C., Kobilarov, G., Lehmann, J., Cyganiak, R., & Ives, Z. (2007). Dbpedia: A nucleus for a web of open data. *The Semantic Web, 4825*, 722–735. doi:10.1007/978-3-540-76298-0_52

Axelrod, R., & Testfatsion, L. (2006). A guide for newcomers to agent-based modeling in the social sciences. In Ammon, H. M., & Kendrick, D. A. (Eds.), *Handbook of computational economics*. Amsterdam, The Netherlands: Elsevier. doi:10.1016/S1574-0021(05)02044-7

Aykin, N. (2005). Overview: Where to start and what to consider. In Aykin, N. (Ed.), *Usability and internationalization of Information Technology* (pp. 3–20). Mahwah, NJ: Lawrence Erlbaum Associates Publishers.

Backstrom, L., Huttenlocher, D., Kleinberg, J., & Lan, X. (2006). Group formation in large social networks: Membership, growth, and evolution. *Proceedings of the 12th ACM SIGKDD International Conference on Knowledge Discovery and Data Mining*, (pp. 44-54).

Bailey, N. (1975). *The Mathematical Theory of Infectious Diseases and Its Applications* (2nd ed.). London: Griffin.

Bainbridge, W. S. (2007). The scientific research potential of virtual worlds. *Science, 317*, 472–476. doi:10.1126/science.1146930

Bakardjieva, M. (2005). *Internet society: The Internet in everyday life*. London, UK: Sage.

Bakardjieva, M., & Smith, R. (2001). 'The internet in everyday life: Computer networking from the standpoint of the domestic user. *New Media & Society, 3*, 67–83.

Baker, R. P. (1992). New technology in survey research: Computer assisted personal interviewing (CAPI). *Social Science Computer Review, 10*, 145–157.

Bakshy, E., Karrer, B., & Adamic, L. A. (2009). Social influence and the diffusions of user-created content. In *Proceedings of the ACM Conference on Electronic Commerce* (pp. 325-334). The ACM Press.

Bandura, A. (1997). *Self-efficacy: The exercise of control*. New York, NY: Freeman.

Barabasi, A. L., & Albert, R. (1999). Emergence of scaling in random networks. *Science, 286*(5439), 509–512. doi:10.1126/science.286.5439.509

Barnes, J. (1954). Class and committee in a Norwegian island parish. *Human Relations, 7*, 39–58. doi:10.1177/001872675400700102

Barnes, J. A. (1954). Class and committees in a Norwegian island parish. *Human Relations, 39*, 39–58. doi:10.1177/001872675400700102

Barnouw, V. (1961). Chippewa social atomism. *American Anthropologist, 63*, 1006–1013. doi:10.1525/aa.1961.63.5.02a00080

Barnouw, V. (1974). On Lieberman's use of the concept of atomism: Comment on *Atomism and mobility among underclass Chippewas and whites* by L Lieberman, with a reply by L Lieberman. *Human Organization, 33*, 418–421.

Barros, S. (2009, September 21). 5 social media disasters. *Penn Olson*. Retrieved September 28, 2010 from http://www.penn-olson.com/2009/09/21/5-social-media-disasters/

Barthélémy, O. T. (2006). *Untangling scenario components with agent based modelling: An example of social simulations of water demand forecasts*. Unpublished doctoral dissertation, Centre for Policy Modelling, Manchester Metropolitan University, Manchester, UK.

Bartlett, C. A., & Mohammed, A. (1995). 3M: Profile of an innovating company. *Harvard Business School Case,* 395-016.

Basile, P., Gendarmi, D., Lanubile, F., & Semeraro, G. (2007). Recommending smart tags in a social bookmarking system. *Bridging the Gap between Semantic Web and Web, 2,* 22-29.

Basile, M. (2004). Going to the source: Why Al Qaeda's financial network is likely to withstand the current war on terrorist financing. *Studies in Conflict and Terrorism, 27,* 169–185. doi:10.1080/10576100490438237

Bastani, S. (2007). Family comes first: Men's and women's personal networks in Teheran. *Social Networks, 29,* 357–374. doi:10.1016/j.socnet.2007.01.004

Bastians, F. (2004). *Die Bedeutung soziaer Netzwerke für die Integration russlanddeutscher Spätaussiedler in der Bundesrepublik Deutschland.* Bissendorf, Germany: Methodos.

Bauman, Z. (1990). *Thinking sociologically.* Oxford, UK: Blackwell.

Bauman, Z. (2007). *Consuming life.* Cambridge, UK: Polity Press.

Beck, U., & Beck-Gernsheim, E. (2002). *Individualization: Institutionalized individualism and its social and political consequences.* London, UK: Sage Publication.

Beenen, G., Ling, K. S., Wang, X., Chang, K., Frankowski, D., Resnick, P., & Kraut, R. E. (2004). Using social psychology to motivate contributions to online communities. *Proceedings of the 2004 ACM Conf. on Computer Supported Cooperative Work* (pp. 212-221). ACM.

Bell, D. (2001). *Introduction to cyberculture.* London, UK: Routledge.

Bell, D. (2007). *Cyberculture theorists: Manuel Castells and Donna Haraway.* New York, NY: Routledge.

Bell, D., Loader, B., Pleace, N., & Schuler, D. (2004). *Cyberculture: The key concepts.* London, UK: Routledge.

Bellotti, E. (2008). What are friends for? Elective communities of single people. *Social Networks, 30,* 318–329. doi:10.1016/j.socnet.2008.07.001

Bender, M., Crecelius, T., Kacimi, M., Michel, S., Neumann, T., & Parreira, J. X. … Weikum, G. (2008). Exploiting social relations for query expansion and result ranking. *IEEE 24th International Conference on Data Engineering Workshop, 2,* (pp. 501-506).

Beresford Research. (2009). *Use of online social networks results of US user survey* [White Paper]. Retrieved September 27, 2010, from http://beresfordresearch. com/_beresfordtest/ pdfdocuments/Use%20of%20 Online%20 Social%20Networks%20White%20Paper% 20%28Beresford%20Research%29.pdf

Bernard, H. R., Killworth, P., Kronenfeld, D., & Sailer, L. (1984). The problem of informant accuracy: The validity of retrospective data. *Annual Review of Anthropology, 13,* 495–517. doi:10.1146/annurev.an.13.100184.002431

Bhadra, A., Jordan, F., Sumana, A., Deshpande, S. A., & Gadagkar, R. (2009). A comparative social network analysis of wasp colonies and classrooms: Linking network structure to functioning. *Ecological Complexity, 6,* 48–55. doi:10.1016/j.ecocom.2008.10.004

Bharwani, S., Bithell, M., Downing, T. E., New, M., Washington, R., & Ziervogel, G. (2005). Multiagent modelling of climate outlooks and food security on a community garden scheme in Limpopo, South Africa. *Philosophical Transactions of the Royal Society B., 360,* 2183–2194. doi:10.1098/rstb.2005.1742

Bidart, C., & Lavenu, D. (2005). Evolutions of personal networks and life events. *Social Networks,* 359–376. doi:10.1016/j.socnet.2004.11.003

Bigné, J. E., Mattila, A. S., & Andreu, L. (2008). The impact of experiential consumption cognitions and emotions on behavioral intentions. *Journal of Services Marketing, 22*(4), 303–315. doi:10.1108/08876040810881704

Bird, G., Blomberg, S. B., & Hess, G. D. (2008). International terrorism: Causes, consequences and cures. *World Economy, 31,* 255–274. doi:10.1111/j.1467-9701.2007.01089.x

Bishop, C. M. (2006). *Pattern recognition and machine learning (Information Science and Statistics).* New York, NY: Springer-Verlag, Inc.

Bitner, M. J., Zeithaml, V. A., & Gremler, D. D. (2010). Technology's Impact on the Gaps Model of Service Quality. *Handbook of Service Science*. pp. 197–218.

Black, D. (2004). The geometry of terrorism. *Sociological Theory, 22*, 14–25. doi:10.1111/j.1467-9558.2004.00201.x

Blanchard, A., & Markus, M. L. (2004). The experienced sense of virtual community: Characteristics and processes. *ACM SIGMIS Database, 35*(1), 64–79. doi:10.1145/968464.968470

Blanchard, C. M., & Prados, A. B. (2007). *Saudi Arabia: Terrorist financing issues*. Washington, DC: Congressional Research Service.

Blau, M., & Fingerman, K. L. (2009). *Consequential strangers: The power of people who don't matter, but really do*. New York, NY: W. W. Norton.

Boellstorf, T. (2008). *Coming of age in Second Life: An anthropologist explores the virtually human*. Princeton University Press.

Boguña, M., Krioukov, D., & Claffy, K. C. (2007). Navigability of complex networks. *Nature Physics, 5*(1).

Boguña, M., Pastor-Satorras, R., & Vespignani, A. (2003). Absence of epidemic threshold in scale-free networks with connectivity correlations. *Physical Review Letters, 90*(02), 8701–8704. doi:10.1103/PhysRevLett.90.028701

Boinski, S., & Campbell, A. F. (1995). Use of trill vocalisations to coordinate troop movement among white-faced capuchins: A second field test. *Behaviour, 132*, 875–901. doi:10.1163/156853995X00054

Boinski, S., & Garber, P. A. (2000). *On the move*. Chicago, IL: University of Chicago Press.

Bollen, A., & Emes, C. (2008). *Understanding customer relationships - How important is the personal touch?* Ipsos MORI Loyalty, London. Retrieved September 20, 2010, from http://www.ipsos.com/loyalty/sites/ipsos.com.loyalty/files/IpsosLoyalty_UnderstandingCustomerRelationships.pdf

Bonabeau, E., Theraulaz, G., Deneubourg, J.-L., Aron, S., & Camazine, S. (1997). Self-organization in social insects. *Trends in Ecology & Evolution, 12*, 188–192. doi:10.1016/S0169-5347(97)01048-3

Bonhard, P., & Sasse, M. A. (2006). 'Knowing me, knowing you' - Using profiles and social networking to improve recommender systems. *BT Technology Journal, 24*(3), 84–98. doi:10.1007/s10550-006-0080-3

Bonini, S. M. J., Hintz, G., & Mendonca, L. T. (2008). Addressing consumer concerns about climate change. *McKinsey Quarterly (March)*. Retrieved September 25, 2010, from https://www.mckinseyquarterly.com/ PDF-Download.aspx?ar=2115

Bonini, S. M. J., McKillop, K., & Mendonca, L. T. (2007). What consumers expect from companies. *McKinsey Quarterly, 2007*(2). Retrieved September 25, 2010, from https://www.mckinseyquarterly.com/ PDFDownload.aspx?ar=1986

Bontis, N. (2001). Assessing knowledge assets: A review of the models used to measure intellectual capital. *International Journal of Management Reviews, 3*(1), 41–60. doi:10.1111/1468-2370.00053

Borgatta, E. F., & Baker, P. M. (1981). Introduction: Updating small group research and theory [Special issue]. *The American Behavioral Scientist,* ▪▪▪, 24.

Borgatti, S. P., Carley, K. M., & Krackhardt, D. (2006). On the robustness of centrality measures under conditions of imperfect data. *Social Networks, 28*(2), 124–136. doi:10.1016/j.socnet.2005.05.001

Borgatti, S. P., & Everett, M. G. (1992). Notions of position in social network analysis. In Marsden, P. (Ed.), *Sociological methodology* (pp. 1–35). doi:10.2307/270991

Borgatti, S. P., & Everett, M. G. (1999). Models of core/periphery structures. *Social Networks, 21*, 375–395. doi:10.1016/S0378-8733(99)00019-2

Borgatti, S. P., Everett, M. G., & Freeman, L. C. (2002). *UCINET for Windows: Software for social network analysis*. Harvard, MA: Analytic Technologies.

Borgatti, S. P., Everett, M., & Freeman, L. C. (Eds.). (1999). *UCINET 5.0 version 1.00*. Natick, MA: Analytic Technologies.

Borgatti, S. P., Mehra, A., Brass, D. J., & Labianca, G. (2009). Network analysis in the social sciences. *Science, 323*, 892–895. doi:10.1126/science.1165821

Borgatti, S. P., & Molina, J. L. (2003). Ethical and strategic issues in organizational social network analysis. *The Journal of Applied Behavioral Science, 39*(3), 337–349. doi:10.1177/0021886303258111

Borges, B. (2009). *Marketing 2.0: Bridging the Gap between Seller and Buyer through Social Media Marketing.* Tucson, Arizona: Wheatmark.

Borzo, J. (2007, February 8). *Serious business: Web 2.0 goes corporate: How Web 2.0 tools and trends are breaking out of the IT industry.* Economist Intelligent Unit. Retrieved July 15, 2010, from http://www.fastforwardblog.com/wp-content/uploads/2007/FASTSEconomist.pdf

Bott, E. (1955). Urban families: Conjugal roles and social networks. *Human Relations, 8,* 345–384. doi:10.1177/001872675500800401

Bott, E. (1957). *Family and social network.* London, UK: Tavistock.

Bott, E. (1971). *Family and social network.* New York, NY: Free Press.

Bourdieu, P. (1986). Forms of capital. In Richardson, J. G. (Ed.), *Handbook of theory and research for the sociology and education* (pp. 241–258). Greenwood, NY.

Bourdieu, P. (1988). *Cosas dichas.* Barcelona, Spain: Gedisa.

Boyack, K., Klavans, R., & Borner, K. (2005). Mapping the backbone of science. *Scientometrics, 64*(3), 351–374. doi:10.1007/s11192-005-0255-6

Boyd, D. M., & Ellison, N. B. (2007). Social network sites: Definition, history and scholarship. *Journal of Computer-Mediated Communication, 13*(1). Retrieved July 13, 2010, from http://jjmc.indiana.edu/vol13/issue1/boyd.ellison.html

Boyd, D. M., & Ellison, N. (2008). Social network sites: Definition, history, and scholarship. *Journal of Computer-Mediated Communication, 13,* 210–230. doi:10.1111/j.1083-6101.2007.00393.x

Bradford, R., & Milstein, S. (n.d.). Best practices. In Twitter (Ed.), *Twitter 101 for business — A special guide.* Retrieved July 15, 2010, from http://business.twitter.com/twitter101/

Brandes, U., Raab, J., & Wagner, D. (2001). Exploratory network visualization: Simultaneous display of actor status and connections. *Journal of Social Structure, 2*(4). Retrieved August 24, 2010, from http://www.library.cmu.edu:7850/JoSS/brandes/index.html

Brandtzaeq, P. B., & Heim, J. (2007). User loyalty and online communities: Why members of online communities are not faithful. *Proceedings of the 2nd Int'l Conf. on INtelligent TEchnologies for Interactive EnterTAINment* (p. 11). ICST.

Breiger, R. L. (2004). The analysis of social networks. In Hardy, M., & Bryman, A. (Eds.), *Handbook of data analysis* (pp. 505–526). London, UK: SAGE Publications.

Brown, I., & Korff, D. (2009). Terrorism and the proportionality of internet surveillance. *European Journal of Criminology, 6,* 119–134. doi:10.1177/1477370808100541

Brown, J. S., Collins, A., & Duguid, P. (1989). Situated cognition and the culture of learning. *Educational Researcher, 18*(1), 32–42.

Brown, J., & Duguid, P. (2000). *The Social Life of Information.* Boston: Harvard Business School Press.

Brown, R. E. (2001). The process of community-building in distance learning classes. *Journal of Asynchronous Learning Networks, 5*(2), 18–35.

Brubaker, R., & Cooper, F. (2000). Beyond identity. *Theory and Society, 29,* 1–47. doi:10.1023/A:1007068714468

Brudner, L., & White, D. R. (1997). Class property and structural endogamy: Visualizing networked histories. *Theory and Society, 25,* 161–208. doi:10.1023/A:1006883119289

Bughin, J. (2008). The rise of enterprise 2.0. *Journal of Direct. Data and Digital Marketing Practice, 9*(3), 251–259. doi:10.1057/palgrave.dddmp.4350100

Buhl, J., Sumpter, D. J. T., Couzin, I. D., Hake, J. J., Despland, E., Miller, E. R., & Simpson, S. J. (2006). From disorder to order in marching locusts. *Science, 312,* 1402–1406. doi:10.1126/science.1125142

Burson-Marsteller. (2010). The global social media check-up (White Paper). *Burson-Marsteller*. Retrieved September 20, 2010, from http://www.burson-marsteller.com/Innovation_and_insights/blogs_and_podcasts/BM_Blog/Documents/Burson-Marsteller%202010%20Global%20Social%20Media%20Check-up%20white%20paper.pdf

Burt, R. (1978). Cohesion versus structural equivalence as a basis for network subgroups. *Sociological Methods & Research, 7*, 189–212. doi:10.1177/004912417800700205

Burt, R. E. (2005). *Brokerage and closure. An introduction to social capital.* Oxford, UK: Oxford University Press.

Burt, R. E. (2010). *Neighbor networks: Competitive advantage local and personal.* Oxford, UK: Oxford University Press.

Burt, R. S. (1980). Models of network structure. *Annual Review of Sociology, 6*, 79–141. doi:10.1146/annurev.so.06.080180.000455

Burt, R. S. (1982). *Toward a structural theory of action: Network models of social structure perception and action.* New York, NY: Academic Press.

Burt, R. S. (1987). Social contagion and innovation: Cohesion versus structural equivalence. *American Journal of Sociology, 92*, 1287–1355. doi:10.1086/228667

Burt, R. S. (1992). *Structural holes: The social structure of competition.* Cambridge, MA: Harvard University Press.

Burt, R. S. (2001). Structural holes versus network closure as social capital. In Lin, N., Cook, K., & Burt, R. S. (Eds.), *Social capital: Theory and research.* New York, NY: Aldine De Gruyter.

Busemeyer, J. R., & Townsend, J. T. (1993). Decision field theory: A dynamic cognitive approach to decision-making in an uncertain environment. *Psychological Review, 100*, 432–459. doi:10.1037/0033-295X.100.3.432

Butko, T. (2006). Terrorism redefined. *Peace Review, 18*, 145–151. doi:10.1080/10402650500510933

Buytendijk, F., Cripe, B., Henson, R., & Pulverman, K. (2008). Business management in the age of Enterprise 2.0: Why business model 1.0 will obsolete you [White paper]. *Oracle.* Retrieved May 20, 2010, from http://www.oracle.com/solutions/business_intelligence/docs/epm-enterprise20-whitepaper.pdf

Caiani, M., & Wagemann, C. (2009). Online networks of the Italian and German extreme right: An explorative study with social network analysis. *Information Communication and Society, 12*, 66–109. doi:10.1080/13691180802158482

Calhoun, C. (1998). Community without propinquity revisited: Communications technology and the transformation of the urban public sphere. *Sociological Inquiry, 63*(3), 373–397. doi:10.1111/j.1475-682X.1998.tb00474.x

Camazine, S., Deneubourg, J. L., Findividuals, N. R., Sneyd, J., Theraulaz, G., & Bonabeau, E. (2001). *Self-organization in biological systems.* Princeton, NJ: Princeton University Press.

Carley, K. M. (2009). *Dynamic network analysis for counter-terrorism.* Unpublished manuscript, Carnegie Mellon University, Pittsburgh, PA.

Carley, K. M. (2002). Smart agents and organizations of the future. In Lievrouw, L., & Livingstone, S. (Eds.), *The handbook of new media.* London, UK: Sage.

Carpenter, T., Karakostas, G., & Shallcross, D. (2004). *Practical issues and algorithms for analyzing terrorist networks.* Morristown, NJ: Telcordia Technologies.

Carrington, P. J., Scott, J., & Wasserman, S. (Eds.). (2006). *Models and methods of social network analysis.* Cambridge, UK: Cambridge University Press.

Case, C. J., King, D. L., & DeSimone, K. (2009). Virtual worlds: An exploratory study of undergraduate behavior. *Proceedings of the Academy for Studies in Business.*

Castells M. (2000-2003). *The information age,* vols. 1-3. London, UK: Routledge

Castells, M. (2002). *La galàxia Internet.* Barcelona, Spain: Rosa dels Vents.

Castells, M. (1996). *The rise of network the society.* Oxford, UK: Blackwell Publishing.

Castells, M. (1996). *The rise of the network society.* Cambridge, MA: Blackwell.

Castells, M. (2003). The power of identity: The information age: *Vol. II. Economy, society, and culture.* Oxford, UK: Wiley-Blackwell.

Castronova, E. (2006). On the research value of large games: Natural experiments in Norrath and Camelot. *CESifo Working Paper Series No. 1621*. Retrieved from http://ssrn.com/abstract=87557

Center for Computational Analysis of Social and Organizational Systems (CASOS) <http://www.casos.cs.cmu.edu/>

Cha, M., Mislove, A., & Gummadi, K. P. (2009). A measurement-driven analysis of information propagation in the flickr social network. *Proceedings of the 18th international conference on World Wide Web*, 721-730.

Chaliand, G., & Blin, A. (Eds.). (2007). *The history of terrorism: From antiquity to Al Qaeda*Schneider, E., Pulver, K., & Browner, J., Trans.). Berkeley, CA: University of California Press.

Chambers, R. (1985). Shortcut methods of gathering social information for rural development projects. In Cernea, M. (Ed.), *Putting people first: Sociological variables in rural development* (pp. 515–537). New York, NY: Oxford University Press.

Chan, K. W., Yim, C. K., Simon, S. K., & Lam, S. S. K. (2010). Is Customer Participation in Value Creation a Double-Edged Sword? Evidence from Professional Financial Services Across Cultures. *Journal of Marketing*, *74*(3). doi:10.1509/jmkg.74.3.48

Chen, P., & Xie, H. (2007). Finding scientific gems with Google's PageRank algorithm. *Journal of Informatrics*, *1*(1), 8–15. doi:10.1016/j.joi.2006.06.001

Chepko-Sade, B. D., Reitz, P. R., & Sade, D. S. (1989). Sociometrics of Macaca mulatta IV: Network analysis of social structure of a pre-fission group. *Social Networks*, *11*, 293–314. doi:10.1016/0378-8733(89)90007-5

Chesbrough, H. W. (2003). The era of open innovation. *MIT Sloan Management Review*, *4*(3), 74–81.

Chevalier, J. A., & Mayzlin, D. (2006). The effect of word of mouth on sales: Online book reviews. *JMR, Journal of Marketing Research*, *43*(3), 345–354. doi:10.1509/jmkr.43.3.345

Chiu, C. M., Hsu, M., & Wang, E. (2006). Understanding staring in virtual communities: an integration of social capital and social cognitive theories. *Decision Support Systems*, *42*, 1872–1888. doi:10.1016/j.dss.2006.04.001

Choudhury, M. D., Lin, Y.-R., Sundaram, H., Candan, K. S., Xie, L., & Kelliher, A. (2010b). How does the data sampling strategy impact the discovery of information diffusion in social media? In *Proceedings of the Fourth International AAAI Conference on Weblogs and Social Media*, (pp. 34-41).

Choudhury, M. D., Mason, W. A., Hofman, J. M., & Watts, D. J. (2010a). Inferring relevant social networks from interpersonal communication. In *Proceedings of the Nineteenth World Wide Web Conference*, (pp. 301-310).

Christakis, N. A., & Fowler, J. H. (2007). The spread of obesity in a large social network over 32 years. *The New England Journal of Medicine*, *357*(4), 370–379. doi:10.1056/NEJMsa066082

Christiansen, K., & Levinson, D. (Eds.). (2003). *Encyclopedia of community: From the village to the virtual world*. Thousand Oaks, CA: Sage Publications.

Chua, V., Madej, J., & Wellman, B. (2011forthcoming). Personal communities: The world according to me. In Carrington, P., & Scott, J. (Eds.), *Handbook of social network analysis*. London, UK: Sage.

Chun-Yuen, T., & Adamic, L. A. (2010). Longevity in Second Life. In *Proceedings of the Fourth International AAAI Conference on Weblogs and Social Media*. AAAI Press.

Chwe, M. S.-Y. (2000). Communication and coordination in social networks. *The Review of Economic Studies*, *67*, 1–16. doi:10.1111/1467-937X.00118

Cicone, A., & Serra-Capizzano, S. (2010). Google PageRanking problem: The model and the analysis. *Journal of Computational and Applied Mathematics*, *234*(11), 3140–3169. doi:10.1016/j.cam.2010.02.005

Clark, L. H., & Shahrokhi, F. (1992). A linear time algorithm for graph partition problems. *Information Processing Letters*, *42*(1), 19–24. doi:10.1016/0020-0190(92)90126-G

Clore, G. L., & Palmer, J. (2009). Affective guidance of intelligent agents: How emotion controls cognition. *Cognitive Systems Research*, *10*(1), 21–30. doi:10.1016/j.cogsys.2008.03.002

Cohen, J. B., Pham, M. T., & Andrade, E. B. (2008). The nature and role of affect in consumer behavior. In Haugtvedt, C. P., Herr, P., & Kardes, F. (Eds.), *Handbook of consumer psychology* (pp. 297–348). Erlbaum.

Cohen, P. R. (1985). *Heuristic reasoning about uncertainty: An artificial intelligence approach*. Boston, MA: Pitman Advanced Publishing Program.

Cohen, S., Doyle, W. J., Skoner, D. P., Rabin, B. S., & Gwaltney, J. M. Jr. (1997). Social ties and susceptibility to the common cold. *Journal of the American Medical Association, 277*, 1940–1944. doi:10.1001/jama.277.24.1940

Cohen, S., Doyle, W. J., Turner, R., Alper, C. M., & Skoner, D. P. (2003). Sociability and susceptibility to the common cold. *Psychological Science, 14*(5), 389–395. doi:10.1111/1467-9280.01452

Coleman, J. S. (1988). Social capital in the creation of human capital. [Supplement.]. *American Journal of Sociology, ▪▪▪*, 4.

Commission on Children at Risk. (2003). *Hardwired to connect: The new scientific case for authoritative communities*. New York, NY: Institute for American Values.

Comscore. (2010). *Facebook captures top spot among social networking sites in India*. Retrieved December 20, 2010, from http://www.comscore.com/Press_Events/Press_Releases/2010/8/Facebook_Captures_Top_Spot_among_Social_Networking_Sites_in_India

Conradt, L., & Roper, T. J. (2003). Group decision-making in animals. *Nature, 421*, 155–158. doi:10.1038/nature01294

Conradt, L., & Roper, T. J. (2005). Consensus decision making in animals. *Trends in Ecology & Evolution, 20*, 449–456. doi:10.1016/j.tree.2005.05.008

Constantinides, E., & Fountain, S. (2008). Web 2.0: Conceptual foundations and marketing issues. *Journal of Direct. Data and Digital Marketing Practice, 9*(3), 231–244. doi:10.1057/palgrave.dddmp.4350098

Costenbader, E., & Valente, T. W. (2003). The stability of centrality measures when networks are sampled. *Social Networks, 25*(4), 283–307. doi:10.1016/S0378-8733(03)00012-1

Couper, M. P., & Nicholls, W. L. (1998). The history and development of computer assisted survey information collection. In Couper, M. (Ed.), *Computer assisted survey information collection* (pp. 1–23). New York, NY: Wiley.

Couzin, I. D., & Krause, J. (2003). Self-organization and collective behaviors in vertebrates. *Advances in the Study of Animal Behavior, 32*, 1–75. doi:10.1016/S0065-3454(03)01001-5

Coviello, N. (2005). Integrating Qualitative and Quantitative Techniques in Network Analysis Qualitative Market Research 8(1): 39-60. *Qualitative Market Research, 8*, 39–60. doi:10.1108/13522750510575435

Coviello, N. (2005). Integrating qualitative and quantitative techniques in network analysis. *Qualitative Market Research, 8*(1), 39–60. doi:10.1108/13522750510575435

Crandall, D., Cosley, D., Huttenlocher, D., Kleinberg, J., & Suri, S. (2008), Feedback effects between similarity and social influence in online communities. In *Proc. of the ACM SIGKDD International Conference on Knowledge Discovery and Data Mining (SIGKDD '08)*, (pp. 160-168). Las Vegas, NV, USA, ACM Press.

Cranford, C. J. (2005). Networks of exploitation: Immigrant labour and the restructuring of the Los Angeles janitorial industry. *Social Problems, 52*(3), 379–397. doi:10.1525/sp.2005.52.3.379

Croft, D. P., James, R., & Krause, J. (2008). *Exploring animal social networks*. Princeton, NJ: Princeton University Press.

Croft, D. P., James, R., Ward, A. J. W., Botham, M. S., Mawdsley, D., & Krause, J. (2005). Assortative interactions and social networks in fish. *Oecologia, 143*, 211–219. doi:10.1007/s00442-004-1796-8

Crooks, A., Hudson-Smith, A., & Dearden, J. (2009). Agent Street: An environment for exploring agent-based models in Second Life. *Journal of Artificial Societies and Social Simulation, 12*(4), 10. Retrieved from http://jasss.soc.surrey.ac.uk/12/4/10.html.

Crossley, N. (2008). Pretty connected: The social network of the early UK punk movement. *Theory, Culture & Society, 25*, 89–116. doi:10.1177/0263276408095546

Cross, R., Borgatti, S. P., & Parker, A. (2002). Making invisible work visible: Using social network analysis to support strategic collaboration. *California Management Review, 44*(2).

Csermely, P. (2008). Creative elements: Network-based predictions of active centres in proteins and cellular and social networks. *Trends in Biochemical Sciences, 33*(12), 569–576. doi:10.1016/j.tibs.2008.09.006

Currarini, S., Jackson, M., & Pin, P. (2009). An economic model of friendship: Homophily, minorities and segregation. *Econometrica: Journal of the Econometric Society, 77*(4), 1003–1045. doi:10.3982/ECTA7528

Danchin, E., Boulinier, T., & Massot, M. (1998). Conspecific reproductive success and breeding habitat selection: Implications for the study of coloniality. *Ecology, 79*, 2415–2428. doi:10.1890/0012-9658(1998)079[2415:CR SABH]2.0.CO;2

Dasgupta, P., & Serageldin, I. (Eds.). (1999). *Social capital: A multifaceted perspective.* Washington, DC: The World Bank.

Davidsson, P. (2002). Agent based social simulation: A computer science view. *Journal of Artificial Societies and Social Simulation, 5*(1). Retrieved from http://jasss.soc.surrey.ac.uk/5/1/7.html.

Davis, A., Gardner, B. B., & Gardner, M. R. (1941). *Deep south. A social anthropological study of caste and class.* Chicago, IL: University of Chicago Press.

Davis, J. (1969). Social structures and cognitive structures. In Abelson, R. (Ed.), *Theories of cognitive consistency.* Chicago, IL: Rand McNally.

De Bruijn, H. (2006). One fight, one team: The 9/11 commission report on intelligence, fragmentation and information. *Public Administration, 84*, 267–287. doi:10.1111/j.1467-9299.2006.00002.x

de Gemmis, M., Lops, P., Semeraro, G., & Basile, P. (2008). Integrating tags in a semantic content-based recommender. In *Proc. of the ACM Conference on Recommender Systems (RecSys '08)*, (pp. 163-170). ACM Press.

De Meo, P., Garro, A., Terracina, G., & Ursino, D. (2003). X-Learn: An XML-based, multi-agent system for supporting "user-device" adaptive e-learning. In *Proc. of the International Conference on Ontologies, Databases and Applications of Semantics (ODBASE 2003)*, (pp. 739-756). Taormina, Italy. Lecture Notes in Computer Science, Springer.

De Meo, P., Quattrone, G., Terracina, G., & Ursino, D. (2007). An XML-based multi-agent system for supporting online recruitment services. *IEEE Transactions on Systems, Man ad Cybernetics - Part A, 37*(4), 467-480.

De Meo, P., Rosaci, D., Sarnè, G., Terracina, G., & Ursino, D. (2003). An XML-based adaptive multi-agent system for handling e-commerce activities. *Proc. of the International Conference on Web Services (ICWS-Europe 2003)*, (pp. 152-166). Erfurt, Germany.

De Meo, P., Quattrone, G., & Ursino, D. (2010). A query expansion and user profile enrichment approach to improve the performance of recommender systems operating on a folksonomy. *User Modeling and User-Adapted Interaction, 20*(1), 41–86. doi:10.1007/s11257-010-9072-6

De Ruiter, J. P., Rossignol, S., Vuurpijl, L., Cunningham, D. W., & Levelt, W. J. M. (2003). SLOT: A research platform for investigating multimodal communication. *Behavior Research Methods, Instruments, & Computers, 35*(3), 408–419. doi:10.3758/BF03195518

De Solla Price, D. J. (1965). Networks of scientific papers. *Science, 149*, 510–515. doi:10.1126/science.149.3683.510

de Souza e Silva, A. (2006). From cyber to hybrid: Mobile technologies as interfaces of hybrid spaces. *Space and Culture, 9*, 261–278. doi:10.1177/1206331206289022

De Souza, C. S., & Preece, J. (2004). A framework for analyzing and understanding online communities. *Interacting with Computers, 16*(3), 579–610. doi:10.1016/j.intcom.2003.12.006

de Tocqueville, A. (2002). *Democracy in America* (Mansfield, H. C., & Winthrop, D., Trans.). Chicago, IL: University of Chicago Press. (Original work published 1835)

Degenne, A., & Forsé, M. (2003). *Introducing social networks* (Borges, A., Trans.). London, UK: Sage Publications.

den Boer, M., Hillebrand, C., & Nolke, A. (2008). Legitimacy under pressure: The European web of counter-terrorism networks. *Journal of Common Market Studies, 46*, 101–124. doi:10.1111/j.1468-5965.2007.00769.x

Denzin, N. K. (1970). *The research act.* Chicago, IL: Aldaline.

Dery, M. (Ed.). (1994). *Flame wars: The discourse of cyberculture.* Durham, NC: Duke University Press.

Detrain, C., & Deneubourg, J. L. (2006). Self-organized structures in a superorganism: Do ants "behave" like molecules? *Physics of Life Reviews, 3*, 162–187. doi:10.1016/j.plrev.2006.07.001

Diani, M. (2009). The structural bases of protest events: Multiple memberships and civil society networks in the 15th February 2003 anti-war demonstrations. *Acta Sociologica, 52*(1), 63–83. doi:10.1177/0001699308100634

Diaz-Bone, R. (2007). *Does qualitative network analysis exist?* Retrieved November 21, 2010, from http://www.qualitative-research.net/index.php/fqs/article/view-Article/224/493

Diewald, M. (1991). *Soziale Beziehungen, Verlust oder Liberalisierung?: Soziale Unterstützung in informellen Netzwerken.* Berlin, Germany: Edition Sigma.

DiMicco, J. M., Geyer, W., Millen, D. R., Dugan, C., & Brownholtz, B. (2009). People Sensemaking and Relationship Building on an Enterprise Social Network Site. *HICSS '09: 42nd Hawaii International Conference on System Sciences,* 1-10

DiMicco, J., Millen, D. R., Geyer, W., Dugan, C., Brownholtz, B., & Muller, M. (2008). Motivations for social networking at work. In *CSCW '08: Proceedings of the 2008 ACM Conference on Computer Supported Cooperative Work,* (pp. 711-720).

DiMicco, J., Millen, D. R., Geyer, W., Dugan, C., Brownholtz, B., & Muller, M. (2008). Motivations for social networking at work. [San Diego, California, USA.]. *Proceedings of CSCW, 08*(November), 8–12.

Dishman, C. (2005). The leaderless nexus: When crime and terror converge. *Studies in Conflict and Terrorism, 28*, 237–252. doi:10.1080/10576100590928124

Doreian, P. (1999). An intuitive introduction to block-modeling with examples. *BMS Bulletin de Methodologie Sociologique, 61*, 5–34.

Dourisboure, Y., Geraci, F., et al. (2007). Extraction and classification of dense communities in the Web. *Proceedings of the 16th International Conference on World Wide Web,* (pp. 461-470). Banff, Canada: ACM.

Dow, M. M., & de Waal, F. B. M. (1989). Assignment methods for the analysis of network subgroup interactions. *Social Networks, 11*, 237–255. doi:10.1016/0378-8733(89)90004-X

Driskell, R. B., & Lyon, L. (2002). Are virtual communities true communities? *City & Community, 1*, 373–390. doi:10.1111/1540-6040.00031

Drury, G. (2008). Opinion piece: Social media: Should marketers engage and how can it be done effectively? *Journal of Direct. Data and Digital Marketing Practice, 9*, 274–277. doi:10.1057/palgrave.dddmp.4350096

DuBois, T., Golbeck, J., Kleint, J., & Srinivasan, A. (2009). *Improving recommendation accuracy by clustering social networks with trust.* ACM Workshop on Recommender Systems & the Social Web.

Ducheneaut, N., Wen, M., Yee, N., & Wadley, G. (2009). *Body and mind: A study of avatar personalization in three virtual worlds.* 27th Annual CHI Conference on Human Factors in Computing Systems (CHI 2009). Boston, USA.

Durante, A., & Goodwin, Ch. (1997). *Rethinking context.* Cambridge, UK: Cambridge University Press.

Durkheim, E. (1984). *The division of labour in society.* London, UK: Macmillan. (Original work published 1893)

Dwyer, C. (2007). Digital relationships in the 'MySpace' generation: Results from a qualitative study. *Proceedings of the 40th HICSS*

Dwyer, C., Hiltz, S. R., & Widmeyer, G. (2008). Understanding development and usage of social networking sites: The social software performance model. *Proceedings of the 41st Hawaii Int'l Conf. on System Sciences* (p. 212). IEEE CS.

Dyer, J. R. G., Ioannou, C. C., Morrell, L. J., Croft, D. P., Couzin, I. D., Waters, D. A., & Krause, J. (2007). Consensus decisions making in human crowds. *Animal Behaviour*, *75*, 461–470. doi:10.1016/j.anbehav.2007.05.010

eBay. (2010). *Online auction website*. Retrieved September 15, 2010, from http://ebay.com

eBizMBA Inc. (2010, September 15). Top 15 Most Popular Social Networking Websitess. *eBizMBA*. Retrieved September 21, 2010, from http://www.ebizmba.com/articles/social-networking-websites

Edelman. (2010). 2010 Edelman Trust Barometer: an annual global opinion leaders study – executive summary. Retrieved September 18, 2010 from http://www.edelman.co.uk/trustbarometer/files/edelman-trust-barometer-2010.pdf

Edmonds, B. (1998). Modelling bounded rationality in agent-based simulations using the evolution of mental models. In Brenner, T. (Ed.), *Computational techniques for modelling learning in economics* (pp. 305–332). Kluwer. doi:10.1007/978-1-4615-5029-7_13

Edmonds, B. (2006). How are physical and social spaces related? Cognitive agents as the necessary glue. In Billari, F. (Eds.), *Agent-based computational modelling: Applications in demography, social, economic and environmental sciences* (pp. 195–214). Berlin, Germany: Springer-Verlag. doi:10.1007/3-7908-1721-X_10

Edmonds, B., & Moss, S. (2011). *Simulation social complexity: A handbook*. Springer.

Edwards, G. (2010). *Mixed-Method Approaches to Social Network Analysis.* Retrieved December 21, 2010, from http://eprints.ncrm.ac.uk/842/1/Social_Network_analysis_Edwards.pdf

Eilstrup-Sangiovanni, M., & Jones, C. (2008). Assessing the dangers of illicit networks: Why Al-Qaida may be less dangerous than many think. *International Security*, *33*, 7–44. doi:10.1162/isec.2008.33.2.7

Elliot, A. J., & Maier, M. A. (2007). Color and psychological functioning. *Current Directions in Psychological Science*, *16*, 250–254. doi:10.1111/j.1467-8721.2007.00514.x

Elliot, A. J., Maier, M. A., Moller, A. C., Friedman, R., & Meinhardt, J. (2007). Color and psychological functioning: The effect of red on performance attainment. *Journal of Experimental Psychology. General*, *136*, 154–168. doi:10.1037/0096-3445.136.1.154

Ellis, D., & Maoz, I. (2007). Online argument between Palestinians and Jews. *Human Communication Research*, *33*(3), 291–309. doi:10.1111/j.1468-2958.2007.00300.x

Ellison, N., Lampe, C. & Steinfield, C. (2009). Social Network Sites and Society: Current Trends and Future Possibilities. *Interactions Magazine*, 16 (1)

Emanuelson, P., & Willer, D. (2009). One-shot exchange networks and the shadow of the future. *Social Networks*, *31*(2), 147–154. doi:10.1016/j.socnet.2009.02.001

Embree, J. (1950). Thailand: A loosely structured social system. *American Anthropologist*, *52*, 181–193. doi:10.1525/aa.1950.52.2.02a00030

Emirbayer, M., & Goodwin, J. (1994). Network analysis, culture, and the problem of agency. *American Journal of Sociology*, *99*, 1411–1451. doi:10.1086/230450

Enders, W., & Jindapon, P. (2010). Network externalities and the structure of terror networks. *The Journal of Conflict Resolution*, *54*, 262–280. doi:10.1177/0022002709355439

Enders, W., & Su, X. (2007). Rational terrorists and optimal network structure. *The Journal of Conflict Resolution*, *51*, 33–57. doi:10.1177/0022002706296155

Entwistle, B., Faust, K., Rindfuss, R., & Kaneda, T. (2007). Networks and contexts: Variations in the structure of social ties. *American Journal of Sociology*, *112*(5), 1495–1533. doi:10.1086/511803

Epstein, J., & Axtell, R. (1996). *Growing artificial societies: Social science from the bottom up*. Boston, MA: The MIT Press.

Ereteo, G., Buffa, M., Gandon, F., Grohan, P., Leitzelman, L., & Sander, P. (2008). State of the Art on Social Network Analysis and its Applications on a Semantic Web. *Proceedings of the 7th International Semantic Web Conference.*

Ernst, A., Krebs, F., & Zehnpfund, C. (2007). Dynamics of task oriented agent behaviour in multiple layer social networks. In Takahashi, S., Sallach, D., & Rouchier, R. (Eds.), *Advancing social simulation* (pp. 319–330). Berlin, Germany: Springer-Verlag. doi:10.1007/978-4-431-73167-2_29

Ertell, K. (2010b, February 9). The key to driving retail success with social media: Focus on Facebook [White Paper]. *ForeSee Results*. Retrieved January 20, 2011, from http://www.foreseeresults.com/research-white-papers/_downloads/foresee-results-how-to-drive-retail-success-social-media-us-2010.pdf

Escobar, A. (2000). Welcome to Cyberia, notes on the anthropology of cyberculture. In Bell, D., & Kennedy, B. (Eds.), *The cybercultures reader*. London, UK: Routledge. doi:10.1086/204266

Estrada, E. (Eds.). (2010). *Network science: Complexity in nature and technology*. London, UK: Springer-Verlag.

Estrada, E., & Hatano, N. (2008). Communicability in complex networks. *Physical Review E: Statistical, Nonlinear, and Soft Matter Physics*, 77(3), 036111..doi:10.1103/PhysRevE.77.036111

European Security Research and Innovation Forum (ES-RIF) <http://www.esrif.eu/>

Evers, H. D. (Ed.). (1969). *Loosely structured social systems: Thailand in perspective*. Cultural Report Series No 17. New Haven, CT: Yale University (Southeast Asia Studies).

Facebook Insights. (2010). *Facebook upgrading "Insights" metrics dashboard for page managers tonight*. Retrieved August 22, 2010, from http://www.insidefacebook.com/2009/05/05 /facebook-upgrading-insights-metrics-dashboard-for-page-managers-tonight/

Facebook. (2007). Facebook Pages. *Facebook*. Retrieved June 20, 2010, from http://www.facebook.com/advertising/FacebookPagesProductGuide.pdf

Facebook. (2010). *Facebook statistics*. Retrieved August 11, 2010, from http://www.facebook.com/press/info.php

Fan Page List. (2010). *Top Facebook fan pages*. Retrieved June 29, 2010, from http://fanpagelist.com/category/top_pages/

Farley, J. (2003). Breaking Al-Qaeda cells: A mathematical analysis of counterterrorism (a guide for risk management and decision making). *Studies in Conflict and Terrorism*, 26, 399–411. doi:10.1080/10576100390242857

Farooqi, M. N. (2010). Curbing the use of hawala for money laundering and terrorist financing: Global regulatory response and future challenges. *International Journal of Business Governance and Ethics*, 5, 64–75. doi:10.1504/IJBGE.2010.029556

Fenicia, T., Gamper, M., & Schönhuth, M. (2010). Integration, Sozialkapital und soziale Netzwerke. Egozentrierte Netzwerke von (Spät-)Aussiedlern. In M. Gamper & L. Reschke (Eds.), *Knoten und Kanten. Soziale Netzwerkanalyse in Wirtschafts- und Migrationsforschung* (pp. 305–332). Bielefeld, Germany: transcript-Verl.

Fenneman, M., & Tillie, J. (2001). Civic community, political participation and political trust of ethnic groups. *Connections*, 24(1), 26–41.

Ferber, J. (1999). *Multi-agent systems: An introduction to distributed artificial intelligence*. Addison Wesley.

Ferron, M., Massa, P., & Odella, F. (2011). Analyzing collaborative networks emerging in Enterprise 2.0: The Taolin Platform. *Procedia Social and Behavioural Science*, 10, 68–78. doi:10.1016/j.sbspro.2011.01.010

Fewell, J. H. (2003). Social insect networks. *Science*, 301, 1867–1870. doi:10.1126/science.1088945

Field, A. (2009). Tracking terrorist networks: Problems of intelligence sharing within the UK intelligence community. *Review of International Studies*, 35, 997–1009. doi:10.1017/S0260210509990416

Fielding, N., Lee, R. M., & Blank, G. (Eds.). (2008). *The Sage handbook of online research methods*. Los Angeles, CA: SAGE.

Figueroa Sarriera, H. J. (2006). Connecting the selves: Computer mediated identification processes. In Silver, D., & Massanari, A. (Eds.), *Critical cyberculture studies: Current terrains, future directions*. New York, NY: NYU Press.

Fischer, C. S., Jackson, R. M., Steuve, A. C., Gerson, K., Jones, L. M., & Baldassare, M. (1977). *Networks and places: Social relations in the urban setting*. New York, NY: Free Press.

Fischhoff, I. R., Sundaresan, S. R., Cordingley, J., Larkin, H. M., Sellier, M. J., & Rubenstein, D. I. (2007). Social relationships and reproductive state influence leadership roles in movements of plains zebra, *Equus burchellii. Animal Behaviour*, *73*, 825–831. doi:10.1016/j.anbehav.2006.10.012

Fisher, D., Smith, M., & Welser, H. T. (2006). You are who you talk to: Detecting roles in Usenet newsgroups. *Proceedings of the 39th Hawaii International Conference on System Sciences*.

Fisher, C. (1977). *Network and places. Social relations in the urban setting.* New York, NY: The Free Press.

Fisher, C. (1982). *To dwell among friends. Personal networks in town and city.* Chicago, IL: University of Chicago Press.

Flap, H. D., & Volker, B. (Eds.). (2004). *Creation and returns of social capital.* London, UK: Routledge.

Flew, T. (2004). New media: An introduction. In Shields, R. (Ed.), *Cultures of Internet.* London, UK: Oxford University Press.

Fogg, B. J. (2008). Mass interpersonal persuasion: An early view of a new phenomenon. *Proceedings of the 3rd International Conference on Persuasive Technology.* Berlin: Springer

Forrester. (2010). *Forrester research.* Retrieved September 29, 2010, from http://www.forrester.com/rb/research

Fortes, M. (1953). The structure of unilineal descent groups. *American Anthropologist, 55*, 17–41. doi:10.1525/aa.1953.55.1.02a00030

Fortino, A., & Nayak, A. (2010). An architecture for applying social networking to business. *2010 Long Island Systems Applications and Technology Conference (LISAT)*, (pp. 1-6).

Fortunato, S. (2010). Community detection in graphs. *Physics Reports*, *486*(3-5), 75–174. doi:10.1016/j.physrep.2009.11.002

Foster, B. L. (1980). Minority traders in Thai village social networks. *Ethnic Groups, 2*(3), 221–240.

Fowler, J. H., & Christakis, N. A. (2008). Dynamic spread of happiness in a large social network: longitudinal analysis over 20 years in the Framingham heart study. *British Medical Journal*, *337*, 1–9. doi:10.1136/bmj.a2338

Fox, M. W. (1972). *Behavior of wolves, dogs and related canids.* New York, NY: Harper and Row.

Franks, N. R., Dornhaus, A., Fitzsimmons, J. P., & Stevens, M. (2003). Speed versus accuracy in collective decision making. *Proceedings of the Royal Society, Series B, 270*, 2457–2463. .doi:10.1098/rspb.2003.2527

Franks, N. R., Pratt, S. C., Mallon, E. B., Britton, N. F., & Sumpter, D. J. T. (2002). Information flow, opinion polling and collective intelligence in house-hunting social insects. *Philosophical Transactions of the Royal Society of London, Series B, 357*, 1567–1583. .doi:10.1098/rstb.2002.1066

Frantz, T. L., & Carley, K. M. (2005). *A formal characterization of cellular networks.* Unpublished manuscript, Carnegie Mellon University, Pittsburgh, PA.

Freeman, L. (1979). Centrality in social networks: Conceptual clarification. *Social Networks*, *1*, 215–239. doi:10.1016/0378-8733(78)90021-7

Freeman, L. C. (1978). On measuring systematic integration. *Connections, 2*(1), 13–14.

Freeman, L. C. (2004). *The development of social network analysis: A study in the sociology of science.* Empirical Press.

Friedkin, N. (1998). *A structural theory of social influence.* Cambridge University Press. doi:10.1017/CBO9780511527524

Fulk, J., & Steinfeld, C. (1990). *Organizations and communication technology.* Newbury Park, CA: Sage.

Gabrilovich, E., & Markovitch, S. (2007). Computing semantic relatedness using Wikipedia-based explicit semantic analysis. *Proceedings of the 20th International Joint Conference on Artificial Intelligence*, (pp. 6-12).

Gajendra, S., & Sun, W. (2010). Second Life: A Computer Mediated Environment for Communication and E Business Management. *2010 International Conference on Challenges in Environmental Science and Computer Engineering*, pp. 431-434.

Galaskiewicz, J. (1979). The structure of community organizational networks. *Social Forces, 57*, 1346–1364.

Galaskiewicz, J., & Krohn, K. R. (1984). Positions, roles, and dependencies in a community interorganization system. *The Sociological Quarterly, 25*(4), 527–550. doi:10.1111/j.1533-8525.1984.tb00208.x

Gallaher, A. (1961). *Plainville fifteen years later*. New York, NY: Columbia University Press.

Gamper, M., & Reschke, L. (2010). Soziale Netzwerkanalyse. Eine interdisziplinäre Erfolgsgeschichte. In M. Gamper & L. Rechke (Eds.), *Sozialtheorie. Knoten und Kanten. Soziale Netzwerkanalyse in Wirtschafts- und Migrationsforschung* (pp. 13–51). Bielefeld, Germany: transcript.

Ganley, D., & Lampe, C. (2009). The ties that bind: Social network principles in online communities. *Decision Support Systems, 47*, 268–274. doi:10.1016/j.dss.2009.02.013

Gans, H. J. (1962). Urbanism and suburbanism as ways of life. In Rose, A. M. (Ed.), *Human behavior and social processes: An interactionist approach*. Boston, MA: Houghton Mifflin.

Garg, N., & Weber, I. (2008). Personalized tag suggestion for flickr. *Proceeding of the 17th International Conference on World Wide Web*, (pp. 1063-1064).

Gautrais, J., Michelena, P., Sibbald, A., Bon, R., & Deneubourg, J. L. (2007). Allelomimetic synchronization in Merino sheep. *Animal Behaviour, 74*, 1443–1454. doi:10.1016/j.anbehav.2007.02.020

Geertz, C. (1987). *La interpretación de las culturas*. Barcelona, Spain: Gedisa.

Gerhard, M., Moore, D., & Hobbs, D. (2004). Embodiment and copresence in collaborative interfaces. *International Journal of Human-Computer Studies, 61*(4), 453–480. doi:10.1016/j.ijhcs.2003.12.014

Geyer, W., Dugan, C., Millen, D. R., Muller, M., & Freyne, J. (2008). Recommending topics for self-descriptions in online user profiles. In *Proc. of the ACM Conference on Recommender Systems (RecSys '08)*, (pp. 59-66). Lausanne, Switzerland.

Ghita, S., Nejdl, W., & Paiu, R. (2005). Semantically Rich Recommendations in Social Networks for Sharing, Exchanging and Ranking Semantic Context. *The Semantic Web - ISWC*. 293-307.

Giarchi, G. G. (2001). Caught in the nets: A critical examination of the use of the concept of networks in community development studies. *Community Development Journal, 36*(1), 63–71. doi:10.1093/cdj/36.1.63

Gibson, D. (2005). Concurrency and commitment: Network scheduling and its consequences for diffusion. *The Journal of Mathematical Sociology, 29*(4), 295–325. doi:10.1080/00222500590957491

Giddens, A. (1991). *Modernity and self-identity: Self and society in the late modern age*. Cambridge, UK: Polity Press.

Giese, J., & Cote, J. (2002). Defining consumer satisfaction. *Academy of Marketing Science Review, 1*, •••. Retrieved from http://www.amsreview.org/amsrev/theory/giese00-01.html.

Gilbert, N. (2002). Varieties of emergence. In *Proceedings of the Agent 2002 Conference: Social agents: Ecology, Exchange, and Evolution*, Chicago, USA.

Gilbert, N. (2004). The art of simulation. In *Proceedings of the Second European Social Simulation Conference (ESSA'04)*, Groningen, The Netherlands.

Gilbert, N., & Troitzsch, K. (2005). *Simulation for the social scientist*. Open University Press.

Girard, A., & Fallery, B. (2009). E-recruitment: new practices, new issues. An exploratory study. *3rd International Workshop on Human Resource Information Systems (HRIS 2009), in conjunction with ICEIS 2009*. Milan, Italy: INSTICC PRESS

Girvan, M., & Newman, M. E. J. (2002). Community structure in social and biological networks. *Proceedings of the National Academy of Sciences of the United States of America, 99*(12), 7821–7826. doi:10.1073/pnas.122653799

Girvan, M., & Newman, M. E. J. (2002). Community structure in social and biological networks. *Proceedings of the National Academy of Sciences of the United States of America, 99*(12), 8271–8276. doi:10.1073/pnas.122653799

Gloor, P. A. (2006). *Swarm creativity. Competitive advantage through collaborative innovation networks.* New York, NY: Oxford University Press.

Golbeck, J., & Hendler, J. (2006). Filmtrust: Movie recommendations using trust in web-based social networks. *Proceedings of the IEEE Consumer Communications and Networking Conference, 42,* (pp. 43-44).

Golder, S., Wilkinson, D., & Huberman, B. (2007). Rhythms of social interaction: Messaging within a massive online network. In *Proc. 3rd International Conference on Communities and Technologies (CT2007)*, East Lansing, MI.

Golder, S., Wilkinson, D., & Huberman, B. (2007). Rhythms of social interaction: Messaging within a massive online network. In *Proceedings of the Third Communities and Technologies Conference,* (pp. 41-66).

Golder, S. A., & Huberman, B. A. (2006). Usage patterns of collaborative tagging systems. *Journal of Information Science, 32*(2), 198–208. doi:10.1177/0165551506062337

Goldschmidt, W. (1947). *As you sow.* New York, NY: Harcourt Brace.

Gori, M., & Numerico, T. (2003). Social networks and web minorities. *Cognitive Systems Research, 4*(4), 355–364. doi:10.1016/S1389-0417(03)00016-0

Gouldner, A. (1957). Cosmopolitans and locals: Toward an analysis of latent social roles. *Administrative Science Quarterly, 2*(3), 281–306. doi:10.2307/2391000

Granovetter, M. (1973). The strength of weak ties. *American Journal of Sociology, 78*(6), 1360–1380. doi:10.1086/225469

Granovetter, M. (1985). Economic action and social structure: The problem of embeddedness. *American Journal of Sociology, 91,* 481–510. doi:10.1086/228311

Granovetter, M., & Soong, R. (1983). Threshold models of diffusion and collective behavior. *The Journal of Mathematical Sociology, 9*(3), 165–179. doi:10.1080/0022250X.1983.9989941

Gratch, J., Marsella, S., & Petta, P. (2009). Modeling the antecedents and consequences of emotion. *Journal of Cognitive Systems Research, 10*(1), 1–5. doi:10.1016/j.cogsys.2008.06.001

Gration, D., Foster, D., & Raciti, M. (2008). *Emotion and place: A consumer perspective in the context of hallmark events.* Council for Australian University Tourism and Hospitality Education.

Gray, D. H., & Stockham, E. (2008). Al-Qaeda in the Islamic Maghreb: The evolution from Algerian Islamism to transnational terror. *African Journal of Political Science and International Relations, 2,* 91–97.

Green, H., & Hannon, C. (2007). *Their space: Education for a digital generation.* London, UK: Demos. Retrieved 3 August, 2009, from http://www.demos.co.uk/files/Their%20 space%20-%20web.pdf

Grieco, M. S. (1982). Family structure and industrial employment: The role of information and migration. *Journal of Marriage and the Family, 44*(3), 701–707. doi:10.2307/351590

Groh, G., & Ehmig, C. (2007). Recommendations in taste related domains: Collaborative filtering vs. social filtering. In *Proc. of the International ACM conference on Supporting Group Work (GROUP '07),* (pp. 127-136).

Gross, B. (2000). *De la cibernética clásica a la cibercultura: Herramientas conceptuales desde donde mirar el mundo cambiante.* Salamanca, Spain: Ediciones Universidad de Salamanca.

Grossetti, M. (2007). Are French networks unique? *Social Networks, 29,* 391–404. doi:10.1016/j.socnet.2007.01.005

Gruhl, D., Liben-Nowell, D., Guha, R., & Tomkins, A. (2004). Information diffusion through blogosphere. In *Proc. 13th International World Wide Web Conference.*

Guimera, R., & Nunes Amaral, L. A. (2005). Functional cartography of complex metabolic networks. *Nature, 433*(7028), 895–900. doi:10.1038/nature03288

Guo, L., Tan, E., Chen, S., Zhang, X., & Zhao, Y. E. (2009). Analyzing patterns of user content generation in online social networks. *Proceedings of the 15th ACM SIGKDD international conference on Knowledge discovery and data mining, 369-378.*

Guo, Y., & Barnes, S. (2007). Why people buy virtual items in Virtual Worlds with real money. *Advances in Information Systems, 38*(4), 69–75.

Gustafson, S., Ma, H., & Moitra, A. (2009). A note on creating networks from social network data. *Connections, 29*(2), 77–84.

Gwinner, K., Gremler, D., & Bitner, M. (1998). Relational Benefits in Services Industries: The Customer's Perspective. *Journal of the Academy of Marketing Science, •••,* 101–114. doi:10.1177/0092070398262002

Haas, J., & Mützel, S. (2010). Netzwerkanalyse und Netzwerktheorie in Deutschland. Eine empirische Übersicht und theoretische Entwicklungspotentiale. In Stegbauer, C. (Ed.), *Netzwerkanalyse und Netzwerktheorie. Ein neues Paradigma in den Sozialwissenschaften* (pp. 49–64). Wiesbaden, Germany: VS Verlag für Sozialwissenschaften.

Hafez, M. M. (2007). Martyrdom mythology in Iraq: How jihadists frame suicide terrorism in videos and biographies. *Terrorism and Political Violence, 19,* 95–115. doi:10.1080/09546550601054873

Hagenbuchner, M., & Sperduti, A. (2009). Graph self-organizing maps for cyclic and unbounded graphs. *Neurocomputing, 72*(7-9), 1419–1430. doi:10.1016/j.neucom.2008.12.021

Hakken, D. (1999). *Cyborgs@Cyberspace?: An ethnographer looks at the future.* New York, NY: Routledge.

Halwani, R. (2006). Terrorism: Definition, justification, and applications. *Social Theory and Practice, 32,* 289–310.

Hampton, K. N. (2003). Grieving for a lost network: Collective action in a wired suburb. *Special Issue: ICTs and Community Networking. The Information Society, 19*(5), 417–428. doi:10.1080/714044688

Hampton, K. N. (2010). Internet use and the concentration of disadvantage: Glocalization and the urban underclass. *The American Behavioral Scientist, 53,* 1111–1132. doi:10.1177/0002764209356244

Hampton, K., & Wellman, B. (1999). Netville online and offline: Observing and surveying a wired suburb. *The American Behavioral Scientist, 43,* 475–492. doi:10.1177/00027649921955290

Hampton, K., & Wellman, B. (2001). Long distance community in the network society: Contact and support beyond Netville. *The American Behavioral Scientist, 45,* 476–495. doi:10.1177/00027640121957303

Han, J., & Kamber, M. (2006). *Data mining: Concepts and techniques* (2nd ed.). Morgan Kaufmann Publishers.

Harary, F., Norman, R., & Cartwright, D. (1965). *Structural models.* New York, NY: Wiley.

Haraway, D. (2003). Cyborgs to companion species: Reconfiguring kinship in technoscience. In Idhe, D., & Selinger, E. (Eds.), *Chasing technoscience: Matrix for materiality.* Bloomington, IN: Indiana University Press.

Harris, H., Bailenson, J. N., Nielson, A., & Yee, N. (2009). The evolution of social behavior over time in Second Life. *Presence (Cambridge, Mass.), 18*(6), 434–448. doi:10.1162/pres.18.6.434

Harris, M. (2001). *The rise of anthropological theory: A history of theories of culture.* London, UK: AltaMira Press.

Harrison, S., & Dourish, P. (1996). Re-place-ing space: The roles of place and space in collaborative systems. In M. S. Ackerman, (Ed.), *Proceedings of the 1996 ACM Conference on Computer Supported Cooperative Work,* Boston, Massachusetts, United States, November 16 - 20, 1996, CSCW '96, (pp. 67-76). New York, NY: ACM.

Hart, J., Ridley, C., Taher, F., Sas, C., & Dix, A. (2008). Exploring the Facebook experience: A new approach to usability. *Proceedings of the 5th Nordic Conf. on Human-Computer Interaction: Building Bridges* (pp. 471-474). ACM.

Hedetniemi, S., Hedetniemi, S., & Liestman, A. (1988). A survey of gossiping and broadcasting in communication networks. *Networks, 18,* 319–349. doi:10.1002/net.3230180406

Helbing, D., Farkas, I., & Vicsek, T. (2000). Simulating dynamical features of escape panic. *Nature, 407,* 487–490. doi:10.1038/35035023

Hemp, P. (2006). Avatar-based marketing. *Harvard Business Review, 84*(6), 48–56.

Henning, M. (2007). Re-evaluating the community question from a German perspective. *Social Networks, 29,* 375–390. doi:10.1016/j.socnet.2007.01.008

Herlocker, J. L., Konstan, J. A., Terveen, L. G., & Riedl, J. T. (2004). Evaluating collaborative filtering recommender systems. [TOIS]. *ACM Transactions on Information Systems, 22*(1), 5–53. doi:10.1145/963770.963772

Herz, A., & Gamper, M. (2011). Möglichkeiten und Grenzen der Erhebung ego-zentrierter Netzwerke via Computer und Internet. In M. Gamper, L. Reschke, & M. Schönhuth (Eds.), *Knoten und Kanten 2.0: Soziale Netzwerkanalyse in Medien- und Kulturforschung.* Bielfeld, Germany: transcript. (forthcoming)

Heymann, P., Ramage, D., & Garcia-Molina, H. (2008). Social tag prediction. *Proceedings of the 31st Annual International ACM SIGIR Conference on Research and Development in Information Retrieval*, (pp. 531-538).

Hickerson, H. (1967). The feast of the dead among the seventeenth century Algonkians of the upper Great Lakes. *American Anthropologist, 62*, 81–107. doi:10.1525/aa.1960.62.1.02a00050

Hiltz, S. R., Coppola, N., Rotter, N., Turoff, M., & Benbunan-Fich, R. (2000). Measuring the importance of collaborative learning for the effectiveness of ALN: A multi-measure, multimethod approach. *Journal of Asynchronous Learning Networks, 4*(2), 103–125.

Hird, J. (2010, August 18). 25 brilliant examples of Facebook brand pages. *eConsultancy*. Retrieved September 10, 2010, from http://econsultancy.com/uk/blog/6438-25-brilliant-examples-of-facebook-brand-pages

Hirschman, E. C., & Holbrook, M. B. (1982). Hedonic consumption: Emerging concepts, methods and propositions. *Journal of Marketing, 46*(3), 92–102. doi:10.2307/1251707

Höfer, R., Keupp, H., & Straus, F. (2006). Prozesse sozialer Verortung in Szenen und Organisationen – Ein netzwerkorientierter Blick auf traditionale und reflexive moderne Engagementformen. In Hollstein, B., & Straus, F. (Eds.), *Qualitative Netzwerkanalyse. Konzepte, Methoden, Anwendungen* (pp. 267–294). Wiesbaden, Germany: VS Verlag für Sozialwissenschaften.

Hofstede, G., & Hofstede, G. J. (2005). *Cultures and organizations: Software for the mind* (rev. 2nd ed.). New York, NY: McGraw-Hill.

Hogan, B., Carrasco, J.-A., & Wellman, B. (2007). Visualizing personal networks: Working with participant-aided sociograms. *Field Methods, 19*(2), 116–144. doi:10.1177/1525822X06298589

Hogan, J., Carrasco, A., & Wellman, B. (2007). Visualizing personal networks: Working with participant-aided sociograms. *Field Methods, 19*, 116–144. doi:10.1177/1525822X06298589

Hogan, J., Carrasco, A., & Wellman, B. (2007). Visualizing Personal Networks: Working with Participant-aided Sociograms. *Field Methods, 19*, 116–144. doi:10.1177/1525822X06298589

Holloway, T., Bozicevic, M., & Borner, K. (2007). Analyzing and visualizing the semantic coverage of Wikipedia and its authors. *Complexity, 12*(3), 30–40. doi:10.1002/cplx.20164

Hollstein, B., & Pfeffer, J. (2010). *Netzwerkkarten als Instrument zur Erhebung egozentrierter Netzwerke.* Retrieved November 14, 2010, from http://www.wiso.uni-hamburg.de/fileadmin/sozialoekonomie/hollstein/Literatur_Betina/Netzwerkkarten_Hollstein_Pfeffer_2010.pdf

Hollstein, B., & Straus, F. (Eds.). (2006). *Qualitative Netzwerkanalyse: Konzepte, Methoden, Anwendungen.* Wiesbaden, Germany: VS Verlag für Sozialwissenschaften.

Holme, P., & Kim, B. J. (2002). Growing scale-free networks with tunable clustering. *Physical Review E: Statistical, Nonlinear, and Soft Matter Physics, 65*(2), 26107. doi:10.1103/PhysRevE.65.026107

Homans, G. C. (1950). *The human group.* New York, NY: Harcourt, Brace and Company.

Hood, M. G. (1993). *After 70 years of audience research, what have we learned? Who comes to museums, who does not, and why? Visitor Studies: Theory, Research and Practice.* Visitor Studies Association.

Horowitz, M. C. (2010). Nonstate actors and the diffusion of innovations: The case of suicide terrorism. *International Organization, 64*, 33–64. doi:10.1017/S0020818309990233

Hosio, S., Kukka, H., & Riekki, J. (2008). Leveraging social networking services to encourage interaction in public spaces. *Proceedings of the 7th International Conference on Mobile and Ubiquitous Multimedia*, (pp. 2-7).

Hotho, A., Jäschke, R., Schmitz, C., & Stumme, G. (2006). BibSonomy: A social bookmark and publication sharing system. *Proceedings of the Conceptual Structures Tool Interoperability Workshop at the 14th International Conference on Conceptual Structures*, (pp. 87-102).

http://www.business.att.com/content/whitepaper/WP-soc_17172_v3_11-10-08.pdf

Hu, X., Zhang, X., Lu, C., Park, E. M., & Zhou, X. (2009). Exploiting Wikipedia as external knowledge for document clustering. *Proceedings of the 15th ACM SIGKDD international conference on Knowledge discovery and data mining*, 16(7), 389-396.

Huang, Y. (2003). *Fishing-dependent communities on the Gulf Coast of Florida: Their identification, recent decline and present resilience.* Master's Thesis, University of South Florida.

Huffaker, D. A., Simmons, M., Bakshy, E., & Adamic, L. A. (2010). Seller activity in a virtual marketplace. *First Monday*, 15(7).

In, K. J., Hye, A. S., & Lee, C. C. (2009). A study on service quality determinants that influence continued success of portal online community services. *Proceedings of the 2ⁿᵈ IEEE Int'l Conf. on Computer Science and Information Technology* (pp. 171-175). IEEE CS.

Infosecurity. (2010 March/April). *RSA 2010 News Coverage: Pitfalls and promise of social networking.* Infosecurity. Retrieved August 30, 2010, from http://www.infosecurity-us.com/view/7761/hot-topic-at-rsa-the-pitfalls-and-promise-of-social-networking/

Intriligator, M. D. (2010). The economics of terrorism. *Economic Inquiry*, 48, 1–13. doi:10.1111/j.1465-7295.2009.00287.x

Ipsos. (2010, May 25). Engaging CPG consumers in the digital space Tuesday. *Ipsos*. Retrieved September 21, 2010, from http://www.ipsos-na.com/news-polls/pressrelease.aspx?id=4789

Iriberri, A., & Leroy, G. (2009). A life-cycle perspective on online community success. [ACM.]. *ACM Computing Surveys*, 41(2), 1–29. doi:10.1145/1459352.1459356

Iyer, B., Lee, C., & Venkatraman, N. (2006). Managing in a small world ecosystem: Lessons from the software sector. *California Management Review*, 48(3), 27–47.

Jackson, B. A. (2006). Groups, networks, or movements: A command-and-control-driven approach to classifying terrorist organizations and its application to Al Qaeda. *Studies in Conflict and Terrorism*, 29, 241–262. doi:10.1080/10576100600564042

Jacobson, M. (2010). Terrorist financing and the internet. *Studies in Conflict and Terrorism*, 33, 353–363. doi:10.1080/10576101003587184

Jacobson, M., & Levitt, M. (2010). Tracking narco-terrorist networks: The money trail. *The Fletcher Forum of World Affairs*, 34, 117–124.

James, R., Croft, D. P., & Krause, J. (2009). Potential banana skins in animal social network analysis. *Behavioral Ecology and Sociobiology*, 63, 989–997. .doi:10.1007/s00265-009-0742-5

Jansen, B. J., Zhang, M., Sobel, K., & Chowdury, A. (2009). Micro-blogging as online word of mouth branding. *Proceedings of the 27th Int'l Conf. on Human Factors in Computing Systems*. (pp. 3859-3864). ACM.

Java, A., Song, X., Finin, T., & Tseng, B. (2007). Why we Twitter: Understanding microblogging usage and communities. *Proceedings of the 9th WebKDD and 1st SNA-KDD 2007 Workshop on Web Mining and Social Network Analysis* (pp. 56-65).

Jeh, G., & Widom, J. (2002). SimRank: A measure of structural-context similarity. In *Proc. of the ACM SIGKDD International Conference on Knowledge Discovery and Data Mining (SIGKDD'02)*, (pp. 538-543). Edmonton, Alberta, Canada.

Jenkinson, A. (2007). Evolutionary implications for touchpoint planning as a result of neuroscience: A practical fusion of database marketing and advertising. *Journal of Database Marketing & Customer Strategy Management*, 14, 164–185. doi:10.1057/palgrave.dbm.3250054

Jones, S. G. (2007). Fighting networked terrorist groups: Lessons from Israel. *Studies in Conflict and Terrorism*, 30, 281–302. doi:10.1080/10576100701200157

Jones, S. G., & Libicki, M. C. (2008). *How terrorist groups end: Lessons for countering Al Qa'ida*. Santa Monica, CA: Rand Corporation.

Jordán, J., & Horsburgh, N. (2005). Mapping jihadist terrorism in Spain. *Studies in Conflict and Terrorism, 28,* 169–191. doi:10.1080/10576100590928089

Jung, J. J., & Euzenat, J. (2007). Towards semantic social networks. *Proceedings of the 4th European conference on The Semantic Web.* 267-280.

Jung, J. J. (2008). Query transformation based on semantic centrality in Semantic Social Network. *Journal of Universal Computer Science, 14*(7), 1031–1047.

Kahn, R. L., & Antonucci, T. C. (1980). Convoys of life course: Attachment, roles, and social support. In Featherman, D. L., Lerner, R. M., & Perlmutter, M. (Eds.), *Life-span development and behaviour* (pp. 253–286). Hillsdale, NJ: Lawrence Erlbaum.

Kapferer, B. (1969). Norms and the manipulation of relationships in a work context. In J. C. Mitchell (Ed.), *Social networks in urban situations. Analyses of personal relationships in Central African towns* (pp. 181–244). Manchester, UK: Published for the Institute for Social Research, University of Zambia, by Manchester U.P.

Kaplan, A. M., & Haenlein, M. (2009). Consumer use and business potential of virtual worlds: The Case of "Second Life". *International Journal on Media Management, 11*(3), 93–101. doi:10.1080/14241270903047008

Kashoob, S., Caverlee, J., & Ding, Y. (2009). A categorical model for discovering latent structure in social annotations. *Proceedings of the International AAAI Conference on Weblogs and Social Media* (pp. 27-35).

Katz, L. (1953). A new status index derived from sociometric analysis. *Psychometrika, 18*(1), 39–43. doi:10.1007/BF02289026

Kaye, J., Levitt, M., Nevins, J., Golden, J., & Schmitt, V. (2005). Communication intimacy one bit at a time. In *CHI Extended Abstracts on Human Factors in Computing Systems.*

Kempe, D., Kleinberg, J., & Tardos, E. (2003). Maximizing the spread of influence through a social network. In *Proc. KDD'03.*

Kermack, W., & McKendrick, A. (1927). A contribution to the mathematical theory of epidemics. *Proceedings of the Royal Society of London. Series A, Containing Papers of a Mathematical and Physical Character, 115,* 700–721. doi:10.1098/rspa.1927.0118

Kernighan, B. W., & Lin, S. (1970). An efficient heuristic procedure for partitioning graphs. *The Bell System Technical Journal, 49*(1), 291–307.

Kim, Y. A., & Srivastava, J. (2007). Impact of social influence in e-commerce decision making. In *ICEC '07: Proceedings of the Ninth International Conference on Electronic Commerce, 258,* (pp. 293-302).

Kim, A. J. (2000). *Community building on the Web: Secret strategies for successful online communities.* London, UK: Addison Wesley.

King, A. J., Johnson, D. D. P., & van Vugt, M. (2009). The origins and evolution of leadership. *Current Biology, 19,* R911–R916. doi:10.1016/j.cub.2009.07.027

Kirby, A. (2007). The London bombers as self-starters: A case study in indigenous radicalization and the emergence of autonomous cliques. *Studies in Conflict and Terrorism, 30,* 415–428. doi:10.1080/10576100701258619

Kirchick, J. (2010). The homegrown-terrorist threat: It can happen here, and it is happening here. *Commentary (New York, N.Y.), 129,* 16–20.

Kitsak, M., Gallos, L., Havlin, S., Liljeros, F., Muchnik, L., Stanley, H., & Makse, H. (2010). Identifying influential spreaders in complex networks. *Nature Physics, 6*(888).

Kleinberg, J. (2008). The convergence of social and technological networks. *Communications of the ACM, 51*(11), 66–72. doi:10.1145/1400214.1400232

Knoke, D. (1988). Incentives in collective action organizations. *American Sociological Review, 53,* 311–329. doi:10.2307/2095641

Knoke, D. (1990). Networks of political action: Toward theory construction. *Social Forces, 68*(4), 1041–1063.

Knoke, D., & Rogers, D. L. (1979). A blockmodel analysis of interorganizational networks. *Sociology and Social Research, 64,* 28–52.

Knoke, D., & Yang, S. (2008). *Social network analysis* (2nd ed.). Thousand Oaks, CA: Sage Publications.

Knopfmacher, A., & Tichy, R. F. (2007). Graphs, partitions and Fibonacci numbers. *Discrete Applied Mathematics*, *155*(10), 1175–1187. doi:10.1016/j.dam.2006.10.010

Kobsa, A. (2001). Generic user modeling systems. *User Modeling and User-Adapted Interaction*, *11*, 49–63. doi:10.1023/A:1011187500863

Kohlmann, E. F. (2008). 'Homegrown' terrorists: Theory and cases in the war on terror's newest front. *The Annals of the American Academy of Political and Social Science*, *618*, 95–109. doi:10.1177/0002716208317203

Köksal, Y. (2008). Rethinking nationalism: State projects and community networks in 19th century Ottoman empire. *The American Behavioral Scientist*, *51*(10). doi:10.1177/0002764208316352

Kolip, P. (1993). *Freundschaften im Jugendalter: Der Beitrag sozialer Netzwerke zur Problembewältigung*. Weinheim, Germany: Juventa.

Koren, Y., Bell, R., & Volinsky, C. (2009). Matrix factorization techniques for recommender systems. *Computer*, *42*(8), 30–37. doi:10.1109/MC.2009.263

Koschade, S. (2007). *The internal dynamics of terrorist cells: A social network analysis of terrorist cells in an Australian context*. Unpublished doctoral dissertation, Queensland University of Technology, Brisbane, Australia.

Koschade, S. (2006). A social network analysis of Jemaah Islamiyah: The applications to counterterrorism and intelligence. *Studies in Conflict and Terrorism*, *29*, 559–575. doi:10.1080/10576100600798418

Kossinets, G., Kleinberg, J., & Watts, D. (2008). The structure of information pathways in a social communication network. In *Proc. KDD'08* (pp. 24–27). Las Vegas, Nevada, USA.

Kossinets, G. (2006). Effects of missing data in social networks. *Social Networks*, *28*, 247–268. doi:10.1016/j.socnet.2005.07.002

Krackhard, D., Blythe, J., & McGrath, C. (1994). Krackplot 3.0: An improved network drawing program. *Connections*, *17*(2), 53–55.

Krause, J., Croft, D. P., & James, R. (2007). Social network theory in the behavioural sciences: Potential applications. *Behavioral Ecology and Sociobiology*, *62*, 15–27. doi:10.1007/s00265-007-0445-8

Krause, J., Lusseau, D., & James, R. (2009). Animal social networks: An introduction. *Behavioral Ecology and Sociobiology*, *63*, 967–973. doi:10.1007/s00265-009-0747-0

Krause, J., & Ruxton, G. D. (2002). *Living in groups*. Oxford, UK: Oxford University Press.

Krebs, V. (2001). Mapping networks of terrorist cells. *Connections*, *24*, 43–52.

Krestel, R., Fankhauser, P., & Nejdl, W. (2009). Latent Dirichlet allocation for tag recommendation. *Proceedings of the 3rd Conference on Recommender Systems*, (pp. 61-68).

Krishnamurthy, B., & Wang, J. (2000). On network-aware clustering of Web clients. *SIGCOMM Comput. Commun. Rev.*, *30*(4), 97–110. doi:10.1145/347057.347412

Kronenwett, M. (2010). *VennMaker 1.0 Anwenderhandbuch*. Retrieved October 21, 2010, from http://www.vennmaker.com

Krotoski, A. K. (2007). *Making e-friends and influencing people: Assessing the perceptions of opinion leaders in a virtual world*. Paper presented at the International Sunbelt Social Network Conference, Corfu, Greece.

Krotoski, A. K. (2009). *Social influence in Second Life: Social network and social psychological processes in the diffusion of belief and behaviour on the Web*. Unpublished doctoral dissertation, University of Surrey, Department of Psychology, School of Human Sciences.

Krueger, A. B. (2008). What makes a homegrown terrorist? Human capital and participation in domestic Islamic terrorist groups in the U.S.A. *Economics Letters*, *101*, 293–296. doi:10.1016/j.econlet.2008.09.008

Krueger, A. B., & Laitin, D. D. (2004). Misunderestimating terrorism: The State Department's big mistake. *Foreign Affairs (Council on Foreign Relations)*, *83*, 8–13. doi:10.2307/20034063

Krumbein, S. (1995). *Selbstbild und Männlichkeit. Rekonstruktion männlicher Selbst- und Idealbilder und deren Veränderung im Laufe der individuellen Entwicklung.* München, Germany: Opladen.

Kumar, R., Novak, J., & Tomkins, A. (2010). Structure and evolution of online social networks. *Link Mining: Models, Algorithms, and Applications, 337-357.*

Kummer, H. (1968). *Social organization of Hamadryas baboons.* Chicago, IL: University of Chicago Press.

Kuramochi, M., & Karypis, G. (2004). An Efficient Algorithm for Discovering Frequent Subgraphs. *IEEE Transactions on Knowledge and Data Engineering, 16*(9), 1038–1051. doi:10.1109/TKDE.2004.33

LaFree, G., & Dugan, L. (2009). Research on terrorism and countering terrorism. *Crime and Justice, 38*, 413–477.

Lakoff, G., & Johnson, M. (1980). *Metaphors we live by.* Chicago: University of Chicago Press.

Lam, H. Y., & Yeung, D. Y. (2007). *A learning approach to spam detection based on social networks.* 4th Conference on Email and Anti-Spam (CEAS).

Lampe, C., Ellison, N., & Steinfield, C. (2006). A Face(book) in the crowd: Social searching vs. social browsing. *Proceedings of the 20th Conf. on Computer Supported Cooperative Work* (pp. 167-170). ACM.

Lange, P. G. (2007). Publicly private and privately public: Social networking on YouTube. *Journal of Computer-Mediated Communication, 13*(1), article 18. Retrieved September 18, 2010 from http://jcmc.indiana.edu/vol13/issue1/lange.html

Langerak, F., Verhoef, P. C., Verlegh, P., & de Valck, K. (2004). Satisfaction and participation in virtual communities. *Advances in Consumer Research. Association for Consumer Research (U. S.), 31*, 56–57.

Langridge, E. A., Franks, N. R., & Sendova-Franks, A. B. (2004). Improvement in collective performance with experience in ants. *Behavioral Ecology and Sociobiology, 56*, 523–529. doi:10. 1007/s00265-004-0824-3

Langridge, E. A., Sendova-Franks, A. B., & Franks, N. R. (2009). How experienced individuals contribute to an improvement in collective performance in ants. *Behavioral Ecology and Sociobiology, 62*, 447–456. doi:10.1007/s00265-007-0472-5

Larson, C. E., & LaFasto, F. (1989). *Teamwork. What must go right/What can go wrong.* Newbury Park, CA: Sage.

Latapy, M., & Magnien, C. (2008). Complex network measurements: Estimating the relevance of observed properties. *IEEE Conference on Computer Communications,* (pp. 1660-1668).

Latour, B. (2001). *La esperanza de Pandora: Ensayos sobre la realidad de los estudios de la ciencia.* Barcelona, Spain: Gedisa.

Laumann, E. O. (1973). *Bonds of pluralism: The form and substance of urban social networks.* New York, NY: J. Wiley.

Laumann, E. O., Galaskiewicz, J., & Marsden, P. (1978). Community structure as interorganizational linkages. *Annual Review of Sociology, 4*, 455–484. doi:10.1146/annurev.so.04.080178.002323

Laumann, E., & Pappi, F. (1976). *Networks of collective action: A perspective on community influence systems.* New York, NY: Academic Press.

Lau, R. Y. K., Song, D., Li, Y., Cheung, T. C. H., & Hao, J. (2009). Toward a Fuzzy Domain Ontology Extraction Method for Adaptive e-Learning. *IEEE Transactions on Knowledge and Data Engineering, 21*(6), 800–813. doi:10.1109/TKDE.2008.137

Lave, J., & Wenger, E. (1991). *Situated learning: Legitimate peripheral participation.* Cambridge, UK: Cambridge University Press.

Layder, D. (2009). *Intimacy and power. The dynamics of personal relationship in modern society.* Basingstoke, UK: Palgrave Macmillan.

Lazarsfeld, P., & Merton, R. K. (1954). Friendship as a social process: A substantive and methodological analysis. In Berger, M., Abel, T., & Page, C. H. (Eds.), *Freedom and control in modern society* (pp. 18–66). New York, NY: Van Nostrand.

Lazer, D., Pentland, A., Adamic, L., Aral, S., Barabasi, A. L., & Brewer, D. (2009). Computational social science. *Science, 323*(5915), 721–723. doi:10.1126/science.1167742

Leary, B. (2010). The social customer engagement index (White Paper). *The Social Customer & The Society of Consumer Affairs Professionals*. Retrieved September 20, 2010, from http://thesocialcustomer.com/sites/default/docs/TSC-76KvzawuvVcXnLoCUUlk/TSC_Whitepaper_v10_083110.pdf

Lehdonvirta, V. (2009). Virtual item sales as a revenue model: Identifying attributes that drive purchase decisions. *Electronic Commerce Research, 9*, 97–113. doi:10.1007/s10660-009-9028-2

Leicht, E. A., Holme, P., & Newman, M. E. J. (2006). Vertex similarity in networks. *Physical Review Part E, 73*(2), 026120. doi:10.1103/PhysRevE.73.026120

Leimeister, J. M., Sidiras, P., & Krcmar, H. (2004). Success factors of virtual communities from the perspective of members and operators: An empirical study. *Proceedings of the 37th Annual Hawaii International Conference on System Sciences* (pp. 70194a). IEEE CS.

Lengel, R. H., & Daft, R. L. (1988). The selection of communication media as an executive skill. *The Academy of Management Executive, 2*, 225–232. doi:10.5465/AME.1988.4277259

Lerman, K. (2007). Social networks and social information filtering on Digg. *Proceedings of International Conference on Weblogs and Social Media*.

Leskovec, J., & Horvitz, E. (2008). Planetary-scale views on a large instant-messaging network. In *Proc. 17th International Conference on World Wide Web* (pp. 915–924). New York.

Levitt, B., & March, J. (1988). Organizational learning. *Annual Review of Sociology, 14*, 319–340. doi:10.1146/annurev.so.14.080188.001535

Lévy, P. (1997). *La cibercultura, el segon diluvi?* Barcelona, Spain: Edicions UOC-Proa.

Lewis, D. (1969). *Convention: A philosophical study*. Cambridge, MA: Harvard University Press.

Lewis, K., Kaufman, J., Gonzales, M., Wimmer, A., & Christakis, N. (2008). Tastes, ties and time: A new social network dataset using Facebook.com. *Social Networks, 30*, 330–342. doi:10.1016/j.socnet.2008.07.002

Liben-Nowell, D., & Kleinberg, J. (2007). The link-prediction problem for social networks. *Journal of the American Society for Information Science and Technology, 58*(7), 1019–1031. doi:10.1002/asi.20591

Li, C., & Bernoff, J. (2008). *Groundswell: Winning in a World Transformed by Social Technologies*. Boston, Massachusetts: Harvard Business Press.

Lindelauf, R., Borm, P., & Hamers, H. (2009). The influence of secrecy on the communication structure of covert networks. *Social Networks, 31*(2), 126–137. doi:10.1016/j.socnet.2008.12.003

Lindelauf, R., Borm, P., & Hamers, H. (2009). The influence of secrecy on the communication structure of covert networks. *Social Networks, 31*, 126–137. doi:10.1016/j.socnet.2008.12.003

Linden, T. (2009). *The Second Life economy - First quarter 2009 in detail*. Retrieved 10th September, 2009, from https://blogs.secondlife.com/community/features/blog/2009/04/16/the-second-life-economy--first-quarter-2009-in-detail

Lin, N. (2001). Building a network theory of social capital. In Lin, N., Cook, K., & Burt, R. S. (Eds.), *Social capital: Theory and research*. New York, NY: Aldine De Gruyter.

Lin, N., Cook, K., & Burt, R. S. (Eds.). (2001). *Social capital: Theory and research*. New York, NY: Aldine de Gruyter.

Lin, N., Son, J., & George, L. K. (2008). Cross-national comparison of social support structures between Taiwan and the United States. *Journal of Health and Social Behavior, 49*, 104–126. doi:10.1177/002214650804900108

Lin, N., & Zhao, H. (2005). Are scale-free networks robust to measurement errors? *BMC Bioinformatics, 6*(1), 119. doi:10.1186/1471-2105-6-119

Linton, R. (1936). *The study of man*. New York, NY: Appleton-Century-Crofts.

Liu, B. (2007). *Web data mining*. Springer.

Li, Y., Lin, C., & Lai, C. (2010). Identifying influential reviewers for word-of-mouth marketing. *Electron. Commer. Rec. App*, *9*(4), 294–304. doi:10.1016/j.elerap.2010.02.004

Lu, C., Hu, X., Chen, X., Park, J. R., He, T., & Li, Z. (2010). The topic-perspective model for social tagging systems. *Proceedings of the 16th ACM SIGKDD international conference on Knowledge discovery and data mining,* 683-692.

Lubbers, M. J., Molina, J. L., & McCarty, C. (2007). Personal Networks and Ethnic Identifications. *International Sociology, 22*, 721–741. doi:10.1177/0268580907082255

Lubbers, M. J., Mollina, J. L., Brandes, U., Ávila, J., & McCarty, C. (2010). Longitudinal analysis of personal networks. The case of Argentinean migrants in Spain. *Social Networks, 32*, 91–104. doi:10.1016/j.socnet.2009.05.001

Luce, R., & Perry, A. (1949). A method of matrix analysis of group structure. *Psychometrika, 14*(2), 95–116. doi:10.1007/BF02289146

Ludford, P. J., Cosley, D., Frankowski, D., & Terveen, L. (2004). Think different: Increasing online community participation using uniqueness and group dissimilarity. *Proceedings of the SIGCHI Conf. on Human Factors in Computing Systems* (pp. 631-638). ACM.

Lusseau, D. (2003). The emergent properties of a dolphin social network. *Proceedings. Biological Sciences, 270*(Suppl 2), S186–S188. doi:10.1098/rsbl.2003.0057

Lusseau, D. (2007). Evidence for social role in a dolphin social network. *Evolutionary Ecology, 21*, 357–366. doi:10.1007/s10682-006-9105-0

Lusseau, D., Wilson, B., Hammond, P. S., Grellier, K., Durban, J. W., & Parsons, K. M. (2006). Quantifying the influence of sociality on population structure in bottlenose dolphins. *Journal of Animal Ecology, 75*, 14–24. doi:10.1111/j.1365-2656.2005.01013.x

Luz, F., Damásio, M. J., & Gouveia, P. (2008). *Realism in gameplay: Digital fiction and embodiment.* In *Proceeding of the 2nd ACM International Workshop on Story Representation, Mechanism and Context.* SRMC '08, (pp. 1-8). New York, NY: ACM.

Lynch, O. M. (1984). *Culture and community in Europe: Essays in honor of Conrad M Arensberg.* Delhi, India: Hindustan Publication Corp.

Lynd, R. S., & Lynd, H. M. (1929). *Middletown: A study in American culture.* New York, NY: Harcourt Brace and Company.

Ma, H., Gustafson, S., Moitra, A., & Bracewell, D. (2009). Ego-centric network sampling in viral marketing applications. In *IEEE International Conference on Computational Science and Engineering,* (pp. 777-782).

Maamar, Z., & Badr, Y. (2009). Social networks as a service in modern enterprises. *2009 International Conference on the Current Trends in Information Technology (CTIT),* (pp. 1-5).

Mackenzie, K., Buckby, S., & Irvine, H. (2009). A framework for evaluating business lead users' virtual reality innovations in Second Life. *Electronic Commerce Research, 9*(3), 183–202. doi:10.1007/s10660-009-9035-3

Macskassy, S. A., & Provost, F. (2007). Classification in networked data: A toolkit and a univariate case study. *Journal of Machine Learning Research, 8*, 935–983.

Macy, M. W., & Willer, R. (2002). From factors to actors: Computational sociology and agent-based modeling. *Annual Review of Sociology, 28*, 143–167. doi:10.1146/annurev.soc.28.110601.141117

Magouirk, J., Atran, S., & Sageman, M. (2008). Connecting terrorist networks. *Studies in Conflict and Terrorism, 31*, 1–16. doi:10.1080/10576100701759988

Ma, H., Gustafson, S., Moitra, A., & Bracewell, D. (2010). Ego-centric network sampling in viral marketing applications. In Ting, I.-H., Wu, H.-J., & Ho, T.-H. (Eds.), *Mining and analyzing social networks. Studies in Computational Intelligence* (p. 288). Springer-Verlag. doi:10.1007/978-3-642-13422-7_3

Maia, M., Almeida, J., & Almeida, V. (2008). Identifying user behavior in online social networks. In SocialNets '08: *Proceedings of the 1st Workshop on Social Network Systems,* 1-6

Maine, H. (1866). *Ancient law.* London, UK: Oxford University Press.

Mandel, T., & Van der Luen, G. (1996). *Rules of the net: Online operating instructions for human beings.* New York, NY: Hyperion.

Marion, R. (1999). *The edge of organization.* Thousand Oaks, CA: Sage.

Marsden, P. V. (1990). Network data and measurement. *Annual Review of Sociology, 16,* 435–463. doi:10.1146/annurev.so.16.080190.002251

Marshall, J. A. R., Bogacz, R., Dornhaus, A., Planqué, R., Kovacs, T., & Franks, N. R. (2009). On optimal decision-making in brains and social insect colonies. *Journal of the Royal Society, Interface, 6,* 1065–1074. doi:10.1098/rsif.2008.0511

Marshall, J. A. R., Dornhaus, A., Franks, N. R., & Kovacs, T. (2006). Noise, cost and speed–accuracy trade-offs: Decision making in a decentralized system. *Journal of the Royal Society, Interface, 3,* 243–254. .doi:10.1098/rsif.2005.0075

Mascarenhas, J. (1991). Participatory rural appraisal and participatory learning methods: Recent experiences from Myrada and South India. *RRA Note, 13,* 26–32.

Maslow, A. H., & Honigmann, J. J. (1970). Synergy: Some notes of Ruth Benedict. *American Anthropologist, 72,* 320–333. doi:10.1525/aa.1970.72.2.02a00060

Matsuo, Y., Mori, J., & Hamasaki, M. (2006). POLY-PHONET: An Advanced Social Network Extraction System from the Web structure and evolution of online social networks. *Proceedings of the World Wide Web Conference,* 262-278.

Matzat, U. (2009). A theory of relational signals in online groups. *New Media & Society, 11,* 375–394. doi:10.1177/1461444808101617

Mayer, A. C. (1966). The significance of quasi-groups in the study of complex societies. In Banton, M. (Ed.), *The social anthropology of complex societies. ASA Monograph no 4.* New York, NY: Praeger.

McCarty, C., Molina, J. L., Aguilar, C., & Rota, L. (2007). A Comparison of Social Network Mapping and Personal Network Visualization. *Field Methods, 19,* 145–162. doi:10.1177/1525822X06298592

McCarty, C., Molina, J. L., Lubbers, M. J., & Gamper, M. (2011forthcoming). Personal networks analysis. In Barnett, G. (Ed.), *Encyclopedia of social networks.* Thousand Oaks, CA: SAGE.

McPherson, M., Smith-Lovin Lynn, & Cook James. (2001). Birds of feather: Homophily in social networks. *Annual Review of Sociology, 27,* 415–444. doi:10.1146/annurev.soc.27.1.415

Mcpherson, M., Lovin, S. L., & Cook, J. M. (2001). Birds of a Feather: Homophily in social networks. *Annual Review of Sociology, 27*(1), 415–444. doi:10.1146/annurev.soc.27.1.415

McPherson, M., Popielarz, P., & Drobnic, S. (1992). Social networks and organizational dynamics. *American Sociological Review, 57,* 153–170. doi:10.2307/2096202

McPherson, M., Smith-Lovin, L., & Brashears, M. (2006). Social isolation in America: Changes in core discussion networks over two decades. *American Sociological Review, 71,* 353–375. doi:10.1177/000312240607100301

McPherson, M., Smith-Lovin, L., & Cook, J. M. (2001). Birds of a feather: Homophily in social networks. *Annual Review of Sociology, 27,* 415–444. doi:10.1146/annurev.soc.27.1.415

Mead, M. (2000). *The study of culture at a distance.* New York, NY: Bregan.

Meharabien, A., & Russell, J. A. (1974). *An approach to environmental psychology.* Cambridge, MA: MIT Press.

Memon, N., Larsen, H. L., Hicks, D. L., & Harkiolakis, N. (2008). Detecting hidden hierarchy in terrorist networks: Some case studies. *ISI Workshops.* 477-489.

Memon, N., Farley, J. D., Hicks, D. L., & Rosenorn, T. (Eds.). (2009). *Mathematical methods in counterterrorism. Vienna, Austria.* Wien: Springer-Verlag. doi:10.1007/978-3-211-09442-6

Merton, R. K. (1957). *Social theory and social structure.* Glencoe, IL: Free Press.

Métivier, Y., & Robson, J. M. (2010). About randomised distributed graph colouring and graph partition algorithms. *Information and Computation, 208*(11), 1296–1304. doi:10.1016/j.ic.2010.07.001

Meunier, H., Leca, J. B., Deneubourg, J. L., & Petit, O. (2006). Group movement decisions in capuchin monkeys: The utility of an experimental study and a mathematical model to explore the relationship between individual and collective behaviours. *Behaviour, 143*, 1511–1527. doi:10.1163/156853906779366982

Michalski, R.S., & Stepp, R. (2009). Automated Construction Of Classifications Conceptual Clustering Versus Numerical Taxonomy. *IEEE Transactions on pattern analysis and machine learning, 4,396-410.*

Microsoft Dynamics. (2009). *CRM and social networking: Engaging the social customer* [White Paper]. Retrieved June 15, 2010, from http://crm.dynamics.com/docs/CRM_and_Social_Networks.pdf

Mihalcea, R., & Csomai, A. (2007). Wikify!: Linking documents to encyclopedic knowledge. *Proceedings of the Sixteenth ACM Conference on Information and Knowledge Management, 7,* (pp. 233-242).

Mika, P. (2005). Flink: Semantic Web technology for the extraction and analysis of social networks. *Web Semantics: Science. Services and Agents on the World Wide Web, 3,* 211–223. doi:10.1016/j.websem.2005.05.006

Mika, P. (2005). Social networks and the Semantic Web: The next challenge. *IEEE Intelligent Systems, 20*(1), 82–85.

Mika, P. (2007). Ontologies are us: A unified model of social networks and semantics. *Web Semantics: Science. Services and Agents on the World Wide Web, 5*(1), 5–15. doi:10.1016/j.websem.2006.11.002

Milgram, S. (1967). The small world problem. *Psychology Today, 1*(1), 60–67.

Miller, D., & Slater, D. (2000). *The Internet: An ethnographic approach.* Oxford, UK: Berg.

Miller, J. H., & Page, S. E. (2007). *Complex adaptive systems: An introduction to computational models of social life.* Princeton University Press.

Milstein, S. (n.d.). What is Twitter? In Twitter (Ed.), *Twitter 101 for business — A special guide.* Retrieved July 15, 2010, from http://business.twitter.com/twitter101/

Mislove, A., Koppula, H. S., Gummadi, K. P., Druschel, P., & Bhattacharjee, B. (2008). Growth of the Flickr social network. *Proceedings of the First Workshop on Online Social Networks,* (pp. 25-30).

Mislove, A., Marcon, M., Gummadi, K. P., Druschel, P., & Bhattacharjee, B. (2007). Measurement and analysis of online social networks. In IMC '07: *Proceedings of the 7th ACM SIGCOMM Conference on internet Measurement, 29-42*

Mislove, A., Marcon, M., Gummadi, K. P., Druschel, P., & Bhattacharjee, B. (2007). Measurement and analysis of online social networks. *Proceedings of the 7th ACM SIGCOMM conference on Internet measurement, 29-42.*

Mitchell, J. C. (Ed.). (1969). *Social networks in urban situations: Analyses of personal relationships in Central African towns.* Manchester, UK: Published for the Institute for Social Research, Manchester U.P.

Mitzenmacher, M. (2004). A brief history of generative models for power law and lognormal distributions. *Internet Mathematics, 1*(2), 226–251. doi:10.1080/15427951.2004.10129088

Molina, J. L., & Borgatti, S. (2005). Toward ethical guidelines for network research in organizations. *Social Networks, 27*(2), 107–117. doi:10.1016/j.socnet.2005.01.004

Moltz, B. (2009, December 15). The 10 customer service trends for 2010. *Small Business Trends.* Retrieved July 30, 2010, from http://smallbiztrends.com/2009/12/customer-service-trends-2010.html

Monge, P. R., & Contractor, N. S. (2003). *Theories of communication networks.* Oxford, UK: Oxford University Press.

Moody, J., & White, D. R. (2003). Structural cohesion and embeddedness: A hierarchical concept of social groups. *American Sociological Review, 68*(1), 103–127. doi:10.2307/3088904

Moore, R. J., Gathman, C., Ducheneaut, N., & Nickell, E. (2007). *Coordinating joint activity in avatar-mediated interaction.* 25th Annual Conference on Human Factors in Computing Systems (CHI 2007). San Jose, USA.

Moore, A., & Newman, M. (2000). Epidemics and percolation in small-world networks. *Physical Review E: Statistical Physics, Plasmas, Fluids, and Related Interdisciplinary Topics*, *61*, 5678–5682. doi:10.1103/PhysRevE.61.5678

Moore, M. G., & Greg, K. (1996). *Distance education: A systems view*. Belmont, CA: Wadsworth Publishing Company.

Morely, D., & Robin, K. (1995). *Spaces of identity*. London, UK: Routledge. doi:10.4324/9780203422977

Moreno Mínguez, A., & Crespo Ballesteros, E. (2007). Critical issue: Ensuring equitable use of education technology. In Cruz-Cunha, M. M., & Putnik, G. D. (Eds.), *Encyclopedia of networked and virtual organizations*. Hershey, PA: Idea Group Reference.

Moreno Mínguez, A., & Suárez Hernan, C. (2009). Online virtual communities as a new form of social relations: Elements for the analysis. In Cunha, M., Oliveira, E. F., Talavera, A. J., & Ferreira, L. G. (Eds.), *Handbook of research on social dimensions of semantic technologies and Web services*. Hershey, PA: Idea Group Reference. doi:10.4018/978-1-60566-650-1.ch022

Moreno, J. L. (1934). *Who shall survive?* Washington, DC: Nervous and Mental Disease Publishing Company.

Morris, M. F. (2005). *Al-Qaeda as insurgency*. Master's thesis. Carlisle Barracks, PA: U.S. Army War College. Retrieved July 31, 2010 from http://www.strategicstudiesinstitute.army.mil/pdffiles/ksil234.pdf

Morris, M. R., Teevan, J., & Panovich, K. (2010). What do people ask their social networks, and why?: A survey study of status message Q&A behavior. *Proceedings of the 28th International Conference on Human Factors in Computing Systems*, (pp. 1739-1748).

Moss, S. (2008). Simplicity, generality and truth in social modeling. In *Proceedings of the Second World Congress on Social Simulation (WCSS'08)*, Fairfax VA, USA.

Moss, S. (1998). Critical incident management: An empirically derived computational model. *Journal of Artificial Societies and Social Simulation*, *1*(4). Retrieved from http://jasss.soc.surrey.ac.uk/1/4/1.html.

Moss, S., & Edmonds, B. (2005). Sociology and simulation: Statistical and qualitative cross-validation. *American Journal of Sociology*, *110*(4), 1095–1131. doi:10.1086/427320

Mullins, S. (2009). Parallels between crime and terrorism: A social psychological perspective. *Studies in Conflict and Terrorism*, *32*, 811–830. doi:10.1080/10576100903109776

Murakami, K. (2008). *Re-imagining the future: Young people's construction of identities through digital storytelling*. London, UK: DCSF/Futurelab. Retrieved 4 August, 2009, from http://www.beyondcurrenthorizons.org.uk/wp-content/uploads/final_murakami_youngpeoplesdigitalstorytelling_20081201_jb2.pdf

Musiał, K., Kazienko, P., & Bródka, P. (2009). User position measures in social networks. *Proceedings of the 3rd Workshop on Social Network Mining and Analysis*, 1-9

Nadel, S. F. (1957). *The theory of social structure*. London, UK: Cohen & West.

Nambiar, K. K. (2001). Theory of search engines. *Computers & Mathematics with Applications (Oxford, England)*, *42*(12), 1523–1526. doi:10.1016/S0898-1221(01)00259-0

National Commission on Terrorist Attacks Upon the United States. (2004). *The 9/11 commission report*. Washington, DC: U.S. Government Printing Office.

National Consortium for the Study of Terrorism and Responses to Terrorism (START) <http://www.start.umd.edu/start/>

Naug, D. (2009). Structure and resilience of the social network in an insect colony as a function of colony size. *Behavioral Ecology and Sociobiology*, *63*, 1023–1028. .doi:10.1007/s00265-009-0721-x

Neill, J. T., Marsh, H. W., & Richards, G. E. (2003). The life effectiveness questionnaire: Development and psychometrics. Sydney, Australia: University of Western Sydney. Retrieved September 16, 2010, from http://wilderdom.com/tools/leq/leqreferences.html

Newman, D. (2005). *Sociology: Exploring the architecture of everyday life*. Pine Forge Press.

Newman, M. E. J. (2001). The structure of scientific collaboration network. *PNA*, *98*(16), 404–409. doi:10.1073/pnas.021544898

Newman, M. E. J. (2003). The structure and function of complex networks. *SIAM Review, 45*, 167–256. doi:10.1137/S003614450342480

Newman, M. E. J., & Girvan, M. (2004). Finding and evaluating community structure in networks. *Physical Review E: Statistical, Nonlinear, and Soft Matter Physics, 69*, 026113. doi:10.1103/PhysRevE.69.026113

News, A. B. C. (2001, December 13). *Transcript of Osama bin Laden video*. Retrieved December 24, 2009, from http://www.globalresearch.ca/articles/BIN112A.html

Niedenthal, P. M. (2007). Embodying emotion. *Science, 316*(5827), 1002. doi:10.1126/science.1136930

Nikolai, C., & Madey, G. (2009). Tools of the trade: A survey of various agent based modeling platforms. *Journal of Artificial Societies and Social Simulation, 12*(2). Retrieved from http://jasss.soc.surrey.ac.uk/12/2/2.html.

Nikolic, D., & Gronlund, S. D. (2002). A tandem random walk model of the SAT paradigm: Response times and accumulation of evidence. *The British Journal of Mathematical and Statistical Psychology, 55*, 263–288. doi:10.1348/000711002760554589

Ning, H., & Xu, W. (2010). Incremental spectral clustering by efficiently updating the eigen-system. *Pattern Recognition, 43*(1), 113–127. doi:10.1016/j.patcog.2009.06.001

Nood, D., & Attema, J. (2006). *Second Life, the second life of virtual reality*. The Hague, The Netherlands: EPN Electronic Highway Platform.

Northway, M. L. A. (1940). Method for depicting social relations by sociometric testing. *Sociometry, 3*, 144–150. doi:10.2307/2785439

Nucleus Research. (2009). *Facebook: Measuring the cost to business of social notworking*. (Report No. J579). Retrieved July 15, 2010, from http://nucleusresearch.com/research/notes-and-reports/facebook-measuring-the-cost-to-business-of-social-notworking/

Núñez, F., Ardèvol, E., & Vayreda, A. (2004). *La actuación de la identidad online: Estrategias de representación y simulación en el ciberespacio*. Bilbao, Spain: Ciberart.

Odella, F. (2006). *Using ego-network in surveys: Methodological and empirical research issues*. Paper presented at NETSCI 06 International Conference on Network Sciences, Bloomington Indiana, USA.

Oegma, D., Kleinnijenhuis, J., Anderson, K., & von Hoof, A. (2008). Flaming and blaming: The influence of mass media content on interactions in online discussions. In Konijin, E. A., Utz, S., Tanis, M., & Barnes, S. B. (Eds.), *Mediated interpersonal communication* (pp. 331–358). New York, NY: Routledge.

Ofcom. (2008). *Social networking: A quantitative and qualitative research report into attitudes, behaviours and use*. Retrieved September 6, 2010, from http://www.ofcom.org.uk/advice/media_literacy/medlitpub/medlitpubrss/socialnetworking/report.pdf

Ohtsuki, H., Hauert, C., Lieberman, E., & Nowak, M. A. (2006). A simple rule for the evolution of cooperation on graphs and social networks. *Nature, 441*, 502–505. doi:10.1038/nature04605

Olson, D. H. L., Sprenkle, D. H., & Russell, C. S. (1979). Circumplex model of marital and family systems: Cohesion and adaptability dimensions, family types, and clinical applications. *Family Process, 18*, 3–28. doi:10.1111/j.1545-5300.1979.00003.x

Osman, A., Lou, L. G., Muller-Gethmann, H., Rinkenauer, G., Mattes, S., & Ulrich, R. (2000). Mechanisms of speed– accuracy trade-off: Evidence from covert motor processes. *Biological Psychology, 51*, 173–199. doi:10.1016/S0301-0511(99)00045-9

Oviatt, S. (1999). Ten myths of multimodal interaction. *Communications of the ACM, 42*(11), 74–81. doi:10.1145/319382.319398

Padgett, J., & Ansell, C. (1993). Robust action and the rise of the Medici, 1400-1434. *American Journal of Sociology, 98*, 1259–1319. doi:10.1086/230190

PageData. (2010). *Page leaderboards*. Retrieved June 29, 2010, from http://pagedata.insidefacebook.com

Page, L., & Brin, S. (1999). *The PageRank Citation Ranking: Bringing Order to the Web*. Stanford University.

Palla, G., Barabasi, A. L., & Vicsek, T. (2007). Quantifying social group evolution. *Nature, 446*(5), 664–667. doi:10.1038/nature05670

Palla, G., & Derenyi, I. (2005). Uncovering the overlapping community structure of complex networks in nature and society. *Nature, 435*(7043), 814–818. doi:10.1038/nature03607

Pantucci, R. (2010). The Tottenham Ayatollah and the hook-handed cleric: An examination of all their jihadi children. *Studies in Conflict and Terrorism, 33*, 226–245. doi:10.1080/10576100903555770

Pape, R. A. (2003). The strategic logic of suicide terrorism. *The American Political Science Review, 97*, 343–361. doi:10.1017/S000305540300073X

Pape, R. A. (2005). *Dying to win: The strategic logic of suicide terrorism*. New York, NY: Random House.

Parsons, C. (2007). Web-based surveys: Best practices based on the research literature. *Visitor Studies, 10*(1), 13–33. doi:10.1080/10645570701263404

Passant, A., Hastrup, T., Bojars, U., & Breslin, J. (2008). Microblogging: A semantic and distributed approach. *Proceedings of the 4th Workshop on Scripting for the Semantic Web*.

Pastor-Satorras, R., & Vespignani, A. (2001). Epidemic spreading in scale-free networks. *Physical Review Letters, 86*(14), 3200–3203. doi:10.1103/PhysRevLett.86.3200

Pawlak, P. (2009). Network politics in transatlantic homeland security cooperation. *Perspectives on European Politics and Society, 10*, 560–581. doi:10.1080/15705850903314833

Pazzani, M., & Billsus, D. (1997). Learning and revising user profiles: The identification of interesting web sites. *Machine Learning, 27*(3), 313–331. doi:10.1023/A:1007369909943

Pedahzur, A., & Perliger, A. (2006). The changing nature of suicide attacks: A social network perspective. *Social Forces, 84*, 1987–2008. doi:10.1353/sof.2006.0104

Pedahzur, A., & Perliger, A. (2009). *Jewish terrorism in Israel*. New York, NY: Columbia University Press.

Pedica, C., & Vilhjálmsson, H. (2009). Lecture Notes in Computer Science: *Vol. 5773. Spontaneous avatar behavior for human territoriality* (pp. 344–357). Berlin, Germany: Springer Verlag.

Penuel, W. R., Sussex, W., Korbak, C., & Hoadley, C. (2006). Investigating the potential of using social network analysis in educational evaluation. *The American Journal of Evaluation, 27*(4), 437–451. doi:10.1177/1098214006294307

Petraeus, D. H., & Amos, J. F. (2006). *Counterinsurgency*. Field manual 3-24. Washington, DC: Headquarters Department of the Army.

Petroczi, A., Nepusz, T., & Baszo, F. (2007). Measuring tie-strength in virtual social networks. *Connections, 27*(2), 39–52.

Pew Research Center. (2010, April). *The people and their government: Distrust, discontent, anger, and partisan rancor.* Washington, DC: Author.

Pfeil, U., Arjan, R., & Zaphiris, P. (2009). Age differences in online social networking – A study of user profiles and the social capital divide among teenagers and older users in MySpace. *Computers in Human Behavior, 25*(3), 643–654. doi:10.1016/j.chb.2008.08.015

Phelan, O., McCarthy, K., & Smyth, B. (2009). Using twitter to recommend real-time topical news. *Proceedings of the Third ACM Conference on Recommender Systems*, (pp. 385-388).

Pinkster, F., & Volker, B. (2009). Local social networks and social resources in two Dutch neighbourhoods. *Housing Studies, 24*(2), 225–242. doi:10.1080/02673030802704329

Pisano, G., Bohmer, M., & Edmondson, A. (2001). Organizational differences in rates of learning: Evidence from the adoption of minimally invasive surgery. *Management Science, 47*, 752–768. doi:10.1287/mnsc.47.6.752.9811

Piselli, F. (2007). Communities, places and social networks. *The American Behavioral Scientist, 50*(7), 867–878. doi:10.1177/0002764206298312

Plumper, T., & Neumayer, E. (2010). The friend of my enemy is my enemy: International alliances and international terrorism. *European Journal of Political Research, 49*, 75–96. doi:10.1111/j.1475-6765.2009.01885.x

Pollet, T. V., Roberts, S. G. B., & Dunbar, R. I. M. (2010). Use of social network sites and instant messaging does not lead to increased offline social network size, or to emotionally closer relationships with offline network members. *Cyberpsychology. Behavior and Social Networking*, *14*(4). doi:.doi:10.1089/cyber.2010.0161

Porter, D. (Ed.). (1996). *Internet culture*. New York, NY: Routledge.

Portes, A. (1998). Social capital: Its origins and applications in modern sociology. *Annual Review of Sociology*, *24*, 2. doi:10.1146/annurev.soc.24.1.1

Portes, A., & Sensenbrenner, J. (1993). Embeddedness and immigration: Notes on the social determinants of economic action. *American Journal of Sociology*, *98*, 1320–1350. doi:10.1086/230191

Pothen, A. (1997). *Graph partitioning algorithms with applications to scientific computing*. Old Dominion University.

Pratt, S. C., & Sumpter, D. J. T. (2006). A tunable algorithm for collective decision-making. *Proceedings of the National Academy of Sciences of U.S.A.*, *103*, 906–15 910. doi:10.1073/pnas.0604801103

Preece, J. (2000). *Online Communities: Designing Usability, Supporting Sociability*. New York: John Wiley & Sons.

Price, D. (2010, September 8). Poll: 60 percent of web users visit social networks - Facebook by far the most popular site. *PC Advisor*. Retrieved September 20, 2010, from http://www.pcadvisor.co.uk/news/index.cfm?newsid=3238832

Prins, H. H. T. (1989). Buffalo herd structure and its repercussions for condition of individual African buffalo cows. *Ethology*, *81*, 47–71. doi:10.1111/j.1439-0310.1989.tb00757.x

Putnam, R. (1993). *Making democracy work: Civic traditions in modern Italy*. Princeton, NJ: Princeton University Press.

Putnam, R. (2000). *Bowling alone: The collapse and revival of American community*. New York, NY: Simon and Schuster.

Putnam, R. D. (1995). Bowling alone. *Journal of Democracy*, *6*(1), 65–78. doi:10.1353/jod.1995.0002

Putnam, R. D. (2000). *Bowling alone: The collapse and revival of American community*. New York, NY: Simon & Schuster.

Qiu, H., & Hancock, E. R. (2006). Graph matching and clustering using spectral partitions. *Pattern Recognition*, *39*(1), 22–34. doi:10.1016/j.patcog.2005.06.014

Qualman, E. (2009). *Socialnomics: How Social Media Transforms the Way We Live and Do Business*. Hoboken, New Jersey: John Wiley & Sons, Inc.

Raab, J., & Milward, H. B. (2003). Dark networks as problems. *Journal of Public Administration: Research and Theory*, *13*, 413–439. doi:10.1093/jopart/mug029

Rambaldi, G., & Callosa-Tarr, J. (2000). *Manual on participatory 3-D modeling for natural resource management. Essentials of protected area management in the Philippines*. Retrieved June 05, 2010, from http://www.iapad.org/publications/ppgis/p3dm_nipap.pdf

Rapoport, D. C. (2001). The fourth wave: September 11 in the history of world terrorism. *Current History (New York, N.Y.)*, (December): 419–424.

Rasa, O. A. E. (1986). *Mongoose watch: A family observed*. New-York, NY: Anchor Press.

Rashid, A. (2008). *Descent into chaos: The United States and the failure of nation building in Pakistan, Afghanistan and Central Asia*. New York, NY: Viking.

Razavy, M., & Haggerty, K. D. (2009). Hawala under scrutiny: Documentation, surveillance and trust. *International Political Sociology*, *3*, 139–155. doi:10.1111/j.1749-5687.2009.00068.x

Reddy, P. K., Kitsuregawa, M., et al. (2002). A graph based approach to extract a neighborhood customer community for collaborative filtering. *Proceedings of the Second International Workshop on Databases in Networked Information Systems*, (pp. 188-200). Springer-Verlag.

Redfield, R. (1960). *The little community and peasant society and culture*. Chicago, IL: University of Chicago Press.

Reed, B. (2007). A social network approach to understanding an insurgency. *Parameters*, (Summer): 19–30.

Reed, B. J., & Segal, D. R. (2006). Social network analysis and counterinsurgency analysis: The capture of Saddam Hussein. *Sociological Focus, 39,* 251–264.

Reid, E. M. (1994). *Cultural formations in text-based virtual realities.* M. A. Thesis, University of Melbourne. Retrieved from http://www.ee.mu.oz.au/papers/emr/work.html

Reitz, K. P., & White, D. R. (1989). Rethinking the role concept: Homomorphisms in social networks. In Freeman, L. C., White, D. R., & Romney, A. K. (Eds.), *Research methods in social network analysis* (pp. 429–488). Fairfax, VA: George Mason University Press.

Resnick, P., & Varian, H. R. (1997). Recommender systems. *Communications of the ACM, 40*(3), 56–58. doi:10.1145/245108.245121

Ressler, S. (2006). Social network analysis as an approach to combat terrorism: Past, present, and future research. *Homeland Security Affairs, 2,* 1-10. Retrieved January 9, 2010, from http://www.hsaj.org

Reviews, C. M. S. (2010). *Content management software review.* Retrieved September 21, 2010, from http://cms-software-review.toptenreviews.com

Rheingold, H. (2000) The Virtual Community: Homesteading on the Electronic Frontier. The MIT Press; Rev Sub edition.

Rheingold, H. (1993). *The virtual community.* New York, NY: Harper.

Rheingold, H. (2000). *The virtual community homesteading on the electronic frontier.* Cambridge, MA: The MIT Press.

Richins, M. L. (1997). Measuring emotions in consumption experience. *The Journal of Consumer Research, 24.*

Riley, S. (2008). *Identity, community and selfhood: understanding the self in relation to contemporary youth cultures.* London, UK: Futurelab/DCSF. Retrieved 4 August 2009, from http://www.beyondcurrenthorizons.org.uk/wp- content/uploads/final_riley_identitycommunityselfhood_20081201_jb.pdf

Rives, A. W., & Galitski, T. (2003). Modular organization of cellular networks. *Proceedings of the National Academy of Sciences of the United States of America, 100*(3), 1128–1133. doi:10.1073/pnas.0237338100

Robins, G. (2009). Understanding individual behaviors within covert networks: The interplay of individual qualities, psychological predispositions, and network effects. *Trends in Organized Crime, 12,* 166–187. doi:10.1007/s12117-008-9059-4

Robinson, E. J. H., Richardson, T. O., Sendova-Franks, A. B., Feinerman, O., & Franks, N. R. (2009). Radio tagging reveals the roles of corpulence, experience and social information in ant decision making. *Behavioral Ecology and Sociobiology, 63,* 627–636. doi:10.1007/s00265-008-0696-z

Roethlisberger, F. J., & Dickson, W. J. (1939). *Management and the worker.* Cambridge, MA: Harvard University Press.

Rogers, E. (1995). *Diffusion of Innovations* (4th ed.). New York: Free Press.

Rogers, J. (2000). Communities of practice: A framework for fostering coherence in virtual learning communities. *Journal of Educational Technology & Society, 3*(3), 384–392.

Romney, A. K., Weller, S. C., & Batchelder, W. H. (1986). Culture as consensus: A theory of culture and informant accuracy. *American Anthropologist, 88*(2), 313–338. doi:10.1525/aa.1986.88.2.02a00020

Rood, V., & Bruckman, A. (2009). Member behavior in company online communities. *Proceedings of the ACM 2009 Int'l Conf. on Supporting Group Work* (pp. 209-218). ACM.

Rothenberg, R. B. (1995). Commentary: Sampling in social networks. *Connections, 18*(1), 104–110.

Rothenbuhler, E. W. (1998). *Ritual communication: From everyday conversation to mediated ceremony.* Thousand Oaks, CA: Sage.

Rowe, R., & Creamer, G. (2007). Automated social hierarchy detection through email network analysis. *Proceedings of the Joint 9th WEB-KDD and 1st SNA-KDD Conference,* (pp. 109-117).

Rowley, J. (1999). Measuring total customer experience in museums. *International Journal of Contemporary Hospitality Management*, *11*(6), 303–308. doi:10.1108/09596119910281801

Rowley, J., Teahan, B., & Leeming, E. (2007). Customer community and co-creation: A case study. *Marketing Intelligence & Planning*, *25*(2), 136–146. doi:10.1108/02634500710737924

Rubicon Consulting, Inc. (2008). Online communities and their impact on business: Ignore at your peril (White paper). *Rubicon Consulting, Inc*. Retrieved June 30, 2010, from http://rubiconconsulting.com/downloads/whitepapers/Rubicon-web-community.pdf

Ruby, C. L. (2002). The definition of terrorism. *Analyses of Social Issues and Public Policy (ASAP)*, *2*, 9–14. doi:10.1111/j.1530-2415.2002.00021.x

Russell, S., & Norvig, P. (2003). *Artificial intelligence: A modern approach* (2nd ed.). Prentice Hall.

Ryan, G., & Bernard, H. (2003). Techniques to identify themes. *Field Methods*, *15*(1), 85–109. doi:10.1177/1525822X02239569

Saarinen, L. (2002). Imagined community and death. *Digital Creativity*, *13*(1), 53–61. doi:10.1076/digc.13.1.53.3212

Sageman, M. (2004). *Understanding terror networks*. Philadelphia, PA: University of Pennsylvania Press.

Sageman, M. (2008). *Leaderless jihad: Terror networks in the twenty-first century*. Philadelphia, PA: University of Pennsylvania Press.

Salem, P. J. (1998, July). *Paradoxical impacts of electronic communication technology*. Paper presented to the National Research Center of the University of Siena, International Communication Association and National Communication Association Conference on Communication: Organizing for the Future, Rome Italy. (ERIC No. ED 420-891, 24p)

Salem, P. J. (2008). *Preliminary observations on the notion of passive constraint*. Paper presented at the Annual Meeting of the Russian Communication Association meeting in Moscow, Russia.

Salem, P. J. (2009). *The complexity of human communication*. Cresskill, NJ: Hampton Press.

San Cornelio, G. (2004). Art i identitat: una relació utòpica amb la tecnologia. *Arnodes*, 1-8. Retrieved from http://www.uoc.edu/artnodes/cat/art/pdf/sancornelio0604.pdf

Sandler, T., & Enders, W. (2007). Applying analytical methods to study terrorism. *International Studies Perspectives*, *8*, 287–302. doi:10.1111/j.1528-3585.2007.00290.x

Santos, F. C., Santos, M. D., & Pacheco, J. M. (2008). Social diversity promotes the emergence of cooperation in public goods games. *Nature*, *454*, 213–216. doi:10.1038/nature06940

Sarfraz, M., & Salah, K. (2003). Internet Computing. *Information Sciences*, *150*(3-4), 119–122. doi:10.1016/S0020-0255(02)00372-9

Schelling, T. (1978). *Micromotives and Macrobehavior*. New York: Norton.

Schenkel, R., Crecelius, T., Kacimi, M., Michel, S., Neumann, T., Parreira, J. X., & Weikum, G. (2008). Efficient top-k querying over social-tagging networks. *Proceedings of the 31st Annual International ACM SIGIR Conference on Research and Development in Information Retrieval*, (pp. 523-530).

Schensul, J. J., LeCompte, M. D., Trotter, R. T. II, Cromley, E. K., & Singer, M. (1999). *Mapping social networks, spatial data, and hidden populations*. Walnut Creek, CA: Altimira Press.

Schields, R. (1996). *Cultures of internet: Virtual spaces, real histories, living bodies*. London, UK: Sage Publications.

Schiffer, E. (2007). *Net-map toolbox. influence mapping of social networks*. Retrieved September 05, 2010, from http://www.ifad.org/english/water/innowat/tool/Tool_2web.pdf

Schiffer, E., & Hauck, J. (2011). (forthcoming). Net-map: Collecting social network data and facilitating network learning through participatory influence network mapping. *Field Methods*.

Schmid-Hempel, P., & Schmid-Hempel, R. (1984). Life duration and turnover of foragers in the ant Cataglyphis bicolor (Hymenoptera, Formicidae). *Insectes Sociaux, 31*, 345–360. .doi:10.1007/BF02223652

Schnegg, M. (2010). Strategien und Strukturen. Herausforderungen der qualitativen und quantitativen Netzwerkforschung. In M. Gamper & L. Rechke (Eds.), *Sozialtheorie. Knoten und Kanten. Soziale Netzwerkanalyse in Wirtschafts- und Migrationsforschung* (pp. 55–75). Bielefeld, Germany: transcript.

Schneirla, T. C. (1953). Modifiability in insect behaviour. In Roeder, K. D. (Ed.), *Insect physiology* (pp. 23–747). New York, NY: Wiley.

Schönhofen, P. (2009). Identifying document topics using the Wikipedia category network. *Web Intelligence and Agent Systems, 7*(2), 195–207.

Schönhuth, M. (2005). *Entwicklung, Partizipation und Ethnologie. Implikationen der Begegnung von ethnologischen und partizipativen Forschungsansätzen.* Retrieved from http://ubttest.opus.hbz-nrw.de/volltexte/2005/300/pdf/habil_schoenhuth.pdf

Schönhuth, M. (2007). Diversity in der Werkstatt – Eine Feldstudie zum Thema Vielfalt und Behinderung. In Jent, N. H., & Steinmetz, B. (Eds.), *Diversity Management und Antidiskriminierung* (pp. 95–114). Weimar, Germany: Bertuch.

Schönhuth, M., & Kievelitz, U. (1995). *Participatory learning approaches: Rapid rural appraisal, participatory appraisal: An introductory guide.* Rossdorf, Germany: TZ-Verlagsgesellschaft.

Schumpeter, J. (1909). On the concept of social value. *The Quarterly Journal of Economics, 23*(2), 213–232. doi:10.2307/1882798

Schweitzer, T. (1996). *Muster sozialer Ordnung.* Berlin, Germany: Reimer.

Schweizer, T., Schnegg, T., & Berzborn, S. (1998). Personal networks and social support in a multiethnic community of southern California. *Social Networks, 20*, 1–21. doi:10.1016/S0378-8733(96)00304-8

Scoble, R., & Israel, S. (2006). *Naked Conversations: How Blogs are Changing the Way Businesses Talk with Customers.* Hoboken, New Jersey: John Wiley & Sons, Inc.

Scott, D. M. (2010). *The New Rules of Marketing and PR: How to Use Social Media, Blogs, News Releases, Online Video, and Viral Marketing to Reach Buyers Directly* (2nd ed.). Hoboken, New Jersey: John Wiley & Sons, Inc.

Scott, J. (2000). *Social network analysis: A handbook* (2nd ed.). Los Angeles, CA: Sage.

Scullin, S. S., Fjermestad, J., & Romano, N. C. (2004). E-relationships marketing: Changes in traditional marketing as the outcome of eCRM. *Journal of Enterprise Information Management, 17*, 410–415. doi:10.1108/17410390410566698

Sedgwick, M. (2007). Inspiration and the origins of global waves of terrorism. *Studies in Conflict and Terrorism, 30*, 97–112. doi:10.1080/10576100601101042

Sen, A., & Deng, H. (1992). On a graph partition problem with application to VLSI layout. *Information Processing Letters, 43*(2), 87–94. doi:10.1016/0020-0190(92)90017-P

Sha, Z., Wen, F., Gao, G., & Wang, X. (2009). Antecedents and consequences of flow experience in virtual brand community. *Proceedings of the Int'l Conf. on e-Business and Information System Security* (pp. 1-5). IEEE CS.

Shen, H. T., Shu, Y., & Yu, B. (2004). Efficient semantics-based content search in P2P network. *IEEE Transactions on Knowledge and Data Engineering, 16*(7), 813–826. doi:10.1109/TKDE.2004.1318564

Shenk, D. (1998). *Data smog: Surviving the information glut (rev.).* San Francisco, CA: Harper Edge.

Shepitsen, A., Gemmell, J., Mobasher, B., & Burke, R. (2008). Personalized recommendation in social tagging systems using hierarchical clustering. *Proceedings of the 2008 ACM Conference on Recommender Systems,* (pp. 259-266).

Shi, J., & Malik, J. (1997). Normalized Cuts and Image Segmentation. Proceedings of the 1997 Conference on Computer Vision and Pattern Recognition (CVPR '97), IEEE Computer Society: 731-737.

Shukla, M., Bessis, N., Conrad, M., & Clapworthy, G. (2009b). *A dynamically adaptive, dimensionalised, experience feedback mechanism within second life.* IADIS International Conference on Computer Science and Information Systems, Web Based Communities. Rome, Italy.

Sigala, M. (2010). Special issue on web 2.0 in travel and tourism: Empowering and changing the role of travelers. *Computers in Human Behavior*.

Sigurbjörnsson, B., & van Zwol, R. (2008). Flickr tag recommendation based on collective knowledge. *Proceeding of the 17th International Conference on World Wide Web*, (pp. 327-336).

Silk, J. B., Alberts, S. C., & Altmann, J. (2004). Patterns of coalition formation by adult female baboons in Amboseli, Kenya. *Animal Behaviour, 67*, 573–582. doi:10.1016/j.anbehav.2003.07.001

Silver, D., & Massanari, A. (2006). *Critical cyberculture studies*. New York, NY: New York University Press.

Simon, H. (1957). *Administrative behaviour: A study of decision-making processes in administrative organization*. New York, NY: Macmillan Press.

Simon, H. (1962). The architecture of complexity. *Proceedings of the American Philosophical Society, 106*(6), 467–482.

Singla, P., & Richardson, M. (2008). Yes, there is a correlation from social networks to personal behavior on the Web. In *Proc. WWW '08*.

Skeels, M. M., & Grudin, J. (2009). When social networks cross boundaries: A case study of workplace use of Facebook and Linkedin. *Proceedings of the ACM 2009 International Conference on Supporting Group Work*, (pp. 95-104).

Smith, A. (2002, 24 October). Mind over matter. *The Guardian*.

Smith, A., Lehman Scholzman, K., Verba, S., & Brady, H. (2009, September). *The Internet and civic engagement*. Report for the Pew Internet and American Life Project, Washington, DC. Retrieved from http://www.pewinternet.org/Reports/2009/15--The-Internet-and-Civic-Engagement.aspx

Smith, H. (2008). Defining terrorism: It shouldn't be confused with insurgency. *American Diplomacy*. Retrieved July 26, 2010, from http://www.unc.edu/depts/diplomat/item/2010/0103/comm/smith_hurtorhelp.html

Smith, B., & Welty, C. (2001). Towards a new synthesis. In *Formal ontology in Information Systems* (pp. iii–x). Ontology.

Snijders, T. A. B. (2001). The statistical evaluation of social network dynamics. In Sobel, M. E., & Becker, M. P. (Eds.), *Sociological methodology* (pp. 361–395). Boston, MA: John Wiley & Sons. doi:10.1111/0081-1750.00099

Snjiders, T., Spreen, M., & Zwaagstra, R. (1995). The use of multilevel modelling for analysing personal networks of cocaine users in a urban area. *Journal of Quantitative Anthropology, 5*, 85–105.

Sokal, R. R., & Sneath, P. H. A. (1963). *Principles of numerical taxonomy*. San Francisco, CA: W. H. Freeman and Co.

Sörensen, J. (2008). *Measuring emotions in a consumer decision-making context – Approaching or avoiding*. Aalborg: Aalborg University, Department of Business Studies.

Specia, L., & Motta, E. (2007). Integrating folksonomies in the Semantic Web. In *The Semantic Web: research and applications*, (pp. 624-639).

Spertus, E., Sahami, M., & Buyukkokten, O. (2005). Evaluating similarity measures: A large-scale study in the orkut social network. In *Proc. of the ACM SIGKDD International Conference on Knowledge Discovery in Data Mining (KDD '05)*, (pp. 678-684). ACM Press.

Spinuzzi, C. (2003). Knowledge circulation in a telecommunications company: A preliminary survey. In *Proc. the 21st Annual International Conference on Documentation* (pp. 178–183). New York.

Steenstrup, M. (2001). *Cluster-based networks. Ad hoc networking* (pp. 75–138). Addison-Wesley Longman Publishing Co., Inc.

Stern, M. J., & Adams, A. E. (2010). Do rural residents really use the internet to build social capital? An empirical investigation. *The American Behavioral Scientist, 53*, 1389–1422. doi:10.1177/0002764210361692

Stewart, G. W. (1998). *Matrix algorithms: Basic decompositions (Vol. 1)*. Society for Industrial Mathematics.

Stone, J. V. (2000). *Public participation in environmental management: Seeking participatory equity through ethnographic inquiry*. Doctoral Dissertation, University of South Florida.

Strater, K., & Lipford, H. R. (2008). Strategies and struggles with privacy in an online social networking community. Paper published online by the British Computer Society.

Strater, K., & Lipford, H. R. (2008). Strategies and struggles with privacy in an online social networking community. *Proceedings of the 22nd British HCI Group Annual Conference on People and Computers: Culture, Creativity. Interaction, 1*, 111–119.

Straus, F. (2002). *Netzwerkanalysen: Gemeindepsychologische Perspektiven für Forschung und Praxis*. Wiesbaden, Germany: Dt. Univ.-Verl.

Strauss, A., & Corbin, J. (1998). *Basics of qualitative research: Grounded theory procedures and techniques*. Thousand Oaks, CA: Sage.

Stutzman, F. (2006). An evaluation of identity-sharing behavior in social network communities. *Journal of the International Digital Media and Arts Association, 3*(1), 10–18.

Subrahmanyam, K., Reich, S. M., Waechter, N., & Espinoza, G. (2008). Online and offline social networks: Use of social networking sites by emerging adults. *Journal of Applied Developmental Psychology, 29*(6), 420–433. doi:10.1016/j.appdev.2008.07.003

Subramony, D. P. (2004). Instructional technologists' inattention to issues of cultural diversity among learners. *Educational Technology*, 19–24.

Suchanek, F. M., Kasneci, G., & Weikum, G. (2008). Yago: A large ontology from Wikipedia and Wordnet. *Web Semantics: Science. Services and Agents on the World Wide Web, 6*(3), 203–217. doi:10.1016/j.websem.2008.06.001

Sueur, C., Deneubourg, J. L., & Petit, O. (2010). Sequence of quorums during collective decision-making in macaques. *Behavioral Ecology and Sociobiology, 64*, 1885–1895. doi:10.1007/s00265-010-0999-8

Sueur, C., Jacobs, A., Petit, O., Amblard, F., & King, A. J. (2011). How can social network analysis improve the study of primate behaviour? *American Journal of Primatology, 73*, 703–709. doi:10.1002/ajp.20915

Sueur, C., & Petit, O. (2008). Organization of group members at departure of joint movements is driven by social structure in macaques. *International Journal of Primatology, 29*, 1085–1098. doi:10.1007/s10764-008-9262-9

Sueur, C., Petit, O., & Deneubourg, J.-L. (2009). Selective mimetism at departure in collective movements of Macaca tonkeana: An experimental and theoretical approach. *Animal Behaviour, 78*, 1087–1095. doi:10.1016/j.anbehav.2009.07.029

Sumpter, D. J. T. (2006). The principles of collective animal behavior. *Philosophical transactions of the Royal Society of London, Series B, 361*, 5-22.

Symeonidis, P., Nanopoulos, A., & Manolopoulos, Y. (2008). Tag recommendations based on tensor dimensionality reduction. *Proceedings of the ACM Conference on Recommender Systems,* (pp. 43-50).

Szell, M., & Thurner, S. (2010). Measuring social dynamics in a massive multiplayer online game. *Social Networks, 32*, 313–329. doi:10.1016/j.socnet.2010.06.001

Szomszor, M., Cattuto, C., Alani, H., O'Hara, K., Baldassarri, A., Loreto, V., & Servedio, V.D.P. (2007). Folksonomies, the semantic web, and movie recommendation. *4th European semantic web conference, bridging the gap between semantic web and web, 2*.

Tang, J., Sun, J., Wang, C., & Yang, Z. (2009). Social influence analysis in large-scale networks. *Proceedings of the 15th ACM SIGKDD international conference on Knowledge discovery and data mining*, 807-816.

Tang, J., Zhang, J., Yao, L., Li, J., Zhang, L., & Zhoung, S. (2008). ArnetMiner: Extraction and Mining of Academic Social Networks. *International conference on Knowledge discovery and data mining*, 990-998.

Tang, L., & Liu, H. (2009). Relation learning via latent social dimensions. *Proceedings of the 15th ACM SIGKDD International Conference on Knowledge Discovery and Data Mining,* (pp. 817-826).

Tang, L., & Liu, H. (2010). Toward predicting collective behavior via social dimension extraction. *IEEE Intelligent Systems, 25*(4), 19–25. doi:10.1109/MIS.2010.36

Tan, P., Steinbach, M., & Kumar, V. (2006). *Introduction to data mining*. Pearson Addison Wesley.

Tao, L., & Sarabjot, S. A. (2009). Exploiting Domain Knowledge by Automated Taxonomy Generation in Recommender Systems. *Proceedings of 10th International Conference on E-comemerce and Web Technologies,* 120-131.

Taylor, C. (1945). Techniques of community study and analysis as applied to modern civilized societies. In Linton, R. (Ed.), *The science of man in the world crisis* (pp. 416–441). New York, NY: Columbia University Press.

Terranova, T. (2004). *Network culture: Politics for the information age*. Basingstoke, UK: Palgrave Macmillan.

The Nielsen Company. (2010). *Social networks*. Retrieved June 19, 2010, from http://blog.nielsen.com/nielsenwire/online mobile/nielsen-provides-topline-u-s-web-data-for-march-2010

The White House. (2010). *Service*. Retrieved May 18, 2010, from http://www.whitehouse.gov/issues/service

Thompson, R. A. (1973). A theory of instrumental social networks. *Journal of Anthropological Research, 29*(4), 244–265.

Thorpe, W. H. (1963). *Learning and instinct in animals* (2nd ed.). London, UK: Methuen.

Tilly, C. (2004). Terror, terrorism, terrorists. *Sociological Theory, 22*, 5–13. doi:10.1111/j.1467-9558.2004.00200.x

Tobias, R., & Hoffman, C. (2004). Evaluation of free Java-libraries for social-scientific agent based simulation. *Journal of Artificial Societies and Social Simulation, 7*(1). Retrieved from http://jasss.soc.surrey.ac.uk/7/1/6.html.

Tomasello, M., & Call, J. (1997). *Primate cognition*. New York, NY: Oxford University Press.

Tönnies, F. (1957). *Community and society*. East Lansing, MI: Michigan University Press.

Tosini, D. (2007). Sociology of terrorism and counter-terrorism: A social science understanding of terrorist threat. *Social Compass, 1*, 664–681. doi:10.1111/j.1751-9020.2007.00035.x

Tripet, F., & Nonacs, P. (2004). Foraging for work and age-based polyethism: The roles of age and experience on task choice in ants. *Ethology, 110*, 863–877. doi:10.1111/j.1439-0310.2004.01023.x

Trotter, R. T. (1999). Friends, relatives and relevant others: Conducting ethnographic network studies. In Schensul, J. J., LeCompte, M. D., Trotter, R. T., Cromley, E. K., & Singer, M. (Eds.), *Mapping social networks, spatial data, and hidden populations*. Thousand Oaks, CA: AltaMira Press.

Tsai, W. (2002). Social structure of "competition" within a multiunit organization: coordination and intra organizational knowledge sharing. *Organization Science, 13*(2), 179–190. doi:10.1287/orsc.13.2.179.536

Tsvetovat, M., & Carley, K. M. (2007). On effectiveness of wiretap programs in mapping social networks. *Computational & Mathematical Organization Theory, 13*, 63–87. doi:10.1007/s10588-006-9009-0

Tuckman, B. (1965). Developmental sequence in small groups. *Psychological Bulletin, 63*(6), 384–399. doi:10.1037/h0022100

Tuckman, B., & Jensen, M. (1977). Stages of small-group development revisited. *Group and Organizational Studies, 2*, 419–427. doi:10.1177/105960117700200404

Turkle, S. (1995). *Life on the screen: Identity in the age of the Internet. London, UK: Weidenfeld & Nicolson. Shepard, J., & Greene, R. W. (2003). Sociology and you. Ohio.*Glencoe: McGraw-Hill.

Twitter. (n.d.) Twitter 101 for business—A special guide. *Twitter.* Retrieved July 15, 2010, from http://business.twitter.com/twitter101/

Tylor, E. (1958). *Primitive culture*. New York, NY: Harper & Row.

U.S. Department of Treasury. (2007). *The Holy Land Foundation for Relief and Development*. Washington, DC: Office of Terrorism and Financial Intelligence. Retrieved August 23, 2010, from www.ustreas.gov/offices/enforcement/key-issues/protecting/charities_execorder_13224e.shtml#h

University of Arizona Artificial Intelligence Laboratory <http://ai.arizona.edu/research/terror/>

Uzzi, B. (1998). The sources and consequences of embeddedness for the economic performance of organizations: The network effect. *American Sociological Review*, ▪▪, 32.

Van Der Gaag, M., & Snijders, T. A. B. (2003). *A comparison of measures for individual social capital. ICS paper for the Research Program SCALE*. Groningen University.

Van Grove, J. (2009, January 21). 40 of the best Twitter brands and the people behind them. *Mashable*. Retrieved September 10, 2010, from http://mashable.com/2009/01/21/best-twitter-brands/

Van Horn, R. C., Buchan, J. C., Altmann, J., & Alberts, S. C. (2007). Divided destinies: Group choice by female chacma baboons during social group fission. *Behavioral Ecology and Sociobiology*, *61*, 1823–1837. doi:10.1007/s00265-007-0415-1

van Vugt, M., Hogan, R., & Kaiser, R. B. (2008). Leadership, followership, and evolution, some lessons from the past. *The American Psychologist*, *63*, 182–196. doi:10.1037/0003-066X.63.3.182

Vascellaro, J. E. (2007, August 28). Social Networking Goes Professional: Doctors, Salesmen, Executives Turn to New Sites to Consult, Commiserate With Peers; Weeding Out Impostors. *Wall Street Journal*, Washington, D.C.

Vayreda, A., Nuéz, F., & Miralles, L. (2001). La interacción mediatizada por ordenador: Análisis del Fòrum d'Humanitats i de Filologia de la Universitat Oberta de Catalunya. *Apuntes de Psicología*, *19*(1), 101–122.

Vehovar, V., & Manfreda, K. L. (2008). Overview: Online surveys. In Fielding, N., Lee, R. M., & Blank, G. (Eds.), *The Sage handbook of online research methods* (pp. 177–194). Los Angeles, CA: SAGE.

Vehovar, V., Manfreda, K. L., Koren, G., & Hlebec, V. (2008). Measuring ego-centered social networks on the web: Questionnaire design issues. *Social Networks*, *30*, 213–222. doi:10.1016/j.socnet.2008.03.002

Victoroff, J. (2005). The mind of the terrorist: A review and critique of psychological approaches. *The Journal of Conflict Resolution*, *49*, 3–42. doi:10.1177/0022002704272040

Viswanath, B., Mislove, A., Cha, M., & Gummadi, K. (2009). On the evolution of user interaction in Facebook. In *Proc. 2nd ACM Workshop on Online Social Networks* (pp. 37–42). New York.

Vitevitch, M. S. (2002). Influence of onset density on spoken word recognition. *Journal of Experimental Psychology. Human Perception and Performance*, *28*, 270–278. doi:10.1037/0096-1523.28.2.270

Vitrue. (2010). *Virtrue social page evaluator*. Retrieved June 29, 2010, from http://evaluator.vitrue.com/

Voelkl, B., & Noë, R. (2008). The influence of social structure on the propagation of social information in artificial primate groups: A graph-based simulation approach. *Journal of Theoretical Biology*, *252*, 77–86. doi:10.1016/j.jtbi.2008.02.002

Von der Lippe. Holger & Gaede, Nina-S (2011). Die Konstitution personaler Netzwerke: ein psycho-logisches Studienprojekt mit VennMaker 0.9.5 VIP. In M. Schönhuth, M. Gamper, M. Kronenwett & M. Stark (Eds.), *Vom Papier zum Laptop – Perspektiven elektronischer Tools zur partizi-pativen Visualisierung und Analyse sozialer Netzwerke*. Bielfeld, Germany: transcript. (forthcoming).

Walter, F. E., Battiston, S., & Schweitzer, F. (2008). A model of a trust-based recommendation system on a social network. *Autonomous Agents and Multi-Agent Systems*, *16*(1), 57–74. doi:10.1007/s10458-007-9021-x

Walther, J., & D'Addario, K. (2001). The impacts of emoticons on message interpretation in computer-mediated communication. *Social Science Computer Review*, *19*(3), 324–347. doi:10.1177/089443930101900307

Wandrip-Fruin, N., & Montefort, N. (Eds.). (2003). *The new media reader*. MIT Press. Webster, F., & Puoskari, E. (Eds.). (2003). *The information society reader*. London, UK: Routledge.

Wang, F. W., & Chen, W. (2003). Complex networks: Small-world, scale-free and beyond. *IEEE Circuits and Systems Magazine,* first quarter 2003.

Wang, J., Li, Q., Chen, Y. P., Liu, J., Zhang, C., & Lin, Z. (2010). News recommendation in forum-based social media. *Proceedings of the Twenty-Fourth AAAI Conference on Artificial Intelligence,* (pp. 1449-1454).

Wang, P., Hu, J., Zeng, H. J., & Chen, Z. (2009). Using Wikipedia knowledge to improve text classification. *Knowledge and Information Systems, 19*(3), 265–281. doi:10.1007/s10115-008-0152-4

Warner, W. L., & Lunt, P. S. (1941). *The social life of a modern community.* New Haven, CT: Yale University Press.

Warner, W. L., & Lunt, P. S. (1942). *The status system of a modern community.* New Haven, CT: Yale University Press.

Wasserman, S., & Faust, K. (1994). *Social network analysis: Methods and applications.* Cambridge University Press.

Waterworth, J. A., & Waterworth, E. L. (2008). Presence in the future. In A Spagnolli & L Gamberini (Eds.), *Proceedings of the 11th International Workshop on Presence* (pp. 61-65). University of Padova, Italy.

Weaver, A. C., & Morrison, B. B. (2008). Social networking. [IEEE.]. *Computer, 41*(2), 97–100. doi:10.1109/MC.2008.61

Weber, M. (1947). *The theory of social and economic organisation,* (transl. by A. R. Hudson and Talcott Parsons).

Weber, M. (1978). *Economy and society: An outline of interpretive sociology.* Berkeley, CA: University of California Press.

Weimann, G. (1980). *Conversation Networks as Communication Networks.* PhD thesis, University of Haifa, Israel.

Weiss, R. S., & Jacobson, E. (1955). A method for the analysis of the structure of complex organizations. *American Sociological Review, 20*(6), 661–668. doi:10.2307/2088670

Welles, F. B., Van Devender, A., & Contractor, N. (2010). *Is a "friend" a friend? Investigating the structure of friendship networks in virtual worlds.* Paper presented at the 28th International Conference on Human Factors in Computing Systems (CHI), Atlanta, GA, USA.

Wellman, B. (2001, October). *The persistence and transformation of community: From neighbourhood groups to social networks.* Report to the Law Commission of Canada.

Wellman, B., Hogan, B., Berg, K., Boase, J., Carrasco, J. A., & Coté, R. ... Tran, P. (2006). Connected Lives: The project. In P. Purcell (Ed.), *The networked neighbourhood* (pp. 161-216). Berlin, Germany: Springer.

Wellman, B. (1979). The community question: The intimate networks of East Yorkers. *American Journal of Sociology, 84*(5), 1201–1231. doi:10.1086/226906

Wellman, B. (1999). *Networks in the global village: Life in contemporary communities.* New York, NY: Westview Press.

Wellman, B. (2002). Little boxes, glocalization, and networked individualism. In Tanabe, M., van den Besselaar, P., & Ishida, T. (Eds.), *Digital cities II: Computational and sociological approaches* (pp. 11–25). Berlin, Germany: Springer-Verlag. doi:10.1007/3-540-45636-8_2

Wellman, B. (2004). Connecting community: On- and offline. *Contexts, 3*(4), 22–28. doi:10.1525/ctx.2004.3.4.22

Wellman, B. (2007). The network is personal: Introduction to a special issue of *Social Networks. Social Networks, 29,* 349–356. doi:10.1016/j.socnet.2007.01.006

Wellman, B. (Ed.). (1999). *Networks in the global village: Life in contemporary communities.* Boulder, CO: Westview Press.

Wellman, B., & Berkowitz, S. D. (Eds.). (1988). *Social structures: A network approach.* Greenwich, CT: JAI Press.

Wellman, B., Carrington, P. J., & Hall, A. (1988). Networks as personal communities. In Wellman, B., & Berkowitz, S. D. (Eds.), *Social structures: A network approach.* New York, NY: Cambridge University Press.

Wellman, B., & Leighton, B. (1979, March). Networks, neighborhoods and communities. *Urban Affairs Quarterly, 14,* 363–390. doi:10.1177/107808747901400305

Wellman, B., Salaff, J., Dimitrova, D., Garton, L., & Gulia, M. (1996). Computer networks: Collaborative work, telework and virtual community. *Annual Review of Sociology*, *22*, 213–238. doi:10.1146/annurev.soc.22.1.213

Wellman, B., Wong, R. Y., Tindall, D., & Nazer, N. (1997). A decade of network change: Turnover, persistence and stability in personal communities. *Social Networks*, *19*, 27–50. doi:10.1016/S0378-8733(96)00289-4

Wenger, E. (1998). *Communities of practice: Learning, meaning, identity*. Cambridge, MA: Cambridge University Press.

Wenger, E. C., & Snyder, W. M. (2000). Communities of practice: The organizational frontier. *Harvard Business Review*, *78*(1), 139–145.

Wessels, B. (2010). *Understanding Internet: A socio-cultural perspective*. Basingstoke, UK: Palgrave Macmillan.

West, J. (1945). *Plainville, USA*. New York, NY: Columbia University Press.

Wey, T., Blumstein, D. T., Shen, W., & Jordan, F. (2007). Social network analysis of animal behavior: A promising tool for the study of sociality. *Animal Behaviour*, *75*, 333–344. doi:10.1016/j.anbehav.2007.06.020

White, D. R. (2003). Ties weak and strong. In Christensen, K., & Levinson, D. (Eds.), *Encyclopedia of community* (*Vol. 4*, pp. 1376–1379). Thousand Oaks, CA: Sage Reference.

White, D. R. (2005). Ring cohesion in marriage and social networks. In Degenne, A. (Ed.), *Social networks, Mathématiques informatique et sciences humaines. Journal of the Ecole des Hautes Etudes en Science Sociales Paris*. doi:10.4000/msh.2940

White, D. R., & Harary, F. (2001). The cohesiveness of blocks in social networks: Node connectivity and conditional density. *Sociological Methodology*, *31*, 305–359. doi:10.1111/0081-1750.00098

White, D. R., & Johansen, U. (2005). *Network analysis and ethnographic problems: Process models of a Turkish nomad clan*. Lanham, MD: Lexington Books.

White, D. R., Owen-Smith, J., Moody, J., & Powell, W. W. (2004). Networks fields and organizations: Microdynamics, scale and cohesive embeddings. *Computational & Mathematical Organization Theory*, *10*(2), 95–117. doi:10.1023/B:CMOT.0000032581.34436.7b

White, D. R., & Reitz, K. (1983). Graph and semigroup homomorphisms on networks of relations. *Social Networks*, *5*(2), 193–234. doi:10.1016/0378-8733(83)90025-4

White, H. C. (1992). *Identity and control: How social formations emerge*. Princeton, NJ: Princeton University Press.

White, H. C. (2005). *Markets from networks: Socioeconomic models of production*. Princeton, NJ: Princeton Univ. Press.

Whitehead, H. (2007). *Programs for analyzing social structure*. Retrieved from http://myweb.dal.ca/hwhitehe/MANUAL.htm

Whitehead, H. (1997). Analysing animal social structure. *Animal Behaviour*, *53*, 1053–1067. doi:10.1006/anbe.1996.0358

Whitmeyer, J. M., & Yeingst, C. N. (2006). A dynamic model of friendly association networks. *Social Science Research*, *35*, 642–667. doi:10.1016/j.ssresearch.2005.05.001

Whitten, N. A., & Wolfe, A. W. (1973). Network analysis. In Honigmann, J. (Ed.), *Handbook of social and cultural anthropology* (pp. 717–746). Chicago, IL: Rand-McNally.

Wikipedia. (2010). *Social network*. Wikipedia, the Free Encyclopedia. Retrieved September 4, 2010, from http://en.wikipedia.org/wiki/Social_network

Wilner, A. S., & Dubouloz, C. (2010). Homegrown terrorism and transformative learning: An interdisciplinary approach to understanding radicalization. *Global Change, Peace & Security*, *22*, 33–51. doi:10.1080/14781150903487956

Wilson, C., Boe, B., Sala, A., Puttaswamy, K., & Zhao, B. (2009). User interactions in social networks and their implications. In *Proc. 4th ACM European Conference on Computer Systems* (pp. 205–218). New York.

Wilson, J. (2009, June 1) Social networking: The business case. *Engineering & Technology Magazine*. Retrieved August 14, 2010, from http://kn.theiet.org/magazine/issues/0910/social-networking-0910.cfm

Wilson, M. (2002). Six Views of Embodied Cognition. *Psychonomic Bulletin & Review*, *9*(4), 625–636. doi:10.3758/BF03196322

Winer, J. M. (2008). Countering terrorist finance: A work, mostly in progress. *The Annals of the American Academy of Political and Social Science*, *618*, 112–132. doi:10.1177/0002716208317696

Winfield, N., & Gatopoulos, D. (2010). European anarchists grow more violent, coordinated. *Yahoo! News*. Retrieved December 28, 2010, from http://news.yahoo.com/s/ap/20101228/ap_on_re_eu/eu_italy_embassy_blasts

Wittemeyer, G., Douglas-Hamilton, I., & Getz, W. M. (2005). The socioecology of elephants: Analysis of the processes creating multitiered social structures. *Animal Behaviour*, *69*, 1357–1371. doi:10.1016/j.anbehav.2004.08.018

Witzel, A. (2000). *The problem-centered interview.* Retrieved September 21, 2010, from http://www.qualitative-research.net/index.php/fqs/article/viewArticle/1132/2521

Witzel, A. (1982). *Verfahren der qualitativen Sozialforschung: Überblick und Alternativen.* Frankfurt, Germany: Campus Verlag.

Wolf, E. R. (1955). Types of Latin American peasantry: A preliminary discussion. *American Anthropologist*, *57*(3, Part 1), 452–471. doi:10.1525/aa.1955.57.3.02a00050

Wolf, E. R. (1957). Closed corporate communities in Mesoamerica and Java. *Southwestern Journal of Anthropology*, *13*(1), 1–18.

Wolf, E. R. (1986). The vicissitudes of the closed corporate peasant community. *American Ethnologist*, *13*(2), 325–329. doi:10.1525/ae.1986.13.2.02a00080

Wolfe, A. W. (1961). *In the Ngombe tradition: Continuity and change in the Congo.* Evanston, IL: Northwestern University Press.

Wolfe, A. W. (1963). The African mineral industry: Evolution of a supranational level of integration. *Social Problems*, *11*(2), 153–164. doi:10.1525/sp.1963.11.2.03a00040

Wolfe, A. W. (1970). On structural comparisons of networks. *The Canadian Review of Sociology and Anthropology. La Revue Canadienne de Sociologie et d'Anthropologie*, *7*(4), 226–244. doi:10.1111/j.1755-618X.1970.tb01296.x

Wolfe, A. W. (1977). The supranational organization of production. *Current Anthropology*, *18*(4), 615–636. doi:10.1086/201973

Wolfe, A. W. (2005). Connecting the dots without forgetting the circles. *Connections*, *26*(2), 107–119.

Wolfe, A. W., Lex, B. W., & Yancey, W. L. (1968). *The Soulard area: Adaptations by urban White families to poverty.* St Louis, MO: The Social Science Institute Washington University.

Wrangham, R. W. (1980). An ecological model of female-bonded primate groups. *Behaviour*, *75*, 262–300. doi:10.1163/156853980X00447

Wu, A., DiMicco, J. M., & Millen, D. R. (2010). Detecting professional versus personal closeness using an enterprise social network site. *Proceedings of the 28th International Conference on Human Factors in Computing Systems*, (pp. 1955-1964).

Wu, L., Majedi, M., Ghazinour, K., & Barker, K. (2010). Analysis of social networking privacy policies. *Proceedings of the 2010 EDBT/ICDT Workshops*, 1-5

Wu, X., Zhang, L., & Yu, Y. (2006). Exploring social annotations for the Semantic Web. *Proceedings of the 15th International Conference on the World Wide Web*, (pp. 417-426).

Xiang, T., & Gong, S. (2008). Spectral clustering with eigenvector selection. *Pattern Recognition*, *41*(3), 1012–1029. doi:10.1016/j.patcog.2007.07.023

Xiao, Z., Guo, L., & Tracey, J. (2007). Understanding instant messaging traffic characteristics. In *Proc. ICDCS'07.*

Xia, T., & Cao, J. (2009). On defining affinity graph for spectral clustering through ranking on manifolds. *Neurocomputing*, *72*(13-15), 3203–3211. doi:10.1016/j.neucom.2009.03.012

Xu, J., Hu, D., & Chen, H. (2009). The dynamics of terrorist networks: Understanding the survival mechanisms of global Salafi jihad. *Journal of Homeland Security and Emergency Management, 6*. Retrieved July 26, 2010, from http://www.bepress.com/jhsem/all.

Xue, Y., Zhang, C., Zhou, C., Lin, X., & Li, Q. (2008). An effective news recommendation in social media based on users' preference. *Proceedings of the 2008 International Workshop on Education Technology and Training & 2008 International Workshop on Geoscience and Remote Sensing, 1*, (pp. 627-631).

Yee, N., & Bailenson, J. N. (2008). A method for longitudinal behavioral data collection in Second Life. *Presence (Cambridge, Mass.), 17*(6), 594–596. doi:10.1162/pres.17.6.594

Yin, Z., Li, R., Mei, Q., & Han, J. (2009). Exploring social tagging graph for web object classification. *Proceedings of the 15th ACM SIGKDD International Conference on Knowledge Discovery and Data Mining*, (pp. 957-966).

Young, H. (2002). The diffusion of innovation in social networks. *Santa Fe Institute working paper* 02-04-018.

Young, P. A. (2008). The culture based model: constructing a model of culture. *Journal of Educational Technology & Society, 11*(2), 107–118.

Young, P. A. (2008a). Integrating culture in designs of ICTs. *British Journal of Educational Technology, 39*(1), 6–17.

Yu, L. (2011). OWL: Web Ontology Language. *A Developer's Guide to the Semantic Web*, 155-239.

Zachary, W. W. (1977). An information flow model for conflict and fission in small groups. *Journal of Anthropological Research, 33*(4), 452–473.

Zanardi, V., & Capra, L. (2008). Social ranking: Uncovering relevant content using tag-based recommender systems. In *Proc. of the International Conference on Recommender Systems (RecSys 2008)*, (pp. 51-58). Lausanne, Switzerland. ACM Press.

Zdanowicz, J. S. (2009). Trade-based money laundering and terrorist financing. *Review of Law & Economics, 5*, 1–24. doi:10.2202/1555-5879.1419

Zhan, J., Loh, H. T., & Liu, Y. (2009). Gather customer concerns from online product reviews - A text summarization approach. *Expert Systems with Applications, 36*(2), 2107–2115. doi:10.1016/j.eswa.2007.12.039

Zhao, F., & Jiao, L. (2010). Spectral clustering with eigenvector selection based on entropy ranking. *Neurocomputing, 73*(10-12), 1704–1717. doi:10.1016/j.neucom.2009.12.029

Zhou, Z., Jin, X. L., Vogel, D., Guo, X., & Chen, X. (2010). *Individual motivations for using social virtual worlds: An exploratory investigation in Second Life*. Hawaii International Conference on System Sciences.

Zinoviev, D., & Duong, V. (2010). A game theoretical approach to modeling full-duplex information dissemination. In *Proc. SCMC'10* (pp. 358–363). Ottawa, Canada.

Zinoviev, D., Duong, V., & Zhang, H. (2010). A game theoretical approach to modeling information dissemination in social networks. In *Proc. IMCIC 2010, volume 1* (pp. 407–412). Florida: IIIS.

# About the Contributors

**Maytham Safar** is currently an Associate Professor at the Computer Engineering Department at Kuwait University. He received his Ph.D. degree in Computer Science from the University of Southern California in 2000. He authored and edited several books, conference, and journal articles. Current research interests include social networks, complex networks, and geographic information systems. He is a Senior Member of IEEE since 2008, and the First Kuwaiti to become an ACM Senior member in 2009. He is also a member of IEEE Computer Society, IADIS, @WAS, SDIWC and INSNA. He was granted over eleven research grants from research administration at Kuwait University, and Kuwait Foundation for the Advancement of Sciences (KFAS). He also served as a member of editorial board, steering committee, organizing committee, publicity committee, and reviewer for over a hundred of conferences and journals. Established the first complex networks research group (Synergy) at Kuwait University, http://synergy.ku.edu.kw, 2010.

**Khaled A. Mahdi** graduated from University of Toronto with BASc in Chemical Engineering in 1993. He received his PhD from Northwestern University in 2000. Currently, he is in the Chemical Engineering Department in Kuwait University. The scope of his research is statistical thermodynamics and dynamics of complex system with specific interest in social and biological networks system. In 2008, Khaled cofounded with Prof. Safar the Synergy group, a complex network research group in Kuwait University.

\* \* \*

**Shah Jamal Alam** is currently a postdoctoral research fellow in the School of Public Health at the University of Michigan. He studied Computer Science at the Universities of Karachi and Saarland and did his PhD in Social Simulation from the Centre for Policy Modelling under Scott Moss and Bruce Edmonds. SJAs' research interests include simulating social complexity, HIV transmission dynamics, dynamical social networks, and models of social movements and conflicts.

**Sadaf Alvi** is a graduate in Computer Science from University of Karachi, where she later on served as a faculty member teaching compiler construction and natural language programming. She has previously worked in the areas of language translation, genetic algorithms, and Urdu poetry's metric system. Current interests include agent-based modeling in the areas of political networks and geographical information systems.

**Nik Bessis** is currently a Head of Distributed and Intelligent Systems (DISYS) research group, a Professor and a Chair of Computer Science in the School of Computing and Mathematics at University of Derby, UK. He is academic member in the Department of Computer Science and Technology at University of Bedfordshire (UK). He obtained a BA (1991) from the TEI of Athens, Greece and completed his MA (1995) and PhD (2002) at De Montfort University (Leicester, UK). His research interest is the analysis, research, and delivery of user-led developments with regard to trust, data integration, annotation, and data push methods and services in distributed environments with focus on the study and use of next generation and grid technologies methods. He is involved in and leading a number of funded research and commercial projects and is the editor of three books and the Editor-in-Chief of the *International Journal of Distributed Systems and Technologies* (IJDST). In addition, he is a regular reviewer and has served as a keynote speaker, conferences/workshops/track chair, Associate Editor, session chair, and scientific program committee member.

**Luca Cagliero** received the Master's degree in Computer and Communication Networks from the Politecnico di Torino in 2008. Since January 2009, he has been a PhD student in Computer Engineering in the Dipartimento di Automatica e Informatica, Politecnico di Torino. His current research interests are in the areas of data mining and database systems. In particular, he is investigating the application of novel classification and association rule mining approaches to very large databases as well the exploitation of generalized patterns to support analyst decision making in different application contexts. He has been a Teaching Assistant in different databases and data mining courses at the Politecnico di Torino since academic year 2009-2010.

**Chung-Hao Chen** received his B.S. and M.S. in Computer Science and Information Engineering from Fu-Jen University, Taiwan 1997 and 2001, respectively. He received his Ph.D. in the department of Electrical Engineering and Computer Science at the University of Tennessee, Knoxville in 2009. Currently he is an Assistant Professor in the department of Mathematics and Computer Science at North Carolina Central University. His research interests include statistical analysis, robotics, and image processing.

**Marc Conrad** (Ph.D.) currently works for the Faculty of Creative Arts, Technology and Science at the University of Bedfordshire as a Senior Lecturer in Computer Science. While being educated as a Mathematician, where he received his PhD, interest in virtual worlds dates back to 1994 when he became engaged with the German MUD Unitopia hosted at the University of Stuttgart. When in 2007 his University acquired the Second Life islands 'Bedfordia' and 'University of Bedfordshire' he utilized both the social and technical aspects of Second Life for his teaching and research. The name of his avatar is Sanf Oh. Other than virtual worlds, he has research interests and publications in areas as diverse as algebraic number theory, software engineering, project management, trust, security, and sound art.

**Angelo Corallo** is an Associate Professor at the Department of Innovation Engineering, University of Salento (Lecce, Italy) and a research fellow at the e-Business Management Section (eBMS), Scuola Superiore ISUFI, University of Salento (Lecce, Italy). His main research interests are technology and organizational strategy in complex industries, knowledge management, and collaborative working environments in project and process-based organizations, with specific reference to the aerospace industry and languages, methodologies, and technologies for knowledge modelling. Starting from 2000 he coordinated for eBMS the following projects, funded by the EC under FP6 or by Italian national research funds: X@Work, DISCORSO (Distributed Information Systems for CooRdinated Service Oriented interoperability), DBE (Digital Business Ecosystem), MAIS (Multi-Channel Adaptive Information system), KIWI (Knowledge-based Innovation for the Web Infrastructure), TEKNE (Towards Evolving Knowledge-based interNetworked Enterprise) X-Net-Lab (Extended Net-Lab), SecureSCM (Secure Supply Chain Management System).

**Marco De Maggio** earned his PhD in "e-business" at eBusiness Management Section of Scuola Superiore ISUFI - University of Salento, Italy, and Bachelor Degree in Economics at University of Lecce, and Chartered Accountant. His research field concerns the development of methodologies for the analysis and management of organizational learning patterns inside organizations and communities of practice. His focus is mainly on the development of tools and methodologies for the monitoring of the organizational behavior responsible for Social Capital creation. Visiting Scholar at MIT – Cambridge, MA, USA, he experimented the application of Content and Social Network analysis supported by computer-aided systems for the improvement in the analysis of Virtual Communities.

**Pasquale De Meo** received the MsC Degree in Electrical Engineering from the University of Reggio Calabria in May 2002 and the PhD in System Engineering and Computer Science from the University of Calabria in February 2006. He was a Marie Curie Fellow at Department of Computer Science, Vrijie Universiteit van Amsterdam, The Netherlands. He is an Assistant Professor (non tenure-track) at University of Messina. His research interests include user modeling, intelligent agents, e-commerce, e-government, e-health, scheme integration, XML, Cooperative Information Systems, Folksonomies, and Social Internetworking.

**Emilio Ferrara** received is M.Sc. degree magna cum laude in Computer Science from the University of Messina in July 2008 and is currently a Ph.D. student of Mathematics and Computer Science at the same University. During his Ph.D. he has been a visiting student at the Vienna Technische Universität and an intern at the Lixto Software. His research interests focus on the Semantic Web, in particular on topics such as adaptive algorithms for automatic extraction of information from Web sources, analysis of online social networks, social communites, folksonomies, and virtual and dynamic environments.

**Alessandro Fiori** received the Master degree in Computer Engineering and the European Ph.D. degree from Politecnico di Torino, Italy. He is a postdoctoral researcher at the Database and Data Mining group of Politecnico di Torino since January 2010. His research interests are in the field of data mining, in particular bioinformatics and text mining. His activity is focused on the analysis of microarray gene expression data and on the summarization of scientific documents to extract correlated information. His research activities are also devoted to social network analysis, particularly the extraction of hidden information in the user-generated content.

**Giacomo Fiumara** is Assistant Professor at the Faculty of Sciences of the University of Messina since 2008. He graduated in Physics in 1989 and took his Ph.D. in Physics in 1992 at the University of Messina. His scientific areas of interest cover: Semantic Web, automatic extraction of data from Web sources, reasoning on Web data, and social networks.

**Markus Gamper,** born 1975, studied at the University of Tübingen and Trier. He did his doctorate in sociology at the University of Trier. His research interests include sociology of religion, migration, and network analysis. Currently he is board member and postdoctoral research fellow at the Cluster of Excellence in Societal dependencies and social networks at the University of Trier.

**Francesca Grippa,** PhD is an Assistant Professor in eBusiness Management at the Scuola Superiore ISUFI, University of Salento (Lecce, Italy). Her current research interest is in applying Social Network Analysis to business and learning communities. Francesca has a Ph.D. in e-Business Management and a MA in Business Innovation Leadership from the University of Salento and a BS in Communication Sciences from the University of Siena, Italy. In 2005 and 2006 she was Visiting Scholar at the MIT Sloan Center for Collective Intelligence, Cambridge, MA, USA. She teaches at undergraduate and graduate levels, both in academic and corporate environments. She is part of the Faculty in several Master's Programs, such as Finmeccanica Master FHINK and the Master in Management of Innovation at Scuola S.Anna in Pisa.

**Steven M. Gustafson,** received a Ph.D. from the University of Nottingham and is a Computer Scientist in the Computational Intelligence Laboratory at GE Global Research, focused on social networks, machine learning, and data mining. He serves as a Technical Editor-in-Chief of *Memetic Computing,* a journal dedicated to heuristic search and optimization. He has been the technical and project lead for several large research projects over the past three years, working in the area of marketing intelligence, data mining, text analysis, and social network analysis and visualization. He has filed 8 patent applications, and has published numerous articles in journals and conferences, including a recent book on systems self-assembly. A major theme to Dr. Gustafson's work has been understanding complex systems and developing heuristic and hybrid technologies to solve challenging problems. In 2006, Dr. Gustafson was awarded the "IEEE Intelligent Systems 10 to Watch in Artificial Intelligence" Award.

**Helen Y. Hadush** is a teacher, software developer, and an entrepreneur at heart. After receiving her first degree with honors in July 2007 from Mekelle Institute of Technology, one of the best in Ethiopia, she started her career as a graduate assistant in the same institute and worked for a year. In August 2008, she went to the USA, North Carolina Central University to pursue her Master's degree in Computer and Information Science and graduated with honors on May 2010. She wrote her Master's thesis in the area of Community Structure Extraction for Social Networks under the supervision of Dr. Gaolin Zheng. Currently she lives in Silver Spring, MD, USA, where she is working as a Software Engineer for Danya International, Inc.

**E-Wen Huang** received his Bachelor's Degree in Chemical Engineering from Chang Gung University in 1998 and his first Master's Degree in Materials Science and Engineering from National Dong Hwa University in 2002, respectively, in Taiwan. He received a second Master's from Texas A&M University in Industrial Engineering in 2005. He received his Ph.D. in the Department of Materials Science and Engineering at the University of Tennessee in 2009. He has been an Assistant Professor in the Department of Chemical & Materials Engineering at National Central University since February 2010. His research interests include mechanical behavior of the metallic systems, experimental designs of neutron & synchrotron x-ray measurements, and statistical analysis.

**Pedro Isaías** is a Professor at the Universidade Aberta (Portuguese Open University) in Lisbon, Portugal, responsible for several courses and director of the Master degree program in Electronic Commerce and Internet since its start in 2003. He holds a PhD in Information Management (in the speciality of information and decision systems) from the New University of Lisbon. Author of several books, book chapters, papers, and research reports, all in the information systems area, he has headed several conferences and workshops within the mentioned area. He has also been responsible for the scientific coordination of several EU funded research projects. He is also member of the editorial board of several journals and program committee member of several conferences and workshops. At the moment he conducts research activity related to Information Systems in general, as well as e-learning, e-commerce, and WWW-related areas.

**David Knoke** (Ph.D. 1972, University of Michigan) is Professor of Sociology at the University of Minnesota. His primary areas of research and teaching are in organizations, networks, and social statistics. He has been a principal investigator on more than a dozen National Science Foundation grants, most recently a project to investigate networks and teamwork of 26 Minnesota Assertive Community Treatment (ACT) teams, a multi-professional mental-health services program. Recent books, some with coauthors, include Comparing Policy Networks: Labor Politics in the U.S., Germany, and Japan (1996), Organizations: Business Networks in the New Political Economy (2001), Statistics for Social Data Analysis 4th ed. (2002), and Social Network Analysis, 2nd ed. (2008). In 2008 Prof. Knoke received the UMN College of Liberal Arts' Arthur "Red" Motley Exemplary Teaching Award.

**Michael Kronenwett**, M.A., is Scientific Assistant at the Cluster of Excellence in Societal dependencies and social networks at the University of Trier. He studied Sociology, Computer Science, and History at the University of Cologne. Since at the end of 2008, he is the project coordinator of the VennMaker project at the Cluster of Excellence in Societal dependencies and social networks.

**Paula Miranda** is an Assistant Professor in the Department of Informatics and Systems at School of Technology at the Polytechnic Institute of Setubal, Portugal. She holds a Master degree from University of Coimbra with the dissertation in the area of Decision Support Systems (DSSs). She has authored several research papers in the aforementioned area of DSSs. Her areas of interest include Information Systems in general, and more specifically, database systems, systems analysis and design, decision support systems, and programming environments. Over the last years her research interests have been concentrated in the Information Society.

**Abha Moitra**, received a Ph.D. from the Tata Institute of Fundamental Research, Mumbai, India and is a Computer Scientist in the Computational Intelligence Lab at GE Global Research. She has developed tools for automated generation of ontologies from technical documents, including clinical medical guidelines. She has also investigated semantic languages for modeling data provenance and information assurance. She developed reliable systems for monitoring and measuring the online discussion and associating it to real-world events. Dr. Moitra also develops algorithms to predict the effects of an event to evaluate and incorporate events in operations planning. She has also developed a multi-level security service that can provide assurance on the source of data, the data transit path and the security of the systems for data storage. Dr. Moitra has filed several patent applications and has published recently in the area of data provenance. Recently, she was invited as a data provenance expert to the National Cyber Leap Year in 2009.

**Almudena Moreno,** Ph.D. in Sociology at the Universitat Autònoma de Barcelona in 2004 and is a Lecturer in Sociology at the University of Valladolid. Specialised in family issues, the welfare state, public policy, and comparative research on gender and sociology of new technologies of the communication. She has been a visiting researcher at the universities of Oxford (United Kingdom), McGill (Canada), Gothenburg (Sweden), Stirling (UK), Turin (Italy), and Chicago (USA). She is currently taking part in two European projects on equality policies on gender and youth, and is a member of AREA as a researcher on different European projects. Her research work has been recognized with the International Award for Young Sociologists, presented by the International Sociological Association in 1998; a research award presented by the Fundación Acción Familiar, in 2004 and the Extraordinary Award for Doctoral Theses in 2006.

**Francesca Odella** is Researcher and Assistant Professor at the University of Trento, Department of Sociology and Social Research. She graduated in Sociology of Work and Organization, as junior member of an international project on organizational perception of risk (Daimler Benz Foundation, 1998), and obtained her PhD in Economic Sociology in 2001. After the PhD she was awarded a Post-Doctoral grant at the Department of Sociology and Social Research at the University of Trento, where, since 2006, she has been working as Assistant Professor in Methodology of the Social Sciences. She had been involved in national and international research projects in the socio-economic areas (social capital, local development) and in the last years working in projects concerning social and organizational impact of advanced and pervasive communication technologies (Discreet European Project, Foundation Bruno Kessler, Trento).

**Eric Pardede** is a Lecturer in the Department of Computer Science and Computer Engineering at La Trobe University, Melbourne, Australia. From the same university, he received his Doctor of Philosophy and Master of Information Technology in 2006 and 2002 respectively. He has research interests in data quality, data security and data privacy in XML and Web Databases, as well as data repository and the development of social networking Websites.

**Sara Pífano** is a Research Assistant at the Information Society Research Lab, in Lisbon, Portugal and is currently completing a PhD devoted to the study of Web 2.0's Critical Success Factors, at the Universidade Aberta (Portuguese Open University) in Portugal. She holds a degree in International Relations from the University of Minho (Braga, Portugal) and a MA in Refugee Studies from City University (London, United Kingdom). Besides her focus on the broad field of the information society, her main research interests and recent publications place an emphasis in Web 2.0 and its repercussions in the several domains of society, particularly education, business, and politics.

**Philip Salem** (Ph. D., University of Denver) is Professor of Communication Studies at Texas State University. His publications include work on organizational communication, interpersonal communication, communication and technology, research methods, and communication theory. He has been investigating communication networks since the 1970s. He has received awards for his work on communication and technology, and he was the third person to receive the Outstanding Member Award from the Organizational Communication Division of the International Communication Association. He wrote The Complexity of Human Communication, a book about nonlinear communication processes published by Hampton Press. He received a Fulbright Senior Specialist fellowship funding collaborative international scholarship through 2012.

**Michael Schoenhuth** is a full Professor for Cultural Anthropology at the University of Trier, Germany. He is also an acting director at the Cluster of Excellence in Societal dependencies and social networks and project leader in the German Science Foundation, branch 600 Foreignness and Poverty. He graduated 1989 with a doctoral thesis on witchcraft in Europe and Africa. He is co-founder of the journal *Entwicklungsethnologie*, the only German-speaking journal on the anthropology of development. Michael's scientific work focuses on participatory methods, migration, social networks, diversity, culture & development, and intercultural issues, and since the 1990s he is consulting governmental and non-governmental agencies and foundations in these fields.

**Mitul Shukla** is currently engaged by the Research Directorate at the University of Bedfordshire, UK. His role there is in evaluating and updating the processes applied to conducting research at the University. His recent work based background has been focused on the facilitation of better communication processes to elicit lessons learned during transformational periods. Mitul Shukla has an educational background in media production as well as in computer science. His research interests lie in the consumption process of virtual goods and the communication processes involved in virtual organisations. Presently he is in part-time study for his PhD, which investigates metrics applicable to consumer satisfaction in virtual worlds such as Second Life.

**Cédric Sueur** is Ethologist and Primatologist affiliated to the Free University of Brussels (Belgium) and to the University of Kyoto (Japan). He works on collective phenomena and social networks. He carried out his doctoral and post-doctoral researches on different species of primates (macaques, lemurs, capuchins, chimpanzees and baboons) with the University of Strasbourg (France) and Princeton University (USA). His studies were about how social network of a group affects collective decision making and specifically the emergence of leadership and the organization of group members during movements. He got two famous French scientist prizes for his thesis.

**Alvin W. Wolfe** is Distinguished University Professor Emeritus, Department of Anthropology, at the University of South Florida. He earned his Ph.D. at Northwestern University in 1957, having done ethnographic field research in the Congo in the early 1950s. Later he began to study the networks formed by the mining companies in southern Africa. Urban anthropological research in the United States led to further network studies. From 1974 to 2003, at the University of South Florida, he directed the Applied Anthropology Internship Project. He developed the Human Services Information System in the Tampa Bay Area. He served as president of the Society for Applied Anthropology, and was among the founders of the Sunbelt Social Network Conference, as well as the International Network for Social Network Analysis.

**Zanita Zahari** received her degree in Computer Science from University Technology Malaysia in 2003. She was a Course Coordinator for ICT course at National Institute of Public Administration, Malaysia from 2004 to 2008. She completed her Master in Information Systems from La Trobe University in 2010. Currently, she is an Information Technology officer at Ministry of Higher Education, Malaysia. She is interested in design, development, and success measurement of social networking websites.

**Gaolin Zheng** received her Bachelor's degree in Biomedical Engineering from Huazhong University of Science and Technology in 1992, and a Master's degree in Environmental Biology from the Chinese Academy of Sciences in 1995. She received her Ph.D. in Computer Science from Florida International University in 2006. She has been an Assistant Professor in Department of Mathematics and Computer Science at North Carolina Central University since 2007. Her research interest includes computational biology, Bayesian statistics, protein structure prediction, and assembly and high performance computing.

**Dmitry Zinoviev** received M.S. in Physics from Moscow State University, Russia, in 1993 and M.S. and Ph.D. in Computer Science from the State University of New York (SUNY) at Stony Brook, USA, in 1994 and 1997, respectively. He worked as a Research Scientist at SUNY in 1997–2000. In 2001, he joined the Departments of Mathematics and Computer Science at Suffolk University, Boston, where he currently works in the rank of Associate Professor. His research interests include social networks, modeling and simulation, human-computer interaction, social informatics, and operating systems. He published 38 papers in *IEEE Transactions* and various conference proceedings, including SCSC and ISEC, and four books. He served as reviewer for several journals, conferences, and books. He is also a co-principal investigator for the NSF Research Experience for Undergraduates grant aimed at promoting research of online social networks among undergraduate students.

# Index

## A

acquaintance networks 91
agent-based modeling 88
agile development 104
agile iteration life cycle 104-106, 108, 117
Althusser, Louis 70
analysis phase 110
animal group 168
animal/human comparison 170
Arensberg, Conrad 26, 30-31, 33
Arensberg's Types of American Communities 31
atomistic society 34

## B

BibSonomy 127
Black, Donald 233
block modelling techniques 13
broad environment 287
business-customer relationship 254

## C

cell structures 236
civic engagement 51-52, 62-63
civic engagement and communication 53
civic engagement study
    conclusion 62
    descriptive results 59
    inferential results 60
classical sociology 70
coding phase 112
collaborative behavior modeling 130
Collaborative Innovation Networks (COIN) 218
collective decisions 172
communication 54
communication technologies 54

communication technology networks 51-52, 55, 62-63
communitarian contexts 4
communities 267
    definition of 27, 36
    development stages 224
    observing evolution of 221
    online - See online communities.
    ranking within 273, 277
    role in today's organizations 217
    social capital 6
    social participation 6
    varieties of 30-31
community detection 13
community development 219, 224
community identification 267
community reconstructing 2
community structure 266, 268
community theory 2
community variations 33
complete network 8
consumer profile/behaviour 249
contemporary personal communities 4
counterterror network analysis 238
cultural based model (CBM) 76
culture 53
customer loyalty 308
customer profile/behaviour 252
customer profitability 308
customer segmentation 308
cyberculture 68-69, 71-72, 75, 77
    identities 75
    socialization 75
cyberculture theorists 72
cybersecurity data 182

# D

data classification 137
decision-making 165
Del.icio.us 126
deliver increment phase 113
design phase 110
de Tocqueville, Alexis 53
diffusion processes 5
Digg 127
digital actor generator 200
digital network maps 197, 200, 205
direct environment 287
Director of National Intelligence (DNI) 239
divisive algorithm 270
dolphins dataset 274

# E

ego-centred networks 8
egocentric network analysis 196, 212
Eliciting Consumer Satisfaction (ECSA) 286, 297-298

# F

Facebook 128, 305
financial networks 237
Flickr 126
folksonomy 133
friendship networks 91

# G

global similarity score 311
Granovetter's Theory 11
graph partitioning 270
grouping principles 8
guerillas - See terrorism.

# H

hierarchical addressing 156
homegrown terrorism 238
homophily 151
human/animal comparison 170
hybrid community 216
hybrid participation 20
hybrid space 290

# I

information adoption 152
information flow 165
information pathways 148, 157
insurgencies - See terrorism.

# K

Katz Coefficient 310, 317
K-means clustering 271
knowledge creation in W.2 17

# L

Lave and Wenger's model 219
Life Effectiveness Questionnaire (LEQ) tool 224
Linden Scripting Language (LSL) 290
Linton, Ralph 28-29
loosely organized social structures 34

# M

Media Sharing Communities 125-126, 128, 139
member communication, predicting 187
message dynamics 155
message routing 156
message taxonomies 148
MicroBlogs 127
modularity based approach 272

# N

Netville research project 16
Network Perspective on Communities 32-33, 37
network pictures 197, 212
network thresholds 187
nexted connectivity 9

# O

online communities 15, 125
online identity 74
online learning communities 218
ontologies 134

# P

PageRank 273
paper-and-pencil approach 198
personal communities 5
planning phase 108
Porter, David 72

Prototype Model 89
Prototyping 104, 121
pure terrorism 233
Putnam, Robert 27

## Q

qualitative network analysis 196
quantitative network analysis 196
query engines 138

## R

Rapid Application Development (RAD) 104, 121
recommender systems 135
    news recommendation 136
    tag recommendation 136
Redfield, Robert 26-27, 31, 33
regression approach 319
research approaches 7

## S

Second Life 85, 87, 283-284
    cognition and emotion 288
    communities 90
    interaction 288
    internal economy 290
    user experience 287
social bookmarking 126
social capital 6
social capital and personal ties 12
social correlation analysis 129
social homophily principle 234
social influence discovery 129
socialization model 69
social knowledge representation 132
social network analysis 168, 195
    egocentric network 196, 212
    qualitative 196
    quantitative 196
    tool prospects 206
    whole network 195
social network developers 115
social network indicators 224
social networking 104
    customers as business reviewers 252
    customer service impact 256
    decision patterns 252
    information searches 252
    success factors 106

success measurement 106
social networking development 113
social network measurements 179
social network metrics 222
    learning community observation 223
social network models 128
social networks 82, 124, 131-132, 135, 138, 142,
    144, 146-152, 158, 160, 162, 180, 234, 249-
    252, 259-260, 264, 268, 289, 304-309
    extracting 182
    measuring 182
Social Network Sites (SNSs) 249
    challenges and best practices 254
    in the corporate arena 251
    using mainstream sites 255
social participation 6
social selective processes 5
social simulation 88
    results 92
    schedule 91
Social Web - See Web 2.0.
sociological thinking 70
Software Development Process Model 104
space-localized conception of community 3
spectral clustering 271
strong and weak ties 11, 147
structured knowledge 134
System Development Life Cycle (SDLC) 104, 121

## T

team development 219
terrorism 232-233
    financial networks 237
    guerillas 233
    insurgencies 233
    pure terrorism 233
    social networking 238
terrorist cells - See cell structures.
terror network analysis 234
terror networks 233-234
testing phase 107, 112
Twitter 127

## U

User Datagram Protocol (UDP) 291
User-Generated Content (UGC) 124-125, 145

# V

Venn-diagrams 198
VennMaker 194-195, 201
virtual participation 18
virtual worlds 284
visual data collection 201
visualised network surveys 196

# W

weak and strong ties 11, 147
Web 2.0 249, 265
Wellman, Barry 3, 28, 34, 36
whole network analysis 195
Wikipedia 126

# Z

Zachary Karate Club Dataset 274